SURVEY OF
American Industry and Careers

SURVEY OF

American Industry and Careers

Volume 2

Coal Mining Industry—Food Retail Industry

The Editors of Salem Press

SALEM PRESS
Pasadena, California   Hackensack, New Jersey

Editorial Director: Christina J. Moose
Project Editor: Rowena Wildin
Manuscript Editors: Stacy Cole, Andy Perry
Acquisitions Manager: Mark Rehn
Administrative Assistant: Paul Tifford, Jr.

Research Supervisor: Jeffry Jensen
Photo Editor: Cynthia Breslin Beres
Design and Layout: James Hutson
Additional Layout: William Zimmerman

Cover photo: ©Pauline St. Denis/CORBIS

∞ The paper used in these volumes conforms to the American National Standard for Permanence of Paper for Printed Library Materials, X39.48-1992 (R1997).

Library of Congress Cataloging-in-Publication Data

Survey of American industry and careers / The Editors of Salem Press.
   v.   cm.
Includes bibliographical references and indexes.
   ISBN 978-1-58765-768-9 (set : alk. paper) — ISBN 978-1-58765-769-6 (vol. 1 : alk. paper) — ISBN 978-1-58765-770-2 (vol. 2 : alk. paper) — ISBN 978-1-58765-771-9 (vol. 3 : alk. paper) — ISBN 978-1-58765-772-6 (vol. 4 : alk. paper) — ISBN 978-1-58765-773-3 (vol. 5 : alk. paper) — ISBN 978-1-58765-774-0 (vol. 6 : alk. paper) 1. Business—Vocational guidance—United States. 2. Industries—United States. 3. Occupations—United States. 4. Vocational guidance—United States. I. Salem Press.
   HF5382.5.U5S87 2012
   331.7020973—dc23
                                                                2011019601

First Printing

Contents

Complete List of Contents

VOLUME 4

VOLUME 5

VOLUME 6

List of Tables and Sidebars

SURVEY OF

American Industry
and Careers

Coal Mining Industry

©Dreamstime.com

INDUSTRY SNAPSHOT

General Industry: Energy

Career Cluster: Agriculture, Food, and Natural Resources

Subcategory Industries: Anthracite Mining; Bituminous Coal and Lignite Surface Mining; Bituminous Coal Underground Mining; Coal Mining Blasting Services on a Contract Basis; Exploration Services for Coal on a Contract Basis; Mine Shaft Sinking Services on a Contract Basis; Mine Tunneling on a Contract Basis; Stripping and Overburden Removal on a Contract Basis; Support Activities for Coal Mining

Related Industries: Electrical Power Industry; Mining Industry; Petroleum and Natural Gas Industry

Annual Domestic Revenues: $22 billion USD (World Coal Institute, 2008, based on an annual production of 1.1 billion tons)

Annual International Revenues: $134 billion USD (World Coal Institute, 2008, based on an annual production of 6.7 billion tons)

Annual Global Revenues: $156 billion USD (World Coal Institute, 2008)

NAICS Numbers: 2121, 213113

INDUSTRY DEFINITION

Summary

The coal mining industry locates coal, extracts it from the earth, processes it, and sells it for use in generating energy and for other industrial purposes. Miners often extract coal from horizontal sedimentary layers in the ground, though the processes used for coal extraction depend on the location of the coal, the type of coal being extracted, and the thickness and lateral extent of the coal bed. Coal close to the surface can sometimes be surface mined by removing overlying sediment to expose it. Coal located deeper underground may require mines to be constructed. Coal is widespread throughout much of the world, so mining is a worldwide industry. Over the course of the twentieth and twenty-first centuries, smaller coal companies have been shutting down or have been incorporated into larger companies, which have been steadily increasing.

History of the Industry

Coal has been used for heating for thousands of years. For example, the Welsh used it for this purpose three to four thousand years ago, while the Romans heated public baths by burning coal in the second century C.E. People in England were using coal for heating by the twelfth century, since some coal was easily obtained at the surface and burning it produced more heat than did burning wood. By the early eighteenth century, industries were heating coal in air-free chambers to produce coke. Coke burns with a much hotter flame than does coal, so it could be used to smelt iron ores into iron. Steam engines were also invented during the eighteenth century, and most of them burned coal to produce steam. By the early nineteenth century, steam engines were used to propel trains and ships, rapidly expanding transportation networks within and among nations.

The United States has abundant coal deposits, and the eastern states began to mine the substance by the mid-eighteenth century to propel ships and trains. Electric generators run by coal-fired steam were developed in the late nineteenth century, and coal became the major fuel for generating electricity in the twentieth century. Thus, much of the coal used during the first half of the twentieth century was used for heating, trains, and electricity. As petroleum and natural gas became more readily avail-

able in the late twentieth century, those substances became more common for heating and powering trains. Most coal use then became devoted to electrical generation. Lesser amounts of coal have also been used by other industries to, for example, produce steel from iron ores.

Initially, coal was mined using hand tools such as picks to break it up and remove it from the surrounding earth, often in underground mines. The coal was then carried away in handcarts. Many coal beds are fairly flat-lying or are layers that can be followed laterally, but some beds may be less than a meter thick. This situation can result in underground mines that are only as thick as the coal beds themselves. Children, because of their small size and the low wages for which they would work, were often used in the nineteenth century to bring out the coal from such mines in many countries, such as England and the United States. Work hours were also long, with miners working as many as sixty hours per week. These hours were gradually reduced in the twentieth century, when heavier ma-

A miner holds excavated coal. (©Grzegorz Kula/Dreamstime.com)

chines came to be used to more readily break up and transport the coal. The unionization of miners in the United States also led to shorter hours and better pay for those workers.

Underground jobs are dangerous, especially in the early years when miners breathed coal dust and silicate dust without protection, resulting in black lung disease and silicosis. The buildup of gases such as methane in some mines resulted in many catastrophic explosions. More than 120,000 miners in the United States alone have been killed by accidents in coal mines since 1870. Most of these deaths occurred in the early twentieth century, and the number of deaths has decreased drastically in contemporary mines as safety measures have been adopted.

The use of large machines to break up, extract, and move coal has brought about a significant reduction in the coal mining workforce in the United States, from around 700,000 persons in the 1920's to around 170,000 persons in the early twenty-first century. Even with fewer workers and coal mines, mechanization has increased total coal production in the United States, from around 300 million tons per year in the early twentieth century to nearly 1.2 billion tons per year in 2005.

The Industry Today

Coal is formed over millions of years from buried swamp plants such as those now found in the Florida Everglades. When such plants die, some of their remains can become preserved in the swamp water if its oxygen content is low enough. As the dead plants are gradually buried by sediment, their remains transform into peat, lignite, and subbituminous, bituminous, and anthracite coal—in that order—as they become buried more deeply and reach higher temperatures. During this process, the amount of volatiles such as water contained by the coal gradually decreases, and its carbon content gradually increases, so each type of coal burns hotter than its precursor. As coal develops, it forms horizontal beds that are associated with other sedimentary rocks, such as mudstones, sandstones (mostly composed of sand), and limestones (mostly composed of calcium carbonate). Coal beds' thickness ranges from a few centimeters to tens of meters or more. Even though the beds are originally horizontal, they may become folded or fractured, requiring some effort on the part of geologists to interpret their distribution.

Coal is widely distributed throughout the world. More than two-thirds of the world's coal reserves occur in China, Russia, and the United States. South Africa, Australia, Germany, Poland, and England also have major coal reserves.

Most coal in the eastern and central United States is either bituminous or anthracite, with high sulfur content, and some of this coal is extensively folded or faulted. Most coal in the nothern Great Plains and the Rocky Mountain region is lignite or subbituminous, with low sulfur content. Wyoming contains large amounts of thick, horizontal coal beds at or near the surface. Such deposits may be surface mined more economically than those in the eastern United States that require underground mines. The size, thickness, and shape of a coal deposit, as well as the kind of coal in the deposit, influence whether the deposit is mined by surface or underground mining.

In 2001 in the United States, 65 percent of coal mines were surface mines, employing 48 percent of miners (34,590 miners), and 35 percent were underground mines, employing about 52 percent of miners (37,180 miners). To engage in surface mining, miners must remove the overburden (noncoal sediment covering the coal), so the coal itself can be extracted with machinery and explosives. Often, the coal is taken in successive strips across the coalface, so the term "strip mining" is used to describe this process. For surface mining to be cost-effective, the overburden cannot be too thick.

Surface mining is usually more economical than underground mining because it is easier to break up and remove coal with large machines at the surface than it is to work with the smaller tools and machines that fit within tunnels—especially if the coal beds are thick as they are in Wyoming. Also, surface mines have fewer air, electricity, and water problems than do underground mines. Underground mines are often smaller operations than surface mines, and they disturb much less land surface than do strip mines, unless they collapse during or after operations.

In underground mines, the coal is often broken into pieces with electric drills and cutters and then moved by conveyor to the surface, where it is loaded onto trucks or railroad cars. Some mines use machines with rotating cutters that move back and forth across coal beds, both breaking up and

A man operates a dragline at a coal mine. Draglines can move up to 130 tons of material in their shovels at one time. (©John Casey/Dreamstime.com)

such as bulldozers, huge shovels, loaders, and draglines to move the fragments. Draglines are two-thousand- to thirteen-thousand-ton machines that can move up to 130 tons of material in their shovels at one time. If the overburden becomes too thick in a surface mine, the operation may proceed underground.

During the early twentieth century, most coal was mined underground, in part because there was no economical way to remove overburdens above even shallow coal beds. Moreover, the coal that was most easily accessible to surface mining was located in Wyoming, too far from the large energy markets in the eastern United States. In the twenty-first century, by contrast, the development of large-scale equipment has made it much more economical to mine near-surface coal with overburden thicknesses as great as thirty meters, and Wyoming's thick, low-sulfur coal beds are now close to many electrical generating plants. As a result, coal mining has shifted from east to west in the United States, with a greater use of the low-sulfur lignite and subbituminous coal in the Great Plains relative to the higher-sulfur bituminous and anthracite coals of the eastern United States. Wyoming's movement to larger surface coal mines has also greatly increased coal production per miner, and mines are safer than they once were, though major accidents do still occur.

A number of environmental problems result from coal mining that can be very costly for mining companies to solve. High-sulfur coals have iron sulfide minerals in them that react with water and the atmospheric oxygen within mines, producing sulfuric acid waters high in iron and some other dissolved elements. These acid waters can contaminate groundwater and streams and kill fish and other organisms, as has happened in Pennsylvania and West Virginia in the eastern United States. The dissolved iron also oxidizes at the surface and produces large amounts of unsightly iron compounds in contaminated streams.

Burning high-sulfur coal produces sulfur dioxide, which reacts with atmospheric water vapor to produce acid rain. Thus, laws have been passed capping the permissible amount of sulfur dioxide emissions from coal burning. These laws have increased the use of low-sulfur coal in electrical generating plants, since it is very expensive to capture or otherwise minimize the sulfur dioxide released

transporting pieces of coal. Enough pillars of coal must be left standing within a mine to support the layers of rock above it, so it does not collapse. Coal beds as thin as sixty centimeters usually can be mined economically.

The greatest hazards within underground mines include methane gas (which can collect locally and explode), falling rock, and mining machines themselves, which can be quite dangerous. Several other gases can cause problems if they build up sufficiently in a mine. Carbon dioxide can suffocate miners by displacing oxygen, and carbon monoxide can cause sickness or death. The well-ventilated underground mines of today often avoid problems with these gases, however.

Overburdens and the coal in surface mines are usually removed first by using explosives to break up the material and then by using large machines

by burning high-sulfur coal. Burning coal also gives off a lot of carbon dioxide, which has possibly contributed to global warming and the acidification of the oceans.

A number of other environmental problems are associated with the coal industry, such as the collapse or burning of coal in old, abandoned underground mines and the destruction of countryside caused by surface mining. Some mining operations in West Virginia have formed massive piles of fine-grained waste, much of which rapidly runs off into streams during major rainfalls. Now, mines are supposed to fix such problems, and the expense of doing so reduces their profit margins.

INDUSTRY MARKET SEGMENTS

The mining industry has moved from smaller mining operations to larger operations, mainly as a result of the higher profit margins that can be achieved with the greater resource investment potential of large mines. Large mines have the resources, for instance, to purchase the larger pieces of equipment needed to move a large amount of overburden and coal from surface mines, thus increasing the total amount of coal produced per worker.

Small Businesses

Small coal mines generally produce less than 500,000 tons of coal per year. Small companies often mine smaller seams of coal of lower quality than those mined by larger companies. Investors are not attracted to put money into smaller mines because of the low probability of realizing a profit, so small companies tend to use smaller and more economical machines than do large companies. Because they have high overhead relative to sales, small coal companies have low profit margins, so many may go out of business if, for example, the price of coal suddenly drops. Smaller companies are also less likely to be unionized.

Potential Annual Earnings Scale. According to the U.S. Bureau of Labor Statistics (BLS), continuous coal-mining machine operators earned an average of $47,550 in 2009, while construction equipment operators earned an average of $43,120 and operators of coal-excavating and -loading machines and draglines earned an average of $42,160. Mining and geological engineers in the coal industry earned $76,580, on average. General and operations managers averaged $105,730. Salaries for all of these positions are likely to be below these averages at small companies.

Clientele Interaction. Most persons working in coal mines have little interaction with clients since the coal is often sold to electrical generating plants or other industries. Small mines may not have their own sales departments, but in some cases one of the mine's personnel may make some sales. Small mines may hire their own sales agents, or they may even conduct sales through the sales departments of larger coal companies. Often, small companies sell their coal locally to minimize transportation costs, so their prices are competitive with larger mines that transport their coal over longer distances.

Amenities, Atmosphere, and Physical Grounds. Underground coal mines are generally not pleasant places for many people to work, and underground mining is one of the most dangerous jobs in the United States, even with the many safety regulations now in effect. Nevertheless, mining conditions are much improved over the horrible conditions common in the early twentieth century—although many small coal mines in China still present poor working conditions.

Underground coal mines make many people feel confined, and the mines are often dark, dusty, and musty. Underground mining machinery is extremely noisy. Even with safety regulations, accidents such as methane explosions, machinery accidents, and roof collapses still occur. Miners often interact in small groups, so they are aware of how to protect themselves and one another. Often, general mine workers come from families in which at least one other person has worked in a mine. Surface coal mines are more pleasant places for most people to work since they are open to the atmosphere, to which dust and gases can escape. Also, the noise of machinery and explosives is not as loud outdoors as it is in underground mines.

Typical Number of Employees. Mining companies seek to minimize labor expenses by employing as few people as possible. Small mines may employ fewer than twenty-five people full time, although they may need to hire supplemental temporary workers at times of high activity.

Traditional Geographic Locations. Coal mines must be located where there is mineable coal either close to or at the land's surface and where it is possible to conduct mining operations to reach that coal. They are almost always in rural areas, since it is not feasible to lease and mine on urban land. Sometimes, small towns comprising mostly miners are built near mines, and they are often largely abandoned once mining operations cease. Coal mines are often developed near coal purchasers to reduce transportation costs.

Pros of Working for a Small Mining Company. Employees of small companies may enjoy closer relationships with their fellow workers. They often must perform more than one task, which appeals to those seeking more varied work experiences.

Cons of Working for a Small Mining Company. While close interactions with coworkers can appeal to some miners, small companies afford few opportunities for employees to avoid any coworkers with whom they do not get along. If relationship problems arise, a worker may have no choice but to leave the company. This issue has arisen, for example, among women facing prejudice or harassment in what has traditionally been a male-dominated industry. Mining, moreover, entails a great deal of overhead, so small companies that are unable to exploit economies of scale may struggle to realize profits. Finally, coal miners in general receive pensions and other benefits through the major mining union, the United Mine Workers of America. Small mining companies are less likely to be unionized than larger companies, so their employees are less likely to have access to these benefits.

Costs

Payroll and Benefits: Most general mine employees are hired at hourly wages, while some professionals, such as engineers, may receive salaries. Other employees, such as electricians, may be hired temporarily on contract to perform specialized work. Generally, wages are lower in most small mines than in larger mines. Health benefits and compensation for injuries may be offered.

Supplies: Coal mining companies require very heavy machinery and explosives, the tools necessary to maintain the machinery, hand-mining tools, safety equipment, lights, surveying equipment, construction materials, storage and trans-portation containers and vehicles, gasoline, and air supplies. Their offices require standard office supplies and equipment.

External Services: Small mining companies may contract electricians, plumbers, explosive experts, geologists, mining engineers, or sales representatives. They may also contract individual independent truckers or large trucking companies, as well as freight railroad companies, to transport coal. Small companies often have limited access to railroad cars, and they may have to pay more for them than do large companies.

Utilities: Mining companies must pay for electricity, water, sewage, heating, telephone, and Internet access.

Taxes: Mining companies must pay local, state, and federal taxes and fees. State taxes may include sales, property, corporate income, or severance taxes. Severance taxes are calculated based on the amount or value of coal extracted. The highest state taxes are levied by Wyoming, at 15 percent of gross revenue (0 percent sales, 10.5 percent severance, 1 percent property, and 3.5 percent corporate income). The lowest are levied by Utah, which charges only a property tax equal to 0.6 percent of gross revenue.

Other Expenses: There are other kinds of costs that influence small coal mines, such as the reclamation and safety costs resulting from the Coal Mine and Safety Act of 1969 and the Mine Control and Reclamation Act of 1977. These costs made it impossible for many small mines to stay in business. The Clean Air Act of 1990 indirectly affects coal mines since it requires that coal-burning electrical power plants emit no more than 1.2 pounds of sulfur dioxide gas per 1 million British thermal units (BTU) of heat produced. This regulation caused some coal mines with high-sulfur coals to go out of business. Finally, most small mining operations are nonunion. If these nonunion mines sell coal to union mining companies, the National Bituminous Coal Wage Agreement (1978) requires that they pay a significant fee per ton of coal sold. This has also helped drive some small mines out of business.

Midsize Businesses

Midsize coal businesses produce between 500,000 tons and 1 million tons of coal per year.

Many of these companies operate intrastate, integrated, or interstate mines. Intrastate mining businesses operate multiple mines in one state. Integrated mining businesses mine coal for their own use. Interstate mining businesses have mines in different states. Investors are more often attracted to invest in midsize coal businesses than to small ones, allowing midsize companies to purchase more and larger equipment to more rapidly and efficiently access, extract, process, and transport coal. Often, midsize coal businesses have the resources to mine coal beds that are thicker or deeper than those that small businesses are able to exploit. Some midsize businesses may have the resources to develop new mines, which typically take up to ten years, from the planning and development stage to the extraction stage, before any money can be made.

Potential Annual Earnings Scale. According to the BLS, continuous coal-mining machine operators earned an average of $47,550 in 2009, while construction equipment operators earned an average of $43,120 and operators of coal-excavating and -loading machines and draglines earned an average of $42,160. Mining and geological engineers in the coal industry earned $76,580, on average. General and operations managers averaged $105,730. Salaries at midsize companies are likely to be roughly in line with these averages.

Hourly workers in the eastern United States generally earn less money than do those working the same job in the western United States. Union mine workers sometimes earn more money than nonunion workers in similar jobs. Finally, hourly employees working in surface mines earn more for a corresponding job than do those in underground mines. By contrast, employees with a yearly salary usually earn more money in underground mines than do those in corresponding jobs in surface mines, with the exception of environmental coordinators.

Clientele Interaction. Most midsize mining company employees have even less opportunity to interact with clients than do those of small companies. Midsize companies are more likely to have their own sales departments to sell directly to buyers such as electrical power generating plants.

Amenities, Atmosphere, and Physical Grounds. Underground mines run by midsize coal companies may be bigger than those run by small companies, but they are still dark, damp, dirty, and noisy. There is still a possibility for accidents, such as roof falls, sudden water intrusions from other mines, or explosions. Many midsize mining companies employ special personnel to implement safety rules for mine workers and to train the workers in such protocols. As a result, there is often a lower rate of accidents at midsize coal companies than at small coal companies. Miners still work together in small groups for safety. Surface coal mines remain more pleasant to work in than underground mines.

Typical Number of Employees. Midsize companies employ from twenty to several hundred persons, most of whom work full time. In 2001 in the United States, there were 823 midsize coal mines, employing a total of nearly sixty thousand miners and twenty-seven hundred office workers. Most

An excavator in action at a coal mine. (©Dreamstime.com)

miners at midsize companies perform only one job function each.

Traditional Geographic Locations. Coal mines must be located where there is mineable coal either close to or at the land's surface and where it is possible to conduct mining operations to reach that coal. They are almost always in rural areas, since it is not feasible to lease and mine on urban land. Sometimes, small towns comprising mostly miners are built near mines, and they are often largely abandoned once mining operations cease. Coal mines are often developed near coal purchasers to reduce transportation costs. Some mines, known as "captive mines," sell all their coal to a single purchaser, such as an electrical power station neighboring a given mine.

Pros of Working for a Midsize Coal Company. Employees of midsize coal companies may work at only one kind of job, rather than having to split their attention among multiple functions as may be necessary at small companies. They tend to have opportunities for satisfying personal interactions with other employees within the same working

group, although a miner may not know everyone else working at the same mine. Salaries paid by midsize companies are likely to be somewhat higher than those paid by small companies. Midsize mines are more likely to be profitable than small mines, while they are less likely to have accidents.

Cons of Working for a Midsize Coal Company. Some miners may not enjoy working at the same job every day, especially in underground mines filled with dust, noise, and the possibility of severe accidents. Midsize companies are still small enough that it may be difficult to avoid coworkers or supervisors with whom one has personal difficulties.

Costs

Payroll and Benefits: General mine employees in midsize coal companies are paid hourly wages, while supervisors and technical employees are paid yearly salaries. As at small mining companies, some people may be hired on short contracts to perform specialized work. Wages for many jobs tend to be higher in midsize coal

A coal mine in Wyoming. (©Phil Augustavo/iStockphoto.com)

companies than in smaller companies. Midsize companies are more likely to be unionized than small companies. If they are, they are required to contribute toward employee benefits and pensions.

Supplies: Coal mining companies require very heavy machinery and explosives, the tools necessary to maintain the machinery, hand-mining tools, safety equipment, lights, surveying equipment, construction materials, storage and transportation containers and vehicles, gasoline, and air supplies. Their offices require standard office supplies and equipment. The machinery employed by midsize companies is often bigger and more expensive than that employed by small companies. This machinery is often custom-made on-site, so replacement parts and repairs can be very expensive.

External Services: Midsize mining companies are more likely to have full complements of workers than are small companies, but they may still contract electricians, plumbers, explosive experts, geologists, mining engineers, or sales representatives as necessary. They may also contract individual independent truckers or large trucking companies, as well as freight railroad companies, to transport coal.

Utilities: Mining companies must pay for electricity, water, sewage, heating, telephone, and Internet access.

Taxes: Mining companies must pay local, state, and federal taxes and fees. State taxes may include sales, property, corporate income, or severance taxes. Severance taxes are calculated based on the amount or value of coal extracted. The highest state taxes are levied by Wyoming, at 15 percent of gross revenue (0 percent sales, 10.5 percent severance, 1 percent property, and 3.5 percent corporate income). The lowest are levied by Utah, which charges only a property tax equal to 0.6 percent of gross revenue.

Other Expenses: Midsize companies must pay the same reclamation and safety costs as small companies.

Large Businesses

Large coal mining businesses produce more than 1 million tons of coal per year; some of them produce considerably more. Many operate interstate and intrastate mines. Large coal businesses

have a great deal of power, and they can, for instance, set coal prices and sell their coal directly to users. Large coal businesses can attract investors to purchase huge pieces of equipment, such as draglines and trucks, to move coal more efficiently and thus make more money. Large coal businesses have large corporate headquarters with many layers of executives and staff. Some of these staff members work to acquire smaller companies, expanding the large companies' holdings and operations. Large companies often serve a number of coal users, especially those on the East Coast.

Potential Annual Earnings Scale. According to the BLS, continuous coal-mining machine operators earned an average of $47,550 in 2009, while construction equipment operators earned an average of $43,120 and operators of coal-excavating and -loading machines and draglines earned an average of $42,160. Mining and geological engineers in the coal industry earned $76,580, on average. General and operations managers averaged $105,730. Salaries at large companies are likely to be equal to or greater than these averages.

Clientele Interaction. Hourly mineworkers and many managers have no interaction with clients. Large companies often have large sales departments that sell coal directly to users such as electrical power generating plants.

Amenities, Atmosphere, and Physical Grounds. Underground mines in large mining companies are still dark, dirty, and noisy. Large companies, however, have better safety training programs than smaller companies, so their accident rates are lower. Surface coal mines operated by large companies are huge compared to those of smaller companies. For example, some such mines use specialized equipment, such as electric shovels and draglines with twenty- to fifty-cubic-meter shovels or 170-ton trucks that are two stories high and ten meters wide with V-16 three-thousand-horsepower engines. Some large mines may operate twenty-four hours per day, seven days per week. Their headquarters are large offices, housing executives and support staff such as secretaries, computer specialists, and various helpers.

Typical Number of Employees. Large companies employ hundreds or thousands of workers. For example, ten large mining operations in 2001 employed 5,500 miners and 174 office staff. Most employees work at only one specialized job. For ex-

A front-end loader picks up a shovel full of coal. (©Jason Doucette/iStockphoto.com)

ample, one miner may drill holes for explosive charges, while another may place the charges, and still others may support these two demolition experts.

Traditional Geographic Locations. Coal mines must be located where there is mineable coal either close to or at the land's surface and where it is possible to conduct mining operations to reach that coal. They are almost always in rural areas, since it is not feasible to lease and mine on urban land. Sometimes, small towns comprising mostly miners are built near mines, and they are often largely abandoned once mining operations cease. Coal mines are often developed near coal purchasers to reduce transportation costs. Some mines, known as "captive mines," sell all their coal to a single purchaser, such as an electrical power station neighboring a given mine.

Pros of Working for a Large Coal Company. Employees of large mines may be quite specialized, allowing them to gain significant experience and expertise in a particular task. They often work together in small groups, developing personal and professional relationships within each group. Pay is generally better at large companies than at smaller ones. Employees who work hard and get along well with others may have greater opportuni-

ties for advancement than are available in smaller companies.

Cons of Working for a Large Coal Company. Some miners may not enjoy working at the same job every day, especially in underground mines filled with dust, noise, and the possibility of severe accidents. Large companies are often heavily regulated; while these regulations may result in better conditions for some workers, they may also represent significant obstacles for managers. In addition to these external regulations, large companies often develop their own internal bureaucracies, which can reduce efficiency and frustrate some workers, especially those in middle management.

Costs

Payroll and Benefits: General mine employees in large coal companies are paid hourly wages, while supervisors and technical employees are paid yearly salaries, and contract workers are hired as necessary to perform specialized work. Large companies are often unionized and provide benefits and pensions accordingly.

Supplies: Coal mining companies require very heavy machinery and explosives, the tools necessary to maintain the machinery, hand-mining tools, safety equipment, lights, surveying equipment, construction materials, storage and transportation containers and vehicles, gasoline, and air supplies. Their offices require standard office supplies and equipment. The machinery employed by large companies is often bigger and more expensive than that employed by smaller companies. This machinery is often custom-made on-site, so replacement parts and repairs can be very expensive.

External Services: Large mining companies are more likely to have full complements of workers than are smaller companies, but they may still contract electricians, plumbers, explosive experts, geologists, or mining engineers as necessary. They may also contract individual independent truckers or large trucking companies, as well as freight railroad companies, to transport coal.

Utilities: Mining companies must pay for electricity, water, sewage, heating, telephone, and Internet access.

Taxes: Mining companies must pay local, state, and federal taxes and fees. State taxes may include sales, property, corporate income, or severance taxes. Severance taxes are calculated based on the amount or value of coal extracted. The highest state taxes are levied by Wyoming, at 15 percent of gross revenue (0 percent sales, 10.5 percent severance, 1 percent property, and 3.5 percent corporate income). The lowest are levied by Utah, which charges only a property tax equal to 0.6 percent of gross revenue.

Other Expenses: Large companies must pay the same reclamation and safety costs as small companies.

ORGANIZATIONAL STRUCTURE AND JOB ROLES

The organization of jobs and tasks is similar at different-sized coal companies, but the way these tasks are implemented may be somewhat different. For example, some coal mining engineers in larger mines may be in charge of mine studies and design, others may oversee the construction of the mine, and others may oversee daily operations. In smaller coal mines, only a few engineers may work on these tasks, so one engineer may have a number of differ-

ent jobs. Some of the best engineers may be promoted into management.

The following umbrella categories apply to the organizational structure of businesses in the coal mining industry:

- Executive Management
- On-Site Management
- Sales
- Operations
- Administration and Human Resources
- Maintenance and Warehouse
- Transportation
- Environmental Control and Safety

Executive Management

The layers of management can be quite extensive in large mining operations, but they are much more limited in smaller ones. In large mining operations, there may be a chief executive officer (CEO), a president, and a number of vice presidents. These managers, for instance, look at the broader aspects of managing many mines, including acquiring new mines, funding, purchasing equipment, ensuring that their companies are working smoothly, and assessing their overall budgets. Smaller companies are more likely to simply have on-site managers for their mines.

Executives are often college graduates with a number of years of experience in management, and they include some mining engineers who have been promoted. Executives earn the most money of anyone in their companies. CEOs of the largest companies, for example, can earn millions of dollars in salaries and stock benefits. The average annual income of a coal mining executive was $103,770 in 2009.

Executive managment occupations may include the following:

- Chief Executive Officer (CEO)
- Chief Financial Officer (CFO)
- Chief Operating Officer (COO)
- President
- Vice President
- Chief Sales Officer

On-Site Management

Each active mine within a company has its own general manager, who is in charge of the entire operation at that mine. Larger companies may also assign each mine its own on-site managers of accounting, engineering, coal processing, personnel, and maintenance. Within each mine, a pit supervisor is usually directly responsible for ensuring that coal extraction is moving smoothly and for resolving any problems that arise. Generally, mining engineers solve major problems that interfere with mining operations, since they are the employees who have planned, developed, and maintained those operations. Other supervisors may oversee processing plants, loading facilities, office buildings, repair buildings, or roads in a given mining area. Some geologists may manage the search for new coal beds, especially if such beds are likely to be folded or fractured rather than horizontal and continuous.

Engineering and geology managers must have at least bachelor's degrees, and some may have master's degrees. They also generally have a number of years of mining experience. Pit supervisors may have begun as general mine workers without any college work and been promoted up the chain of command. Engineering managers earned an average of $107,370 in 2009.

On-site management occupations may include the following:

- General Manager
- Chief Engineer
- Mining Engineer
- Construction Engineer
- Pit Engineer
- Geologist
- Pit Supervisor

Sales

Sales personnel attempt to negotiate the best price for their companies' coal through short-term and long-term contracts. Smaller companies may employ their own sales staffs, or they may sell their coal through larger companies. Sales personnel may also negotiate transportation contracts. Sales managers, for example, may establish contacts with

---

OCCUPATION PROFILE

Geologist and Geophysicist

Considerations	Qualifications
Description	Studies the physical composition and structure of the Earth.
Career clusters	Agriculture, Food, and Natural Resources; Science, Technology, Engineering, and Math
Interests	Data; things
Working conditions	Work both inside and outside
Minimum education level	Bachelor's degree; master's degree; doctoral degree
Physical exertion	Light work; medium work
Physical abilities	Unexceptional/basic fitness
Opportunities for experience	Military service; part-time work
Licensure and certification	Usually not required
Employment outlook	Faster-than-average growth expected
Holland interest scores	IRE; IRS

Note: See volume 1, "Publisher's Note," for an explanation of the Holland interest score.

electrical power generating companies or other industrial purchasers to determine the types and quantities of coal that they desire. They must take into account the locations of prospective purchasers and the anticipated expenses of supplying coal to each purchaser when negotiating prices. Managers may also need to train the sales representatives who will have the most direct contact with users.

Salespeople usually have college degrees in marketing, business, or related fields and should be able to speak and write well and use word-processing, spreadsheet, and statistical computer programs. Coal mining sales staff members earned an average of $78,260 in 2009.

Sales occupations may include the following:

- Sales Manager
- Sales Representative

Operations

Operations personnel perform the actual mining and extraction of coal. In surface mines, these personnel may include various kinds of explosives experts, as well as equipment operators who break up and move overburden and coal. Some, for instance, may operate scrapers, wheeled vehicles that can scrape and move overburden to another location. Powder crews can also use explosives to break up overburden and coal, so they can then be removed by large machines. Smaller coal mines may employ outside contractors to perform such tasks, but large mines employ their own scraper and powder crews. Any size company can use bulldozers or front-end loaders to move overburden and coal. Both machines have front shovels to push or carry material, but bulldozers run on treads, whereas front-end loaders have wheels. Loading shovels and draglines have huge scoops to move material directly into large trucks. Loading shovels move on treads, but draglines can be moved only slowly. Loading shovels and draglines are usually too expensive to be used by small mines.

Other specialized equipment is used to remove coal in the confined spaces of underground mines. For instance, coal plows with moving blades can shear off underground coal in pieces and move them by conveyor belt to where they can be transported out of the mine. Rotary drum shearers have even larger rotating blades that break up coal. As in surface mines, explosives may be used to break up coal into pieces that can be picked up with loaders and moved to conveyors or mining cars. Alternately, another kind of machine with vertical rotating drums, a "dash three miner," may break up the coal and move the coal pieces to a conveyor.

The general coal mine workers who operate these machines are often high school graduates with mechanical skills, and they are trained at coal mines upon employment to operate heavy machinery. The most successful workers are those who are willing to work hard, who can get along with co-workers and supervisors, and who precisely follow managers' rules for operating equipment. The mean hourly wages for the most common operations occupations in 2009 ranged from $20.73 to $22.86.

Operations occupations may include the following:

- Scraper Operator
- Powder Crew Worker
- Bulldozer/Front-End Loader Operator
- Shovel/Dragline Operator
- Coal Plow/Rotary Drum Operator
- Conveyor Operator
- General Laborer

Administration and Human Resources

A variety of office personnel support coal mining executives, managers, and sales staff. These include secretaries, clerks, human resources administrators, computer specialists, and accountants. They help their superiors perform such necessary chores as filling out government forms, balancing the books, paying taxes, and running errands. Human resources personnel administer employee benefits, fill out paperwork for hiring and dismissal, and oversee employee relations. The mean annual income of a coal mining office or administrative support worker was $36,150 in 2009.

Administration and human resources occupations may include the following:

- Secretary
- Clerk
- Accountant
- Computer Specialist
- Human Resources Manager
- Human Resources Coordinator

Maintenance and Warehouse

A mine's equipment, electrical lines, plumbing, water supply, and air supply need to be maintained, and any problems in these systems must be fixed quickly so that coal production is not stopped. Mechanics, welders, electricians, and plumbers carry out these tasks. Smaller mining operations may hire some of these workers on a contract basis as needed to fix a given problem. Larger mining operations, however, may have full-time employees who can respond to problems as they arise. Mining personnel may also make some spot repairs on some of the bigger machines, but major repairs may need to be made by the manufacturers. Mechanics may also be hired to fix trucks and other coal-transport vehicles.

Maintenance personnel should have the mechanical abilities and training necessary to repair any problems within their areas of responsibility. Many are high school graduates. Pay ranges are similar to those of machine operators.

Maintenance and warehouse occupations may include the following:

- Electrician
- Plumber
- Welder
- Mechanic
- Helper
- Laborer
- Warehouse Worker

Transportation

Coal must be transported out of mines by conveyors, carts, and loaders and into trucks that take it to and from railroads to its destination. Coal companies generally contract with railroads to transport coal, and larger mines are generally able to negotiate better prices and easier access to coal cars than the smaller mines. Truck drivers and other transportation employees should have enough mechanical ability to perform their assigned tasks. Drivers also require commercial driving licenses. Most are high school graduates. Pay ranges are similar to those of the other machine operators.

Transportation occupations may include the following:

- Conveyor Operator
- Freight Loader/Unloader
- Truck Driver

Environmental Control and Safety

Environmental control and safety personnel address environmental and safety problems: They seek to decrease acid drainage, avoid accidents, and ensure that overburdens are placed back over surface mines after the coal has been removed. For example, some of the bulldozer and front-end loader operators who initially remove the overburden and coal may need to use their machines to backfill mine pits with overburden material and soil and to plant vegetation on top of it. Safety experts attempt to train miners to avoid accidents and to check for poisonous or explosive gases in underground mines. Environmental specialists attempt, for example, to reduce acid mine drainage. Some of these personnel may not work directly for mining companies; instead, they may be employed as consultants.

Environmental specialists and safety experts are likely to have some college education and further training in their specialties. Environmental engineers in the coal industry earned an average of $79,490 in 2009, while environmental engineering technicians earned an average of $45,940.

Environmental control and safety occupations may include the following:

- Environmental Coordinator
- Environmental Science Technician
- Safety Trainer
- Bulldozer/Front-End Loader Operator

INDUSTRY OUTLOOK

Overview

The outlook for coal mining suggests that coal production will increase worldwide between 2010 and 2030 by nearly 50 percent. This projected increase contrasts with other mining industries, which are expected to decline in production over the same period. In the United States, the energy produced by coal is expected to increase from 22 quadrillion BTU in 2006 to 26.6 quadrillion BTU in 2030. Coal in the United States is mostly used for electrical generation; lesser amounts are employed for industrial applications such as steel and cement production. Electrical production is expected to grow in the future, so coal use is likely to become even more important. Western states such as Wyoming and Montana are expected to increase their coal production, while eastern states such as West Virginia are expected to decrease production.

The expected increase in coal use for energy is subject to change as technology and markets change. Natural gas, nuclear energy, wind, solar energy, and hydroelectric facilities can also be used to produce electricity. Natural gas prices have fluctuated and have generally increased more than coal prices, making coal use more attractive. Nevertheless, these other fuel sources are expected to increase in use alongside coal.

Fuel cells are also being used by some major companies, such as Google and Walmart, in some of their plants to reduce the amount of outside electricity used. If the use of fuel cells or other alternative energy sources increases drastically, the amount of coal required by electrical plants could decrease. Moreover, environmental problems may decrease or hamper the growth of coal, especially in the United States, where energy reform is an ongoing concern of the federal government.

Most of Canada's domestic coal use, like that of the United States, is dedicated to electrical generation. Canada also exports about 40 percent of its coal to coal-poor countries such as Japan. Canada's coal production is expected to increase between 2010 and 2030.

Increased energy use in China is expected to increase coal production in that country by over 100 percent by 2030, as annual production goes from 24.9 quadrillion BTU in 2006 to 57 quadrillion BTU in 2030. This growth rate is markedly higher than that of the United States or Canada. The predicted increase in coal production in China is partly due to the country's lack of natural gas and petroleum resources, forcing it to rely more heavily on coal. China also plans greatly to expand electrical production and other industries that use coal, such as the steel industry. It also plans rapidly to increase production of synthetic liquids derived from the processing of coal. China is investing significant resources in improving its coal production and building new railroads to meet the expected higher demand for coal.

Coal use in Europe and Russia is not likely to grow as much as in China, and in some European countries coal use may actually decrease by 2030. Environmental problems arising from the use of coal will contribute to this possible decrease. Some countries plan to more rapidly increase their use of renewable resources and natural gas. Australia and New Zealand are expected slowly to increase coal use, from 2.6 quadrillion BTU in 2006 to 2.9 quadrillion BTU in 2030.

South Africa uses most of the coal in Africa. Its coal use is expected to increase slowly between 2010 and 2030. Several old electrical generating plants that use coal have been reopened, and a number of other plants are being planned. The use of coal in Central and South America is also expected slowly to increase. Brazil is the largest coal producer in this region, with much of its coal being used in large steel mills.

Employment Advantages

Coal production is expected to grow in the United States through 2018, according to the BLS, especially in the light of the projected increased use of coal to generate electricity. However, the continued demand for coal is expected to raise industry employment by only 4 percent, less than the average increase of 11 percent across all industries. Miners, on average, are in their early fifties, so many miners are expected to retire soon, increasing the number of available positions.

A wide range of jobs is available in the coal industry, especially for those persons who enjoy working outside in surface mines or underground in subsurface mines. Those who like technical work, science, and mathematics can gain college degrees in mining engineering, geology, or environmental science. Those who like working or repairing machines, have high school diplomas, and enjoy working hard can obtain specialized training, often at mine sites, to become equipment operators, truck drivers, or repair personnel. Those who like to work in office buildings can seek work as secretaries, computer specialists, accountants, or general office workers. These jobs likely will require some advanced training beyond high school. Other office jobs include administrators and managers, but these positions require significant work experience in mining and often college degrees in business or engineering.

Annual Earnings

Coal mining, like other types of mining and the petroleum industry, has experienced a number of changes in production in response to issues of supply and demand. Coal production, however, has seen less fluctuation than metal or petroleum production. For example, coal production in the United States varied from about 600 million to 675 million tons from 1944 to 1949, but production decreased to 450 million to 475 million tons between 1950 and 1965. Then coal production increased to about 1.1 billion tons in 2005, with a net worth of over $18 billion. Of that total, surface coal mines produced over $8 billion worth of coal, and subsurface mines produced over $9 billion worth of coal. The price per ton of coal has also varied signifiantly with time: In 1950, coal cost about $5 per ton, rising to nearly $20 per ton in 1975. Since 1975, coal prices have ranged from $17 to $25 per ton.

RELATED RESOURCES FOR FURTHER RESEARCH

ENERGY INFORMATION ADMINISTRATION
1000 Independence Ave. SW
Washington, DC 20585
Tel: (202) 586-8800
http://www.eia.doe.gov

MINE SAFETY AND HEALTH ASSOCIATION
1100 Wilson Blvd., 21st Floor
Arlington, VA 22090-3939
Tel: (201) 693-9400
http://www.nsga.gov

NATIONAL MINING ASSOCIATION
101 Constitution Ave. NW, Suite 500 East
Washington, DC 2001-2133
Tel: (202) 463-2600
Fax: (202) 463-2666
http://www.nma.org

SOCIETY FOR MINING, METALLURGY, AND
EXPLORATION
8307 Shaffer Parkway
Littleton, CO 80127
Tel: (800) 763-3132
http://www.smenet.org

UNITED MINE WORKERS OF AMERICA
8315 Lee Hwy.
Fairfax, VA 22031

Tel: (703) 208-7200
http://www.umwa.org

WORLD COAL ASSOCIATION
5th Floor, Heddon House
149-151 Regent St.
London
W1B 4JD
United Kingdom
Tel: 44-20-7851-0052
Fax: 44-20-7851-0061
http://www.worldcoal.org

ABOUT THE AUTHOR

Robert Cullers has carried out research and taught geology and geochemistry for more than thirty years at Kansas State University, including courses in natural resources, mineralogy, petrology, and water chemistry. He received a bachelor's degree in geology in 1959 and a master's degree in chemistry in 1962 from Indiana University, as well as a Ph.D. in geology-geochemistry from the University of Wisconsin, Madison, in 1971.

FURTHER READING

Brister, Brian S., and L. Greer Price. *New Mexico's Energy, Present, and Future.* Socorro: New Mexico Bureau of Geology and Mineral Resources, 2002.

Burke, D. Barlow, and Robert E. Beck. *The Law and Regulation of Mining: Minerals to Energy.* Durham, N.C.: Carolina Academic Press, 2010.

Craig, James R., David J. Vaughn, and Brian J. Skinner. *Resources of the Earth: Origin, Use, and Environmental Impact.* Upper Saddle River, N.J.: Prentice Hall, 2001.

Godell, Jeff. *Big Coal: The Dirty Secret Behind America's Energy Future.* New York: Houghton Mifflin, 2006.

Gore, Tony, et al. *Coalfields and Neighbouring Cities: Economic Regeneration, Labour Markets, and Governance.* York, North Yorkshire, England: Joseph Rowntree Foundation, 2007.

Kolker, Allan, et al. *Emissions from Coal Fires and Their Impact on the Environment.* Reston, Va.: U.S. Geological Survey, 2009.

Parker, Philip M. *The 2009-2014 World Outlook for Coal Mining*. San Diego, Calif.: ICON Group, 2008.

Rouse, Michael J., and Usher Fleising. "Miners and Managers: Workplace Cultures in a British Columbia Coal Mine." *Human Organization* 54 (1995): 238-248.

Schmidt, Richard A. *Coal in America: An Encyclopedia of Reserves, Production, and Use*. New York: McGraw-Hill, 1979.

Simpson, David. *Productivity in Natural Resource Industries: Improvement Through Innovation*. Washington, D.C.: Resources for the Future, 1999.

Thomas, Larry. *Coal Geology*. Hoboken, N.J.: John Wiley & Sons, 2002.

U.S. Bureau of Labor Statistics. *Career Guide to Industries*, 2010-2011 ed. http://www.bls.gov/oco/cg.

U.S. Census Bureau. North American Industry Classification System (NAICS), 2007. http://www.census.gov/cgi-bin/sssd/naics/naicsrch?chart=2007.

U.S. Department of Commerce. International Trade Administration. Office of Trade and Industry Information. Industry Trade Data and Analysis. http://ita.doc.gov/td/industry/otea/OTII/OTII-index.html.

Complementary and Alternative Health Care Industry

©Dreamstime.com

INDUSTRY SNAPSHOT

General Industry: Health Science
Career Cluster: Health Science
Subcategory Industries: Acupuncturists' Offices;
Chiropractors' Offices; Herbalists' Offices; Homeopaths'
Offices; Hypnotherapists' Offices; Midwives' Offices;
Naturopaths' Offices
Related Industries: Health and Fitness Industry; Hospital
Care and Services; Medicine and Health Care Industry;
Personal Services
Annual Domestic Revenues: $33.9 billion USD (National
Health Statistics Report, 2009)
NAICS Numbers: 62131, 621399

INDUSTRY DEFINITION

Summary

The complementary and alternative health or medical care (CAM) industry produces and applies a wide range of herbal, vitamin, and food remedies; patient-practiced therapies; and practitioner services. They are not considered part of conventional medical practice, although complementary care may be used along with it. Alternative health care, by contrast, is used in place of conventional medical care and can interfere with it. For example, herbal therapy could interact with conventional medications. Patients turn to CAM therapies when conventional medical care is not relieving their symptoms, such as chronic pain. In the United States, these therapies are most often used by well-educated Caucasian women.

History of the Industry

Some CAM therapies have been in practice since the beginning of human civilization. Herbs have been used to treat and prevent illness for at least as long as the concept of an herb has existed. Midwives, or their ancient equivalent, were most likely the first non-family members to assist in the delivery of infants. The ancient Chinese developed a medical system that included acupuncture for the treatment of their health problems.

Early physicians were not interested in delivering infants. As a result, untrained midwives delivered all infants until the 1700's. If a mother had complications of delivery, she often died because midwives lacked medical skills. In the 1700's, surgeons began to deliver infants for the wealthy. New York City began to require that midwives be licensed. In 1799, doctors Valentine Seaman and William Shippen opened a school to train midwives. In the early 1800's, physicians began to take over the delivery of infants for the middle class. The practice of midwifery declined. Increasingly, mothers delivered their infants in hospitals.

In the 1970's, women clamored for the opportunity to demedicalize childbirth and to deliver their infants at home. Nursing schools began to offer programs in nurse-midwifery. Both nurse-midwives and nonnurse midwives received formal training. Physicians fought to hold onto childbirth, and laws were created to limit the practice of midwifery. Many states required that midwives practice only under the supervision of physicians. Other states licensed nonnurse midwives and permitted them to practice independently.

There is evidence that acupuncture has been practiced for at least eight thousand years. From 650 to 692 c.e., the development and practice of acupuncture increased, and acupuncture schools were established. In 1911, Western medicine was introduced to China, and acupuncture and herbal medicines experienced a decline. In 1950, the Chinese merged Western medicine with acupuncture. Gradually, acupuncture came to the United States. Starting in 1971, acupuncture began to be well known in the United States, and by 1997, it was widely available.

Chiropractic care was recognized as a medical treatment in 1895. It was introduced by Daniel David Palmer. Spinal adjustment is the basis of chiropractic medicine, and it is used to treat a wide variety of conditions. It is thought that spinal adjustment has been practiced since ancient times. Palmer defined the practice of chiropractics and started a training school. In the early 1900's, states began regulating and licensing chiropractors.

Homeopathy was developed by a German physician, Samuel Hahnemann, in 1796. It was introduced to the United States in 1828 by John Franklin Gray. It was quite popular with patients in the early 1900's, in part because conventional medical treatments were often ineffective. Homeopathy is frequently criticized by conventional medicine as being ineffective. Very little research has been done to establish its effectiveness.

Naturopathy was introduced to the United States in the late 1800's by Benedict Lust, although it had been practiced in Germany earlier. In the early 1900's, it was widely accepted, but after that it experienced a decline in popularity. Beginning in the 1970's, there has been increased interest in natural treatments such as those proposed by naturopaths.

Hypnosis was originally performed as part of the system of Chinese medicine. It was not studied and practiced until the 1800's. James Braid, a Scottish surgeon, began this exploration. Subsequently, the study of hypnosis became popular in France. One of the students of the French school of hypnosis was Sigmund Freud. Hypnosis was first studied in the United States in 1933 by Clark L. Hull.

The Industry Today

CAM is fairly popular today, in part because conventional medical care is sometimes impersonal and fragmented. Consumers want to be treated as whole people, not just body parts. Stress-related symptoms are common in contemporary society. Some conventional medical treatments do not cure patients or treat their symptoms effectively. CAM practitioners practice holistic medicine, meaning

Acupuncture is used to treat a wide variety of conditions, such as depression, chronic pain, and the nausea caused by chemotherapy. (©Dreamstime.com)

that they base their treatments on the total needs of each individual patient, rather than concentrating only on the particular system or body part that demonstrates symptoms. Patients' medical and psychological histories, body types, and family histories are all considered when treating them. CAM providers have been successful in treating some health issues that conventional medicine has been unable to cure.

Acupuncture is used to treat a wide variety of conditions, such as depression, chronic pain, and the nausea caused by chemotherapy. An acupuncturist inserts many very fine needles into various locations on the body to assist the flow of chi, or life energy. Acupuncturists work in individual or group practices, and some are employed by hospitals in their integrative therapy clinics. Persons with no medical training must have at least two thousand hours of acupuncture training in order to practice acupuncture. Some physicians, dentists, and other medical practitioners train in the practice of acupuncture. If they use it in their regular practices,

they need one to two hundred hours of training. If they plan to devote their practices solely to acupuncture, they require fifteen hundred hours of training. Most states require licensure for acupuncturists.

Most midwives choose to become nurse-midwives to avoid the legal limitations placed upon nonnurse midwives. Nurse-midwives have master's degrees in nursing with majors in midwifery. They are usually employed by either physician practices or hospitals. In physicians' offices, nurse-midwives provide pre- and postnatal care, and they also assist in delivery rooms. They perform only normal vaginal deliveries. If there appears to be a complication during childbirth, a physician takes over the delivery. Nurse-midwives do not perform surgery. They are permitted to prescribe medications in some states. Some states permit nurse-midwives and nonnurse midwives to have their own practices and to participate in home childbirth.

Chiropractors practice either alone or with other chiropractors. They can also practice as part

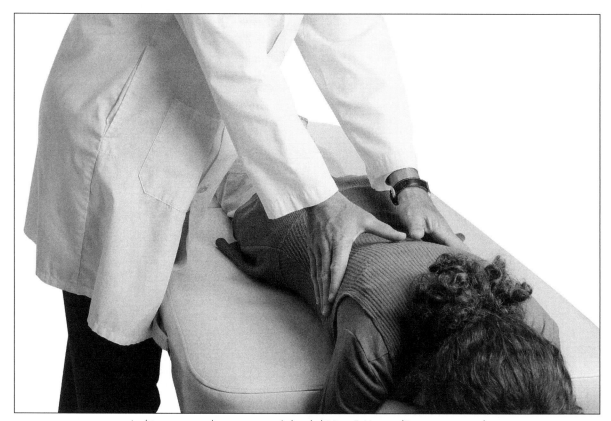

A chiropractor adjusts a woman's back. (©Lisa F. Young/Dreamstime.com)

This traditional Chinese herbalist works in a Chinatown neighborhood of New York City. (Getty Images)

of hospital-based integrative medical clinics, but this is not as common. Chiropractors work on the musculoskeletal and nervous systems. Frequently, they use spinal realignment as a treatment to improve nerve conduction. Potential chiropractors must have at least ninety semester hours of undergraduate study, or bachelor's degrees, before they can enter chiropractic programs. Such programs provide four years of training in the medical sciences and public health, and they grant the degree of doctor of chiropractic (DC). Licensure is required for the practice of chiropractic in all U.S. states and the District of Columbia.

The basis of the practice of homeopathy is the belief that "like cures like" and that the body is able to heal itself of symptoms by confronting similar symptoms. Homeopaths use very dilute solutions of substances that come from plants, minerals, or animals to treat their patients. Homeopathy is often used to treat allergies, rheumatoid arthritis, irritable bowel syndrome, minor injuries, and muscle sprains. It is never used to treat persons with severe, acute injuries or serious illnesses such as heart disease or cancer. Homeopaths may be medi-

cal doctors who have taken homeopathy courses, or they may be nonphysicians who have taken four-year courses in homeopathy. Only three states license homeopaths: Arizona, Connecticut, and Nevada. Licensure for homeopathy does not include standards for practice.

Naturopaths believe that an imbalance in one's life is the cause of illness and that by restoring a natural balance, the illness can be cured. The balance is restored by natural treatments and improvements in lifestyle. Naturopaths do not perform any surgical procedures. They are trained as general practitioners or primary care providers and are able to treat a wide range of conditions. A bachelor's degree, including completion of premedical courses, is required for admission to a school of naturopathy. Naturopathy students study for four to five years. Often, the fifth year of study is devoted to a specialty such as obstetrics. There are only three or four schools of naturopathy in the United States and Canada. A number of states have licensure requirements and standards for practice. These standards include education and passing the Naturopathic Physicians Licensing Examina-

Pills used in homeopathy. The basis of the practice of homeopathy is the belief that "like cures like." (©Frank Pieth/ iStockphoto.com)

tions (NPLEX). The areas requiring licensure are Alaska, Arizona, California, Connecticut, Hawaii, Idaho, Kansas, Maine, Montana, New Hampshire, Oregon, Utah, Vermont, Washington, the District of Columbia, Puerto Rico, and the U.S. Virgin Islands.

Hypnosis consists of guided relaxation and focused attention that induces a trancelike state in which the subject blocks out external stimuli. It is thought that hypnosis increases suggestibility and helps subjects change their thoughts. Not everyone is susceptible to hypnosis. Hypnosis is used to achieve weight loss and to treat addictions to cigarettes, alcohol, and drugs; insomnia; anxiety; asthma; and irritable bowel syndrome. Hypnosis has been successfully used to alleviate the pain of childbirth. There are no educational requirements for hypnotists in the United States, so consumers must evaluate hypnotists themselves. Some psychologists, counselors, psychiatrists, and dentists are trained in hypnosis. Four states—Colorado, Connecticut, Indiana, and Washington—require licensure for hypnotists, and some other states regulate their practice.

An important issue for CAM providers and recipients is health insurance coverage. Many health insurance plans do not cover any CAM therapies. Of the classes of those therapies, chiropractic and acupuncture are the most likely to be covered by health insurance, but insurance plans may limit the number and frequency of treatments for which they will pay. Other plans may contract with specific CAM providers and obtain discounts for their members. Most CAM treatments must be paid for directly by patients.

In the past, some animosity has existed between CAM providers and conventional medical providers. While some research has been done to evaluate CAM practices, it has not been adequate to reach definitive conclusions. Moreover, some existing studies do not validate their hypotheses. If a patient chooses a CAM treatment over conventional medical treatment for a serious condition, the patient's life can be at risk. Some efforts are being made by the National Center for Complementary and Alternative Medicine (NCCAM) to increase CAM research. Meanwhile, some conventional medical institutions such as hospitals are setting up CAM clinics in order to integrate CAM therapies with conventional medicine, and some conventional medical providers use CAM treatments in their practices.

INDUSTRY MARKET SEGMENTS

Unlike most industries, CAM providers fall entirely within two segments: small or large. CAM providers either operate small practices of one or several providers or they operate as part of hospitals or hospital systems. Thus, there are no midsize businesses in this industry.

Small Businesses

The majority of CAM providers are employed in small businesses. The typical model for a CAM practice is an office with one to five providers of the same type of CAM care and, possibly, some support staff. Some CAM providers go into practice with other CAM providers in holistic care clinics. CAM provider offices are most commonly located in cities. Nurse-midwives may work in physician practices, which are also small businesses.

Potential Annual Earnings Scale. Salaries for CAM providers in the United States vary with provider type, provider experience, office size, the number of patients seen per week, and office location. Chiropractors earn from $32,380 to $159,640 per year. Naturopaths earn from $50,000 to $100,000 per year. Acupuncturists earn from $25,000 to $100,000 per year. Homeopaths earn from $45,710 to $156,000 per year. Hypnotists earn from $60,000 to $125,000 per year. Midwives working in physician practices earn from $55,000 to $80,000 per year. Nonnurse midwives are typically paid by birth, often about $2,000.

Clientele Interaction. CAM providers tend to form close relationships with their patients because of the holistic nature of their practices. One of the draws of these practitioners is the time that they spend with their patients and the individualized treatment they provide. Typically, CAM providers spend thirty minutes or more getting to know their patients. Since they often provide regular, frequent services, they rely on having good relationships with their clients to maintain their businesses.

Amenities, Atmosphere, and Physical Grounds. CAM providers usually have small, comfortable offices with some amenities—such as relaxing music or freshly cut flowers—but limited decorations. Offices are usually clean, but there may be only one or two examination rooms, and the waiting room may be small. Chiropractors and nurse-midwives are likely to have larger offices. Chiropractors may have radiology equipment and exercise equipment. Physician offices where nurse-midwives work may have larger waiting rooms, larger back offices, and larger examination rooms.

Typical Number of Employees. In order to keep business costs low, CAM providers have few employees. A practice usually consists of one to five providers and three or fewer support staff. Providers may have receptionists to make appointments, or they may make their own appointments. They may use answering machines in lieu of phone staff. With the exception of nurse-midwives and possibly chiropractors, many CAM providers operate cash-only businesses, so they do not require billing staffs either. Those providers that need to bill health insurers generally must hire billing persons and purchase computer software to keep track of their bills. They are likely to order their own supplies and equipment and perform their own marketing. They are likely to advertise on the Internet, at health fairs, at grocery stores, at health food stores, at beauty salons or day spas, or in smaller, alternative newspapers or magazines.

Nurse-midwives who are employed by physicians are not involved with running their offices unless they are very small. Many physician practices have staffs of six to ten persons who work as receptionists, billing staff, and medical assistants to each physician. Some practices may have business managers. Each physician practice either has a single billing person or uses a professional billing service, depending on its size. Larger physician groups may have their own billing services. They send claims to health insurers for most of the services that they provide. Chiropractors tend to operate in a similar manner to physicians. They usually have receptionists and several medical assistants. They accept cash payments from some patients, but they also require either billing persons or billing services.

Traditional Geographic Locations. CAM providers tend to have offices in locations where physicians and other medical providers have offices.

Most of their offices may be in cities, but they also may be in the suburbs. They are less likely to be located in rural areas, since they want to be conveniently accessible to their clients. Holistic health clinics with multiple CAM providers are frequently located in college towns, where residents are thought to be more open-minded about nontraditional health care providers. Hospital-based CAM clinics are usually in separate office buildings owned by their parent hospitals, usually on or near the hospitals' campuses. Physician offices where nurse-midwives may be employed are often in large medical office buildings near hospitals.

Pros of Working for a Small Practice. Practitioners working in small practices have significant control over their business. They are, generally speaking, their own bosses. Even in partnerships of five or six providers, few decisions—such as hiring receptionists or choosing a location—need to be made jointly. Otherwise, each provider maintains responsibility for his or her own patients and is ultimately answerable only to him- or herself. They set their own hours and determine their own workloads—although nurse-midwives and chiropractors are more likely to work typical business hours. In addition, practitioners working in small practices usually are able to develop closer and better relationships with their clients, since they are not insulated from them by office staff. Nurse-midwives who work in physician practices and chiropractors in practice with more than three other chiropractors are exceptions to this principle because such practices usually place several staff members between clients and their providers.

Cons of Working for a Small Practice. The owners of a small practice are at significant risk of financial loss if they cannot operate profitably. One- or two-person practices cannot afford to hire many staff. As a result, they must fulfill many business roles, including accountant, secretary, receptionist, supply clerk, marketer, business manager, and possibly housekeeper. These additional responsibilities increase practitioners' working hours. All CAM practitioners must meet state licensing requirements, including those for education. Malpractice insurance is necessary for all medical providers, including CAM providers, and it can be a significant expense. In the provision of health care, malpractice is always a risk.

Costs

Payroll and Benefits: CAM support staff are usually paid hourly wages, whereas practitioners hired by a practice's owners to help with the workload earn annual salaries and may become business partners. Partners and owners pay themselves out of their profits; if there are no profits, they receive no pay. Very small practices may offer no benefits, but practices attempt to offer standard benefits when feasible to retain qualified support staff.

Supplies: CAM practitioners require examination tables, pillows, paper or linens to cover them, and hospital gowns. Acupuncturists need acupuncture needles, Chinese herbs, and audio systems or players to play music during treatment. Midwives require gynecological examination tables with stirrups, paper or sheets to line the tables, sterile and unsterile gloves, tools for patient examination, and stethoscopes. Hypnotists do not require any specific equipment for their practice. A homeopath needs either a supply of homeopathic solutions or a relationship with a homeopathic pharmacy. Naturopaths need stethoscopes and other patient care supplies. Chiropractors need X-ray machines, hot and cold packs, possibly small whirlpool baths, infrared and ultraviolet lights, ultrasound machines, electrical stimulation machines, and traction. All CAM providers need office supplies, antiseptic solutions, sterilizing machines (autoclaves), telephones, computers, and cleaning supplies. If the providers own their office buildings, they may require landscaping equipment and snow removal equipment.

External Services: CAM practices may contract laundry, landscaping and snow-removal, accounting, credit-card processing, patient billing, and computer maintenance services. Smaller practices use as few external services as possible. Some may wash their own laundry, maintain their own accounting books, and fix their own computers. They may not accept credit cards. Larger practices are likely to employ more of these services. Most practices purchase malpractice insurance.

Utilities: Utilities used by CAM providers include water, telephone, gas or oil, sewage, cable television, and Internet access. Smaller offices may not use cable or require Internet access. If offices are rented, water, sewage, heat, and cooling may be included in the rent.

Taxes: The taxes paid by CAM providers include local, state, and federal income and property taxes. Small practices may pay these as corporate taxes, or practitioners may report their business income on their personal returns, in which case they must also pay self-employment taxes. In some states, taxes are applied on medical services. In such states, providers must apply these taxes to patients' bills, collecting the taxes from patients and passing them on to the state government.

Other Expenses: Additional costs of doing business as a CAM provider include paying fees for state licensure and possibly fees for national certification within professional organizations. Some states require continuing education credits for nurse-midwives, in which case those practitioners must bear the costs of the requisite seminars or classes.

Large Businesses

CAM providers are much less likely to be employed by large businesses. When they are, they are usually employed by hospitals in integrative care departments. Some types of CAM providers are more likely to be employed by hospitals. Nurse-midwives may work in the labor and delivery departments of hospitals. Acupuncturists, hypnotists, and naturopaths are the most likely to be employed by hospitals in their integrative care departments. Chiropractors usually practice with other chiropractors in offices. It is uncommon for them to work in hospitals. Unless homeopaths are also physicians, they are unlikely to be employed by hospitals. A 2007 survey performed by Optimal Healing Environments for the American Hospital Association found that 37 percent of respondent U.S. hospitals had integrative care departments. Most of these departments provided only outpatient services, but some also provided inpatient services.

Potential Annual Earnings Scale. Pay scales for CAM providers who work in hospital integrative care clinics vary according to whether the integrative care department is intended to be self-supporting, whether the hospital is supporting the department, or whether the department is supported by outside grants. If the integrative care department is intended to be self-supporting, the CAM providers

are paid based on the number of patients seen. If the hospital is supporting the department or the department is supported by outside grants, the CAM providers are paid either an hourly wage or an annual salary. Some integrative care departments may employ volunteer CAM providers on a part-time basis. CAM providers working in a hospital often earn less than providers with their own offices. Nurse-midwives who work in hospital labor and delivery departments earn an average of $55,000 to $80,000 per year. They may be paid salaries or hourly wages. As employees of hospitals, CAM providers are usually but not always given government-mandated benefits, vacation time, and sick time.

Clientele Interaction. CAM providers strive to achieve supportive and caring relationships with their patients. The goal of CAM providers is to care for patients as complex, whole entities, and this can only be achieved if they take the time to get to know each patient individually. Typically, patient care sessions are scheduled to last thirty minutes to one hour. Much CAM business is repeat business, and new patients are often referred by friends who use the provider, so maintaining good relationships is necessary.

Amenities, Atmosphere, and Physical Grounds. Hospital buildings are usually clean and well kept, inside and out. They attempt to create a quiet and calming atmosphere. The most common amenity is soothing and relaxing music that is played during treatments. Many hospitals have paintings of country or other outdoor scenes to foster a relaxing atmosphere. Clean bathroom facilities are available, and they may be locked so that they will only be used by patients and family members. Most physician office buildings and hospital buildings have information desks and security guards in their lobbies. Grounds around hospital buildings are well kept and frequently have decorative flower gardens.

Typical Number of Employees. Hospitals have hundreds to thousands of employees, depending on the number of beds they provide. On average, small hospitals employ five or six persons per bed, while larger hospitals employ eight or nine persons per bed. Hospitals are in the business of providing care twenty-four hours per day, seven days per week, particularly emergency care. They must employ sufficient staff to cover all of these hours. Hospital employees, such as nurse-midwives, often work rotating shifts to provide coverage for their departments. Integrative care departments may have providers on call for emergencies, but they typically provide treatments only during the work week and during the day. Some may have evening or Saturday hours. Their staffs are much smaller than those of other hospital departments. They may have six to ten employees, depending on the types of services that they provide.

Traditional Geographic Locations. Usually, hospitals are located in large cities, but some may be located in small towns. Large city hospitals are more likely to have integrative care departments, but smaller community hospitals may also have such departments. City hospitals are often located in some of the less affluent sections of a city. They are often located in residential areas of cities or towns.

Pros of Working for a Hospital. Large businesses such as hospitals are departmentalized, al-lowing each employee to perform a single job role and concentrate on a narrow area of expertise. CAM providers at such facilities need only provide care and need not attend to financial record keep-ing, patient scheduling, or ordering supplies. CAM providers working in hospitals usually enjoy gov-ernment-mandated benefits, paid vacation, and sick time. Nurse-midwives can count on consistent paychecks, and, in integrative care departments, providers may also receive consistent paychecks, depending on their contracts. Hospitals provide continuing education for their staffs, so employees may have access to free classes on a wide variety of topics, including computer software. Hospitals al-ways have employee cafeterias, and they sometimes subsidize the cost of the food.

Cons of Working for a Hospital. Hospital workloads may be inconsistent. Employees in labor and delivery units may wait with nothing to do at some times, only to find themselves facilitating multiple simultaneous births at other times. Simi-

OCCUPATION PROFILE

Chiropractor

Considerations	Qualifications
Description	Treats people for various illnesses through manipulation of the spine; often incorporates other alternative health practices such as nutritional therapy.
Career cluster	Health Science
Interests	Data; people; things
Working conditions	Work inside
Minimum education level	Doctoral degree
Physical exertion	Medium work
Physical abilities	Unexceptional/basic fitness
Opportunities for experience	Part-time work
Licensure and certification	Required
Employment outlook	Faster-than-average growth expected
Holland interest score	ISR

Note: See volume 1, "Publisher's Note," for an explanation of the Holland interest score.

larly, in integrative care departments, providers may not be very busy part of the day, but then, at other times, they may be overloaded, forcing patients to wait for care. This occurs because hospitals experience peak hours, as patients often come before or after work, or on their lunch hour. Hospital employees must all generally work on-call shifts, and they may not be able to leave work on schedule.

Hospitals are dramatically more bureaucratic than small practices. Business decisions are made by administrators at a level that is unrelated to direct patient care. Thus, staffing may be reduced, and hours and policies may be changed by hospital executives without consulting providers. Individual employees in large organizations may have relatively little control over their work lives. It is unusual for professional providers, such as CAM providers, to be unionized, even if other hospital employees are.

Costs

Payroll and Benefits: Nurse midwives may be paid either annual salaries or hourly wages. Hospitals usually provide government-mandated benefits, vacation time, and sick time. CAM providers working in hospital integrative care departments may earn salaries, hourly wages, or payments for each patient seen. Some may even be volunteer workers. If they are considered hospital employees, some will receive government-mandated benefits, vacation, and sick time. Other CAM providers may be independent contractors, in which case they will not receive such benefits.

Supplies: Hospitals require many different types of supplies, including landscaping and snow-removal equipment, cleaning supplies, office supplies, computers and software, telephones, food and dinnerware, beds and bed linens, towels, autoclaves, dressing supplies, personal care supplies, acupuncture needles, examination tables, medications, intravenous fluids, physical therapy equipment, electronic patient care equipment, medication administration equipment, operating- and delivery-room equipment, scrub uniforms, hospital gowns and pants, dialysis equipment, and laboratory equipment and supplies. They also require radiology equipment, including computed tomography (CT) scanners, magnetic resonance imaging (MRI) scanners, and fluoroscopy machines, as well as medication administration machines, patient care supply machines, infant beds, isolette infant beds (for premature or ill newborns), cribs, wheelchairs, and stretchers.

External Services: Hospitals may contract lawn and grounds care services, parking vendors, computer maintenance services, computer software trainers, vending machine companies, cleaning services, security services, MRI or CT scanner rental services, medical engineering services, billing services, and oxygen and other gas vendors. Larger hospitals may use their own staff for some or all of these services.

Utilities: Hospitals must pay for water, sewage, oil or gas, telephone service, cable television, Internet access, and electricity.

Taxes: As large businesses, private for-profit hospitals must pay local, state, and federal income taxes, as well as property taxes. Nonprofit hospitals may be exempted from these taxes. Some states charge for-profit hospitals additional taxes per patient.

Other Expenses: CAM providers are required to pay for their own state licensing fees, malpractice insurance, and board certification when necessary. Some states and individual hospitals require ongoing continuing education credits for professional employees, who must pay for their own continuing education. Although professional employees should have their own malpractice insurance, hospitals must also have institutional malpractice insurance.

ORGANIZATIONAL STRUCTURE AND JOB ROLES

There are two settings where CAM providers are employed, private practices and general hospitals. In smaller offices, either providers themselves or office managers must fulfill multiple roles to keep the businesses running. In larger offices, several staff members will fulfill these roles. A majority of CAM practitioners work in private practices.

Some CAM practitioners are employed by general hospitals. Some work in integrative medicine departments, while nurse-midwives are generally employed in labor and delivery departments. In hospitals, most business functions are performed by hospital staff.

The following umbrella categories apply to the organizational structure of businesses in the complementary and alternative health care industry, including general hospitals that employ CAM providers:

- Management
- Public Relations
- Marketing
- Human Resources
- Housekeeping
- Maintenance
- Information Technology
- Nursing
- Billing

Management

In small CAM provider offices, usually one provider manages the practice. Managers may meet periodically with the other providers in their practices to make major decisions. Larger CAM offices may hire dedicated business managers; the owners or partners nevertheless retain ultimate authority in such practices. Different types of CAM providers have different educational backgrounds. Acupuncturists require at least fifteen hundred to two thousand hours of acupuncture study. Naturopaths require four to five years of study in naturopathy. Nurse-midwives require master's degrees in nursing with specialties in midwifery. Nonnurse midwives must have midwifery training. Chiropractors require four years of study in chiropractic medicine. Most homeopaths are either medical doctors or osteopathic physicians with additional training in homeopathy. Office managers usually have bachelor's degrees in business, but experience may be more important than education, especially in smaller practices. Office managers are usually paid annual salaries.

The management team of a hospital is responsible for high-level decisions and usually consists of four or five executives. The persons in these positions oversee operations, set institutional goals, work with physicians, and make strategic plans. Most executive management team members have master's degrees in business administration, accounting, or nursing. They are paid annual salaries.

Management occupations may include the following:

- Owner/Sole Practitioner
- Managing Partner
- Office/Business Manager
- Chief Executive Officer (CEO)
- Chief Financial Officer (CFO)
- Chief Operating Officer (COO)
- Director of Patient Care Services
- Controller
- General Counsel

Public Relations

In CAM provider offices, any public relations work is performed by providers or business managers. It is performed as needed only, although CAM providers work hard to maintain good relationships with their patients. Public relations includes responding to patient complaints or problems, as well as soliciting patient feedback.

Hospitals have dedicated public relations departments that respond to patient complaints and solicit feedback, as well as maintaining media and government relations and issuing press releases as necessary. If patients or former patients complain about their treatment by phone or by mail, public relations personnel must follow up with them. Any valid problems are then communicated to the appropriate departments, so changes can be made. In order to get feedback, some hospitals send questionnaires to discharged patients or participate in national surveys of hospital patients. In a fairly competitive hospital market, feedback is important to ensure that patients are satisfied with their care. Hospital public relations departments can vary in size and type of personnel. Generally, there is a director, a clerical person, and one or more representatives. Directors have bachelor's degrees and sometimes master's degrees, as do representatives. Secretary require at least high school educations. Directors are paid annual salaries. Representatives and clerical staff are usually paid hourly wages.

Public relations occupations may include the following:

- Business Manager
- Public Relations Director
- Spokesperson

- Public Relations Representative
- Administrative Assistant

Marketing

In CAM provider offices, marketing is performed by providers or office managers. Usually, marketing consists of placing advertisements in newspapers, on the Internet (particularly on CAM Web sites), in local advertising magazines, in supermarkets, at health fairs, at day spas, or in alternative newspapers. Private practices look for ways to market their services that are low in cost yet effective. This type of marketing does not reach a very large number of people.

A given hospital may employ one marketing person or a whole marketing department, depending on the hospital and how competitive its market is. Hospital marketing budgets are much larger than those of private practices. They include money for advertising through television, radio, the Internet, large local newspapers, and billboards. Some hospitals may publish newsletters about their services, either on paper or online. This kind of marketing reaches a wide range of persons. Marketing personnel generally have bachelor's degrees in marketing and may have master's degrees as well. Marketing directors often have master's degrees in marketing or business. Clerical personnel have at least high school educations. Directors are paid annual salaries, while their staffs may also be paid salaries or may be paid hourly wages. Clerical staffs are paid hourly.

Marketing occupations may include the following:

- Marketing Director
- Marketing Assistant
- Market Research Analyst
- Administrative Assistant

Human Resources

CAM private practices lack formal human resources staffs. Either providers or office managers hire and fire staff. They also interview prospective staff, check references and previous employers, and negotiate salaries. Usually, the partners in a given practice make the ultimate hiring or firing decisions for that practice. In addition, office managers or practice managers advertise for job applicants, conduct performance appraisals, and deal with any personnel problems. If there is no office staff except the providers, there is little to do in the area of human resources.

Hospitals have human resources departments whose staff members advertise for employees, hire them, respond to employee grievances, check prospective employees' references and previous employers, and conduct exit interviews. Support staff members work as receptionists, give out employment applications, check that submitted applications are complete, and answer questions. Typically, human resources departments have directors, representatives, and clerical staffs. Directors have bachelor's degrees, may have master's degrees, and are paid annual salaries. Human resources representatives have bachelor's degrees and are generally paid hourly wages. Clerical staff members have high school educations and are paid hourly wages.

Human resources occupations may include the following:

- Human Resources Director
- Human Resources Generalist
- Payroll Clerk
- Benefits Manager
- Administrative Assistant

Housekeeping

For private CAM offices, housekeeping is a required service. Offices must be cleaned, as must lobbies, hallways, elevators, and common restrooms. Provider offices located within larger office buildings generally need not worry about spaces outside the offices proper, which are cleaned by building cleaning staff. Cleaning staff may clean only common areas, however, requiring practices to engage their own cleaning services. CAM providers pay either hourly rates or set per-visit fees. Cleaning services do not have educational requirements for their workers, who generally earn hourly wages.

Most hospitals have housekeeping departments that clean all areas within the hospitals themselves, as well as their attached medical office buildings. Some smaller hospitals outsource this function, but this is uncommon. It is critical that hospital patient care areas be spotlessly clean, and cleaning personnel must be trained in the handling of medical waste and the sterilizing of medical equipment and surfaces. Employing their own staffs allows hospitals to exercise more control over their cleanliness. Housekeeping staff are responsible for cleaning patient beds after discharge, so they have some control over how soon the beds are available for admissions. Housekeeping managers or supervisors oversee crews. Managers and supervisors may or may not have bachelor's degrees, but they usually have high school educations. There are no educational requirements for housekeeping personnel. Usually, managers and supervisors are paid annual salaries, and their staffs are paid hourly wages.

Housekeeping occupations may include the following:

- Housekeeping Manager
- Housekeeper
- Custodian/Janitor

Maintenance

Private practices may rely on their office buildings' maintenance staff for routine problems. However, problems requiring greater expertise, such as plumbing problems or medical equipment repairs, may require the use of external vendors.

Hospital maintenance departments are usually called "engineering departments." Department personnel maintain plumbing; electrical systems; and heating, ventilation, and air-conditioning (HVAC) systems, as well as performing major equipment repairs and renovations. Medical engineers maintain their hospitals' patient care equipment. Most hospital maintenance workers have trained either in vocational schools or with other maintenance professionals to learn their trade. Some may have engineering degrees. They are paid based on their experience and education. Chief engineers usually have master's degrees and are paid annual salaries. Plumbers, HVAC technicians, electricians, and medical engineers are paid hourly wages.

Maintenance occupations may include the following:

- Office Building Maintenance Person
- Chief of Engineering
- Plumber
- Heating, Ventilation, and Air-Conditioning (HVAC) Technician

- Electrician
- Medical Engineer

Information Technology

Private CAM practices may or may not use computers. Large physician practices usually use computers, as do chiropractors. They often keep their patients' medical records on their systems, as well as their office finances and patient billing accounts. Other providers may not see the need for computers or feel their expense is justified. Some offices rely on computers for patient billing and record keeping. Others do not use them at all.

Modern hospitals use computers throughout their buildings and departments. They generally have dedicated information technology (IT) departments. IT personnel assist with computer access and troubleshooting, back up computer data, and maintain data security. Directors of IT are paid annual salaries and usually have undergraduate or graduate degrees in information technology. IT assistants and help desk staff assist hospital staff with their computer problems. They usually have some college training or bachelor's degrees in information technology. They are paid hourly wages.

IT occupations may include the following:

- Information Technology Director
- Information Technology Assistant
- Help Desk Staff

Nursing

Some CAM providers employ nurses to assist them in caring for patients in their offices. Not all CAM offices have nursing staffs. CAM office nurses may be registered nurses (RNs), licensed practical nurses (LPNs), or nurses' aides.

Hospital nursing staffs provide direct patient care throughout their hospitals. Hospitals employ nurse managers, nursing supervisors, staff nurses, and patient care assistants. Nursing supervisors and nurse managers must have bachelor's and master's degrees in nursing or related fields, as well as experience in nursing, usually including emergency care. Nurse clinicians and nurse midwives have master's degrees in nursing. Staff nurses have completed accredited nursing programs. Nurses are usually paid by the hour, although some nursing supervisors and nurse managers are paid annual salaries.

Patient care assistants are trained by hospitals to assist nursing staffs. They are taught technical skills, such as taking electrocardiograms and drawing blood for testing. They also provide direct care to patients. LPNs are trained in one-year programs and lack the medical science knowledge that RNs have. Nurses' aides are trained by hospitals, nursing homes, or technical schools in programs that last several months. Patient care assistants, LPNs, and nurses' aides are paid by the hour.

Nursing occupations may include the following:

- Office Nurse
- Nursing Supervisor
- Nurse Manager
- Nurse Clinician/Nurse Midwife
- Registered Nurse
- Licensed Practical Nurse
- Patient Care Assistant

Billing

If CAM practitioners provide services that are covered by their patients' health insurance, they need personnel to handle insurance billing. Some CAM providers operate on a cash-only basis because their services are not covered by health insurance. They do not need billing departments because they are generally paid for their services at the time they are administered. Some providers receive insurance payments from some patients and cash payments from others. Most health care billing personnel have high school educations and are paid hourly wages.

Hospitals usually have dedicated billing departments with billing managers, billing staffs, and clerical staffs. A majority of hospital patients have some type of health insurance, so it is necessary for hospitals to bill insurers. Those patients without health insurance must pay deposits for their hospital stays before they are admitted, unless they are emergency admissions. Billing managers may have high school educations or bachelor's degrees, as well as billing experience. Managers are paid annual salaries. Billing staff and clerical staff have high school educations and possibly associate's degrees. They are paid hourly wages.

Billing occupations may include the following:

- Billing Manager
- Billing Specialist
- Accounts Receivable Clerk
- Office Manager
- Administrative Assistant

INDUSTRY OUTLOOK

Overview

The outlook for this industry shows it to be in decline in the United States. From 1997 through 2007, the use of CAM practitioners decreased by about 50 percent, although self-care CAM measures increased. CAM practitioner visits, among survey respondents in 2007, totaled 1,592 visits per 1,000 adults. One-third of out-of-pocket dollars spent on CAM services were for practitioner visits. Acupuncture did not follow this general downward trend: Acupuncturist office visits increased during the same period and reached a total of 17.6 million visits in 2007. This rise in the number of acupuncture treatments may be due to an increase in the number of acupuncturists, as well as increased media discussion of acupuncture and increased health insurance coverage for acupuncture.

Several factors could affect the long-term outlook of the CAM industry. The U.S. population continues to age, and large numbers of baby boomers are turning 62 and becoming eligible to receive Social Security payments. The recession of 2007-2009 significantly decreased the retirement savings of many Americans. The Patient Protection and Affordable Care Act of 2010 (PPACA) is expected to lead to more than 30 million uninsured Americans gaining health insurance. More than 20 million Americans will still lack insurance, however. Because CAM treatments may be less expensive than conventional treatments but may also be ineligible for health insurance coverage or reimbursement, these events may have unpredictable and conflicting effects upon the CAM market. However, in general, health care utilization of all sorts is expected to increase after 2014 when the major provisions of the PPACA go into effect.

Market analyses may also be distorted by a lack of data on nurse-midwives and nonnurse midwives. Nurse-midwives, who most often work within the realm of traditional medicine, may not be perceived as CAM practitioners. Surveys may also be distorted if they include only participants who are either middle- or upper class. Working-class Americans are less likely to respond to surveys, and they are more likely to use nonnurse midwives, than are members of other classes. Survey respondents may also be reluctant to admit to visiting CAM practitioners as a result of social stigmas against those practitioners in some groups. Nevertheless, it appears that the demand for treatment by CAM providers other than acupuncturists and possibly midwives is in decline.

In other countries, the use of herbal medicines represents the highest percentage of CAM treatments. International data on CAM use, other than herbal treatments, is limited, particularly for less affluent countries. The World Health Organization reports that in countries other than the United States, traditional medicine is responsible for at least 80 percent of medical care. China embraces the practice of acupuncture. Great Britain and Australia provide some data on their use of CAM practitioners.

Employment Advantages

Americans' consumption of acupuncture is increasing, and acupuncture is increasingly being covered by health insurers, as research is published demonstrating its effectiveness. Acupuncturists require significantly less training and less financial investment than do medical doctors, and they may be able to develop better relationships with their patients than many doctors are able to. Careers in midwifery may appeal to people who wish to support maternity patients who dislike conventional medical techniques for delivery. It can be very exciting to assist women in childbirth and witness one of the major events of life. Nurse-midwives may have significantly greater career options than nonnurse midwives, however, especially given that nonnurses are not allowed to practice midwifery in many states.

While other CAM providers are less in demand, people who are able to succeed in such careers may find them rewarding. CAM providers help people with health problems who cannot or do not wish to seek conventional medical treatment. They often develop close relationships with their patients because they are committed to treating whole people rather than symptoms.

Annual Earnings

The demand for complementary and alternative care services, with the exception of midwifery,

is related to the availability of disposable income, since services must often be paid for in cash, and to the incidence of chronic health problems. Americans, particularly educated Americans, have a fair amount of disposable income. As the U.S. population ages and health reforms mandated by the PPACA are implemented, the demand for CAM services is likely to increase. With annual expenditures at $33.9 billion in the United States, there appears to be a continued demand for CAM providers.

It is difficult to determine the demand for CAM services in the international health care market. There are few data on current expenditures on CAM services. Developing countries are unlikely to increase their use of CAM services. They are also unlikely to report the use of these services. Lack of education and scarcity of conventional medical care make it unlikely that interest in alternative medicine will increase. Countries such as Australia, Great Britain, Japan, and China may demonstrate increased interest in CAM services as their populations increase in wealth, education, and age.

RELATED RESOURCES FOR FURTHER RESEARCH

AMERICAN HOLISTIC MEDICINE ASSOCIATION
23366 Commerce Park, Suite 101B
Beachwood, OH 44122
Tel: (216) 292-6644
Fax: (216) 292-6688
http://www.holisticmedicine.org

GLOBAL INSTITUTE FOR ALTERNATIVE MEDICINE
3822 Lake Ave.
Wilmette, IL 60091
Tel: (800) 410-0612
Fax: (888) 201-4186
http://www.gifam.org

NATIONAL ASSOCIATION FOR INTEGRATIVE
HEALTH CARE PRACTITIONERS
9201 Edeworth Dr.
P.O. Box 5631
Capital Heights, MD 20791
Tel: (757) 292-7710
http://aihcp-norfolkva.org

National Center for Complementary and
  Alternative Medicine, National
  Institutes of Health
9000 Rockville Pike
Bethesda, MD 20892
Tel: (888) 644-6226
Fax: (866) 464-3616
http://nccam.nih.gov

ABOUT THE AUTHOR

Christine M. Carroll has a diploma in nursing from Massachusetts General Hospital, a bachelor of science in nursing from Boston University, and master of business administration in health care administration from the University of Connecticut. She has experience in medical-surgical nursing, nursing education, and health insurance. She has published articles in nursing journals and has performed peer review for several nursing journals, as well as contributing to medical reference works, including *Magill's Medical Guide, Salem Health: Cancer, Salem Health: Psychology and Mental Health*, and *Salem Health: Genetics and Inherited Disorders*.

FURTHER READING

American Association of Professional Hypnotists. "How Profitable a Career Is Hypnotherapy?" http://www.aaph.org/node/166.

Anath, Sita. "CAM: An Increasing Presence in U.S. Hospitals." *Hospitals and Health Networks*, January 20, 2009. http://www.hhnmag.com/hhnmag_app/jsp/articledisplay.jsp?dcrpath=HHNMAG/Article/data/01JAN2009/090120HHN_Online_Ananth&domain=HHNMAG.

_____. "A Steady Growth in CAM Services." *Hospitals and Health Networks*, March 31, 2009. http://www.hhnmag.com/hhnmag_app/jsp/articledisplay.jsp?dcrpath=HHNMAG/Article/data/03MAR2009/090331HHN_Online_Ananth&domain=HHNMAG.

Brody, Jane E., et al. *The New York Times Guide to Alternative Health*. New York: Henry Holt and Company, 2001.

Cohen, Michael H. *Complementary and Alternative Medicine: Legal Boundaries and Regulatory Perspectives*. Baltimore: The Johns Hopkins University Press, 1998.

Ernst, Edzard, ed. *Healing, Hype, or Harm? A Critical Analysis of Complementary or Alternative Medicine*. Charlottesville, Va.: Societas Imprint Academic, 2008.

FeldHusen, Adrian E. "The History of Midwifery and Childbirth in America: A Time Line." http://www.midwiferytoday.com/articles/timeline.asp.

French, Nancy. *Complementary and Alternative Medicine*. Colleyville, Tex.: CAM, 2002.

Hartford Hospital. *Building Bridges Between Conventional and Complementary Medicine: A Manual*. Hartford, Conn.: Hartford Hospital, 2003.

Nahin, Richard L., et al. *National Health Statistics Report: Cost of Complementary and Alternative Medicine (CAM) and Frequency of Visits to CAM Practitioners—U.S., 2007*. Washington, D.C.: U.S. Department of Health and Human Services, 2009.

Santa, Colleen F. "The Adoption of Complementary and Alternative Medicine by Hospitals: A Framework for Decision Making." *The Journal of Health Care Management* 46 (July, 2001): 250-260. http://www.allbusiness.com/management/3604702-1.html.

Tierney, Gillian. *Opportunities in Holistic Medical Careers*. Rev. ed. New York: McGraw Hill, 2007.

U.S. Bureau of Labor Statistics. *Career Guide to Industries*, 2010-2011 ed. http://www.bls.gov/oco/cg.

_____. "Chiropractors." In *Occupational Outlook Handbook*, 2010-2011 ed. http://www.bls.gov/oco/ocos071.htm.

U.S. Census Bureau. North American Industry Classification System (NAICS), 2007. http://www.census.gov/cgi-bin/sssd/naics/naicsrch?chart=2007.

U.S. Department of Commerce. International Trade Administration. Office of Trade and Industry Information. Industry Trade Data and Analysis. http://ita.doc.gov/td/industry/otea/OTII/OTII-index.html.

Weil, Andrew. *Health and Healing*. Rev. ed. New York: Houghton Mifflin, 2004.

White House Commission on Complementary

and Alternative Medicine Policy. *Final Report.* Washington, D.C.: Government Printing Office, 2002. http://www.whccamp.hhs.gov/finalreport.html.

World Health Organization. *National Policy on Traditional Medicine and Complementary/*

Alternative Medicine. Geneva, Switzerland: Author, 2005.

———. *National Policy on Traditional Medicine and Regulation of Herbal Medicines: Report of a WHO Global Survey.* Geneva, Switzerland: Author, 2005.

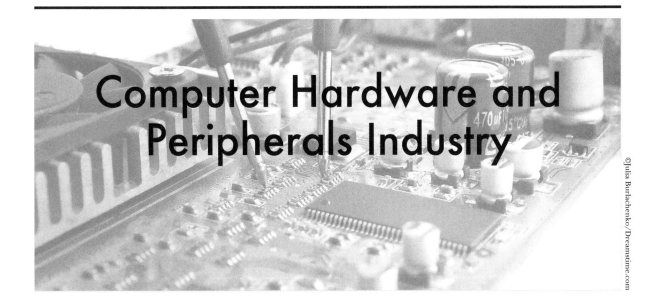

Computer Hardware and Peripherals Industry

©Julia Burlachenko/Dreamstime.com

INDUSTRY SNAPSHOT

General Industry: Manufacturing

Career Clusters: Manufacturing; Science, Technology, Engineering, and Math

Subcategory Industries: Computer Display Manufacturing; Computer Printer Manufacturing; Computer Storage Device Manufacturing; Computer Workstation Manufacturing; Integrated Circuit Manufacturing; Mainframe Computer Manufacturing; Personal Computer Manufacturing; Semiconductor and Other Electronic Component Manufacturing

Related Industries: Computer Software Industry; Computer Systems Industry; Internet and Cyber Communications Industry; Retail Trade and Service Industry; Telecommunications Equipment Industry; Video, Computer, and Virtual Reality Games Industry

Annual Domestic Revenues: $110 billion USD (Research and Markets, 2009)

Annual Global Revenues: $411 billion USD (Research and Markets, 2009)

NAICS Numbers: 3341, 33441

INDUSTRY DEFINITION

Summary

The computer hardware and peripherals industry affects nearly every aspect of modern life, from Web sites and e-commerce applications to medicine and telecommunications. The industry manufactures computers and their peripherals. (A peripheral is any computer part or device other than the central processing unit, or CPU, and the working memory. Common peripherals include printers, external storage devices, keyboards, and mice.) Companies active in the computer hardware and peripherals industry range from small start-ups offering just a few niche products to international corporations, such as International Business Machines (IBM) and Hewlett-Packard (HP), that have manufacturing and engineering operations across the globe and employ tens of thousands of people.

History of the Industry

The earliest counting device was the abacus, a tablet of stone, wood, or metal upon which stones were moved along grooves or painted lines. These were used perhaps as early as 3000 B.C.E. by ancient civilizations such as the Sumerians and the Babylonians. (Later versions consisted of framed devices using freely moving beads.) Similar counting tables were later created to simplify such specialized and diverse fields as navigation, astronomy, and trigonometry. By the nineteenth century, the term "computer" referred to a person who performed complex calculations for a living using mechanical devices. The term applied particularly to astronomers and surveyors.

In 1821, English inventor Charles Babbage grew frustrated with the inaccuracies in the mathematical tables then available. He began experimenting with automatic calculating machines. In 1834, Babbage designed the analytical engine, the first true forerunner to modern computing systems. Babbage's device was to be steam-powered and capable of completing complex computations that went beyond numbers. Supporter Ada Lovelace wrote an article about the analytical engine in 1843 that foreshadowed the era of modern computing. She imagined utilizing numbers to represent letters of the alphabet, allowing the analytical engine to store many different types of data. However, a working version of the ambitious project never materialized.

A computer mainboard with a microprocessor. (©Dreamstime.com)

Just a few decades later, United States Census Bureau employee Herman Hollerith developed the punch-card system, which was used by the bureau to calculate population data as early as 1890. Hollerith further refined his punch-card system after 1896, when he founded the Tabulating Machine Company, the precursor to IBM. Punch-card technology formed the basis for many early computer models.

In 1937, physicists John V. Atanasoff and Clifford Berry created the first digital electronic computer at Iowa State University. This breakthrough was soon followed by a rapid expansion in technology during World War II, as governments poured money into computer research. In 1946, this research led to the creation of the Electronic Numerical Integrator and Computer (ENIAC), a general-purpose computer that was developed to assist the U.S. military in calculating weapon trajectories. The project was led by John P. Eckert and John W. Mauchly at the University of Pennsylvania. The enormous computer took up eighteen hundred square feet of space, weighed thirty tons, and used nearly eighteen thousand vacuum tubes. It relied on removable plug boards to communicate instructions. Reprogramming the computer involved rewiring the entire system, a process that took days.

A team of engineers at Texas Instruments created the first integrated circuit, or computer chip, in 1959. This extremely advanced miniature electronic circuit revolutionized computer science. In 1968, Robert Noyce, Gordon Moore, and Andrew Grove founded Intel Corporation with the intention of developing an affordable silicon-based memory chip. Intel would become one of the largest manufacturers of integrated circuits. By 1971, the invention of the floppy disk allowed computer programmers easily to store and transfer data. The earliest modern personal desktop computer was the Apple I, developed by Steve Wozniak in 1976. Wozniak and his partner, Steve Jobs, sold the Apple I as a complete unit. It was the first computer to feature a full keyboard and could be plugged directly into a standard television.

In 1981, IBM introduced the personal computer, or PC, which utilized the Microsoft Disk Operating System (MS-DOS) to run all of its applications. Every personal computer in the world can trace its lineage directly to IBM's first model. Just three years later, Apple launched the Macintosh, the first popular computer system to use a mouse to control an advanced graphical user interface (GUI). Since then, computers have become a ubiquitous part of modern life. Because of the constantly evolving nature of technology, the computer hardware and peripherals industry continues to offer creative entrepreneurs many opportunities to form successful new businesses. There are also many established companies that employ thousands of people, including engineers, scientists, production workers, and administrative staff.

The Industry Today

Computers are utilized in nearly every modern industry and have become a necessity for most households. The hardware and peripherals industry builds physical computer components in cooperation with the software industry, which develops programs that run on and control those components. In some instances, a single company may offer both hardware and software, either separately or as part of a single integrated computer system.

The term "peripherals" refers to devices that either allow users to input information or allow computers to make information externally available to users. Common peripherals include keyboards, monitors, computer mice, external storage devices, cameras, microphones, speakers, headphones, and projectors. Modern computer components require such precision in their design and construction that computer modeling and automated manufacturing techniques are necessary to create them. The testing of finished components is also handled through automated processes. Because of this high level of automation, the hardware industry hires few production workers. Moreover, the physical

Inputs Consumed by the Computer and Electronic Products Industry

Input	Value
Energy	$2.3 billion
Materials	$131.2 billion
Purchased services	$63.9 billion
Total	$197.4 billion

Source: U.S. Bureau of Economic Analysis. Data are for 2008.

manufacturing process is increasingly being outsourced overseas. However, most research, design, and development of computers by American companies is still based in the United States.

Some computer hardware and peripherals, such as the specialized servers utilized by schools or hospitals, can be offered only by midsize or large firms because developing new products requires high expenditures on both research and manufacturing. Hardware and peripheral manufacturers often work closely with companies in the information technology and cyber communications sectors to develop products for database systems, Web servers, and computer networks. Hardware manufacturers also commonly produce specialized components and integrated circuits for use in other products, including automobiles, aircraft, medical devices, toys, and personal electronics.

The largest firms manufacture the majority of all computer components, such as integrated circuits and hard drives. Components usually require "clean-room" manufacturing facilities. In such facilities, employees are required to wear full-length coveralls and face masks and often pass through airlocks before entering. The atmosphere in clean rooms is carefully controlled with air filtration systems and particulate monitors. Commonly manufactured components requiring clean-room facilities include integrated circuits and hard drives.

The Computer and Electronic Products Industry's Contribution to the U.S. Economy

Value Added	Amount
Gross domestic product	$195.2 billion
Gross domestic product	1.4%
Persons employed	1.25 million
Total employee compensation	$129.8 billion

Source: U.S. Bureau of Economic Analysis. Data are for 2008.

Integrated circuits, also known as microchips, are created by blending multiple layers of semiconductor materials, such as silicon and germanium compounds, into a base structure. Transistors, which are capable of amplifying electrical signals and turning them on or off, are installed on the structure, and microscopic pathways are etched into the structure, connecting multiple transistors in the same manner that streets connect buildings in a city. Information is passed along these pathways as bursts of electrical impulses. Many different computer components rely on integrated circuits, including CPUs, motherboards, and video cards.

Hard drives store digital data for long periods of time. These data can be easily and quickly accessed at any time. Inside a disk drive, an actuator arm locates and reads data stored on magnetic disks as binary ones and zeroes. The actuator arm also contains recording elements that can write data to the disk by turning the magnetic charge of a tiny segment of the disk on or off. This segment represents one binary digit, or bit.

In both large and small firms, employees from many different departments, including research and development, engineering, manufacturing, and sales and support, work together closely to develop and perfect new products. A company may sell its products directly to consumers, or it may sell them wholesale to electronics or big-box retailers. In the competitive computer marketplace, companies succeed based on their dedication to innovative design and manufacturing techniques. As computers continue to become fully integrated in people's daily lives, the hardware and peripherals industry will play an increasingly important role in all sectors of the global business community.

INDUSTRY MARKET SEGMENTS

The computer hardware and peripherals industry includes companies of all sizes. Most manufacturing activities are concentrated in midsize and

Inside a hard disk drive, an actuator arm locates and reads data stored on magnetic disks as binary ones and zeroes. (© Jean-Francois Vermette/iStockphoto.com)

large companies, while smaller companies may produce niche products or build and repair customized computer systems for a local community.

Small Businesses

There are many small computer firms based in the United States, although midsize and large firms employ a greater percentage of the workers in the hardware and peripherals manufacturing industry. Small firms sometimes employ just a single owner-operator. Many small companies focus on manufacturing a few peripheral products, such as customizable universal serial bus (USB) flash drives or game controllers.

Some small companies focus on manufacturing a few peripheral products, such as customizable USB flash drives. (©Brian Jackson/iStockphoto.com)

These niche products can be developed and manufactured with a small staff and have low start-up costs. Other small companies purchase components built by larger firms and use them to build and repair computers for individuals or local small businesses. Most established computer hardware manufacturers were founded as small, niche companies, and many small computer hardware and peripherals companies are founded every year.

Potential Annual Earnings Scale. For small computer hardware manufacturing and consulting firms, employee earnings may vary widely depending on geographical location and technical expertise. Small start-up firms often run at a loss for the first few years, but they stand to earn substantial profits if the company goes public or is bought by a larger firm. Other small computer hardware firms may hire few full-time employees, and part-time employees are usually paid hourly wages.

At small local retail and repair firms, full-time computer sales representatives or sales clerks, whose main function is to obtain new accounts for their company, can expect to earn between $17,180 and $27,760 per year. Experienced technicians tasked with repairing and building computer systems may earn between $37,000 and $45,000 per year, on average. According to 2009 data compiled by Salary.com, highly experienced computer hardware engineers working at boutique consulting

firms in high-tech hot spots such as San Francisco may earn up to $160,000 per year.

Clientele Interaction. Many owners and employees of companies in the computer hardware and peripherals industry have direct contact with their clients. For small, Internet-based hardware and peripherals manufacturers, telecommunications may be the only form this contact takes. On the other hand, employees at small computer firms with storefront locations frequently meet with customers to give them hands-on demonstrations of products or to train them to operate new products. Customers may also visit storefront locations to drop off items for repair. In addition, many small computer firms offer on-site repair services, giving employees the opportunity to visit clients at their homes or businesses. Employees of boutique computer consulting firms often travel to the headquarters of large clients and make business proposals in person.

Amenities, Atmosphere, and Physical Grounds. Many computer hardware manufacturers were formed by entrepreneurs working from home. Some, including such well-known brands as Dell and Apple, have gone on to dominate the industry, while others have remained small and focus on niche products, consulting services, or serving the local community. Working from home reduces start-up costs but may also limit options for attracting customers. However, for companies that make the majority of their sales through the Internet, it is a viable strategy for optimizing financial stability during the early stages of development. A home office may also be a good starting option for owner-operators of small local firms that focus on hardware repair.

Once a company has reached a certain stage, it is usually necessary to rent warehouse or office space. Small businesses focusing on Internet sales may need minimal rental space, only enough to store overflow retail products. Small companies usually outsource their production work to overseas facilities or purchase components directly from larger manufacturers and assemble them on site. Computer hardware firms that serve the local community often rent small storefront locations, where they offer repair services; sell an assortment of hardware, peripherals, and software; and custom-build computers to customer specifications. Small consulting firms and niche manufacturers that focus on attracting larger clients usually rent urban office space near industry hot spots.

Typical Number of Employees. Most start-up computer hardware design and manufacturing firms are founded as very small companies, although some successful firms grow quite large over time. Small start-ups will begin with a minimal staff. Some consulting firms, manufacturers of niche products, and computer hardware companies with a local focus purposely maintain small staffs to keep their overhead low and retain flexibility. The staff may consist of a single owner-operator, but it is also common for small firms to hire part-time, full-time, or contract workers as needed.

Traditional Geographic Locations. Thanks to the growth of electronic commerce (or e-commerce) and the increased ability of companies to outsource production work overseas, computer hardware firms can be located throughout the world, in urban, suburban, or rural locations. Companies focused on Internet sales can be especially flexible, since most customers will never visit their facilities. Small computer firms catering to residents and local small businesses can likewise be founded in any location, though many are concentrated in urban and suburban areas. Small consulting firms catering to large clients in the computer and hardware industry are usually located near cities with high concentrations of high-tech compa-

nies, including San Francisco, Seattle, Boston, New York City, and Austin, Texas.

Pros of Working for a Small Computer-Manufacturing Firm. As major manufacturing and production activities continue to move overseas, it becomes easier to launch small computer start-ups with low overhead and a minimal staff. Some of these small start-ups will eventually become prominent in the industry, and early employees may reap great financial rewards. At start-ups, the atmosphere may feel more creative, exciting, and ambitious than at larger firms, particularly as small teams work closely together in the hope of achieving success.

For consulting and manufacturing firms, a minimal staff offers greater flexibility and allows them to maintain much smaller profit margins while remaining viable. Owner-operators of small firms enjoy the freedom to determine their own schedule, select their own employees, and maintain direct control over their businesses. Employees at these companies usually enjoy the benefits of a much less rigid office hierarchy. They may also benefit from greater creative input in all stages of research, design, development, and testing for new products. This allows employees at small firms to gain substantial experience that may give them significant advantages when seeking future job opportunities.

Cons of Working for a Small Computer-Manufacturing Firm. While some computer hardware start-ups attain great success in the industry, the majority of small start-ups eventually fail. According to the U.S. Small Business Administration, an estimated seven out of ten new firms last at least two years, and about half of them survive for five years. Because of this, prospective employees at small start-ups need to take into serious consideration the lack of job security. Also, since many start-ups may have very limited funds at their inception, wages and employee benefits may be reduced. Employees at small local firms and niche computer manufacturing companies also face decreased wages, and part-time and contract workers rarely receive benefits such as health insurance. Owner-operators face unique challenges, since they often have very narrow profit margins. A serious slowdown in business for just a few months can put their company out of business. In addition, small local firms specializing in building customized computers and making hardware repairs face severe competition from larger manufacturing firms and electronics retailers, which increasingly offer their own warranties and repair services.

Costs

Payroll and Benefits: Full-time employees at small companies usually receive benefits and a salary or hourly wages. Part-time employees are normally paid by the hour and usually do not receive benefits. Contract workers may be paid by the project or by the hour and rarely receive benefits.

Supplies: Since small computer companies generally outsource production duties or utilize off-the-shelf components manufactured by larger firms, supply needs are minimal. If the company or consulting firm has offices or storefront space, requirements will include standard office and telecommunication supplies and equipment, repair equipment, and possibly cash registers and credit-card readers. For small owner-operator firms specializing in on-site hardware repairs or building customized computer systems, requirements may be as minimal as a personal computer or laptop, a portable computer repair kit, and a cellular phone.

External Services: Small computer start-ups and hardware and peripherals firms usually outsource production duties to overseas manufacturing firms, focusing instead on creating innovative product designs. They may also establish wholesale retail arrangements with larger manufacturing firms, allowing them to purchase basic computer components at a reduced cost. In addition, they may hire Web site programmers and graphic designers on a contractual basis. Small firms are likely to hire external accountants or bookkeepers.

Utilities: For owner-operators running home-based businesses, utilities costs are comparable with basic household utility costs, although they must include high-speed Internet access. Computer firms that rent offices and storefront locations require high-speed Internet and telephone service. Electricity, water, and sewer services are also required, but some or all of these utilities may be included in the rental agreement.

Taxes: Tax rates vary widely for small firms, depending on many factors. Small manufacturing firms that outsource production duties overseas may pay high import taxes and tariffs. While most small businesses are required to pay local, state, and federal taxes, some states do not charge sales tax for Internet purchases. Rarely, small firms may own their own commercial property, while others are home-based businesses. In these cases, companies are required to pay all applicable property taxes.

Midsize Businesses

Most midsize computer-manufacturing firms are run in a manner similar to their larger counterparts. They have between 100 and 999 employees, and the midsize sector employs the majority of workers in the computer hardware and peripherals industry. However, midsize firms are less likely to own and operate their own international production facilities than are large firms. Instead, they frequently contract with overseas manufacturing companies or maintain their own domestic production facilities.

Midsize firms are more likely to focus on manufacturing peripherals or specialized components than on complete computer systems, although some do manufacture niche computers, such as high-end computer gaming systems. Some midsize firms become large firms by overtaking their competitors. Successful midsize firms may also be taken over by larger companies interested in acquiring their product lines, design expertise, or other intellectual property or capabilities.

Potential Annual Earnings Scale. Employees at successful midsize computer firms can earn wages comparable to those of their colleagues at larger companies. Wages are likely to vary internally between different job descriptions and levels of responsibility. According to the U.S. Bureau of Labor Statistics (BLS), production workers may earn $40,000 per year, while hardware engineers can expect to earn between $50,000 and $100,000 per year.

Clientele Interaction. Some employees of midsize computer firms, such as technical support specialists or sales representatives, interact extensively with clients. Marketers and sales representatives may work closely with electronic retailers to offer their companies' products at big-box retailers such as Best Buy or smaller chains such as Radio Shack. Other employees may interact with clients over the Internet, processing order forms and answering customer e-mails.

Technicians use probes to test a computer circuit board. (©Julia Burlachenko/ Dreamstime.com)

Amenities, Atmosphere, and Physical Grounds. Midsize computer firms normally have headquarters housing executive and administrative offices. Headquarters may also house research and development labs and sales-and-marketing offices. Production and warehouse facilities may be located on site, or they may be located elsewhere, sometimes in different states or overseas. Customers will rarely visit the headquarters of midsize firms, since they will most likely purchase products at retailers or over the Internet. The atmosphere in midsize businesses is usually very professional, although some companies may have a more relaxed attitude and dress code.

Typical Number of Employees. Midsize computer hardware and peripherals manufacturers usually employ between 100 and 999 people. The majority are full-time employees, although midsize firms also hire some workers, such as freelance technical writers, on a temporary contract basis.

Traditional Geographic Locations. Many midsize firms are clustered in traditional industry hot spots near colleges and universities. These include Silicon Valley, Boston, Austin, Seattle, and the Research Triangle area, comprising the cities of Raleigh, Durham, and Chapel Hill, North Carolina.

Pros of Working for a Midsize Computer-Manufacturing Firm. Job competition at large, established hardware manufacturers may be very in-

tense, and prospective employees must have extensive experience and are often educated at Ivy League schools. Midsize firms offer employees a chance to gain valuable job experience in a more relaxed atmosphere, where competition is less intense and employers may be more likely to hire graduates from public colleges. Employees may choose to spend their entire careers working in midsize firms, which may often provide more opportunities for upward mobility. At midsize firms, employees may also be able to establish a more direct rapport with fellow employees in different divisions as they work together closely to develop and market products. Most computer hardware and peripherals manufacturers provide their full-time employees with generous benefits, including health care, profit sharing, and retirement funds.

Cons of Working for a Midsize Computer-Manufacturing Firm. Although wages at midsize firms may be comparable with those at larger firms, they are normally, on average, at the lower end of the pay scale. Midsize firms may only have one or a few locations, so employees may not be able to transfer to another position if they need to relocate for personal reasons. They are also less likely to provide extensive research and development funding, so engineers and scientists hoping to work on the cutting edge of computer science may be more satisfied working at larger companies.

Costs

Payroll and Benefits: Full-time employees at midsize companies usually receive generous benefits and a salary or hourly wages. Contract workers may be paid by the project and rarely receive benefits.

Supplies: Midsize companies either have their own production facilities or outsource production duties, usually overseas. If companies have their own production facilities, they must purchase manufacturing equipment, often including clean-room technology. Research and development divisions usually require laboratory facilities, as well as specialized computers used for computer-aided design applications. They must also provide standard office supplies for their workers.

External Services: Midsize computer firms may outsource technical writing duties to freelancers. They may also outsource production duties and end-user technical support, often overseas. Sometimes they hire marketing firms and Web designers on a contractual basis.

Utilities: Midsize companies may rent or own their production facilities and headquarters. They must normally pay for Internet services, electricity, water, and sewer services. Research and development departments may require special disposal services for semiconductor equipment or exotic compounds.

Taxes: Tax rates vary for midsize firms, depending on their geographical location. Manufacturing firms that outsource production duties overseas may pay high import taxes and tariffs. They are also required to pay all applicable local, state, federal, and property taxes, although some states do not charge sales tax for Internet purchases.

Large Businesses

Large computer hardware and peripherals firms are usually established companies with long histories of developing many innovative products and providing customers with extensive technical support. Large companies such as IBM and Apple may inspire a loyal following of dedicated customers and electronic hobbyists. They may also host and participate in major computer technology conferences, such as EMC World and the MacWorld Expo, which are attended by thousands of industry insiders and devoted customers. They usually have very large research and development divisions and often take the lead in developing innovative new technologies that are implemented worldwide.

Many large computer companies have elaborate, centralized corporate headquarters, as well as far-flung domestic and international locations, in-

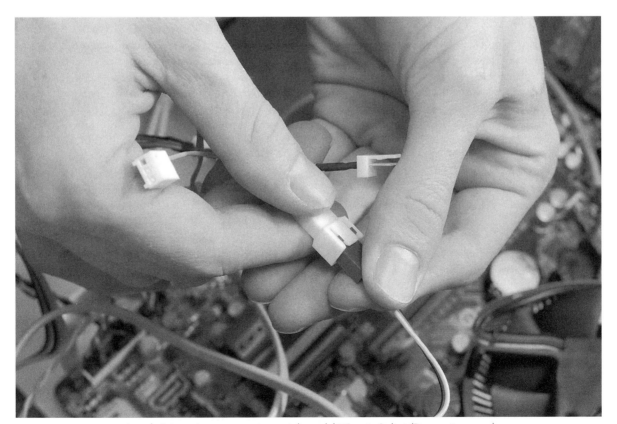

A technician wires a computer mainboard. (©Farzin Salimi/Dreamstime.com)

cluding training centers, multiple production facilities, and dedicated research and development laboratories. A few also have retail locations, where customers can purchase their products directly or drop off items for repair.

The largest computer hardware firms have become very diversified, often offering not just hardware components, peripherals, and complete computer systems but also software, online data storage, installation services, and personal electronics such as MPEG-1 Audio Layer 3 (MP3) players and even cell phones. They can also form joint ventures with other large companies and may acquire smaller competitors and other businesses whose niche products they may want to add to their own product lines.

Potential Annual Earnings Scale. Large computer hardware and peripherals companies pay the highest wages in the industry. It is common for employees in research and development, marketing, and sales departments to earn six-figure salaries, and high-powered executives earn even higher salaries. In addition, large firms often provide their employees with generous benefits, including health insurance, profit sharing, stock options, bonuses, and retirement benefits.

Clientele Interaction. Many employees in large computer firms interact extensively with individual customers and corporate clients. Large computer hardware and peripherals manufacturers often have an extensive sales force that may form close professional relationships with business clients. Marketers and sales representatives also make arrangements with big-box retailers such as Target, Best Buy, and Walmart to sell their products in stores, sometimes exclusively. Their sales force may also sell products directly to customers via phone or through the Internet. In addition, technical support employees often directly assist customers over the phone or via e-mail. A handful of large computer hardware and peripherals manufacturers have opened their own retail locations. Apple, for example, owns and operates its chain of Apple Stores. In these instances, employees make recommendations directly to customers in person and may also provide on-site training and repair services.

Amenities, Atmosphere, and Physical Grounds. Large computer firms often have luxurious campus headquarters, extensive research and development labs, multiple production facilities, training centers, and sales offices. Individual customers rarely visit company headquarters, although a few iconic campuses, such as Apple's headquarters in Cupertino, California, have become minor tourist attractions in their own right. Important clients may also visit the headquarters of large firms for business meetings. Large companies have multiple production facilities, including overseas production factories in countries such as Ireland and China. They may outsource individual components to various factories and then assemble the final product at a single location. The atmosphere at large firms varies widely. Large firms expect a high level of professionalism from their employees, but company standards and dress codes may be more relaxed in certain divisions. Many large companies also offer their employees on-site amenities, including day care, cafeterias, and even exercise facilities.

Typical Number of Employees. Large computer firms usually employ thousands or tens of thousands of people, often at numerous facilities across the globe. Most are full-time employees.

Traditional Geographic Locations. Large computer hardware and peripherals manufacturers often have multiple locations around the globe. Many have production facilities in China, Taiwan, Costa Rica, and Ireland. However, many have headquarters or facilities in high-tech hot spots near major universities, including Silicon Valley, Seattle, Boston, Austin, and the Research Triangle area in North Carolina.

Pros of Working for a Large Computer-Manufacturing Firm. Employees at large computer hardware and peripherals manufacturing companies are usually paid the highest wages in the industry, as well as receiving extremely generous benefits, stock options, retirement plans, vacation time, and on-site amenities. There is also a certain amount of prestige for employees of iconic firms. The possibility of developing groundbreaking technology is especially attractive to many employees interested in research and development.

Large companies usually provide extensive funding to research and development departments, allowing scientists and engineers to experiment with many different types of technology and brainstorm new products that may completely change the way human beings interact with technology. Iconic hardware firms such as Intel, IBM, and Apple attract the very top talent in the computer hardware and peripherals industry.

Cons of Working for a Large Computer-Manufacturing Firm. Competition for jobs at large computer hardware and peripherals manufacturers can be very intense. Prospective employees often have extensive experience in the field and advanced degrees from highly prestigious universities. Even once they are hired, employees feel intense pressure to succeed, and competition for internal promotions can be fierce. The work can be exhilarating but extremely stressful. Employees often work many hours of overtime per week, especially when preparing for new-product rollouts. They often have to work late nights and on weekends and may have to travel extensively for business. While some thrive on the constant pressure, burnout is very common among employees at large computer hardware firms.

Costs

Payroll and Benefits: Full-time employees at large companies are paid the most generous wages in the industry. They also receive generous benefits, including stock options, retirement funds, vacation time, health insurance, and possibly even on-site amenities, such as child-care and exercise facilities.

Supplies: Large companies often have their own production facilities and must purchase and maintain expensive manufacturing equipment and facilities, often utilizing clean-room technology. Large firms have well-funded research and development divisions with extensive laboratories and high equipment costs. They must also provide standard office supplies for their workers.

External Services: Large computer hardware and peripherals manufacturers may hire outside consulting firms and sometimes hire marketing firms to produce commercials and advertisements. They may also outsource some technical support duties or the manufacturing of certain components, often to overseas facilities.

Utilities: Large companies usually own their own production facilities and headquarters. They are normally required to pay for Internet services, electricity, water, and sewer services. These costs can be quite high for firms with extensive campuses or multiple locations. Research and development departments may require special disposal services for semiconductor equipment or exotic compounds.

Taxes: Since large firms may have far-flung domestic and overseas facilities, they often face very complicated tax structures. They may have to pay import and export tariffs and taxes in multiple countries. They are also required to pay all applicable local, state, federal, and property taxes.

ORGANIZATIONAL STRUCTURE AND JOB ROLES

Midsize and large hardware and peripherals manufacturing firms often share a similar organizational structure. Large computer firms may have divisions specializing in research and development, quality control, customer support, sales, and marketing. By contrast, smaller firms may vary widely in their organizational structure and hierarchy. Small, local firms dedicated to building customizable computer systems and repairing hardware, as well as niche hardware and peripherals manufacturing firms, may have just a handful of employees, or even a single owner-operator. Owners and employees may need to work together to perform any necessary duties, regardless of hierarchy or official position. Start-up hardware manufacturers and small consulting firms face unique challenges. While consulting firms may remain small and still earn profits, ambitious start-up firms often lose money in their first few years but may grow very rapidly if they prove successful. In these instances, developing a stable organizational structure is a key to remaining viable in the rapidly evolving computer hardware and peripherals manufacturing industry.

The following umbrella categories apply to the organizational structure of companies in the computer hardware and peripherals industry:

- Executive Management
- Research and Development
- Technical Writing Staff
- Marketing
- Sales

- Information Technology
- Technical Support
- Production
- Administrative Staff

Executive Management

Executives in the computer hardware and peripherals industry usually have advanced degrees, training, and experience in the field. In small companies and start-ups, the executive team may consist of just the owner or founder. The founders may also run midsize and large firms, continuing to serve as lead executives until their retirement. Some executives have legal backgrounds, but most work their way up from the sales or engineering side of the business. Either way, successful executives must have a firm understanding of the technical aspects of the business in order to serve in any leadership role within their companies.

In midsize or large firms, executives may work closely with a board of directors, especially in companies that are publicly traded. Executives normally earn very high salaries in comparison to other employees and are directly responsible for determining the future direction of their companies. They usually set goals and priorities, determine market segment focus, decide which products to release, and oversee other employees.

Executive management occupations may include the following:

- Chief Executive Officer (CEO)
- Board Chair
- Chief Financial Officer (CFO)
- Chief Technology Officer (CTO)
- Chief Information Officer (CIO)
- General Counsel
- Vice President
- General Manager/Managing Director

Research and Development

A company's research and development division creates new products. Normally, researchers bring new ideas to the table, while development teams refine, test, and implement these ideas. Both usually work closely together and in conjunction with marketing and sales departments to create and test prototypes that will ultimately be released as new products. They also improve existing technology, developing new models for existing prod-

uct lines. The original founders of small start-up companies often engage in their own independent research and development before launching their first products.

Research and development departments usually look for experienced scientists and engineers with extensive training and master's or doctoral degrees, although some entry-level positions may be available for experienced candidates with bachelor's degrees. According to the BLS, in 2007, research and development workers, depending on their degrees and experience, earned an average of between $50,000 and $100,000. Companies and government organizations also fund theoretical research conducted in university settings that may have practical applications for consumers.

Research and development occupations may include the following:

- Engineer
- Computer Scientist
- Physicist
- Engineering Technician
- Project Manager
- Development Manager

Technical Writing Staff

Technical writers and editors play a vital role in the computer hardware and peripherals industry. They are responsible for documenting the features of the industry's products and how to use them. Technical writers produce manuals both for end users, explaining the features of a computer or peripheral in plain language, and for technical specialists such as software engineers, explaining in specialized jargon how best to produce programs to control and utilize a company's products. They also produce in-house manuals that centralize information needed by the rest of their company's staff, providing all employees with standardized descriptions of both the company's products and the tools used to create those products.

Technical writers and editors need excellent writing skills and a firm understanding of complex computer technology and infrastructure. They usually have advanced degrees in English, technical writing, or journalism, as well as additional expertise, experience, and training in computer technology.

While some industries produce products that

may be easy to identify, many computer hardware products seem very similar on the surface. Technical writers help explain the differences between various products and also develop user manuals and other documentation materials. They may work closely with sales and marketing departments to ensure accuracy in their companies' written marketing materials. According to the BLS, computer hardware and peripherals companies are among the highest-paying employers of specialized technical writers and editors, with wages normally averaging between $45,130 and $73,750 per year.

Technical writing occupations may include the following:

- Technical Writer
- Editor

Marketing

Marketing employees are responsible for adver-tising their brands and attracting clients. They usually work closely with research and development departments, the sales force, and technical writers and editors to craft advertisements, brochures, and other related materials. Marketers in midsize and large firms may also suggest new products based on their marketing research. Some travel to conventions to interact with prospective clients and other firms in the computer industry.

Employees working in the marketing divisions of midsize and large computer hardware and peripherals manufacturers usually hold degrees in marketing, advertising, or public relations. They must also have specific expertise and training in the computer sciences, since they must be able to explain detailed technical specifications in ways that make these details easy for prospective customers to understand. Companies in the computer industry pay high wages to marketing employees, with managers earning $119,000 per year, on average, according to 2009 figures from the BLS.

OCCUPATION PROFILE

Computer Engineer

Considerations	Qualifications
Description	Designs, researches, and develops computers and computer peripherals.
Career clusters	Finance; Information Technology; Manufacturing; Science, Technology, Engineering, and Math
Interests	Data
Working conditions	Work inside
Minimum education level	Bachelor's degree; master's degree
Physical exertion	Light work
Physical abilities	Unexceptional/basic fitness
Opportunities for experience	Military service; part-time work
Licensure and certification	Usually not required
Employment outlook	Slower-than-average growth expected
Holland interest score	IRE

Note: See volume 1, "Publisher's Note," for an explanation of the Holland interest score.

Marketing occupations may include the following:

- Marketing Manager
- Advertising Copywriter
- Graphic Designer
- Public Relations Specialist

Sales

Employees working in sales departments usually interact directly with clients and customers. In large and midsize firms, sales representatives may spend significant time traveling to visit clients and potential customers at their offices. Others may call or e-mail prospective clients. Sales representatives in midsize and large firms often work on commission, meaning their pay may vary widely depending on how successful they are at selling products.

According to 2009 BLS figures, successful sales managers can expect to earn between $65,000 and $141,000 per year. Smaller firms with storefront locations may hire part-time retail sales clerks to interact with customers. However, they may instead depend on technicians to handle any sales needs. In the case of companies run by a single owner-operator, the owner usually handles all sales duties.

Sales occupations may include the following:

- Sales Representative
- Sales Manager
- Retail Sales Clerk

Information Technology

Companies in the computer hardware and peripherals industry must have a highly skilled information technology (IT) staff. This staff is responsible for maintaining the extensive computer networks and Web sites utilized by companies to communicate both internally with their employees and externally with their customers. IT professionals are also responsible for securing computer networks and protecting against viruses and attacks by hackers. Other responsibilities may include updating computer hardware and software and providing technical support for other employees within an organization. IT employees usually possess advanced training and computer expertise, and midsize and large firms tend to prefer candidates with graduate-level degrees. According to the BLS, highly skilled IT workers can expect to earn between $79,000 and $129,000 per year.

IT occupations may include the following:

- Network Specialist
- Web Designer
- Computer Systems Analyst
- Information Technology Director
- Computer Security Specialist

Technical Support

Technical support representatives are responsible for troubleshooting problems encountered by customers, either in person or over the phone. They may also install new products for customers, instruct customers on the proper use of their companies' products, and diagnose hardware and software errors. They must closely document customer requests and complaints and ensure that products work as intended. Technical support representatives play an increasingly vital role in the computer hardware and peripherals industry; as computer products become more complex, customers place added value on receiving extra support from manufacturers.

Training or preparation in technical support offers many opportunities for entry-level positions. Prospective employees often hold associate's degrees, bachelor's degrees, or technical certificates. According to 2007 BLS estimates, they can expect to earn an average of between $32,000 and $54,000 per year. Some manufacturers and retailers directly employ technical support representatives, while others outsource technical support duties to external companies, including overseas firms. For small, local computer hardware companies, technical support and computer repairs can make up a significant percentage of their overall earnings.

Technical support occupations may include the following:

- Technical Support Specialist
- Help Desk Specialist
- Computer Maintenance and Repair Technician

Production

Production duties in the computer hardware and peripherals industry are increasingly being outsourced overseas. The opportunities available for production work within in the United States are generally very specialized and may involve clean-room facilities. Production workers usually receive extensive technical training on the job, but most firms also expect prospective employees to have obtained associate's degrees or be certified in high-tech manufacturing techniques.

In small, local computer hardware companies, repair specialists may also serve as assembly workers, putting together new computers for customers from components purchased from larger manufacturers. Production workers in the computer hardware and peripherals industry can expect to earn approximately $40,000 per year, on average, which is more than most production workers earn in other sectors.

Production occupations may include the following:

- Assembly Worker
- Quality Assurance Tester
- Production Supervisor
- Bench Technician

Administrative Staff

The administrative staff is responsible for coordinating day-to-day schedules and appointments, greeting visitors, resolving personnel issues, and keeping financial records. Educational requirements vary widely, especially in larger firms. Receptionists, for example, may need only a high school degree, while accountants are usually expected to have at least an associate's degree, and human resources (HR) professionals should have at least a bachelor's degree. HR managers can expect to earn between $67,000 and $107,000 per year, while administrative assistants may earn $30,000 to $46,000 per year. In small firms, administrative duties may be contracted out. For example, accountants may be hired only on a temporary basis during tax time.

Administrative occupations may include the following:

- Human Resources Manager
- Administrative Assistant
- Accountant
- Receptionist

INDUSTRY OUTLOOK

Overview

The computer has revolutionized the world, allowing nearly instantaneous access to almost limitless amounts of information and becoming a necessary component of the operations of almost all businesses. Businesses all over the world must stay current with modern trends in the computer hardware and peripherals industry or face being left behind by their competitors. Many older products that were once the standard have been replaced by better, faster, more efficient technologies. For example, vacuum tubes were replaced by transistors, and floppy disk drives by hard drives and flash drives. Data once held in massive libraries of paper punch cards can now be stored at a fraction of the cost in much smaller storage devices, such as hard drives.

While spending on computer hardware and peripherals tends to fall during recessions, the computer industry is very resilient and tends to bounce back as soon as the economy begins to turn around. The computer hardware and peripherals industry has continued to grow overall, despite slowdowns and the recession caused by the crash of the dot-com boom in 2000-2001. The 2001 recession following the dot-com crash proved especially punishing to the computer industry overall, since much of the rapid growth in that sector ultimately proved unsustainable. During the global recession of 2007-2009, most of the industry again suffered major slowdowns in hardware and peripherals sales. However, not every company was affected, and earnings at manufacturing firms such as Intel and EMC had already begun to rise by late 2009. For the foreseeable future, computer hardware will be necessary for the growth of almost any business, so the industry can be expected to grow with the economy.

The first integrated circuit was created in 1959. In 1965, Intel cofounder Gordon Moore made a startling prediction. According to the so-called Moore's law, the number of transistors on an integrated circuit (and thus the rough computing power of the chip) will double every two years. Surprisingly, what may have seemed to be an overly ambitious forecast has held true into the twenty-first century.

PROJECTED EMPLOYMENT FOR SELECTED OCCUPATIONS

Computer and Electronic Products Manufacturing

Employment		
2009	Projected 2018	Occupation
27,150	23,000	Computer hardware engineers
33,890	27,800	Computer software engineers, applications
50,850	45,900	Computer software engineers, systems software
34,860	30,200	Electrical and electronic engineering technicians
104,230	82,700	Electrical and electronic equipment assemblers
24,780	20,100	Semiconductor processors

Source: U.S. Bureau of Labor Statistics, Industries at a Glance, Occupational Employment Statistics and Employment Projections Program.

As transistors have continued to shrink and integrated circuits have become more powerful and more compact, new devices have been developed that blur the boundaries between computers, telecommunications equipment, consumer electronics, and even medical devices. For example, so-called smart phones have more in common with computers than they do with Alexander Graham Bell's original telephone. Many devices, including personal digital assistants (PDAs), touch-screen video gaming systems, satellite navigation devices, digital video recorders (DVRs), and multitouch tabletop computers (such as the Microsoft Surface), are becoming harder to categorize as computers, personal electronics, or household appliances.

In addition, the U.S. military, which initially funded much of the research that led to the development of early computers such as ENIAC, is increasingly dependent on computer hardware technology. Modern warfare involves constant communication among soldiers utilizing computers and digital satellite technology. Computers are also used by the military to control unpiloted aerial vehicles that perform rescue and reconnaissance missions and launch attacks into dangerous combat zones. Even police officers increasingly carry computers in their squad cars, and specially designed heavy-duty laptops have been created for use by police and military personnel in the line of duty.

If Moore's law continues to hold true, transistors will shrink to the size of an atom by 2020. Research is currently being conducted into new experimental technologies, such as quantum computing, that would make such transistors possible, and quantum computers may one day be able to store data on a subatomic scale. Another experimental hardware technology that may one day revolutionize the field of computer science is the deoxyribonucleic acid (DNA) computer, which uses biomechanical genetic coding to store information. While these technologies are still in the early stages of development, it is likely that if they come to fruition they will become as firmly integrated into modern life as is the personal computer. In addition, many computer hardware and peripherals firms are researching new ways to minimize energy consumption and use environmentally sustainable manufacturing techniques.

Many of the computing innovations that are now taken for granted began as simple ideas of entrepreneurs, researchers, scientists, and even amateur hobbyists. Because of the rapid, ceaseless innovation that is the hallmark of this industry, there will always be new opportunities for creative advancement. Nobody can predict what the next great technological leap forward in computer hardware and peripherals will be, but it is certain that the industry will continue to evolve dramatically and its effect on daily life will continue to increase.

Employment Advantages

The amount of digitally encoded information will continue to increase exponentially for the foreseeable future, so demand for computer hardware and peripherals will continue to rise overall. In addition, computer usage is skyrocketing in many countries throughout the developing world, including China, India, and Brazil. This trend will further increase global demand for computer hardware and peripherals.

Despite rising demands, 2009 projections by the BLS indicate that U.S. employment in the industry is expected to drop by 12 percent by 2016. This expected drop is mostly due to productivity gains and intense competition from international firms. Production workers, in particular, can expect steep drops in employment as manufacturing duties continue to move overseas. However, employment trends in research, design, sales, and marketing are expected to remain strong. In addition, new innovations on the horizon may further increase demand and provide new start-up companies with many opportunities for future growth.

Annual Earnings

With domestic revenues of $110 billion, the computer hardware and peripherals industry is extremely cyclical and is frequently affected by economic bubbles and downturns. Because computer hardware and peripherals represent a major investment for most companies, sales usually drop during recessions. However, as the economy improves, demand for hardware products rises dramatically.

During the 2007-2009 global recession, computer hardware and peripherals manufacturing firms proved surprisingly resilient compared to other economic sectors. Both Intel and Hewlett-Packard forecast substantial revenue growth in the early 2010's. The *Denver Post* has reported that Intel beat its own predictions for second-quarter growth in 2009, increasing its earnings by $879 million, the highest jump in twenty-one years.

RELATED RESOURCES FOR FURTHER RESEARCH

ASSOCIATION FOR COMPUTING MACHINERY
2 Penn Plaza, Suite 701
New York, NY 10121-0701

Tel: (800) 342-6626
Fax: (212) 944-1318
http://www.acm.org

COMPTIA
1815 S Meyers Rd., Suite 300
Oakbrook Terrace, IL 60181-5228
Tel: (630) 678-8300
Fax: (630) 678-8384
http://www.comptia.org

COMPUTER SOCIETY
Institute of Electrical and Electronics Engineers
2001 L St. NW, Suite 700
Washington, DC 20036
Tel: (202) 371-0101
Fax: (202) 728-9614
http://www.computer.org

INFORMATION TECHNOLOGY ASSOCIATION OF AMERICA
1401 Wilson Blvd., Suite 1100
Arlington, VA 22209
Tel: (703) 522-5055
Fax: (703) 525-2279
http://www.itaa.org

INSTITUTE FOR CERTIFICATION OF COMPUTING PROFESSIONALS
2400 E Devon Ave., Suite 281
Des Plaines, IL 60018
Tel: (800) 843-8227
Fax: (847) 299-4280
http://www.iccp.org

SOCIETY FOR INFORMATION MANAGEMENT
401 N Michigan Ave.
Chicago, IL 60611
Tel: (312) 527-6734
http://www.simnet.org

SOCIETY FOR TECHNICAL COMMUNICATION
9401 Lee Hwy., Suite 300
Fairfax, VA 22031
Tel: (703) 522-4114
Fax: (703) 522-2075
http://www.stc.org

USENIX, the Advanced Computing Systems
    Association
2560 9th St., Suite 215
Berkeley, CA 94710
Tel: (510) 528-8649
Fax: (510) 548-5738
http://www.usenix.org

ABOUT THE AUTHOR

Elizabeth Fernandez took apart her first computer when she was very young. As a result of her early fascination with technology, she began working in the computer industry in 2002, serving as a Webmaster and a hardware and software repair specialist. For the past ten years, she has also worked as a writer and editor specializing in computer science and technology trends. She has been published online, in newspapers, and in local magazines, and has edited several books focusing on the computer, aviation, and transportation industries. She graduated with a degree in journalism from the University of Central Florida.

FURTHER READING

Allan, Roy A. *A History of the Personal Computer: The People and the Technology*. 2d ed. London, Ont.: Allan Publishing, 2001.

Burns, Julie Kling. *Opportunities in Computer Careers*. Chicago: VGM Career Books, 2002.

Campbell-Kelly, Martin, and William Aspray. *Computer: A History of the Information Machine*. 2d ed. Boulder, Colo.: Westview Press, 2004.

Computer History Museum. "Timeline." http://www.computerhistory.org/semiconductor/timeline.html.

Cortada, James W. *The Digital Hand: How Computers Changed the Work of American Manufacturing, Transportation, and Retail Industries*. New York: Oxford University Press, 2004.

Eberts, Marjorie, and Margaret Gisler. *Careers for Computer Buffs and Other Technological Types*. 3d ed. New York: McGraw-Hill, 2006.

Morley, Deborah. *Understanding Computers in a Changing Society*. Boston: Cengage Learning, 2009.

Swade, Doron. "The Babbage Engine." Computer History Museum, 2008. http://www.computerhistory.org/babbage.

U.S. Bureau of Labor Statistics. *Career Guide to Industries*, 2010-2011 ed. http://www.bls.gov/oco/cg.

_____. "Computer and Information Systems Managers." In *Occupational Outlook Handbook*, 2010-2011 ed. http://www.bls.gov/oco/ocos258.htm.

U.S. Census Bureau. North American Industry Classification System (NAICS), 2007. http://www.census.gov/cgi-bin/sssd/naics/naicsrch?chart=2007.

U.S. Department of Commerce. International Trade Administration. Office of Trade and Industry Information. Industry Trade Data and Analysis. http://ita.doc.gov/td/industry/otea/OTII/OTII-index.html.

Yost, Jeffrey R. *The Computer Industry*. Westport, Conn.: Greenwood Press, 2005.

Computer Software Industry

```
main()
_setvideomode(0x13);                              /* set

for (i=0; i<=64; i++) {                           /* as
    if ((i & 32) == 32) R=21; else R=0;
    if ((i & 16) == 16) G=21; else G=0;
    if ((i &  8) ==  8) B=21; else B=0;
    if ((i &  4) ==  4) R+=42;
    if ((i &  2) ==  2) G+=42;
    if ((i &  1) ==  1) B+=42;

    vgacolor(i,R,G,B);
}
```

©Dreamstime.com

INDUSTRY SNAPSHOT

General Industry: Information Technology
Career Cluster: Information Technology
Subcategory Industries: Computer Applications;
Computer Gaming Software; Computer Operating
Systems; Computer Programming Languages and
Compilers; Computer Utility Software; Custom Computer
Programming Services
Related Industries: Computer Hardware and Peripherals
Industry; Computer Systems Industry; Internet and Cyber
Communications Industry; Video, Computer, and Virtual
Reality Games Industry
Annual Domestic Revenues: $180 billion USD (Computer
Software Development, 2009)
Annual Global Revenues: $303.8 billion USD (Software:
Global Industry Guide, 2009)
NAICS Numbers: 511210, 541511

INDUSTRY DEFINITION

Summary

In modern computing terms, software usually refers to nearly all aspects of a computer except for the physical hardware or components. Thus, software includes a computer's operating systems and graphic user interfaces, firmware designed to control electronic hardware components, Web browsers, and stand-alone programs called applications, such as Microsoft Word or Apple's Garage Band. The software industry developed in parallel with the computer hardware industry. The two industries depend on each other to survive, and many companies offer both hardware and software products. With the development of cloud computing, Internet-based firms such as Google have begun to develop software that users can access online without downloading code permanently onto their own computers.

History of the Industry

Throughout history, people have searched for more efficient ways of organizing useful information. By the early 1800's, mathematical calculation tables had become standard tools adopted by many professions, including accountants, astronomers, sailors, and mathematicians. However, such tables were frequently inaccurate and difficult to use. This situation led inventor Charles Babbage to design several automatic calculating machines, culminating in his design for the analytical engine in 1834. According to Babbage's original designs, punch cards would have been used to program the analytical engine. Although the project was never completed, Babbage's design inspired mathematician Ada Lovelace to write an extremely perceptive article describing how numbers could be used to represent other forms of data, such as musical notes or the letters of the alphabet. Lovelace also developed a rudimentary computer program for the analytical engine and is considered by many to be the world's first computer programmer.

Punch-card technology represents another forerunner that would lead to the development of modern software. In 1890, former United States Census Bureau employee Herman Hollerith started the Tabulating Machine Company, later known as International Business Machines (IBM). Hollerith had previously developed a punch-card system that allowed thin paper punch cards to store popula-

tion statistics. Early punch cards had been used to control automated looms in the textile industry, but Hollerith was the first person to perfect the use of punch cards to store many different types of data.

As engineers, scientists, and physicists began experimenting with computer technology, they also developed new methods for storing and manipulating information. Early computers such as the Electronic Numerical Integrator and Computer (ENIAC), one of the world's first electronic computers, used a mixture of vacuum tubes, plug boards, and punch cards to store and input computer instructions. Developed in 1937, the 1,800-square-foot ENIAC was so large and complex that it weighed 30 tons and took days to reprogram.

In 1944, IBM unveiled the Automatic Sequence Controlled Calculator (ASCC) at Harvard University, where it was known as the Harvard Mark 1. Early computer scientists such as Grace Murray

A Google employee drives through the streets of Palo Alto, California, shooting street views for its map software. (AP/Wide World Photos)

Hopper and Howard Aiken soon began creating programs for the Mark 1, working together to write complex mathematical codes that were input into the computer through a series of punch cards. These computer scientists are considered the first programmers in the United States.

Throughout the 1950's, early computer scientists frequently collaborated to develop a standard computer-programming language that would be compatible with specific computer hardware. For example, some groups focused on sharing common programming routines for IBM computers, while others concentrated on models manufactured by Digital Equipment Corporation (DEC). In 1959, Hopper led a team assembled by the U.S. Department of Defense in designing (the Common Business-Oriented Language (COBOL), one of the earliest universal programming languages. COBOL is still used by businesses, governments, and military organizations worldwide. In addition, elements of COBOL continue to be used commonly in computer operating systems such as Microsoft's Windows and Unix.

As computer hardware continued to evolve, software programming became more widespread, thanks in part to the development of the integrated circuit in 1959 and the invention of the floppy disk. These important milestones helped bring the computer widespread acceptance in the business world, and in 1976, Steve Wozniak began to market the Apple I, the world's first personal desktop computer. As computers became fully integrated into homes and businesses, programmers simplified the graphic user interface (GUI), leading to the development of Microsoft Windows in 1983 and the Mac OS in 1984. Software has since become an increasingly important aspect of modern life, as specialized programs have been developed for every type of industry and electronic product, from household robotic devices such as the Roomba to smart phones such as the iPhone.

Although the software industry suffered as a result of the collapse of the dot-com bubble during the late 1990's and early 2000's, as did most computer-based industries, the continued rise of the Internet has offered companies in the software industry many new opportunities to expand their business. Thanks to powerful new computers and low-cost, or even free, online distribution methods, new developers can sell their software directly to customers online, bypassing wholesalers and retail locations. Delivering software to customers through the Internet has dramatically reduced the costs incurred by software developers. This reduced cost has led to an explosion of low-cost shareware and free, open-source software projects such as Linux or the popular Firefox browser. Countless people are involved in the software industry, from software engineers and beta testers to hobbyists who create software for free in their spare time.

The Industry Today

As computers have become ubiquitous in modern life, so has software. Without software, computers would be practically unusable to the average consumer. Software allows consumers of any age and skill range, from children to the elderly, to have access to the Internet, play games, connect with other people for work or play, and even edit films and photos. Meanwhile, as advanced smart phones and netbook computers allow more people to access the Internet, software developers have gained many new platforms through which to offer their products.

The growing and thriving software industry has evolved to meet the ever-changing requirements of a global society that is constantly utilizing such advanced technology. From handheld gaming systems and electronic appliances to cellular phones and personal computers, software is included in countless devices and utilized by practically every profession. The right software, for example, makes it much easier for architects to design buildings, for doctors to keep track of their patients' medical records, for teachers to contact parents and students, and for investors to trade stocks. Because of software, businesses and individuals have become increasingly dependent on computers to store and manage information.

On the Internet, software is what makes it possible for people to communicate online. Web designers use software to create Web sites and online content, and Web browsers allow users easy access to nearly unlimited amounts of information in a plethora of formats, including social networking sites, newspapers, online government records, and e-mail. However, the popularity of the Internet has also caused a skyrocketing number of dangerous computer viruses, malware, and spyware. Individuals may hack into home networks, businesses intranets, and school and government records, often in an attempt to change records, defraud banks, or launch denial-of-service attacks, which have crippled numerous Web sites and led to many instances of identity theft. These malicious activities have led to the growth of many companies such as Norton, McAfee, and Trend Micro that specialize in antivirus software designed to block and remove malicious programs while repairing infected files. These companies also provide software designed to protect businesses and users from hacking attacks that may disrupt computer systems or allow malicious access to personal or confidential information.

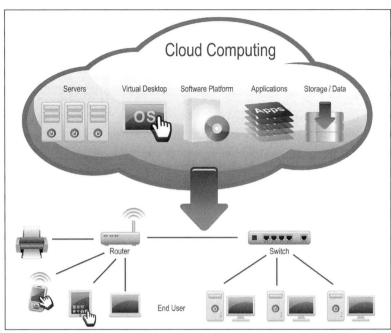

Cloud computing makes available at any site with Internet access both users' information and software capable of manipulating that information. (©Arrow/Dreamstime.com)

Software is sold in many different retail stores, including electronics, office-supply, and video-game stores. Most new computers come with some software preinstalled, including the operating system, Web browsers, and word processors, as well as trial versions of premium software products such as Microsoft Office. In addition, countless software companies and individual entrepreneurs offer their products online. Some individuals create software as a hobby in their spare time. For example, the word-processing application Scrivener was originally developed as a hobby by an aspiring writer. However, after founder Keith Blount released Scrivener as shareware (proprietary software that can be downloaded and tried out for free—sometimes in a limited or trial version), the application gained a strong following among novelists and screenwriters. By 2009, its publisher, Literature & Latte, had grown into a successful two-person company, allowing Blount to work on his software full time.

The first decade of the twenty-first century has also seen the growth of open-source software, including such popular programs as Linux and Firefox. Open-source software is software whose source code is made freely available for use, study,

and modification. As a result, it is developed and improved by an extended community of programmers that may include company employees, hobbyists, and professionals working in their spare time. Even profitable companies such as Google have developed and released free open-source software, such as Google's Chromium project, which includes much of the code behind the company's free Chrome Web browser. Major corporations also make use of open-source software developed elsewhere. For example, Mac OS X includes code taken from FreeBSD, an open-source version of Unix.

The development of cloud computing (a model for delivering hosted services over the Internet) has also altered the software landscape. Companies such as Google and Microsoft have begun to offer users the ability to access software programs directly through the Internet, including database software and word processors. Users can also store information in a fashion that makes it available through the "cloud." Thus, cloud computing makes available, at any site with Internet access, both users' information and software capable of manipulating that information. This availability frees users from needing to use a dedicated machine or to carry their data with them. For example, students writing essays can use Google Docs to write and edit their work, accessing their documents from computers at their local libraries, homes, or schools. They need not worry about whether these computers utilize particular software applications, nor must they carry data-storage devices to transport their files. As long as a computer is installed with a relatively current version of a common Web browser, it can access and modify the students' files.

Other companies have begun to offer cloud computing software for specialized applications and businesses, including human resources software and accounting programs. This software has made it much easier for employees and small-business owners to access their data at any time. A local contractor, for example, can access spreadsheets with account information from an office computer, a laptop, or even a smart phone while on a job site. Cloud computing as a technology is still in its inception, but it has already experienced wide adoption by many different types of users, and creative software programmers can take advantage of this evolving technology to create new and unique programs.

INDUSTRY MARKET SEGMENTS

Computer software companies can be of any size. Most software companies are founded by very small groups of people. Microsoft, for example, was founded by just two people. In fact, more than half of all software companies have fewer than five employees, although more than 76 percent of software jobs are located in firms with more than fifty employees, according to the U.S. Bureau of Labor Statistics (BLS).

Small Businesses

Small businesses in the computer software industry usually employ fewer than fifty people, and many firms employ four or fewer. In addition, amateur programmers and hobbyists, as well as professionals in the field working in their spare time, create many software programs. Because of the low entry costs for software publishing, anybody with a good idea can enter the field and have a chance at

lasting success. Even failed early attempts should not dissuade aspiring programmers, many of whom can eventually build portfolios of software programs that may help them obtain jobs at larger firms.

Potential Annual Earnings Scale. Because of the varied nature of small software firms, potential earnings vary widely. Some software programmers work for free, while others may consider the earnings from their small software company a secondary income. On average, according to 2008 estimates by the BLS, the average annual salary for full-time software engineers can range from $52,000 to $122,720.

Clientele Interaction. Small software companies usually release their products online, often as shareware or freeware through sites such as CNET.com or MacUploads.com. In addition, many smart phones such as the iPhone or the Motorola Droid have thriving online application stores that allow programmers to offer their software to prospective customers for a small fee. Since small firms mostly sell their products online, they usually have very little direct customer interaction. Instead, they normally handle most communication through e-mail, forums, chat rooms, and instant messages. In very small firms, such as those with fewer than five employees, nearly everybody helps provide customers with technical assistance. Small firms often have loyal niche followings, with many clients offering suggestions for future products and helping the companies identify bugs in their products.

Amenities, Atmosphere, and Physical Grounds. Small computer software firms often have a single small office location, often rented, while many others are run from a home office. Employees often telecommute, working from their homes to answer customer queries or create new software programs and submitting their work online.

The atmosphere at small firms is usually casual and laid back. Often, these companies are founded by friends, classmates, or relatives, with a very small and intimate staff. However, employees may be required to work extremely long hours under strict deadlines, whether they are working from home or from an office location, especially in the run-up before a new software release.

Typical Number of Employees. Most small computer software firms have very few employees, typically less than fifty, with the majority of firms employing fewer than five people. However, most small firms, especially nonprofit firms, also employ a large army of volunteers willing to beta test their software free of charge. In the case of nonprofit firms, unpaid collaborators may actually do most of the programming. Mozilla, for example, allows unpaid collaborators to write the majority of the code, beta test the software for errors, and suggest new features, all within an interactive community forum. Working on free software can provide aspiring programmers with valuable experience that they can later use in launching their own businesses or pursuing employment at for-profit firms.

Traditional Geographic Locations. Because small software firms are founded by people from all walks of life—often working from home and collaborating online—they exist throughout the United States. However, there are several high-tech hot spots where many software firms have their headquarters. These include Silicon Valley, in California's San Francisco Bay Area; Los Angeles, California; Portland, Oregon; and Seattle, Washington. Often, once a small start-up software company has attained a certain level of success, it will relocate its headquarters to one of these high-tech hot spots in order to attract top employees and more easily obtain funding to expand. Microsoft, for example, was founded in Albuquerque, New Mexico, but moved to the Seattle suburb of Redmond, Washington, in 1979.

Pros of Working for a Small Software Company. Many small software companies have been founded by amateur programmers who began developing software as a hobby. Others have been founded by full-time programmers during their off hours. Because these company founders often develop their original software programs as hobbyists, they may start their businesses with a sense of freedom. They may develop new software programs simply for themselves, to solve a dilemma or to entertain themselves and their friends. Many consider programming simply a lucrative hobby at the start of their careers.

In addition, since many small software firms have fewer than five employees, they generate a very strong sense of camaraderie. These companies may have a more relaxed atmosphere than larger firms, and employees are usually encouraged to make new product suggestions or even to experiment with their own projects. Small firms sometimes release successful "killer apps"—applications that alone justify the purchase of the platform on which they run. Such applications can create real paradigm shifts in the way people use computers. Early employees of these companies often receive substantial stock options and may reap great financial benefits if the small company is sold or becomes publicly traded.

Cons of Working for a Small Software Company. Because most small software companies have very few employees, each member of the staff must take on multiple responsibilities. This is especially true of the many software firms with fewer than five employees, who may be required to work very long hours. Since small computer software firms are often founded by one or two people, sometimes simply as a hobby, their initial software offerings may need to achieve a certain level of success and develop a strong following before the founders can quit their day jobs and focus all their attention on their new business. Aspiring programmers launching their own products must often work long hours for months at a time, without pay. They reap financial rewards only if their software manages to gain a following. If a particular piece of software proves unpopular, then individual programmers must start from scratch on new programs or attempt to refine their products in the hope that new features will attract new customers.

Software piracy is also a huge concern in the industry, and, since small companies and individual programmers usually have slim profit margins, they may feel the effects of piracy more strongly than do larger companies, which are more easily able to absorb such costs. Also, small software companies may be less stable to work for than larger companies, since the popularity of software can be quite cyclical. Smaller companies are usually less diversified, with much smaller software portfolios than those of larger companies. A company that relies on a single program for its income is in a more precarious position than a company that sells several different—or even different categories of—applications.

Costs

Payroll and Benefits: Many small software companies are founded by individuals working on projects in their spare time. In this scenario, benefits are most likely not available. However, once established, even small software companies usually offer generous benefits in order to attract talented employees. Benefits often include stock options, health insurance, and paid sick days.

Supplies: Small businesses and entrepreneurs in the software industry require up-to-date computer systems and software, as well as other standard office supplies.

External Services: Small software companies, hobbyists, and entrepreneurs developing their own software via the Internet typically outsource their Web hosting and server needs. They may also hire accountants and other financial specialists on a contractual basis—during tax time, for example.

Utilities: Small software companies with office locations must pay rent, which may include water and sewer service, as well as electricity, which may be a significant cost depending on the number of computers located on the property. They also must pay for high-speed Internet.

Taxes: Individuals and small businesses must pay all applicable local, state, federal, and property taxes.

Midsize Businesses

Midsize computer software companies have between fifty and two hundred employees. These companies usually focus on specialized niches, such as converting (or "porting") Windows games and software to run on Apple computers. Some companies offer only a single popular software title, while others offer a selection of related software titles that appeal to their specific customer base. Usually, midsize software firms start as small firms and grow as their software becomes more popular. However, entrepreneurs with strong and successful business records may be able to raise enough venture capital or invest enough of their own profits from previous ventures to launch midsize businesses.

Potential Annual Earnings Scale. Midsize software firms usually pay good wages and offer generous benefits. The majority of employees in this industry work full time, though firms may employ part-time employees for software testing or customer support purposes. Earnings vary by position, experience, and education. General managers in this industry earn more than the average for other industries; the BLS estimates that their average annual salary is around $126,000.

Clientele Interaction. Midsize software companies usually have separate divisions or departments related to sales and technical support. These are normally the departments that spend the most time interacting with clients. They typically answer customer queries via phone, e-mail, or live chat. In addition, sales associates and marketers often interact directly with large electronics retailers to offer their products to consumers. They also may negotiate deals with businesses, schools, or organizations that purchase software in bulk.

Amenities, Atmosphere, and Physical Grounds. Midsize software companies normally have professional office locations, though some employees may telecommute from home, either for a portion of the workweek or full time. Unlike large software companies, they usually do not own large campus facilities, instead renting office space. In addition, they do not require extensive manufacturing facilities, since nearly all software is sold either online or on compact discs (CDs) or digital versatile discs (DVDs). They usually outsource the printing of their software and reference materials, as well as packaging.

The atmosphere in midsize firms varies tremendously, often depending on the type of software they manufacture. Some firms have a casual atmosphere. For example, a company that manufactures computer games will usually have a laid-back office environment. However, a firm that develops accounting software, for example, will usually be more businesslike, with a more structured atmosphere and strict dress code.

Typical Number of Employees. Nearly all employees in the computer software industry work full time. Most midsize firms have between 50 and 250 full-time employees. However, they may also utilize a strong task force of unpaid volunteers involved in beta testing software and offering suggestions for improvement. In addition, they may occasionally outsource technical support.

Traditional Geographic Locations. Software firms can be located anywhere in the world, since much of the programming duties, and even software distribution, can take place easily via the Internet. However, there is a very strong concentration of midsize software firms on the West Coast, especially in Silicon Valley, Portland, and Seattle.

Locating in one of these high-tech hot spots makes it easier for software companies to find the most talented and experienced employees.

Pros of Working for a Midsize Software Company. Midsize software companies are usually more established than smaller companies, so employees may have more job security than those at smaller firms. They normally have more well-defined roles and duties than employees at smaller companies, where a very small staff must do a little bit of everything. As a result, midsize companies may be less stressful workplaces in some ways than smaller companies, allowing employees to focus more completely on the tasks at hand. They also usually offer more generous perks and benefits than do smaller companies and often provide generous stock options and higher salaries. Midsize software companies also offer more opportunities for career flexibility and advancement than smaller firms, while maintaining a more intimate environment than larger firms can offer. With less office hierarchy than at larger companies, workers at midsize firms can take their ideas directly to their superiors.

Cons of Working for a Midsize Software Company. Midsize companies often make attractive takeover targets for larger companies interested in expanding or diversifying their software offerings; although employment in midsize firms is usually more stable than at smaller firms, employees in midsize firms may face job insecurity because of acquisitions. In addition, wages may be lower than at larger firms, and midsize companies are normally unable to provide as many opportunities for research and development as larger firms. Midsize firms may also lack the strong sense of intimate camaraderie and freedom found at smaller firms. Although employees may receive stock options or join in profit-sharing plans, they usually own a less significant share of the company than do their counterparts at smaller firms, so they may not benefit as much if the company is sold or goes public. Lastly, because midsize firms have narrower profit margins than larger firms, employees may also be more affected by downturns in the economy or the technology sector.

Costs

Payroll and Benefits: Midsize companies in the computer software industry typically offer employees generous salaries and full benefits, such as health and life insurance and stock options. They usually also offer perks, often including paid vacations.

Supplies: Midsize software companies must purchase basic office equipment and supplies. They also require specialized, high-end computer systems and may occasionally host their own Web servers if they have a significant online presence. All computers must be up-to-date, especially computers used by programmers and software testers.

External Services: Most employees at midsize firms work full time. However, the companies may occasionally hire external firms or consultants, often hiring financial consultants or marketing and advertising firms. They may also outsource technical support services and manufacturing duties, since midsize firms usually offer CDs or DVDs of their products in stores as well as online.

Utilities: Midsize firms normally rent office locations, often in corporate office parks. They also require high-speed Internet service, often including dedicated fiber-optic data lines if they conduct much of their business online. Operations utilities include telephone services, electricity, and rent, which may include water and sewage.

Taxes: Midsize companies must pay all usual taxes, including state, local, federal, and property taxes.

Large Businesses

The computer software industry includes few large companies, which have more than 250 employees. According to the BLS, large firms make up just 1.3 percent of all software firms. However, in 2008 they employed more than 49 percent of all workers in the industry. These few large and influential companies often attract a significant proportion of the most talented and experienced employees in the technology sector. They are usually diversified, with companies such as Apple and Google offering software, hardware, and Internet services such as cloud computing.

Potential Annual Earnings Scale. Employees at large computer firms are often among the highest paid in the industry, especially at the executive level. For example, software giant Microsoft reports that Steven Ballmer, the company's chief executive officer (CEO), earned more than $1.3 million in 2008. In addition, large companies usually offer very lucrative benefits, including health benefits and paid vacations. They also often provide employees with perks such as gym memberships and child care, and will usually offer generous stock options.

Clientele Interaction. As is the case in midsize software companies, most of large companies' clientele interaction is limited to employees in the sales, marketing, and customer-support departments. These departments usually handle all customer queries and concerns and interact with representatives from large software and electronics vendors and retailers. They also arrange large software purchases with businesses, schools, and organizations. In addition, employees in the sales and marketing departments often work closely with hardware manufacturers to determine which software to include in new computers. Most hardware

manufacturers, for example, must purchase their computers' operating systems from large companies such as Microsoft, which makes Windows. However, a minority of hardware manufacturers may include free operating systems such as Linux with their computers, or they may not include any operating system at all, leaving it up to consumers to install their own software.

Other companies, such as Apple, bundle their proprietary software with their own hardware, selling them together as a single unit. Apple acts as both a hardware and a software company, offering a proprietary operating system that works only on its hardware. The company employs a vast army of software programmers, software testers, and technical support staff who specialize in developing and supporting the company's own line of popular software products. Some of these products are sold over the Internet, at Apple Store retail locations, and by big-box retailers. Others are free. Apple's free products serve two functions. Some, such as

Apple Stores, like this one in New York , offer instructions, workshops, and assistance with software issues. (AP/Wide World Photos)

the Safari Web browser, simply build the company's brand. By exposing consumers to software that the company believes is superior in user experience, Apple hopes to motivate them to purchase Apple's other products. Other free Apple applications drive sales more directly. For example, iTunes is a free program for managing audio and video content, as well as iPhone and iPad applications and electronic books (e-books). Through iTunes and the iTunes Store, Apple sells music, television programs, games, podcasts, e-books, and a plethora of other content. By making the program itself free, Apple maximizes the number of consumers who may purchase this content.

Amenities, Atmosphere, and Physical Grounds. Large software companies usually have expansive campus headquarters and often have offices in multiple locations, both domestic and international. They may outsource their technical service needs or open satellite offices overseas or in multiple states. They also normally host their own Web servers and often have a significant online presence. Large software companies are also more likely to open overseas research and development facilities. If large firms also manufacture hardware products, they may have extensive manufacturing facilities as well.

Typical Number of Employees. Large software companies usually have more than 250 employees, sometimes far more depending on how diversified the company's operations are. Microsoft, for example, makes video-gaming systems and computer operating systems—as well as some of the most popular software titles in the world—and has more than ninety-three thousand employees in more than one hundred countries all over the globe.

Traditional Geographic Locations. Large software companies usually have multiple offices in many different countries. However, many of the world's largest software companies maintain central headquarters in high-tech hot spots such as Silicon Valley, Portland, and Seattle. Many also have a significant presence in countries such as China and India, often in the form of major centers employing thousands of programmers, software testers, and technical support specialists.

Pros of Working for a Large Software Company. Compared to small and midsize software firms, large computer companies pay extremely competitive wages to most of their employees.

They also offer very generous benefits and stock options. In addition, workers frequently have much more flexibility and are often able to transfer to other facilities and to engage in business travel. Large companies usually offer their employees many opportunities for career advancement, and they are normally much more stable than their smaller counterparts.

Large software companies also offer many more research and development opportunities for their employees, allowing them to create and test many new products in a diversified setting. Large companies usually attract the most talented workers in the industry, so employees are able to work with other extremely capable and creative people to craft software that will be used by hundreds of thousands, even millions, of people across the globe.

Cons of Working for a Large Software Company. At large software companies, it can be very easy to get lost in the crowd. With such a large staff, much of the intimate camaraderie of smaller firms is lost. Most employees are not able to suggest new products or services directly to executives. The larger the operation, the more likely it is that bureaucratic hurdles will cause employees strife, simply because of the increased complexity of an organization with thousands or tens of thousands of workers scattered across the globe. At the same time, large software companies are extremely competitive in their hiring and promotion practices. It can be very difficult to find a job at a large company, with potentially thousands of applicants vying for positions at large firms such as Microsoft, and prospective employees usually have advanced degrees from prestigious schools. Most have already gained significant experience in the industry.

Costs

Payroll and Benefits: Employees at large companies in the software industry usually enjoy generous salaries and many benefits, such as health insurance, vacation time, and stock options, and even perks such as child care and gym memberships.

Supplies: Large software companies usually have extensive on-site Web servers and many research and development facilities. They must maintain state-of-the-art computer systems for their employees, especially those involved in software development and engineering.

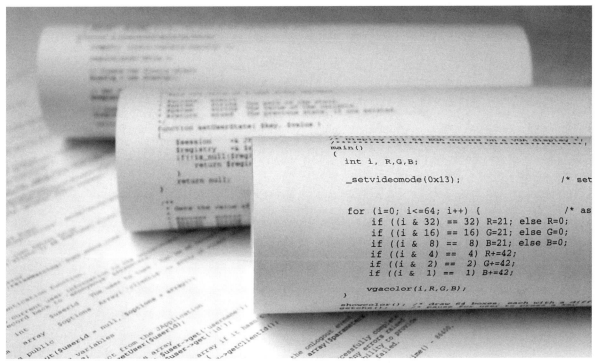

A printout of a computer program, as seen by the developer. (©Dreamstime.com)

External Services: Most employees in large software companies work full time. However, these companies may hire external businesses to clean and maintain their facilities, and they may also hire external firms to handle advertising and sales efforts. For example, they may hire external firms to produce television commercials or full advertising campaigns for their products. They may also outsource technical support services, especially overseas.

Utilities: Large businesses pay mortgages or rent for their facilities, as well as paying for water, sewage, and telephone services. They also usually require extensive dedicated fiber-optic Internet services and massive amounts of electricity. Indeed, Google has attempted to purchase electricity wholesale directly from power plants, bypassing public utilities in order to save money.

Taxes: Large software companies pay all required local, state, and federal, and property taxes. In addition, since many large companies have a significant international presence, they may be required to pay additional taxes for their overseas operations.

ORGANIZATIONAL STRUCTURE AND JOB ROLES

Software companies vary widely in their organizational structure. For example, in smaller firms a single person may handle almost every task related to the company, while in larger firms there may be entire departments devoted to just a few software products in a vast portfolio.

The following umbrella categories apply to the organizational structure of companies in the computer software industry:

- Executive Management
- Software Development
- Marketing and Sales
- Information Technology
- Human Resources
- Technical Support
- Administrative Staff

Executive Management

Most executives in the software industry have advanced degrees, although many individual programmers without degrees have founded successful software companies. Bill Gates, for example, dropped out of college before founding Microsoft. The job of a company's management team is to guide the overall direction and vision of the company, determining what products are developed, how they are developed, and how they and the company as a whole are branded. CEOs are usually the highest-paid employees in their companies, often earning between $58,230 and $128,580 per year, not including stock options, bonuses, or other perks, according to Top Executives. CEOs at a few top companies earn more than $1 million per year.

Executive management occupations may include the following:

- Chief Executive Officer (CEO)
- Board Chair
- Chief Financial Officer (CFO)
- Chief Technology Officer (CTO)
- Chief Information Officer (CIO)
- General Counsel
- Vice President

Software Development

Software developers create a software company's products. They plan, code, and test software, as well as build the architecture necessary for a program to run smoothly. They often engage in research and development, as well as in perfecting final products for release. They usually work closely with the technical support department to address customer concerns and fix bugs discovered by customers during testing and shortly after a product is released. According to the BLS, software engineers earn annual salaries averaging around $79,780.

OCCUPATION PROFILE

Computer Programmer

Considerations	Qualifications
Description	Writes step-by-step instructions for computers in special computer languages, telling the computers exactly what to do to perform specific tasks.
Career clusters	Architecture and Construction; Finance; Information Technology; Science, Technology, Engineering, and Math
Interests	Data
Working conditions	Work inside
Minimum education level	On-the-job training; junior/technical/community college; bachelor's degree
Physical exertion	Light work
Physical abilities	Unexceptional/basic fitness
Opportunities for experience	Internship; military service; part-time work
Licensure and certification	Recommended
Employment outlook	Decline expected
Holland interest score	IRE

Note: See volume 1, "Publisher's Note," for an explanation of the Holland interest score.

OCCUPATION PROFILE

Software Designer

Considerations	Qualifications
Description	Creates and designs computer software programs, outlining general formats, writing necessary code, and developing graphics, animation, and sound effects to enhance user experience and functionality.
Career cluster	Arts, A/V Technology, and Communications; Information Technology
Interests	Data; things
Working conditions	Work inside
Minimum education level	Junior/technical/community college; bachelor's degree
Physical exertion	Light work
Physical abilities	Unexceptional/basic fitness
Opportunities for experience	Internship; apprenticeship; military service; part-time work
Licensure and certification	Recommended
Employment outlook	Faster-than-average growth expected
Holland interest score	AES; IRE

Note: See volume 1, "Publisher's Note," for an explanation of the Holland interest score.

Software development occupations may include the following:

- Software Engineer
- Software Programmer
- Computer Systems Analyst
- Software Tester

Marketing and Sales

Sales and marketing departments publicize their companies' products. They may develop advertisements and work directly with retailers and high-volume customers to increase their companies' sales. Companies of all sizes, even the largest, frequently outsource major advertising campaigns to independent public relations firms. However, even when such campaigns are outsourced, the company's marketing staff will liaise with the relevant team at the contracting company to help coordi-

nate the campaign. On average, advertising managers earn approximately $73,060 per year, sales managers earn $91,560 per year, and public relations managers earn $82,180 per year.

Sales and marketing occupations may include the following:

- Marketing Manager
- Sales Executive
- Sales Manager
- Account Manager
- Market Research Analyst
- Marketing Strategist

Information Technology

Software companies depend on their information technology (IT) staff to keep their computer networks running smoothly and efficiently, especially if they run their own Web hosting servers. IT staff are also responsible for cyber security, which includes preventing hackers from accessing sensitive corporate information, protecting corporate systems against viruses, fighting back against denial-of-service attacks, and securing both external and internal computer networks. They are very highly trained, often possessing bachelor's or master's degrees. IT specialists can earn between $79,240 and $129,250 per year on average.

Information technology occupations may include the following:

- Network Specialist
- Computer Systems Analyst
- Information Technology Director
- Support Specialist
- Computer Security Specialist

Human Resources

Human resources (HR) managers recruit, train, and support employees. The size of HR departments varies widely depending on the scope of their companies, ranging from a single person to a staff of hundreds. HR managers earn an average of between $67,710 and $114,860 per year.

Human resources positions may include the following:

- Human Resources Manager
- Human Resources Representative
- Training Specialist
- Recruitment Officer

Technical Support

Technical support employees play a major role at software companies. At small firms, technical support duties may be shared among all employees, while larger companies usually organize technical support services into separate departments or outsource those duties to an external firm. Technical support staff usually interact with customers over the phone, on message boards and forums, and in chat rooms, and each worker may respond to hundreds of messages a day.

Often, technical support positions are offered as entry-level positions. Depending on employees' education and skill level, they may later be promoted to more prominent roles within the organization. Technical support representatives earn between $32,110 and $53,640 per year.

Technical support occupations may include the following:

- Technical Support Specialist
- Help Desk Specialist
- Customer Service Representative

Administrative Staff

The administrative staff is responsible for scheduling meetings and appointments, providing accounting services, keeping financial records, greeting visitors, and assisting executives. Education requirements for members of the administrative staff vary depending on the individual position. Income may vary depending on position and training. Receptionists for software companies have average salaries of between $18,800 and $28,100 per year.

Administrative occupations may include the following:

- Administrative Assistant
- Accountant
- Receptionist

INDUSTRY OUTLOOK

Overview

From the earliest computer program proposed by mathematician Ada Lovelace in the 1800's, software has grown to control many aspects of the technology people use daily. The software industry plays a tremendous role in nearly every other industry, in schools and governments, and, increasingly, in daily life. As computer use continues to grow, software will remain necessary to allow users access to the information encoded within. Thus, computer software is closely tied to most economic activities in the Information Age, including both business and leisure. As a result, despite periodic alterations in revenue models that may cause temporary deviations, the software industry is expected to continue its rapid growth.

Software offerings have become increasingly robust, and many new programs are being created for specialized purposes within specific industries. For example, architectural firms use computer-aided design (CAD) software to design new homes; artists, photographers, and graphic designers use image-editing software such as Photoshop; and filmmakers use programs such as Final Cut Pro to edit films. In addition, many businesses employ software programmers or hire external firms and consultants to develop specialized software to meet each company's individual needs. This is especially true for Internet-based businesses and companies engaged in extensive e-commerce transactions. E-commerce is becoming increasingly important for a growing number of businesses, and Standard and Poor's estimated that online retail sales reached $141.3 billion in 2008.

As e-commerce has grown, online criminal activity has grown alongside it. By 2009, such activity had skyrocketed, as online criminal enterprises accounted for up to $1 trillion in global revenues, surpassing the amount of money exchanged through drug trafficking. This development has led in turn to a robust $10.5-billion industry engaged in blocking hacker attacks, e-mail spam, and industrial espionage and in deleting or repairing infected computer files. The security software industry is expected to grow rapidly, with global revenues expected to reach $13.1 billion by 2012. Antivirus software is widely used by businesses, governments, schools, and individuals.

Many new software firms are created every year, with up to ten thousand software companies established by 2006 according to the BLS. As the price of developing software has fallen for many firms, individual entrepreneurs, software publishers, and hardware manufacturers have continued to develop innovative new technologies. At the same time, however, major operating systems and professional-grade business suites have become extremely complex. A major new release of the Mac OS or Windows requires years of effort and untold millions of dollars in development costs. Thus, even as much of the software market has become more accessible to start-ups, one segment remains more dominated by large companies. Nevertheless, many computer hardware companies, software publishers, Internet firms, and even cell-phone manufacturers release specialized software development kits to encourage software engineers to develop new products and services, since they know that a platform is only as good as the software that runs on it.

New software products are increasingly being released through open-source platforms and non-profit organizations such as the Mozilla Foundation. These groups release free, open-source software online. They have very few paid employees—fewer than ten in the case of Mozilla. Instead, these organizations rely on an army of volunteer programmers, software engineers, and beta testers to perfect and refine their software offerings. Even without a focus on profits, many free software products have become extremely popular. Firefox, released by the nonprofit Mozilla Foundation, was used by 47 percent of Internet users as of late 2009, challenging Microsoft's Internet Explorer for dominance and far surpassing Google's Chrome and Apple's Safari.

Software has become a global enterprise. Many software companies, including large firms such as Microsoft, have opened overseas development, testing, and customer-support facilities. Other companies outsource duties such as beta testing and technical support to overseas firms. At the same time, as computer usage expands—especially in the developing world—many new overseas companies are being formed to meet the specific needs of their home countries. In fact, even when Japan is excluded, the Asia-Pacific region is expected to experience the fastest growth in global software revenues. The demand for software will undoubtedly continue to expand as people become more dependent on computer technology. Software is also increasingly used for educational purposes, with schools and universities offering many Web-based software options, as well as traditional software programs that help students learn important new skills.

New growth in the software industry is also taking place in the field of video games and mobile phone services. Smart phones such as the Motorola Droid, which uses Google's Android operating system, and Apple's iPhone, which uses a modified operating system similar to Mac OS X, offer entrepreneurs new avenues to develop and market software. Such offerings frequently include mobile games, as well as music players, Web browsers, e-mail clients, and maps. They also include business tools such as the Transaction application by SkorpiosTech, which allows users to accept credit card payments directly from their iPhone. Mobile phones and digital music players are also increasingly used to distribute educational software. There are even applications that provide workers in the health care industry with important information, including medical dictionaries, anatomy guides, and diagnosis codes.

The software industry will continue to grow, with many opportunities for entrepreneurs to develop successful new software. As the barriers for entry into the lucrative industry continue to fall away, many new software companies will be founded by innovative programmers and even amateur hobbyists. In fact, as of 2006, more than half of all software firms employed five workers or fewer. By developing a niche following, even small software companies can become astounding successes. For example, just two people—Bill Gates and Paul Allen—founded Microsoft, which eventually produced the most popular operating system on the planet. Anybody with the right dedication and imagination can learn software programming and, with the right mix of innovative creativity, hard work, and a little luck, can prosper in the computer software industry.

Employment Advantages

The computer software industry is expected to experience exponential growth, even in the wake of the 2007-2009 global economic downturn. The BLS projects employment in the industry to grow by 32 percent between 2006 and 2016, with 52 percent of all employees in the industry working as computer specialists. In fact, the software industry is expected to grow three times faster than the economy as a whole.

Prospective employees in the computer software industry are usually professionals with advanced degrees, although entrepreneurs of every educational background can find success by developing innovative software on their own. In either case, people working in this field need to pursue educational opportunities as part of their efforts to keep up with the constant evolvution of software technology. Because the modern development of software is such a recent phenomenon, most workers in the software industry are quite young: The average worker is between twenty-five and forty-five years old, according to the BLS.

Annual Earnings

The computer software industry is expected to continue its rapid growth, regardless of the economic climate. Growth projections for the industry are very high, with 32 percent growth predicted by 2016; thus, it is expected that employment opportunities in the software industry will be higher than average. As a result, software companies frequently offer more generous benefits and salaries than do companies in other industries. According to the BLS, the average annual salary for nonsupervisory employees in the software industry is $75,000, much higher than the average of $29,000 for all other industries. Long-term prospects for the industry are very favorable, with projected revenues of $457 billion by 2013.

RELATED RESOURCES FOR FURTHER RESEARCH

COMPUTER SOCIETY
Institute of Electrical and Electronics Engineers
2001 L St. NW, Suite 700
Washington, DC 20036
Tel: (202) 371-0101
Fax: (202) 728-9614
http://www.computer.org

INSTITUTE FOR CERTIFICATION OF COMPUTING PROFESSIONALS
2400 E Devon Ave., Suite 281
Des Plaines, IL 60018
Tel: (800) 843-8227
Fax: (847) 299-4280
http://www.iccp.org

NATIONAL WORKFORCE CENTER FOR EMERGING TECHNOLOGIES
Bellevue College
3000 Landerholm Circle SE, N211
Bellevue, WA 98007-6484
Tel: (425) 564-4229
Fax: (425) 564-6193
http://www.nwcet.org

SOFTWARE AND INFORMATION INDUSTRY ASSOCIATION
1090 Vermont Ave. NW, 6th Floor
Washington, DC 20005-4095
Tel: (202) 289-7442
Fax: (202) 289-7097
http://www.siia.net

ABOUT THE AUTHOR

Elizabeth Fernandez began working in the computer industry in 2002, serving as a Webmaster and a hardware and software repair specialist. For the past ten years, she has also worked as a writer and editor specializing in computer science and technology trends. She has been published online, in newspapers, and in local magazines, and she has edited several books focusing on the computer, aviation, and transportation industries. She graduated with a degree in journalism from the University of Central Florida.

FURTHER READING

Arora, Ashish, and Alfonso Gambardella, eds. *From Underdogs to Tigers: The Rise and Growth of the Software Industry in Brazil, China, India, Ireland, and Israel.* New York: Oxford University Press, 2005.

Convergence Plus Journal. "InfoSecurity: F-Secure, VSNL Offer Internet Security Solutions for SMEs." January 22, 2007. http://www .convergenceplus.com/jan07%20infosec %2002.html.

Dale, Nell, and John Lewis. *Computer Science Illuminated.* 3d ed. Sudbury, Mass.: Jones and Bartlett, 2007.

D'Costa, Anthony P., and E. Sridharan, eds. *India in the Global Software Industry: Innovation, Firm Strategies, and Development.* New York: Palgrave Macmillan, 2004.

Hall, Pat, and Juan Fernández-Ramil. *Managing the Software Enterprise: Software Engineering and Information Systems in Context.* London: Thomson Learning, 2007.

Hoch, Detlev J., et al. *Secrets of Software Success: Management Insights from One Hundred Software Firms Around the World.* Boston: Harvard Business School Press, 2000.

Johnston, Jessica. *Technological Turf Wars: A Case Study of the Antivirus Industry.* Philadelphia: Temple University Press, 2009.

Lightstone, Sam. *Making It Big in Software: Get the Job—Work the Org—Become Great.* Upper Saddle River, N.J.: Prentice Hall, 2010.

Lopp, Michael. *Being Geek: The Software Developer's Career Handbook.* Sebastopol, Calif.: O'Reilly Media, 2010.

Mozilla.org. "About Mozilla." http://www.mozilla .org/about.

Qing, Liau Yun. "APAC to See Fastest Software Revenue Growth." ZDNet Asia, November 9, 2009. http://www.zdnetasia.com/news/ business/0,39044229,62059188,00.htm

Robat, Cornelis, ed. *The History of Computing Project.* http://www.thocp.net/index.html.

U.S. Bureau of Labor Statistics. *Career Guide to Industries,* 2010-2011 ed. http://www.bls.gov/ oco/cg.

_____. "Computer and Information Systems Managers." In *Occupational Outlook Handbook,* 2010-2011 ed. http://www.bls.gov/oco/ ocos258.htm.

_____. "Computer Support Specialists and Systems Administrators." In *Occupational Outlook Handbook,* 2010-2011 ed. http:// www.bls.gov/oco/ocos268.htm.

U.S. Census Bureau. North American Industry Classification System (NAICS), 2007. http:// www.census.gov/cgi-bin/sssd/naics/ naicsrch?chart=2007.

U.S. Department of Commerce. International Trade Administration. Office of Trade and Industry Information. Industry Trade Data and Analysis. http://ita.doc.gov/td/industry/ otea/OTII/OTII-index.html.

Yu, Eileen. "Global Security Software Revenue to Hit US$10.5 billion." ZDNet Asia, April 24, 2008. http://www.zdnetasia.com/news/ security/0,39044215,62040592,00.htm.

Computer Systems Industry

©Chromatika Multimedia/iStockphoto.com

INDUSTRY SNAPSHOT

General Industry: Information Technology

Career Cluster: Information Technology

Subcategory Industries: Computer Disaster Recovery Services; Computer Facilities Management Services; Computer Software Installation Services; Computer Systems Design Services; Custom Computer Programming Services

Related Industries: Computer Hardware and Peripherals Industry; Computer Software Industry; Internet and Cyber Communications Industry

Annual Domestic Revenues: $285 billion USD (Research and Markets, 2010)

Annual International Revenues: $293 billion USD (Research and Markets, 2010)

Annual Global Revenues: $578 billion USD (Research and Markets, 2010)

NAICS Number: 5415

INDUSTRY DEFINITION

Summary

The computer systems industry provides goods and services designed to enhance the storage, manipulation, and transfer of digital data through computer networks. Such networks may exist within single buildings or other limited areas, constituting local area networks (LANs), or may span much larger areas or connect disparate, widely separated locations in the world, constituting wide area networks (WANs). In the vast majority of cases, the Internet provides the connection for these networks. The Internet has rapidly evolved from its beginnings in the late 1960's as a research project funded by the Department of Defense to become an indispensable tool for many types of businesses involved in electronic commerce (e-commerce). Along with this evolution of communication networks, there have been countless technological advances involving the physical components of computers and communications, called hardware, and the written computer code in programming languages, called software. These devices drive and facilitate the storage and communication systems—such as databases, Web pages, and other interactive Internet information portals—that constitute computer systems. All these computer components are interrelated and compose the computer systems industry.

History of the Industry

It was during World War II that computers such as the Electronic Numerical Integrator and Computer (ENIAC), developed by John P. Eckert and John W. Mauchly, began to be used to help decide which enemy targets to bomb. To decide on a location, many factors needed to be considered, including any differences in height between the bomb launcher and the intended target, wind speeds, and the shapes of the bombs, which required a complex mathematical calculation involving several equations. Calculators had not been invented yet. Although the ENIAC was huge by present-day standards, using over twenty thousand vacuum tubes and filling entire rooms, this was the birth of the computer systems industry.

Throughout the 1940's and 1950's, computers continued to decrease in size while increasing in speed and capacity as a result of technological advances, such as the invention of the transistor in 1947 by John Bardeen, Walter Brattain, and Wil-liam Shockley; magnetic ink character recognition (MICR), used by the banking industry to read checks; and the integrated circuit chip by Jack Kilby and Robert Noyce in 1958. During this time, the first useful high-level programming language, the IBM Mathematical Formula Translating System (or FORTRAN), was developed primarily for scientific applications. It was soon followed by the development of the second useful high-level programming language, the Common Business-Oriented Language (or COBOL), for business applications.

The application of computers to the banking industry gained importance, and in 1962 the first computer game was invented by Steve Russell at the Massachusetts Institute of Technology. In the 1960's, silicon microchips became available that allowed the large mainframe computers to decrease in size and led to their manufacture by many companies, including International Business Machines (IBM). The RAND Corporation developed a fully

A computer engineer working on a network data center server consults with a colleague by cell phone. (©Benis Arapovic/ Dreamstime.com)

The Computer Systems Industry's Contribution to the U.S. Economy

Value Added	Amount
Gross domestic product	$169.7 billion
Gross domestic product	1.2%
Persons employed	1.458 million
Total employee compensation	$149.1 billion

Source: U.S. Bureau of Economic Analysis. Data are for 2008.

distributed, packet-switched network to facilitate military communication, and researchers at the National Physical Laboratory developed hardware to physically connect computers so that they could transmit digital information between them. Improvements in the hardware of these microcomputers throughout the 1970's led to their mass production, thus creating a rapid-growth segment of the computer industry.

Meanwhile, the linking of computers became available in 1969 with the creation of the Advanced Research Project Agency Network, or ARPANET, developed by the U.S. Department of Defense. ARPANET originally linked the Stanford Research Institute with the University of California at Santa Barbara, the University of Utah, and the University of California, Los Angeles. It expanded to establish communication destinations, called nodes, at fifteen locations, including the National Aeronau-

Inputs Consumed by the Computer Systems Industry

Input	Value
Energy	$0.9 billion
Materials	$6.2 billion
Purchased services	$65.2 billion
Total	$72.3 billion

Source: U.S. Bureau of Economic Analysis. Data are for 2008.

tics and Space Administration (NASA), the Massachusetts Institute of Technology (MIT), RAND Corporation, and Harvard.

In 1973, Bob Metcalfe invented Ethernet, in order to allow multiple computers to share digital information and computer resources, such as printers and files, while he was working at Xerox. Two years later, Larry Roberts developed Telnet, which was the first commercial packet-switching network to link customers in seven cities. In 1979, Metcalfe left Xerox and persuaded the companies of Intel, Digital Equipment, and Xerox to promote Ethernet as an international standard for the computer industry, causing it to become the most widely installed LAN. Metcalfe later went on to form 3Com Corporation. Numerous pieces of computer hardware were developed to facilitate Ethernet, and one of the most successful companies producing such hardware, Cisco Systems, shipped its first product in 1986. By 1990, Cisco achieved annual revenues of $69 million, and by 1998, these revenues had reached $8.46 billion. ARPANET had been the predecessor of today's Internet, and by 1993 the Internet was used to link WANs into a "network of networks," which became known as the World Wide Web and was facilitated by the innovations of Tim Berners-Lee of MIT and Marc Andreessen of Netscape.

The Industry Today

Computer information systems generally complete tasks by using computer systems that can range from a single personal computer and its software to networks linking thousands of computers to share resources, including printers, Internet access, and databases. The computer systems industry has led the way in the establishment of the digital economy because it has developed into a facilitator of business via the growth of e-commerce and of computer systems designed to support business objectives by facilitating communication and collaboration. Modern businesses use databases and computational abilities to improve decision making and productivity, reduce costs, enhance customer relationships, and develop strategic applications. These strategic applications include online services for health care, insurance, banking, auctions, electronic payments, travel, and even online

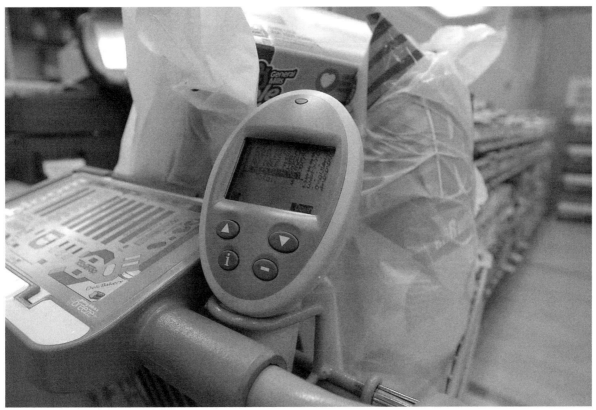

In this Laurel, Maryland, grocery store, customers can use a handheld scanner as they shop to save time when they check out. (AP/Wide World Photos)

social networking Web sites and online dating sites that can earn money by selling advertising space.

The digital economy allows the U.S. online population of approximately 250 million users to communicate and conduct transactions involving graphics (including photographs, maps, and X-ray images), audio recordings (including music, audio books, podcasts, and lectures for online classes), videos (including television programs, films, and original material), and many types of computer software applications. In addition, Internet users can purchase nondigital goods and services, from airline tickets to books to almost any other product, and they can participate in online auctions and gambling. The wealth of digital information available on the Internet and the vast array of goods and services available for purchase have caused search engines allowing users to find what they are looking for online to become increasingly important. The companies that develop these search engines have grown significantly, as have companies that

optimize Web sites' code to ensure that they appear near the top of search engine results, a field known as search engine optimization, or SEO.

Today, handheld devices allow workers to update inventory counts, print shelf-tags anywhere within a store, and enter order information for out-of-stock items. Handheld devices are sometimes given to customers to provide information regarding price comparisons and recommended products. A cell-phone-sized portable device called a mobile manager facilitates communication and supervision of employees. Cart-mounted tablet personal computers (PCs) can allow customers to check prices while shopping, and employees can also use tablet PCs to communicate with one another and with managers wirelessly. Personal scanners are given to customers at Food Lion grocery stores. When a customer picks up an item, it is scanned before being placed into a shopping cart, and the final tally is downloaded to the cash register when the customer is ready to check out.

An employee of Ernst & Young's Advanced Security Center tries to hack into a Honolulu bank's computer system to uncover possible weaknesses. (AP/Wide World Photos)

More than 50 million people in 2008 participated in social networking on Web sites such as Facebook, MySpace, YouTube, and LinkedIn, causing these companies, along with Google, Apple, and Yahoo!, to become major economic driving forces and making the computer systems industry one of the few growth industries today. These companies are leading the way in growth for health care, commerce, travel, politics, finance, and entertainment. Enterprise resource planning (ERP) and customer relationship management (CRM) combine business management tools with the technological tools of the computer systems industry to facilitate countless, routine daily transactions including banking, purchases of goods, and rental of films and other media.

The explosive growth in Internet-based businesses resulted in approximately 1.5 million people being employed in the computer systems industry in 2008. Because the technology of the computer systems industry has continued to de-

velop and find an increasing number of applications in recent years, the workforce for the computer systems industry is considerably younger than those of other types of industries, with more than 60 percent of the workers in the computer systems industry being age forty-four or younger. Less than 50 percent of the workers in all other industries fall within this age demographic.

Approximately 78 percent of companies within the computer systems industry employ fewer than five workers. Thus, small companies are a significant component of the industry. However, the majority of jobs can be found within companies that employ at least fifty employees. Many employees within the computer systems industry with job positions such as computer support specialists, programmers, consultants, and systems analysts are able to work from home by linking directly to computers at the location of the employer or client via the Internet.

With so many e-commerce and social networking sites allowing users to share a great deal of personal information, there has been an increase in identity theft and the need for network security systems to protect against hackers. Maintaining the security of computer systems has become an important discipline, with several certificate programs available to train employees for this growing job market. These security certifications include Security+, Red Hat, Network+, and Certified Network Associate (CNA) certifications. Some certificates are vendor-specific, such as Cisco's CNA certification, while others are vendor-neutral, such as the Security+ and Network+ certificates.

Numerous other certificate programs exist for network administrators, database administrators, software engineers, and network engineers. The wireless transmission of data has become especially susceptible to theft by hackers. Many certificate programs are offered by Microsoft to address this problem. These certificate programs are so important and widespread that they have developed into an industry of their own, with many opportunities for educators and trainers in various security, network, database, and software applications.

The computers systems industry could not function without specialized computer hardware that enables computers to communicate. Manufacturing such hardware is another area within the industry that has seen explosive growth, providing numerous opportunities for employment to support the design, manufacture, and sales of constantly evolving computer hardware, as well as for electronic consumer gadgets to play music and videos and to share e-mail and photos between any geographic location. A network interface card (NIC) is a device that is inserted into a computer's motherboard to provide the physical, electrical, and electronic connections to network media that allow various peripheral components to be attached electronically.

Traditionally, coaxial cable has been used to connect several computers or other network nodes, including printers, to central communication devices called hubs.

Switches, bridges, routers, and gateways are examples of additional hardware devices that are manufactured by companies within the computer systems industry and are used to connect network segments. The Open Systems Interconnect (OSI) model was developed as a guideline to describe the protocols, or rules of communication, followed by various hardware manufacturers to ensure that their products will be compatible with the systems into which they will be integrated. This model is still used today, and it makes it possible to replace one piece of equipment made by one manufacturer with a similar piece made by a different manufacturer. The model has greatly facilitated the growth of the computer systems industry worldwide.

INDUSTRY MARKET SEGMENTS

Companies within the computer systems industry can be categorized as small, midsize, or large, based on their net annual sales or number of employees. Their geographic scope can range from local to global, and the largest corporations have thousands of employees located in dozens of countries.

A router and a network interface card, which is inserted into a computer's motherboard to provide the physical, electrical, and electronic connections to network media. (©Dreamstime.com)

Small Businesses

A small computer systems company is one with net annual sales of less than $950,000 or fewer than one hundred employees. Typically, these small businesses try to focus on a relatively limited number of products or services. The computer systems industry spans a range of products, including database software, servers, network hardware, and systems software. A small company might produce only network hardware, without offering any database or systems software products.

Potential Annual Earnings Scale. The earnings potential in a small business is generally significantly less than the earnings potential within a large business, and the range from the lowest paid employee to the highest paid employee is not as wide as the range within a large company. According to the U.S. Bureau of Labor Statistics (BLS), sales representatives at service-oriented computer systems businesses earned an average of $79,830 in 2009, while their supervisors earned an average of $105,760. On average, computer support specialists earned $47,850, programmers earned $76,110, systems analysts earned $85,460, application software engineers earned $91,130, system software engineers earned $95,150, and computer and information system managers earned $130,000. Generally speaking, salaries for all these positions at small companies tend to be lower than these averages.

Clientele Interaction. Small companies are dependent on a customer base of repeat, loyal customers, who have the potential within a relatively small, local area to either "make or break" a business based on word of mouth. Therefore, direct clientele interactions tend to be much more important than at larger companies. More emphasis is placed on ongoing, long-term customer relationships. Sales representatives might routinely call customers just to check on how they are doing and to see if they have any questions or are in need of any help. They attempt to maintain strong relationships with customers and may interact with them on a first-name basis. Technical support to customers could include visits to the customer's home or business and may be available on weekends.

Amenities, Atmosphere, and Physical Grounds. The atmosphere of a small company is often more casual than that of a larger company, with a more casual dress code. There is less paperwork required for requests for vacation days and time off from work. Usually, the physical grounds are quite pleasant and personal in overall feeling. While amenities such as an on-site cafeteria for lunch may be available, the food selection and hours are likely to be less than those available in a larger company, and the extra benefits, such as an on-site fitness center, may not be available at all within a small company. These small companies are located within relatively small, new buildings that consist of only one or two stories and may not even have elevators. Typically, though, they are quite pleasant, having many windows with views of greenery and central air-conditioning, along with carpeted rooms containing cubicles. Often, the computer equipment must be securely stored in locked rooms that are temperature controlled, so they will not become warm enough to cause their wiring or electronic components to deteriorate.

Typical Number of Employees. A small computer systems company has fewer than one hundred employees, and 78 percent of companies in the industry employee five persons or fewer.

Traditional Geographic Locations. Because the computer systems industry is a relatively new industry, these small businesses are usually located in new buildings with modern plumbing and facilities. Often, they are located in suburban business parks, and many are within close proximity to malls convenient to customers. Because these small companies are often sole proprietorships or limited liability corporations with only a few partners, they are quite dispersed geographically, in all sizes of cities and small towns. However, a higher proportion of small computer systems companies are located within the United States than that of larger companies, which tend to have large facilities in other countries. The start-up costs for international facilities are prohibitive for small companies.

Pros of Working for a Small Business. A somewhat more relaxed and personal atmosphere is considered by many to be a positive aspect of working in a small business. Because there are relatively few employees, opportunities exist for co-workers to get to know one another quite well and for the company to develop a family feeling. Workers' families often know one another and interact outside work. Another potential benefit of a small business is the higher probability of being more "hands-on" with a larger number of products and the ability to have more knowledge of the activities of the entire business. Smaller businesses are sometimes willing to train new, inexperienced employees on the job in an informal manner. Also, the chain of command has less depth than that of a larger, more rigidly structured corporation. In other words, the overall management structure for a smaller company is flatter than the tiered management structure for a larger company.

Cons of Working for a Small Business. Some of the unique characteristics that are often advantages of working in a small company can also have drawbacks. For example, although an individual may have a higher probability of being more "hands-on" in a small company and be able to participate in more projects, there is also more stress associated with the greater responsibility and visibility. Opportunities for advancement within a small company may be significantly limited by the flat management structure.

Costs

Payroll and Benefits: Payroll and benefits are often completed within a single office, with only a handful of employees who must be able to complete many different tasks. As a result, there is not always the level of expertise present with a larger company, where an individual worker can specialize in one area. Also, few benefit options are available to workers in small businesses. Opportunities for group insurance and investment plans may be available, but the options involved are fewer than at larger companies.

Supplies: Depending on their specific products or services, computer systems companies may require computer workstations, software development environments, engineering and computer-assisted design (CAD) software, hardware construction and development laboratories, or production equipment. They all require office equipment and supplies.

External Services: Computer systems companies may contract for the manufacture of products they design or the distribution of products they manufacture. They may also contract for such business support services as accounting and tax preparation, legal counsel, advertising, maintenance, and custodial services.

Utilities: The typical utilities for a small company

include water, sewage, electricity, gas or oil, telephone, cable television, and Internet access.

Taxes: Small companies are required to pay local, state, and federal corporate and property taxes. If they are sole proprietorships or partnerships, they may report corporate income on personal returns, in which case owners or partners must also pay self-employment taxes.

Midsize Businesses

Midsize computer systems companies have net annual sales of between $950,000 and $7.5 million.

Potential Annual Earnings Scale. The earnings potential at midsize companies is generally more than the earnings potential within small companies, and it may be comparable to that at large companies for some occupations, particularly for the job roles that require the most specific and technical training. However, managers usually earn significantly less at midsize companies than they do at large companies. Also, the range from the lowest paid employees to the highest paid employees is not as wide as the range within a large company. According to the BLS, sales representatives at service-oriented computer systems businesses earned an average of $79,830 in 2009, while their supervisors earned an average of $105,760. On average, computer support specialists earned $47,850, programmers earned $76,110, systems analysts earned $85,460, application software engineers earned $91,130, system software engineers earned $95,150, and computer and information system managers earned $130,000.

Clientele Interaction. Midsize companies are less dependent on repeat customers than are small companies. Therefore, clientele interactions tend to be somewhat more limited, with a great deal more e-mail information exchange and less emphasis on visits to customers' homes or businesses. Project managers assist with the assessment of customer and clientele interactions.

Amenities, Atmosphere, and Physical Grounds. The atmosphere of a midsize company is somewhat more casual than that of a large company. There is less paperwork required for requests for vacation days and time off from work. Usually, the physical grounds are quite pleasant and personal in overall feeling. Extended work periods looking at a computer screen can lead to eye problems, and repetitive work while sitting at a computer can lead to carpal tunnel syndrome or other musculoskeletal strain issues. While amenities such as an on-site cafeteria for lunch may be available, the food selection and hours are likely less than those available in a larger company, and the extra benefits, such as an on-site fitness center, may be limited within a midsize company.

These midsize companies are located within relatively small, new buildings that consist of only a few stories. There may be one centralized location that maintains constant contact via an intranet with branch locations, most within the same state or country. Typically, they are quite pleasant, containing windows with views of greenery and central air-conditioning for carpeted rooms containing cubicles. The offices are generally clean and quiet. Often, the computer equipment must be securely stored in locked rooms that are temperature controlled so as to not become warm enough to cause their wiring or electronic components to deteriorate.

Typical Number of Employees. A midsize computer systems company has between 100 and 250 employees.

Traditional Geographic Locations. Because the computer systems industry is a relatively new industry, midsize businesses are usually located in new buildings with modern plumbing and facilities. Often, they are located in suburban business parks. Because they are often limited liability corporations with only a few partners, they are quite dispersed geographically, in all sizes of cities and small towns. However, a higher proportion of these midsize companies are located within the United States than are large companies, which tend to have large facilities in other countries.

Pros of Working for a Midsize Business. A somewhat more relaxed, while also structured, atmosphere is considered by many to be a positive aspect of working in a midsize business. Interactions with fellow employees are not as abundant as they are in many small businesses, so relationships among coworkers are often not as close. Interactions outside work may be more limited than for employees of a small company. An individual worker has less knowledge of the activities of the entire business, but instead focuses more attention on a more structured range of tasks. Because of the presence of some management structures within midsize companies, there are more opportunities for advancement than there are at small companies.

Cons of Working for a Midsize Business. Because there is greater pressure to compete for customers within a larger geographic area than at small businesses, there can be more pressure and an overall less personal feeling within a midsize company. Individuals do not have as much ownership of projects. Teams are often created to accomplish specific tasks rather than complete entire projects. This strategy can be efficient, but it can also alienate workers from those projects. It can also lead to so-called group-think, which may limit both creativity and productivity.

Costs

Payroll and Benefits: Payroll and benefits are often completed within a single office, but with a larger number of employees than present within a small company. Generally, there are more benefit options available than at small companies, and some midsize companies may offer retirement plans with matching contributions. There are still fewer benefit options available to workers in midsize businesses than are available to those working in large companies. Opportunities for group insurance and investment plans are available, with more options than present for employees of a small company.

Supplies: Depending on their specific products or services, computer systems companies may require computer workstations, software development environments, engineering and computer-assisted design (CAD) software, hardware construction and development laboratories, or production equipment. They all require office equipment and supplies.

External Services: Computer systems companies may contract for the manufacture of products they design or the distribution of products they manufacture. They may also contract for such business support services as accounting and tax preparation, legal counsel, advertising, maintenance, and custodial services.

Utilities: The typical utilities for a midsize company include water, sewage, electricity, gas or oil, telephone, cable television, and Internet access.

Taxes: Midsize companies are required to pay local, state, and federal corporate and property taxes.

Large Businesses

Large computer systems companies have net annual sales in excess of $7.5 million. They employ more than 250 persons, and some employ thousands.

Potential Annual Earnings Scale. According to the BLS, sales representatives at service-oriented computer systems businesses earned an average of $79,830 in 2009, while their supervisors earned an average of $105,760. On average, computer support specialists earned $47,850, programmers earned $76,110, systems analysts earned $85,460, application software engineers earned $91,130, system software engineers earned $95,150, and computer and information system managers earned $130,000. Salaries at large companies are likely to be significantly higher than these averages.

Clientele Interaction. Large companies can have dozens of locations in different countries. Therefore, interactions with clientele tend to be much more limited to specified channels dedicated to communication, such as a toll-free phone number to interact with help desk technicians or sales representatives. Interactions with clients via the Internet is generally much more important than the personal visits that can take place with clients in small companies. Each country and each department within a large company can have sales representatives dedicated to a particular product, and a great deal of formal paperwork is required for interactions with large companies.

Amenities, Atmosphere, and Physical Grounds. Because the computer systems industry is a relatively new industry, these large businesses are usually located in new buildings with modern plumbing and facilities. Often, they are located in suburban business parks. Many employees work from home, or telecommute, especially in these larger companies where there is a great enough division of labor and segmentation of job responsibilities to make such telecommuting feasible. For example, programmers and consultants often can work either from home or from a client's location. A computer support specialist could log into a client's computer remotely to work with the client, and systems analysts often can work from home via an Internet connection. Large companies are located either in new, modern, high-rise buildings with many stories or, more often, in campuses of several buildings located in close proximity to

one another, often with beautiful grounds with benches and sidewalks, to encourage employees to feel as if they are members of the corporate community and to spend more time at work.

Typical Number of Employees. Large computer systems companies have more than 250 employees. The largest companies within the computer systems industry include hardware manufacturers Intel, Cisco, Hewlett-Packard, Dell, and Apple; database software producer Oracle; and systems-related software manufacturers Microsoft, Sun Microsystems, and (again) Apple. These companies each employ thousands of people in dozens of countries worldwide.

Traditional Geographic Locations. Many of the large companies have global headquarters in the United States, with many of these located on the East Coast and on the West Coast. These global companies also have facilities located in dozens of countries throughout the world, especially in India, Germany, and Sweden.

Pros of Working for a Large Business. Higher salaries and greater opportunities for advancement are significant advantages of working in a large business. Employees of large companies also enjoy much greater access to educational advancement programs than those of smaller companies. Large companies may provide training within the company, or they may pay for formal higher educational programs and other external training programs for employees. These programs make it possible for workers to gain technical expertise that can then be transferred to a new job role within the same company.

Cons of Working for a Large Business. Employees of large companies may experience more stress associated with a less personal atmosphere and having less control over their projects than do employees of smaller companies. Large teams are much more common in large companies, and massive, corporation-wide layoffs are possible. For example, Cisco Systems has over twenty-five thousand employees worldwide and is the world's leading manufacturer of computer systems, networking products, and services, with a product line that includes Internet services devices, networking management software, remote access devices, routers, and switches. It has had several cycles of layoffs worldwide because of fluctuations in the economy. Employees of a large business often have less freedom in their work schedules than do employees at smaller companies.

Costs

Payroll and Benefits: Payroll and benefits are handled by several individuals who have specific, defined job responsibilities and therefore can provide a higher level of expertise. There are usually several choices for group insurance and investment plans for retirement, with some type of company matching plan to match employee contributions toward retirement, often 6 percent or higher. Benefit packages can include additional features, such as access to on-site gourmet cafeterias and fitness centers.

Supplies: Depending on their specific products or services, computer systems companies may require computer workstations, software development environments, engineering and computer-assisted design (CAD) software, hardware construction and development laboratories, or production equipment. They all require office equipment and supplies.

External Services: Computer systems companies may contract for the manufacture of products they design or the distribution of products they manufacture. They may also contract for such business support services as accounting and tax preparation, legal counsel, advertising, maintenance, and custodial services.

Utilities: The typical utilities for a large company include water, sewage, electricity, gas or oil, telephone, cable television, and Internet access.

Taxes: Large corporations are required to pay local, state, federal, and international corporate and property taxes, as well as all relevant tariffs and other import and export fees.

ORGANIZATIONAL STRUCTURE AND JOB ROLES

The computer systems industry contains the same general categories for organizational structure and job roles that are found in most other types of industries, as well as an additional emphasis on technology. In small businesses, a single individual may handle all or almost all of these job roles, while large departmentalized companies assign a different role to each employee.

The following umbrella categories apply to the organizational structure of businesses within the computer systems industry:

- Business/Executive Management
- Customer Service
- Sales and Marketing
- Facilities and Security
- Technology, Research, Design, and Development
- Production and Operations
- Distribution
- Human Resources
- Information Technology

Business/Executive Management

A management information system (MIS) is a tool used by managers, and business intelligence (BI) is another technology tool used to acquire and analyze data to assist with development of budgets and to assist with investment analysis. Interorganizational information systems (IOSs) facilitate the sharing of data between two organizations that are business partners, and global information systems can connect IOSs in different countries. Most business and executive managers, as well as personnel within other functional areas such as customer service and human resources, use these computer systems technologies to enhance productivity.

The role of an administrative assistant in the computer systems industry is very similar to this role in many other industries. Assistants spend approximately 60 percent of their work time providing administrative support to managers and other staff in their daily duties. Approximately 20 percent of their time may be spent on special projects, while another 20 percent may be spent on routine daily supportive tasks, including arrangement of interviews and relocation of prospective employees, scheduling of meetings and arranging of travel, and faxing, taking phone messages, and photocopying. This entry-level position may or may not require a bachelor's degree but definitely requires skills using common office software packages such as Microsoft Word, Excel, PowerPoint, e-mail programs, and messaging tools.

A senior administrative assistant typically spends less time on routine, supportive tasks and spends much more time on special projects, which can account for at least 8 percent of their work time. These special projects can include analysis of spreadsheet models, monitoring of projects, creation of administration manuals, training new hires on policies and procedures, acting as liaisons to human resources, and managing equipment. This position requires several years of experience and proficiency in software such as Microsoft Word, Excel, PowerPoint, and e-mail and messaging programs.

An information technology business implementation analyst spends time on nonroutine and highly complex tasks and also configures settings for computer information systems and develops plans to solve business problems using automated computer systems. This position also provides consultation in the application of automated computer systems to users and serves as a cross-functional team leader to ensure that computer systems are developed to meet the business requirements for e-commerce applications. At least a bachelor's degree is required. Often, a master's degree is preferred.

Business and executive management occupations may include the following:

- Administrative Assistant
- Information Technology Business
    Implementation Analyst
- Accountant/Auditor
- General Manager
- Management Analyst
- Controller
- Assistant Information Technology Officer
- Computer and Information Systems
    Manager
- Chief Financial Officer (CFO)
- Chief Executive Officer (CEO)
- Chief Technology Officer (CTO)
- Chief Operating Officer (COO)

Customer Service

Customer service personnel, such as computer support specialists and help desk technicians, may have very little education or training. Others, with more specific product training and at least associate's degrees, may serve as network administrators. A network administrator typically builds networks that can both communicate data within an organi-

zation and communicate information to external organizations via the World Wide Web. Often, network administrators work under the supervision of project managers. Routine duties for a network administrator include overseeing system backups to protect the company's information and performing daily maintenance of computer networks and operating systems for customers. Additional job responsibilities include installation and configuration of new computer systems for customers. Appropriate preparation can include either two-year or four-year degrees, which can be enhanced by obtaining industry-recognized computer systems certification, such as through the Microsoft Certified Systems Engineer program. However, sometimes on-the-job training and hands-on experience may be sufficient preparation. Average salaries range from $56,829 to $71,254.

Customer service occupations may include the following:

- Technical Support Representative
- Help Desk Specialist
- Technical Support Specialist
- Computer Support Specialist
- Network Administrator
- Project Manager

Sales and Marketing

Sales and marketing personnel are responsible for creating demand for the product, often through the analysis of market requirements, creating technical programs to help customers with product definition and development, and developing communications with end users. Press relations and advertising are important tasks for this department.

Sales and marketing occupations may include the following:

- Corporate Sales Manager
- Marketing Director
- Sales Director
- District Sales Manager
- Senior Sales Manager
- Technical Sales Representative
- Administrative Assistant
- Services Sales Representative
- Wholesale and Manufacturing Sales
    Representative

Facilities and Security

Facilities and security personnel are often responsible for providing mechanical, electrical, and chemical infrastructure support in the areas of environmental health and safety, landscaping, ergonomic engineering, industrial hygiene, cafeteria services, and security. Security personnel are responsible not only for protecting a company's physical property and employees but also for safeguarding its intellectual property. Thus, they must guard against both physical theft and electronic theft through computer networks.

Occupations within this department may include the following:

- Chief Engineer
- Building Maintenance Manager
- Heating, Ventilation, and Air-Conditioning (HVAC) Specialist
- Custodian/Janitor
- Network Security Specialist
- Investigator

Technology, Research, Design, and Development

Computer systems companies' technical research and development staffs are generally among the most highly trained in technology and drive innovation for their companies. Computer systems analysts test and maintain computer systems in an organization. They coordinate the installation of computer programs and systems software to facilitate the sharing of information. Typical daily responsibilities include the analysis of all data processing problems in electronic data processing systems, which includes the analysis of user requirements and the design and modification of computer systems to improve workflow. These tasks often require the use of object-oriented programming languages, as well as client

---

OCCUPATION PROFILE

Computer Systems Analyst

Considerations	Qualifications
Description	Decides how data are collected, prepared for computers, processed, stored, and made available for users.
Career clusters	Business, Management, and Administration; Finance; Information Technology; Science, Technology, Engineering. and Math
Interests	Data; people
Working conditions	Work inside
Minimum education level	Bachelor's degree; master's degree
Physical exertion	Light work
Physical abilities	Unexceptional/basic fitness
Opportunities for experience	Military service; part-time work
Licensure and certification	Recommended
Employment outlook	Faster-than-average growth expected
Holland interest score	IER

Note: See volume 1, "Publisher's Note," for an explanation of the Holland interest score.

and server applications, multimedia, and Internet technology. To accomplish these tasks, knowledge of hardware, such as chips, circuit boards, and processors, is required, as is knowledge of software, including applications and programming.

Database administrators design, create, modify, and maintain databases by implementing various relational database tools. Maintenance of the databases involves planning for backup, recovery, and allocation of system storage to plan for future storage of data. These database administrators often are required to write short computer programs and scripts using Structured Query Language (SQL), develop database objects, design interfaces, and implement other relational database tools.

Technology, research, design, and development occupations may include the following:

- Computer Systems Analyst
- Product Life Cycle Management (PLM) Consultant/Analyst
- Applications Computer Software Engineer
- Systems Software Computer Engineer
- Computer Programmer
- Network System Analyst
- Data Analyst
- System Programmer
- Project Manager
- Research Director

Production and Operations

Production and operations personnel are involved with the manufacture of hardware components such as circuit boards, routers, modems, hubs, switches, and various types of cables. The number of job positions within production, operations, and manufacturing has been declining and is predicted to continue to decline through 2018, according to the BLS.

Production and operations occupations may include the following:

- Project Manager
- Chief Operating Officer (COO)
- Manufacturing Technician
- Laboratory Technician
- Facility Technician

Distribution

Distribution personnel manage supplier relations and assist with the optimization of inventory and supply lines through the use of statistics, information systems, and supply-chain management.

Distribution occupations may include the following:

- Distribution Planner
- Delivery Technician
- Supply Chain Analyst
- Warehouse Manager
- Truck Driver
- Shipping and Receiving Clerk
- Freight Loader/Unloader

Human Resources

Human resources personnel include consultants and specialists who assist employees with benefits and compensation paperwork, as well as managers and senior managers who supervise variable numbers of employees within the human resources department, depending on the size of the company. Typically, these managers may be required to travel often and may be involved with leading and implementing various training programs. The collection of applications that facilitate work within human resources is called the human resources information system (HRIS), and many of the job roles within the human resources functional area use it.

A human resources senior manager develops company-wide programs, such as programs dealing with performance management, training assessment, benefits, and reviews of salaries and bonuses. This manager is a member of the line management staff that specifically manages employee relations issues and is responsible for conducting any investigations related to corporate ethics and values. The human resources senior manager is also responsible for following government specifications related to staffing needs. This position typically requires at least five years of experience as a general human resources manager and a bachelor's degree.

A recruitment representative needs to have strong project management and communication skills along with experience using spreadsheet software and HRIS computer systems to assess employees and maintain employee information within database software, such as Oracle's Web tool called i-Recruitment that is specifically designed to assist with recruitment activities. Individuals in this position must be independent self-starters who enjoy travel. This position also requires a bachelor's degree or a master's degree.

A compensation and benefits consultant assists with the design and implementation of policies, procedures, and programs pertaining to various compensation programs and may also participate in salary administration, data analysis, and job evaluations. This position typically requires a bachelor's degree, several years of experience with compensation and benefits, and sometimes a Certified Computing Professional designation.

Human resources occupations may include the following:

- Administrative Assistant
- Compensation and Benefits Specialist
- Recruitment Specialist
- Administrative Assistant
- Human Resources Specialist
- Human Resources Coordinator
- Human Resources General Manager
- Human Resources Director
- Human Resources Senior Manager

Information Technology

Computer and information systems managers coordinate and direct activities in information systems, systems analysis, programming, and electronic data processing. Their routine tasks include management of the backup of data, security, and

Computer backup tapes. (©Amy Walters/Dreamstime.com)

user help systems. They develop computer information resources, provide for data security, and provide for strategic computing and disaster recovery, as well as providing users with technical support. They are also responsible for the evaluation of data processing proposals to assess project feasibility and requirements.

Computer software engineers for systems software are responsible for the design and testing of compilers, operating systems, and network distribution of software for medical, industrial, military, communications, aerospace, scientific, business, or general computing applications. A system administrator controls the system configurations from a network hub, using hardware and software, local area and wide area networking, information system security, disk space traffic load monitoring, data backup, and allocation of resources.

Webmasters and Web developers develop and maintain Web servers and hosted Web pages at Web sites. Their tasks often include server installation and maintenance, Internet applications of information systems security, computer systems and networks, design and editing of Web pages, Web policy, Web procedures, and usability of user interfaces.

Information technology occupations may include the following:

- Information Technology Director
- Database Administrator
- Web Developer
- Webmaster
- Computer Software Engineer
- Computer Programmer
- Network System Analyst
- System Programmer
- System Administrator

INDUSTRY OUTLOOK

Overview

The outlook for this industry shows it to be dramatically on the rise. According to the BLS, the computer systems industry is one of the twenty-five fastest-growing industries in the United States, and employment within this industry is projected to increase by 45 percent between 2008 and 2018, more than four times the 11 percent growth rate of the overall job market during that time. Electronic commerce grew from $75 billion in 2002 to more than $204 billion in 2008 and is projected to reach $335 billion in 2012.

High-speed Internet connections in the United States increased from 5 million connections in 2002 to more than 80 million connections in 2008, increasing the demand for the many peripherals and Internet connectivity devices that make use of such connections. Wireless Internet connectivity is also increasing dramatically, driven by the proliferation of handheld computers and smart phones. These new devices continuously lead to increases in both available positions and salaries within the computer systems industry. As the Internet and its use for e-commerce become even more important, businesses will continue to increase their application of computer systems, including the most recent technological advances that can be affordably purchased. Thus, the integration of new hardware, software, and communications tools will drive the industry and will also increase the need for experts in network security and support services.

E-commerce is becoming increasingly dependent on the use of wireless technology to operate. Devices developed by an increasing number of computer systems technology companies such as wireless personal digital assistants (PDAs) and smart phones continue to transform the way that companies and individuals communicate. These wireless devices pose additional security problems, and much research and development is aimed at making wireless communications more secure. The cost of wireless devices to consumers is expected to continue to decrease, and this decrease will lead to increasing availability and sales.

Wireless devices will find increasing applications in all kinds of industries, ranging from the health care industry to real estate to education. Online Webinar training is gaining in popularity, and many computer systems consulting jobs will assist the implementation of wireless devices into education, health care, and real estate. Thus, the demand for computer and information systems managers, computer systems programmers, computer systems software engineers, computer systems analysts, computer scientists, computer systems support specialists, and computer systems administrators is expected to remain higher than average, according to the BLS.

Employment Advantages

Because all industries are becoming more dependent on computer information systems, employment opportunities within the computer systems industry are expected to continue to be excellent, especially for those with specialist certifications and higher levels of training. For example, the BLS projects that job opportunities for computer systems analysts will grow much faster than the average for all occupations through 2018. Also according to the BLS, the computer systems industry will add approximately 656,400 new jobs between 2008 and 2018, which makes this industry one of the top five industries in terms of growth.

Because of the high demand for skilled workers, employees in this industry experience less gender and age bias, tend to have more lucrative benefit packages along with salaries, and have more potential for advancement. Typically, entry into the industry is less restrictive than it is in many other industries. Although most employees have either bachelor's or associate's degrees in computer science, information technology, or information systems, it is possible for job seekers to enter the computer systems industry with a degree in an entirely different field, as long as they have the required job skills. There are many certification programs representative of these job skills that can substitute for a specific computer science degree. Thus, careers within the industry are potentially ideal for those who want to make a career change.

Annual Earnings

According to Research & Markets, the U.S. computer systems industry earned revenues of $285 billion in 2009, while the global industry earned revenues of $578 billion. The average annual earnings for computer systems analysts were $78,830 in 2008, according to the BLS. The top 10 percent of computer systems analysts in the United States earned more than $99,180 in 2004, while 50 percent earned between $52,400 and $82,980, and the lowest 10 percent earned less than $41,730. Earnings for various project managers with certifications tend to be higher, with managers who have the Project Management Professional certification earning $101,695 annually and managers with the Certified Associate in Project Management designation earning $101,103 annually.

Earnings for other certifications within the computer systems industry are also quite high, with the average annual earnings for the Certified Information Systems Security Professional being $94,018, the Microsoft Certified Solution Developer being $84,522 annually, the Cisco Certified Network Professional being $84,161 annually, and the Red Hat Certified Engineer being $83,692. Earnings for additional certifications for professionals within the computer systems industry are $82,941 for a Microsoft Certified IT Professional, $80,000 for a Cisco Certified Security Professional, $79,444 for a Microsoft Certified Applications Developer, $77,000 for a Microsoft Certified IT Database Professional, and $76,960 for a Microsoft Certified Database Administrator. Salaries for those without certifications are approximately 20 percent lower than these annual earnings but are still higher than salaries in most other industries. In 2008, the average earnings of all production or nonsupervisory employees in the computer systems industry was $72,852, compared to the average of $31,616 for all industries combined.

RELATED RESOURCES FOR FURTHER RESEARCH

ASSOCIATION FOR COMPUTING MACHINERY
2 Penn Plaza, Suite 701
New York, NY 10121-0701
Tel: (800) 342-6626
Fax: (212) 944-1318
http://www.acm.org

COMPUTER SOCIETY
Institute of Electrical and Electronics Engineers
2001 L St. NW, Suite 700
Washington, DC 20036
Tel: (202) 371-0101
Fax: (202) 728-9614
http://www.computer.org

NATIONAL CENTER FOR WOMEN AND INFORMATION TECHNOLOGY, UNIVERSITY OF COLORADO
Campus Box 322
Boulder, CO 80309-0322
Tel: (303) 735-6671
Fax: (303) 735-6606
http://www.ncwit.org

NATIONAL WORKFORCE CENTER FOR EMERGING TECHNOLOGIES
Bellevue College
3000 Landerholm Circle SE, N211
Bellevue, WA 98007-6484
Tel: (425) 564-4229
Fax: (425) 564-6193
http://www.nwcet.org

UNIVERSITY OF WASHINGTON COMPUTER SCIENCE AND ENGINEERING DEPARTMENT
AC101 Paul G. Allen Center
Box 352350, 185 Stevens Way
Seattle, WA 98195-2350
Tel: (206) 543-1695
Fax: (206) 543-2969
http://www.cs.washington.edu/WhyCSE

ABOUT THE AUTHOR

Jeanne L. Kuhler has more than fifty-five publications and eight years of industrial experience within the areas of pharmaceutical chemistry research, cheminformatics, computer programming, and data management, including four years at American Home Products and over three years at General Electric. She fell in love with teaching while teaching part time and has been sharing her enthusiasm for technology with students for the past seven years. She was awarded the Auburn Montgomery School of Sciences Teaching Award for 2008-2009. She earned a Ph.D. from Texas Tech University, an M.S. from Yale University, and an Honors B.S. from Indiana University.

FURTHER READING

Bayles, D. L. *E-Commerce Logistics and Fulfillment.* Upper Saddle River, N.J.: Prentice Hall, 2001.
Chesbrough, H. W. *Open Business Models.* Boston: Harvard Business School Press, 2006.
Conference Board of Canada. *Canada's Computer Systems Design Industry: Industrial Outlook, Spring, 2010.* Ottawa, Ont.: Author, 2010.
Cowhey, Peter F., Jonathan David Aronson, and Donald Abelson. *Transforming Global Information and Communication Markets: The*

Political Economy of Innovation. Cambridge, Mass.: MIT Press, 2009.

Fisher, Eran. *Media and New Capitalism in the Digital Age: The Spirit of Networks.* New York: Palgrave Macmillan, 2010.

Forrester Business Data Services. *Enterprise Network and Telecommunications Survey.* Boston: Author, 2007.

Gronstedt, A. *Training in Virtual Worlds.* New York: ASTD Press, 2008.

Hunter, R. *World Without Secrets: Business, Crime, and Privacy in the Age of Ubiquitous Computing.* New York: Wiley, 2002.

Kalakota, R., and M. Robinson. *E-Business 2.2 Roadmap for Success.* Boston: Addison Wesley, 2001.

Khosrow-Pour, M., ed. *Encyclopedia of E-Commerce, E-Government, and Mobile Commerce.* Hershey, Pa.: Idea Group Reference, 2006.

Prahalad, C. K., and M. S. Krishnan. *The New Age of Innovation.* New York: McGraw-Hill, 2008.

Sadeh, N. *M-Commerce.* New York: Wiley, 2002.

SalaryList.com. "Manager of Information Technology Jobs Salary, Ranked by Salary." http://xxx.salarylist.com/all-manager-of-information-technology-real-jobs-salary.htm.

Turban, E., et al. *Decision Support Systems and Intelligent Systems.* 8th ed. Upper Saddle River, N.J.: Prentice Hall, 2007.

U.S. Bureau of Labor Statistics. *Career Guide to Industries,* 2010-2011 ed. http://www.bls.gov/oco/cg.

U.S. Census Bureau. North American Industry Classification System (NAICS), 2007. http://www.census.gov/cgi-bin/sssd/naics/naicsrch?chart=2007.

U.S. Department of Commerce. International Trade Administration. Office of Trade and Industry Information. Industry Trade Data and Analysis. http://ita.doc.gov/td/industry/otea/OTII/OTII-index.html.

Construction Equipment Industry

INDUSTRY SNAPSHOT

General Industry: Manufacturing
Career Cluster: Manufacturing
Subcategory Industries: Bulldozer Manufacturing; Crane Manufacturing; Crushing Machinery Manufacturing; Dredging Machinery Manufacturing; Excavator Manufacturing; Grader, Roller, and Compactor Manufacturing; Mixer and Paver Manufacturing; Pile Driver Manufacturing, Front Loader Manufacturing, Tractor Manufacturing
Related Industries: Heavy Machines Industry; Highway, Road, and Bridge Construction Industry
Annual Domestic Revenues: $36 billion USD (Hoovers, 2009)
Annual International Revenues: $45 billion USD (Freedonia, 2009)
Annual Global Revenues: $81 billion USD (Freedonia, 2009)
NAICS Number: 333120

INDUSTRY DEFINITION

Summary

Construction equipment comprises a large variety of powered, heavy machines, which perform specific construction (or demolition) functions. The power plant is usually an integral part of the machine; however, it is sometimes a separate piece of equipment, such as a towed grader or cement mixer. Construction equipment is classified by its function: drilling, excavating, grading, hauling, hoisting, paving, or pile driving. No new categories have evolved since the middle of the twentieth century. Present-day design emphasis is on modifications that increase speed, efficiency, and accuracy. In addition, new machines have reduced emissions, lower noise levels, and increased operator comfort and safety. Virtually every industrialized nation on the planet has a significant construction equipment industry, employing individuals in a wide variety of career paths.

History of the Industry

The use of construction equipment began as early as ancient times, in Rome. In *De architectura* (c. 27 B.C.E.; *The Architecture*, 1771), the Roman engineer Marcus Vitruvius Pollio provided detailed descriptions of construction equipment, cranes, and hoists, as well as war machines such as catapults and siege engines. He also described the aeolipile, which was the precursor of the steam engine.

The modern industry, however, can be traced back to the nineteenth century. Various sectors of the construction equipment appeared or expanded following the Industrial Revolution, which had its onset in the eighteenth century in Europe. The industry then spread throughout Europe, North America, and the rest of the globe. It was marked by major changes in agriculture, mining, manufacturing, and transport; this phenomenon had a profound impact on socioeconomic and cultural conditions, as much of the world's population began to migrate from the country to urban areas for industrial occupations.

In 1836, John Deere manufactured a polished-steel plow for use by pioneer farmers in the American Midwest. By 1870, his company was producing plows, cultivators, harrows, drills, planters, wagons, and buggies. In the 1880's, steam tractors appeared; they were replaced thirty years later by gasoline-powered tractors. In 1931, the first diesel-powered tractor rolled off the assembly line at Deere & Company in East Peoria, Illinois. By 1940, the Caterpillar Tractor Company produced mo-

tor graders, generators, and a special tank engine used by the United States during World War II. In 1963, Caterpillar and Mitsubishi Heavy Industries formed one of the first joint ventures in Japan, Caterpillar Mitsubishi. The company, later known as Shin Caterpillar Mitsubishi, is the second largest producer of construction and mining equipment in Japan. In the 1960's, Deere & Company also took steps to become multinational, establishing small tractor plants in Mexico, France, Argentina, and South Africa.

A basic piece of earth-moving equipment is the bulldozer. It is not known for certain who invented the first bulldozer; however, the bulldozer blade antedates any form of earth mover. Before the Industrial Revolution, two mules were harnessed to a frame with a blade attached to the front. The mules pushed the blade into a pile of dirt, which was dumped from a cart. The dirt was spread over a depression in the earth to fill it. In 1904, American inventor Benjamin Holt patented and manufactured the first crawler type of tread tractor, which was powered by a steam engine. The continuous tread

Excavators, like this backhoe, dig up earth and rock and place it in a dump truck or other device for transportation to another location. (©Eti Swinford/Dreamstime.com)

spread the weight of heavy earth-moving equipment over a large area, thus preventing it from sinking into the ground. Richard Hornsby, an English inventor, improved on the design. In 1914, the Hornsby Company manufactured its powered tractor, known as a "chain track," which was steered by controlling the speed of each track. This was a marked improvement over Holt's machine, which was steered by a tiller wheel located in front of the treads. Hornsby's steering method is used by modern bulldozers and military tanks.

One of the key developments in the production of all machines was the assembly line, which made it possible to produce equipment more efficiently. Before 1900, machinery was produced at one location, one unit at a time. Although the origin of the assembly line is often linked with Henry Ford, Ransom Olds patented an assembly line concept, which he implemented in his Olds Motor Vehicle Company factory in 1901.

The concept was, however, vastly improved on by Ford. His improvement of the assembly line involved moving work, via conveyor belts, from one worker to another while the worker remained stationary; each worker had a particular task to complete on the building of a unit, or part, of an automobile, and he became expert at that task and would perform it repeatedly. As the work moved forward, each task was completed by its expert worker or workers, until the unit was completely assembled. These units were then moved, at the right time and the right place, to a final assembly line, which produced the finished product. As a result of Ford's assembly line improvements, an automobile came off the line every three minutes. Previous assembly lines had produced vehicles at a rate of about two per hour and required significantly more manpower. Ford also implemented safety procedures, which involved assigning each worker to a specific location rather than allowing him to roam about the work area; this dramatically reduced the rate of injuries.

Front-end loaders (also known as skip loaders) are a motorized device with a digging/carrying bucket on the front end. (©Dreamstime.com)

Graders are vehicles with a leveling blade mounted between large front and rear wheels. (©Vladimir Bryzgin/ Dreamstime.com)

The Industry Today

The construction equipment industry is dominated by large, multinational companies that produce a wide range of products. More than 80 percent of the industry's revenue is generated by these large companies. In the early 1900's, construction equipment was primarily produced in the United States and Western Europe; however, much of this production has shifted to Asia, including India. The industry is highly susceptible to the state of the economy and rates of economic growth. Inasmuch as the equipment is designed for construction, when new construction experiences a slowdown, these companies are affected. Strong export sales are essential for the survival and growth of companies in the industry, and hence the market is extremely competitive. However, many companies that manufacture construction equipment also manufacture agricultural equipment. Equipment produced for farm use is affected to a lesser degree because of the ongoing need for agricultural products worldwide.

Technology has markedly affected the industry, which is emphasizing manufacturing high-quality machinery. Machines being introduced to the marketplace feature modifications that make them more efficient and faster than older models. Operator comfort and safety are stressed, harmful emissions are being reduced, and the machines are quieter. Many of these machines are expensive and can cost from $100,000 to well in excess of $1 million. Thus, selection of a piece of construction equipment is affected by economics. Price, efficiency, and the ability of a machine to accomplish a needed task have to be considered before purchase. Availability can be a major factor for larger and more specialized pieces of equipment. Transportation costs can be more than $1 million if the product must travel a significant distance from manufacturer to purchaser.

Major subindustries supported by the construction equipment industry are maintenance and repair, sales, leasing, engine manufacturing, and tire manufacturing. Some products (such as tractors)

Dump trucks, a type of hauling equipment, can move materials over large distances and are designed for road and off-road use. (©Billy Gadbury/Dreamstime.com)

can be used for a variety of tasks; others (such as pipe layers) are designed for specific tasks. As of 2010, the top ten construction equipment companies were Caterpillar (Peoria, Illinois); Komatsu (Tokyo, Japan); Terex (Westport, Connecticut); Case New Holland (CNH; Amsterdam, the Netherlands); Volvo Construction Equipment (Götenburg, Sweden); Deere & Company (Moline, Illinois); Doosan Group (Bobcat Company; Seoul, South Korea); Hitachi Construction Machinery (Tokyo, Japan); Bell Equipment (Rochester, New York); and Hitachi Construction Machinery Europe (Oosterhout, the Netherlands). These companies primarily produce earth-moving, construction, and farming equipment. Many of these companies manufacture their own engines, which are primarily diesel. Some, like Caterpillar, market their engines as a separate product. Although the mention of Caterpillar brings to mind earth-moving equipment, the company has a large presence in the marine engine industry as well.

Construction equipment manufactured by these companies requires either continuous tracks or specialized tires. The equipment with more severe service requirements uses continuous tracks; however, tires are preferable when greater speed and mobility are required. Because of this need, the construction equipment industry is a significant source of revenue for the sub-industry of tire manufacturing. Selecting the proper tire for the lifetime use of the equipment is important, because it can have a major impact on per-unit production costs.

Construction equipment is often categorized by its function: drilling, excavating, grading, hauling, hoisting, paving, or pile driving.

Drilling equipment bores holes into the earth's surface. It includes augers, bore-tunneling machines, compactors, and pile hammers. Drills are classified according to how they penetrate: rotary, percussion, or rotary percussion. These machines range in size from small, portable equipment that can be operated by a single person to massive structures containing drilling equipment that can bore a passageway for the extraction of water, oil, or natural gas. This equipment can be used for sampling mineral deposits as well as installing underground utilities.

When drilling rigs first appeared in the nineteenth century, they were often left in place after the completion of drilling. In modern times, the equipment is frequently moved from one work site to the next. The smaller machines are mobile and moved intact from one location to the next. The larger rigs must be disassembled for relocation. The process often takes weeks. A life-saving use of drilling equipment received international attention on August 15, 2010, when thirty-three Chilean miners were trapped 700 meters (2,300 feet) below the earth's surface. Initially, holes were bored to provide food and water to the miners; a larger hole was bored to allow extraction of the miners on October 13, 2010.

Excavating equipment is manufactured for either land or marine use. Land excavation involves the use of machines that dig up earth and rock and place it in a dump truck or other device for transportation to another location. Types of excavators include backhoes, cranes with attached buckets, continuous bucket excavators, draglines, excavating belt loaders, power shovels, and trenchers. Some equipment involves both excavation and relocation of rocks and earth. Examples are bulldozers, scrapers, and front-end loaders (also known as skip loaders, motorized devices with a digging/carrying bucket located on the front end). Dump trucks can move materials over large distances and are designed for road and off-road use. Some dump trucks have a bottom dump, which allows for the slow release of material so that it is dispersed over an area. Conveyer belts are sometimes used to move materials between areas too small to permit the passage of even a small truck.

Marine excavators are commonly referred to as dredges. They are mounted on a barge or a boat. Clamshell and bucket excavators are similar to their land counterparts. Some dredges employ a movable suction pipe, which is lowered to the bottom. The pipe usually contains a sharp cutting head, which dislodges material for suction as the dredge is propelled forward.

Graders are vehicles with a leveling blade mounted between large front and rear wheels. They are commonly used for the fine grading of an area. They can also produce an inclined surface and a V-shaped channel for drainage. Another use of graders is for snow removal.

Hauling equipment includes dump trucks, which transport loads of materials, and excavating equipment, which also transports the material it dislodges from the earth. Examples include skip loaders, backhoe loaders, and skid steer loaders.

Hoisting equipment raises or lowers objects from one elevation to another or moves materials from one location to another over an obstruction. The main types of hoisting equipment are cableways, cranes, conveyors, derricks, and elevators. Hoisting devices range in size from small cranes for lifting an automobile engine out of a vehicle to large devices that can lift very heavy loads for construction of ships and large buildings. Some of these devices are fixed to one location; however, most are mobile (on tracks or wheels). An extreme example of a mobile crane is the aerial crane, which is a specialized type of helicopter.

Pavers apply paving materials, then smooth and compact them. Paving material is usually fed to them from a dump truck. Concrete pavers use a vibrator to level the surface. Asphalt pavers contain tamping pads to compress the applied material. After asphalt is laid, a separate machine, the roller, is used to further smooth the surface.

Pile-driving equipment drive piles into the earth; they include both land- and water-based machines. The three main types of pile drivers are the diesel hammer, the hydraulic hammer, and the vibratory pile driver. The diesel hammer is a very large two-cycle diesel engine, which transfers the combustion energy to the pile head. The hydraulic hammer elevates water, which then falls in an enclosed cylinder; the force drives the pile downward. The

Hoisting equipment, such as a crane, raises or lowers objects from one elevation to another or moves materials from one location to another over an obstruction. (©Martijn Mulder/Dreamstime.com)

vibratory pile driver consists of an electric motor, which turns unbalanced weights that produce a vibratory, downward force.

Although some smaller companies with fewer than one thousand employees compete in the marketplace, this industry is dominated by large companies with a global presence. Their products are large and complicated; thus, large facilities are necessary for their production.

Small Construction Equipment Businesses

Small businesses in this industry are concentrated in the subindustry of maintenance and repair, sales, and leasing. However, some produce components for large companies and some produce complete machines. Those that produce complete machines are in direct competition with midsize and large companies.

An example of a small equipment sales company is Eberhard Equipment, located in Santa Ana, California. The company occupies a two-acre site, has nineteen employees, and generates annual sales of approximately $7 million. Upper-level employees include the owner, an office manager, a parts manager, a service manager, and a sales/rental manager. The company is a dealer for equipment manufactured by Kubota, Terex, Walker Equipment, Deere & Company, Massey Ferguson, and Mustang Skid Steer. The company leases the equipment and also services construction equipment. The company distributes about one-third of its profits to its employees.

Potential Annual Earnings Scale. The average earnings for a small construction equipment business owner vary from region to region but usually are usually less than $100,000 annually.

Clientele Interaction. Small businesses tend to favor more interaction with customers, and the personal touch can foster consumer satisfaction. However, clientele interaction can vary widely. The owner might have direct contact with his or her customers or market the product over the Internet with contact limited to telephone and e-mail. A Web site is essential to a small business. A well-designed site can successfully compete with that of a large company. For example, a small company's Web site can mimic the appearance or style of a much larger company's site; it can not only market the product but also offer technical advice and serve as a vehicle for customer feedback.

Amenities, Atmosphere, and Physical Grounds. Amenities of small businesses are often limited. Inasmuch as the owner has extensive control over the business, the working environment can be tailored to personal taste and budget. An owner interested in a favorable working environment might have a facility with extremely pleasant working conditions; however, most facilities are utilitarian, no-frills structures.

Typical Number of Employees. The number of employees can range from one to several dozen.

Traditional Geographic Locations. Small construction businesses are usually located near the owner's home.

Pros of Working for a Small Construction Equipment Business. The owner is often responsible for all operational decisions. The owner might consult with staff members regarding these decisions or have the option of complete autonomy. A staff member usually has a closer working relationship with the owner than would be the case in a larger company. Part-time employment and flexible hours are usually easier to arrange than they would be in a larger company. A small-business owner can control waste and unnecessary expenditures to a greater degree than the manager of a larger company, because all expenditures are subject to his or her approval; furthermore, less bureaucracy exists in these small businesses.

If the company fosters teamwork and group decision making, the employee can be more involved in the company's growth. In some cases, partnership opportunities exist for an exceptional employee. If the company flourishes, the company might grow in both size and profit margin; this could lead to expansion or purchase by a larger company. If either occurs, the financial return could be significant. Some small-business owners have sold their company at a large profit and have generated enough income to retire with an extremely comfortable lifestyle. This large profit might be shared among key or long-term employees.

Cons of Working for a Small Construction Equipment Business. The construction equipment industry is extremely competitive. Even if the company produces a good product (or products), it may not be able to compete successfully with a large company that can produce a comparable product at a lower price. A small business is less resilient if an unexpected major expense—such as major equipment failure or a worker's compensation lawsuit—arises. Such situations can bankrupt a small business. The owner and staff generally will not have the variety of skills that the staff and management of a larger company will possess. For example, the staff may have technical expertise but lack marketing skills. Furthermore, with a small staff, the owner and employees will be responsible for a wide range of duties. For example, a technician might be asked to sweep the floor or clean the restroom. Interemployee relationships can become strained, and small companies rarely have dedicated human resources departments to handle such matters. In a large company, if two employees do not get along, one can be relocated to another area. This is not possible in a small company, confined to a small area. Finally, loss of a key employee can slow or even halt production until a suitable replacement is found.

Costs

Payroll and Benefits: Small companies often place all employees on an hourly wage and usually do not provide the same level of benefits as a large company; these benefits can be at the discretion of the owner. However, most small companies offer sick pay, health insurance, and paid vacation time.

Supplies: Supplies will usually cost a small business more than a large business, which has the clout to negotiate lower prices with large bulk purchases. Both supplies directly related to the construction of the machinery and office supplies necessary for the business will be more expensive.

External Services: Costs for external services for a small business are typically minimal and might include such things as Web site development and maintenance or billing services. If a small business becomes involved in a legal dispute, an attorney usually must be retained. In this situation, the small-business owner might incur significant costs.

Utilities: Utility usage may be comparable to that of a residence; however, the manufacturing of some equipment might involve significantly more use of electricity or natural gas.

Taxes: Small businesses are obligated to pay local, state, and federal taxes. If the business is a sole proprietorship, these taxes may be similar to those of an individual taxpayer. If the business is incorporated, state corporate taxes must also be paid. In addition, small businesses must pay federal and state payroll taxes and social security contributions for their employees.

Midsize Construction Equipment Businesses

Midsize businesses tend to favor smaller types of equipment; they often serve niche markets with a limited product line. These products may compete with products produced by large businesses. Some produce products that complement the product lines of large businesses. Midsize companies are also involved in maintenance and repair, leasing, and sales.

An example of a midsize construction business is Klein Products, which maintains facilities in Ontario, California, and Jacksonville, Texas. The company was founded in the 1950's by Richard Klein, who transitioned from a store manager for JCPenney to a welder and truck mechanic. He then went on to found his company. Klein Products employs more than one hundred individuals and manufactures small to midsize construction and water-distributing machinery. The products are marketed worldwide.

Potential Annual Earnings Scale. Salaries vary from region to region; however, the pay for a mechanical engineer is about $32 per hour; sales representatives earn about $28 per hour and may receive commissions for sales; first-line supervisors or managers of production and operating workers earn about $26 per hour; tool and die makers earn about $21 per hour; machinists earn about $18 per hour; computer-controlled machine tool operators (for metals and plastics) earn about $17 per hour; inspectors, testers, sorters, samplers, and weighers earn about $17 per hour; welders, cutters, solderers, and brazers earn about $16 per hour; cutting, punching, and press machine setters, operators, and tenders (metals and plastics) earn about $14 per hour; and team assemblers earn about $14 per hour. Incomes for managers in the manufacturing arm vary widely, from less than $50,000 to more than $100,000 annually.

Clientele Interaction. Vendors can foster long-term relationships, which can generate repeat business. All midsize businesses will have a Web site for both marketing and clientele interaction. The site will offer customer service, provide technical support, and often supply downloadable Adobe PDF copies of user's manuals.

Amenities, Atmosphere, and Physical Grounds. Manufacturing facilities are typical of factories and are customarily spartan and utilitarian.

Typical Number of Employees. A manufacturing facility consists of a management staff, assembly supervisors, and assemblers.

Traditional Geographic Locations. Manufacturers are typically in the industrial area of a city and are commonly located in areas near rail or ocean cargo service.

Pros of Working for a Midsize Construction Equipment Industry. The owner of a midsize manufacturing business often has more control over operational decisions than he or she would in a large company. Employee-management interaction is often at a higher level than a large company. Midsize manufacturing businesses can employ individuals with a variety of skills; these employees include technicians, assemblers, and marketing personnel. Employees of a midsize company may have closer relationships with management than employees in a larger firm and may have a greater sense of being part of a team. Midsize companies may have one or only a few locations; thus, an employee who prefers to remain in one location usually will not be confronted with the threat of a transfer to another location, as he or she would in a large, global company.

Cons of Working for a Midsize Construction Equipment Industry. Many midsize businesses produce a limited product line or specialty products. In times of economic downturn, these companies are more susceptible to failure. The limited number of management positions in a midsize company decreases opportunities for advancement, particularly to positions commanding a high salary.

Costs

Payroll and Benefits: Midsize companies can usually offer benefits comparable to those of a large company; these benefits include sick pay, health insurance, and paid vacations.

Supplies: Midsize companies can often negotiate discounts from suppliers; however, the unit production cost may be higher than for a comparable product produced by a large company.

OCCUPATION SPECIALTIES

Computer-Controlled Machine Tool Operators

Specialty	*Responsibilities*
Drill-press operators	Set up and operate numerically controlled drill presses that automatically perform machining operations such as drilling, reaming, counter-sinking, spot-facing, and tapping of holes in metal workpieces.
Jig-boring machine operators	Set up and operate numerically controlled jig-boring machines to perform such jigging operations as boring, drilling, and counter-sinking holes in metal workpieces.
Milling-machine operators	Set up and operate multiaxis, numerically controlled milling machines to mill surfaces on metallic and nonmetallic workpieces.
Router set-up operators	Set up and operate multiaxis, numerically controlled routing machines to cut and shape metallic and nonmetallic workpieces.

External Services: Manufacturing companies often use accounting services and billing services; however, they might also maintain employees that can perform these services. They also often use outside legal services rather than in-house services.

Utilities: Manufacturing of construction equipment often entails major costs for utilities, particularly gas and electricity.

Taxes: Midsize businesses must pay local, state, and federal income taxes as well as applicable property taxes. Almost all businesses in the United States are incorporated; thus, they pay state and federal taxes at the corporate level. They must also collect state sales taxes for retail sales. Midsize businesses must pay federal and state payroll taxes and social security contributions for their employees.

Large Construction Equipment Businesses

Large manufacturing businesses market their products internationally. The large companies in the United States compete directly with companies whose headquarters are in other nations. For example Deere & Company, headquartered in Moline, Illinois, maintains facilities in Canada, Europe, China, Australia, South America, and Russia. These companies often market a variety of products, including light equipment and products in other market segments (such as televisions or even life insurance). They profit from brand recognition. Most consumers recognize these brand names when considering a purchase and will often favor a product that they deem to have a good reputation for reliability and features. Some equipment manufactured by non-U.S. companies, specifically Asian companies, may have less brand recognition in the United States; however, brand recognition is increasing for these products as well.

An example of a large, global construction equipment industry is Mitsubishi Heavy Industries (Tokyo), which is one of the core companies of the Mitsubishi Group. The Mitsubishi Group markets an extensive variety of products, including automobiles, televisions, Nikon cameras, beer breweries, and life insurance. A division of Mitsubishi Heavy Industries is located in the United States. Products marketed by Mitsubishi Heavy Industries include airplanes, ships and other marine structures, steel structures and construction, power systems, turbochargers, forklifts, military combat tanks, wind turbines, air-conditioning and refrigeration systems, industrial machinery, paper and printing machinery, machine tools, and light rail vehicles. An example of a large construction equipment industry with a narrower, but still impressive, product range is Caterpillar, which manufactures equipment for construction and farming, including trucks, compacters, harvesters, graders, bulldozers, excavators, pipe layers, front loaders, and pavers. Both Mitsubishi and Caterpillar began as small companies in the nineteenth century. Caterpillar was founded in 1890 by Benjamin Holt and Daniel Best in the United States. Mitsubishi was founded in 1837 by Yataro Iwasaki in Japan. Caterpillar's first product was a steam tractor for farm use. Mitsubishi began on a grander scale, as a shipbuilder.

Potential Annual Earnings Scale. Salaries vary from region to region. The salaries for top management positions, such as a chief executive officer, can be well over $1 million per year. On average, the pay for a mechanical engineer is $32 per hour; sales representatives earn about $28 per hour and may receive commissions for sales; first-line supervisors or managers of production and operating workers earn about $26 per hour; tool and die makers earn about $21 per hour; machinists earn about $18 per hour; computer-controlled machine tool operators (metals and plastics) earn about $17 per hour; inspectors, testers, sorters, samplers, and weighers earn about $17 per hour; welders, cutters, solderers, and brazers earn about $16 per hour; cutting, punching, and press machine setters, operators, and tenders (metals and plastics) earn about $14 per hour; and team assemblers earn about $14 per hour. Many large companies offer dealership franchises. A motivated individual with capital to invest has an opportunity to develop a dealership into a multimillion-dollar business providing tremendous personal financial benefits. These dealerships can operate with a high degree of autonomy, provided that they generate adequate revenues for the parent company.

Clientele Interaction. Vendors can foster long-term relationships, which can generate repeat business. All large businesses will have a Web site for both marketing and clientele interaction. The site will offer customer service, provide technical support, and often supply downloadable Adobe PDF files of operator's manuals.

OCCUPATION PROFILE

Computer-Controlled Tool Programmer

Considerations	Qualifications
Description	Develops programs to control computer numerically controlled machines that precisely cut metal, plastic, or glass.
Career cluster	Manufacturing
Interests	Data; things
Working conditions	Work inside
Minimum education level	On-the-job training; high school diploma/technical training; junior/technical college; apprenticeship
Physical exertion	Light work
Physical abilities	Unexceptional/basic fitness
Opportunities for experience	Apprenticeship; military service
Licensure and certification	Recommended
Employment outlook	Decline expected
Holland interest score	IRC

Note: See volume 1, "Publisher's Note," for an explanation of the Holland interest score.

Amenities, Atmosphere, and Physical Grounds. Manufacturing facilities are customarily spartan and utilitarian. Dealerships, however, can range from utilitarian to luxurious. Corporate headquarters are luxurious and state of the art. The headquarters may have a large area devoted to displaying examples of the company's product line. For example, Deere & Company's world headquarters is located on fourteen hundred acres of manicured land, which is home to a variety of wildlife, including white-tailed deer, ducks, geese, and swans. Visitors can view displays of John Deere equipment, ranging from antiques to the company's latest offerings.

Typical Number of Employees. The number of individuals employed by many companies in this industry had dropped as of 2010 as a result of the impact of the widespread economic downturn. Deere & Company reported 56,653 employees for 2008, for example, but only 51,262 employees in 2009—a 10 percent drop. Mitsubishi Heavy Indus-

tries states that the company initiated a plan in 2008 to reduce the average number of employees in Japan from 3,500 to 2,000 over the following two years. However, over that same period, the company planned to increase the workforce in overseas companies, particularly in growth businesses, from 8,450 to 15,000 employees. The company predicted that its consolidated workforce would number 72,000 by March, 2015.

Traditional Geographic Locations. Corporate headquarters can be located in virtually any large or small city; large retail outlets also can be located in any area with a reasonable population density. Manufacturing facilities are typically in the industrial areas of large cities and located in areas near rail or ocean cargo services.

Pros of Working for a Large Construction Equipment Business. A wealth of career opportunities exists within large manufacturing companies as well as their dealerships. Positions include high-paying management jobs, as well as engineering and other technical opportunities, and positions in information technology, marketing, and sales. Upper-management positions can be extremely lucrative in regard to salaries, bonuses, and retirement benefits. Even lower-level employees may be entitled to generous bonuses, retirement, and profit-sharing benefits. Large corporations can also offer summer internships for college students and training for those employees wishing to advance in their position or career. Lateral transfers are possible. For example, a marketing employee could transfer to a management position in human resources. Large corporations promote a "we are a big, close-knit family" approach to foster good employee-management relationships.

Moreover, large manufacturers offer a wide range of products; thus, they are more likely to survive an economic downturn than a small or midsize company. Also, a large company often can offer a wider range of price points for specific products,

ranging from full-featured to economy; thus, during economic downturns, the company's businesses may continue to generate revenues from its economy lines.

Cons of Working for a Large Construction Equipment Business. Large businesses are profit driven and must answer to a board of directors and, if they are public companies, shareholders. Despite a company's attempt to foster good employee-employee and employee-management relationships, an employee in a large corporation with thousands of employees might have a sense that his or her opinion does not matter and that his or her position could be readily filled by another individual. Upper-management personnel might be urged to relocate to another state or even another country at regular intervals to ensure a promotion. For some individuals, a relocation might not be seen as a negative; some might welcome living in different areas. However, others might feel

OCCUPATION PROFILE

Computer-Controlled Machine Tool Operator

Considerations	Qualifications
Description	Sets up and operates computer numerically controlled machines that precisely cut metal, plastic, or glass.
Career cluster	Manufacturing
Interests	Data; things
Working conditions	Work inside
Minimum education level	On-the-job training; high school diploma or GED; high school diploma/technical training; junior/technical college; apprenticeship
Physical exertion	Medium work
Physical abilities	Unexceptional/basic fitness
Opportunities for experience	Apprenticeship; part-time work
Licensure and certification	Recommended
Employment outlook	Slower-than-average growth expected
Holland interest score	REI

Note: See volume 1, "Publisher's Note," for an explanation of the Holland interest score.

that it is disruptive to their families. Spouses can be forced to move to a new home and, if employed outside the home, to seek a new position; children may have to change schools and form new friendships. Performance goals sometimes imposed on employees, even those in lower positions, might be extremely stressful to the individual. If a company loses market share or profitability, the chief executive officer might be terminated. The same holds true of the manager of one of the company's departments if revenue for that department drops.

Costs

Payroll and Benefits: Large companies usually offer many benefits; these benefits include sick pay, health insurance, vacations, and family leave. In the United States, for example, some of these benefits are mandated by law for companies of a particular size. Minimum compensation and benefits also can be mandated by state laws for large companies.

Supplies: Large companies can achieve economies of scale because they purchase large quantities of supplies and can benefit from reduced per-unit prices for volume sales. Large companies often strive for just-in-time delivery of supplies (with supplies arriving just before they are needed) to avoid maintaining a large inventory. This just-in-time concept, however, can pose problems, since a breakdown in the supply chain (caused by weather, natural disasters, or strikes) can slow or halt production. For example, the 2010 volcanic eruption in Iceland halted air shipments of many products when concerns over the effect of particulates disbursed by the volcano on aircraft passing through the area required a temporary cessation of flights to ensure safety.

External Services: Large companies usually have in-house departments for most services, which include accounting, payroll, legal, and even urgent-care medical services; therefore, the use of external services is often much less than it is with small or midsize companies.

Utilities: Manufacturing of construction equipment often entails major costs for utilities, particularly gas and electricity.

Taxes: Large businesses, both manufacturing plants and dealerships, must pay local, state, and federal income taxes as well as applicable property taxes. These businesses are incorporated; thus, they pay state and federal taxes at the corporate level. They must also collect state sales taxes for retail sales. In addition, large businesses must pay federal and state payroll taxes and social security contributions for their employees.

ORGANIZATIONAL STRUCTURE AND JOB ROLES

Although responsibilities for different functions are often shared in small businesses, large businesses have departments for each division of their organization, and midsize companies will often have a department or at least an individual focused on each division. The following umbrella categories apply to the organizational structure of businesses in the construction equipment industry:

- Business Management
- Customer Service
- Legal Services
- Medical Services
- Sales and Marketing
- Information Technology
- Facilities and Security
- Technology, Research, Design, and Development
- Production and Operations
- Distribution
- Human Resources
- Accounting and Finance

Business Management

Management of a heavy equipment company usually consists of hundreds of top-level individuals; however, some midsize companies might have a few dozen top positions. A large company will consist of a hierarchy headed by the chief executive officer; under the chief executive officer will be upper-management personnel who are in charge of operations for a facility in another country or a region of the United States. Below these upper-management positions are middle-management positions, which in turn are followed by low-level managers.

A large dealership may have a similar hierarchy. Individuals in the upper-management positions command high salaries ranging from several hundred thousand to well over a million dollars a year. These individuals have a college degree and usually have majored in a business-related curriculum. Most also have a master of business administration degree (M.B.A.). These high positions are usually held by motivated individuals who work their way up the corporate ladder. In some cases, after achieving a high level in one company, a manager will be recruited to work for a rival company or a company with another but related focus, such as the automobile industry. Included in management are assistants such as secretaries and clerks.

Occupations in this area of the business may include the following:

- Chief Executive Officer (CEO)
- Chief Financial Officer (CFO)
- Controller
- Administrative Assistant
- Secretary

Customer Service

Customer service is an essential element for both manufacturing companies and dealerships. Individuals working in this capacity must possess excellent people skills. When a customer issues a complaint, customer service personnel must handle it in a competent and cheerful manner. The customer may be an individual or a representative of another company that may purchase thousands of units annually. A large company may employ managers, assistant managers, and representatives who communicate with customers through the telephone or Internet. Customer service is usually augmented by automated telephone messages as well as Web-based services to handle common questions. It is imperative that such services be well designed and capable of handling many common customer issues. These automated services can result in extreme customer frustration if the customer must invest significant time without getting an answer or being able to talk to a human. Customer service is a link between the customers and the company; thus, the division obtains invaluable information regarding a product such as likes, dislikes, and suggestions for improvement.

Occupations in this area of the business may include the following:

- General Manager
- Director
- Administrative Assistant
- Customer Service Representative
- Webmaster

Legal Services

Large companies incur significant expenses for legal services. Legal issues can arise with companies of any size and can include product liability issues (issues arising from injury related to a product defect), patent infringement (an accusation that an innovative idea was stolen from another company), employee issues (such as job discrimination, wrongful termination, or sexual harassment), and illegal business practices. Large companies have more vulnerability to large settlements because of their financial standing. However, lawsuits ranging from the frivolous to multimillion-dollar cases must all be handled. Small and some midsize businesses must retain an outside attorney in these instances. Larger companies will maintain in-house counsel (a full-time attorney employee) or a team of attorneys. The attorneys must be specialists in or have some expertise in the following areas: mergers and acquisitions; patents; contracts; and labor law. When a company is exploring a merger with another company or dissolution of a business segment, the in-house consul is involved in the negotiations. These teams will also consist of other legal assistants, such as legal secretaries and paralegals. Even large companies may be required to obtain outside legal services in the event of a high-profile case. Lawsuits have the potential to financially devastate even the largest corporations.

Occupations in this area of the business may include the following:

- General Counsel
- Paralegal
- Legal Secretary
- Administrative Assistant

Medical Services

Large companies might maintain in-house health care professionals, who can handle urgent care issues such as job injuries and health care issues that arise during the workday. When physicians are employed, they usually are family practitioners, emergency medicine specialists, or doctors with specialized training in industrial medicine. This department might also promote preventive health care, including weight loss and smoking cessation programs. These measures may result in reduced health insurance costs for the company as well as decreased employee sick days.

Occupations in this area of the business may include the following:

- Physician
- Nurse Practitioner
- Registered Nurse
- Physician Assistant
- Medical Assistant
- Administrative Assistant

Sales and Marketing

Manufacturing companies maintain a staff of vendors: salespeople who call on businesses or individuals to promote their product line. These vendors often invite customers to lunches or dinners to explain and promote the company's product line; other incentives (that comply with federal and state relations) may also be offered.

Dealerships maintain a staff of in-house salespeople. Marketing is conducted by advertising in trade magazines, newspapers, television, and radio. The Internet is a common vehicle for promoting products. Potential customers can obtain product specifications, compare products (including those of rival manufacturers), and purchase products (either through the Web site or by referral to dealerships in their area).

The marketing department includes graphic designers who can develop illustrations for a Web site, brochure, or magazine display. This department includes photographers and videographers. The photographers take pictures for sales brochures, magazines, and newspapers. The videographers prepare video clips for television and the company's Web site. Writers are also employed to prepare text for publications. The marketing department also employs public relations (PR) specialists. These personnel prepare press releases of new products; these press releases are supplied to newspaper, magazine, television, and radio media.

Large companies will employ specialists in the aforementioned areas. Smaller companies will outsource that work. Occupations in this area of the business may include the following:

- Sales Manager
- Assistant Sales Manager
- Sales Representative
- Administrative Assistant
- Webmaster
- Photographer
- Videographer

Information Technology

Computer networks are present in all businesses, and hence all businesses have individuals familiar with computer maintenance and operation. Computers are involved in many aspects of a business, including inventory, payroll, sales, and production. A breakdown in a computer network can bring production or sales to a halt. The information technology (IT) department consists of information system technicians who maintain the computer network and communication systems within a company at one or more locations (locations may be global). They usually have a bachelor's degree in computer science or management information systems. The department may also include IT assistants who usually receive their training at a vocational school or a city college. These lower-level positions include installation, wiring, and maintenance of computer equipment (hardware), whereas higher-level positions include the design and management of networks, operating systems, and other software, including recommendations for upgrades.

Occupations in this area of the business may include the following:

- Information Technology Manager
- Information Technology Director
- Information Technology Technician
- Information Technology Assistant
- Data Entry Clerk

Facilities and Security

Maintenance of larger facilities requires housekeeping personnel, painters, and repair workers. A large manufacturing corporation may often have a large security department headed by one or more managers. Security personnel are responsible for preventing unwanted entry to areas where research and development is being conducted. They are also responsible for the safety of workers by guarding against entry by individuals who could pose a threat. Identification tags are almost universally a requirement for all personnel, from top management down to janitorial personnel. Entries into many portions of the building are restricted by a variety of devices, including card slots, key pads, and a guard posted at a desk. Video surveillance is often present, with a central location from which portions of the building can be viewed by security personnel and recorded on tape.

Dealerships also often have video monitoring. Theft is a much greater problem for mobile equipment than it is for fixed equipment. The size and weight of these products limits theft; however, their per-unit value is high. Theft can also be perpetrated by employees. Larger establishments will maintain an on-site security force during nonbusiness hours.

Occupations in this area of the business may include the following:

- Security Supervisor
- Housekeeping Manager
- Housekeeper
- Security Guard
- Custodian/Janitor

Technology, Research, Design, and Development

Ongoing research and development are vital to a construction equipment company. Even midsize businesses must devote time in this arena to remain competitive. Although engineers and technicians are responsible primarily for the development of a new product, this department also includes a large number of support personnel.

Before a new machine is ready for the production line, an extensive process of development and testing must be completed. For complicated equipment, this process can take several years. Engineers with a variety of specialties are employed by this department. Mechanical engineers design the machine's moving parts (such as its hydraulics, gears, levers, and engine pistons). They also oversee the work of technicians, who run tests on materials and parts before they are assembled into the final product. After assembly, this department tests products before they are released to the marketplace. Equipment is run through repeated duty cycles, knobs are twisted, buttons are pushed, and doors are slammed. Mechanical devices rather than employ-

ees usually perform these functions. If a construction defect surfaces after a product is released, the company might incur a major expense in product recall. Electrical and electronics engineers are required for the development of machines with complicated electric or electronic systems; these engineers also assist in the design and testing process. The responsibility of industrial engineers is to optimize production of the product; they determine how to best allocate the factory's resources, both workers and equipment. Once the design process and testing are completed, draftsmen prepare the plans that production workers use for assembly of the machine. For each part, draftsmen provide specifications and diagrams; they also produce assembly instructions for the final product.

Occupations in this area of the business may include the following:

- Research and Development Director
- Engineering Manager
- Electrical Engineer
- Mechanical Engineer
- Industrial Engineer
- Mechanical Drafter
- Production Worker
- Assembly Worker

Production and Operations

Production is overseen by managers, assistant managers, and supervisors. The bulk of the workforce consists of a hierarchy ranging from experienced workers with expertise in one or more production areas to inexperienced new hires. Large companies offer training programs to help workers advance to the next level.

Large and many midsize companies assemble their products on a production line similar to that of an automobile company. Robots are increasingly being employed in heavy equipment manufacturing in place of human workers, although workers are still required to control these devices. The use of robots reduces operational costs and lowers the number of injuries. However, conflicts have arisen between management, which is interested in improving production with robotics, and labor unions, which are focused on preserving jobs. Employee safety is a major concern; the production line is equipped with features to ensure safety. Specialized clothing and goggles may be required for workers. The primary responsibility of some of a large company's supervisors is to ensure employee safety.

Small companies often have fewer than a dozen workers responsible for the entire production process. However, large companies often have a multi-stage production process consisting of separate teams of workers for design and testing, parts manufacturing, and product assembly. Despite this segmentation, considerable interaction takes place between the teams. For example, to promote worker interaction, the design offices are often located near the assembly line.

Occupations in this area of the business may include the following:

- Chief Operating Officer (COO)
- Assistant Chief Operations Manager
- Administrative Assistant
- Assembly Line Supervisor
- Assembly Worker
- Wireman
- Assembly Line Maintenance Worker

Distribution

Construction equipment companies own or lease distribution centers to warehouse and distribute products. Because many companies are global in nature, they will have distribution centers located in various areas around the globe. These centers are often located near rail lines, ports, and the interstate highway system. Distribution centers are overseen by managers who are in charge of a workforce consisting primarily of warehouse workers who move products in and out of the facility. Managers must also ensure that the inventory remains at an appropriate level. The distribution center may employ truck drivers or contract with a trucking company for transporting items.

Occupations in this area of the business may include the following:

- Supply Chain Manager
- Warehouse Supervisor
- Dispatcher
- Warehouse Worker
- Truck Driver
- Freight Loader/Unloader

Human Resources

The human resources department of a construction equipment company or retail outlet is responsible for all personnel. It handles the employee hiring and dismissal, employee relations (handling employee disputes or grievances), employee benefits (such as health care insurance, retirement plans, profit-sharing plans, interdepartment or interfacility transfer requests), and on-the-job-training. The human resources department is involved with recruiting employees via the Internet or personal contact and interviews at college campuses or job fairs. This department often interacts with the legal department for such matters as alleged sexual harassment or an accusation of wrongful termination.

Human resources managers are typically college graduates. Clerical personnel and assistants with less educational experience are also employed in this department. Occupations in this area of the business may include the following:

- Human Resources Manager
- Administrative Assistant
- Employee Counselor
- Legal Liaison
- Employee Training Director
- Interviewer

Accounting and Finance

The accounting and finance department is often overseen by a certified public accountant (CPA) with management experience. Other CPAs, clerical personnel, and assistants are also employed. The financial department keeps track of a company's cash flow and participates in company decisions such as equipment purchase, business expansion, and mergers/acquisitions. A function of this department is payroll, which often is a major expenditure. Large companies have a computerized, automated system to generate paychecks; however, some human intervention on a daily basis is required.

Occupations in this area of the business may include the following:

- Chief Financial Officer (CFO)
- Assistant Financial Officer
- Payroll Director
- Accounts Payable Director

- Accounts Receivable Director
- Administrative Assistant
- Data Entry Clerk

INDUSTRY OUTLOOK

Overview

The outlook for this industry shows it to be in decline both in the United States and globally. However, in September 2010, *The Wall Street Journal* reported that the Institute for Supply Management, which surveys U.S. purchasing managers, noted that its manufacturing index rose from 55.5 in July, 2010, to 56.3 in August, 2010. *The Wall Street Journal* also reported that new orders for factory goods rose in July, 2010, and the number of unemployment claims dropped in the last two weeks of August, 2010. Another positive sign reported by the newspaper in July was a decrease in the U.S. trade deficit. In that month, exports increased by $2.8 billion and imports decreased by $4.2 billion. As a result, the trade deficit shrank from $49.8 billion to $42.8 billion. It was believed that, if this trend continued, hiring would increase.

Many companies reduced their number of employees between 2008 and 2010. This was accomplished by hiring freezes, layoffs, and incentives for early retirement. Augmenting this process was increased efficiency of operation through robotics and other technologies that reduced the demand for labor. Even if the upsurge noted in September, 2010, did not continue, many openings were expected to occur because of the need to replace workers retiring or moving to other industries. Production workers accounted for more than 50 percent of the workers in this industry; those with greater technical skills were expected to have a significant advantage in obtaining and maintaining a position over those who did not. Training beyond high school is often necessary for these positions.

The presence of midsize and small businesses will most likely decrease, particularly with a prolonged economic downturn leading to insolvencies. In such a scenario, these companies will either disappear or be acquired by other companies. Furthermore, mergers and acquisitions will result in an increase in size of the dominant companies. Large companies are increasing not only in size but also in level of globalization. A symptom of this growth is the typical requirement of Japanese businesses that their personnel become fluent in English, which is prevalent around the globe, so that they can compete more successfully in the international marketplace.

One sector of the industry will profit if an economic downturn continues: the repair sector. In this economic situation, consumers will be much more likely to have existing equipment repaired rather than to replace it with a new device sporting state-of-the-art features.

Robotics will increasingly be used for manufacturing, although their use will most likely be opposed by labor unions, which will fight to preserve jobs. A number of companies outside the United States that use robotics heavily have an improved profit margin, and their products have a competitive advantage over those manufactured in the United States. Technology features will also increase with the design of new products. Energy efficiency will be stressed, and new equipment may combine diesel, electrical, or natural gas usage with renewable energy sources such as solar panels incorporating photovoltaic cells, which can convert solar energy into electricity.

Considerable research is focused on increasing energy efficiency and reducing emissions. As greener products are released on the market, end users ranging from companies to individuals will be motivated to purchase them if they have an interest in using a machine that is both more efficient and less polluting. An example of a machine that is undergoing modification to be more ecologically beneficial is the diesel engine. Many products are diesel-powered. Diesel engines are powerful and reliable, and they can yield a significantly higher number of miles per gallon than gasoline engines; however, they release high levels of greenhouse gases (including carbon dioxide, methane, and nitrous oxide) as well as particulate matter into the atmosphere. Engines are being designed to run on cleaner diesel fuel; emission-reducing techniques, such as removing pollutants with urea before they exit the exhaust system, have been developed.

Employment Advantages

According to the U.S. Bureau of Labor Statistics, "machinery manufacturing has some of the most highly skilled—and highly paid—production jobs in manufacturing." Even though this industry is in a decline, it can be a good career choice. Heavy equipment is an essential component of any industrialized nation, and a demand for construction equipment will always exist. These machines are subject to heavy use, and over time, components will need to be replaced or a new unit purchased. Most of these companies are large, global, and produce a wide variety of products; thus, they offer a degree of stability not found in smaller companies and those that do not produce essential products. The industry can support workers in a wide variety of careers, including managerial, technical, and sales professionals as well as skilled laborers. In addition, this large industry allows employees to make lateral transfers within a company, should they desire an alternative career path. An employee of a company may also derive satisfaction when he or she passes a construction site and can point to a piece of heavy equipment and say, "My company builds those."

Annual Earnings

Whether annual earnings will continue to decline or experience growth remains, as of 2010, uncertain. Most companies reported a decline in net sales between 2008 and 2009. For example, net sales declined for Deere & Company from $25.8 million in 2008 to $20.8 million in 2009, a 26 percent decrease. Komatsu also reported a decline, from $22.4 million in 2008 to $20.4 million in 2009, a 9 percent decrease. The Doosan Group (Seoul) bucked the trend and reported a small increase in net sales, from $18.1 million in 2008 to $18.4 million in 2009, a 2 percent increase.

The decline for most companies was attributed to a slowdown in both the U.S. and the global economy, as well as a concomitant slowdown in the U.S. construction, housing, and home improvement markets. Of greatest effect on the construction equipment industry is the dearth of new home construction, which began in 2009. Some building resumed in the first quarter of 2010; however, that resurgence did not continue through the next two quarters. The economy improved to a degree during the first quarter of 2010, but consumer spending for all products in the United States fell 1.2 percent from April to May, 2010.

The relative stability of the U.S. and European economies will benefit this industry, and the U.S. construction equipment industry will no doubt sur-vive and perhaps grow. However, both U.S. and European companies continue to face ever-increasing competition from Asian manufacturers. A significant portion of the construction equipment industry is already based in Asia, and these companies market their products throughout the globe and hold significant market share in the United States. China—which exports light machines and manufactures components for construction equipment—is likely to join Japan and South Korea as a leading manufacturer as the twenty-first century progresses.

RELATED RESOURCES FOR FURTHER RESEARCH

CATERPILLAR
  100 NE Adams St.
  Peoria, IL 61629
  Tel: (309) 675-1000
  Fax: (309) 675-4332
  http://www.cat.com

DEERE & COMPANY
  Deere & Company World Headquarters
  1 John Deere Place
  Moline, IL 61265
  Tel: (309) 765-8000
  Fax: (309) 765-7283
  http://www.deere.com

EQUIPMENT WORLD
  3200 Rice Mine Rd.
  Tuscaloosa, AL 35406
  Tel: (800) 633-5953
  Fax: (205) 349-3765
  http://www.equipmentworld.com

FREEDONIA
  767 Beta Dr.
  Cleveland, OH 44143
  Tel: (440) 684-9600
  Fax: (440) 646-0484
  http://www.freedoniagroup.com

INSTITUTE FOR SUPPLY MANAGEMENT
  P.O. Box 22160
  Tempe, AZ 85285
  Tel: (480) 752-6275, (800) 888-6276

Fax: (480) 752-7890
http://www.ism.ws

KOMATSU
2-3-6 Akasaka, Minato-ku
Tokyo 107-8414
Japan
Tel: 81-3-5561-2616
http://www.komatsu.com

MARKETRESEARCH.COM
11200 Rockville Pike, Suite 504
Rockville, MD 20852
Tel: (240) 747-3000
Fax: (240) 747-3004
http://www.marketresearch.com

MITSUBISHI HEAVY INDUSTRIES
16-5 Konan 2-chome Minato-ku
Tokyo 108-8215
Japan
Tel: 81-3-6716-3111
Fax: 81-3-6716-5800
http://www.mhi.co.jp/en

TECHNIK MANUFACTURING
1005 17th St.
Columbus, NE 68601
Tel: (800) 795-8251
Fax: (402) 564-0406
http://www.technikmfg.com

ABOUT THE AUTHOR

Robin L. Wulffson, M.D., is a board-certified specialist in obstetrics and gynecology. In 1997, he transitioned to a writing career. He has written analytic reports on major corporations and industries and has analyzed hospital systems and medical device manufacturers. He is familiar with the heavy machines industry in the United States, Europe, and Asia. For the past fifteen years, he has closely followed the business sector in the United States and abroad.

FURTHER READING

Harris, Frank. *Modern Construction and Ground Engineering Equipment and Methods*. 2d ed. New York: Longman, 1994.

Huzij, Robert, Angelo Spano, and Sean Bennett. *Modern Diesel Technology: Heavy Equipment Systems*. Detroit: Delmar Cengage Learning, 2008.

Levy, Sidney M. *Construction Databook: Construction Materials and Equipment*. 2d ed. New York: McGraw-Hill, 2010.

Stearns, Peter. *The Industrial Revolution in World History*. 3d ed. Boulder, Colo.: Westview Press, 2007.

Stonehouse, Tom, and Eldon Brumbaugh. *J. I. Case: Agricultural and Construction Equipment, 1956-1994*. St. Joseph, Mich.: American Society of Agricultural Engineers, 1996.

U.S. Bureau of Labor Statistics. *Career Guide to Industries*, 2010-2011 ed. http://www.bls.gov/oco/cg.

_____. "Construction Trades and Related Workers." In *Occupational Outlook Handbook*, 2010-2011 ed. http://www.bls.gov/oco/oco1009.htm.

Vorster, Michael C. *Construction Equipment Economics*. Christiansburg, Va.: Pen, 2009.

Corporate Education Services

INDUSTRY SNAPSHOT

General Industry: Education and Training

Career Cluster: Education and Training

Subcategory Industries: Computer Training; Management Development Training; Professional Development Training; Quality Assurance Training

Related Industries: Business Services; Private Education Industry

Annual Domestic Revenues: $56.2 billion USD (Bersin and Associates, 2008)

Annual Global Revenues: Between $110 billion and $130 billion USD (BME Global, 2008)

NAICS Numbers: 611420, 611430

INDUSTRY DEFINITION

Summary

Corporate education services are provided by external firms or internal corporate divisions to provide workers with knowledge and skills that are helpful or necessary in fulfilling their tasks. An estimated two thousand corporate training programs are currently housed within larger companies in the United States—an approximate figure nearly equal to the number of the nation's colleges and universities. This number alone is indicative of the importance that companies place on internal training and education. In fact, according to a 2004 study from Accenture, a global management consulting and outsourcing company, many executives list training and development as one of the three most important initiatives within their respective organizations.

Corporate training programs and staff have a high level of accountability toward their employers and clients. Companies expect that investments in training and corporate education will contribute to their overall growth and profitability. The success of a training initiative, in fact, is no longer measured by the number of employees who receive training in a given time period. Instead, executive management teams evaluate training programs based on their quantifiable contributions to their organizations' success.

Measuring the financial return on corporate training (return on investment, or ROI) is the most common way of measuring a training program's effectiveness. Corporate education providers may themselves be tasked with measuring the long-term benefits of the training they provide. Training and development (T&D) groups find that measuring the ongoing effectiveness of training demonstrates the contribution of corporate education to their organizations over time. As employees apply new skills gained through corporate education to their work, continued education will further increase their skill level and cumulative knowledge, advance their organization, and elevate individual employees within a company. Corporate training, therefore, adds to the comprehensive institutional knowledge of companies, as well as to the career advancement of individual employees. The more a corporation invests in growing the knowledge and skills of its employees, the greater an interest the employer has in retaining those employees, both to maximize its ROI and to capitalize on the knowledge and skills the employees have acquired.

History of the Industry

The concept of learning and the organized teaching and acquisition of skills from one individual to another dates back to antiquity. Before reading and writing were ubiquitous skills, people acquired skills by watching others perform a task. After an individual achieved a certain level of competency, it was possible for that individual to train a less-skilled person. Training was thus accomplished through demonstration. It evolved into the practice of apprenticing, in which individuals observed others until their competency increased to the point of independence. Children often followed in the same profession as their parents, who trained their offspring in a particular trade or craft from an early age. Each generation took responsibility to pass along the necessary skills to the next generation so that the family could sustain itself.

For centuries, apprenticeship was, by and large, the sole means by which skills were passed on. As the printed word became more widely used and the literacy of whole populations increased, it became possible to supplement visual, verbal, and tactile training with written instructions. Much of

Corporate education, as an industry, is represented both by training specialists within larger organizations and by third-party consulting firms. (©Dmitriy Shironosov/Dreamstime.com)

modern training still involves demonstration combined with oral and written instruction. The advent of print also made it easier for one teacher to train multiple students. Instead of relying on pure demonstration, the teacher could provide supplemental printed materials to convey lessons to a group too large to conveniently train through demonstration alone.

In time, particularly after the advent of industrialism, the search for prosperity superseded subsistence living, and populations shifted from rural to urban areas. Large numbers of people left agricultural jobs and agrarian lifestyles to settle in urban areas and labor in mass, mechanized manufacturing industries. In contrast to a craft-based, artisan business or a traditional farm, an industrial factory employed far more people but gave each one a far less complex, often repetitive task. As the nature of labor changed, the nature of training changed as

well. Lengthy apprenticeships were unnecessary to impart the limited skills required to work on a factory assembly line, and one-on-one training was insufficient to instruct the number of workers needing basic instruction. Thus, it became apparent that large groups of workers required more skilled managers to train and oversee them. The managers themselves required a certain level of training, both in manufacturing skills and in management. Much of modern-day corporate education emphasizes the need to train future organizational leaders, a trend that largely began during the Industrial Revolution of the eighteenth and nineteenth centuries.

Vocational education was introduced during the era that followed the American Civil War (1861-1865) and preceded World War I (1914-1918). It was during this time that the term "working class" emerged, as men and women alike joined

A trainer with the Disney Institute conducts a training session with Miami International Airport employees in 2007. The airport hoped to improve customer service. (AP/Wide World Photos)

the urban, mechanized workforce in increasing numbers. Vocational training, which combined classroom and on-site training, was largely employed as a means to impart job-specific skills. Vocational education continues to be widely used as a means to train tradespeople such as plumbers and electricians.

The Great Depression of the 1930's—the first great economic downturn of the twentieth century—created a surplus of workers. With too few jobs and too many workers, job-specific training became unnecessary and was largely abandoned. However, the lack of workforce preparedness after the Great Depression left many American workers ill-equipped to participate in the next economic boom. The larger the gap in preparedness, the longer it takes to train workers to appropriate levels

The Second City improvisational troupe performs a routine for IntraNet employees in 2004. The troupe uses improvisation to polish the skills of business people. (AP/Wide World Photos)

of competency. Training is most effective when it is incremental and continuous, and employees benefit from using new skills immediately after they learn them. These lessons became apparent with the onset of World War II (1939-1945), which helped end the Great Depression.

America's entry into World War II in 1941 required a great deal of training. New military recruits underwent so-called basic training, while the manufacturers supporting the war effort with materiel had to train a great many people to work in their factories—including the women who entered the workforce to replace male draftees. The decrease in training caused by the Great Depression was felt acutely by industries that suddenly needed skilled line workers and the managers to supervise them. As more workers joined companies and prosperity reigned in the latter half of the twentieth century, training became commonplace at many companies. Manufacturing workers required training in new production processes, and much of this training was classroom-based.

After World War II, America and many other countries entered a period of unprecedented economic growth and prosperity. It was only toward the end of the twentieth century that manufacturing jobs started to shift offshore, where labor costs were much lower. Much of America's economic prosperity was built on high-paying manufacturing jobs, such as those offered by the automobile industry. These jobs required extensive employee training at all levels—and increasingly to a white-collar workforce.

The Industry Today

The twenty-first century has ushered in a new kind of economy—the knowledge economy. It is an economy that is fueled as much by the transmission of knowledge and data as it is by the manufacture of goods and services. Workers no longer perform the same task on a daily basis, as they did on assembly lines. Instead, a typical worker is likely to undertake work that requires learning and applying new skills on an almost daily basis. It is often the responsibility of the worker to learn new skills independently. Problem solving and knowledge creation are the mainstays of knowledge jobs.

In the knowledge economy, the training of employees requires a broad-level approach. It emphasizes skills that help employees improve workplace relationships and manage projects and time lines. Additionally, the global marketplace requires that employees be more culturally aware, as their colleagues are just as likely to live in another country or region as they are to be situated down the hall. Often, companies employ labor forces in emerging markets such as India and China, where communication is paramount. This changing corporate landscape, in which projects and people are managed around the globe, is driving a new model of corporate education.

The delivery of corporate education services has been transformed radically in the early twenty-first century. As manufacturing continues to shift to countries where labor costs are much lower, such as India and China, the United States and other mature economies will focus on the creation of knowledge rather than the creation of goods. Corporate education will be essential to support this new type of economy. The advent of the Internet and the ability to deliver information quickly and inexpensively through a digital medium has redefined many aspects of corporate education and helped meet this growing need for education. While many companies still offer in-house or on-site classroom training, the training room now extends to a virtual space that is often accessible twenty-four hours a day, seven days a week.

Corporate educators face the challenge of determining how to train a very diverse workforce. The baby-boom generation has already begun to retire, and the pace of retirements will continue to increase into the second decade of the twenty-first century. Moreover, the generations following the baby boomers are far less likely to have the same occupation throughout their lives. As they continue to change jobs, they will need to acquire new skills sets to work effectively in new occupations. Thus, as skilled workers and workers experienced in a given industry retire, companies will need to rely on corporate education services to train their replacements. Without such training, there would be a skills void that could be detrimental to many industries.

When compared to the production-line-based structure of the manufacturing economy, the current knowledge economy is much more complex. Time-to-market pressure and competition among businesses to be first to release new products to market require a highly trained and motivated workforce. As a result, corporate education and continuous job training are no longer considered to be merely an employee benefit. Rather, they are seen as having a large impact on a company's financial health. Because many employees now work with ideas and knowledge rather than with tangible products, employees are in a state of constant learning. Processes and practices change rapidly, so employees must continuously develop their skills and maintain the agility to multitask and move rapidly from one project to another.

INDUSTRY MARKET SEGMENTS

Corporate education, as an industry, is represented both by training specialists within larger organizations and by third-party consulting firms. Some companies have corporate education or T&D departments, while others employ trainers within broader departments, usually human resources. Third-party consulting firms often offer a broad range of corporate training and management consulting services, often contracting with other organizations to use an off-the-shelf product or a customized training solution. The following sections discuss the internal training programs of small, midsize, and large businesses, followed by a general assessment of third-party firms.

Small Businesses

Definitions of a small business vary in different industries. In general, a small business employs fewer than one hundred persons, generates revenue of less than $1 million annually, and serves relatively local markets. Consequently, because of limited staff and revenue, individual small businesses typically have less of an impact on the marketplace than do larger firms. Small organizations also generally have limited financial resources available for formal training. As a result, they may lack a dedicated staff responsible for training new employees. That task is generally handled by the owner or another experienced employee. This training is mostly accomplished through demonstration and passed along from peer to peer.

While many small and midsize enterprises hire a third-party provider to perform corporate training, they are becoming increasingly aware of the impact that corporate education can have on a business's success. Many small companies are therefore beginning to designate in-house staff as trainers, some in a part-time capacity. These corporate education employees and trainers in the small business sector are responsible for providing employee education, but they often have other responsibilities as well.

Potential Annual Earnings Scale. According to the U.S. Bureau of Labor Statistics (BLS), the average annual salary for T&D specialists in 2006 was $47,830, while the median for T&D managers was $80,250. The average salary for human resources managers, who are sometimes tasked with corporate education and job training, was $88,510. According to Salary.com, the starting salary for a corporate trainer in 2009 ranged from $32,000 to $57,500.

Clientele Interaction. In-house trainers' clients are also their colleagues. Thus, in a business with relatively few employees, trainers are likely to know all of their trainees. Part-time trainers with additional duties may work alongside their fellows to accomplish other tasks, which may create a sense of camaraderie between trainers and trainees but which may also diminish the trainers' authority within educational settings. In a small business, it is unlikely that an employee would be tasked solely with preparing materials for training to be conducted by others. Thus, all in-house trainers in a small business are likely to interact directly with their trainees. If it becomes necessary for the business to contract additional external training services, in-house trainers are responsible for coordinating and administering that supplemental training with the third-party company.

Amenities, Atmosphere, and Physical Grounds. As a way to keep costs low, small businesses refrain from renting more space than is necessary. Most space is taken up by employees who are directly involved in operations, though there may be a cafeteria or other small common areas. Training space at small businesses is also limited. Training is likely to take place in a conference room or cafeteria, or even at an employee's workstation.

Typical Number of Employees. The typical number of employed trainers at a small organization is relatively low, perhaps as few as one person.

Traditional Geographic Locations. Small businesses can be found anywhere, depending on the industry and the customer base. Those businesses dealing heavily in goods usually need inexpensive space in low-cost areas to house goods and facilitate access to major roadways. Other small businesses rely on a steady flow of customers and locate themselves where they are easily accessible. The success of companies that sell their goods online is less dependent on location than is that of traditional storefront companies. Most training for small businesses takes place on site at a company's primary location.

Pros of Working for a Small Company. Trainers at small companies have a significant influence on the design and delivery of their curricula. They often have the opportunity to create content from whole cloth—which may be a pro or a con, depending on the aptitudes and attitudes of particular trainers. Trainers also enjoy high levels of interaction with their fellow employees and have a direct impact on building skills and knowledge within their organizations. While advancement opportunities may be limited, working in a small business as an educator may help prepare a trainer for a related role in a larger organization.

Cons of Working for a Small Company. At small organizations, training budgets are limited, and most training personnel have responsibilities beyond their training duties. As the people responsible for providing company education, trainers must create and deliver all or most content on their own—possibly including content that is outside their areas of expertise. Training staff at small companies do not have the benefit of working with other professional trainers and gaining from their mentorship. Moreover, the lack of a formal training division or dedicated staff makes it less likely that a company will maintain an archive of training materials from which newer trainers may draw when planning curricula.

In small organizations, where employees often have multiple responsibilities, training is also often not given a high priority on the business agenda. Resources, including a part-time trainer's time, may be reallocated to accomplish higher-priority goals. Training budgets are often among the first to be cut, and small companies may attempt to compensate for lack of resources by transferring or redistributing training duties among available staff.

Costs

Payroll and Benefits: Trainers employed by small businesses are paid hourly wages or salaries, depending on the extent of their work. Benefits such as vacation and sick days, health insurance, and 401(k) plans are offered at employers' discretion.

Supplies: Trainers generally need computers and training or presentation software, as well as standard supplies such as office consumables, telephones, and office furniture.

External Services: In-house training may be supplemented with third-party corporate education providers. Such providers may provide full-time or part-time service, or they may be called on to produce content that is then used by in-house training personnel. Outsourced training may be conducted at a third-party training facility, at a public facility such as a nearby hotel's conference room, on site at the contracting company's premises, or via the Internet.

Utilities: Typical utilities for a small business include electricity, air-conditioning and heating, water, telephone, and Internet access. Specialist resources and utilities depend on the type of organization and its activities.

Taxes: State and federal taxes are payable according to business revenue.

Midsize Businesses

Midsize businesses are defined as those having between one hundred and one thousand employees. Operations at most midsize organizations are divided into different functional areas and may include sales, marketing, human resources, and operations. Some midsize firms may be managed by an owner or company founder, but they more often have an executive team to manage operations. Midsize businesses can have significant local, regional, or global influence in the marketplace but are generally limited in market reach.

Many midsize companies employ T&D staff to enhance communications, as well as to deliver specialized education offerings. At midsize companies, training is an important initiative for company executives who understand that effective learning contributes to increased revenue and profitability. While the training needs of specific departments may differ, companies often have common training needs across an entire organiza-

tion. The cost of recruiting and hiring employees is significant, and most employers therefore wish to hold onto employees and their institutional knowledge as long as possible. Effective corporate training helps retain employees, in addition to increasing their value.

Potential Annual Earnings Scale. According to the BLS, the average annual salary for T&D specialists in 2006 was $47,830, while the median for T&D managers was $80,250. The average salary for human resources managers, who are sometimes tasked with corporate education and job training, was $88,510. According to Salary.com, the starting salary for a corporate trainer in 2009 ranged from $32,000 to $57,500.

Clientele Interaction. In-house trainers' clients are also their colleagues. In a midsize business, trainers are likely to know many of their trainees. Some midsize businesses may have employees in training departments or in human resources departments who are tasked solely with researching and producing content for training that will be conducted by others or conducted primarily online. Such content providers interact with trainees far less than trainers do, but they may conduct surveys or otherwise communicate with trainees in order to evaluate and improve their training materials.

Amenities, Atmosphere, and Physical Grounds. Most midsize companies rent or own office space that can accommodate the majority of employees at one location. While some employees (such as sales personnel) may work remotely, the majority of employees work out of a central office. Employees at midsize companies can enjoy a collaborative work environment where it is possible to know many of their colleagues personally. Employees are usually grouped on the floor by functional area.

Amenities at midsize companies may include a company cafeteria, fitness center, or day-care center. These amenities are perks that midsize companies offer to attract and retain employees. Midsize organizations also generally offer employee training as a benefit. Often, this training is marketed as a way to advance career options. Midsize companies generally have dedicated training spaces that include computer workstations. Projectors and sound systems may also be used to improve the classroom learning experience.

Typical Number of Employees. The number of training staff at midsize companies is generally between four and seven trainers per one thousand employees.

Traditional Geographic Locations. Midsize companies can be located in any geographic area but are generally located near urban areas. Many midsize companies are headquartered near regional or national airports and position their operational centers near interstate highways. Corporate education at most midsize companies takes place on site and within dedicated training areas. However, it is also common for organizations to send employees off site for training.

Pros of Working for a Midsize Company. Training services at midsize organizations often entail much more than general employee training, providing opportunities for those who seek full-time employment as trainers. Typically, operations are diverse, and different functional areas have specific training requirements. For example, employees who deal directly with customers may need training in customer satisfaction and retention, while employees who develop software applications may need training in using a new coding environment. Thus, the breadth of curricula that need to be developed is likely to be significantly greater than at small businesses.

The diversity of a midsize company's training needs may require training managers to enlist subject-matter experts from specific areas of the company or to hire third-party vendors with the necessary expertise. Such experts may be called on to conduct training, but they may also be asked to train the trainers, enhancing the knowledge of training specialists who will use their expertise in educational techniques to pass it on to other workers. While training materials may be drawn from different sources, training managers or coordinators usually oversee all aspects of company training, functioning as the point of contact for all division managers within the organization who need training for themselves or their staffs. Midsize organizations offer better opportunities for career advancement for corporate educators.

Cons of Working for a Midsize Company. While midsize companies offer more opportunities for those in the corporate education field than do small companies, the scope of training may still be limiting for those who seek executive-level positions. In addition, trainers are most often responsible for training at local or regional offices, so they may not have the opportunity to work with particularly diverse or international constituents. Corporate educators who seek to work at global or international levels or who seek executive-level positions will probably find greater opportunities in larger companies.

Costs

Payroll and Benefits: Depending on the extent of their work, trainers employed by midsize businesses are paid either hourly wages or salaries. Benefits such as vacation and sick days, health insurance, and 401(k) plans are offered at employers' discretion.

Supplies: Trainers generally need computers and training or presentation software, as well as standard supplies such as office consumables, telephones, and office furniture.

External Services: In-house training may be supplemented with third-party corporate education providers. Such providers may provide full-time or part-time service, or they may be called on to produce content that is then used by in-house training personnel. Outsourced training may be conducted at a third-party training facility, at a public facility such as a nearby hotel's conference room, on site at the contracting company's premises, or via the Internet.

Utilities: Typical utilities for a midsize business include electricity, air-conditioning and heating, water, telephone, and Internet access. Specialist resources and utilities will depend on the type of organization and its activities.

Taxes: State and federal taxes are payable according to business revenue.

Large Businesses

Large organizations employ more than one thousand people, many of whom may work at locations other than the corporate headquarters. Large organizations may also have several levels of executive management, including department and line managers. Corporate education plays a significant role in most large organizations, and it is generally well funded in strong economic times. There is ample evidence that corporate education yields a significant return on investment; organizations that are committed to top-notch training, development, and education benefit from increased market share and profitability. In addition, organizations that support employees through corporate education services are more likely to attract and retain top talent.

During lean economic times, companies often cut funding to corporate education budgets but not necessarily more than from other functional areas. In fact, large companies often see training as more important in tough economic times, especially if they must lay off some workers and cross-train their remaining employees to take on multiple new responsibilities. Companies must also position themselves strategically during a recession so they will be prepared to ramp up production when the economic outlook improves.

Potential Annual Earnings Scale. According to the BLS, the average annual salary for T&D specialists in 2006 was $47,830, while the median for T&D managers was $80,250. The average salary for human resources managers, who are sometimes tasked with corporate education and job training, was $88,510. According to Salary.com, the starting salary for a corporate trainer in 2009 ranged from $32,000 to $57,500.

Clientele Interaction. Large organizations typically have a significant impact in the marketplace, generally at a global level, and may employ tens of thousands of employees. Providing support and education for such a large and diverse group can be challenging. Within a large organization, the corporate education department is likely to oversee training of the global workforce, and it is very likely to administer training for customers as well. In such an organization, the T&D group may be dispersed geographically and may spend significant time traveling to other locations to provide training. Because the needs of large organizations are so diverse, trainers are likely to be assigned to functional areas in which they have high levels of interaction with specific groups of employees.

Amenities, Atmosphere, and Physical Grounds. Larger organizations can provide many amenities for employees that are not available at smaller organizations. They are also generally able to provide in-house corporate education services at a reduced per capita cost. Often, a large company will have its own on-site headquartered training facility, and it may choose to send employees to a central location or to provide in-house classroom

training. Global companies, however, may find it useful to bring trainees to a third-party location, such as a hotel, to conduct training weeks or weekends—particularly if they need to find a central location in a region far removed from the corporate headquarters. In addition, larger companies also handle some corporate training online, although online training is more commonplace for smaller companies.

Typical Number of Employees. For large organizations, the number of trainers averages between three and five per one thousand employees, which is slightly less than the ratio at midsize organizations.

Traditional Geographic Locations. Large businesses are usually located near large urban or metropolitan areas where there is access to a larger number of skilled workers. Large organizations are likely to have operations run from several locations, with partners or divisions outside domestic borders. As the globalization of business increases, larger organizations will continue to move production operations offshore, where labor costs are lower and corporate training is necessary to train new employees.

Pros of Working for a Large Company. Since the beginning of the twenty-first century, large organizations have enjoyed robust training budgets and ample personnel to plan, create, and conduct educational initiatives. Learning departments at large organizations offer substantial opportunities for advancement in the corporate education industry. New graduates entering the field can gain extensive experience while being mentored by more experienced and professional staff. Likewise, trainers can advance to more senior positions as higher-level trainers, curriculum or content specialists, or training managers. Staff at large organizations are also likely to have access to professional development through conferences and professional associations.

Many companies have created executive-level positions to oversee corporate learning. For example, positions such as chief learning officer (CLO) or chief knowledge officer (CKO) focus on the strategic value of corporate learning. Positions at this senior level require ten or more years of experience within corporate learning, as well as an advanced degree in human resources, business, or a related field.

Cons of Working for a Large Company. Large companies may respond to tight budgets by outsourcing repetitive administrative tasks, eliminating staff positions, and refocusing in-house training staff to concentrate on more key initiatives. Economies of scale make this course of action more attractive to large companies than it would be to a small firm, for which an employee whose multiple duties include training is much more affordable than a third-party solution. Many large companies are comfortable outsourcing generic training to vendors but retain industry-specific training within their organizations. Companies with highly proprietary knowledge or processes benefit less from outsourcing than do companies with more generic processes.

Costs

Payroll and Benefits: Corporate educators employed by large businesses will generally be paid salaries. Benefits such as vacation and sick days, health insurance, and 401(k) plans are typical.

Supplies: Trainers generally need computers and training or presentation software, as well as standard supplies such as office consumables, telephones, and office furniture.

External Services: In-house training may be supplemented with third-party corporate education providers. Such providers may provide full-time or part-time service, or they may be called on to produce content that is then used by in-house training personnel. Outsourced training may be conducted at a third-party training facility, at a public facility such as a nearby hotel's conference room, on site at the contracting company's premises, or via the Internet. Large businesses in particular may elect to hire third-party specialist trainers, including technology experts to develop training delivery methods, educational consultants, and skills assessment professionals.

Utilities: Typical utilities for a large business include electricity, air-conditioning and heating, water, telephone, and Internet. Specialist resources and utilities will depend on the type of organization and its activities.

Taxes: State and federal taxes are payable according to business revenue.

Third-Party Training Vendors

Third-party T&D firms gained ground in the last decades of the twentieth century. These firms offer a broad range of services and largely market themselves as knowledge management firms, offering documentation of organizational processes, policies, and products, as well as training for internal and external clients. Third-party firms may be given fairly extensive responsibilities. For example, if an external T&D firm is contracted to develop a training program for an in-house system (for instance, a new point-of-sale product), the firm may first be asked to work with the product's developers to ensure that it meets the needs of the organization. If the product is determined to be satisfactory, the firm may then work with its designers and engineers to document its operation, develop a training program to teach employees to use it, and plan a roll-out schedule for transitioning the contracting company to the new system. Some companies outsource software training regularly, to ensure that their software engineers and technology staff are well versed in the latest software on the market.

Alternatively, a training company may be contracted by an organization to develop similar programs for a new product line. In that case, it may have some input into functionality and develop documentation and training for the product after its release—which may necessitate multiple forms of training (online, paper-based, classroom, and interactive) depending on the customer base. In this case, the T&D firm has a vested interest in making sure that the product functions as the company intended and that the customers are aware of the full range of its capabilities.

T&D vendors that offer corporate education services claim that it is possible for companies to save up to 30 percent by outsourcing their in-house training functions. A company that outsources its training does not necessarily have to maintain floor space for training facilities, computers, or software. Vendors, moreover, can offer savings by charging for training on a pay-per-use basis.

Potential Annual Earnings Scale. According to the BLS, the average annual salary for T&D specialists in 2006 was $47,830, while the median for T&D managers was $80,250. According to Salary.com, the starting salary for a corporate trainer in 2009 ranged from $32,000 to $57,500.

Clientele Interaction. Unlike the T&D divisions of larger companies, in which almost all employees are likely to interact directly with clients, third-party training vendors are often organized into divisions or departments with disparate levels of client interaction. Thus, trainers spend much of their time interacting with trainees, but content developers, executives, human resources managers, and other staff members may seldom or never interact directly with a company's clients. Additionally, sales and marketing personnel do not often interact with trainees, but they have a high level of interaction with the decision makers at client companies who determine whether to engage third-party vendors.

Amenities, Atmosphere, and Physical Grounds. Third-party training vendors come in all sizes. A self-employed consultant may work out of his or her home and conduct all training at clients' facilities or rent public space when necessary. Large training companies have offices similar to those of other large companies, but they may make a point of featuring state-of-the-art on-site training facilities, including high-tech classrooms and auditoriums. Some vendors that specialize in executive development expend a great deal of money and energy developing their physical grounds, as executives may well plan their training retreats based as much on on amenities and location as on services offered. Some executive-training vendors, for example, locate their training facilities in the south of France or on Lake Como, Italy.

Typical Number of Employees. A third-party vendor may be a sole practitioner or may employ hundreds of trainers, curriculum developers, and support staff.

Traditional Geographic Locations. A third-party vendor may be located anywhere, but the choice of location must take into account the company's business model. A consulting firm that sends trainers to clients need not be physically accessible to those clients, whereas a company that conducts its training on site must locate itself either near potential clients or in a location that is attractive or is a desirable travel destination, such as a retreat facility or an urban center of national or international business.

Pros of Working for a Corporate Education Company. Corporate education companies are virtually guaranteed to understand the value of corporate education—a feature that is not always true of other companies with corporate education departments or positions. Workers in this field may appreciate being employed at a firm wholly dedicated to the mission of their job description. Vendors may also have significantly more resources to devote to developing trainers and curricula than even large companies' training divisions can muster. They are also able to repurpose materials they have already generated to meet the needs of new clients, thereby decreasing costs and increasing profitability. T&D personnel who work for learning vendors can expect to command salaries similar to those at larger organizations. These salaries pay 10 to 20 percent more than do similar positions at midsize companies.

In the past, companies have relied on experienced managers to train employees, but trainers are now increasingly required to have classroom experience. They must also be knowledgeable or experienced in teaching adults. Creating and maintaining a training program takes a lot of time, and relying on employees with a broader set of responsibilities, such as department or human resources managers, can be problematic. Often, managers are too busy managing outcomes to take the time to thoroughly train their staff. A dedicated or full-time training staff can build momentum and refine training based on past experiences, both successful and not. Trainers also have the time and expertise to evaluate existing training programs to build knowledge.

Trainers with a particular interest or expertise in executive development may find opportunities at third-party vendors that do not exist elsewhere. It may not be in the best interests of a company for its executive-level employees to participate in on-site training delivered by the people they manage. Thus, these executives often join other executives at off-site training facilities to further develop their executive management skills. These opportunities allow executives to speak freely about what they are learning, share ideas and strategies with their peers, and network with other executives.

Cons of Working for a Corporate Education Company. It is not unusual for a training vendor to recruit personnel from an organization with which they have a training agreement. In such cases, the intellectual capital held by former trainers can be invaluable to the vendor to foster a successful outsourcing relationship. However, the vendor may be seen as a threat to in-house training departments, coloring trainers' relationships with their clients, who sometimes view them as "hired guns" within the corporate education space.

Costs

Payroll and Benefits: Corporate educators may be self-employed or may be employed by businesses that pay them hourly wages or salaries, depending on the size and business model of the company. They may receive standard benefits such as vacation and sick days, health insurance, and 401(k) plans.

Supplies: Trainers generally need computers and training or presentation software, as well as standard supplies such as office consumables, telephones, and office furniture. High-quality office consumables are necessary to produce professional-quality materials such as booklets and training packets.

External Services: Learning vendors may work with independent contractors to assemble and deliver training solutions. Subcontracting allows these companies more flexibility and access to the latest technology for content creation and delivery without requiring them to purchase that technology or maintain all relevant skills among their full-time staff. In addition, third-party training firms may choose to outsource such services as printing, accounting, advertising and marketing, information technology, technical support, or building maintenance and security.

Utilities: Corporate education firms require electricity, air-conditioning and heating, water, telephone, and Internet service.

Taxes: State and federal taxes are payable according to business revenue.

ORGANIZATIONAL STRUCTURE AND JOB ROLES

There are many differences between a corporate education company, a dedicated department within a larger company, and a small group of employees with education responsibilities in addition to their other duties. However, the process of education and the core requirements for effectiveness are largely the same in each case. All trainers must determine or be told the needs of the client, acquire or create content to meet those needs, impart that content to trainees, and assess the effectiveness of their training.

The following umbrella categories apply to the organizational structure of businesses and departments within the corporate education services industry:

- Training Personnel
- Content Creation
- Training Administration
- Training Strategy and Development

Training Personnel

The front lines of corporate education services are staffed by an organization's trainers. Of all positions within corporate education, trainers have the highest level of contact with trainees. There can be several levels of trainers within an organization, each with an increasing amount of requisite experience. Trainers at small companies may have on-the-job experience, as opposed to previous experience with training or teaching in a classroom. Larger organizations recruit trainers with backgrounds in education or human resources. Companies, both large and small, need to hire outside subject-matter experts from time to time. It is nearly impossible for a company to have in-house staff with knowledge in every area for which it requires training.

In addition to other types of training, businesses need educators who can teach their employees about working with diverse populations and different cultures. In one example, a North American software firm planning to provide professional services to customers in Japan hired a "culturalist" to provide insights on doing business with Japanese customers. Heightening cultural awareness is one of the best ways to ensure that customer expectations are met and that staff are sensitive to the many cultural differences that exist in the global business world.

Another common role in many businesses is that of a deployment trainer, who is responsible for training a company's customers or partners, typically in the use of software or services. For example, a company that manufactures high-end graphics workstations for use in the motion picture industry may have a deployment training department whose job is to teach special effects crews to use the company's hardware and software. While this type of training position is not found at every organization, it is becoming more common as companies sell knowledge to their customers.

Training personnel occupations may include the following:

- Trainer
- Senior Trainer
- Training Consultant
- Deployment Training Specialist
- Subject Matter Expert

Content Creation

Depending on the size and scope of a company's corporate education program, one or more individuals may be made responsible for developing training materials. Many small organizations may choose to purchase ready-made materials if they lack the staff or budget to create their own content, while a larger organization is likely to employ experienced content developers or instructional designers on staff.

Instructional designers have expertise in creating training materials for adult learners and other specialized populations. They propose new and innovative training methods by studying and analyzing existing educational models and relating them to particular audiences and instructional content. In any size organization, it may be more cost-effective to purchase ready-made content than to create it from scratch. For example, if a company needs to train employees to use a common software package, purchasing standard training from a vendor could save considerable time and money. Similarly, some content will require input if a company does not have the requisite skills within its organization.

Content-creation occupations may include the following:

- Content Developer
- Instructional Designer
- Instructional Content Consultant

OCCUPATION PROFILE

Career/Technology Education Teacher

Considerations	Qualifications
Description	Instructs students in vocational or occupational subjects such as how to operate industrial machinery and communications, transportation, or medical equipment.
Career cluster	Education and Training
Interests	Data; people
Working conditions	Work inside
Minimum education level	Bachelor's degree; master's degree
Physical exertion	Light work
Physical abilities	Unexceptional/basic fitness
Opportunities for experience	Internship; military service; part-time work
Licensure and certification	Required
Employment outlook	Average growth expected
Holland interest score	SEC

Note: See volume 1, "Publisher's Note," for an explanation of the Holland interest score.

Training Administration

The administration, scheduling, and tracking of training initiatives can require significant work, depending on the number of employees at an organization and the number of educational offerings available. In many cases, employees need to complete a number of required training sessions, either as a condition of employment, to meet job-specific requirements, or to gain professional certification. At a small company, the same individual who delivers training may also be responsible for tracking training offerings and completion targets. Alternatively, the task of tracking employee training may be handled by an administrative assistant. At a large company with thousands of employees, scheduling and tracking training is a substantial job. Beyond logistics, it is also necessary for a company to manage its training staff. This role may fall to a more experienced manager who will ensure that trainers are meeting their own professional requirements for continuing education and performance standards.

Training administration occupations may include the following:

- Training Coordinator
- Training Manager
- Training Administrator

Training Strategy and Development

Every organization, regardless of size, that offers training to employees does so with a goal in mind. Training is a benefit to employees because it teaches them new skills, thus helping them advance their careers. To the company, training helps with employee retention, increases productivity, and—if executed correctly—helps increase a company's market share and profitability. Within every company that offers corporate education services, at least one individual is responsible for approving the budget for training. That same individual or others are also responsible for the overall vision for training. At a small organization, the owner or founder is likely to decide what training is needed to support the organization. While the owner of a small company is accountable only to himself for the success of the education program, at larger companies, the chief learning officer or a similar executive must report to the executive team or board of directors.

Training strategy and development occupations may include the following:

- Chief Learning Officer
- Vice President of Human Resources
- Training Director
- Management Consultant

INDUSTRY OUTLOOK

Overview

According to the BLS, training and development positions are expected to grow by 17 percent between 2006 and 2016. This figure represents a higher than average rate of growth. The projections for growth include mixed projections in the near term, as T&D adapts to cyclical and technological developments. Computerized information applications for tracking administrative functions in human resources are expanding to encompass T&D and will eliminate some of the more administrative T&D positions. Mergers and acquisitions will also cause a number of redundant positions to disappear. However, an increased need for specialized training and trainers will increase jobs within the industry. As the general complexity of jobs increases across the national and global workforce, so does the need for job-specific training. The rapid pace at which technology and computer applications have developed has also increased the need to keep employees abreast of emerging technologies. Without continuous training, employees are often easily and quickly left behind, especially in terms of technology.

The increased demand for specialized training is not the only factor increasing the proportion of such training offered by the industry. In addition to this increase, more general training tends to be outsourced or eliminated when company budgets are cut, decreasing not only the percentage but also the absolute amount of generalized corporate education. Companies learned a hard lesson during the recession of 2001, when many training budgets were slashed. During the 2000 downturn, companies abandoned training as a nonessential function. However, when the recession ended, the cuts left a tremendous amount of training ground to recover.

Based on this experience, most contemporary

companies believe that the preferred course of action in tough economic periods is to reevaluate their training needs and to retrench. This strategy is likely to be superior in the long run to cutting training completely. Nevertheless, training budgets were again slashed in the recession of 2007-2009. On average, two to three positions per one thousand employees were eliminated. In the wake of the recession, however, many companies are identifying training best practices to maximize the value of their continued investments in corporate education. These best practices include retaining skilled high performers and taking advantage of mentoring and informal coaching from one employee to another.

In the future, core competencies for T&D personnel will include an understanding of how adults from different generations learn, as well as an in-depth knowledge of technology and learning applications across generations and cultures. Teaching to a group with diverse social, cultural, and technological experiences will continue to be an exciting challenge for corporate educators.

Employment Advantages

Corporate training offers better pay than traditional teaching positions, but it is also more competitive. Corporate trainers, like any good teachers, must be engaging, entertaining, and knowledgeable of their subject matter. Individuals who are interested in a teaching career, but prefer to teach adults, may enjoy careers as corporate trainers. The BLS projects that college graduates with certification in human resources will be the most in demand to meet corporate education challenges. Course work in technology and business will also provide students with skills that are sought after by companies hiring training staff.

Trainers must be comfortable with technology and constant interaction, specifically through video and chat. The learning experience exists on a continuum and is no longer necessarily an event that takes place in a classroom on a given day. A discussion may start prior to training and continue long after the formal training ends. Despite this rise in technology and the fact that many companies are taking advantage of outsourced and online training, surveys indicate that 67 percent of training was instructor-led in 2008. Reliance on e-learning, in fact, decreased from 30 percent to 24 percent

in 2008. This change indicates that many companies may have leveraged all they can from available e-learning content. The future of corporate education will possibly leverage traditional classroom instruction, where it is most effective, and supplement employee knowledge with online training when that is the best option.

Annual Earnings

According to the *Corporate Learning Factbook*, the amount spent by U.S. companies for training fell by the largest margin in a decade between 2007 and 2008—from $58.5 billion to $56.2 billion. During lean times and tight budgets, companies seek opportunities to cut costs in all functional areas, and T&D is no exception. Efficiency in the delivery of training is nearly unanimously accepted as a cost-saving measure. Many organizations report that off-site training and conferences and any travel related to training have been curtailed as a result of budget constraints. Decreases in training budgets have taken the form of cuts not only in the money allotted for training itself but also in the payroll costs associated with training staff. Trends in growth and earnings figures across the globe are similar to those seen in the American market.

In mature markets, such as Europe and Japan, trends in corporate learning are following those in the United States. Companies are cutting back on in-house training as a way to weather the declining global economy, and nearly all developed countries are taking advantage of inexpensive labor in emerging markets. India, for example, has a large, inexpensive workforce with many English speakers. Companies that can take advantage of outsourcing some training functions are generally doing so. However, while many manufacturing jobs have moved to places where labor costs are low, this is not expected to happen in the corporate learning industry to the same extent. Nonetheless, outsourcing has become a reality for the corporate education services industry.

In recent years, government funds have been made available for training state, federal, and private-sector workers. State and federal training has gotten a boost of nearly $5 billion as part of the American Recovery and Reinvestment Act (2009). This money is earmarked for training and retraining to aid in the economic recovery. The enormous loss of jobs in specific sectors such as financial services and the automobile industry is likely to require millions of Americans to be trained or retrained in new jobs or even new occupations. It is now acknowledged that many of the jobs lost in 2007-2009 are unlikely to return, so many who lost jobs will find themselves working in vastly different industries and jobs in the future. Many predict that the domestic and global workforce will look very different at the end of the next decade, as manufacturing jobs continue to move overseas and some once-stable jobs diminish in number or cease to exist entirely. If this is indeed the case, then the need for trainers within private industry and the government may grow even faster than predicted.

RELATED RESOURCES FOR FURTHER RESEARCH

AMERICAN SOCIETY OF TRAINING AND
DEVELOPMENT
1640 King St., Box 1443
Alexandria, VA 22313-1443
Tel: (703) 683-8100
http://www.astd.org

CONFERENCE BOARD
845 3d Ave.
New York, NY 10022-6679
Tel: (212) 759-0900
http://www.conference-board.org

HUMAN CAPITAL INSTITUTE
1250 Connecticut Ave. NW, Suite 200
Washington, DC 20036
Tel: (866) 538-1909
http://www.humancapitalinstitute.org

INTERNATIONAL SOCIETY FOR PERFORMANCE
IMPROVEMENT
1400 Spring St., Suite 400
Silver Spring, MD 20910-2753
Tel: (301) 587-8570
http://www.ispi.org

SOCIETY FOR HUMAN RESOURCE MANAGEMENT
1800 Duke St.
Alexandria, VA 22314
Tel: (800) 283-7476
http://www.shrm.org

WORLD AT WORK
1100 13th St. NW, Suite 800
Washington, DC 20005
Tel: (202) 315-5500
http://www.worldatwork.org

ABOUT THE AUTHOR

Carolyn Sprague holds a bachelor of arts degree from the University of New Hampshire and a master's degree in library science from Simmons College. She has worked in numerous library and information settings within the academic, corporate, and consulting worlds. Her operational experience as a manager at a global high-tech firm and work as a Web content researcher have afforded her insights into today's quickly changing business climate and the ways that companies and individuals access and utilize information. Sprague has written on numerous topics in the areas of business, human capital, and social networking and related technologies.

FURTHER READING

Analoui, Farhad. *The Changing Patterns of Human Resource Management.* Burlington, Vt.: Ashgate, 2002.
Brakeley, Harry H., and Jeanne C. Meister. "Greater Expectations: How Corporate Education Can Boost Company Performance." *Outlook,* February, 2005. http://www.accenture.com/Global/Research_and_Insights/Outlook/By_Issue/Y2005/ToAdvantage.htm.
Craig, Robert L., ed. *The ASTD Training and Development Handbook: A Guide to Human Resource Development.* 4th ed. New York: McGraw-Hill, 1996.
Greeno, Nathan J. *Corporate Learning Strategies.* Alexandria, Va.: American Society for Training and Development, 2006.
Haskell, Robert E. *Reengineering Corporate Training: Intellectual Capital and Transfer of Learning.* Westport, Conn.: Quorum Books, 1998.
Noe, Raymond A. *Employee Training and Development.* 4th ed. New York: McGraw-Hill/Irwin, 2008.

Paradise, Andrew. "Learning Remains Steady During the Downturn." American Society for Training and Development, State of the Industry Report, November, 2009. http://www.astd.org/TD/Archives/2009/Nov/Free/0911_SOIR.htm.

Rothwell, William J., John E. Lindholm, and William G. Wallick. *What CEOs Expect from Corporate Training: Building Workplace Learning and Performance Initiatives That Advance Organizational Goals.* New York: AMACOM, 2003.

Tyler, Kathryn. "Carve Out Training? Outsourcing the Entire Training Function Is a Huge Change That—When Handled Properly—Can Yield Improved Services and Decreased Costs." *HR Magazine*, February, 2004.

U.S. Bureau of Labor Statistics. *Career Guide to Industries*, 2010-2011 ed. http://www.bls.gov/oco/cg.

———. "Human Resources, Training, and Labor Relations Managers and Specialists." In *Occupational Outlook Handbook*, 2010-2011 ed. http://www.bls.gov/oco/ocos021.htm.

U.S. Census Bureau. North American Industry Classification System (NAICS), 2007. http://www.census.gov/cgi-bin/sssd/naics/naicsrch?chart=2007.

U.S. Department of Commerce. International Trade Administration. Office of Trade and Industry Information. Industry Trade Data and Analysis. http://ita.doc.gov/td/industry/otea/OTII/OTII-index.html.

Counseling Services

©Alexander Raths/Dreamstime.com

INDUSTRY SNAPSHOT

General Industry: Personal Services
Career Clusters: Health Science; Human Services
Subcategory Industries: Individual and Family Services; Offices of Mental Health Physicians; Offices of Nonphysician Mental Health Practitioners; Outpatient Mental Health and Substance Abuse Centers; Psychiatric and Substance Abuse Hospitals
Related Industries: Medicine and Health Care Industry; Personal Services; Pharmaceuticals and Medications Industry; Residential Medical Care Industry
Annual Domestic Revenues: $33 billion (IBISWorld, 2009)
Annual Global Revenues: $4.5 trillion (total health care expenditures; The Medica)
NAICS Numbers: 6222, 6241, 62133, 621112, 621420

INDUSTRY DEFINITION

Summary

Counseling services are health care services that are essentially nonmedical, compared to physician-driven medical treatment. In contrast to historical Western medical practice, which treats patients through medical, procedural, and pharmaceutical means, counseling services typically assess and treat by helping clients understand their own challenges and find opportunities to help themselves to wellness. The fundamental goal of the industry is to enable people to function at their highest level of capability and desire. There are many areas of specialization in counseling. Some professions that fall under the umbrella of counseling include mental health and substance abuse counselors, behavioral disorder counselors, family counselors, marriage counselors, rehabilitation counselors, social workers, clinical psychologists, and grief counselors. All counseling professions exist in both the private and the public sectors, and some counselors are employed by corporations and universities to serve their populations' counseling needs.

History of the Industry

Early in the twentieth century, Austrian neurologist Sigmund Freud helped found psychoanalytic psychology, believing that behavior therapy was a means to interpersonal connectedness between counselor and patient. Talking and listening were primary modalities of psychoanalysis, and Freud

Counseling services typically assess and treat by helping clients understand their own challenges and find opportunities to help themselves to wellness. (©Alexander Raths/Dreamstime.com)

documented much success in this noninvasive communication-based form of therapy.

In the early 1940's, psychiatrist Carl Jung founded analytical psychology, which focuses on the exploration of the human unconscious as a means of understanding behavior. Closer in design to the modern-day dominant treatment models, Jung's inclusive, patient-centered approach was successful because it pulled deep emotion from patients and appeared to lead to recovery more rapidly than had earlier practices based on long, drawn-out counseling sessions.

Following World War II, veterans faced an unprecedented need for personal mental health services to deal with the psychological stress of combat. The need to bring the U.S. workforce back to optimal productivity presented a challenge to the business sector, while society's understanding of veterans' postwar mental health needs was lacking. President Harry Truman signed the Mental Health Act in 1946, which provided funding for psychiat-

ric research and education in the United States. The National Institute of Mental Health (NIMH) was founded in 1949. By the 1950's, in recognition of the growing counseling industry, many organizations dedicated to research, education, and standards in applied psychology had been created. These included the American Psychological Association (APA), the American Association of Applied Psychology, and the American Association of Clinical Psychologists (AACP).

Because the postwar need for psychology and mental health support was so great, the federal government, through its Veterans Administration hospitals and clinics, began to fund training for clinical counselors to better serve the needs of veterans, as well as to reduce costs. It was clear that quality behavioral rehabilitation needed to be available for veterans so that they could return to being productive contributors to society and the economy. In the 1950's, the terms "counselor" and "psychologist" became more closely linked. The roles and parameters of each were increasingly formalized, and people seeking those positions required and received greater professional training than they had earlier. Moreover, the formalization and professionalization of counseling occupations enhanced counselors' abilities to leverage resources and operate cost-effectively, while simultaneously increasing access to counseling for the people who needed it.

In 1963, the Community Mental Health Act was passed. This law provided funding for community mental health centers. It also provided training programs to encourage and support the counseling profession, as well as financial support for those

OCCUPATION SPECIALTIES

Psychologists

Specialty	Responsibilities
Clinical psychologists	Help mentally and emotionally disturbed people adjust to life.
Counseling psychologists	Use such techniques as interviewing and testing to advise people on how to deal with problems of everyday living—personal, educational, vocational, and social.
Educational psychologists	Design, develop, and evaluate psychological programs that are applicable to educational problems.
Engineering psychologists	Research, develop, apply, and evaluate psychological principles relating human behavior to characteristics, design, and the use of environments and systems within which human beings work and live.
Experimental psychologists	Conduct experiments with human beings and animals, such as rats, monkeys, and pigeons, in the prominent areas of experimental research that include motivation, thinking, learning and retention, sensory and perceptual processes, and genetic and neurological factors in behavior.
Industrial organizational psychologists	Develop and apply psychological techniques to solve administration, management, and marketing problems. They are involved in policy planning, applicant screening, training and development, psychological test research, counseling, and organizational development.
Psychometrists	Administer, score, and interpret tests to measure intelligence, aptitude, achievement, and other psychological characteristics.
School psychologists	Evaluate children within an educational system and plan and implement corrective programs. They work with teachers, parents, and administrators to resolve students' learning and behavioral problems.
Social psychologists	Investigate the psychological aspects of human interrelationships to gain understanding of individual and group thought, feeling, and behavior, using observation, experimentation, and survey techniques.

interested in pursuing postgraduate counseling degrees.

The Industry Today

When managed care insurance companies joined traditional payers such as Medicare and Medicaid, focus was placed on cost-conscious, expeditious care. As this managed model of care grew in popularity, so did its focus on cost and time. This model continues to be favored. Counselors commonly provide several sessions, limited to an hour or less, that constitute a baseline therapy that generally incorporates plans for closure and discharge from the practice.

Counseling has become socially accepted; most employed workers with health insurance have mental health coverage, which they value alongside medical coverage. As social acceptance of counseling has increased, so has the amount of money spent on it. The road to recovery is not necessarily mechanical or pharmaceutical but behavioral, cost-effective, and delivered by caring professionals.

INDUSTRY MARKET SEGMENTS

In the counseling services industry, service can be delivered by individual practitioners in small private practices or by one or more clinicians in midsize ambulatory (outpatient) centers. Counseling practitioners are also employed by schools; long-term care facilities (nursing homes); large academic, nonprofit hospitals and clinics; large for-profit hospitals and clinics; school guidance offices; college career planning offices; prisons; and corporate businesses.

Small Businesses

A growing number of counselors are working in their own private practices, providing services from their homes or offices. Some contract with schools or employers as consultants to supplement their private-practice income, especially in more rural areas where individuals' demand may be insufficient to sustain private practices. Because licensed professional counselors can enroll with mental health insurance plans and be paid for their services, the private-practice model is attractive to

many. In contrast to working in a salaried position for someone else, private practice offers more autonomy, the ability to work for oneself, and the potential to enhance earnings by simply providing more services to more customers.

Potential Annual Earnings Scale. According to the U.S. Bureau of Labor Statistics (BLS), the mean annual salary of all nonphysician mental health care providers in 2009 was $77,300. Counselors who work in their own private practices generally receive the highest salaries in the industry.

Clientele Interaction. Client interaction constitutes the central activity of a counselor. Private-practice clinicians see clients for sessions lasting between fifty and sixty minutes. Documentation and followup work for each client can take as long as the session itself. Private clinicians must also deal directly with insurance companies for billing and must discuss billing and insurance information with their clients, unless they employ administrative assistants.

Counselors must be trained and alert not only to creating a comfortable environment for their clients but also to modulating their own body language: Intonation and verbal cues that minimize patients' anxiety and maximize their ability to engage in their own assessment and treatment will lead to better outcomes. Maintaining a client base is critical to keeping a counseling business solvent.

Amenities, Atmosphere, and Physical Grounds. Private clinicians may practice within offices within their own residences, or they may rent or purchase separate office space. Privacy during counseling sessions, as well as assurance of anonymity in patient receiving areas, must be guaranteed. A quiet and relaxed atmosphere without telephones, pagers, or other potential interruptions is essential for clients' comfort and for the reputation of providers' practices.

Typical Number of Employees. Many private clinicians have no employees, attending themselves to all business operations, including billing, collections, scheduling, and client communication. Some are able to employ one or more support staff, and joint practices of a few clinicians are more likely to be able to afford such staff, since the clinicians can pool their resources and share expenses.

Traditional Geographic Locations. Behavioral health counseling is equally in demand across socioeconomic and ethnic groups, and practices ex-

OCCUPATION PROFILE

Marriage Counselor

Considerations	Qualifications
Description	Diagnoses and treats mental and emotional problems within the context of a marriage.
Career cluster	Human Services
Interests	Data; people
Working conditions	Work inside
Minimum education level	Master's degree; doctoral degree
Physical exertion	Light work
Physical abilities	Unexceptional/basic fitness
Opportunities for experience	Internship; military service
Licensure and certification	Required
Employment outlook	Faster-than-average growth expected
Holland interest score	SEC

Note: See volume 1, "Publisher's Note," for an explanation of the Holland interest score.

ist in all areas. Rural areas, however, may not have sufficient population density to sustain practices, so they are rarer in such areas than in suburban and urban centers.

Pros of Working for a Private Practice. A small operation such as a counseling practice may not require a large start-up investment. Small business grants and financial aid are available from federal government sources, and even loans may be attained through government support. While a business remains small, the accounting and management functions tend to be fairly manageable; a home computer and basic accounting software can usually offer what is needed to maintain sufficient record keeping. Private clinicians usually have full control over their schedules and workloads, and they have the freedom to limit their practice to paying customers. They may pick and choose which insurers they wish to deal with, and they may seek to negotiate better reimbursement rates without having to ask someone else's permission. (There are no guarantees, though, that private practitioners

will be in a position strong enough to negotiate better rates.)

Cons of Working for a Private Practice. Health care reimbursement structures and mechanisms are vast and complex bureaucratic systems. It is not by coincidence that major medical practices have full-time staff devoted to wrangling with insurance companies. Private clinicians operating without support staffs must expend a serious proportion of their time and energy negotiating payments with insurance companies seeking to deny or minimize every claim they receive. Each hour spent dealing with insurance companies over payments is an hour not spent treating patients and earning income.

Private clinicians, moreover, may find it challenging to maintain relations with their colleagues, to meet continuing professional development requirements, and to take advantage of peer- and case-review opportunities in order to maintain their clinical proficiency and currency. It is therefore important for them to belong to relevant professional organizations and to make a point of devoting time and resources to continuing education. Professional and personal growth for counselors can come from expanding practices with individual clients to include group or family therapy or contracting privately with high schools. Solid relationships with referring physicians form an important cornerstone of a stable counseling business. Counselors may need to advertise and visit referring providers to keep their services visible, but doing so costs time and money.

Private clinicians must develop business plans, as well as finance (or arrange financing for) their start-up costs. Those who have employees have no human resources department, so clinicians must hire, fire, and manage their own staffs. As business owners, they are responsible for paying any employees first before they pay themselves. They must also take responsibility for conducting, contracting, or purchasing all marketing; payroll administration; accounting, tax withholding, and payments; legal services; and health, property, liability, and malpractice insurance required by their practices. Private clinicians are self-employed, so they have no guaranteed salary, and their costs stand to be greater than those of large firms because they have little bargaining power.

Clinicians must be available on call for their patients, depending on the contracts in place with mental health insurance companies. Medical record documentation is a core function of counseling work; its safe storage and retention are significant obligations for private clinicians. Liability and even lawsuits can ensue from negligence in these areas. Patients are often very concerned about the safety of their medical information, and private clinicians are responsible for any breach of confidentiality regarding their clients' behavioral and mental health records.

Costs

Payroll and Benefits: Private practitioners do not earn specific salaries. Rather, they draw their incomes from the revenues generated by their businesses. Taking such paychecks requires that there be monies left in a practice's account after all other obligations have been paid. Once these obligations are paid, however, all profits of the practice are available as income for its owner.

Supplies: Private clinicians require pagers, computers, medical record-keeping software, and business and financial software, as well as all other standard office supplies, such as paper, pens, a copier and fax machines, and so forth. It is still relatively common for small practices to keep paper medical records. Such practices must have secure, locking cabinets or other storage facilities to maintain these files.

External Services: Clinicians may contract cleaning, maintenance, and landscaping services as necessary to maintain a professional atmosphere. They may also hire accountants, lawyers, answering services, or marketing consultants.

Utilities: Clinicians must pay for electricity, water, heat, air-conditioning, telephone service, and Internet access.

Taxes: Clinicians must pay income taxes, including self-employment taxes where appropriate, as well as property taxes. Those who maintain office space at home are able to deduct a percentage of their home expenses from their taxes, subject to applicable laws and regulations.

Midsize Businesses

Midsize counseling businesses include large private practices and small specialized mental health clinics and hospitals. These may be public facilities, or they may operate within the confines of a larger institution and serve only that institution's population. An example of the latter arrangement would be a college's mental health center. Midsize counseling businesses may employ anywhere from ten to over one hundred persons.

Potential Annual Earnings Scale. Average earnings for counselors (including behavioral psychologists) working in midsize facilities fall between $45,000 and $65,000 per year, depending on education level and geography. The revenues generated by such facilities vary, depending on the number of clients and employees. When considering counseling work in a midsize facility, it is important to look closely at the terms of employment and to be well informed about any financial risk sharing, productivity expectations, and malpractice coverage.

Clientele Interaction. Counselors are both employees and ambassadors of their home organizations. They must display professional attire, attitudes, and attention to detail. Patient satisfaction information may be collected regularly, and clinicians are evaluated by their employers based on such information. Being accessible to both new and current patients will encourage referrals from other providers. A solid referral base is key to a counselor's success at a midsize facility. Productivity data for a clinician's practice are likely to be monitored, and sometimes salary may be affected either positively or negatively by these data, depending on the terms of a clinician's contract.

Amenities, Atmosphere and Physical Grounds. Mental health centers and clinics cultivate both professional and calm atmospheres in order to attract and reassure patients. Reception areas and counselors' offices may resemble those of medical doctors, although counselors often eschew overly clinical settings for more reassuring surroundings. Facilities must include secure storage for medical records, privacy in waiting areas, and white noise or other sound protection in order to maintain the privacy of counseling conversations.

Typical Number of Employees. The number of employees in a midsize health care facility varies by facility size and the service lines offered. In a community-based mental health facility, there might be a nurse for client care management, a receptionist, and other support staff. In small hospitals, the number of employees could be in the hundreds. Billing staff are critical to a facility's success, as they handle claims submission and reimbursement. They should be approachable and ready to instruct counselors on policies for documentation, billing, and claims-filing requirements.

Traditional Geographic Locations. Midsize counseling facilities include small ambulatory centers, residential facilities, and counseling center offices that are typically located near populated areas, often in professional districts near hospitals, labs, or outpatient clinics. Referrals from other providers are the lifeblood of these organizations. Counselors must engage professionally with hospitals' physician staff and private-practice physicians. Socioeconomic aspects of a facility's location should be considered, as areas with low unemployment will attract more insured clients and therefore entail less hassle collecting direct payments from patients.

Pros of Working for a Midsize Counseling Facility. Well-established organizations provide employment security and more freedom from finan-

cial constraints than private practice ownership can. They provide the infrastructure for efficient scheduling, human resources oversight, contracting, billing, and day-to-day facility operations, as well as management of financial performance. Employees in this setting generally have access to group health insurance for themselves and their families. Investments in capital and facilities are made by the facility rather than the individual provider. Pay incentives may be available, usually based on productivity and expense controls.

Billing and collections are the concerns primarily of the employer and less of the individual provider. Clinicians can focus their energy on client care and not on pursuing clients or insurance companies for payment. Additionally, responsibility for being on call at night and on weekends is more likely to be shared among professionals than to be borne entirely by one individual.

Cons of Working for a Midsize Counseling Facility. Employees of counseling facilities, including clinicians, may have their hours and workload determined by their employers. Autonomy is compromised to a degree. Counselors must also compete with colleagues and other units for limited resources, such as medical record systems, staffing, and capital. Employed professionals need to be strong advocates for themselves and for their patients, particularly in times of economic challenge. Pressures to see more clients and to increase productivity will likely wax and wane, also depending on the economy and the financial state of a given organization. At the same time, midsize facilities may share some of the potential risks of private practices, including lack of feedback on performance, few colleagues with whom to collaborate, long hours, and even emotional fatigue.

Costs

Payroll and Benefits: Counselors working in community hospitals or ambulatory midsize facilities are usually salaried, meaning their paychecks and benefits (if any) are guaranteed. There may also be incentive salary available for meeting certain workload benchmarks. Benefits may include employer-sponsored malpractice insurance coverage and reimbursement for professional membership dues and travel.

Supplies: Midsize counseling facilities require paper or electronic medical records, office supplies, computers, telephones, décor conducive to a health care setting, billing software, fax machines, and current billing and coding manuals for compliance and maximum reimbursement.

External Services: Midsize counseling facilities may contract such services as answering services, office cleaning and maintenance, and security.

Utilities: Mental health facilities must pay for electricity, gas or oil, water, sewage, telephone, and Internet access.

Taxes: Nonprofit facilities are often exempt from many taxes. For-profit facilities must pay corporate and property taxes. All facilities must pay payroll taxes and withhold applicable taxes from employee paychecks.

Large Businesses

Large counseling businesses include mental hospitals and clinics located in densely populated areas that have sufficient referral bases to support varied services. Such facilities can be for-profit or not-for-profit and can see annual revenue in the millions of dollars, depending on size. Typically, such businesses employ hundreds or even thousand of people, including physicians and nurses, administrators, support staff, security personnel, and housekeeping personnel. Because of their size and centralized locations, large mental health facilities draw business from a large area, depending on competition and patient willingness to travel for services.

Potential Annual Earnings Scale. According to the U.S. Bureau of Labor Statistics (BLS), the mean annual salary of all nonphysician mental health care providers in 2009 was $77,300.

Clientele Interaction. Large facilities offer more diversity and opportunity for professionals than do their smaller counterparts. Inpatient (hospital) care, long-term care, ambulatory care, or contract work for schools and others may be options for professionals operating in large facilities. An example of a large counseling or mental health facility is an academic medical center with an imbedded psychiatry department that offers both inpatient and outpatient services to adults, children, and employees.

Counselors at large facilities work as members of teams or groups of similar professionals. It can be challenging to coordinate schedules among the members of such groups, especially at times of holidays or school vacations. Professionals represent their organizations and their colleagues, and they are expected to be available and responsive when they are on call.

Amenities, Atmosphere, and Physical Grounds. Large organizations are typically freestanding and feature sizeable grounds. As large facilities employ many people, parking can be an issue, particularly for facilities located in cities. Some may even charge employees for parking on site, thereby encouraging them to use public transit or form car pools. An aesthetically pleasing, well laid out, and safe environment will help ensure a facility's success. Counselors should be alert to these amenities when considering joining large organizations.

Typical Number of Employees. Large health care facilities can employ thousands of staff, although behavioral counseling staff have historically been only a small percentage of the total employed. Mental health services, though immeasurably valuable, are often not reimbursed well by insurance companies, making them less profitable for organizations with high overhead. That said, behavioral health services are being integrated with primary care medical services as a means to demonstrate improved outcomes in physical and cognitive function.

Traditional Geographic Locations. Large health care facilities with integrated behavioral services divisions are generally located in densely populated areas. A sufficient population base with potential for growth is critical to the livelihood of a large medical facility. Unlike a business that relies on product sales through the Internet, for example, a health care facility provides a face-to-face service to its clientele. Counselors are one of the best representations of this service model.

Pros of Working for a Large Counseling Facility. Generally, large health care facilities offer more opportunities for advancement than do smaller facilities. Throughout their careers, counselors can develop leadership skills and move into partial or total administrative roles, such as teaching, mentoring, overseeing quality improvement, or conducting research. Large organizations tend to have the financial capacity to promote these activities, particularly if their mission includes academics alongside clinical care. The counseling industry, embedded in the huge health care industry, offers job security and a steady state of work.

Cons of Working for a Large Counseling Facility. Internal politics can be an issue in large facilities. Clinicians at such facilities may encounter increased bureaucracy, and they may sometimes feel they have to fight for resources. Money does play a role, and because behavioral health services produce less revenue than other services, they are often understaffed and allocated fewer resources than are more lucrative units. Counselors at these facilities are therefore under pressure to see more clients in order to bring in more money.

Costs

Payroll and Benefits: Large organizations hire counselors under salary structures, ideally one designed to accommodate the peaks and valleys of a variable workload and to pay a fair, consistent rate. Benefits may include health and dental insurance, disability coverage, Family Medi-

The National Health and Nutrition Examination Survey, 2005-2006, found that in any two-week period, 5.4 percent of Americans twelve years of age and older experienced depression. (©Stephanie Swartz/Dreamstime.com)

cal Leave Act (FMLA) protection, retirement plans, malpractice coverage, continuing medical education (covering expenses related to travel, time, and registration for courses), and even tuition reimbursement for additional degree work.

Supplies: Mental health facilities require paper or electronic medical records, office supplies, computers, telephones, décor conducive to a health care setting, billing software, fax machines, and current billing and coding manuals for compliance and maximizing reimbursement.

External Services: Large facilities may hire internal staff to handle support functions, but many contract external vendors to provide janitorial, maintenance, or security services. They may also contract cafeteria service and independent auditors. While larger organizations may have public relations staff, they often contract dedicated firms when launching major advertising campaigns.

Utilities: Mental health facilities must pay for electricity, gas or oil, water, sewage, telephone, and Internet access.

Taxes: Nonprofit facilities are often exempt from many taxes. For-profit facilities must pay corporate and property taxes. All facilities must pay payroll taxes and withhold applicable taxes from employee paychecks.

ORGANIZATIONAL STRUCTURE AND JOB ROLES

Mental health practitioners must fill a variety of job roles. Sole practitioners must perform most of these tasks themselves or must contract external support for any they cannot handle. Large organizations, by contrast, are segmented and organized hierarchically to ensure that each task is handled by a specialist in the relevant field.

The following umbrella categories apply to the organizational structure of businesses in the counseling industry:

- Counseling Staff
- Business and Operations Management
- Contracting and Reimbursement

- Human Resources
- Customer Service
- Marketing and Public Affairs
- Facilities and Security

Counseling Staff

Counselors work in a variety of diverse settings, in both the public and private sectors, depending on their specialization, preference, education level, and licensure. The type and number of positions within a counseling staff varies depending on the size, focus, and structure of the parent organization. A psychiatric hospital, a drug rehabilitation center, a university, and an elementary school will each have different counseling staff needs.

There are several predominant counseling specializations. Social workers, for example, serve counseling needs within communities such as nursing homes, schools, and hospitals. They earned an average of between $35,000 and $55,000 per year in 2009, according to the BLS. Mental health counselors help clients deal with mental and emotional issues such as depression, and they also work with couples and families who need counseling. In 2008, the median annual salary for mental health counselors was $36,810. School counselors work in elementary and high schools and colleges, counseling students about issues such as vocation, continuing education, and mental health issues such as depression. In 2008, the median wage of school counselors was around $51,000. Counselors specializing in substance abuse and behavioral disorders help clients with issues such as eating disorders and addiction. In 2008, they earned a median annual salary of around $37,000.

Counseling occupations may include the following:

- Social Worker
- Mental Health Counselor
- School Counselor
- Vocational Counselor

OCCUPATION PROFILE

Medical Social Worker

Considerations	Qualifications
Description	Provides people with psychosocial support needed to cope with sudden, terminal, or chronic illness; educates patients and caregivers; and refers patients to other social services as needed.
Career clusters	Health Science; Human Services
Interests	Data; people
Working conditions	Work inside
Minimum education level	Bachelor's degree; master's degree
Physical exertion	Light work
Physical abilities	Unexceptional/basic fitness
Opportunities for experience	Volunteer work; part-time work
Licensure and certification	Required
Employment outlook	Faster-than-average growth expected
Holland interest score	ESA

Note: See volume 1, "Publisher's Note," for an explanation of the Holland interest score.

The American School Counselor Association says a student-counselor ratio of 250:1 is optimal, but the national average is closer to 460:1. (©Chris Schmidt/iStockphoto.com)

zations that disseminate information about changes in regulations and the tax codes.

In larger organizations, operations management is usually centralized and accomplished by accountants, front-line operations managers, and other white-collar professionals whose work is intellectual in nature. Such professionals are experts in finance, operations, and strategy and develop relationships with key stakeholders. Particularly large organizations are directed by chief operating officers (COOs), who set their organizational vision, strategy, and goals. The salary of top executives and management varies depending on the size, focus, and structure of the organization; however, according to the BLS, the median annual salary for operations managers was $91,000 in 2008.

Business and operations management occupations may include the following:

- Chief Operating Officer (COO)
- Operations Manager
- Office Manager
- Logistics Manager
- Purchasing Manager
- Facility Coordinator

- Grief Counselor
- Substance Abuse Counselor
- Rehabilitation Counselor
- Art Therapist
- Music Therapist

Business and Operations Management

Day-to-day operational managers support clinicians, so they may focus on treating clients. They provide financial management and budgeting for revenues, expenses, and capital investments. Private-practice clinicians must become adept in areas of operational management until they are able to hire support staff to assume some of these duties. Operations managers of smaller practices, often called office managers, generally have business degrees and belong to professional organi-

A six year old whose father died in the World Trade Center attacks on September 11, 2001, works with an art therapist in 2004. (AP/Wide World Photos)

OCCUPATION PROFILE

Music Therapist

Considerations	Qualifications
Description	Plans, organizes, and directs instrumental and vocal music activities and experiences to help patients with their communication, social, daily living, or problem-solving skills.
Career cluster	Health Science
Interests	Data; people
Working conditions	Work inside
Minimum education level	Bachelor's degree
Physical exertion	Light work
Physical abilities	Unexceptional/basic fitness
Opportunities for experience	Volunteer work; part-time work
Licensure and certification	Recommended
Employment outlook	Faster-than-average growth expected
Holland interest score	ESI

Note: See volume 1, "Publisher's Note," for an explanation of the Holland interest score.

Contracting and Reimbursement

Reimbursement in the counseling industry varies by insurance carrier and by geography. Generally, reimbursement for these services is executed through a contracted fee schedule. Often, if not always, prior authorization through insurance carriers is required. Often, documentation must be presented, and limits on the number of covered sessions are set by carriers. Counseling businesses must devote significant time and resources to negotiating, claiming, and coordinating payments from these carriers. This role may be filled by individual providers or by support staff, and in either case it is a crucial function in keeping a business financially solvent. Actions such as running afoul of contractual obligations or providing services when coverage is not approved or has run out can devastate a business's bottom line.

Contracting and reimbursement staff should be strong negotiators with the ability to understand billing processes and documentation requirements. Larger organizations centralize this function because of its need for highly specialized expertise. Medical and health care contracts and reimbursement mechanisms are highly complex and changeable. They must be monitored and kept current at all times to protect businesses' livelihood. Moreover, not all services rendered are covered by insurance. Some clients pay for services out of pocket, while others receive work-related service. The former can be particularly challenging, as clinicians and billing staffs become the collectors of debt from their clients.

Contracting and reimbursement occupations may include the following:

- Billing Manager
- Contract Reimbursement Specialist

- Medical Coding Specialist
- Medical Billing Assistant
- Administrative Assistant

Human Resources

Human resources staff recruit, hire, manage, pay, and fire employees. They also handle employee training and development, as well as employee performance appraisals. They administer payrolls and benefits, as well as responding to employee grievances. At small practices, owners are responsible for all these tasks. At large facilities, the human resources function is generally centralized, with some autonomy within individual departments or business units. Entry-level salaries within human resources average around $45,000 per year for those with bachelor's degrees, according to the National Association of Colleges and Employers, while human resources managers earn between around $85,000 and $100,000 per year.

Human resources occupations may include the following:

- Human Resources Director
- Payroll Manager
- Benefits Manager
- Diversity Coordinator
- Benefits Specialist
- Recruitment Specialist
- Human Resources Administrator

Customer Service

Customer service personnel address customer concerns and needs professionally, promptly, and thoroughly. Patients concerned with the care they receive from private clinicians may express these concerns directly to their counselors or through their attorneys. In larger organizations, client-relations professionals provide service recovery and resolutions to customer issues. Risk management and patient relations professionals are available to support clinicians and customers. In all counseling services, a strong customer service ethic is mandatory. Customer service personnel address customer inquiries, complaints about billing practices, confidentiality concerns, and legal issues. Specialized skill sets, including strong emotional intelligence, are required in this role. Customer service representatives are generally paid by the hour; the 2008 median hourly wage of a representative was $14.36.

Customer service occupations may include the following:

- Customer Service Director
- Customer Service Representative

Marketing and Public Affairs

Advertising for a small private practice can be relatively inexpensive and take the form of newspaper or other print advertisements. Private clinicians can also utilize professional groups as referral sources. Larger organizations advertise broadly, particularly if the referral base for their clients is in a competitive environment. Competition for any kind of clients, but particularly for those who are insured or can pay out of pocket, is a challenge in virtually every geographic location.

Liaisons to outside physician practices and businesses can play a substantial role in growing clinicians' referrals. Sometimes individual counselors make outreach visits to referring providers because face-to-face interactions increase the likelihood of referrals. When advertising and outreach become priorities, professional marketing and public affairs staff, holding a minimum of undergraduate or advanced degrees, target market share and determine where best to spend valuable resources in order to gain the most return on advertising investments. According to the BLS, marketing managers in 2008 earned a median annual salary of around $108,000, while the 2008 median annual salary of market research analysts was $61,000.

Marketing and public affairs occupations may include the following:

- Marketing Manager
- Physician Liaison
- Market Research Analyst
- Business Analyst
- Marketing Administrator

Facilities and Security

Individual clinicians operating out of homes or private offices must recognize that their clients may have behavioral, relationship, or social issues. They must plan their office environments with this in mind and include mechanisms for getting prompt help when necessary. Precautions might be as simple as having a second staff person on site at all times or housing a practice within a professional building in a populated area.

In larger organizations, centralized security is provided. Service hours should be well defined, and client interaction outside of the normal business day must be routinely reported to security personnel. Most of the time, the need for security is minimal, but its proximity and availability should always be a strong consideration for the clinician. Training for security staff is centralized in midsize and large organizations. Some security personnel have backgrounds in law enforcement. According to the BLS, the mean annual wage for security guards was around $26,000 in 2008.

Facilities and security occupations may include the following:

- Security Director
- Hospital Security Analyst
- Security Guard

INDUSTRY OUTLOOK

Overview

The outlook for the counseling services industry shows it to be on the rise. Researchers have projected long-term growth (through 2018) in the demand for counseling professions, including mental health and substance abuse counselors, behavioral disorder counselors, rehabilitation counselors, and marriage and family counselors. According to the Substance Abuse and Mental Health Services Administration, over 24 million Americans reported suffering from "serious psychological distress" in 2008. According to the BLS, the demand for counselors of most specializations will increase since the number of available jobs exceeded the national enrollment in counseling degree programs as of 2009. Revenue from the family counseling and social services industry in the United States grew by 4.3 percent in 2009 according to IBISWorld.

There are many indications that the counseling services industry will continue to grow. As the baby-boomer population ages, demand for counselors is likely to increase. Aged populations face issues such as disease, pain, and loss of independence, and the counseling services industry will grow to meet the rising mental health needs of this group. Another key client base of the counseling industry

is people struggling with substance abuse and addiction. Research from the U.S. Substance Abuse and Mental Health Services Administration has found that illicit drug use is increasing, a trend that strengthens the need for substance abuse and addiction counseling.

Employment Advantages

Health care services professions are vast and disparate. In an industry of increasing federal oversight and legal compliance regulations, specialization in counseling careers is inevitable. In fact, counselors are increasingly focusing on specific patient populations, strengthening fields such as geriatric counseling, adolescent counseling, substance abuse counseling, and marriage counseling. Despite such specialization, the fundamental basis of counseling services remains the same: helping people. Professional evaluations, teaching, and professional research in academic settings are all intriguing opportunities that counselors can explore and enjoy in most any area of specialization.

People who are strong communicators, who like helping others, and who are emotionally competent enough to offer quality counsel are ideally suited for counseling careers. Counselors may work in a variety of settings, such as medical facilities and hospitals, elementary and high schools, colleges and universities, and private practices. This career path provides great satisfaction to professionals who enjoy working face-to-face with customers. The pleasures of working with adults, children, couples, and groups are but a few of the advantages to this vocation. Counselors also find work within the academic realm, performing research and publishing on topics of interest to them.

Annual Earnings

In 2008 in the United States, the counseling services industry generated around $33 billion in revenue. Generally, health care and social assistance industries are experiencing growth. From 2006 to 2007, for instance, the industry grew by 6.8 percent. Parsing out earnings in the counseling field, nationally or globally, is difficult since counseling is delivered in so many settings. Because billing data are the primary means by which revenue data are collected, it is best to look at the health care industry in aggregate. According to the BLS, counselors can generally earn between around $30,000 and $60,000, depending on specialization, level of education, preference, and employer. This salary range presents a challenge in recruiting candidates to the industry. However, in part because of relatively low salaries, there is no glut of providers and demand from clients has historically exceeded supply. That trend, combined with the growth of populations who will seek out counseling services, ensures job security in the counseling field.

RELATED RESOURCES FOR FURTHER RESEARCH

AMERICAN COLLEGE OF MEDICAL PRACTICE
    MANAGEMENT
    Crossville Commons
    560 W Crossville Rd., Suite 103
    Roswell, GA 30075
    Tel: (770) 649-7150
    Fax: (770) 649-7552
    http://www.epracticemanagement.org

AMERICAN COUNSELING ASSOCIATION
    5999 Stevenson Ave.
    Alexandria, VA 22304
    Tel: (703) 823-9800
    Fax: (800) 473-2329
    http://www.counseling.org

HEALTHCARE FINANCIAL MANAGEMENT
    ASSOCIATION
    2 Westbrook Corporate Center, Suite 700
    Westchester, IL 60154
    Tel: (800) 252-4362
    Fax: (708) 531-0032
    http://www.hfma.org

MEDICAL GROUP MANAGEMENT ASSOCIATION
    104 Inverness Terrace East
    Englewood, CO 80112-5306
    Tel: (303) 799-1111
    http://www.mgma.com

ABOUT THE AUTHOR

Nancy Sprague holds a bachelor's degree from Granite State College of the University System of New Hampshire and a master's degree in health policy from the Dartmouth Institute, Dartmouth College. She is a member of the National Medical Group Managers' Association, the Healthcare Financial Management Association, and the American College of Healthcare Executives. She is also a fellow in the American College of Healthcare Executives, a registered nurse, and a health care operations consultant. Sprague has spent her career in medical practice and hospital operations, both in private practice and in a large academic tertiary hospital setting.

FURTHER READING

Broskowski, Anthony, and Shelagh Smith. *Estimating the Cost of Preventive Services in Mental Health and Substance Abuse Under Managed Care.* Rockville, Md.: U.S. Department of Health and Human Services, Substance Abuse and Mental Health Services Administration, Center for Mental Health Services, Office of Managed Care, 2001.

Cummings, Nicholas A., William T. O'Donohue, and Michael A. Cucciare. *Universal Healthcare: Readings for Mental Health Professionals.* Reno, Nev.: Context Press, 2005.

Levin, Bruce Lubotsky, Kevin D. Hennessy, and John Petrila. *Mental Health Services: A Public Health Perspective.* New York: Oxford University Press, 2010.

Mark, Tami, et al. *National Expenditures for Mental Health Services and Substance Abuse Treatment, 1993-2003.* Rockville, Md.: U.S. Department of Health and Human Services, Substance Abuse and Mental Health Services Administration, 2007.

Munley, Patrick H., et al. "Counseling Psychology in the United States of America." *Wes Counselling Psychology Quarterly* 17, no. 3 (2004): 247-271.

Pedrini, Laura, et al. "Burnout in Nonhospital Psychiatric Residential Facilities." *Psychiatric Services* 60 (November, 2009): 1547-1551.

Pistole, M. Carole. "Mental Health Counseling: Identity and Distinctiveness." ERIC Digest. http://www.ericdigests.org/2002-4/mental-health.html.

Reinhardt, Uwe E., et al. "U.S. Health Care Spending in an International Context." *Health*

Affairs: The Policy Journal of the Health Sphere 23, no. 3 (2004): 10-25.

U.S. Bureau of Labor Statistics. *Career Guide to Industries*, 2010-2011 ed. http://www.bls.gov/oco/cg.

U.S. Census Bureau. North American Industry Classification System (NAICS), 2007. http://www.census.gov/cgi-bin/sssd/naics/naicsrch?chart=2007.

U.S. Department of Commerce. International Trade Administration. Office of Trade and Industry Information. Industry Trade Data and Analysis. http://ita.doc.gov/td/industry/otea/OTII/OTII-index.html.

Walfish, Steven, and Jeffrey E. Barnett. *Financial Success in Mental Health Practice: Essential Tools and Strategies for Practitioners.* Washington, D.C.: American Psychological Association, 2009.

Williams, Ruth F. G., and D. P. Doessel. *The Economics of Mental Health Care: Industry, Government, and Community Issues.* Burlington, Vt.: Ashgate, 2001.

Criminal Justice and Prison Industry

INDUSTRY SNAPSHOT

General Industry: Law, Public Safety, and Security

Career Cluster: Law, Public Safety, and Security

Subcategory Industries: Correctional Institutions; Courts; Parole Offices and Probation Offices

Related Industries: Civil Services: Public Safety; Federal Public Administration; Local Public Administration

Annual Domestic Revenues: Private prisons: $2.7 billion USD (Correctional Corporation of America and GEO Group, 2009); annual expenditures by U.S. Department of Justice: $25.7 billion (U.S. Department of Justice, 2009)

NAICS Numbers: 92211, 92214-92215

INDUSTRY DEFINITION

Summary

Prisons are places where persons convicted of crimes are held in order to meet the goals of punishment or rehabilitation. Persons are physically confined, so they cannot harm others, and they are deprived of freedom, so they will be deterred from future crime. The prison industry has also become a business where prisoners are used for work. Prison-run programs for inmates can be public or private and bring in revenue for the industry.

History of the Industry

Prisons constitute one subsection of the criminal justice system, which is made up of three major parts: police, courts, and corrections. The act of imprisoning individuals is based on the notion of incapacitation, or making one physically unable to commit a crime. Imprisonment throughout history has been used to confine criminals, who would be subject to corporal punishment or even death.

Prisons were established in London under the ideas of Jeremy Bentham, who was a classical theorist. He believed, along with Cessare Beccaria, that crime could be deterred if the punishment for violations of the law were swift, certain, and severe. They both believed that punishment could prevent persons from committing crime if the consequences outweighed the benefits. During the nineteenth century, prison became a form of punishment, rather than a place to hold a criminal until he was punished.

The first prison in the early nineteenth century was based on the penitentiary movement. Individuals were supposed to reflect upon their behavior, and do penance for their crimes. The term "prison" is often used interchangeably with "jail." However, they really are different terms, associated with the

Keys hang on the belt of a guard at California's San Quentin State Prison for men, which has three levels of security, from minimum to maximum, including death row. (AP/Wide World Photos)

severity of the crime and the length of time for which one is incarcerated. A prison can be run by the state or federal government and is a place where criminals are held for more than a year. State prisons are reserved for serious criminals, and federal prisons are reserved for those who violate federal laws, such as white-collar criminals. Jails are run by municipalities or counties and are reserved for individuals who have been convicted of less serious crimes or for those awaiting trial. The longest amount of time spent in jail is one year.

While incarcerated, prisoners are required to work and exercise. They also have the option of participating in recreational activities. This not only keeps them busy and out of trouble but also gives them skills they can use on release. In addition, they can obtain high school equivalency credits and get the therapy and treatment necessary for success outside the prison walls. Prisoners have to earn the right to work in the more desirable areas of the prison and are paid (very little) for their work. They can use their earnings to buy items for themselves at the commissary.

The prison industry has become an important revenue stream for prisons. Often, inmates are hired out to work in factories, where they produce goods to be sold to the federal government. They are cheap labor, so profit margins increase at com-panies that use them, and prisons earn money by lending out their inmates as laborers. In addition, the work helps inmates feel they are accomplishing something during the course of their day, and sometimes they learn usable skills. Even if they are performing tedious labor, the more they work, the lower the likelihood they will be involved in criminal behavior.

The Industry Today

Prisons and jails continue to hold those awaiting trial and those convicted criminals serving time as part of their sentences. Some facilities have thousands of beds, while others have only two cells. Many have education, vocational, and treatment programs that help meet the special needs of inmates. Since jails hold prisoners for relatively short periods of time, the therapeutic and recreational programs offered in such facilities are minimal. Jails must still provide care and treatment in a safe environment, however. Thus, they need employees, food service, laundry service, attorneys, therapists, and other workers, as well as security personnel and managers. The physical environment ranges in size from small, one-to-two-cell local jails to massive prisons run like hotels at the state and federal level. Prisons may operate through public or private funding.

Some jails are found in small towns and municipalities and offer few services. They typically have relatively small staffs, comprising local police officers. These locations are used only to hold offenders for twenty-four to forty-eight hours. In mid-2009, local jails held 767,620 persons awaiting trail or serving sentences, according to the Bureau of Justice Statistics (BJS).

Midsize prisons might be found in larger counties and smaller states. They must provide for all of the basic needs of offenders, although they may not be able to offer all of the services of a large prison. For example, larger prisons might offer drug treatment and counseling, as well as vocational training in many areas. Midsize prisons might not have the room or the budget for such services. Facilities for women only, tend to offer even fewer services. Although food, security, and medical services are imperative, treatment opportunities and useful vocational training might be lacking.

Large institutions, especially those located in states with a high number of inmates, such as California, are run as big businesses. They have all the necessary housekeeping services, as well as administrative, educational, and vocational programs. These prisons can house serious violent offenders in separate locations on the prison grounds and offer opportunities for offenders to work on-site or have inmates hired out by private companies to produce goods to be sold or services to be offered outside the prison walls.

Prisons have undergone a significant evolution since the 1700's. They operate more like businesses and even earn profits by selling products made by inmates. Prisons are now focused on rehabilitation and deterrence, in addition to retribution and punishment. Today's prisons have better criminal record keeping, forensic analysis, fingerprint analysis, quicker access to records, and auto-

mation of records, as well as decreased delays in processing information. At midyear 2008, state and federal prison authorities had over 1.6 million prisoners under their jurisdiction. Today, there are more than 2.3 million people behind bars. Those numbers are expected to go up as the penalties for certain crimes, especially drug offenses, go up. In addition, tougher state and federal sentencing laws have increased the population of minority offenders in particular.

Another major change has been the use of private prisons. Today, about 10 percent of U.S. prisons and jails have been privatized. They have become for-profit businesses that reduce essential services within the prison. The private contracting of prisoners for work is a booming business because it allows prison workers to supply the market with goods that are cheap to produce. Federal prison industry workers produce almost all U.S. military and war supplies and assemble many products and appliances. The three major private firms in the United States that offer security services to private corporations are the Corrections Corporation of America, Wackenhut, and Esmor. There

This minimum-security federal correctional facility for women is located in Bryan, Texas. (AP/Wide World Photos)

are a few others that operate correctional or detention facilities, and the big three also have facilities in Australia, England, and Puerto Rico.

Interestingly, private prisons were common over one hundred years ago. Prisoners were hired out as slave labor and were exposed to horrible conditions. They were worked to death, and there was no concern for their physical safety. Today, legislation regulates private contractors running correctional facilities. Most of those run by private firms are low- to medium-security level. The number of private prisons is likely to increase in the near future.

According to the BLS *Occupational Outlook Handbook*, employment of correctional officers is expected to grow by 9 percent between 2008 and 2018. There will be an increased demand for officers as the prison population grows as a result of "get tough" policies and mandatory minimum sentences. Employment opportunities are expected to increase even more in the private sector, as public authorities contract with private companies to staff correctional facilities and offer services to those facilities. Further, there will be an increase in not only state corrections agencies but also federal corrections agencies, using private prisons.

Changes in the programs offered to inmates have occurred during the early twenty-first century. Faith-based programs have been added, and restorative justice efforts are being incorporated into the prison mentality. Programs that promote positive behavior, as opposed to punishing deviant behavior, are projected to be a new focus. In addition, technological changes will play a major role in communication and offender tracking, detection, and monitoring. Biometrics—the identification or verification of identities via measurable physiological and behavior traits—will be used more. Examples could include retinal and facial recognition, voice- and fingerprint identification, and thermal imagery. Global Positioning System devices will begin to be used with more regularity as well.

INDUSTRY MARKET SEGMENTS

Prisons can be designated as minimum-security, medium-security, and maximum-security facilities. Sometimes, a prison has sections devoted to one or another security level, but these designations are used to protect offenders from one another and to make management of the prison run more smoothly.

Minimum-Security Facilities

Minimum-security prisons are reserved for the least serious offenders. They are often set up like small camps and might be located in or near military bases. The prisoners live in less secure dormitories, and they are usually surrounded by a single fence. The facilities are most often located in rural areas, and the offenders are usually nonviolent. Inmates usually participate in community-based work assignments and in prerelease transition programs.

Potential Annual Earnings Scale. According to the U.S. Bureau of Labor Statistics (BLS), the average salary for probation officers and correctional treatment specialists in 2009 was $51,100. Correctional officers and jailers earned an average of $43,150, while their supervisors earned an average of $60,160.

Clientele Interaction. Small and local facilities have high rates of turnover. Often, local jails hold offenders for only twenty-four to forty-eight hours, and the longest they can be held is for seventy-two hours. In minimum-security locations, the staff-to-inmate ratio is low, and inmates live in dormitory housing or private rooms. Because minimum-security institutions allow for more freedom of movement, correctional officers might be able to interact on a bit more of a personal level with inmates.

Amenities, Atmosphere, and Physical Grounds. Minimum-security facilities offer more privileges but not more amenities. Because many offenders are nonviolent, the focus is less on security and violence prevention and more on treatment and education. Many inmates are assigned to private rooms, and the atmosphere is less restrictive than it is at medium- and maximum-security facilities.

The atmosphere in minimum-security facilities is a bit more relaxed. The facility is usually located in a rural area, with lots of grass and trees. Activities are often planned for outside, and services might include educational programs, counseling, recreational activities, and work details. Staff are responsible for inmate accountability, including their conduct, personal hygiene, and noise level.

The physical grounds are often set up like a college. There is an area where classes are held, an

An inmate at Blackburn Correctional Complex, a minimum security prison in Lexington, Kentucky, works with a thoroughbred that he trained during a prison program. (AP/Wide World Photos)

area where there is counseling, an area where the inmates eat, and an area where they sleep. There is laundry service, medical staff, and administrative staff. Sometimes, inmates are sent to programs in the community for treatment.

Typical Number of Employees. There are approximately 370 minimum-security prisons in the United States, and about 17 percent of the prison population is confined at this level. One of the largest issues facing minimum-security facilities is expenses. Because they are small and located in rural areas, they are often expensive to run. In addition, they often offer fewer services and activities. Staff would include a warden or director, staff for security, educational and vocational staff, counselors, and service staff.

Traditional Geographic Locations. Minimum-security facilities tend to be located in rural areas, often on or near military bases. Although they are not as stringent, and might be located in a picturesque community, they offer fewer opportunities for visitation because the locations are often very far from home.

Pros of Working for a Minimum-Security Facility. Because they operate under less secure conditions, one of the positive aspects of minimum-

security facilities is more freedom of movement. There could be no fence or only one fence around the facility, and inmates are often free to roam about the facilities, as long as they behave as instructed. Correctional officers therefore work in conditions that are a bit less restrictive than at other facilities. There is less risk of violence or attack because the inmates they are watching are low risk and nonviolent. In addition, they are not cooped up in an institution for the course of their day because the facilities are more open in nature. Staffs are usually smaller than at higher-security facilities because open institutions have less need for officers to enforce the more stringent rules and confinement protocols of medium- and maximum-security facilities. Inmates need to participate in educational, recreational, and vocational activities as part of the requirements of their sentences, and the correctional officers need to make sure they arrive at their destination safely. Higher job satisfaction has been found among correctional officers at lower-security facilities than among those at higher-security facilities.

Cons of Working for a Minimum-Security Facility. Since there are only a few correctional officers on staff, only a small number of persons are responsible for most operational duties. Any neglect of duties could lead to security breaches and direct accountability. Correctional officers might also experience stress because they are working with criminals, sleep disturbances because they are working odd hours, and alienation because they might be seen as adversaries by inmates. Further, because minimum-security facilities are located in rural areas, many employees have long commutes to and from work.

Costs

Payroll and Benefits: The mean average wage for correctional officers is $20.49 per hour, but hourly wages can range from $12.48 to $21.18 depending on the region. In September of 2007, a 5 percent annual salary increase for officers became effective. Health benefits cover officers and their eligible dependents.

Supplies: Minimum-security prisons require medical supplies, cleaning supplies, food, linens, hardware (for maintenance), office supplies, information technology (telephones and computers), outdoor supplies (such as lawn mowers and snow shovels), bedding, and toiletries.

External Services: Prisons may contract some of the staff who work with prisoners, such as teachers or counselors, as well as food services. Private prisons may contract accounting services or lobbying services as necessary.

Utilities: Typical utilities for a minimum-security institution include water, sewage, electricity, gas or oil, telephone, cable television, and Internet access. Many states allow inmates in minimum-security facilities access to the Internet.

Medium-Security Facilities

Medium-security prisons house offenders who require more secure facilities than those housed in minimum-security facilities. They are often set up like maximum-security facilities but have fewer controls over the freedom of the inmates. The prisoners live in secure, barred cells within fortified perimeters. The rooms can be set up in dormitories or bunk beds, with communal showers, toilets, and sinks. Medium-security facilities often house fifty inmates per officer, and some might be designed with "dry cells," with no toilet fixtures in the dormitory. There is a single cell unit set aside for punishment of inmates. The facilities are most of-

ten located in rural areas, and the offenders are less violent than maximum-security inmates. Inmates usually participate in work assignments, education, and vocational training, as well as faith-based programs and prison industry. There is less supervision in regard to internal movement of prisoners, but the dormitories are locked at night (and are thus more secure than minimum-security facilities).

Potential Annual Earnings Scale. According to the BLS, the average salary for probation officers and correctional treatment specialists in 2009 was $51,100. Correctional officers and jailers earned an average of $43,150, while their supervisors earned an average of $60,160.

Clientele Interaction. Staff-to-inmate ratios are lower than at maximum-security facilities but higher than at minimum-security facilities, and inmates live in dormitory housing or private rooms. Because medium-security institutions allow for some freedom of movement, correctional officers might be able to interact on a bit more of a personal level with inmates.

Amenities, Atmosphere, and Physical Grounds. Medium-security facilities offer more privileges than maximum-security facilities and more amenities than minimum-security facilities. The focus is less on security and more on treatment and work programs. However, the layout is similar to that of a maximum-security facility. The atmosphere in medium-security facilities is a bit more relaxed than in maximum-security facilities. The facility is usually located in a rural area, and activities might include educational programs, counseling, recreational activities, and work details.

The physical grounds are set up like maximum-security facilities. There is an area where classes are held, an area where there is counseling, an area where the inmates eat, and then an area where they sleep. There are laundry service, medical staff, and administrative staff. Sometimes, inmates work in prison industry while incarcerated.

Typical Number of Employees. There are approximately 506 medium-security prisons in the United States, and about 48 percent of the prison population is confined at this level. One of the largest issues facing medium-security facilities is balancing security with treatment and education. Staff include a warden or director, staff for security, educational and vocational staff, counselors, and service staff. Perimeter security and yard officers are necessary.

Traditional Geographic Locations. Medium-security facilities tend to be located in rural areas. They are more stringent than minimum-security facilities and offer fewer opportunities for visitation because the locations are often far from home.

Pros of Working for a Medium-security Facility. Because they operate under more secure conditions, one of the positive aspects of a medium-security facility is more freedom of movement than at maximum-security facilities. Correctional officers therefore work in conditions that are a bit less confining and a bit more safe. There is less risk of violence or attack because the inmates they are watching are lower risk than maximum-security inmates. In addition, staff-to-inmate ratio is low. Inmates participate in educational, recreational, and vocational activities as part of the requirements of their sentences, and the correctional officers make sure they arrive at their destination safely. Industrial and shop security are necessary, as well as yard and perimeter security.

Cons of Working for a Medium-Security Facility. Because the inmates prison employees supervise are more dangerous than minimum-security inmates, any neglect of duties could lead to security breaches and direct accountability. Guards need to keep the perimeter and yard safe via regular patrol. Satisfaction with the job may be decreased by the risks employees face. Studies find that correctional officers are happier in minimum-security facilities, where they have more control or influence regarding the policies of the facilities.

Further, because medium-security facilities are located in rural areas, correctional officers often commute long distances to work. The amenities at the medium-security level tend more plentiful than at minimum-security facilities, but the inmates might be more violent and more dangerous to work with. Correctional officers might also experience stress because they are working with criminals, sleep disturbances because they are working odd hours, and alienation because they might be seen as adversaries by inmates.

Costs

Payroll and Benefits: The mean average wage for correctional officers is $20.49 per hour, but hourly wages can range from $12.48 to $21.18 depending on the region. Health benefits cover officers and their eligible dependents.

Supplies: Medium-security prisons still need medical supplies, cleaning supplies, food, linens, hardware (for maintenance), office supplies, information technology (telephones and computers), outdoor supplies (such as lawn mowers and snow shovels), bedding, and toiletries.

External Services: Prisons may contract some of the staff who work with prisoners, such as teachers or counselors, as well as food services. Private prisons may contract accounting services or lobbying services as necessary.

Utilities: Typical utilities for a medium-security institution include water, sewage, electricity, gas or oil, telephone, and cable television.

Maximum-Security Facilities

Maximum-security prisons are reserved for the most serious offenders. They are often set up to confine the most dangerous offenders, for long periods. Thus they need to have a highly secure perimeter. The facilities are most often located in rural areas, and the offenders are usually violent. Inmates have strict controls placed on them, and routines are highly regimented.

Potential Annual Earnings Scale. According to the BLS, the average salary for probation officers and correctional treatment specialists in 2009 was $51,100. Correctional officers and jailers earned an average of $43,150, while their supervisors earned an average of $60,160.

Clientele Interaction. In maximum-security locations, the staff-to-inmate ratio is high, and inmates live in single- or multiple-occupancy barred cells. Because maximum-security institutions are most concerned about security, correctional officers might have to interact on an impersonal level with inmates.

Amenities, Atmosphere, and Physical Grounds. Maximum-security facilities offer fewer privileges than lower-security facilities and fewer amenities. Because many offenders are violent, the focus is on security and violence prevention. Inmates are usually required to remain in their cells for twenty-three hours per day. A shower and some exercise for a short time are allowed.

The atmosphere in maximum-security facilities is very structured and regimented. The facility is usually located in a rural area. Services might include educational programs and counseling, but there are constant custody and security concerns. When out of their cells, prisoners must remain in the exterior part of the institution (still part of the cell block). Any movement outside of the cell block is severely restricted.

The physical grounds are often set up like a fortress. There is a highly secure perimeter with watchtowers and high walls. There are laundry service, medical staff, and administrative staff. Security needs to be maintained in the yard and the perimeter. The cells are operated from a remote-control station, so there is little contact between the inmates and the correctional officers. Because the inmates are high risk, each cell has its own toilet and sink, so there are fewer reasons for them to leave their cells. Inmates may leave for work assignments or programs, so there needs to be supervision at the work detail area, and block officers are necessary in the housing areas.

Typical Number of Employees. There are approximately 332 maximum-security prisons in the United States, and about 36 percent of the prison population is confined at this level. One of the largest issues facing maximum-security facilities is safety. Because they are large and because the inmates are dangerous, they are often expensive to run. In addition, they often offer fewer services and activities. Staff include a warden or director, staff for security, educational and vocational staff, counselors, and service staff.

Traditional Geographic Locations. Maximum-security facilities tend to be located in rural areas. They are very stringent and regimented, and offer fewer opportunities for visitation because the inmates are so dangerous. The inmates pose a risk to others, as well as to the guards, so the facilities need watch towers.

Pros of Working for a Maximum-Security Facility. Because they operate under very secure conditions, one of the positive aspects of a maximum-security facility is its lock-down capabilities. There are high walls and watchtowers, and inmates cannot roam about the facilities. Correctional officers therefore work in conditions where there is a constant watch over the inmates. Staff numbers are usually higher because of the risk level associated with maximum-security inmates. Thus, correctional officers always have backup. Some inmates are not allowed access to activities because of their risk

level. Others are allowed to participate in activities but need direct supervision.

Cons of Working for a Maximum-Security Facility. Since the inmates are high risk, correctional officers have to be on high alert at all times. Any neglect of duties could lead to security breaches and direct accountability. Further, because maximum-security facilities are located in rural areas, most correctional officers work far from home. Amenities at the maximum-security level tend to be lacking, as are privileges. Thus, there might be disgruntled inmates that the officers have to deal with. Correctional officers might also experience stress because they are working with criminals, sleep disturbances because they are working odd hours, and alienation because they might be seen as adversaries by inmates.

Costs

Payroll and Benefits: The mean average wage for correctional officers is $20.49 per hour, but hourly wages can range from $12.48 to $21.18 depending on the region. Health benefits cover officers and their eligible dependents.

Supplies: Maximum-security prisons require medical supplies, cleaning supplies, food, linens, hardware (for maintenance), office supplies, information technology (telephones and computers), outdoor supplies (such as lawn mowers and snow shovels), bedding, and toiletries.

External Services: Prisons may contract some of the staff who work with prisoners, such as teachers or counselors, as well as food services. Private prisons may contract accounting services or lobbying services as necessary.

Utilities: Typical utilities for a maximum-security institution include water, sewage, electricity, gas or oil, telephone, and cable television.

ORGANIZATIONAL STRUCTURE AND JOB ROLES

The organizational structure within a prison is typically based on law and policy. Wardens are likely to handle most of the major decision making because they are prisons' administrators. Wardens make arrangements for prisoners to be placed in certain positions, based on trust, qualifications, and need. They delegate to assistant wardens and to correctional officers the coordination of moving prisoners. Correctional officers keep their sites safe. In addition, there are companies that provide private correctional and detention management.

The following umbrella categories apply to the organizational structure of institutions in the criminal justice and prison industry:

- Administration
- Correctional Officers
- Clerical Support
- Program Staff
- Maintenance
- Food, Beverage, and Laundry
- Groundskeeping

Administration

Administrators handle the general operations of prisons. Wardens run their institutions, and assistant wardens assist them. These individuals oversee major operations, goal-setting, and the implementation of plans for the institution. They also manage the administration and business aspect of the institution (or, in the case of the warden, oversee all departments). Many wardens have advanced degrees; they must possess leadership qualities and

be able to implement public policy. Wardens and assistant wardens generally earn higher salaries than correctional officers and support staff. Their job is to manage the overall functions of prisons, address systemic issues, and ensure that all departments are functioning smoothly and safely. Prison administrators must respond to emergencies, supervise and direct the work of correctional officers to ensure the institution is run in a safe manner—they must ensure that inmates are held in secure conditions and that correctional officers are working in secure conditions. Administrators are responsible for planning, developing, implementing, supervising, and coordinating programs. They might need to review and sign reports, make referrals, determine visitation and phone privileges, and conduct disciplinary action.

Administrative occupations may include the following:

- Warden
- Assistant Warden

Correctional Officers

Correctional officers are responsible for individual contact with inmates in their institutions. They can be assigned to different locations depending on the security level and size of the institution. They are responsible for the safety of the institution from the front lines and report to upper-level management. They do not establish the rules, but they enforce them.

Block officers supervise in the housing areas of a prison, and safety is their main concern. They are also responsible for inspecting property and conducting head counts. They interact directly with inmates and hold significant power because they can give rewards or punishment for behavior they observe. Work detail officers supervise crews in their institutions as they go back and forth and while they are working inside prisons. They also supervise work details out-

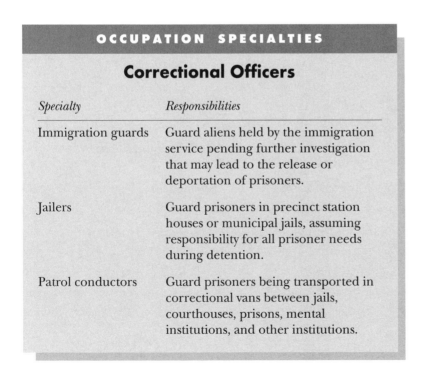

OCCUPATION SPECIALTIES

Correctional Officers

Specialty	Responsibilities
Immigration guards	Guard aliens held by the immigration service pending further investigation that may lead to the release or deportation of prisoners.
Jailers	Guard prisoners in precinct station houses or municipal jails, assuming responsibility for all prisoner needs during detention.
Patrol conductors	Guard prisoners being transported in correctional vans between jails, courthouses, prisons, mental institutions, and other institutions.

side prisons and keep track of supplies. They may also supervise laundry, kitchen, and maintenance work performed by inmates.

Industrial shop or school detail officers ensure efficient use of equipment in these areas. They protect and work with instructors to ensure that they are safe and that inmates are attending their assigned classes. Yard officers supervise the yard and the movement of inmates to and from it. Perimeter officers supervise the walls and towers in order to prevent escape from and intrusions into the prison. Tower officers review information about inmate movement and are responsible for opening and closing gates. Relief officers replace officers who are out sick or on vacation. Some officers are responsible for transporting inmates from one area to the next. Others are responsible for making sure that those who are in need of protective custody get it and that those who pose a danger to the rest of the institution get their needs met from their cells (such as by having food brought to them).

Regardless of their details, correctional officers must maintain order and follow the rules and regulations of the prison administration. They may need to restrain and control offenders and occasionally use force to gain compliance. Only a high school diploma is required for this position, as on-the-job training is expected to be of more use than formal education. Those expecting to move on to managerial or administrative positions should probably obtain advanced degrees.

All correctional officers need to conduct searches. In the housing areas, they need to search the showers for contraband and make sure cells are cleaned. In the cafeteria, they must inspect all food carts and trays. Outside, the gates, fences, radios, cameras, and other areas and devices must be monitored. In the visiting areas, visitors and inmates need to be searched and monitored. Disciplinary

OCCUPATION PROFILE

Correctional Officer

Considerations	Qualifications
Description	Guards inmates in prisons, jails, and other correctional institutions; also may guard prisoners during transfers between jails, courts, prisons, and other institutions.
Career cluster	Law, Public Safety, and Security
Interests	People
Working conditions	Work inside; work both inside and outside
Minimum education level	On-the-job training; high school diploma or GED; high school diploma/technical training; apprenticeship
Physical exertion	Light work; medium work
Physical abilities	Unexceptional/basic fitness
Opportunities for experience	Apprenticeship; military service
Licensure and certification	Required
Employment outlook	Average growth expected
Holland interest score	SER

Note: See volume 1, "Publisher's Note," for an explanation of the Holland interest score.

OCCUPATION PROFILE

Parole and Probation Officer

Considerations	Qualifications
Description	Supervises probationer or parolee during period specified by the terms of probation or parole.
Career cluster	Law, Public Safety, and Security
Interests	Data; people
Working conditions	Work inside
Minimum education level	Bachelor's degree; master's degree
Physical exertion	Light work
Physical abilities	Unexceptional/basic fitness
Opportunities for experience	Apprenticeship; volunteer work
Licensure and certification	Usually not required
Employment outlook	Faster-than-average growth expected
Holland interest score	SEC

Note: See volume 1, "Publisher's Note," for an explanation of the Holland interest score.

officers are responsible for fact-finding hearings regarding the legal issues surrounding an inmate's incarceration. Morning-shift workers are responsible for cleaning the visiting room, assisting unit officers in screening mail, monitoring phone calls, conducting fire and security checks, and providing training to new officers.

Correctional officer occupations may include the following:

- Shift Manager
- Block Officer
- Work Detail Officer
- Industrial Shop/School Officer
- Yard Officer
- Perimeter Officer

Clerical Support

Although clerical support staff do not work hand-in-hand with inmates, their jobs are very important for the smooth running of prisons. They answer phones, manage keys, schedule and log vis-

its, type, and make contact with the public. They are responsible for record keeping, human resources, scheduling program staff, room assignments, and paperwork. The average pay for clerical support workers is low, and an advanced degree is not required. Personnel must be able to use computer programs and have good communication skills. They might need to make photocopies, send faxes, and provide support to the warden and assistant warden through scheduling, data entry, word processing, managing files, keeping records, and conducting stenography and transcription. Administrative personnel manifest a wide range of backgrounds and professional training experience. Many are temporary employees, while others are brought in as entry-level staff for managers and other personnel. The business office oversees accounting, budgeting, purchasing, accounts payable, credit-card processing, outside contracting, purchasing, travel expenses, inventory management, fiscal operations, payroll, salary expenditures, and projections.

Clerical support occupations may include the following:

- Administrative Assistant
- Secretary
- Records Clerk
- Business Clerk
- Accountant

Program Staff

Program staff in prisons are responsible for encouraging prisoners to participate in educational, vocational, and recreational opportunities. Advanced degrees are required for teachers and counselors, who generally have teaching certificates, and possibly master's or Ph.D. degrees. Teachers need to have knowledge of curriculum design, and if they are teaching English as a second language (ESL), they need knowledge of the English language, including grammar and spelling. Inmates can also be taught the skills necessary to run a business, how to apply for jobs, or how to improve parenting skills. Teachers must be able assess learning styles and work with the resources available in prisons. They also need to keep the environment safe by monitoring the inmates' behavior.

Therapists and counselors need to have doctoral degrees in their areas of expertise. They have to understand human behavior, and they must be able to assess personality and treat behavioral and affective disorders. Psychologists must examine inmates for suicide risks and assist in treating inmates with mental illnesses or mental retardation or other developmental disabilities. They review records and hold crisis-intervention sessions as needed.

As with prison teachers, psychologists need to know how to keep the environment safe, so they may be trained in how to handcuff and transport inmates. Therapists and correctional counselors develop and implement programs to meet the needs of individual inmates. They perform intake, interviewing newly admitted inmates, and plan for counseling sessions. Sometimes there is a need for immediate counseling or guidance, and other times there can be sessions for self-improvement.

Health services are extremely important in prison. Legally, inmates have the right to adequate medical care, so the staff must make sure inmates get medical, dental, and psychiatric care in a safe environment. The prison must make every effort to prevent the spread of contagious diseases and reduce on-site injuries. Medical supplies and equipment must be available, and guards must know cardiopulmonary resuscitation (CPR) techniques. Practitioners provide primary care for inmates, and they are useful in promoting good health, disease prevention, medical evaluation, and treatment of inmates and staff in a safe and secure environment. Medical staff need medical or nursing degrees.

Those providing religious education need to be trained as clerics. Religious services can be utilized to enhance spirituality and rehabilitate criminals. Chaplains can organize programs and offer counseling, emergency interventions, and worship services.

Those who provide recreation need to be trained in their field. Most such personnel have training and certification in physical fitness. They also have first-aid and CPR training or certification. They are usually paid hourly wages. Recreation offers a way to reduce idleness. Recreational instructors can offer programs that improve the physical and emotional well-being of inmates. They might need to purchase equipment and develop special programs that meet the needs of the inmate population. They must also make sure conditions are secure by performing searches and making sure inmates play fair so as not to incite altercations.

All program staff members offer opportunities for inmates to learn skills they can apply upon release. Correctional officers are responsible for keeping the staff safe. Clerical staff make sure that program staff members have proper credentials. Inmates can earn general education diplomas (GEDs) and college credits by taking classes from program staff. They can get the drug treatment and mental health counseling they need to be healthy and emotionally secure. Depending on the security level of their facilities, inmates can also obtain vocational skills in construction, heating, air-conditioning, landscaping, or even painting in the community. Programs are offered in small-appliance repair, culinary arts, forklift operations, floor care, pest control, typing, and even certification in alcohol and substance abuse counseling. In addition, inmates can participate in prison industry, making goods to be used by the government.

Program staff occupations may include the following:

- Psychologist
- Psychiatrist
- Physician
- Nurse
- Teacher
- Counselor
- Recreational Instructor
- Religious Counselor/Chaplain

Maintenance

Maintenance and building engineering staff repair malfunctioning building systems such as air-conditioning, plumbing, electrical hardware, and similar devices. They may also play an important role in renovation planning and implementation. Building maintenance personnel are alternately called engineers, environmental services personnel, and facilities managers. Salaries are commensurate with experience. Most personnel in this department have vocational education and training, if not advanced degrees in engineering or related fields. Facilities personnel provide management oversight, planning, maintenance, and construction programs that ensure maximum efficiency of physical plants and compliance with all appropriate codes and standards. Facilities staff supervise all institutional utilities, existing and new construction projects, and repair and improvement projects. A foreman is responsible for maintenance and repairs of buildings, vehicles, roads, and grounds. There might be a foreman for other services such as heating, ventilation, and air-conditioning (HVAC) repair and maintenance.

Maintenance occupations may include the following:

- Heating, Ventilation, and Air-Conditioning (HVAC) Technician
- Plumber
- Chief Engineer
- General Maintenance and Repair Worker

Food, Beverage, and Laundry

Food and beverage personnel must meet the meal and beverage needs of inmates, although inmates often earn the work detail of serving and preparing meals. Some prisons have gardens where they grow fresh produce for the prisoners to eat, although this is much more rare now than it once was. In such institutions, food personnel include

master gardeners who instruct inmates in tending the garden.

Food and beverage personnel oversee the setting up and cleaning up of eating areas. This is a job of considerable responsibility because eating areas can be extremely dangerous if inmates are not properly screened and supervised. Almost any eating utensil can be fashioned into a lethal weapon.

Although inmates assist the food service staff in preparing and serving food, a supervisory crew is necessary to ensure that the prison food meets health and safety standards, as well as religious, dietary, and medical needs. The quality of prison food is very important to the contentment of inmates. Thus, a food service supervisor plans, controls, and evaluates the food service. Supervisors need to make sure supplies are available and manage food distribution.

The inmates are assigned laundry detail, but again coordination is necessary with support staff and correctional officers. Support staff need to make sure the proper supplies are available: safe working conditions, with a heavy-duty washer and dryer, laundry detergent and baskets. In addition, correctional officers need to make sure the most trusted inmates are assigned this duty, since they could attempt to smuggle goods in this way, or damage a fellow inmate's property if a grudge is being held against someone. Even if laundry service is privatized, and sent out for cleaning, persons would need to be assigned to collecting and loading the soiled clothing, as well as labeling and distributing it upon return. Guards need to make sure inmates are following all the rules, and inmates need to know they must be responsible for cleaning, folding, and storing all bed and bathroom laundry, as well as any laundry from the kitchen and vocational programs. Laundry personnel do not have advanced educations, but they need to be knowledgeable enough to understand the prison rules and comply with them (for example detergent usage, folding techniques, and other tasks).

Food, beverage, and laundry occupations may include the following:

- Food Service Supervisor
- Chief Cook
- Master Gardener
- Laundry Supervisor

Groundskeeping

The maintenance of the property surrounding a prison falls to the institution's groundskeeping crew. Groundskeepers maintain the area and other outdoor amenities. They must be familiar with the equipment necessary to maintain the prison's horticultural features. They may not have advanced educations, but they generally have solid gardening experience, some ability to maintain sprinkler and other mechanical systems, and an eye for the aesthetic quality of the prison's natural resources.

Although they need not possess a postsecondary education, groundskeepers are expected to be familiar with the property's external real estate. They may also be called upon to clear debris, snow, and other seasonal elements that may hinder the operations of the prison.

Groundskeepers are usually paid hourly, at a rate commensurate with their experience and skills. They work closely with those in the maintenance and engineering departments in order to ensure that they have the proper resources to tend to the prison's grounds. Some of this work can be privatized, and some can be performed by inmates doing work details.

Groundskeeping occupations may include the following:

- Head Groundskeeper
- Landscaping Worker
- Assistant Groundskeeper

INDUSTRY OUTLOOK

Overview

The performance of the prison industry has long been an indicator of economic conditions in the United States and around the globe. There is a close link between the number of jail and prison facilities, as well as the number of inmates held in those facilities, and the strength of the economy.

Inmates walk through the Tent City Jail in Phoenix, Arizona, created by Maricopa County Sheriff Joe Arpaio. (AP/Wide World Photos)

High rates of incarceration also reflect the political and government demand for punishment of criminals. Following the terrorist attacks of September 11, 2001, the economic downturn harmed the prison industry. Virtually every type of business establishment saw significant losses during the 2001 recession, and crime rates rose. Some prison staff positions were cut, and new prison construction stagnated.

By 2007, the industry had largely returned to its pre-September 11 growth rate, as the number of prisons and the number of inmates both surged. This resurgence was largely because of more stringent penal policies and changes in criminal laws. Determinate sentencing, tougher drug laws, and truth in sentencing have led to overcrowded prisons and poor conditions. With the 2007-2009 global economic crisis, concern over the prison industry returned. Prisons saw drops in revenues, leading to hiring freezes, layoffs, and a slowdown in the construction of new prisons.

Several factors will contribute to the continued growth of the prison industry over the long term. The first is changes in legislation, such as mandatory minimum sentences. When legislators push for stricter and longer sentences, the need for prison space increases. Second, the focus on drug offenders and offenses will lead to the need for better security and more correctional officers to supervise those inmates.

Alleviating the overcrowding problem will strengthen the prison industry. Overcrowded conditions lead to safety concerns. If there are too few staff, there will be gaps in security. Fewer cell checks and counts can be conducted. This situation can snowball into a dilemma for the prison industry. To control overcrowding, accreditation to mandate acceptable staff-inmate ratios would be of great assistance. Increased attention needs to be paid to victim rights and inmate rights. Specifically, better management of the death penalty, more programs, and better management and treatment of juveniles are necessary.

One of the most important keys to the recovery of the prison industry is the government. The government needs to focus on meeting the needs of elderly inmates, the mentally ill, the drug addicted, and other inmates in need of assistance. Those who have acquired immunodeficiency syndrome (AIDS) and those who are in need of therapeutic community-based residential treatment programs within the prison, must have their needs met. In addition, correctional officers need to be prepared to manage gangs and assaults. One helpful way to improve the prison industry would be better classification of inmates in the first place. Maybe some criminals (those who are less dangerous), would benefit from community sentences. Then, more prisons would not need to be built. Instead, better use of those facilities is a way to more efficiently manage the prison industry. In fact, there are doubts about the effectiveness of mandatory sentencing. Thus, an evaluation of the most successful management techniques is needed yearly.

Also invaluable to the prison industry is the hiring of well-qualified staff. Administratively, there needs to be well-qualified, fair, and knowledgeable upper management. On the front lines, correctional officers need to be knowledgeable and capable as well. Fair wages and proper conditions within the institutions go a long way.

Much of the success of the prison industry relies on the ability to manage costs. The widespread impact of the global economic crisis has kept energy costs largely in check. However, the lack of federal aid to states—and, in turn, the lack of state aid to municipalities—has led governments on all levels to look into other options to fund their facilities. Further, the privatization of the prison industry could be another route to examine. Many analysts say a cost-effective technique is to contract out to private bidders who perform government activities. A private entity could take over full-scale management of the jails and prisons or be utilized for some services. However, it needs to be well-managed so that the services are not sub-par.

Additionally, the pursuit of additional revenues has led officials to seek taxes on inmates. They can be charged for some services and programs they receive while incarcerated, and afterward for some aftercare. Medicine, food, housing, telephone, haircuts, drug testing, program participation, and work release are all examples of inmate fees that can be assigned.

The punitive nature of our society is the main element driving the continued growth of the prison industry, even in times of recession. To be sure, the significant drop in financing during the economic recession of 2007-2009 had a severe impact on industry at large. However, there is always a need for a place to hold prisoners. In addition, there will always be a need for correctional officers to oversee the prisoners. Even if some leave the industry, or are transferred, those officers will need to be replaced, especially those who retire. The prison industry will most likely continue to see growth in both the short and long terms.

Employment Advantages

According to the BLS, the prison industry will continue to grow well into the 2010's. Wages and salaries are expected to grow at about the economy-wide average rate of 7 to 13 percent, and industry-wide construction growth is also anticipated to continue. Employment opportunities for correctional officers are expected to be favorable, and growth is expected to be as fast as the average for all occupations. There will be rising employment demand and thus more job openings.

Projections from the National Employment Matrix indicate that employment of correctional officers, first-line supervisors, managers of correctional officers, bailiffs, and jailers, should see a 9 percent increase from 2008 to 2018. The median wage was $38,380 in May, 2008, and ranged from $29,660 to $51,000. For those employed in privately operated prisons, the median annual wage was $28,790. Bailiffs earned $37,820 on average. Interestingly, it is estimated that one in nine state government employees works in the field of corrections.

The industry may experience difficulty finding and keeping qualified employees, since the salaries for correctional officers are not very high. In addition, most prisons are located in rural areas, far from where most of the potential workforce lives or wishes to live. Further, few people want to work in a prison all day or perform shift work. The work can be stressful and hazardous, and correctional officers have one of the highest rates of nonfatal on-the-job injuries.

The diversity of the industry in terms of the broad range of career paths continues to be a great benefit to those seeking advancement. Most employees begin at a basic, entry-level position in a correctional institution, moving upward either within the prison itself or at prisons in other states. Prisons offer management training, certification, and other programs designed to give employees the opportunity to thrive in their current positions and advance in the future.

Additionally, those in the service sectors of the prison industry, such as housekeepers, food servers, and custodial staff, may see personal development in light of an ever-changing industry. For example, better benefits for employees have been offered to entice them to work in a stressful environment.

Annual Earnings

The prison industry is strongly influenced by politics. If the political environment supports controlling crime, more severe sanctions will be assigned to crimes (such as mandatory minimum sentences and "three strikes" legislation), and the prison population will rise. More prisons would need to be built to hold the greater inmate population. Thus, there would be a larger need for correctional officers to staff the prisons. If the trend is to decrease the number of persons in prison by enhancing community sanctions, there would be a smaller need for correctional officers. In 2011, state spending on prisons is projected to reach $40 billion. Spending was $35.6 billion in 2006. Taxes for prison construction are around $6 billion a year, and $2 billion a year for payroll.

According to the U.S. Department of Justice, $3.314 billion was earned in revenue in 2009, and the net cost of operations was $27.959 billion. The most expensive jail budget is found in New York ($1.1 billion), and the lowest is found in North Dakota ($3.5 million). The compound annual growth rate of the industry in the period 2008-2013 is predicted to be 7-13 percent. The median wage for 2009 was $27.74 an hour, or $57,690 annually, and 19,400 job openings are projected from 2008-2018. There were 44,000 employees in 2008. Overall, the jail and prison population changes constantly. Some prisoners are released, some are convicted and transferred to prison, and new offenders are arrested and enter the system. Thus, there will always be a need for correctional officer oversight.

RELATED RESOURCES FOR FURTHER RESEARCH

AMERICAN CORRECTIONAL ASSOCIATION
  206 N Washington St., Suite 200
  Alexandria, VA 22314
  Tel: (703) 224-0000

Fax: (703) 224-0179
http://www.aca.org

AMERICAN JAIL ASSOCIATION
1135 Professional Ct.
Hagerstown, MD 21740
Tel: (301) 790-3939, ext. 24
http://www.corrections.com/aja

FEDERAL BUREAU OF PRISONS
320 1st St. NW
Washington, DC 20534
Tel: (202) 307-3198
http://www.bop.gov

U.S. BUREAU OF JUSTICE STATISTICS
810 7th St. NW
Washington, DC 20531
Tel: (202) 307-0765
http://bjs.ojp.usdoj.gov

U.S. DEPARTMENT OF JUSTICE
950 Pennsylvania Ave. NW
Washington, DC 20530-0001
http://www.justice.gov

ABOUT THE AUTHOR

Gina M. Robertiello has more than fifteen years of professional experience in the education industry. She is a 1991 graduate of Rutgers University and a 1993 graduate of the School of Criminal Justice-Rutgers University, from which she received a Ph.D. in criminal justice in 2000. She has been associated with criminal justice education in New Jersey since 1993, publishing extensively in the areas of police, domestic violence, research methods, victimology, and criminology. She teaches courses at the introductory and advanced levels in the Criminal Justice Department and the Sociology Department at Felician College, in Lodi, New Jersey, where she is a professor and chair of the Criminal Justice Department.

FURTHER READING

ASIS International. *Career Opportunities in Security.* Alexandria, Va.: Author, 2005. Available at http://www.asisonline.org/careercenter/careers2005.pdf.

Barlow, Hugh D., and Scott H. Decker. *Criminology and Public Policy: Putting Theory to Work.* Philadelphia: Temple University Press, 2010.

Culp, Richard F. "The Rise and Stall of Prison Privatization: An Integration of Policy Analysis Perspectives." *Criminal Justice Policy Review* 16, no. 4 (December, 2005): 412-442.

Federal Bureau of Prisons. *Employment Information Handbook.* Washington, D.C.: Author, 2010.

Kerle, Ken E. *Exploring Jail Operations.* Hagerstown, Md.: American Jail Association, 2003.

Lamont, Christopher K. *International Criminal Justice and the Politics of Compliance.* Burlington, Vt.: Ashgate, 2010.

Maguire, Mary, and Dan Okada. *Critical Issues in Crime and Justice: Thought, Policy, and Practice.* Los Angeles: Sage, 2011.

Pelaez, Vicky. *The Prison Industry in the United States: Big Business or a New Form of Slavery.* New York: El Diario-La Prensa, 2005.

Pew Charitable Trusts. *Public Safety, Public Spending: Forecasting America's Prison Population, 2007-2011.* Philadelphia: Author, 2007.

Shoham, S. Giora, Paul Knepper, and Martin Kett. *International Handbook of Criminology.* Boca Raton, Fla.: CRC Press, 2010.

Spivak, Andrew L., and Susan F. Sharp. "Inmate Recidivism as a Measure of Private Prison Performance." *Crime and Delinquency* 54, no. 3 (July, 2008): 482-508.

Sumpter, Melvina. "Faith-Based Prison Programs." *Criminology and Public Policy* 5, no. 3 (August, 2006): 523-528.

Tewksbury, Richard, and Elizabeth Ehrhardt Mustaine. "Insiders' View of Prison Amenities: Beliefs and Perceptions of Correctional Staff Members." *Criminal Justice Review* 30, no. 2 (September, 2005): 174-188.

U.S. Bureau of Justice Statistics. *Jail Inmates at Midyear.* Washington, D.C.: Author, 2009.

_____. *Prison Inmates at Midyear.* Washington, D.C.: Author, 2009.

U.S. Bureau of Labor Statistics. *Career Guide to Industries,* 2010-2011 ed. http://www.bls.gov/oco/cg.

U.S. Census Bureau. North American Industry Classification System (NAICS), 2007. http://

www.census.gov/cgi-bin/sssd/naics/naicsrch?chart=2007.

U.S. Department of Commerce. International Trade Administration. Office of Trade and Industry Information. Industry Trade Data and Analysis. http://ita.doc.gov/td/industry/otea/OTII/OTII-index.html.

Walmsley, Roy. *World Prison Population List.* London: International Center for Prison Studies, 2009.

Day-Care Services

INDUSTRY SNAPSHOT

General Industry: Education and Training

Career Clusters: Education and Training; Human Services

Subcategory Industries: Activity Centers and Day-Care Centers for Disabled Persons, Elderly Persons, and Persons Diagnosed with Mental Retardation; Adult Community Centers (Except Recreational Only); Adult Day Health Care Centers; Adult Day-Care Centers; Babysitting Services; Child Day-Care Centers; Child Day-Care Services; Group Day-Care Centers; Head Start Programs, Separate from Schools; Infant Day-Care Centers; Infant Day-Care Services; Nursery Schools and Preschools; Senior Citizens Centers

Related Industries: Hospital Care and Services; Personal Services; Private Education Industry; Public Elementary and Secondary Education Industry; Residential Medical Care Industry

Annual Domestic Revenues: Child day-care services: $31 billion USD (Research and Markets, 2009); adult day-care services: $25 billion USD (U.S. Census Bureau, 2007)

NAICS Numbers: 6244, 624120

INDUSTRY DEFINITION

Summary

The day-care industry provides care and supervision to persons who require such services for less than twenty-four hours a day. Care receivers include children, adults with physical or mental disabilities, and seniors. The child day-care industry comprises establishments that offer paid care mainly for infants, toddlers, and preschoolers, as well as independent before- and after-school programs for older children. Adult day care provides assistance with the tasks of daily living for a portion of each day. It represents a viable alternative to placement in residential institutions.

History of the Industry

Caring for children outside the home was not viewed as a significant occupation until the mid-seventeenth century, when John Amos Comenius outlined his vision of early childhood education in *Didactica magna* (1633-1638; *The Great Didactic of John Amos Comenius: Now for the First Time Englished*, 1896; better known as *The Great Didactic*). Facilities that cared for children outside their parents' homes emerged in Europe in the late eighteenth and early nineteenth centuries. These precursors of modern day care were mainly charitable institutions, known as "day nurseries." or "crèches." The Société des Crèches was recognized by the French government in 1869.

Some debate surrounds the timing of the first American day care's establishment. A Quaker day nursery existed in Philadelphia in 1795, and a Boston infant school is mentioned in a document from 1828. One of the earliest facilities, the New York Day Nursery, was established in 1854. Founded by charitable institutions, early day-care facilities had primarily custodial characters and served working mothers. Supervision was emphasized over education.

Historical circumstances and new research in education and psychology brought an expansion of the child-care system in the twentieth century. The Great Depression sent more mothers into the workforce and changed the prevailing attitude toward day care. Nursery schools became involved in education. At the time, large-scale institutionalized day care was employed in the Soviet Union. In the United States, the Lanham Act of 1941 provided funds for the construction and operation of day-care centers serving the children of female defense workers. World War II had turned child day care into a public issue.

The postwar years saw a greater involvement of the day-care system in the intellectual development of children. In the mid-1960's, Head Start was introduced and began subsidizing day care for underprivileged children. The program further strengthened the association between day care and education. Between 1970 and 1995, the proportion of U.S. women who had children and participated in the workforce grew from 30 percent to over 60 percent and the need for child day-care arrangements increased. The end of the twentieth century and the beginning of the twenty-first brought several scientific studies emphasizing the need for high-quality care that supports children's development. Adequate regulation and supervision of day-care operations became a priority. In the 1990's, the National Association for Family Child Care was formed. Together with similar associations abroad, this organization helped move family day care toward better standards of care and professionalism.

Adult day care originated in Europe and initially took the form of daily hospitalization. Doctor Lionel Cosin pioneered this form of care, both in Great Britain and in the United States, in the 1960's. A therapeutic day program at the Cherry Hospital in Goldsboro, North Carolina, prepared patients for discharge and taught them independent living skills. The system expanded and gained adherents, mainly through grassroots efforts to obtain recognition and funding. In California, adult day-care establishments emerged in the 1970's. In 1985, the state began requiring such facilities to acquire specialized licenses, distinct from those required by child day-care facilities. Adult day-care program managers recognized the need to establish national, standardized criteria that would allow caregivers to rate and better describe the services they provide. The National Adult Day Services Association (NADSA) was founded in 1979. Since then, these services have become valuable, community-based care options for seniors and people with disabilities.

The Industry Today

The number of families with two working parents has increased dramatically during the late twentieth and early twenty-first centuries. A major concern for these working parents is identifying quality child care, especially for children under the age of five. The child day-care industry fills this growing need for nonrelative care through several types of services. Children too young to attend school can be cared for in dedicated child day-care centers or in providers' homes (known as "family day care"). Older children may receive day-care services when they are not in school, attending before- or after-school programs or private summer school programs. Formal child day-care centers include preschools (part- and full-day), child-care centers, school- and community-based prekindergartens, and Head Start and Early Head Start centers. Family child-care services are provided in private homes, for a fee, and include most of the self-employed workers in this industry. (Unpaid care providers, such as friends and relatives, are not part of the industry. Child-care providers working in their charges' homes, such as nannies, are part of the personal services industry.)

The rapidly growing for-profit sector of the day-care industry includes independent centers that function as parts of local or national companies. Nonprofit child day-care establishments may function within religious institutions, colleges, public schools, the Ys (formerly Young Men's Christian

Associations, or YMCAs), other social and recreation centers, social service agencies, or various worksites. The federally funded Head Start and Early Head Start programs are strong nonprofit programs that provide underprivileged children with educational, social, and health services. Before- and after-school programs may be operated by public school systems, local community centers, or private organizations.

According to the U.S. Bureau of Labor Statistics (BLS), preschool teachers, teacher assistants, and child-care workers represented almost 78 percent of wage and salary jobs in the day-care industry in 2008. Approximately 44 percent of workers in the industry had high school diplomas or less education, reflecting the minimal training requirements for most jobs in this field. About 29 percent of all employees worked part time in 2008. Dissatisfaction with pay, minimal benefits, and stressful working conditions cause many workers to leave the industry, leading to a high turnover rate and the need constantly to recruit new workers into the industry.

Over twenty federal funding and regulatory avenues for early childhood education exist, and every state has one of a spectrum of differently funded and coordinated programs. There are no structures similar to school districts for early childhood education programs, no federal laws that set uniform expectations for teacher qualifications, and no uniform accountability or reporting systems. The quality of American child care represents a significant problem. Several European countries set high standards of training for early childhood education personnel, such as requiring the majority of caregivers to have college degrees, and strongly emphasize family child care. The United States, by contrast, struggles with a short supply of high-quality programs, as well as limited state requirements and monitoring. Close monitoring of this sector—which has such a profound impact on children's cognitive, social, and emotional development—is acutely necessary but lacking.

Given the high rate of turnover in the U.S. industry, a lack of continuity of care—which can have profound psychological repercussions for young children—has become a particularly serious problem. Improving wages, benefits, and education opportunities for caregivers is critical for improving staff retention and increasing continuity of care. At present, working parents are the main funders of child care, but their budgets are often stretched thin. The question of how to ensure their children grow up in stable, competent, well-paid day-care environments has no easy answer.

In general, three main types of adult day centers exist: social centers (providing meals, recreation, and minimal or no health-related services), medical or health centers (providing social activities, as well as more intensive health and therapeutic services), and specialized cen-

A woman at an adult day-care center in Chino, California, hugs a therapy dog. (AP/Wide World Photos)

ters (dedicated to specific adult populations, such as those with dementias or developmental disabilities). The National Adult Day Services Association (NADSA) has identified over forty-six hundred day programs operating in the United States. According to a study conducted by the Wake Forest University School of Medicine, adult day centers provide care for 150,000 recipients each day. Even so, there is a shortage of such centers in most parts of the United States. The demand for them is expected to increase as the baby boomers age and more of them require care. Approximately 78 percent of adult day centers are operated on a nonprofit or public basis; the remaining 22 percent are for-profit facilities.

Adult day programs provide their charges with structured schedules in safe, supportive environments; they help functionally impaired seniors and disabled adults remain in their communities, retain a degree of independence, and maintain self-worth. They also provide respite for caregivers, in addition to the possibility of maintaining employment. Adult day services that are organized according to a medical model provide medical and rehabilitation day treatment—including physician visits; nursing care; podiatric exams; and physical, occupational, and speech therapy—in a secure environment. The recipients of these services are often individuals with dementia (including Alzheimer's), diabetes, cardiovascular conditions, Down syndrome, and mental illnesses, as well as those who have suffered strokes. Frail elderly people and people recovering from traumatic injuries can also benefit from these services.

The social model offers supervised activities, group support, and companionship. Participants in this model generally require some assistance with daily activities (such as dressing, eating, or bathing), but they do not need skilled nursing care. These social programs also provide transportation, meals, caregiver support groups, referral services, and community outreach programs. If participants require medication during the day, it is usually self-administered.

Approximately thirty-five states license adult day programs, of which twenty require all such programs to be licensed. A center may be licensed as a social or a medical center, or both. Each program determines which level of licensure is most appropriate.

INDUSTRY MARKET SEGMENTS

Child day-care establishments are found across the United States, mirroring the distribution of the population. However, they are less common in rural areas, where there are fewer children to support distinct facilities. Child day-care operations vary in size, from self-employed persons each caring for a few children in private homes to large corporate-sponsored centers with numerous employees and children. Almost 86 percent of all wage and salary jobs in 2008 were located in establishments with fewer than fifty employees. Adult day-care facilities have variable enrollment numbers but on average host twenty-five to thirty participants each day. Such programs may be provided in family homes, freestanding centers, or multiuse facilities such as churches, schools, and senior centers.

Small Businesses

According to the BLS, opportunities for self-employment in the day-care industry are among the best in the economy. Approximately 430,000 persons are self-employed or unpaid family day-care workers. This number reflects the ease of entering the child day-care business. Small businesses are generally single-establishment companies that meet specified minimum annual sales (usually $1,000). This segment of the industry comprises mainly family day-care operations caring for up to ten or fifteen clients. Most family child-care establishments are small, one-person operations that care for one to six children. These providers are self-employed and account for approximately 33 percent of child-care workers. Some hire a small number of additional workers, such as drivers, aides, and substitute caregivers. All states and many municipalities have their own regulations governing the maximum number of children and the number of children of a specific age that a home facility can host. In New York City, for example, a maximum of six children are allowed in a family day-care establishment—five if any of the children are under the age of two.

Many home day-care facilities are licensed and proven to meet certain standards with respect to caregiver-to-child ratio, space (for example, minimum square footage and the presence of fences), sanitation, and so on. Some states do not require these facilities to be licensed, and, in consequence, some facilities do not apply for licenses. Each state publishes minimum standards for health and safety at licensed centers. These include medical information that must be on file, as well as rules involving communicable diseases, hygienic practices, and storage of chemicals, among other factors. States also issue guidelines for serving balanced meals and nutritional snacks to children or adults at day-care facilities. Licensing is often required for family-care establishments accommodating more than six children.

An adult day-care home is a program operating in a single-family dwelling that is lived in by its owner. Such programs provide care, services, and supervision to at least three but not more than eight to fifteen elderly or disabled adults (depending on the state). Small adult commercial day-care centers with similar capacities also exist; they are either private, for-profit, or part of organizations. The demand for these facilities is very high, and their number is insufficient.

Emergency medical care can be provided in these home-based facilities, but routine medical care is usually not available. Depending on their model of operation, commercial and organization-based facilities may hire nurses and therapists. Many medical day-care centers are small businesses. They are licensed to administer medications, make medical assessments, and provide various forms of therapy. While home health care may be appropriate for some seniors, adult day health care is often preferable for a variety of reasons, including the fact that it allows primary caretakers to work or get a break.

Potential Annual Earnings Scale. According to the BLS, the average annual income of a child day-care provider in 2009 was $18,900, and the average annual income of an adult care provider was $20,560.

Clientele Interaction. In family child-care homes, children are cared for by the same persons and share the premises with one or two other children of similar age and perhaps three or four others in different age groups. Family child-care and adult day-care providers need to have excellent social and leadership skills. Children's relationships with their parents or caregivers are inherently close. Caring for children and disabled adults involves a high level of responsibility and dedication.

A genuine love of children is often described as an obligatory trait for family child day-care operators. Interacting with clients requires friendliness and tolerance, in addition to tact and discipline in following the established rules of one's facility. A pleasant and professional demeanor is a valuable asset. Workers have the unique opportunity to influence children's development and become important, memorable parts of their lives. Lasting relationships are often forged with adult charges and their families.

Care providers often describe their professional lives as combining business relationships with parents or caregivers and family-like connections with the children or adults in their care. However, court cases highlight the need for day-care providers to have substantial knowledge of relevant laws. Providers can ask parents to sign consent forms that outline their policies and the procedures to be followed in special situations and emergencies. In addition, the responsibilities and expectations of both parties should be clearly outlined.

Amenities, Atmosphere, and Physical Grounds. Because home day-care facilities may or may not be licensed or meet state and local standards, their physical grounds and atmosphere vary widely. Some homes are minimally modified to accommodate a large number of children, while others undergo extensive changes that turn them into miniature versions of formal commercial day-care centers. More extensive remodeling is usually needed in houses for children with special needs. Multiple beds are required to accommodate clients of night-care facilities. Providers are responsible for purchasing furnishings such as high chairs, infant seats, booster chairs, child-sized tables and chairs, shelves, cribs, cots, and mats, blankets, sheets, pillows, diaper-changing tables, swings, sand boxes, and diaper pails.

The homelike, less institutional atmosphere of small home day-care facilities is sought by many parents and caregivers. Their grounds most resemble those of family residences, often with renovations or added amenities. A provider's home generally reflects the age of the charges it serves. Children respond well to brightly lit, stimulating, colorful environments that are stocked with a variety of age-appropriate toys and games. Outdoor play areas are often available. Childproofing is a priority, as are amenities designed to ensure senior safety. Some owners make their entire homes available to their charges, while others use only specific areas, maintaining a separation between business areas and dwelling space. This decision depends on state regulations, as well as an owner's preference. Designated activity, eating, bathing, and changing or toilet-training areas should exist. Small offices are usually also needed. Owners may or may not provide transportation for their clients.

Keeping educated and abreast of new developments in the day-care field is important, both for clients and for providers. Providers should be certified in first aid and cardiopulmonary resuscitation (CPR). Facilities are usually wheelchair accessible. In small adult day-care facilities, meals are prepared according to each participant's individual needs and served in special dining rooms. Medications are supervised. A garden or outdoor patio usually exists.

Typical Number of Employees. Most small day-care businesses employ from one to four people. Usually, one adult can supervise up to six children. If a business has more than six charges, it requires additional staff.

Traditional Geographic Locations. Small day-care facilities for children or adults are present in most locations, although they are more common in cities and towns than in rural areas.

Pros of Working for a Small Day-Care Facility. Day-care owner-operators have the freedom to decide on many parameters of their businesses, such as the age and number of their charges, fees, hours of operation, and amenities. They can establish their reputations with different categories of working parents or caregivers. Many caregivers, for example, may not work traditional nine-to-five jobs, so they may have distinct day-care needs that small flexible facilities are well equipped to serve. Researching the market in a particular area can help a business owner decide what type of program to implement. For example, facilities may operate full time during weekday hours, after school, regu-

The limited number of children served by small facilities ensures that each will receive more individualized attention. (©Dreamstime.com)

The workday for those caring for preschoolers and infants is often longer than ten hours. (©Christopher Futcher/iStock-photo.com)

lar but nontraditional hours, or on demand. Small day-care facilities may also offer more freedom in terms of curricula and lesson plans than do some larger facilities, in which curricula may be already in place.

Start-up costs for day-care businesses are generally modest (as low as a few hundred dollars), unless a provider's home requires substantial remodeling. Providers may care for their own children or relatives alongside their paying customers, generating a comfortable income and filling a need in the community. Some providers enjoy integrating their work with domestic activities such as cooking and gardening, which can also be beneficial for their charges. The limited number of children or adult charges served by small facilities ensures that each will receive more individualized attention and makes it easier for workers to respond to specific care needs than at larger facilities. The likelihood of contamination and sickness may also be lower in a small facility.

Cons of Working for a Small Day-Care Facility. According to the BLS, self-employed day-care workers tend to work longer hours than their salaried counterparts. For those caring for preschoolers and infants, the normal workday is longer than ten hours. Because the start-up costs in this industry are low, qualifying for a bank loan can prove difficult. In addition to providing quality care for children, family care providers must often concern themselves with the financial, administrative, and marketing aspects of their businesses. In small adult day-care businesses, center directors often function as social workers and nurses, in addition to their management duties.

Businesses need solid financial record-keeping systems, which may require them to hire consultants or accountants. In addition, day-care providers who work out of their homes must purchase their own supplies and provide (or commission) their own advertising. They may have little time to devote to educating their charges or developing curricula.

The income of family day-care facilities is limited by state laws that cap the number of individuals for whom they can care. For this reason, many small day-care operators ultimately decide to open additional facilities, thus expanding their client bases and incomes. Providers must make sure their immediate families are supportive and understand the time and energy commitment their businesses require. Young children may have difficulty sharing their parents' attention with others. Care must be taken so that neighbors are not inconvenienced by the arrival and departure of clients. In addition, they should be made aware of the possibility of increased noise levels during activity times and informed of the steps taken to reduce them. While this type of business fosters a close interaction between providers and clients, it may be difficult to maintain a balance between business and friendship.

Costs

Payroll and Benefits: Small day-care facilities with more than one employee usually pay hourly wages. These vary according to employees' expertise and the type of work involved, but they are generally minimal, and workers receive few if any benefits. Some owners, however, do offer medical and dental plans, training allowances, and subsidized child care. Owner-operators of day-care facilities receive their facilities' profits as income.

Supplies: Depending on the age of their charges, small day-care facilities may need toys, books, games, musical instruments, art and craft items, food, bedding, office supplies, medical supplies, and information technology. Fuel is needed for field trips or daily transportation, if provided.

External Services: Day-care businesses may contract legal, accounting, maintenance, or advertising services. They must also pay for insurance against lawsuits, accidents, and other unexpected liabilities.

Utilities: Day-care businesses typically pay for water, sewage, electricity, gas, telephone, cable television, and Internet services.

Taxes: Small facilities often pay few taxes directly. Instead, their owners may report the businesses' income as personal income and pay business-related taxes (including self-employment taxes) on their personal returns. Owners of home-based businesses may also be able to write off a portion of their rent or mortgage payments and other home expenses, including utilities, as business expenses.

Midsize Businesses

Midsize facilities include child day-care centers, school- and community-based prekindergarten establishments, and Head Start and Early Head Start centers. Many adult day-care centers operate at this level, on a for-profit, nonprofit, or public basis. Some of them are affiliated with multiservice entities such as home care, assisted living, or nursing facilities or hospitals. These entities may offer elder care as an outpatient service to the neighboring population on a daily basis. They also provide respite care for the duration of a week or weekend. Senior centers may also offer senior day care as one of their services.

Potential Annual Earnings Scale. According to the BLS, the average annual income of a child day-care provider in 2009 was $18,900, and the average annual income of an adult care provider was $20,560. Supervisors of adult care staff earned an average of $34,680, while preschool day-care teachers earned an average of $24,560. Median annual wages for most occupations in the child day-care industry range between $17,000 and $38,000. With the possible exception of public school-based and prekindergarten programs and some unionized centers, early childhood education teachers usually work for much lower wages than do teachers in grades K-12, and formal pay scales are infrequent. Their compensation comes from various funding sources and often includes no provision for professional development. Adult day-care providers are similarly relatively poorly compensated, although registered nurses in the field earned an average of $60,740 in 2009. The median expected salary for a typical adult day-care director in the United States is $73,852.

Clientele Interaction. Early childhood education teachers have an important and rewarding mission: to help children grow and learn. Their work is oftentimes both routine and challenging. They must continuously stand, bend, stoop, lift, and walk, while trying to divide their attention equitably among several children; their only real respite is naptime. Workplace injuries are not uncommon. Interactions with parents are somewhat more formal than in small family day-care establishments.

One mission of an adult day-care program is to promote social and personal interaction. Each client's schedule is outlined in an individual plan of care. By interacting with participants and staff, functionally or mentally disabled clients can develop new skills and improve their self-esteem. In such programs, personal service, a supportive atmosphere, and strong community spirit are the norm. Staff emphasize forming enduring friendships and integrating clients into their centers' communities. Nursing, various forms of therapy, activities, counseling, socialization, nutritious meals, and transportation to and from such centers are designed to help adult charges retain the maximum possible degree of independence.

Amenities, Atmosphere, and Physical Grounds. Early childhood education facilities can function as freestanding centers or as parts of other organizations. They often occupy a portion of a larger building, including a different room for each age group, and they may also include separate play and dining spaces, bathrooms, changing areas, activity areas, fenced-in playgrounds, offices, and kitchens. All spaces should be child-safe, bright, clean, and decorated in engaging colors. A variety of age-appropriate toys, books, and games is typically provided.

Adult day-care programs are offered in many types of settings, including stand-alone facilities, storefront properties in shopping centers and strip malls, senior centers, nursing facilities, churches, hospitals, and schools. Regardless of the location, all must be accessible for persons with disabilities, well-lit, and barrier-free. They should include dining spaces, activity areas, staff offices, libraries, bathrooms (a minimum of one toilet for every ten participants, according to NADSA), therapy and nursing rooms, bathtub or shower rooms, kitchens, and laundry areas. NADSA recommends a minimum of sixty square feet of space per participant. Provisions for participants' independence and privacy should be made. Activity spaces comprise areas for both big and small groups and are generally supplied with games and craft items that support mental acuity. Outdoor areas facilitate gardening and relaxation. The overall goal is to achieve a noninstitutional feel, while minimizing client risk.

Typical Number of Employees. Midsize day-care businesses employ approximately five to twenty workers and care for fifteen to sixty charges. States have specific guidelines governing the ratio of caregivers to children in each age group; usually, the desirable ratio varies between one to three for infants and one to eight for four-year-olds (the lower, the better). Staff turnover rates in early childhood education facilities are often very high, mainly because those facilities pay low wages. In adult day care, a minimum staff-to-participant ratio of one to six is recommended by NADSA. This ratio is likely to be smaller (for example, one to four) for participants with more severe impairments, such as dementia.

Traditional Geographic Locations. Midsize day-care facilities can be found in a variety of locations, including cities, suburbs, and small towns. They are less common in rural areas, because those areas have smaller pools of potential participants. Studies indicate that rural areas tend to be disadvantaged with respect to community-based health services, but few rigorous reports are available on adult day care. Using data from a national survey of 822 adult day-care centers, one study found significant differences between urban and rural centers in structure, process, and client measures. Rural adult day-care centers tend to have lower enrollment rates and a significantly less impaired client population that requires fewer clinical services. Rural centers also reported less involvement of the family and community in various activities.

Pros of Working for a Midsize Day-Care Facility. Part-time jobs are often available at midsize facilities, expanding the options for those seeking flexible employment. In fact, according to the BLS, approximately 29 percent of day-care workers are employed part time. In addition, midsize facilities may provide opportunities for workers to concentrate on particular age groups, in well-defined age-specific classrooms. Many private and public preschool programs operate during the usual school year, that is, for nine or ten months out of each year. Family child-care providers, by contrast, may have more flexible hours and daily routines, but they may work long or unusual hours and need to make special provisions in order to take vacations.

At midsize facilities, it is often easier than it is at small facilities for workers to take breaks during the day, as they are more likely to have colleagues that can cover for them. Staffs at such facilities are relatively small, but they generally have at least one dedicated director or administrator. Thus, care-givers can focus on providing care and teaching and can leave their facilities' administrative duties to their administrative staffs.

Cons of Working for a Midsize Day-Care Facility. In a formal day-care center, the children are divided by age into "groups" or "rooms." A staff member and one or two other caregivers attend to the needs of five to fifteen children in each room. (The number of children in a room varies, depending on the children's age group.) If they are not self-employed, workers may not be able to adjust their working hours or make significant decisions regarding wages, program activities, and amenities. Salaries are generally low. Curricula for each age group at a facility may be approved and imple-mented by administrators or by previous employ-ees, so individual teachers and caregivers have less freedom to implement their own ideas. There are no opportunities to integrate domestic and curric-ular activities. The high staff turnover rate at most facilities can prove stressful for workers and chil-dren alike. Obstacles cited by adult day-care provid-ers include inadequate funding, difficulty recruit-ing and retaining staff, and problems maintaining enrollment and attendance at the levels needed to cover operating costs.

Costs

Payroll and Benefits: Day-care facilities often pay hourly wages, although some pay annual sala-ries, especially to administrators. Salaries are generally quite low in this field, and benefits are usually not provided—particularly given the high percentage of part-time employees in the industry. Nonprofit and religiously affiliated centers generally pay higher wages and offer more generous benefits than do for-profit estab-lishments.

Supplies: Day-care facilities require a multitude of items, including toys, books, games, paper prod-ucts, musical instruments, art and craft items, newspaper and magazine subscriptions, food, linens, medical supplies, cleaning supplies, of-fice supplies, personal care accessories, and in-formation technology products. Fuel is needed for field trips and daily transportation. The

Child and Adult Care Food Program (CACFP) reimburses public, nonprofit, and for-profit nonresidential child-care centers; Head Start and Early Head Start centers; preschool pro-grams; before- and after-school hours programs; and after-school programs in low income areas at free, reduced-price, or paid rates for eligible meals and snacks served to enrolled children.

External Services: Day-care businesses may con-tract legal, accounting, laundry, maintenance, transportation, catering, or advertising services. Specialists such as podiatrists, therapists, and personal grooming personnel are periodically present in some adult day-care facilities. Insur-ance is needed to cover the potential costs of lawsuits, accidents, and other unexpected liabil-ities.

Utilities: Utilities typically include water and sew-age, electricity, gas, telephone, cable television, and Internet access.

Taxes: For-profit facilities pay local, state, and fed-eral income taxes, as well as applicable property taxes.

Large Businesses

Large day-care centers may operate indepen-dently or as part of business chains. According to the U.S. Business Administration, some of the lead-ing day-care chains are KinderCare, founded in 1969, with more than 850 locations in forty states and Canada; LaPetite Academy, started in 1970, with 358 centers in twenty states; ARA Services, with 142 schools in eleven states; and Gerber Products with 57 Gerber Children's Centers in six states. Em-ployer-operated day-care facilities may also feature sizable staffs. Fewer adult day cares are large enter-prises, however some do accommodate one hun-dred to two hundred participants. Most states re-quire licensing processes to operate adult day health care businesses, as well as a state licensing process to be approved for Medicare or Medicaid reimbursement.

Potential Annual Earnings Scale. According to the BLS, the average annual income of a child day-care provider in 2009 was $18,900, and the av-erage annual income of an adult care provider was $20,560. Supervisors of adult care staff earned an average of $34,680, while preschool day-care teach-ers earned an average of $24,560. Median annual wages for most occupations in the child day-care industry range between $17,000 and $38,000. With the possible exception of public school-based and prekindergarten programs and some unionized centers, early childhood education teachers usually work for much lower wages than do teachers in grades K-12, and formal pay scales are infrequent. Their compensation comes from various funding sources and often includes no provision for professional development. Adult day-care providers are similarly relatively poorly compensated, although registered nurses in the field earned an average of $60,740 in 2009. The median expected salary for a typical adult day-care director in the United States is $73,852.

Clientele Interaction. Caregivers and teachers have a duty to respond to their charges' needs promptly and efficiently. A group of workers cares for a number of children, according to highly variable state regulations governing adult-to-child ratio. Typically, younger children are cared for in smaller groups, with higher ratios. One worker may be responsible for three or four infants, or even more toddlers, preschoolers, or school-aged children. Policies and rules regarding operating hours are strictly enforced. Parents receive daily reports of their children's activities, food intake, and sleep.

Adult day-care programs facilitate age-appropriate activities for their charges, designed to promote mental acuity through stimulating challenges coupled with social interaction. Seniors and other categories of participants have access to puzzles, board games, bingo, indoor golfing, arts and crafts projects, book clubs, holiday celebrations, intergenerational programs, lectures, and other cultural events.

Program assistants and nurses focus on preserving and enhancing the functional status of their charges, while improving their social interactions and self-esteem. Caregiver groups and seminars support family members. Programs are available up to eight hours per day, usually five days per week. Some facilities may offer half-day services on Saturdays.

Amenities, Atmosphere, and Physical Grounds. Large facilities often operate in multilevel buildings and feature separate classrooms for various age groups, miniature art centers, reading centers, sensory play areas, kitchens, and staff offices. All indoor spaces should be child-safe, bright,

clean, and decorated in engaging colors. Various age-appropriate toys, books, and games are provided. Outdoor areas are equipped with safety barriers, soft materials (rubber, sand, or mulch) to cushion falls, and a variety of play stations. Regularly scheduled activities or curricula are in place. Work environments and their inherent difficulties are analogous to those present in midsize businesses.

Adult day-care centers also have many characteristics in common with midsize facilities. Their goal is to provide warm, homelike environments for their charges. These centers may occupy stand-alone buildings or be part of multibusiness developments. They usually feature enclosed courtyards or gardens, dining rooms, big and small activity rooms, libraries, therapy rooms, kitchens, bathrooms, shower rooms, laundry areas, and staff offices. Some centers include special areas for individuals with memory loss. Most spaces are accessible for persons with disabilities. Gift, beauty, and barber shops may be present on their premises.

Typical Number of Employees. Most large day-care businesses employ between twenty and sixty people, although few child-care facilities employ more than fifty. The typical number of charges cared for by such facilities is greater than sixty.

Traditional Geographic Locations. Large child day-care facilities are located in urban and suburban areas. Adult day-care facilities have a similar distribution, with a relatively small number of centers operating in rural settings.

Pros of Working for a Large Day-Care Facility. Large facilities offer staff members more opportunities for part-time work. Curricula, supplies, and materials are provided. Workers can concentrate their efforts on specific age groups, and they generally have few or no administrative duties to fulfill. Employers often offer incentives for their employees to participate in college courses, seminars, or workshops. Although the general day-care industry profit margin averages only 5 percent, the profit margin potential is actually much higher for large organizations; these have a cost advantage and can take advantage of economies of scale.

Cons of Working for a Large Day-Care Facility. Large child day-care facilities have very high staff turnover rates, which can hinder collaboration among staff members and add to the stress levels inherent in their jobs. Bonuses and raises are infrequent. Many large adult day-care programs have difficulty ensuring adequate funding and attendance, as well as recruiting and retaining staff. Maintaining a homelike feel in a large facility may be difficult.

Costs

Payroll and Benefits: Day-care facilities often pay hourly wages, although some pay annual salaries, especially to administrators. Salaries are generally quite low in child day-care facilities, and benefits are usually not provided—particularly given the high percentage of part-time employees in the industry. Some businesses offer free or discounted child care to their employees, others provide funds for college courses or seminars.

Employees of adult day-care facilities generally receive somewhat higher compensation, especially registered nurses. Benefits are often offered to full-time staff. Employers may also provide training opportunities.

Supplies: Day-care facilities require a multitude of items, including toys, books, games, paper products, musical instruments, art and craft items, newspaper and magazine subscriptions, food, linens, medical supplies, cleaning supplies, office supplies, personal care accessories, and information technology products. Fuel is needed for field trips and daily transportation. The CACFP reimburses public, nonprofit, and for-profit nonresidential child-care centers; Head Start and Early Head Start centers; preschool programs; before- and after-school hours programs; and after-school programs in low-income areas at free, reduced-price, or paid rates for eligible meals and snacks served to enrolled children.

External Services: Day-care businesses may contract legal, accounting, laundry, maintenance, transportation, catering, or advertising services. Specialists such as podiatrists, therapists, and personal grooming personnel are periodically present in some adult day-care facilities. Insurance is needed to cover the potential costs of lawsuits, accidents, and other unexpected liabilities.

Utilities: Utilities typically include water and sewage, electricity, gas, telephone, cable television, and Internet access.

Taxes: For-profit facilities pay local, state, and federal income taxes, as well as applicable property taxes.

ORGANIZATIONAL STRUCTURE AND JOB ROLES

The organizational structure and distribution of tasks in a day-care facility depend on several factors, such as the size of the establishment, age of the participants, and model of operation. Small facilities are frequently operated by their owners, who may or may not employ a small number of aides. At the other end of the spectrum, large adult centers are staffed by multidisciplinary teams that include nurses, therapists, social workers, and caregivers.

The following umbrella categories apply to businesses in the day-care industry:

- Business Management
- Caregiving and Health Services
- Education and Activities
- Social Assistance
- Facilities and Security
- Food Services
- Transportation Services
- Marketing

Business Management

Child day-care directors fulfill administrative duties, such as processing enrollments, keeping attendance, maintaining health and safety records, ordering supplies, and keeping billing records. In some centers, directors create snack and meal menus in accordance with federal guidelines. In addition, they manage staff, create work schedules, ensure that the proper child-to-caregiver ratios are maintained, and communicate with parents. Directors may have advanced degrees in education. In some instances, experience can compensate for the absence of a pertinent degree. According to the Center for the Study of Child Care Employment, only twenty states have some type of director credential requirement, and many set few or no preservice training or education requirements. Large day-care centers also employ support personnel such as assistant directors, administrative assistants (bookkeepers), and receptionists. Assistants and book-keepers, who usually hold at least an associate's degree, help directors maintain center records.

Some of the overseeing duties for adult day-care directors are similar to those of child day-care directors. They often have degrees in nonprofit management, health care, social work, or geriatric care, which enable them to hire nurses experienced in working with seniors or disabled clients and to keep their facilities safe and secure. Managers or the activities directors develop program activities and tailor them to the needs of individual participants. In large adult heath day-care facilities, it is the responsibility of the health services coordinator (usually a registered nurse) to manage the array of health services provided, including internal or external medical staff and caregivers. The average annual compensation for these positions is approximately $60,000.

Business management occupations may include the following:

- Owner-operator
- Child Day-Care Director
- Adult Day-Care Director
- Adult Day-Care Activity Coordinator
- Adult Day-Care Health Services Coordinator
- Marketing Coordinator
- Assistant Director
- Administrative Assistant
- Bookkeeper

Caregiving and Health Services

Each state regulates adult day-care centers differently, but NADSA provides overall directions in its Standards and Guidelines for Adult Day Care. Health day-care centers employ or arrange for the participation of a full range of licensed, reliable health care professionals who care for elderly and disabled individuals. These establishments often employ experienced full-time registered nurses with degrees from reputable universities, who pro-

---

OCCUPATION PROFILE

Occupational Therapist

Considerations	Qualifications
Description	Assesses disabled or injured people and creates and implements rehabilitation plan to restore independence and ability to work and function.
Career cluster	Health Science
Interests	Data; people; things
Working conditions	Work inside
Minimum education level	Bachelor's degree
Physical exertion	Medium work
Physical abilities	Unexceptional/basic fitness
Opportunities for experience	Military service; volunteer work
Licensure and certification	Required
Employment outlook	Faster-than-average growth expected
Holland interest score	SRE

Note: See volume 1, "Publisher's Note," for an explanation of the Holland interest score.

vide and supervise the necessary nursing services for each charge, review service plans, keep patient records, educate clients, conduct assessments, and attend to emergencies. They often supervise licensed practical nurses.

Day-care nurses administer medications, change wound dressings, and monitor overall health. Many nurses concentrate on mental or physical health care services for certain patient categories, such as Alzheimer's care. Some nurses and aides help provide transportation services to and from their facilities. Others work with nutritionists and cooks to ensure that participants receive adequate meals and snacks throughout the day. Registered nurses in the industry earned mean annual salaries of $60,740 in 2009, while licensed practical and vocational nurses earned $40,210 on average. Hands-on help with bathing, changing, and eating is provided by certified nursing assistants and other program assistants. Such health care support staff earned an average of $21,000 in 2009. Additional caregivers and companions may have minimal training but play important roles in assisting program participants at all times.

Ideally, therapists who participate in adult day-care programs have degrees from accredited programs and are certified in their respective fields through national certifying programs. Physical therapists develop programs, games, and activities for elderly clients. Mental health therapists use music and art to communicate with participants and encourage them to socialize. Speech therapists work on improving communication skills through vocal exercises and cognitive methods. Occupational therapists use multiple methods to support and teach participants to lead more independent, productive lives. Mean annual wages for these professionals range from $42,780 for occupational therapists to $62,700 for speech-language pathologists. Some child day-care programs also have in-house nurses, but this is not common.

Caregiving and health services occupations may include the following:

- Adult Day-Care Health Services Coordinator
- Registered Nurse
- Licensed Practical Nurse
- Physical Therapist
- Speech-Language Therapist
- Mental Health Therapist
- Occupational Therapist
- Program Assistant
- Nursing Assistant

Education and Activities

Teaching is considered an important mission of child day-care centers. Usually, a group of adults coteaches a number of children. Depending on the age of the children in a particular classroom, the duties of child-care workers and teachers may include the following:

- Keeping daily records on each child's meals, activities, sleep, and medications
- Directing and monitoring children's play activities
- Reading to children and providing basic painting, drawing, crafts, and music instruction
- Introducing mathematical and scientific concepts
- Teaching personal hygiene and habits such as dressing, eating, resting, and toilet use
- Changing diapers
- Helping prepare food (including formula) and serve meals
- Coordinating rest periods
- Organizing, storing, and sanitizing toys and other play materials
- Helping children with homework
- Supporting children's social and emotional development
- Employing discipline methods
- Identifying signs of emotional or developmental problems in children and informing parents

Workers in before- and after-school programs help students with their homework or engage them in extracurricular activities, including field trips, sports, computer learning, and art projects. Some child-care workers take children to school in the morning and pick them up from school in the afternoon.

Standards for early childhood education teacher qualifications vary widely among different geographic areas, program types, and funding situations. Each state sets its own early childhood education teacher standards, but federal programs such as Head Start are governed by their own, national standards. Some facilities require only a high school diploma and little preservice preparation, while others recommend at least a bachelor's degree. Early childhood education is generally characterized by an emphasis on in-service training. Instructors without bachelor's degrees are encouraged to attend college part time while teaching, in order to earn such degrees. Community colleges and community-based training organizations play important roles in teacher preparation. Many workers enroll in formal programs to receive training in education, nutrition, and psychology. Some two-year colleges offer associate's degrees in preschool or early childhood education. Teaching certification is often required to attain higher-level positions. Average wages for early childhood education workers vary between $9 and $13 per hour, depending on training and facility.

Activities such as painting are an important part of both child and adult day care. (©Orangeline/Dreamstime.com)

Both models of adult day care provide therapeutic activities. Many facilities employ activity coordinators and staff. Their mission is to lead, teach, and encourage clients to participate in games, crafts, cooking, gardening, exercise, field trips, films, community projects, intergenerational programs, and other mentally or physically stimulating activities. Ideally, activity directors have associate's or bachelor's degrees in therapeutic recreation or gerontology. Working closely with their program managers, they evaluate the needs of program members, develop appropriate activity plans, help train and evaluate program assistants and drivers, supervise the program assistants, develop driver schedules, oversee client transportation, and supervise volunteers. Program assistants help with all activities. Their qualifications are set by each center and not specified by regulations. Some are certified nurse assistants (CNAs). Their compensation varies according to training and level of expertise.

Education and activities occupations may include the following:

- Early Childhood Education Teacher
- Teacher Assistant
- Child-Care Worker
- Activity Director
- Activity Assistant
- Recreational Therapist
- Physical Therapist
- Program Assistant

Social Assistance

Some day-care centers employ child or family social workers. These professionals handle a variety of child- and family-related situations, including different cultures and congenital disabilities. They aim to improve the social and emotional functioning of children and their families.

Adult day-care centers generally have licensed social workers on site. Director-managers and assistant managers may fulfill social work roles, if they have the necessary degrees in social work or nursing. They may visit new clients at home, assess their needs, and facilitate their access to services, such as counseling and care plans. Specialized counselors are also available. Rehabilitation counselors help

OCCUPATION PROFILE

Child-care Worker

Considerations	Qualifications
Description	Dresses, feeds, bathes, and supervises children at schools, businesses, and child-care facilities.
Career clusters	Education and Training; Human Services
Interests	People; things
Working conditions	Work inside
Minimum education level	No high school diploma; on-the-job training; high school diploma or GED; high school diploma/technical training; apprenticeship
Physical exertion	Medium work
Physical abilities	Unexceptional/basic fitness
Opportunities for experience	Internship; apprenticeship; volunteer work; part-time work
Licensure and certification	Usually not required
Employment outlook	Average growth expected
Holland interest scores	RES; SCR; SEC

Note: See volume 1, "Publisher's Note," for an explanation of the Holland interest score.

patients cope with the social and personal effects of health conditions. They assist with adjustment to disabilities caused by injury, illness, or developmental conditions. Mental health counselors work with individuals and families to treat mental disorders, through individual or group therapy. Geriatric social workers help elderly persons live healthier, more productive lives. They assess the needs of their clients, coordinate their medical care, and help them deal with end-of-life issues and other age-related concerns. These professionals generally have bachelor's degrees in social work, and some hold master's degrees. Their salary depends on education level and experience.

Many adult day-care facilities provide counseling for family members caring for elderly or disabled individuals. Additional personnel, such as gerontology and mental health social work assistants (or aides), usually work under the direction of social workers and nurses. Their education level varies, as does the amount of responsibility they receive.

Social assistance occupations may include the following:

- Child-Care Social Worker
- Gerontology Social Worker
- Rehabilitation Counselor
- Mental Health Counselor
- Social Work Assistant
- Gerontology Aide

Facilities and Security

Large facilities often employ security personnel. Their duties include making sure that patients with dementia or developmental disorders do not leave the facilities unaccompanied. With a minimum of formal training required, experience and reliability are emphasized. Midsize and large day-care facilities also employ full- or part-time housekeeping personnel, who clean classrooms, day rooms, bathrooms, hallways, and kitchen areas; maintain supplies; report repairs needed and perform minor repairs themselves; and help sanitize furniture, appliances, and toys. Housekeepers and janitors are usually trained according to their facilities' standards and often work at minimum wage.

Maintenance personnel, if present, repair plumbing, air-conditioning, electrical hardware, and various devices. Large establishments may employ groundskeepers, who perform landscaping activities, control insects and pests, trim grass, and maintain dumpsters and recycling areas. They usually have vocational training and are paid according to their experience.

Facilities and security occupations may include the following:

- Security Guard
- Housekeeper
- Custodian/Janitor
- Maintenance and Repair Technician
- Groundskeeper

Food Services

Many facilities rely on food provided by caterers or by parents. In medium and large child day-care centers, though, food service personnel prepare meals and snacks, order and maintain food supplies, ensure kitchen cleanliness, and store ingredients. They should be familiar with nutritional principles, including the correct food portions for children of various ages, and potential allergies. Experience in the food services industry, whether as a cook, waiter, or counter attendant, is the most common background for food service employees. Child day-care cooks may be required to have experience working with children. Both adult day-care and adult day health care centers provide meals and snacks, making special dietary accommodations as necessary for charges with diabetes, renal problems, or other conditions.

Licensing is required for any employee who prepares food for clients, feeds them, assists them in eating, or administers oral medications to them. A food manager and a dietician are often employed by large facilities. The mean annual income of salaried food service managers in this industry was $41,040 in 2009. Such managers have course work in food safety and have demonstrated their knowledge by passing exams. Most food service managers have less than a bachelor's degree; however, some postsecondary education, including a college degree, is increasingly preferred for many such positions.

Food services occupations may include the following:

- Food Service Manager
- Dietician
- Cook
- Kitchen Aide

Transportation Services

Some adult day-care programs arrange for transportation through external agencies; others employ drivers to provide door-to-door transportation in vans. If a program arranges its own transportation system, a transportation coordinator is often employed to supervise its operations by working with families, drivers, and other personnel. For driver positions, holders of high school diplomas are often preferred. Familiarity with operating lifts, CPR training, and sensitivity to the needs of seniors are recommended. An attendant or aide should be present in each vehicle. Drivers and aides plan routes together with coordinators, walk participants to and from vehicles, assist them on and off vans, and ensure their safety during transport. Personnel are often paid hourly wages. Some child day-care centers may also provide transportation to and from their facilities.

Transportation services occupations may include the following:

- Transportation Coordinator
- Driver
- Transportation Attendant

Marketing

Activity directors and marketing coordinators facilitate community awareness of their programs via informal interaction with community members, as well as structured outreach. They must choose niches or other target audiences, position their facilities to appeal to such targets, advertise, organize open houses, obtain "earned" (or free) media coverage, develop promotional tools, and plan events. When enrollment is not at full capacity, marketing personnel and program managers plan and implement strategies to increase awareness and enrollment figures. Marketing personnel usually require bachelor's degrees.

Marketing occupations may include the following:

- Marketing Coordinator
- Marketing Communications Director
- Activity Coordinator
- Program Manager

INDUSTRY OUTLOOK

Overview

Demand for child care is growing, both in North America and in Europe, as more mothers of young children work full time. A 2006 report by Third-Wave Research estimated the total potential market for U.S. day-care centers and preschools to be more than $24 billion. By 2009, industry revenues had risen to $31 billion. Key Note estimates that in the United Kingdom the total child-care market (comprising formal and family establishments) grew by 30.1 percent between 2004 and 2008, to £4.79 billion. The U.S. Department of Labor outlook for the day-care industry shows it to be on the rise.

Many opportunities for employment in the industry are expected: Increased demand will create new jobs, and existing jobs will also need to be filled as experienced workers leave their positions to continue their education or join other industries. Demand for child-care facilities could increase further if more states implement preschool programs for three- and four-year-old children. Subsidies for children from low-income families, legislation requiring welfare recipients to work, and an increasing number of employer-funded day-care centers could

result in more children being enrolled in formal centers.

Over 40 percent employment growth is expected in the overall family and personal services sector. The adult day-care industry is growing at a 5 to 15 percent pace, depending on location; its revenues in the United States were expected to reach $26 billion in 2011. As health care evolves and the longevity of the population increases, the role played by adult day-care facilities will become more and more prominent. An increasing number of local governments are investing in adult day-care centers. Colleges offer degrees in senior recreation and leisure management, to fuel the need for qualified staff. Job openings in social assistance should be abundant as a result both of workers leaving the industry and of a growing demand stemming from the aging of the American population. As baby boomers age, they will require adult day-care services. Facilities that allow them to lead more productive, independent lives outside of nursing homes or hospitals will expand. This growth will depend on the amount of governmental and managed care funding available. More growth in the

PROJECTED EMPLOYMENT FOR SELECTED OCCUPATIONS

Social Assistance

Employment		
2009	Projected 2018	Occupation
269,000	312,100	Child care workers
76,740	92,500	Child, family, and school social workers
313,030	515,300	Personal and home care aides
41,670	51,300	Social and community service managers
120,830	181,100	Social and human service assistants

Source: U.S. Bureau of Labor Statistics, Industries at a Glance, Occupational Employment Statistics and Employment Projections Program.

private segment might occur if state and local government agencies contract out some of their social services operations.

According to a MetLife Mature Market Institute national survey, the national average daily rate for adult day-care services is $64—far less than the cost of hiring a home health nurse or moving to a nursing facility. Medicare does not usually cover the costs associated with adult day care, but if a center is a licensed medical or Alzheimer's facility and a care recipient meets state qualifications, some of the expenses may be covered by Medicaid. Long-term care insurance may cover some of the costs if medical providers are involved.

Employment Advantages

The mission of early childhood educators and caregivers is difficult to achieve but crucial to the health of a society. Patience and strength are required, in addition to a genuine love for children. A moderate increase in the number of child day-care jobs is expected, as well as increases in wages and salaries. Salary and wage jobs are expected to grow by approximately 15 percent during the 2008-2018 period.

Adult day-care providers help the elderly and disabled stay in their homes longer; prevent or delay institutionalization; provide respite to caregivers; decrease emergency-room visits and hospitalization; and offer medical monitoring, care, food service, therapeutic activities, social services, and transportation. As projected by the BLS, the number of social and human service assistants is expected to grow by almost 23 percent between 2008 and 2018. This is a higher rate than the average for all occupations. More social and human service assistants, who are involved in providing day services for the elderly and mentally ill, will be needed to meet an ever-increasing demand. The competition will be more significant for jobs in urban areas, but qualified workers (especially those with postsecondary education) will probably obtain jobs with relative ease.

Annual Earnings

Global day-care industry trends are difficult to predict because of high variability in economic and cultural conditions. As funding is reduced in the wake of the economic crisis of 2007-2009, many U.S. adult day-care programs will experience difficulties, despite growing steadily in the first decade of the twenty-first century. Experts predict that formal day-care centers will expand in the coming years. Family care operations, however, will continue to thrive slowly and steadily domestically and abroad and will be preferred by many parents for the more personal attention they provide.

Despite substantial demand and growing personnel-replacement needs, recession woes—such as parental or caregiver unemployment—will probably cause the short-term expansion of the industry to be modest. After several boom years, with possibly five thousand new day-care centers established annually (as estimated by the National Child Care Association), an increase in child-care center vacancies has been noted across the United States. A 2008 study by the National Association of Child Care Resource and Referral Agencies reported decreased enrollment in 65 percent of child-care centers in forty states. Over 74 percent of these facilities reported that most of their clients had difficulty making payments on time or were not making payments at all. As the U.S. economy recovers, this trend is expected to reverse. The industry is still fragmented: large players with the highest earning potential represent only a small percentage of the market; tremendous growth potential exists.

RELATED RESOURCES FOR FURTHER RESEARCH

Center for the Study of Child Care Employment, Institute for Research on Labor and Employment
2521 Channing Way, Suite 5555
Berkeley, CA 94720-5555
Tel: (510) 643-8293
Fax: (510) 642-6432
http://www.irle.berkeley.edu/cscce/index.html

National Adult Day Services Association
85 S Washington, Suite 316
Seattle, WA 98104
Tel: (877) 745-1440
Fax: (206) 461-3218
http://www.nadsa.org

NATIONAL ASSOCIATION FOR THE EDUCATION OF
    YOUNG CHILDREN
    1313 L St. NW, Suite 500
    Washington, DC 20005
    Tel: (866) 623-9248
    Fax: (202) 328-1846
    http://www.naeyc.org

NATIONAL ASSOCIATION OF CHILD CARE
    RESOURCE AND REFERRAL AGENCIES
    3101 Wilson Blvd., Suite 350
    Arlington, VA 22201
    Tel: (703) 341-4100
    Fax: (703) 341-4101
    http://www.naccrra.org

NATIONAL CHILD CARE ASSOCIATION
    1325 G St. NW, Suite 500
    Washington, DC 20005
    Tel: (800) 543-7161
    http://www.nccanet.org

NATIONAL RESOURCE CENTER FOR HEALTH AND
    SAFETY IN CHILD CARE AND EARLY
    EDUCATION, UNIVERSITY OF COLORADO
    HEALTH AND SCIENCES CENTER AT FITZSIMONS
    UCD-CON Campus Mail Stop F541
    Education 2 North
    13120 E 19th Ave.
    P.O. Box 6511
    Aurora, CO 80045
    Tel: (800) 598-5437
    Fax: (303) 724-0960
    http://nrckids.org

ABOUT THE AUTHOR

Mihaela Avramut trained at the University of Pittsburgh Medical School and the University of California, San Francisco. Her research focused on neurodegenerative disorders, including Alzheimer's disease and Parkinson's disease. As a physician, she has observed firsthand the beneficial effects of skilled adult day-care programs on various categories of patients. She is the president of Verlan Medical Communications and, since 1995, has lectured and written on a variety of medical, sci-entific, and public health topics. As a mother, she has researched child day care extensively.

FURTHER READING

Gestwicki, Carol, and Jane Bertrand. *Essentials of Early Childhood Education.* Toronto: Thomson Nelson, 2008.

Goldsmith, Seth M. *Long-Term Care Administration Handbook.* New York: Aspen, 1994.

Hearron, Patricia F., and Verna Hildebrand. *Management of Child Development Centers.* 7th ed. Boston: Pearson, 2011.

Institute for Career Research. *A Career as a Teacher: Early Childhood Education, Nursery Schools—Daycare.* Chicago: Author, 2004.

Leach, P. *Day Care Today: Getting It Right for Everyone.* New York: Random House, 2010.

Lynn, Jacquelyn, and Charlene Davis. *Start Your Own Senior Services Business.* 2d ed. Irvine, Calif.: Entrepreneur Press, 2010.

Moore, Keith Diaz, Lyn Dally Geboy, and Gerald D. Weisman. *Designing a Better Day: Guidelines for Adult and Dementia Day Services Centers.* Baltimore: The Johns Hopkins University Press, 2006.

Pruissen, Catherine A. *Start and Run a Home Daycare.* 3d ed. North Vancouver, B.C.: Self Counsel Press, 2002.

Schmitt, E. M., et al. "Adult Day Health Center Participation and Health-Related Quality of Life." *Gerontologist,* February 10, 2010.

U.S. Bureau of Labor Statistics. *Career Guide to Industries,* 2010-2011 ed. http://www.bls.gov/oco/cg.

_____. "Child Care Workers." In *Occupational Outlook Handbook,* 2010-2011 ed. http://www.bls.gov/oco/ocos170.htm.

U.S. Census Bureau. North American Industry Classification System (NAICS), 2007. http://www.census.gov/cgi-bin/sssd/naics/naicsrch?chart=2007.

U.S. Department of Commerce. International Trade Administration. Office of Trade and Industry Information. Industry Trade Data and Analysis. http://ita.doc.gov/td/industry/otea/OTII/OTII-index.html.

Defense Industry

Department of Defense

INDUSTRY SNAPSHOT

General Industry: Manufacturing
Career Clusters: Manufacturing; Science, Technology, Engineering, and Math
Subcategory Industries: Combat Logistics; Combat Simulators; Defense Contractors; Military Manufacturing; Military Procurement; Missile Systems Design and Manufacturing; Naval Engineering; Radars and Sensors; Satellite Technology; Systems Engineering
Related Industries: Airline Industry; Computer Hardware and Peripherals Industry; Computer Systems Industry; Federal Public Administration; Heavy Machines Industry; National and International Security Industry; Nuclear Power Industry; Political Advocacy Industry; Telecommunications Infrastructure Industry
Annual Domestic Revenues: $214 billion USD (combined aerospace and defense industry; Hoovers, 2002)
Annual Global Revenues: $674.6 billion USD (Datamonitor, 2008)
NAICS Number: 333-336

INDUSTRY DEFINITION

Summary

The defense industry designs and manufactures the vehicles, systems, and weapons used by military organizations around the world. The industry builds airborne weapons, such as military planes and helicopters; naval vessels; land-based vehicles; and the integrated systems and weaponry on board such craft. The primary clients for such hardware and vehicles are governments, which may purchase defense systems from either native or foreign manufacturers.

History of the Industry

Throughout human history, civilizations, nations, and states have relied on military technology to defend their interests. In ancient Egypt, for example, the introduction of the chariot represented an important turning point in battles, providing soldiers with an advantage in speed, mobility, and armor over their enemies. During the thirteenth century, the Chinese first used gunpowder in battle (although they had invented it hundreds of years prior), defeating the Mongols with "fire arrows."

In the fourteenth century, gunpowder and ordnance (military supplies such as guns and bullets) became dangerous partners. The first such weap-

Defense contractors produce navigational equipment, including Global Positioning System devices, compasses, maps, and two-way radios and other communications equipment. (©Urszula Sawicka/Dreamstime.com)

ons were cannons, but it was not long before weapons producers began to make lighter cannons, first for the battlefield and later for individual soldiers to use. In the seventeenth century, the introduction of the flintlock musket helped bring in a new era of battlefield weaponry. Rifles and, ultimately, revolvers and rapid-fire guns (such as the Gatling gun) further changed the landscape of military technology.

The evolution of military technology was not limited to individual weapons. In 1862, during the American Civil War, the USS *Monitor* engaged the CSS *Merrimack* at Hampton Roads, off the coast of Virginia. The two ships represented a major development in military history—both were cloaked in thick armor (all other ships at that point were made with wood) and able to withstand a considerable

amount of enemy firepower. After that battle (in which there was no clear winner), both the Union and the Confederate governments turned their attention to constructing "ironclad" ships. Wooden combat ships had been rendered obsolete.

In 1905, the success of Orville and Wilbur Wright's airplane prompted entrepreneurs and military leaders alike to develop aircraft of their own. Commercial airlines were born of this technology, as was the notion of aerial warfare. At first, the military used planes solely for reconnaissance, although some strategists envisioned using them to deliver bombs. In 1915, French pilot Roland Garros mounted a machine gun to his plane and, more important, steel deflectors to his propellers, turning the plane into an offensive weapon. The Germans quickly countered with a Dutch-made "interrupter," which made firing through propellers even easier. These developments added the skies over Europe to the many other battlefields of World War I.

World War I also witnessed the birth of a new naval weapon: The German U-boat, capable of operating underwater and attacking its targets clandestinely by firing torpedoes instead of guns, gave the Germans a considerable advantage. The defeat of the Germans in 1918 temporarily halted the development of submarines, but other countries worked quickly to develop their own versions of the U-boat, and at the dawn of World War II Adolph Hitler's Germany restarted its program.

World War II represented another pivotal period of evolution for military technology. In addition to improvements to naval vessels and aircraft, radar (which uses radio waves to detect the presence of such craft) became a critical piece of land-, sea-, and air-based military technology. Sonar had already been introduced during World War I, and it was also used commonly to detect submerged enemy submarines and torpedoes.

At the end of World War II, the most devastating weapon in history was deployed. The atomic bomb brought the war to a close and simultaneously began a new era of military history. It—and its successor, the hydrogen bomb—became the focal point of the Cold War, which continued until the early 1990's.

Upon the close of the Cold War, the focus among the world's major military powers turned away from nuclear technologies. Much attention was instead paid to communications, such as computer networks and satellite technologies. The rise of the Internet (which was itself the product of military research in the mid-twentieth century) added to this pursuit, fueled by perceived and real threats to countries' information resources. The terrorist attacks launched on the World Trade Center and the Pentagon on September 11, 2001, further challenged the perception that an enemy must be met on a battlefield—a perception that had defined almost all previous conflicts. Technology needed for surveillance and intelligence-gathering became a very high priority for the military policy makers responsible for assigning defense contracts.

Many modern military weapons and technologies have been designed and built, not by the military itself but by private corporations contracted by governments. The German Fokker, the fighter plane used in World War I, was built by a Dutch aircraft manufacturer, Anthony Fokker. Private contractors have worked with governments to develop the systems and weapons they need. The driving force behind this development remains market demand. As the need to create or counter new military technologies has become manifest, the industry's growth has been spurred.

During the Cold War, the defense industry received consistent infusions of government money, not just in the United States and the Soviet Union but in other industrialized countries as well. In the United States, this tremendous investment in military manufacturing created what President Dwight D. Eisenhower famously dubbed "the military-industrial complex," an intricate and highly connected collective of military agencies, political leadership, and private enterprise. The military-industrial complex declined somewhat after the fall of the Soviet Union, but it was so significant during its apex that its roots still run deep in the post-Cold War era, giving the current defense industry a strong foundation and durability in the twenty-first century.

The Humvee, or high mobility multipurpose wheeled vehicle, is a four-wheel-drive motor vehicle created for the military by AM Genera, a subsidiary of American Motors. (©Kiraly Istvan Daniel/Dreamstime.com)

The Industry Today

The defense industry today is a vast, diverse, and complex collection of military contractors spanning three general fields: aviation, naval systems, and land-based weaponry. Generating hundreds of billions of dollars in the United States and the international marketplace, the defense industry is one of the world's largest industries, and it sustains millions of jobs around the globe. The industry manufactures and sells military technologies, not just ordnance and weaponry but computer and communications systems as well.

The defense industry is multifarious, spanning a number of areas. The first of these is land-based weaponry, including small arms such as rifles and similar, individually operated weapons. In addition to small arms, this subsector produces field artillery, mines, ground-based radar, troop transport vehicles, tanks, and other hardware.

The individual soldier is an important beneficiary of military contracts. Helmets, night-vision goggles, travel packs, footwear, and other personal equipment are all manufactured by military contractors for soldiers' comfort and utility. Additionally, defense contractors produce integrated systems for land-based weaponry, including Global Positioning System (GPS) devices, cellular technology, radios, and other communications equipment. Finally, armored personnel vehicles (APVs), smaller utility vehicles, tanks, and other vehicles are all produced under military contracts with private companies.

Naval warfare and operations have evolved steadily over recent decades, and the defense industry has played a central role in their evolution. Beyond merely designing and constructing ships, the industry produces integrated ship-defense systems that combine guns, missiles, electronic countermeasures and radar. It also manufactures battle-group communications devices and vehicles (such as helicopters, smaller watercraft, and shipboard vehicles).

The third important industry sector is aviation. The defense industry has consistently developed and strengthened aircraft technologies. In addition to jets, transport planes, helicopters, and bombers, the industry develops each craft's onboard computer and communications system. It has also worked to strengthen the links between ground systems and air systems, and contractors continue to modify radar and similar systems in response to the post-Cold War era's technological transformation. In fact, many of the twenty-first century's most well-used air vehicles are unpiloted. These so-called drones are increasingly popular for reconnaissance, intelligence gathering, and even automated bomb and missile delivery over remote locations in Afghanistan, for example.

Furthermore, the defense industry develops satellite technology that helps military and civilian users track developments around the world. Satellites enable military personnel to monitor and track enemy elements. Airborne and orbiting military systems are better able to assess battlefield actions and environments, as well as track terrorists' movements and activities. This field, in particular, has developed rapidly in recent years.

Central to the defense in-

General Dynamics Land Systems has produced many M1A1/2 Abrams main battle tanks for the U.S. Army: 3,273 of the M1, 4,796 of the M1A1, and 77 of the M1A2. (©Anita Patterson Peppers/Dreamstime.com)

The defense industry has consistently developed and strengthened aircraft technologies, such as those used in the CH-53 Super Stallion transport helicopter. (©Dreamstime.com)

dustry is the system of government contracts. Governments determine their areas of need and seek out solutions from defense companies, using a request for proposal (RFP) or similar statement. Companies are awarded contracts based on their responses to such solicitations. Government contracts are the lifeblood of the defense industry, and contactors stand to earn millions of dollars on many different types of projects, providing jobs to a diverse and often large workforce.

Defense projects vary in size and scope. Some contractors work on large-scale projects, incorporating a number of integrated systems into one major piece of technology, while other companies work on much narrower, more tightly focused projects. Competition among defense contractors is intense, and many companies expend significant resources on their proposal teams, which win contracts based on their ability to combine high quality with cost-effectiveness. In the twenty-first century, cost is one of the most important factors in winning contracts.

Employment at defense contractors is subject to overall fluctuations in government spending, as well as to the ability of employers to attract that spending. If contracts expire or are awarded to competitors, a given company may lose millions of dollars in potential revenues, and many of its employees may lose their jobs. It is for this reason that proposal teams (and the project teams they propose) are so important to a company's success. In many cases, a military agency will give more credence to a proposed project team that has familiar faces, such as former military officers and prominent engineers. Thus, the defense industry is very difficult to break into unless a new company is able to hire such familiar and experienced personnel. The industry's dependence on winning a limited number of contracts, moreover, makes it vulnerable to both economic and political fluctuations.

INDUSTRY MARKET SEGMENTS

The defense industry includes contractors of various sizes. The largest contractors are often diversified multinational corporations that produce both military and civilian equipment and have annual budgets in the billions of dollars. Small firms, by contrast, may work on only a single contract at a time. Such firms must be sure to dedicate resources to constantly seeking their next contracts, as they often cannot afford to have down time between the end of one project and the beginning of the next.

Small Defense Contractors

Small defense contractors generally employ one hundred people or fewer. They tend to be tightly focused operations, working on a limited number of projects at any given time. Because of the importance of connections and established expertise in the defense industry, small contractors are often run by either retired military officers or well-known engineers, and an entire small company may trade on the reputation of its senior management team, as well as its success in delivering contracted projects on time and on budget.

Potential Annual Earnings Scale. Defense project managers and directors may earn as much as $110,000 per year. The lower end of the pay scale includes administrators and hourly employees, some of whom work only part time and therefore do not receive benefits.

Clientele Interaction. Smaller, more specialized defense contractors have varying degrees of client contact, based on the type of position held. Manufacturing engineers, for example, may not have as much interaction with clients as do program managers and customer-service representatives. Still, by virtue of the business's size, most small contractors take great pains to communicate their attention to customer service and interaction.

Amenities, Atmosphere, and Physical Grounds. Small defense contractors operate within professional environments with open work spaces. Such companies may not necessarily be located in a sprawling complex of buildings; in fact, some contractors may be found in relatively small office spaces just large enough to conduct the work at hand. The small number of employees may foster an atmosphere of camaraderie and informality among workers. However, the company's size and minimal number of project employees may require each employee to work longer hours and handle multiple tasks. Defense companies often operate in high-security environments, requiring identification badges, key cards to access sensitive areas, and other standard security protocols.

Typical Number of Employees. Some small defense contractors have fewer than one hundred employees, who focus their energy on production and distribution rather than administrative management and other services. The small number of personnel enables the company to work on a given project without significant overhead costs for salaries.

Traditional Geographic Locations. Small defense contractors are located in a wide range of geographic venues. Many are located in or near capital cities, where they may work closely with a country's military leadership (such as the Pentagon). Others are located on or near military bases, thereby facilitating quick testing and application of the product being manufactured and providing the high security of the base without the contractor itself needing to pay for extensive security measures. Smaller contractors have a wider range of locations to choose from, as they take up less space than larger corporations.

Pros of Working for a Small Defense Contractor. Employees of small defense companies enjoy the benefit of working in small teams in what is often a friendlier, more relaxed environment than may be found in a larger contractor. The companies' projects may be smaller in scope, enabling employees to focus more on their completion rather than take into consideration their application in larger systems under production. Paperwork and payments may also move more quickly through smaller contractors, allowing employees to receive compensation and reimbursement checks in a timely fashion.

Cons of Working for a Small Defense Contractor. Small defense contractors are often limited in resources when compared with much larger, international firms. They are thus always at risk of losing bids for contracts to those larger companies. Employees at small firms may have larger workloads and work longer hours than do members of larger organizations. Furthermore, small contractors may be somewhat obscure, so employees may be less able to advance in their careers than are employees of large firms with much greater reputations, both within and beyond the industry. Finally, small companies may have limited budgets or self-imposed budgeting limitations designed to reduce overhead. These limitations may preclude them from occupying work space in areas with high rents, taxes, or utility costs, even if such spaces would be the most conducive to conducting their business. If small contractors cannot afford to locate near major military centers, their employees will have to travel further to visit clients and work on off-site projects.

Costs

Payroll and Benefits: Defense contractors pay employees on an hourly, annual, or contract basis. Small contractors in particular may pay by the project, as their operating budgets may be tied more closely to the vagaries of individual contracts than are those of larger firms that handle a greater number of projects simultaneously. Most employees of even small firms receive standard benefits.

Supplies: Small defense companies require a number of different types of supplies, including heavy and light manufacturing machinery and parts, as well as computer systems, office supplies, audiovisual equipment, and presentation software.

External Services: Defense contractors with fewer than one hundred employees often require the support of external vendors. They contract such services as accounting, legal counsel, marketing, and public relations. In many cases, these companies hire consultants, both to advise them on the general conduct of business and to provide technical expertise necessary to complete specific projects.

Utilities: Small defense contractors must pay for electricity and other energy utilities, as well as land-based and cellular telephones and Internet access.

Taxes: Defense contractors must pay state, regional, and national corporate income taxes and withhold the taxes of full-time employees. Additionally, they may pay real estate taxes if they own their own manufacturing facilities. Some of these taxes may be lower than those paid by other industries in the same jurisdiction as a result of tax incentive programs designed to

attract defense contractors to a given geographic area.

Midsize Defense Contractors

Midsize defense contractors generally employ between one hundred and one thousand workers, although this figure is somewhat variable. Midsize contractors may operate at more locations than do small contractors, but they usually remain within one country rather than positioning themselves as multinational entities.

Potential Annual Earnings Scale. Defense project managers and directors may earn as much as $110,000 per year. The lower end of the pay scale includes administrators and hourly employees, some of whom work only part time and therefore do not receive benefits.

Clientele Interaction. At midsize defense contractors, senior-level project managers and business development managers are likely to have high degrees of client interaction, while engineers and project administrators are more likely to spend their time in production. However, in the light of the importance of reporting and accounting, some of these latter individuals make client presentations and give periodic reports on goals met and test results.

Amenities, Atmosphere, and Physical Grounds. Midsize defense companies tend to operate in two types of interconnected environments. The first of these is an office environment, in which administrative functions and client presentations take place. The second is a production facility, where all research, development, and construction take place. Each of these environments is professional in nature. Because the projects taken up by midsize contractors are larger than single components, a team dynamic is expected among workers who are developing different parts of this larger system. Defense companies often operate in high-security environments, requiring identification badges, key cards to access sensitive areas, and other standard security protocols.

Typical Number of Employees. Some midsize companies employ between one hundred and one thousand people; others employ fewer than that (and therefore are considered midsize based on their annual revenues).

Traditional Geographic Locations. Midsize defense contractors are often located either in or near cities that house military headquarters, such as national capital cities. Many are also located near or on military bases, giving them easy access to key client personnel and to testing and demonstration facilities, as well as providing them with a free source of added security and access control. Because the projects on which they typically work require more personnel or resources than do small contractors' programs, midsize contractors may offset their costs by locating in suburban or less-expensive urban areas that have lower rents or utility fees.

Pros of Working for a Midsize Defense Contractor. Employees of midsize defense contractors are able to enjoy many of the resources accessible to larger companies without experiencing those companies' high operating costs. Similarly, potential clients may be drawn to midsize contractors by their low overhead and a customer-service-oriented reputation that distinguishes smaller companies from industry giants. The relatively small volume of contracts acquired by midsize companies may enable workers to focus more closely on each project than they can at large corporations.

Cons of Working for a Midsize Defense Contractor. One of the most daunting aspects of a midsize defense contractor is the fact that it is difficult to define and therefore to support with government funding. Small businesses receive some government support, and large companies are usually self-sufficient, but midsize contractors are considered to be squeezed between the other two layers. They may encounter difficulty winning contracts as a result, and they are often targeted by larger companies for acquisition.

Costs

Payroll and Benefits: Pay and benefits for employees of midsize defense contractors depend largely on the monetary size of the contract on which employees are working. Some employees may be paid by the contract, whereas others receive annual salaries or hourly wages. Most full-time employees of midsize defense firms receive full benefits.

Supplies: Midsize defense manufacturers require a number of key supplies. On the production floor and in research facilities, heavy machinery and parts, as well as safety equipment and computer modeling hardware and software are necessary.

In the corporate environment, basic office supplies, as well as personal computers, portable phones, personal digital assistants (PDAs), and laptop computers are also vital for meeting the needs of potential and current clients.

External Services: Midsize contractors require a number of external services during the course of their operations. They may contract public relations, accounting, and general counsel services, as well as custodial and security services. They may also use government agencies to conduct background checks of candidates for positions with access to sensitive materials.

Utilities: Midsize contractors require a great deal of electricity for their operations, as well as water, heating, telephone service, and Internet access. They may also pay for wastewater treatment, trash removal, and sewage fees.

Taxes: Midsize defense and aerospace contractors withhold, report, and collect personal income taxes from full-time employees. They may also be required to pay regional and national unemployment insurance taxes, along with corporate income taxes and property taxes. Some of these taxes may be lower than those paid by other industries in the same jurisdiction as a result of tax incentive programs designed to attract defense contractors to a given geographic area.

Large Defense Contractors

Large defense contractors are massive multinational operations employing as many as tens of thousands of people. Many, including the world's largest aircraft manufacturers, produce a wide range of equipment and vehicles for both military and civilian purposes and sell their products to multiple governments and private corporations throughout the world. It was these large and politically powerful corporations that President Eisenhower had in mind when he devoted his farewell speech to the dangers posed by the military-industrial complex.

Potential Annual Earnings Scale. The executive managers of large defense corporations may earn salaries in the millions of dollars per year, while production-floor workers—while well compensated relative to other manufacturing personnel—often earn hourly wages. According to the U.S. Bureau of Labor Statistics (BLS), the mean annual salary of a production manager overseeing an aerospace defense production project, for example, was $66,610 in 2009, whereas an aircraft assembler earned an average of $44,890. Aerospace engineers earned an average of $87,730, and general managers earned an average of $130,000.

Clientele Interaction. Client interaction between large defense contractors and the government is usually limited to the senior managers who oversee programs and other executive-level employees. Mid-level professionals may be called upon to meet with and present to clients about specific technical developments concerning their projects. Administrative personnel may also be in contact with their client counterparts, scheduling meetings and transmitting important information.

Amenities, Atmosphere, and Physical Grounds. Large-scale defense contractors operate on sprawling, high-security industrial campuses that manufacture equipment of all sizes, from side arms to aircraft carriers. They may also maintain separate corporate headquarters where business executives and design staff work from traditional offices, or such offices may be located in separate buildings on industrial campuses. Contractors must maintain a considerable degree of professionalism, particularly in the light of the large number of military clients who are often on site for meetings and reviews. The environment is usually compartmentalized by program or by technical area, with a strong sense of teamwork within each department.

Typical Number of Employees. The employee populations of large defense manufacturers vary based on the number of contracts in operation and the companies' respective budget status. The U.S.-based Raytheon Company, for example, has more than 66,500 employees at its six major facilities. BAE Systems, based in the United Kingdom, has more than 106,400 employees worldwide.

Traditional Geographic Locations. Large defense contractors are found throughout the world, occupying a number of different geographic locations. Many are located in or near major capital cities, enabling better access to military and government leaders. Others are located in large facilities and campuses in remote or open-space locations that allow for discreet or private testing and demonstrations of missiles and explosive weaponry. Still others are located on or near military bases, again offering close access to military clients who operate at those facilities.

Pros of Working for a Large Defense Contractor. Because of their reputations and long-standing relationships with military establishments, the large defense contractors tend to win and retain many major government contracts. As a result, employees of these corporations enjoy both a degree of job security and a level of prestige (along with higher salaries) that they may not experience in smaller companies. Additionally, opportunities for upward mobility are more readily available within large companies. Furthermore, the opportunity to work on an entire integrated system or weapon (such as a fighter jet or submarine) instead of a smaller, localized system or device, is enticing for many engineers and project workers.

Cons of Working for a Large Defense Contractor. Some individuals may not like the atmosphere at large defense firms with thousands of employees, preferring smaller settings where it is easier to develop personal relationships with co-workers. Additionally, some companies are located in remote locations to maximize opportunities for weapons testing and capitalize on cheap and plentiful real estate. Workers at such sites have limited access to cultural and social centers. Furthermore, like other defense contractors, large companies are beholden to government contracts. If legislatures or executive agencies cease development of a major program, even the largest companies may be forced to lay off workers.

Costs

Payroll and Benefits: Large defense corporations generally pay full benefits to all full-time employees, who may work for hourly, annual, or contract-based wages.

Supplies: Large defense contractors require a great deal of supplies, including industrial manufacturing machinery and parts, as well as all manner of office supplies, including computers, computer servers, and communications devices such as smart phones. In some cases, large companies require food and beverage supplies to support staff and visiting dignitaries, as well as vehicles for travel within the company's campus.

External Services: Large defense companies are often self-sufficient, but they may call upon external vendors for certain services. Some contract lobbyists and legal teams form major firms for government-relations activities. They may also contract transportation companies, such as private air charters and limousines, for local and long-distance employee travel. Many contract security, and some may even contract on-site public safety companies, such as fire departments and emergency medical technicians. Those companies that produce significant volumes of toxic materials may contract an external hazardous material disposal company.

Utilities: Large defense companies use a great deal of energy, including electricity and water, and a great deal of telephone and Internet services. They may also pay for wastewater treatment, particularly at those facilities that have large numbers of people working under one roof.

Taxes: Large defense contractors pay taxes on property and corporate income, as well as withholding income taxes from full-time employees' salaries. They may also be required to pay corporate taxes to cover unemployment insurance pools and health care funding.

ORGANIZATIONAL STRUCTURE AND JOB ROLES

The defense industry is compartmentalized, based on both contracted projects and the arena in which the manufacturing takes place. For example, multiple radar systems projects may be found in development within the same section of the industry. However, there are several general areas that are common to nearly all defense companies.

The following umbrella categories apply to the organizational structure of businesses within the defense industry:

- Executive Management
- Business Development
- Research and Development
- Manufacturing
- Public Relations
- Legal Counsel
- Marketing
- Human Resources
- Accounting
- Administrative Support

Executive Management

At the top of a defense company is its executive team, which manages its overall operations and endeavors. This group develops the company's mission and goals, as well as ensuring that all activities of the company are running smoothly. Executive managers are broken down in terms of the various departments within a company, including certain projects and proposals, as well as day-to-day operations such as human resources and accounting.

Executive managers set corporate goals and strategies; assess, approve, or pass on requests for proposals; and develop and implement budgets. They occasionally assist in high-profile proposals, lending their own experience to the success of a given proposal. They are generally highly experienced, with strong educational backgrounds as well. In many cases, defense executives have military backgrounds, having retired prior to entering the private sector. They are well-educated, either through the military academies or in colleges and universities after their active service. Others received their schooling via on-the-job training or by familiarizing themselves with relevant systems.

Executive management occupations may include the following:

- President/Chief Executive Officer (CEO)
- Chief Operating Officer (COO)
- Chief Financial Officer (CFO)
- Chief Information Officer (CIO)
- Vice President of Government Relations
- Vice President of Marketing

Business Development

The business development department pursues government and military contracts. It monitors government outlets for requests for proposals relevant to its company's expertise, and, once those opportunities arise, it organizes proposal teams to pursue them. The proposal teams then create responses and proposals tailored to the specifications outlined in the requests for proposals, including scope of work, timetables for project completion, and personnel to be assigned.

Business development staff have considerable experience in their companies' areas of capability. They must be well-organized, capable of assembling and managing strong proposal teams and of putting together complex proposals. Business development personnel are usually college educated, although some are former military personnel with strong and relevant experience.

Business development occupations may include the following:

- Vice President of Business Development
- Business Development Manager/ Coordinator
- Team Leader
- Analyst
- Recruiter

Research and Development

Research and development personnel analyze the applications and capabilities of their companies' products. They create computer models and run diagnostic assessments and tests of product operations prior to final distribution. They are primarily concerned with testing products during development and final production.

Personnel in this field must carefully assess their products' design effectiveness, as well as any adverse elements created by the products (such as health or environmental risk factors). They must be detail-oriented in their ability to conduct their assessments. Research and development personnel are typically engineers and have advanced degrees in engineering, environmental science, or other mechanical sciences. According to the BLS,

engineers in the aerospace industry earned a median hourly wage of $44.27 in 2008; mechanical engineers earned $39.01 per hour, and industrial engineers earned $36.79 per hour. Computer programmers earned a median hourly wage of $44.41 for the same year.

Research and development occupations may include the following:

- Research Director
- Quality Assurance Manager
- Engineer
- Programmer
- Clinical Trial Manager

Manufacturing

Defense manufacturing personnel are responsible for building the products sought by military agencies. Following the designs of architectural engineers and the client, manufacturing personnel integrate the necessary systems, assemble parts, and produce final products. They strictly follow established time lines and benchmarks set forth by military clients, working with research and development, systems designers, and senior personnel to complete projects on time.

Manufacturing requires a broad range of mechanically oriented staff. From engineers, to assembly line workers, to painters, members of manufacturing departments work as teams, adhering to clear

---

OCCUPATION SPECIALTIES

Inspectors and Testers

Specialty	Responsibilities
Airplane inspectors	Examine aircraft to see that repairs match specifications and certify airworthiness.
Assemblies and installations inspectors	Inspect assemblies, major structures, and complete aircraft for safety and correct detail.
Electronics inspectors	Examine parts, subassemblies, and assemblies for conformance to specifications.
Exhaust emissions inspectors	Inspect and test automobile emission control systems.
Metal fabricating inspectors	Check materials for conformance with work orders and specifications.

production phases. Some of them have advanced or vocational degrees. Others are less educated, hired to assemble or paint parts on an assembly line following specific instructions from department management. According to the BLS, machinists in the aerospace industry earned a median hourly wage of $19.49 in 2008. Production workers, in the same year, earned an average $1,305 per week.

Manufacturing occupations may include the following:

- Project Director
- Project Manager
- Engineer
- Systems Operator
- Machinist
- Painter
- Assembly Line Worker

Public Relations

The management of all external communications, press statements, interviews, promotions, and other forms of information dissemination falls to a defense company's public relations department. Public relations personnel promote the interests and activities of their companies to the general public, as well as targeted media outlets. They are the primary vehicle through which a company's official positions and its responses to emergency situations, political issues, and other time-sensitive matters are transmitted to the public. In the light of this fact, they must be effective communicators and able to react quickly to sensitive or controversial events in an even-handed, diplomatic manner. In many cases, a defense company's political endeavors, such as lobbying and government relations, are conducted through the public relations department.

Public relations personnel are typically college educated, and many have advanced degrees in such fields as public relations, communications, public affairs, law, and public policy. They must be professionally experienced in the defense industry, demonstrating a strong understanding of relevant issues and the relationship of those issues to their companies' stated goals and activities. They are compensated on the high end of the scale for workers in their field.

Public relations occupations may include the following:

- Public Relations Director
- External Affairs Coordinator
- Government Relations Manager
- Lobbyist
- Event Planner
- Marketing Manager
- Administrative Assistant

Legal Counsel

Defense companies (particularly midsize and large corporations) often employ teams of legal

---

OCCUPATION SPECIALTIES

Precision Assemblers

Specialty	Responsibilities
Aircraft power plant assemblers	Analyze blueprints and other materials to put together and install parts of airplanes such as wings or landing gear.
Electromechanical assemblers	Prepare and test devices such as tape drives and magnetic drums. They also examine parts for surface defects.
Electronics assemblers	Assemble electronics equipment, such as missile control systems, radio and test equipment, and computers.
Machine builders	Analyze blueprint assembly instructions and manuals to construct, assemble, or rebuild engines and turbines.

OCCUPATION PROFILE

Precision Assembler

Considerations	Qualifications
Description	Analyzes blueprints and assembles equipment or parts.
Career cluster	Manufacturing
Interests	Things
Working conditions	Work inside
Minimum education level	No high school diploma; on-the-job training; high school diploma or GED; high school diploma/technical college
Physical exertion	Medium work
Physical abilities	Unexceptional/basic fitness
Opportunities for experience	Part-time work
Licensure and certification	Usually not required
Employment outlook	Decline expected
Holland interest scores	CRE; CRS; CSR; RCE; RCI; RCS; REC; REI; RES; RIC; RIE; RSE

Note: See volume 1, "Publisher's Note," for an explanation of the Holland interest score.

experts to advise them. One of the most important roles legal counsel plays is reviewing government contracts to ensure that they meet their companies' best interests. Additionally, legal counsel are frequently called on to review any local, state, regional, and national regulatory or statutory changes that may affect company operations or obligations. Furthermore, legal counsel may respond to internal employee complaints or external civil suits.

Legal counsel must be fully versed in the law. They must know and understand all federal laws pertaining to the defense field, and they must also carefully observe local ordinances that may apply to the work performed in a given area by their companies. In the light of the complexities of legal statutes and regulations, legal counsel must pay an extraordinary amount of attention to detail.

Legal counsel team members must have advanced degrees in law. Many are also former military personnel, with insights into military protocols. They must also have extensive understanding of how the laws in a given region affect corporate activities in that region.

Legal occupations may include the following:

- Chief Counsel
- Staff Attorney
- Associate Attorney
- Paralegal
- Administrative Assistant

Marketing

A defense contractor always needs to advertise itself in relevant media and in the proper venues in order to generate potential business. For smaller and midsize companies, such efforts may enable them to compete with better-established and better-known companies. The responsibility for this area of operations falls to the company's marketing department.

Marketing personnel put together promotional brochures, create advertising campaigns and strategies, and even establish partnerships with other companies and trade associations in order to generate the maximum amount of visibility. They must therefore be very well educated, not only in marketing but also in defense manufacturing and the overall functioning of the military-industrial complex. This knowledge helps them ensure that marketing materials go to the right groups and individuals. Marketing personnel tend to have undergraduate and advanced degrees in such fields as marketing, advertising, communications, and business management.

Marketing occupations may include the following:

- Marketing Director
- Marketing Manager
- Marketing Coordinator
- Communications Manager
- Administrative Assistant

Human Resources

Defense contractors, like other government contract companies, must recruit two types of employees: full-time employees who manage the day-to-day operations of the company and consultants who work on specific contractual projects. To this end, defense contractors maintain active human resources and recruitment departments.

Human resources personnel recruit, hire, and terminate employees. They administer employee benefits packages, insurance programs, and training programs for full-time employees. They may also be involved in conducting background checks or coordinating with law enforcement investigators to ensure that potential employees have no criminal backgrounds and are otherwise assigned proper security clearances. They play active roles on proposal teams, reviewing the best internal and external personnel for contract positions and, if a proposal is accepted, applying the specified personnel to their proposed positions.

Human resources professionals must be highly conversant in issues pertaining to federal and state employment practices, as well as protocols for hiring and terminating employees. They are typically college educated, and many have advanced training or degrees in business management, human resources, and similar fields.

Human resources occupations may include the following:

- Human Resources Director
- Human Resources Coordinator
- Recruitment Manager
- Administrative Assistant

Accounting

The responsibility of overseeing the financial operations, including accounts payable (money that is owed by a company) and accounts receivable (money that is owed to a company) falls to a defense contractor's accounting department. This area of the company must carefully review and record employee expenses within the context of a given project, as well as in terms of overall company operations.

Accounting departments are extremely vital elements of defense contractors, particularly in light of the fact that their customers, military agencies, are constantly concerned with budget constraints. Accounting personnel must be extremely organized and pay strong attention to detail. Many have military experience, which is useful for managing military contracts and projects. In fact, accountants are oftem asked to join proposal teams. Accountants are typically college educated, while some have advanced degrees in related fields. In the United States, most of them are licensed as certified public accountants (CPAs) as well.

Accounting occupations may include the following:

- Accounting Director
- Accounts Payable Manager
- Accounts Receivable Manager
- Office Manager

Administrative Support

Defense contractors employ administrative assistants to handle a wide variety of administrative tasks in various departments. Administrative personnel answer phones and direct calls, organize accounting records, take meeting minutes, and coordinate visitor protocols. They must have strong organizational skills, as well as an ability to communicate effectively with internal and external personnel. They must also become quickly familiar with office computer, telephone, and filing systems. Many have high school diplomas, although some administrative support personnel are relatively new to the workforce, having recently graduated from undergraduate programs.

Administrative support occupations may include the following:

- Receptionist
- File Clerk
- Administrative Assistant
- Executive Assistant
- Paid Intern

INDUSTRY OUTLOOK

Overview

The defense industry has long been subject to the demands of the consumer. In this case, the consumer is the global military community and its perceived need for new systems, technology, weapons, and vehicles. The modern military-industrial complex took shape as the Cold War began to intensify. Over the next several decades, the United States and its allies worked to develop military technologies that could theoretically counter threats from the Soviet Union (which was in turn developing its own weaponry). When those threats ended with the Soviets' collapse, this intense pursuit of military

buildup lessened, as policy makers believed taxpayer money should be directed elsewhere.

The decline in military expenditures during the 1990's reversed dramatically with the September 11 attacks. The threat from international terrorists gave rise to new security systems, as well as military weaponry to use in the wars in Afghanistan and Iraq. The military-industrial complex in the United States saw renewed interest thereafter.

Although American troops are stationed in Iraq and Afghanistan, it is believed that the administration of President Barack Obama will usher in another period of evolution for the defense industry. Because the president has extended the U.S. engagement in Afghanistan and the commitment to Iraq still requires the presence of U.S. troops at some level, the future of defense industry spending is uncertain. Certainly, the anticipated decline in military investment will not be across the entire industry. Rather, it is predicted that manufacturers that produced large-scale weaponry and vehicles during the Cold War, such as state-of-the-art fighter jets, advanced missile defense systems, and heavy battlefield vehicles, may see a decline in such programs. These weapons systems, useful for battles of nation against nation, will be replaced by systems

A U.S. Air Force RQ-1 Predator unmanned aerial vehicle takes off. (Department of Defense)

that are more useful in fighting nationless threats, including more versatile multipurpose aircraft, automated drones, and so on. Thus, defense contractors already building such devices or well positioned to repurpose their assembly lines will be best positioned to receive the most lucrative contracts of the coming decade.

The demise of the Soviet Union and the 2001 terrorist attacks did not signal the end of the military-industrial complex, nor does it appear that the industry will suffer significantly over the long term. Rather, the industry merely needs to shift its focus to support technologies rather than traditional, battlefield-oriented weaponry. In many cases, military organizations are eschewing the development of new weapons in favor of upgrades to existing technologies. Such shifts in policy are causing many contractors to shift accordingly.

Even the largest of contractors are faced with the reality of needing to cut personnel and programs that have long been the cornerstones of their business. This trend has already begun. Aerospace giant Lockheed Martin had been working on a long-term contract to produce a special helicopter known as the VH-71. In 2009, the Pentagon terminated its contract, citing its exorbitant costs and eliminating the six hundred jobs that accompanied it. Another industry icon, Boeing, cut one thousand jobs that were attached to its missile defense program.

While these cuts were occurring, these companies were succeeding in other areas. In November of 2009, Lockheed Martin won a major military contract to develop a new electronic warfare system for U.S. naval ships (such systems are defensive in nature, protecting a ship from long- and short-distance attacks). Boeing, meanwhile, won a major contract to upgrade the U.S. Air Force's B-1 bomber avionics software, giving a reliable weapon new, cutting-edge technology, rather than expensively developing entirely new planes.

Fallout from the global economic crisis of 2007-2009 is expected to continue to cause declines in revenues within the defense industry in the short term, and this fall in profits is likely to be exacerbated by the winding down of military operations in Iraq and Afghanistan. These two major factors are driving some studies to suggest that total government investment in military procurement could decline by as much as 40 percent over three years.

The United States is not the only country to undergo this shift in its defense industry. In 2010, France cut fifty-four thousand positions within its own industry. The money saved from these layoffs was redirected toward an integrated European security system. In early 2009, South Africa canceled its order for eight A400M military transport planes, which were to be produced by British contractor Airbus. That cancellation placed a project that was already experiencing significant cost overruns in even further jeopardy.

The reduction of large-scale programs poses great opportunities for small companies and the more relevant technologies they offer to the twenty-first century world. Demand for more cost-effective weapons systems, many of which are integrated and interchangeable with other systems, is steadily increasing. In addition, governments around the world are seeking delivery on such systems with greater speed in order to avoid cost overruns in a down economy. As a result, they look for greater communications, computer modeling, and other systems that help expedite production and better facilitate client-manufacturer interaction. Smaller companies are becoming important partners in this pursuit, producing such systems and technologies.

Although smaller companies that produce new technologies have become increasingly popular in the pursuit of expedited and more efficient systems, it is likely that the trend of larger companies acquiring midsize and small companies will continue. This trend may cause jobs in the overall defense industry to remain competitive.

Employment Advantages

The defense industry offers a great number of opportunities for those who seek to help develop the systems and weapons that protect a nation's security and interests. Most of these technologies are state-of-the-art, giving those who work on them a sense of pride and discovery. In fact, many of the nonweapons technologies developed in the defense industry—such as radar, sonar, communications, satellite systems, and computer software—have potential applications in the nondefense world. This point represents a great advantage for employees.

In addition, this industry represents an ideal arena for former military personnel to enter upon retirement from service. A great many former officers and personnel from every branch of a country's military are now part of the defense industry, adding a significant presence to contract teams and giving themselves a boost in income. Finally, there is an element of stability in the defense industry, bolstered by the fact that the industry's primary client is the government. While the current environment necessitates both cost-effective and less traditional weaponry and technology, the defense industry continues to adapt to that environment. Employees and potential employees may need to expand their knowledge of the systems of the twenty-first century in order to compete for jobs.

Annual Earnings

Overall, the defense industry generates hundreds of billions of dollars in revenue around the world. The United States is the largest contributor to this number, as the American military-industrial complex comprises about 45 percent of the global industry. Hoovers' analysis of U.S. Census Bureau data indicates that in 2002, the U.S. defense and aerospace industries earned $214 billion. In 2008, according to Datamonitor, the global industry was worth $674.6 billion.

The 2007-2009 worldwide recession had a significant impact on the defense industry in virtually every country. However, the recession only slowed the industry's growth rather than causing bankruptcies. Although faced with weaker revenues brought about by changes in governments' defense priorities and the economic realities of the twenty-first century, the industry still shows signs of growth. In the United States, the industry generated a mild increase in revenues of about 3.9 percent in 2008, after growing by 9 percent and 10 percent in 2007 and 2006, respectively.

The growth areas of the defense industry are likely to be those that have applications wider than simply to homeland defense. For example, it is believed that the cyber security arena will see a $50 billion increase in U.S. government contract spending. Similar growth in earnings may be seen in other areas. In general, the defense industry is expected to falter in terms of earnings, but it is likely to grow nonetheless, as demand from governments seeking to bolster their national security interests remains consistent.

RELATED RESOURCES FOR FURTHER RESEARCH

AeroSpace and Defence Industries
  Association of Europe
  270 Ave. de Tervuren
  B-1150 Brussels
  Belgium
  Tel: 32-2-775-8110
  Fax: 32-2-775-8112
  http://www.asd-europe.org

Aerospace Industries Association
  1000 Wilson Blvd., Suite 1700
  Arlington, VA 22209-3928
  Tel: (703) 358-1000
  Fax: (703) 358-1151
  http://www.aia-aerospace.org

American Institute of Aeronautics and
  Astronautics
  1801 Alexander Bell Dr., Suite 500
  Reston, VA 20191-4344
  Tel: (703) 264-7500
  Fax: (703) 264-7551
  http://www.aiaa.org

BAE Systems
  6 Carlton Gardens
  London SW1Y 5AD
  United Kingdom
  Tel: 44-1252-37-3232
  http://www.baesystems.com

Defence Manufacturers Association
  Marlborough House
  Headley Rd.
  Greyshot, Hindhead, Surrey GU26 61G
  United Kingdom
  Tel: 44-1428-60-7788
  Fax: 44-1428-60-4567
  http://www.the-dma.org.uk

Lockheed Martin
  1725 Jefferson Davis Hwy., Suite 403
  Arlington, VA 22202-4127
  Tel: (301) 897-6000
  http://www.lockheedmartin.com

National Defense Industry Association
2111 Wilson Blvd., Suite 400
Arlington, VA 22201
Tel: (703) 522-1820
http://www.ndia.org

ABOUT THE AUTHOR

Michael P. Auerbach has over sixteen years of experience in government, defense, and public policy. He is a 1993 graduate of Wittenberg University and a 1999 graduate of the Boston College Graduate School of Arts and Sciences. He is a former analyst for the U.S. Navy's international cooperation programs and has written a number of papers on international security, defense, and military policy, including an in-depth study of NATO's Partnership for Peace program. He is a veteran of state and federal government, having worked for seven years in the Massachusetts legislature and four years as a federal government contractor.

FURTHER READING

Anderson, Guy, and Keri Wagstaff-Smith. "Analysis: Can the Defence Industry Re-ignite the Economy." Jane's Information Group, November 26, 2008. http://www.janes.com/news/defence/business/jdi/jdi081126_1_n.shtml.

Ben-Ari, Guy, and Pierre A. Chao. *Organizing for a Complex World: Developing Tomorrow's Defense and Net-Centric Systems.* Washington, D.C.: Center for Strategic and International Studies, 2009.

Bialos, Jeffrey P., et al. *Fortresses and Icebergs: The Evolution of the Transatlantic Defense Market and the Implications for U.S. National Security Policy.* Washington, D.C.: Center for Transatlantic Relations, 2009.

Bitzinger, Richard. *The Modern Defense Industry: Political, Economic, and Technological Issues.* Santa Barbara, Calif.: Praeger Security International/ABC-CLIO, 2009.

"Boeing Wins $84 Million Contract from U.S. Air Force for B-1 Bomber's Avionics Software Upgradation." *Defense World,* October 30, 2009. http://www.defenseworld.net/go/defense news.jsp?gcatid=2&id=3767&h=Boeing %20wins%20$84%20million%20contract %20from%20US%20Force%20B-1%20Bomber %20avionics%20'software%20upgradation.

Finnegan, Philip. "U.S. Defense and Aerospace Industry Weakens During Worldwide Recession." Teal Group Corporation, October 14, 2009. http://www.tealgroup.com/index.php?option=com_content&view=article&id=59:us-aerospace-and-defense-industry-weakens-in-face-of-worldwide-recession-&catid=8:blogmain&Itemid=100004.

Lasou, Damien. "Five Key Trends Impacting the Aerospace and Defense Industry Amid Challenging Economic Times." *Aviation Spectator,* June 9, 2009. http://www.aviationspectator.com/blogs/admin/guest-post-five-key-trends-impacting-the-aerospace-and-defense-industry-amid-challenging.

Markowski, Stefan, Peter Hall, and Robert Wylie. *Defence Procurement and Industry Policy: A Small Country Perspective.* London: Routledge, 2010.

PayScale.com. "Salary Survey for Industry: Aerospace and Defense." http://www.payscale.com/research/US/Industry%3DAerospace_and_Defense/Salary.

Simply Hired. "Average Defense Industry Salaries." http://www.simplyhired.com/a/salary/search/q-Defense+Industry.

Smith, Ron. *Military Economics: The Interaction of Power and Money.* New York: Palgrave Macmillan, 2009.

Sorenson, David S. *The Process and Politics of Defense Acquisition: A Reference Handbook.* Westport, Conn.: Praeger Security International, 2009.

U.S. Bureau of Labor Statistics. *Career Guide to Industries,* 2010-2011 ed. http://www.bls.gov/oco/cg.

U.S. Census Bureau. North American Industry Classification System (NAICS), 2007. http://www.census.gov/cgi-bin/sssd/naics/naicsrch?chart=2007.

U.S. Department of Commerce. International Trade Administration. Office of Trade and Industry Information. Industry Trade Data and Analysis. http://ita.doc.gov/td/industry/otea/OTII/OTII-index.html.

Dental and Orthodontics Industry

INDUSTRY SNAPSHOT

General Industry: Health Science

Career Cluster: Health Science

Subcategory Industries: Dental Hygienists' Offices; Dental Laboratories; Denturists' Offices; Offices of Dental Surgeons and Doctors of Dental Medicine; Offices of Dentists; Offices of Oral Pathologists; Offices of Orthodontists; Offices of Periodontists; Offices of Prosthodontists; Orthodontic Appliance Makers

Related Industries: Medicine and Health Care Industry; Pharmaceuticals and Medications Industry; Public Health Services; Scientific, Medical, and Health Equipment and Supplies Industry; Veterinary Industry

Annual Domestic Revenues: $94.18 billion USD (U.S. Census Bureau, 2007 Economic Census)

NAICS Numbers: 6212, 339166, 621399

INDUSTRY DEFINITION

Summary

Dentistry is defined by the American Dental Association as the evaluation, diagnosis, prevention, and surgical or nonsurgical treatment of diseases, disorders, and conditions of the oral cavity, maxillofacial area, and the adjacent and associated structures and of the effects of those conditions on the human body. It is a branch of medicine that addresses oral health, including the appearance and function of the teeth, gums, tongue, palate, and jaws. Dental professionals treat oral infections, cancers, malformations, malfunctions, and traumatic injuries that may affect a person's ability to eat, drink, talk, breathe, and sleep, thus affecting overall health.

History of the Industry

Perhaps the earliest known written dental text is a Sumerian cuneiform document from 5000 B.C.E. that attributes tooth decay to "tooth worms." Egyptians described dentistry in the Ebers Papyrus (wr. about 1550 B.C.E., found 1872). This papyrus listed toothache remedies made from common ingredients such as incense, cloves, and fennel. In the fifth century B.C.E., the Greeks Hippocrates and Aristotle wrote about dentistry in a more scientific fashion, noting the eruption pattern of teeth, the extraction of teeth with forceps, and the use of wires to stabilize loose teeth and broken jaws. Also about this time, the Greek physician Diocles instructed people to rub their teeth and gums with crushed mint leaves to remove food remains and freshen breath.

In the tenth century C.E., the Islamic Moor surgeon Abulcasis of Cordova provided illustrations of numerous crude dental instruments, including scalers, elevators, and forceps. In 1530, the anonymous German book *Artzney Buchlein der kreutter* (also known as *The Little Medicinal Book for All Kinds of Diseases and Infirmities of the Teeth*) devoted its forty-four pages exclusively to dentistry. It was written for barbers and surgeons and covered such topics as oral hygiene and methods for filling dental cavities. In 1563, Italian anatomist Bertolomeo Eustachi published *Libellus de dentibus* (*A Little Treatise on the Teeth*, 1999), the first accurate dental anatomy textbook. In 1575, French barber-surgeon Ambroise Paré, known as the father of modern surgery, published *Les Oeuvres de M. Ambroise Paré, conseiller et premier chirurgien du roy* (26 vols.), a practical handbook written in French vernacular. It explained his surgical techniques, including extracting teeth and repairing jaw fractures. Paré was interested in providing artificial body parts to soldiers and designed individual gold and silver replacement teeth.

In the seventeenth century, a new profession arose, known as "operators for the teeth." Members of this professonion did more than extract teeth; they built artificial teeth and concocted dentifrices for keeping teeth clean and white. One such operator in London, Charles Allen, wrote the first dental book in English, *The Operator for the Teeth* (1685).

In 1728, French physician Pierre Fauchard, known as the father of modern dentistry, published *Le Chirurgien dentiste* (*The Surgeon Dentist: Or, Treatise on the Teeth*, 1946), a two-volume treatise on dentistry. In it, he described pyorrhea and tartar, an extraction instrument called a pelican, replacing missing teeth with dental prostheses, and straightening teeth with tension using linen, silk, or fine gold-wire threads.

In 1780, in England, William Addis began mass-producing toothbrushes fashioned from pig or badger bristles glued into small holes drilled into animal bone. Within sixty years, toothbrushes were being produced in England, France, Germany, and Japan. Mass production in the United States began in 1885.

In the nineteenth century, dental chairs that reclined and could be otherwise adjusted were designed by James Snell in London in 1832 and

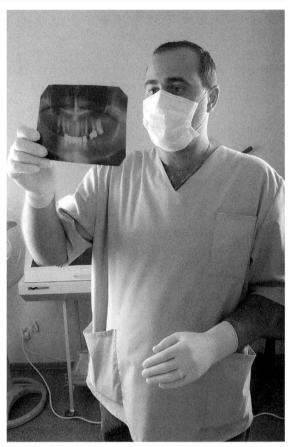

Dentists are trained to identify pathological conditions such as tooth decay, gum disease, and oral cancers, using diagnostic tools such as X rays. (©Andrey Kiselev/Dreamstime.com)

American dentist James Beall Morrison in 1867. Morrison also invented the foot-treadle drill, which allowed dentists to remove dental caries more efficiently. Anaesthetics were developed from nitrous oxide, ether, and cocaine; their use in dentistry was controversial. In 1839, American inventor Charles Goodyear discovered a process for hardening rubber with sulphur and heat, called vulcanization. The resulting product, called vulcanite, became popular as a moldable, durable, and inexpensive base for dentures.

The twentieth century brought more advancements in the dental industry, such as the use of dental X rays, novocaine as a local anaesthetic, high-speed handpieces, and amalgam fillings. Daily tooth brushing came into practice during World War II, first with toothbrushes made from synthetic bristles (which were more hygienic than animal bristles) and then, decades later, with electric toothbrushes. Public health services studied the effects of fluoride on tooth decay, and by 1960, most public drinking-water supplies in the United States were fluoridated, and many toothpastes contained fluoride.

The Industry Today

Dentists are no longer barbers or trade apprentices. Their present profession has evolved as an accredited, independent specialty of surgery and medicine. Modern dental schools confer the degrees of doctor of dental surgery (D.D.S.) and doctor of dental medicine (D.D.M.). The first dental school anywhere was the Baltimore College of Dental Surgery, established in November, 1840. To-

day's dentists typically spend four years in college and then four years in dental school. Once they graduate, they must pass a board exam to receive a license to practice. While most begin to practice general dentistry, some choose to pursue a dental specialty, such as endodontics (diseases of the dental pulp), periodontics (diseases of the gums), orthodontics (the straightening of teeth), and prosthodontics (the replacement of teeth). Such pursuits require several more years of specialized training. Dentists work in private practices, hospitals, public health clinics, and universities. Other than caring for patients, some dentists teach, conduct research, or promote the profession.

Dentists look after the oral health of their patients. This begins with a thorough examination of the oral cavity, including the teeth, gums, and tongue. Dentists are trained to identify pathological conditions such as dental caries (tooth decay), gum disease, and oral cancers. They use diagnostic tools such as radiographs, disclosing solutions, and articulating paper. They probe the relationship between the teeth and gums, the surfaces of the teeth, and the conditions of the oral mucosa.

To maintain a patient's oral and overall health, along with the abilities to eat, swallow, talk, and breathe, dentists treat the appearance and function of the teeth, gums, tongue, palate, and jaws. They practice preventive dentistry by methods including fluoride treatments, placing sealants over vulnerable areas of teeth, conducting regular oral exams, and recommending professional cleanings every six months. They practice ameliorative dentistry by prescribing antibiotics and analgesics for painful conditions, extracting badly decayed or impacted teeth, and performing root canal procedures to remove exposed nerves. They practice restorative dentistry by placing fillings, crowns, and bridges after removing compromising tooth decay and in patients without teeth, they fit dentures. Dentists also adjust occlusion

A technician checks the alignment of a dental prosthesis. (©Vadim Kozlovsky/Dreamstime.com)

so that the teeth and jaws meet in proper alignment. Orthodontics, a dental specialty, is the practice of straightening teeth, reshaping the palate, and realigning the jaws using tension appliances to create a more functional oral cavity as well as a more attractive smile. Cosmetic dentistry, another specialty, compensates for unattractive and misshapen teeth and gums with procedures such as bleaching, gum surgery, and bonding or veneers.

As dental procedures became more complex and time-sensitive, dentists began training dental assistants to work with them, passing instruments to the dentist and keeping the patient's oral field dry and free from debris with water, air, and suction lines. This teamwork is often referred to as "four-handed dentistry." Dental assistants may also set up procedure trays, prepare immediate-use dental materials, and sterilize instruments.

A subprofession of dentistry arose in the late 1800's: Dental hygienists (once called dental nurses) were trained in oral health and the prevention of oral disease. Health care providers had

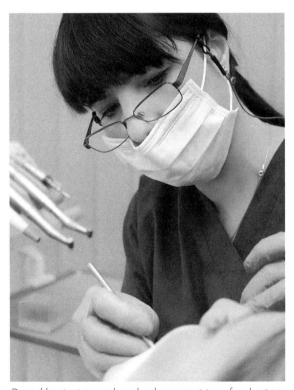

Dental hygienists work under the supervision of a dentist to professionally clean and polish patients' teeth. (©Viktor Levi/Dreamstime.com)

come to realize that dental pain and destruction could be avoided by maintaining a clean mouth. Dental hygienists work under the supervision of a dentist to professionally clean and polish patients' teeth, examine and chart the depth of the pockets between the gums and the teeth and bring to the dentist's attention any unusual conditions that may require further treatment, such as cavities, broken teeth, bleeding gums, or sores. They also provide patient education on the techniques and importance of brushing and flossing.

The twentieth century saw an increased understanding of infectious diseases, especially viral diseases such as hepatitis and human immunodeficiency virus (HIV). Because such diseases may be transmitted in bodily fluids such as blood and saliva and because such fluids are present and even aerosolized during dental procedures, dental personnel now wear eye shields, as well as disposable masks and gloves. Many wear uniforms that are made to withstand tough washing, and those uniforms often remain in the office to avoid introducing potential pathogens into the car and home. Stringent health precautions, such as hand-washing, disinfecting countertops, sterilizing instruments, and using disposable supplies for each patient are followed to protect patients and dental personnel alike.

Dentists work in conjunction with physicians and pharmacists. Dentists have learned the importance of taking a complete medical history, not only to learn about any patient conditions that may potentially complicate dental treatment and results but also to find out what medications a patient is taking or is allergic to and thus avoid negative interactions. Patients with joint or heart-valve replacements may be told to take penicillin before and after dental treatment because such treatment releases bacteria from the mouth into the bloodstream and these patients are more susceptible to infections. Resistance to antibiotics is increasing in the population, so prescribers must be conscious of which antibiotic is appropriate and how long the course of treatment must be to be effective without encouraging resistance. Bisphosphonates used in cancer therapy and the treatment of osteoporosis have been linked to impaired wound healing after tooth extraction or periodontal surgery due to bone death. Dentists began reporting cases of this complication in the professional literature, and in

2005 the U.S. Food and Drug Administration (FDA) issued a statement that osteonecrosis of the jaw was a recognized complication of bisphosphonate treatment.

Dentists also work closely with dental laboratories, which manufacture crowns, bridges, dental implants, dentures, and other custom oral appliances in accordance with dentists' models and specifications. These products are regulated by the FDA as medical devices and thus must meet federal manufacturing and quality standards. The communication of specifications has become more timely with the use of digital photography and radiography that may be transmitted online and has become more precise with the use of three-dimensional imaging technology.

INDUSTRY MARKET SEGMENTS

Dental practices range in size from single-dentist operations in niche practices to community dental health centers employing multiple practitioners and hygienists. The following sections provide a comprehensive breakdown of three different segments.

Small Businesses

Dentists who operate niche or boutique practices deliver high-quality elective procedures and excellent customer service in return for high fees. They limit the services they offer and refer dental hygiene, emergency care, and simple restoration cases to other offices. Insurance companies do not pay for such elective procedures, so these boutique practices require payment in full from patients.

Potential Annual Earnings Scale. Boutique practices command the highest fees of any private practice in general dentistry. While no exact figures are available because of the exclusive nature of these practices, the top 25 percent of general dentists earned more than $166,400 in 2009, according to the U.S. Bureau of Labor Statistics (BLS). The top 10 percent of dental hygienists, who may assist in such practices, earned more than $92,860.

Clientele Interaction. Patients are greeted warmly by receptionists at boutique practices and are immediately made to feel that their care and comfort are important upon their arrival. Many have been referred by friends and come with preconceived notions of the caliber of service they will receive. In some offices, the same dental assistant is assigned to a given patient at every visit to provide continuity of care. This person becomes a familiar and comforting presence and remains readily available to answer questions and to escort the patient through the office. With the patient comfortably seated, the dentist engages in conversation and listens carefully for the patient's desired outcome of dental treatment. The dentist's goal is not merely to meet but to exceed the patient's expectations for both results and experience. A patient's dignity and privacy are carefully guarded, and financial discussions with an administrator are conducted discreetly.

Amenities, Atmosphere, and Physical Grounds. Dental boutique practices strive to create a spalike atmosphere because patients are paying for personal attention in addition to high-quality dental care. The reception area frequently contains large, fresh flower arrangements and attractive art. Soothing instrumental music may be played throughout the office. Patients may be treated to specialty coffees and other beverages; some offices even offer fresh baked goods, which also provide an inviting aroma.

Because these dentists see fewer patients in a day, they are less likely to be running behind schedule and keeping patients waiting. Staff members are trained to pay attention to details that ensure patient comfort and ease. The atmosphere is one of stress-free pampering, which provides relief from the noise and impersonal crowds of a city. Some practices provide patients with thank-you gift baskets containing premium dental products such as toothpaste, a toothbrush, floss, mouthwash, and lip balm, along with a handwritten note of appreciation.

This type of practice is found in an urban setting, typically in a building with other professional offices or in a small converted house. The office must have appropriate electrical and water supplies to meet dental purposes, and it must be accessible to people with special needs, in compliance with the Americans with Disabilities Act. Boutique practices typically employ state-of-the-art equipment and have exquisite interior designs and décor. Some office designs include a patient checkout station, where patients can freshen themselves (reapply makeup, clean eyeglasses) after treatment and admire their newly completed dental work.

Typical Number of Employees. To provide personal attention and expert service, boutique practices require at least one dentist, one chairside assistant, and one receptionist who also oversees billing. There may be additional dental assistants and administrative assistants to ensure attention to customer service.

Traditional Geographic Locations. Niche practices survive only in metropolitan areas in which large numbers of people have discretionary income to spend on high-quality dentistry. With the need for only one or two treatment rooms, these dental offices fit well in city buildings and converted houses.

Pros of Working for a Niche Practice. Patients pay top dollar for top-quality service, so employees of niche dental practices earn high incomes while working comfortable schedules and seeing select patients. Dentists who choose to run boutique practices enjoy the reputation of being exclusive and having patients seek out their dental skill and expertise. They are able to pursue their full potential, work in an elegant environment, work with their hands to produce both art and science, and serve appreciative patients.

Cons of Working for a Niche Practice. Niche practices require sufficient populations of patients with sufficient discretionary income and the willingness to spend it on dentistry in order to be viable businesses. Their high fees must be justified by high-quality dentistry because anything less would compromise the practice's reputation. The customer service they provide must impress patients enough to motivate them to refer new patients to the practice. Overhead expenses may rise with the acquisition of the latest equipment and best materials. Staff-related expenses and location costs (such as rent and renovation) may also be relatively high. As business owners, dentists in such practices bear the responsibility of keeping abreast of applicable federal, state, and local regulations, in addition to developments in dentistry.

Costs

Payroll and Benefits: Staff members in niche practices are typically paid higher-than-average

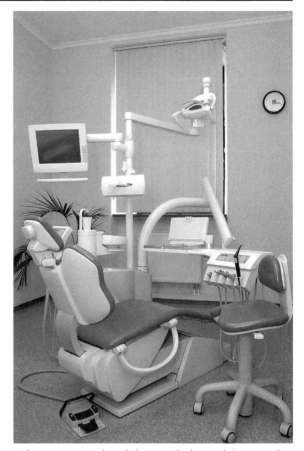

Advancements in dental chairs and other tools have made a visit to the dentist a more comfortable experience. (©Vitaliy Hrabar/Dreamstime.com)

salaries. Dental assistants may also have higher continuing-education allowances than at other practices to fund training in the use of state-of-the-art materials, equipment, and technology. Benefits may include medical insurance and dental care.

Supplies: Fixtures include an adjustable dental chair, adequate adjustable lighting for illuminating the oral cavity, an instrument-tray delivery system, and a system of retractable air, water, and suction lines. Equipment pieces include a sterilization system (autoclave), a high-speed handpiece, a curing light, and assorted dental instruments. The radiography system is commonly digital. Computer hardware and software may be used for both clinical and administrative functions. Many supplies are disposable, such as masks, gloves, patient bibs, cotton rolls, and gauze. Others are consumable, such as dental materials, bleaching reagents, and anaesthetics.

External Services: Outsourced services typically include housekeeping and janitorial services, facilities maintenance, and dental laboratory services. Dentists may also contract marketing, information technology support, and financial services such as billing, bookkeeping, and tax planning. Biohazardous waste disposal, including surgical sharps and bloody gauze, must be handled by licensed contractors. Building owners may contract yard care (lawn mowing, landscaping, and snow removal). Boutique practices aim to create a spalike atmosphere and may contract external services such as florists, beverage suppliers, and bakeries. Some even bring in massage therapists to relax patients before tedious procedures and reduce patient anxiety during injections.

Utilities: Dental practices depend on reliable electrical and water supplies and appropriate wastewater drains. Other utilities include telephone and Internet access lines.

Taxes: Dental practices are required to pay local, state, and federal income and property taxes. Some municipalities also collect annual personal property taxes on dental equipment, computers, compressors, and other assets. Others may impose business privilege taxes based on gross receipts. Some states impose an occupations tax on persons holding professional licenses or registrations to practice dentistry.

Licenses and Continuing Education: Dentists must pay for their licenses and the continuing education credits necessary to maintain those licenses.

Midsize Businesses

In 2008, of all dentists in general private practice, 83.1 percent worked in solo practices or two-dentist practices. Most accept payment from private dental benefits plans, with the balance due from the patients.

Potential Annual Earnings Scale. According to the BLS, the average salary for a general dentist employed by a dental office in 2009 was $159,350. Orthodontists earned an average of $208,910, oral and maxillofacial surgeons earned an average of $212,680, and dental hygienists earned an average of $68,160. These wages are dependent on geographic location, number of hours worked, and years of experience.

Clientele Interaction. Receptionists greet each patient upon arrival for an appointment. Dental assistants escort patients into the operatory and make them comfortable before treatment begins. For prophylaxis appointments, dental hygienists often perform the cleaning, scaling, and polishing, take X rays, and offer patient education. Dentists then perform oral examinations. For diagnostic, ameliorative, and restorative appointments, dentists review patients' medical histories and ask about present dental concerns before beginning their examinations and treatment. At an appointment's conclusion, a patient checks out with a receptionist or financial secretary to make payment arrangements and schedule the next appointment.

Amenities, Atmosphere, and Physical Grounds. Midsize dental offices are clean and comfortably decorated. Music may be playing to create a calm atmosphere and mask the sounds of the handpieces. A water cooler or bottles of drinking water may be available in the reception area. Patients may be given toothbrushes and spools of floss at the end of their visits.

These offices make an effort to remain on a firm schedule so that their patients do not have to wait and will not grow more anxious. Also, practitioners perform better without time pressures. General dentistry practices serve patients of all ages and often have a subsection of the reception area with toys for younger children to keep them busy. Reception areas typically provide appropriate reading materials (such as magazines, newspapers, and brochures) to entertain visitors.

Depending on the number of operatories, these practices may be found in buildings with other professional offices or in dedicated buildings. The offices must be in compliance with the Americans with Disabilities Act, providing such things as wide doorways and handicapped-accessible bathrooms.

Typical Number of Employees. A practice run by one or two dentists typically employs at least two full- or part-time hygienists, at least two full- or part-time assistants, and at least two full- or part-time receptionists. It may also employ an office manager to assume business management and human resources duties and a financial secretary to oversee billing, insurance claims, and other financial arrangements.

Traditional Geographic Locations. These practices are found in urban, suburban, and rural areas of every state. The national average density of dental practices is 60.4 dentists per 100,000 population; Washington, D.C., at the far end of the spectrum, has 144.7 dentists per 100,000 population, while Nevada, at the other, has only 39.2 dentists per 100,000 population.

Pros of Working for a Midsize Practice. General practice dentists perform a variety of procedures that employ their artistic and mechanical talents as well as their problem-solving skills. They enjoy the benefits of self-employment, including control of their time and the freedom to set fees. They have flexibility, especially in two-dentist practices, to balance work and family life. Similarly, partners and associates share the responsibilities for administering emergency care outside of regular business hours. They have the satisfaction of diagnosing diseases and enhancing the oral health of their patients. They have opportunities to pursue professional development, learn and apply advanced technologies, and determine the direction of their practices.

Cons of Working for a Midsize Practice. To reach a target income and minimize overhead expenses, dentists must balance fees with patient volume; to keep fees reasonable, dentists must attract and retain new patients. To do so, they must provide an appreciable level of customer service that may include offering emergency care after regular hours, accepting interruptions of their nights, weekends, and holidays. Dentists must also attract and retain competent dental hygienists and dental assistants by offering reasonable pay and benefits and maintaining sufficient patient loads to keep these staff members productive. Dentists must be proficient in a wide range of skills and keep up with advancements in their field. As business owners, they must also keep abreast of applicable federal, state, and local regulations.

Costs

Payroll and Benefits: Dental hygienists receive an hourly wage, typically between $26.74 and $38.46, with a median of $32.38. In some offices, they may also earn bonuses for exceeding production goals. Dental assistants receive an hourly wage, typically between $13.23 and $19.12, with a median of $15.98. Benefits may include medical insurance and dental care. Some offices provide vacation time, retirement plans, uniform allowances, and continuing education allowances.

Supplies: Required fixtures include an adjustable dental chair, adequate adjustable lighting for illuminating the oral cavity, an instrument-tray delivery system, and a system of retractable air, water, and suction lines in each operatory. Required equipment includes a sterilization system (autoclave), a high-speed handpiece, an ultrasonic cleaning unit, an electrosurgical unit, a curing light, and assorted dental instruments. Radiography systems are commonly automated and take panoramic as well as focal bite-wing X rays. Computer hardware and software may be used for both clinical and administrative functions. Most dental practices have discontinued placing silver amalgam fillings in favor of tooth-colored composite fillings and no longer have a need for amalgam separator systems. Fewer than half of midsize practices use lasers, computer-aided design and computer-aided manufacturing (CAD/CAM) technology, digital radiography, or nitrous oxide anaesthesia. Many supplies are disposable, such as masks, gloves, patient bibs, cotton rolls, and gauze. Others are consumable, such as dental restoration materials, prophy paste, and anaesthetics.

External Services: Outsourced services typically include housekeeping and janitorial services, facilities maintenance, and dental laboratory services. They may also include marketing, information technology, and financial services such as billing, bookkeeping, and tax planning. Biohazardous waste disposal, including surgical sharps, bloody gauze, and extracted teeth, must be handled by licensed contractors. Building owners may contract yard care (lawn mowing, landscaping, and snow removal) or may perform these duties themselves.

Utilities: Dental practices depend on reliable electrical, water, and air supplies and appropriate wastewater drains. Other utilities include telephone and Internet access lines.

Taxes: Dental practices are required to pay local, state, and federal income and property taxes. Some municipalities also collect annual personal property taxes on dental equipment, computers, compressors, and other assets. Others may impose business privilege taxes based on gross receipts. Some states impose occupations taxes on persons holding professional licenses or registrations to practice dentistry.

Licenses and Continuing Education: Dentists must pay for their licenses and the continuing education credits necessary to maintain those licenses.

Large Businesses

Practices with multiple dentists and hygienists may include per diem specialists to establish one location, a community dental health center, in which a patient may have all dental needs met. They typically operate under health-maintenance-organization (HMO) or preferred-provider-organization (PPO) plans, which means that the dental care providers have signed contracts with plan providers to provide treatment and services to members enrolled in their plans in exchange for fees paid from fee schedules determined by the plan providers. These plans are commonly part of benefits packages offered by employers. Dental practitioners in community centers may also treat adults with special needs and children on Medicaid. In some practices, individuals who qualify may be eligible to pay for services on a sliding fee scale.

Practitioners deliver preventive services such as X rays, cleanings, fluoride treatments, and sealants, as well as simple restorations. Per diem specialists may provide extractions, stainless steel crowns, space maintainers, and dentures. Some centers do not offer emergency dental care.

Potential Annual Earnings Scale. Large community practices usually receive lower fees than other private practices in general dentistry. While no exact figures are available because of the charitable nature of these practices, the bottom 25 percent of general dentists (in which community health practitioners may be assumed to be) earned an hourly wage below $48.23 and an annual wage below $100,330 in 2009, according to the BLS. The average annual income of a dentist employed at an outpatient care center was $138,750, and the average annual income of a dentist employed at a general hospital was $109,560. Older dentists who do not want to retire completely may choose to work part time in community practices. New dentists who want to increase their skills, experience, and confidence may also choose to work at such facilities.

Clientele Interaction. Community dental health centers serve children, adolescents, adults, and individuals with special needs. Patients seeking dental treatment are often asked to make initial appointments in person so they can fill out paperwork with a receptionist without taking time away from their treatment. Depending on the population being served, centers may have translators available to facilitate communication in languages such as Spanish or Korean. Dentists are available to perform initial examinations and treatment planning and, later, to provide restorations, but patients spend most of their visits with hygienists, who perform preventive treatment and then teach patients and their families how to maintain a clean mouth. Dental assistants may work chairside with hygienists, as well as with dentists.

Amenities, Atmosphere, and Physical Grounds. Because community dental health centers operate on a tight budget, they offer basic services to as many patients as they can and forego unnecessary expenses. Their offices are clean but not fancy, and they are typically bustling and noisy. They are equipped to accommodate young children, as well as individuals with special needs. Depending on the population being served, patient education literature may be offered in multiple languages and may be written for readers with low levels of literacy. Each patient may receive a basic toothbrush at the end of each visit to encourage proper oral hygiene.

Centers commonly have ample reception areas to accommodate large families and adequate parking lots to accommodate transport vans and staff vehicles. Their buildings may be simple, new construction to ensure adequate electrical and water conduits and meet the measurements, such as doorway widths and ramp angles, specified in the Americans with Disabilities Act. Retrofitting an existing building is difficult and often more costly than renting or purchasing one that already satisfies such requirements.

Typical Number of Employees. The number of employees is dependent upon what a given area can support. There are typically more hygienists than dentists and more assistants than hygienists. There are often many support staff members to handle the paperwork of patient records and service claim forms.

Traditional Geographic Locations. Community health centers are commonly found in underserved areas. The national average density is 60.4 dentists per 100,000 population, but many states are below this average. States in the east south central and west south central regions have fewer than 50 dentists per 100,000 residents, and Mississippi and Nevada have fewer than 40 dentists per 100,000 residents. Community dental health centers typically serve large geographical areas, such as entire counties. In some instances, dental screenings, referrals, and education are presented in mobile dental vans that travel to schools and churches.

Pros of Working for a Large Community Practice. Dental care providers can take great satisfaction in knowing that they are caring for underserved patients by improving their oral health and thus their quality of life. The dental education they offer their patients often has a significant effect. The need for community dental care in the United States is unlikely to decrease. Dentists whose centers do not provide emergency dental care are able to work regular hours, without interruptions of nights, weekends, and holidays.

Cons of Working for a Large Community Practice. Practitioners do not have great earning potential and cannot raise fees of their own volition. Therefore, they must see a larger number of patients to balance income and expenses. They perform a reduced range of services, depending on what HMOs and PPOs will cover, so the work may become monotonous. They have fewer opportunities to learn and incorporate advanced dental techniques because of the expense. As business owners, they must keep abreast of applicable federal, state, and local regulations.

Costs

Payroll and Benefits: Dental hygienists and assistants in community practices are typically paid lower-than-average salaries because of the fixed and sliding fees charged to patients. Employees are frequently part time, with few if any benefits.

Supplies: Required fixtures include an adjustable dental chair, adequate adjustable lighting for illuminating the oral cavity, an instrument-tray delivery system, and a system of retractable air, water, and suction lines in each operatory. Required equipment includes a sterilization system (autoclave), a high-speed handpiece, a curing light, and assorted dental instruments. The radiography system may be wet process or digi-

tal. Patient records are often kept as paper charts. Many supplies are disposable, such as masks, gloves, patient bibs, cotton rolls, and gauze. Others are consumable, such as prophy paste, sealant materials, and anaesthetics.

External Services: Outsourced services typically include housekeeping and janitorial services, facilities maintenance, and dental laboratory services. Biohazardous waste disposal, including extracted teeth, bloody gauze, and filters from an amalgam separator system, must be handled by licensed contractors. If a community center includes an on-site pharmacy, additional security services may be hired. Building owners may contract yard care (such as lawn mowing and snow removal) or may perform these duties themselves.

Utilities: Dental practices depend upon reliable electrical and water supplies and appropriate wastewater drains. Another utility cost is telephone lines.

Taxes: Dental practices are required to pay local, state, and federal income and property taxes. Some municipalities also collect annual personal property taxes on dental equipment, computers, compressors, and other assets. Others may impose business privilege taxes based on gross receipts. Some states impose occupations taxes on persons holding professional licenses or registrations to practice dentistry.

Licenses and Continuing Education: Dentists must pay for their licenses and the continuing education credits necessary to maintain those licenses.

ORGANIZATIONAL STRUCTURE AND JOB ROLES

Three out of four dentists are solo practitioners. In a typical dental office, one dentist operates with one or more dental hygienists, one or more dental assistants, and one or more administrative support personnel. The dentist, as the business owner, often assumes many of the operating responsibilities. Larger, group practices have larger staffs and may employ people to perform more specialized functions, such as an appointment secretary, a billing clerk, or a treatment coordinator. Other functions are outsourced to specialists, such as tax planners, dental laboratory technicians, and information technology experts.

Additional jobs may be found in peripheral fields, such as sales and marketing (to dentists, not just for dentists), continuing education, research, and promotion of the profession. While professions such as dentist and dental hygienist require formal education and state licensure, other employment positions do not, although a college degree in science may be necessary. For positions such as receptionist and dental assistant, dental practices may prefer to train a motivated employee on the job rather than seeking someone with previous training and experience.

The following umbrella categories apply to the organizational structure of businesses in the dental and orthodontics industry:

- Business Management
- Customer Service
- Sales and Marketing
- Technology, Research, Design, and Development
- Dental Care
- Human Resources

Business Management

A dental practice is a business like other businesses and must keep accurate financial records, send bills and insurance claims, record and deposit payments, pay taxes, and manage employee payrolls and benefits. Dental schools by their nature teach many more classes in dental science than in business management, so dentists often feel unprepared to run a private practice in which they must take on corporate duties in addition to performing dentistry. Dentists have been trained to be specialized technicians rather than managers or business owners. Therefore, many of them hire employees and consultants who have the appropriate skills and experience to run the practice as a sound and profitable business.

Services such as bookkeeping, accounting, billing, and payroll may be outsourced or they may be handled in-house by a business manager or office manager. An employee or contractor in this role may also track income versus expenses to monitor an annual budget, make quarterly income tax payments, make employee retirement contributions,

and manage the insurance plans. Dental offices must comply with federal regulations, particularly regarding privacy issues and chemical and biohazard waste containment and disposal, so manuals of safety procedures and policies must be written and maintained in compliance.

A dentist who is an employee of a hospital or other health agency must support good business practices but frequently does not have administrative responsibilities. However, the dentist may be responsible for maintaining a related budget.

Business management occupations may include the following:

- Owner/Partner
- Business Manager
- Office Manager
- Safety Officer
- Billing Clerk
- Payroll and Benefits Manager
- Bookkeeper
- Accountant
- Tax Manager

Customer Service

Customer service is extremely important in a dental office because patients often feel vulnerable, whether because they have a fear of dental treatment, they are embarrassed about the state of their oral hygiene, they are embarrassed about their financial situation, or they are in pain. Patients judge an office by how they are treated before, during, and after their visits.

Dental offices typically have at least one receptionist at a front desk to greet patients as they walk in and to answer telephone calls. Receptionists may schedule new and follow-up appointments, although some practices employ a dedicated secretary for managing the appointment schedule, especially for multiple providers. Dentists are not responsible for their own schedules, although they must specify how much time should be allotted for each procedure. Staff members who make every effort to keep the dentist seeing patients on time show respect to each patient as well as the dentist.

Dental assistants provide customer service by escorting patients into the operatory, seating them comfortably, and preparing the room for the dentist, facilitating efficient treatment. Dental assistants may also review and update the patient's medical history and take current vital signs, showing concern for the whole person, not just the mouth. They are frequently social and may converse with patients to put them at ease before treatment begins.

After treatment is complete and a dental assistant has escorted the patient back to the front desk, a receptionist may accept a patient's payment for services. Some practices may have a billing clerk or financial secretary who assists patients with making payment arrangements and submitting insurance claims. A patient's privacy and dignity should be protected in both the administrative and clinical areas of the dental office.

Customer service occupations may include the following:

- Receptionist
- Dental Assistant
- Financial Secretary

Sales and Marketing

In the past, health care professionals were discouraged from advertising. It was seen as contrary to the medical and dental fields' value of altruism. However, in the present-day competitive market, dentists must promote their services to attract a sufficient patient base to sustain their practice.

Dental offices may have Web sites on which they present their hours, office policies, directions for finding their location, and services offered. These Web sites frequently contain photos of dental personnel at work, so prospective patients have a sense of what to expect in that office. Dentists may even regularly post educational articles to draw return traffic to their Web sites. While the Internet is an effective marketing tool, if the Web site is set up to be interactive, such as to accept appointments or payments made online, there must also be stringent safeguards on the server to protect confidential patient information from computer hackers. Some dental offices choose to sell dental products directly to their patients as a convenience. However, in general, direct sales are not part of a dental practice.

Sales and marketing occupations may include the following:

- Dental Products Salesperson
- Dental Supplies Salesperson
- Information Technology Specialist

Technology, Research, Design, and Development

Significant advancements in dentistry include lasers, three-dimensional imaging systems, and novel adhesives and restoration materials. Dentists are becoming increasingly able to provide more effective treatments more efficiently. However, they must become aware of the latest information and learn to apply it in their practices to offer competitive services in a competent and ethical manner.

Dentists must earn a minimum number of continuing education credits annually as part of their licensing requirements, which vary from state to state. Large continuing education forums are often held in conjunction with trade shows or sponsored by dental product companies so that attendees are exposed to new commercially available products and methods for their use. Dentists who belong to national organizations receive professional journals and other dental magazines that keep them apprised of state-of-the-art materials, techniques, and equipment. State dental associations and local study groups are other networks of information.

The National Institute of Dental and Craniofacial Research (NIDCR), a branch of the National Institutes of Health, oversees scientific research on oral, dental, and craniofacial diseases and disorders. Created in 1948 as the National Institute of Dental Research, it has since supported numerous scientific contributions with significant public health benefits, including the fluoridation of drinking water supplies and the recognition of dental caries and periodontal disease as infectious diseases.

Ongoing research projects funded by NIDCR grants are aimed at not only continuing to improve oral health but also detecting abnormal conditions throughout the body by monitoring biomarkers in the saliva. New biomaterials are being developed, such as bone and tissue regeneration matrices for implant systems, artificial saliva to relieve xerostomia that results from medications and autoimmune diseases, and rinses that prevent the formation of biofilm and thus prevent dental caries. Imaging devices will continue to improve for even earlier identification and treatment of head, neck, and oral cancers.

Technology, research, design, and development occupations may include the following:

- Dental Researcher
- Dental Technology Engineer/Inventor
- Dental Biomaterials Developer
- Dental Appliance Designer
- Dental Appliance Manufacturing Technician
- Technical Writer/Editor
- Instructor

Dental Care

In a dental office, the dentists, dental hygienists, and dental assistants perform billable services. Administrative support staff are auxiliary, meaning that they do not actively generate revenue for the practice.

Dental procedures are coded for documenting, billing, and insurance purposes. The standard coding system is the American Dental Association's Current Dental Terminology (CDT) system. Dental procedure codes are grouped into categories of service: diagnostic, preventive, restorative, endodontics, periodontics, prosthodontics (removable), maxillofacial prosthetics, prosthodontics (fixed), oral surgery, orthodontics, and adjunctive general services. Dental assistants perform diagnostic and information-gathering procedures, as well as reversible procedures. For example, they can manufacture temporary crowns, clean and polish removable appliances, and place and later remove orthodontic brackets and bands.

OCCUPATION SPECIALTIES

Dentists

Specialty	Responsibilities
Endodontists	Examine diseases of the teeth and gums and perform root canals.
Oral and maxillofacial surgeons	Perform surgical operations on the mouth and jaws to remove teeth, tumors, and other abnormal growths or to correct abnormalities in the jaw.
Oral pathologists	Study the nature and causes of diseases of the mouth and determine the best plan of treatment.
Orthodontists	Diagnose and correct or prevent irregularities and deviations in the position of teeth and the development of the jaws, as well as design and fabricate appliances.
Pedodontists	Specialize in treating infants, children, and adolescents; treat primary and secondary teeth and construct suitable appliances for growing mouths.
Periodonists	Treat diseased tissues that support the teeth by cleaning and polishing teeth, eliminating the irritating margins of fillings, and correcting occlusions.
Prosthodontists	Specialize in making artificial teeth or dentures to correct deformations of the mouth and jaws.
Public health dentists	Concern themselves with community dental health; plan, organize, and maintain dental health programs of public health agencies and analyze the dental needs of a community to determine necessary changes.

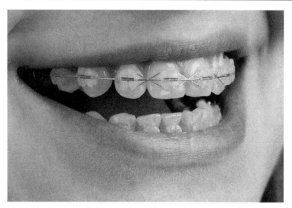

Orthodontics is the practice of straightening teeth, reshaping the palate, and realigning the jaws using tension appliances to create a more functional oral cavity as well as a more attractive smile. (©Dreamstime.com)

In addition to tooth cleaning and periodontal probing, dental hygienists may perform limited irreversible procedures, such as gingival curettage, periodontal scaling, and administration of anaesthetics. Dental hygienists must be licensed to practice, and the licensing state's regulations determine the range of services that may be performed.

Only dentists are allowed to perform irreversible procedures that involve tissue cutting with a high-speed handpiece. Dentists may surgically remove tooth and bone when performing extractions, root canal therapy, and even placing fillings because the preliminary removal of dental caries and the preparation of the tooth to receive restorative material involve the removal of tooth. Dentists may also surgically biopsy lesions. They are responsible for clinical diagnosis and treatment planning and are licensed to write prescriptions.

Dental care occupations may include the following:

- Dentist
- Oral/Maxillofacial Surgeon
- Orthodontist

OCCUPATION PROFILE

Dental Hygienist

Considerations	Qualifications
Description	Cleans teeth and examines mouth, head, and neck for signs of disease; may also educate patient on oral hygiene and take X rays.
Career cluster	Health Science
Interests	Data; people; things
Working conditions	Work inside
Minimum education level	Junior/technical college
Physical exertion	Light work
Physical abilities	Unexceptional/basic fitness
Opportunities for experience	Internship; apprenticeship; military service
Licensure and certification	Required
Employment outlook	Faster-than-average growth expected
Holland interest score	SAI

Note: See volume 1, "Publisher's Note," for an explanation of the Holland interest score.

OCCUPATION SPECIALTIES

Dental Laboratory Technicians

Specialty	Responsibilities
Crown and bridge technicians	Make crowns, inlays, and teeth for fixed bridges according to a dentist's prescription.
Dental ceramists	Apply layers of porcelain paste or acrylic resins over metal framework to form crowns, bridges, and tooth facings.
Metal dental technicians	Lay out designs of metal framework and clasps for partial dentures on plastic models.
Orthodontic technicians	Construct and repair appliances for straightening teeth according to an orthodontist's prescription; shape, carve, and assemble metal and plastic appliances, such as retainers, tooth bands, and positioners using special equipment.

- Dental Hygienist
- Dental Assistant
- Dental Laboratory Technician

Human Resources

Larger dental offices may have office managers who provide human resources services such as administering benefits, hiring and firing, and arranging for employee training. In smaller offices, these duties fall to the dentist. The person responsible for human resources management must maintain the morale of the staff, address performance issues, and ensure that policies and regulations are being upheld in the workplace. The dentist and the office manager may conduct employee appraisals together and budget for appropriate bonuses or additional training opportunities.

As business owners, dentists determine which benefits to offer to employees. These may include complimentary dental treatment, health insurance enrollment, paid vacation time, retirement plan contributions, a uniform allowance, and continuing education funding.

Continuing education is available for clinical and administrative personnel on a wide variety of topics, from infection control, radiology, and tobacco cessation to practice management, communication skills, and serving patients with special needs. Courses may be available online, at local venues, or as part of regional and national dental conventions.

Professional organizations are often the leading source of information regarding professional development. Dentists may join the American Dental Association, founded in 1859. Dental hygienists may belong to the American Dental Hygienists' Association, which held its first annual meeting in 1923. Dental assistants may join the American Dental Assistants Association, established more than 80 years ago.

Human resources occupations may include the following:

- Office Manager
- Payroll and Benefits Manager
- Professional Organization Staff Member

INDUSTRY OUTLOOK

Overview

The outlook for this industry shows it to be on the rise. The BLS projects that the number of dental positions will grow by 16 percent between 2008 and 2018, faster than the average growth rate of 11 percent for all occupations combined. The number of positions for dental hygienists is projected to increase by 36 percent during the same period; the same is true for dental assistants, making these among the fastest-growing occupations.

Employment opportunities should continue to be readily available, as a large number of dentists reach retirement age. Older dentists who do not leave the profession are reducing their work hours and no longer accepting new patients, so they are also creating opportunities for new dentists. In 2010, there were fifty-eight dental schools in the United States, and they produced just over five thousand graduates. This was the highest number in nearly twenty years; the most recent low was less than four thousand graduates in 1993. However, even this high number of graduates is not enough to keep up with the growing demand for dental services.

The need for dental care is continuing to grow because people are living longer, taking better care of themselves, recognizing the importance of dental care, and keeping their teeth longer. Because people are living longer, there are more patients to serve. As people take better care of themselves, they often improve their diets, which not only strengthens teeth but also increases the importance of oral function for chewing whole, unprocessed foods. People have begun to appreciate the value of dental care and are no longer requesting dentures for their convenience. They are choosing to invest in their mouths and spending discretionary funds. Because they want to keep their teeth longer, they are considering restorative procedures rather than settling for extractions without further treatment.

Although water fluoridation and fluoride toothpastes have reduced the incidence of dental caries, teeth still break, gums still recede, and jaws may not align properly. People still care about the appearance of their smiles; increasing numbers of adults are getting braces and bleaching their teeth. New intraoral appliances have been designed to reduce sleep apnea and relieve jaw pain from bruxism (tooth grinding). The need for dentistry is not waning.

As dentists become busier, more responsibilities and expanded skills will fall to dental hygienists and dental assistants. Colleges and universities are beginning to train dental personnel to become "expanded function dental auxiliaries," licensed positions based on education rather than years of experience. This license allows someone other than a dentist to apply sealants; take impressions; place temporary fillings, crowns, and bridges; and place and carve direct restoration materials. In addition, workforce studies have recommended that dental hygienists have expanded responsibilities with less direct supervision to care for underprivileged children and underserved populations away from a traditional dental office.

Medicine and dentistry are continuing to overlap. An emerging field of common interest is called neuromuscular dentistry, which studies the nerves and muscles of the head and neck to determine their relationship to migraines, neuropathic pain (persistent overstimulation of nerves in response to a medical condition, with a burning or electric sensation), and nociceptive pain (time-limited, localized, and constant pain in response to irritation or injury). Dentists are seeking to find and treat the underlying causes of headaches, temporomandibular joint pain, and myofascial pain and are developing new injection techniques to deliver nerve blocks as well as intraoral appliances to balance muscle stress and bring relief. Dentists are also studying the relationship between jaw position and sleep apnea and fabricating intraoral devices to open airways and avert snoring. Such novel scientific pursuits and treatments will give patients new reasons to seek dental care.

Employment Advantages

In a 2008 survey of graduating dentists, five important reasons for going into dentistry as a profession were listed: control of time, service to others, self-employment, income potential, and working with one's hands. Additional reasons reported by practicing dentists were the flexibility to balance family and career, the satisfaction of patient education and fostering change, the significance of disease detection, opportunities for using creativity and problem-solving skills, and the respect accorded the profession. New dentists are able to begin generating meaningful income directly after graduation and licensing and thus may begin to pay back student loans more quickly than new physicians, who must complete internships and residencies at minimal pay before establishing medical practices. As a profession, dentists earn more income than physicians, with more independence and less bureaucracy. However, because dental fees are often paid directly by patients, in some cases assisted by private insurance companies, in times of economic difficulty, the demand for dental services may be reduced.

Dental assistants and dental hygienists may work full time or part time, allowing them to balance work with home and children. They often report satisfaction from working closely with patients, especially in the areas of oral health education and reducing anxiety about dental treatment.

Annual Earnings

According to the U.S. Census Bureau, the dental and orthodontics industry earned revenues of $94.18 billion in 2007. The economic recession of 2007-2009 affected the industry, however. A quarterly survey of economic confidence conducted by the American Dental Association in January, 2010, found that the net income of dentists surveyed had decreased by 5 percent from 2008 to 2009. However, the last quarter of 2009 showed some upturn in dental economic indicators such as net income, gross billings, collections, treatment acceptance rates, and numbers of new patients. Dentists who had been practicing less than ten years were the only ones to report that their net income had increased from 2008 to 2009. These data suggest that the natural increase in income that comes with increasing experience is outpacing the economic decline. In addition, younger dentists may work more hours on average than older, more experienced dentists, thereby generating more income. The survey also reported decreases in adjustments and write-offs, open appointment times, and average days of accounts receivable.

RELATED RESOURCES FOR FURTHER RESEARCH

ACADEMY OF GENERAL DENTISTRY
211 E Chicago Ave., Suite 900
Chicago, IL 60611-1999
Tel: (888) 243-3368
Fax: (312) 444-0559
http://www.agd.org

AMERICAN ASSOCIATION OF ORTHODONTISTS
401 N Lindbergh Blvd.
St. Louis, MO 63141-7816
Tel: (800) 424-2841

Fax: (314) 997-1745
http://www.braces.org

AMERICAN DENTAL ASSOCIATION
211 E Chicago Ave.
Chicago, IL 60611-2678
Tel: (312) 440-2500
http://www.ada.org
http://jada.ada.org

AMERICAN DENTAL HYGIENISTS' ASSOCIATION
444 N Michigan Ave., Suite 3400
Chicago, IL 60611
Tel: (312) 440-8900
http://www.adha.org

NATIONAL INSTITUTE OF DENTAL AND
    CRANIOFACIAL RESEARCH
National Institutes of Health
9000 Rockville Pike
Bethesda, MD 20892-2190
Tel: (301) 496-4261
http://www.nidcr.nih.gov

ABOUT THE AUTHOR

Bethany Thivierge is a biomedical technical writer and editor with a B.S. in biology from the University of Michigan and an M.P.H. in health promotion and education from the Loma Linda University School of Public Health. She began her career in dental research at the University of Michigan Dental School and the Dental Research Institute; her work was published in *Infection and Immunity*. She has written numerous dental education articles for publications such as *The Gale Encyclopedia of Medicine* and *Magill's Medical Guide*.

FURTHER READING

American Dental Association. *Two Thousand Seven Survey of Dental Practices: Characteristics of Dentists in Private Practice and Their Patients.* Chicago: Author, 2007.
American Dental Education Association. *Trends in Dentistry and Dental Education.* Washington, D.C.: Author, 2008.
Bremner, M. D. K. *The Story of Dentistry.* 3d ed.

Brooklyn, N.Y.: Dental Items of Interest, 1954.

Gelbier, S. "125 Years of Developments in Dentistry, 1880-2005." *British Dental Journal* 199 (2005): 470-473.

Hoffmann-Axthelm, Walter. *The History of Dentistry*. Berlin: Quintessential Books, 1990.

Levin, Roger P. "The Boutique Dental Practice." *Dental Angle*, July, 1996. http://www .dentalangle.com/07.96/levin-archived .html.

National Institute of Dental and Craniofacial Research. "Oral Health: Past, Present, and Future." http://www.nidcr.nih.gov/Research/ ResearchPriorities/StrategicPlan/ pastPresentFuture.htm.

Ring, Malvin E., and Neal Hurley. "James Beall Morrison: The Visionary Who Revolutionized the Practice of Dentistry." *Journal of the American Dental Association* 131, no. 8 (2000): 1161-1167.

Spielman, Andrew I., et al. "Dentistry, Nursing, and Medicine: A Comparison on Core Competencies." *Journal of Dental Education* 69, no. 11 (2005): 1257-1271.

U.S. Bureau of Labor Statistics. *Career Guide to Industries*, 2010-2011 ed. http://www.bls.gov/ oco/cg.

_____. "Dentists." In *Occupational Outlook Handbook*, 2010-2011 ed. http://www.bls.gov/ oco/ocos 072.htm.

U.S. Census Bureau. North American Industry Classification System (NAICS), 2007. http:// www.census.gov/cgi-bin/sssd/naics/ naicsrch?chart=2007.

U.S. Department of Commerce. International Trade Administration. Office of Trade and Industry Information. Industry Trade Data and Analysis. http://ita.doc.gov/td/industry/ otea/OTII/OTII-index.html.

U.S. Department of Health and Human Services. Bureau of Health Professions. National Center for Health Workforce Analysis. *U.S. Health Workforce Personnel Factbook, 2002*. http:// bhpr.hrsa.gov/healthworkforce/reports/ factbook.htm.

World Salaries. "Dentist Salaries: International Comparison." http://www.worldsalaries.org/ dentist.shtml.

Electrical and Gas Appliances Industry

©Dreamstime.com

INDUSTRY SNAPSHOT

General Industry: Manufacturing

Career Cluster: Manufacturing

Subcategory Industries: Audio and Video Equipment Manufacturing; Electric Housewares and Household Fan Manufacturing; Household Cooking Appliance Manufacturing; Household Hot Water Heater Manufacturing; Household Laundry Equipment Manufacturing; Household Refrigerator and Home Freezer Manufacturing; Household Vacuum Cleaner Manufacturing; Kitchen Appliance Manufacturing; Major Appliance Manufacturing; Radio Receiving Set Manufacturing; Small Electrical Appliance Manufacturing; Television Set Manufacturing; Trash and Garbage Compactor Manufacturing

Related Industries: Batteries and Fuel Cells Industry; Broadcast Industry; Electrical Power Industry; Home Maintenance Services; Household and Personal Products Industry; Light Machinery Industry; Motion Picture and Television Industry; Music Industry; Petroleum and Natural Gas Industry; Retail Trade and Service Industry; Telecommunications Equipment Industry; Video, Computer, and Virtual Reality Games Industry; Water Supply Industry

Annual Domestic Revenues: $25 billion USD (Hoover's, 2009)

Annual International Revenues: $143.2 billion USD (Research and Markets, 2008)

Annual Global Revenues: $168.2 billion USD (Research and Markets, 2008)

NAICS Numbers: 3343, 3352

INDUSTRY DEFINITION

Summary

The electrical and gas appliance industry is dominated by large companies. For example, in the United States, the twenty largest companies hold about 95 percent of the market share. The three largest companies are Whirlpool, General Electric, and Electrolux. Globally, the two market leaders are Whirlpool and Electrolux. Major products are refrigerators, freezers, ovens, stoves, laundry equipment, and vacuum cleaners. Manufactur-

The modern American kitchen is filled with small electric appliances like these. (©Carolyn Woodcock/iStockphoto.com)

ers often produce several models of a particular product that are tailored to specific market segments. For example, a manufacturer might market a basic model, a full-featured model, and a commercial model. Virtually every industrialized nation on the planet has a significant appliance industry, employing individuals in a wide variety of career paths.

History of the Industry

The history of appliance manufacturing is inextricably linked to, and arose precipitously after, the harnessing of energy from natural gas and electricity. Natural gas was first discovered and used in ancient China around 600 B.C.E. The first recorded use of natural gas in the home was in 100 B.C.E. in Persia (now Iran). The first gas utility, the London-based Gas Light and Coke Company, was incorporated by royal charter in 1812. Subsequently, other gas utilities were formed in England, the rest of Europe, and the United States. These utilities sold gas that was manufactured, not extracted from natural sources, and that was used primarily for street lighting. Manufactured gas was produced by gasifica-tion of a combustible substance, usually coal but sometimes wood or oil. The combustible substances were gasified by heating them in enclosed ovens in an atmosphere low in oxygen. They emitted gases—including hydrogen, methane, and ethylene—that could be burnt for heating and lighting purposes.

In the second half of the nineteenth century, the primary application of gas transitioned from lighting to heating and cooking. This transition was propelled by the development of electric lighting. As the nineteenth century drew to a close, pipelines from oil fields in Texas and Oklahoma were built; these lines supplied gas to distant cities such as Chicago. Natural gas initially supplemented, and eventually completely replaced, manufactured gas. The gas oven was invented by James Sharp, a British inventor, in 1826. By the 1920's, most households in the United States contained a gas appliance consisting of top burners and an interior oven.

Benjamin Franklin's investigations into the properties of electricity in the mid-eighteenth century served as a foundation for the accomplishments of his successor, Thomas Alva Edison. Edison invented the electric lightbulb in 1879; in 1892, he established the first electric plant in New York City. Precursors of today's batteries were also developed in that century. In 1859, the lead-acid battery was produced; this type of rechargeable battery is currently used in today's automobiles. In the early 1890's, the Reverend Marcel Audiffren, a French monk, constructed a refrigerator. Refrigerators were subsequently manufactured in the United States by the General Electric Company.

In 1902, Willis Carrier invented the electric air-conditioner, which in essence is an application of the refrigerator for cooling a room or building. In 1905, Earl Richardson manufactured the Hotpoint electric iron. In 1908, the Hoover Company manufactured the first vacuum cleaner, which had attachments and a cloth filter bag. In 1912, the U.S.-based Electrolux Company manufactured vacuum cleaners. In 1910, William Hadaway designed the first toaster, which was manufactured by Westinghouse. Electric ovens were first produced in the 1890's; by the 1920's, they became competitive with their gas counterparts.

In 1911, the Upton Machine Company in St. Joseph, Missouri, began producing electric motor-driven wringer washers. In 1922, the Maytag Company introduced the first modern washing machine. The device used an agitator to force water through the clothes; previous machines merely dragged the clothes through water. In 1947, the Upton Machine Company introduced the top-loading washing machine. In 1989, the Hoover Company was acquired by Maytag. In 1946, Percy Spencer, an engineer with the Raytheon Company, noted that a new vacuum tube used for radar-related research melted a candy bar in his pocket. He then tried other experiments: He popped popcorn and exploded an egg. In 1947, Raytheon manufactured the first microwave oven for restaurant use; it weighed about 750 pounds, stood 5.5 feet tall, and cost $5,000.

Homes in the mid-twentieth century contained many labor-saving appliances, such as refrigerators, washers, dryers, and stoves; however, before the early 1950's, they did not contain a popular entertainment appliance: the television set. Crude devices that could transmit still images over wires were developed in the latter half of the nineteenth century. In 1929, a Russian inventor, Vladimir Zworykin, developed the kinescope, which was a precursor of the modern picture tube. In 1927, Philo Farnsworth transmitted a television image that comprised sixty horizontal lines. The first commercial television broadcast in the United States aired on December 17, 1953.

The Industry Today

The bulk of the gas and electric appliance industry produces refrigerators, laundry equipment, ovens, ranges, vacuum cleaners, and electronic products such as televisions and radios. The vast majority of the U.S. market is held by large companies, such as Whirlpool, General Electric, and Electrolux. For decades, the market was dominated by large U.S. and European companies; however, since the 1980's, Japanese and Korean companies such as Sony, Sanyo, and Samsung have gained significant market shares. A wide range of large and small appliances is produced by Asian companies. Sony televisions and other electronic devices are popular worldwide. Samsung washers and dryers compete with those of U.S.-based Whirlpool and German-based Robert Bosch LLC.

Smaller companies produce specialty products that fall outside the spectrum of popular consumer products. These include massage devices, coffee roasters, and espresso machines. These products

The Electrical Equipment, Appliances, and Components Industry's Contribution to the U.S. Economy

Value Added	Amount
Gross domestic product	$50.3 billion
Gross domestic product	0.3%
Persons employed	422,000
Total employee compensation	$30.6 billion

Source: U.S. Bureau of Economic Analysis. Data are for 2008.

may compete with similar products produced by large manufacturers. The industry is highly competitive, and profit margins are often narrow. One exception is products produced for the medical and dental industry; these appliances are usually built to exacting standards and are typically sold at a high markup. A number of these products retail for more than $1 million per unit.

Most appliance manufacturers buy components—such as heating elements, electric motors, and electronics—from suppliers and assemble these components in metal or plastic housings. Many of today's appliances incorporate computer technology. For example, a dryer may contain a computer-controlled sensor to ensure proper drying. The addition of computer technology to appliances increases the likelihood that they will require servicing. Appliance repair companies constitute a major subindustry within the electrical and gas appliance industry, and they generate considerable income. When an appliance fails, its owner is confronted with the choice of paying for repairs or replacing the appliance. In a number of cases, it is more cost-effective to replace the item than to repair it, particularly if the appliance is inexpensive (so that the cost of repair might exceed the purchase price of a new appliance) or older (so that replacement parts may be difficult to acquire).

Driving the replacement-versus-repair issue is the industry's promotion of new features. In the early twenty-first century, dryer manufacturers began offering a steam feature, which has been pur-

The Energy Star is a trusted, government-backed symbol for energy efficiency to help Americans save money and protect the environment. (AP/Wide World Photos)

ported to remove stains and reduce wrinkling. In the past, appliances were usually painted white, but they have come to be marketed in a variety of colors. Many appliances are also available with stainless-steel or wood-paneled exteriors to match home décor. Tankless water heaters are available in which water is heated upon demand, thus eliminating the need to maintain a large tank of hot water.

In the realm of electronics (such as television sets), new model lines are introduced frequently. Modern appliances are also geared for efficiency. Newer washers are designated as high efficiency (HE). HE appliances must meet strict industry guidelines and use less water, less energy, and less detergent. Many contemporary appliances are designed to comply with the international Energy Star standard for energy efficiency. This standard for consumer products was created as a U.S. government program by the Bill Clinton administration. Subsequently, the European Union, Australia, Canada, Japan, New Zealand, and Taiwan adopted the program. Noncompliant appliances have waned in popularity. For example, purchases of plasma televisions have decreased because they consume much more electricity than liquid crystal

Inputs Consumed by the Electrical Equipment, Appliances, and Components Industry

Input	Value
Energy	$1.0 billion
Materials	$53.2 billion
Purchased services	$13.3 billion
Total	$67.5 billion

Source: U.S. Bureau of Economic Analysis. Data are for 2008.

displays (LCDs) or light-emitting diode (LED) units.

The appliance industry is consumer driven; when unemployment increases and wages decrease, the industry suffers. New home sales also affect the industry; decreases in home sales decrease the demand for new appliances. For a company to succeed and remain competitive, it must be efficient in production, marketing, and distribution of its products. Innovations that attract consumer interest help gain market share. When one company develops a new feature, competitors usually add similar features to their product lines.

Many appliances are produced on automated assembly lines. Small companies tend to be less automated than midsize or large companies. In many cases, the manufacturing process involves shaping metal (usually steel) into a framework, then assembling the components. Aluminum and plastic are also molded into housings and components for appliances. Some appliances, such as water heaters

and refrigerators, have insulation added. Painting is often part of the assembly process. Manufacturing plants for large appliances are often located near rail lines or harbors to facilitate shipping.

Retail outlets that offer appliances often offer a variety of brands and types of appliances. Some offer a range of items, including refrigerators, freezers, stoves, ovens, washers, dryers, barbecues, and televisions; some focus on a specific product category, such as gas barbecues; and most focus on only some of the many available brands. Although today's consumers often visit appliance stores after conducting their own research (by searching on the Internet or soliciting the advice of friends), they are often receptive of knowledgeable salespeople who can help them select the right product. Appliance stores often offer delivery and installation of new appliances, as well as removal of old appliances. These services may be included in the purchase price or offered at additional cost.

Consumers can also buy products via the Inter-

Appliance stores can carry only a fraction of the many models of washers, dryers, and stoves created to meet the specific needs of customers. (©Serghei Starus/Dreamstime.com)

net. Appliances are sold through the Web sites of manufacturers (such as Whirlpool or Sony), of brick-and-mortar retailers (such as Sears or Best Buy), and of Internet-only vendors (such as Amazon). Web sites often offer product reviews and ratings from experts and from other consumers. Some consumers visit appliance stores to research products in person, then purchase their selected items online if they are offered by Web sites at lower prices than they are by physical stores. Therefore, savvy appliance salespeople must promote the benefits of in-store purchasing over those of e-commerce.

Many appliances are purchased by people other than consumers. In the case of new home or commercial construction, for example, they may be purchased by home builders, contractors, electrical services, or plumbing services. These items include water heaters, stoves, ovens, and refrigerators. A home purchaser becomes involved in the purchase of these items only when a replacement is needed. Plumbing, heating, and air-conditioning companies often recommend specific product lines. Vendors affiliated with an appliance manufacturer call on such companies to promote the vendors' product lines. They also call on appliance stores.

Appliance repair is a major subindustry of appliance manufacturing and sales. Small appliances can be shipped back to their manufacturers for repairs or taken to appliance repair shops. In some cases, these repairs are covered by warranties. Some companies offer extended warranties for onetime fees. Large appliances also usually have warranties with specific time limits, and the consumer can purchase extended warranties from manufacturers or third parties. Because of their weight and semipermanent installation, large appliances must be repaired where they are installed. Large-appliance repair technicians must be knowledgeable about a variety of appliances and carry common replacement items in their service vans.

These old, discarded vacuum cleaners hint at the vast variety, even among upright models. (©Brad Wieland/iStockphoto.com)

Repair costs for large appliances are higher than those of smaller items because technicians must spend much of their time traveling among repair locations.

Some appliances require consumables to operate, and these consumables may be manufactured by third parties. Washing machines and dishwashers, for example, use detergents, stain-removing agents, and fabric softeners. Often, appliance manufacturers recommend certain products or types of products for use with their appliances. For example, some laundry detergents are designed specifically for use in HE washers, and manufacturers encourage owners of HE washers to use that class of detergent.

Although many gas appliances are designed to be attached to city gas lines and many electrical appliances are designed to be attached to the power grid, some are designed for portable use or for use in locations where city gas and electrical power are not available. Examples include portable gas barbecues, which use liquid propane gas (LPG), and battery-powered radios. These products not only support various subindustries, such as those that refill LPG tanks and those that produce batteries, but also expand appliance companies' product lines.

INDUSTRY MARKET SEGMENTS

The electrical and gas appliance industry is dominated by large companies. In the United States, the twenty largest companies hold about 95 percent of the market share. Although small and midsize companies have limited market share, they still provide career opportunities that can generate good economic returns and job satisfaction.

Small Businesses

Small businesses usually offer specialty products designed for niche markets. They may offer a single product or a product line of several related products. These products are primarily small appliances. Examples of small business products are beauty aids, massage devices, and personal hygiene items. Some small businesses produce unique products, while others produce products similar to those of larger companies.

Potential Annual Earnings Scale. According to the U.S. Bureau of Labor Statistics (BLS), the average annual salary of an industrial engineer in the household appliance industry was $75,210 in 2009, while the average salary of a mechanical engineer was $73,260. Industrial engineering technicians earned an average of $48,140, and mechanical engineering technicians earned an average of $42,900.

Clientele Interaction. Small businesses tend to favor more interaction with customers, and the personal touch can foster consumer satisfaction. Owners often are the developers of their products; thus, they are completely familiar with those products. However, clientele interaction can vary widely. Owners may have direct contact with their customers, or they may market their products over the Internet, with contact limited to telephone and e-mail. A Web site is essential to a small appliance business. A well-designed site can successfully compete with that of a large company. A small company's Web site can mimic the appearance of a much larger company's site. Thus, it can give the impression of representing a larger company. The Web site can not only market products but also offer technical advice and serve as a vehicle for customer feedback.

Amenities, Atmosphere, and Physical Grounds. Amenities of small businesses are often limited. Owners may operate their businesses out of their homes or from small rental spaces. Working environments can be tailored to personal taste and budget. An owner interested in a favorable working environment might have a facility with extremely pleasant working conditions; others may house their businesses in spartan, no-frills buildings.

Typical Number of Employees. The number of employees can range from one to several dozen. A small business could consist solely of an owner and family members.

Traditional Geographic Locations. Geographic locations of small businesses are unlimited. They are usually located near or even in their owners' homes.

Pros of Working for a Small Appliance Company. The owner is often responsible for all operational decisions. If there is a staff, the owner might consult with them regarding these decisions or retain complete autonomy. Staff members of small businesses usually have closer working relationships with owners than they do at larger companies. Part-time employment and flexible hours are usually easier to arrange than they are in larger companies. Small-business owners can control waste and unnecessary expenditures to a greater degree than can owners or managers of larger companies because all expenditures at small businesses are subject to owners' approval.

If a company fosters teamwork and group decision making, its employees can be more involved in the company's growth. In some cases, partnership opportunities exist for exceptional employees. If a company flourishes, it can grow in size and profits, expanding into (or being purchased by) a larger company. If either occurs, the financial return could be significant. Some small-business owners have sold their companies at large profits and generated enough income to retire with extremely comfortable lifestyles. Such large profits might be shared among key or long-term employees.

Cons of Working for a Small Appliance Company. The electrical and gas appliance industry is extremely competitive. Even if a company produces good products, it may not be able to compete successfully with large companies that can sell comparable products for lower prices. Small businesses are less resilient to unexpected major expenses, such as lawsuits or major equipment replacement costs, which can bankrupt them. Owners and staffs of small businesses generally do not have the variety of skills that the staffs and management of larger companies possess. For example, a given staff may have technical expertise but lack marketing skills. Furthermore, because there are fewer employees, each worker is typically responsible for a wide range of duties. A technician might be asked to sweep the floor or clean a restroom. Relationships among coworkers can become strained. In a large company, if two employees do not get along, one can be relocated to another area. This is not possible in a small company that is confined to a small area. Loss of a key employee could slow or even halt production until a suitable replacement is found.

Costs

Payroll and Benefits: Small companies often pay all employees hourly and often do not provide the same level of benefits as large companies. Benefits are at the discretion of the owner and could include sick pay, health insurance, and vacations.

Supplies: Small appliance companies may require raw materials and component parts, industrial machinery, tools, laboratory equipment, and office equipment and supplies. Supplies usually cost small businesses more than they cost large businesses, which have the clout to negotiate lower prices for large bulk purchases.

External Services: Small appliance manufacturers often outsource appliance housing construction—either custom-designed or ready-made—from external manufacturers. They may also contract Web design, accounting or billing services, legal counsel, cleaning, and maintenance.

Utilities: Small companies must pay for electricity, water, sewage, gas or oil, telephone, and Internet access.

Taxes: Small businesses must pay local, state, and federal income and property taxes, as well as payroll taxes. Partners and owners—especially owners of home businesses—may report income from their businesses on their personal tax returns, in which case they must also pay self-employment taxes. Home businesses can also claim a portion of their home expenses, such as utilities and mortgage, as business deductions.

Midsize Businesses

Midsize manufacturing businesses are often former small businesses that have expanded. On occasion, they may be former large businesses that have fragmented or simply shrunk. Like small businesses, they tend to favor small appliances tailored for niche markets. Some products manufactured by midsize businesses include gas barbecues, ceiling fans, saunas, and coffeemakers. These products often compete with products produced by large businesses.

Potential Annual Earnings Scale. According to the BLS, the average annual salary of an industrial engineer in the household appliance industry was $75,210 in 2009, while the average salary of a mechanical engineer was $73,260. Industrial engineering technicians earned an average of $48,140, and mechanical engineering technicians earned an average of $42,900. Engineering managers earned an average of $107,150. The average income of all production workers combined was $32,110, while production supervisors earned an average of $50,760 and production managers earned an average of $93,040. Sales managers earned an average of $119,140, while sales representatives earned an average of $70,880. General and operations managers earned an average of $125,650, and chief executives earned an average of $191,360.

Clientele Interaction. Appliance salespeople usually have short-term but intense relationships with customers. Vendors serving homebuilders can foster long-term relationships that can generate repeat business. All midsize businesses have Web sites for both marketing and clientele interaction. Such sites offer customer service and technical support, and they often provide downloadable electronic copies of product user's manuals.

Amenities, Atmosphere, and Physical Grounds. Appliance manufacturing facilities are customarily spartan and utilitarian. Retail facilities often lack frills. One notable exception is the home theater area of a retail outlet. These areas usually have dim lighting and comfortable seating where customers can view large-screen televisions and listen to high-end sound systems. The areas help sell not only the products but also the lifestyle those products are meant to symbolize and help consumers attain.

Typical Number of Employees. A manufacturing facility may consist of a management staff and assemblers. Retail outlets usually consist of a manager and several salespeople.

Traditional Geographic Locations. Manufacturers of small appliances can be situated in a wide range of locations, but they are typically located in urban industrial areas. Manufacturers of large appliances are commonly located in areas near rail or ocean cargo service. Retail outlets are located in areas with sufficient populations to generate adequate sales.

Pros of Working for a Midsize Appliance Company. Owners of midsize manufacturing businesses often have more control over operational decisions than do owners of large companies. Employee-management interaction is often at a higher level at midsize companies than it is at large companies. Unlike a small business, a midsize manufacturing business can employ individuals with a variety of skills. These employees include technicians, assemblers, and marketing personnel.

Cons of Working for a Midsize Appliance Company. Many midsize businesses produce specialty or luxury products. In times of economic downturn, these items are more likely to experience decreased sales than are more essential items. For example, if a refrigerator fails, its owner is likely to purchase a replacement. However, a nonessential item such as a ceiling fan is less likely to be purchased during an economic downturn. Also, midsize companies often produce a narrower range of products than do large companies, so their success is more closely tied to specific market segments. The limited number of management positions in midsize companies decreases employees' opportunities for advancement.

Costs

Payroll and Benefits: Midsize companies generally pay some staff hourly, while others receive annual salaries. They can usually offer benefits comparable to those of large companies. These benefits include sick pay, health insurance, and vacations.

Supplies: Midsize appliance companies may require raw materials and component parts, industrial machinery, tools, laboratory equipment, and office equipment and supplies. They are likely to produce more component parts than do small companies, so their need for raw materials is likely to be greater. They can often negotiate discounts from suppliers, enjoying lower per-unit costs than small appliance manufacturers. However, these costs are usually higher than those of comparable products produced by large companies.

External Services: Midsize companies often contract accounting services and billing services, although some perform these services in-house. They also often use outside legal services. They may commission external manufacturers to create component parts for their products, especially parts far outside their area of expertise (such as computer chips incorporated into rice cookers).

Utilities: Midsize companies must pay for electricity, water, sewage, gas or oil, telephone, and Internet access.

Taxes: Midsize businesses must pay local, state, and federal corporate taxes, as well as applicable property taxes.

Large Businesses

Large manufacturing businesses market their appliances internationally. The twenty largest appliance companies in the United States are in direct competition with companies whose headquarters are in other nations. These companies often manufacture both small and large appliances. They profit from brand recognition. Consumers often favor products whose brands they associate with reliability, features, or other desirable qualities. Some foreign companies, specifically Asian companies, have less brand recognition, but such recognition is increasing for these manufacturers as well. In some market segments, such as televisions and electronics, Asian manufacturers such as Sony enjoy extremely strong branding and reputations.

Large appliance companies market a range of products, from bargain to full-featured models. They may market a number of brands. For example, the Whirlpool Corporation markets Whirlpool, Maytag, Kitchen-Aid, Jenn-Air, Amana, Brastemp, Consul, Baknecht, and Gladiator appliances. Whirlpool, Maytag, Kitchen-Aid, Jenn-Air, and Amana are familiar appliance products in the United States and abroad. Brastemp and Consul appliances are marketed in Brazil. Baknecht appliances are marketed in Germany. Gladiator appliances are designed for garages and include workbenches, tool storage units, and cabinets. Whirlpool maintains headquarters in Michigan; São Paulo, Brazil; Comerio, Italy; and Shanghai, China. It produces many different models of its products. For example, it offers twenty different models of home washing machine.

Potential Annual Earnings Scale. According to the BLS, the average annual salary of an industrial engineer in the household appliance industry was $75,210 in 2009, while the average salary of a mechanical engineer was $73,260. Industrial engineering technicians earned an average of $48,140, and mechanical engineering technicians earned an average of $42,900. Engineering managers earned an average of $107,150. The average income of all production workers combined was $32,110, while production supervisors earned an average of $50,760 and production managers earned an average of $93,040. Sales managers earned an average of $119,140, while sales representatives earned an average of $70,880. General and opera-

tions managers earned an average of $125,650, and chief executives earned an average of $191,360. The salaries for top management positions at the largest firms can be well over $1 million per year.

Clientele Interaction. Appliance salespeople have short-term but intense relationships with customers. Vendors serving homebuilders can foster long-term relationships that can generate repeat business. All large businesses have Web sites for both marketing and clientele interaction. These sites offer customer service and technical support, and they often provide downloadable digital copies of product user's manuals.

Amenities, Atmosphere, and Physical Grounds. Large appliance manufacturing facilities are customarily spartan and utilitarian. Retail facilities usually are large warehouse-like structures. Corporate headquarters, on the other hand, often are luxurious and state of the art.

Typical Number of Employees. Whirlpool reported 66,900 employees in 2009, down from 69,600 in 2008. Large appliance corporations offer a wide range of career opportunities, including sales, marketing, engineering, and management at the store as well as the corporate level.

Traditional Geographic Locations. Corporate headquarters can be located in virtually any large or small city; large retail outlets also can be located in any area with a reasonable population density. Manufacturing facilities are typically in urban industrial areas and located near rail or ocean cargo service.

Pros of Working for a Large Appliance Company. A wealth of career opportunities exists within large appliance-manufacturing corporations. Positions include high-paying management positions, as well as technical, engineering, information technology, marketing, and sales positions. Upper management positions can be extremely lucrative in terms of salaries, bonuses, and retirement benefits. Even lower-level employees may be entitled to generous bonuses and retirement benefits. Large corporations offer summer internships for college students and training for employees wishing to advance their positions. Lateral transfers are possible. For example, a marketing employee could transfer to a management position in human resources. Large corporations encourage employees to think of themselves as members of large, close-knit corporate families in order to foster good employee-management relationships.

Large manufacturers generally offer a wide range of products. Thus, they are more likely to survive an economic downturn than are smaller companies, as they do not depend on a single market segment for success. They are generally diversified both in the class of products they offer (such as refrigerators, ovens, and small appliances) and the target demographic for those products (such as bargain-seeker, middle-class family, or luxury consumer).

Cons of Working for a Large Appliance Company. Despite large companies' attempts to foster good employee-employee and employee-management relationships, their employees may feel anonymous or insignificant within operations of such great size. They may feel that their opinions are not valued or that they are easy to replace. Upper-management personnel may be urged to relocate to another state or even another country at regular intervals to ensure promotion. While some might welcome the opportunity to relocate, others may feel that moving would be disruptive to their lives and those of their family members. Performance goals sometimes imposed on employees, even those in lower positions, can cause significant stress. Large businesses are profit-driven and managers must answer to boards of directors and shareholders. If a company loses market share or profitability, the chief executive might be terminated. The same holds true of the manager of an underperforming department.

Costs

Payroll and Benefits: Large companies pay annual salaries and hourly wages depending on the position. They usually offer many benefits, including sick pay, health insurance, vacations, and maternity leave (even for a husband).

Supplies: Large appliance companies may require raw materials and component parts, industrial machinery, tools, laboratory equipment, trucks and maintenance supplies, and office equipment and supplies. They are likely to create the majority of their components internally.

External Services: Large companies usually have in-house departments for most services, which include accounting, payroll, legal, and even urgent-care medical services. They may contract external auditors when necessary, and they often contract advertising and public relations firms to work with their internal staffs to help launch major advertising campaigns.

Utilities: Large companies must pay for electricity, water, sewage, gas or oil, telephone, and Internet access.

Taxes: Large businesses must pay local, state, federal, and international corporate and property taxes, as well as applicable tariffs and other import and export fees.

ORGANIZATIONAL STRUCTURE AND JOB ROLES

Large businesses have departments for each division of their organization. Midsize companies often have a department or at least an individual focused on each division. In small companies, one individual may handle several and sometimes all of the different business segments.

The following umbrella categories apply to the organizational structure of businesses in the electric and gas appliance industry:

- Business Management
- Customer Service
- Legal Services
- Sales and Marketing
- Information Technology
- Facilities and Security
- Technology, Research, Design, and Development
- Production
- Distribution
- Human Resources
- Payroll

Business Management

Management of an appliance company can consist of a single individual at a small company or hundreds of top-level executives at a large company. Large companies are organized into hierarchies headed by chief executive officers (CEOs). Under a CEO are upper-management personnel who are in charge of operations for a given facility. Below these upper-management positions are middle-management positions, which in turn are followed by low-level managers. Individuals in the upper-management positions command high salaries, ranging from several hundred thousand to well over a million dollars a year. These individuals have college degrees, usually in business-related fields. Most also have master of business administration (M.B.A.) degrees. These high positions are usually achieved by motivated individuals who work their way up the corporate ladder. In some cases, after achieving a high level in one company, a manager will be recruited to work for a rival company or a company with another focus, such as automobile manufacturing. Included in management are assistants such as secretaries and clerks.

Business management occupations may include the following:

- Owner/Partner
- Chief Executive Officer (CEO)
- Chief Financial Officer (CFO)
- Chief Operating Officer (COO)
- Controller
- General Counsel
- Vice President of Sales and Marketing
- Vice President of Business Development
- Executive Assistant
- Administrative Assistant
- Secretary

Customer Service

Customer service is an essential element for both manufacturing companies and retail outlets. Individuals working in this capacity must possess excellent people skills. When a customer issues a complaint, customer service personnel must handle it in a competent and cheerful manner. The customer may be an individual or a representative of another company that may purchase thousands of units annually. A large company may employ managers, assistant managers, and representatives who communicate with customers via the telephone or Internet. Customer services are usually augmented by automated telephone messages as well as Web-based services to handle common questions. It is imperative that these services be well designed and capable of handling many common customer service issues. These automated services can result in extreme customer frustration if the customer must invest significant time without getting an answer or being able to talk to a human. Customer services are a link between the customers and the company; thus, these personnel obtain invaluable information regarding an appliance such as likes, dislikes, and suggestions for improvement.

Customer service occupations may include the following:

- Customer Service Manager
- Customer Service Assistant Manager
- Customer Service Supervisor
- Customer Service Representative
- Technical Writer

Legal Services

Large companies incur significant expense for legal services. Legal issues can arise with companies of any size and can include product liability, copyright infringement, illegal business practices, and employee issues such as job discrimination, wrongful termination, or sexual harassment. Large companies have more vulnerability to large settlements because of their financial standing. However, lawsuits ranging from the frivolous to multi-million-dollar cases must all be handled. Small and some midsize businesses must retain outside counsel in these instances. The larger companies maintain in-house counsel. These attorneys must be specialists in or have some expertise in mergers and acquisitions, patents and intellectual property, contracts, and labor law. When a company is exploring a merger with another company or dissolution of a business segment, in-house counsel are involved in the negotiations. These teams also consist of legal assistants, such as legal secretaries and paralegals. Even large companies may be required to obtain additional legal services in the event of a high-profile case. Lawsuits have the potential to devastate even the largest corporations.

Legal services occupations may include the following:

- General Counsel
- Staff Attorney
- Contracts Attorney
- Intellectual Property Attorney
- Litigator
- Lobbyist
- Paralegal
- Legal Secretary
- Administrative Assistant

Sales and Marketing

Manufacturing companies maintain staffs of salespeople who call on businesses or individuals to promote their product lines. They often invite customers to lunch or dinner to explain and promote their companies' products. Other incentives that comply with federal and state regulations may also be offered. Marketing is conducted by newspaper, magazine, television, and radio advertising. The Internet is a common vehicle for promoting products. Potential customers can go online to obtain product specifications, compare products (including those of rival manufacturers), and purchase products (either on a company's Web site or by referral to retailers in the consumer's area). Marketing departments include graphic designers who develop illustrations for Web sites, brochures, magazine displays, and other materials. Photographers take pictures for sales brochures, magazines, and newspapers. Videographers prepare video clips for television and company Web sites. Writers prepare text for publications. Marketing departments also employ public relations specialists. These personnel prepare press releases about new products and supply them to newspapers, magazines, and television and radio stations.

Sales and marketing occupations may include the following:

- Sales Director
- Marketing Director
- Public Relations Director
- Sales Manager
- Marketing Manager
- Sales Representative
- Market Research Analyst
- Graphic Designer
- Copywriter
- Photographer
- Videographer
- Spokesperson
- Press Representative

Information Technology

Information Technology (IT) personnel design, install, and maintain computer systems. Computer networks are present in all midsize and large businesses. Computers are involved in many aspects of a business, including inventory, payroll, sales, and production. A breakdown in a computer network can bring production or sales to a halt. The IT department of a large company consists of individuals with college degrees in computer science, as well as technicians trained in vocational schools or community colleges. The lower-level positions include installation, wiring, and maintenance of computer equipment.

IT occupations may include the following:

- Chief Information Officer (CIO)
- Information Technology Manager
- Network and Systems Administrator
- Database Designer
- Database Administrator
- Help Desk Staff
- Web Designer
- Software Engineer/Computer Programmer
- Information Technology Technician
- Network Security Specialist

Facilities and Security

Maintenance of larger facilities requires housekeeping personnel, painters, and repair personnel. A large manufacturing corporation may often have a large security department headed by one or more managers. Security personnel are responsible for preventing unwanted entry to areas where research and development is conducted. They are also responsible for ensuring the safety of other employees by guarding against entry by individuals who could pose a threat. Identification tags are almost universally required for all personnel, from top management to janitors. Entry into many portions of buildings may be restricted by a variety of devices, including card slots, key pads, and posted guards. Video surveillance is often present in a central location, where portions of the building can be viewed by security personnel and recorded on tape.

Facilities and security occupations may include the following:

- Security Manager
- Security Guard
- Maintenance Director
- Machinery Maintenance Worker
- Mechanic
- Heating, Ventilation, and Air-Conditioning (HVAC) Specialist

OCCUPATION PROFILE

Electrical and Electronics Engineer

Considerations	Qualifications
Description	Researches, designs, and develops electrical and electronic devices and equipment.
Career clusters	Architecture and Construction; Manufacturing; Science, Technology, Engineering, and Math
Interests	Data; things
Working conditions	Work inside
Minimum education level	Bachelor's degree; master's degree; doctoral degree
Physical exertion	Light work
Physical abilities	Unexceptional/basic fitness
Opportunities for experience	Internship; apprenticeship; military service; part-time work
Licensure and certification	Usually not required
Employment outlook	Slower-than-average growth expected
Holland interest score	IRE

Note: See volume 1, "Publisher's Note," for an explanation of the Holland interest score.

- General Maintenance and Repair Worker
- Custodian/Janitor

Technology, Research, Design, and Development

Ongoing research and development is a vital element of an appliance company. Even small and midsize businesses must devote time in this arena to remain competitive. The research team comprises engineers, scientists, and laboratory assistants. This department not only designs products but also designs the equipment that manufactures those products, and it tests them before they are released to the marketplace. Appliances are run through repeated duty cycles, knobs are twisted, buttons are pushed, and doors are slammed. If a construction defect surfaces after a product is released, the company might incur a major expense in product recall. Research often focuses on increasing energy efficiency and producing new features that will attract consumer interest.

Technology, research, design, and development occupations may include the following:

- Research and Development Director
- Engineering Manager
- Industrial Engineer
- Electrical Engineer
- Mechanical Engineer
- Industrial/Electrical/Mechanical Engineering Technician

Production

Production is overseen by managers, assistant managers, and supervisors. The bulk of the workforce operates within a hierarchy ranging from experienced workers with expertise in one or more production areas to inexperienced new hires. Large companies offer training programs to help workers advance to the next level. Their production personnel assemble products on production lines. Robots are increasingly being employed in appliance manufacturing. These devices replace workers; however, personnel are still required to control them. A conflict often arises between management, which is interested in improving production with robotics, and labor unions, which are focused on preserving jobs. Employee safety is a major concern in appliance production, and the production line is equipped with features to ensure safety. Specialized clothing and goggles may be required for workers. The primary responsibility of some of a large company's supervisors is to ensure employee safety.

Production occupations may include the following:

- Production Manager
- Production Line Supervisor
- Team Assembler
- Machine Operator
- Welding, Cutting, Soldering, and Brazing Worker

- Inspector, Tester, Sorter, Sampler, and Weigher
- Production Worker

Distribution

Appliance companies own or lease distribution centers to warehouse and distribute products. These centers are often located near rail lines, ports, and the interstate highway system. Distribution centers are overseen by managers who are in charge of a workforce consisting primarily of warehouse workers who move appliances in and out of the facility. Managers must also ensure that the inventory remains at an appropriate level. The distribution center may employ truck drivers or contract with a trucking company to transport items.

Distribution occupations may include the following:

- Distribution Manager
- Warehouse Manager

OCCUPATION PROFILE

Electromechanical Equipment Assembler

Considerations	Qualifications
Description	Assembles or modifies electromechanical equipment.
Career cluster	Manufacturing
Interests	Data; things
Working conditions	Work inside
Minimum education level	On-the-job training; high school diploma or GED; high school diploma/technical training
Physical exertion	Light work; medium work
Physical abilities	Unexceptional/basic fitness
Opportunities for experience	Internship; apprenticeship; part-time work
Licensure and certification	Usually not required
Employment outlook	Decline expected
Holland interest score	RIE

Note: See volume 1, "Publisher's Note," for an explanation of the Holland interest score.

- Dispatcher
- Shipping and Receiving Clerk
- Truck Driver
- Freight Loader/Unloader

Human Resources

The human resources department of an appliance company is responsible for all personnel. It hires and dismisses employees, responds to employee grievances, administers benefits (such as health insurance, retirement plans, and profit-sharing plans) responds to interdepartment or interfacility transfer requests, and oversees employee training. The department recruits employees, advertising positions via classified ads and the Internet and making personal contacts at college campuses and job fairs. Managers are typically college graduates. Clerical personnel and assistants with less educational experience are also employed in this department.

Human resources occupations may include the following:

- Human Resources Director
- Human Resources Manager
- Human Resources Generalist
- Benefits Specialist
- Payroll Clerk

According to the California Energy Commission, a gas stove with an electronic ignition costs half as much to operate as an electric stove. (©Dreamstime.com)

- Administrative Assistant
- Recruiter/Interviewer

Payroll

A dedicated payroll department is often overseen by a certified public accountant (CPA) with management experience. Other CPAs, clerical personnel, and assistants are also employed. Large companies have computerized, automated systems to generate paychecks; however, some human intervention on a daily basis is required.

Payroll occupations may include the following:

- Payroll Manager
- Payroll Clerk
- Accountant/Auditor
- Administrative Assistant

INDUSTRY OUTLOOK

Overview

The outlook for this industry shows it to be in decline both in the United States and globally. Experts in the field disagree as to whether this trend will continue. In June, 2010, James Campbell, president and CEO of General Electric's appliances unit, told *The Wall Street Journal* that he foresaw rising revenues and profits for 2010 and 2011 for the appliance industry. However, he attributed this projected growth to government stimulus programs rather than direct private-sector recovery. He added that the consumer appliance sector was probably "behind the curve" in terms of the broad economic recovery. Campbell and other experts are cognizant that the home appliance industry is strongly tied to the housing market. If home prices rise, homeowners are likely to invest in appliances. Until the housing market recovers, the market for large appliances is likely to remain somewhat unstable. One sector of the industry will profit from continued economic weakness: the repair sector. During economic downturns, consumers are likely to repair existing appliances rather than purchase new ones.

The dominance of large businesses is expected to continue. They may even grow to control more than 95 percent of the market. Despite the supremacy of large businesses, however, the industry will always contain small and mid-size segments. Small-business owners who can design innovative products or improve existing products are likely to find success in the appliance industry.

Consumer awareness of energy-efficient appliances is increasing via a variety of sources. Appliance manufacturers and sales personnel are promoting their Energy Star lines of products, the Federal Government is promoting green products, and utilities companies are encouraging energy-efficient appliances as well. As energy costs increase, consumers are motivated to replace inefficient appliances with ones of greater efficiency. This trend supports sales of newer, energy-efficient products.

Robotics will be used increasingly in manufacturing. This increase may be hampered by labor unions, which will fight to preserve jobs. Currently, a number of manufacturing plants outside the United States utilize robotics to a great degree. Many appliances are produced with narrow profit margins, so robotics can increase a company's bottom line. High-technology features will also increase with the introduction of new products. The addition of such features to appliances is expected to decrease. Energy efficiency will be stressed with new products; furthermore, new appliances may combine electrical or natural gas usage with renewable energy sources such as solar. Solar panels can heat water; thus, they can reduce the usage of natural gas by a water heater. Photovoltaic panels are also available, which convert solar energy into electricity.

Government regulation of the health care industry is expanding. This may cause a decrease in the present large profit margin enjoyed by manufacturers of medical and dental appliances.

PROJECTED EMPLOYMENT FOR SELECTED OCCUPATIONS

Electrical Equipment, Appliance, and Component Manufacturing

Employment		
2009	Projected 2018	Occupation
8,750	7,900	Coil winders, tapers, and finishers
8,440	8,000	Cutting, punching, and press machine setters, operators, and tenders, metal and plastic
38,470	36,400	Electrical and electronic equipment assemblers
12,740	12,400	First-line supervisors/managers of production and operating workers
11,410	11,200	Inspectors, testers, sorters, samplers, and weighers
54,290	51,800	Team assemblers

Source: U.S. Bureau of Labor Statistics, Industries at a Glance, Occupational Employment Statistics and Employment Projections Program. Available at http://www.bls.gov.

Employment Advantages

Even though the appliance industry is in decline, the industry may be a good career choice for some candidates. Appliances have become essential components for both home and commercial use. A demand for them will always exist, and over time components will fail. Even during times of economic slowdown, consumers will consider purchase or replacement of essential appliances such as washing machines or refrigerators over a less essential items such as entertainment or dining out. The industry can support a wide variety of careers, including managerial, technical, and sales positions. In addition, this large industry allows one to make lateral transfers within a company should a change in interest occur. An employee of a company may also derive satisfaction when he or she visits a friend's or relative's home and can point to an appliance and say, "My company builds those."

Annual Earnings

According to Hoover's, the U.S. appliance industry earned revenues of $25 billion in 2009. Global industry revenues were $168.2 billion in 2008, according to Research and Markets. Sales have been declining since 2007. This decline is attributable to the recession of 2007-2009, particularly to the downturn in the housing, construction, and home improvement markets. Those markets began to experience modest improvements in 2010.

The relative stability of the U.S. and European economies will affect the appliance industry. The U.S. economy has fared somewhat better than the European economy during the global financial crisis. If this trend continues, the U.S. appliance industry will grow. Even if the U.S. industry perseveres over the European economy, however, it faces increasing competition from Asian manufacturers. Many of the components in today's appliances are built with parts manufactured in Asia. The companies that make those components have begun assembling them into finished products. Japanese and Korean manufacturers hold a significant market share in the United States; however, a greater threat is that of China, which exports small appliances. The large appliance industry in the United States is likely to face major competition from China.

RELATED RESOURCES FOR FURTHER RESEARCH

AIR-CONDITIONING, HEATING AND
    REFRIGERATION INSTITUTE
2111 Wilson Blvd., Suite 500
Arlington, VA 22201-3042
Tel: (703) 524-8800
Fax: (703) 528-3816
http://www.ahrinet.org

APPLIANCE DESIGN
2401 Big Beaver Rd., Suite 700
Troy, MI 48084

Tel: (440) 886-1210
http://www.appliancedesign.com

APPLIANCE MAGAZINE
11444 W Olympic Blvd.
Los Angeles, CA 90064
Tel: (310) 445-4200
Fax: (310) 445-4299
http://www.appliancemagazine.com

APPLIANCE SERVICE NEWS
P.O. Box 809
St. Charles, IL 60174
Tel: (630) 845-9481
http://www.asnews.com

ASSOCIATION OF HOME APPLIANCE
    MANUFACTURERS
1111 19th St. NW, Suite 402
Washington, DC 20036
Tel: (202) 872-5955
http://www.aham.org

BROOM, BRUSH, AND MOP
204 E Main St.
Arcola, IL 61910
Tel: (217) 268-4950
http://www.rankinpublishing.com

ENERGY STAR, U.S. ENVIRONMENTAL PROTECTION
    AGENCY
1200 Pennsylvania Ave. NW
Washington, DC 20460
Tel: (888) 782-7937
http://www.energystar.gov

KITCHENWARE NEWS & HOUSEWARES REVIEW
15 Runnell St.
Portland, ME 04103
Tel: (207) 780-8656
http://www.kitchenwarenews.com

NATIONAL ELECTRICAL MANUFACTURERS
    ASSOCIATION
1300 N 17th St., Suite 1752
Rosslyn, VA 22209
Tel: (703) 841-3200
Fax: (703) 841-5900
http://www.nema.org

ABOUT THE AUTHOR

Robin L. Wulffson is a medical doctor and a board-certified specialist in obstetrics and gynecology. In 1997, he transitioned to a writing career. He has written analytic reports on major corporations and industries. He has analyzed hospital systems and medical device manufacturers. He is familiar with appliance markets in the United States, Europe, and Asia. For the past fifteen years, he has closely followed the business sector both in the United States and globally.

FURTHER READING

Barnes Reports. *U.S. Major Appliance Manufacturing Industry Report*. Woolwich, Maine: Author, 2008.

_____. *Worldwide Household Appliance Stores Industry Report*. Woolwich, Maine: Author, 2009.

_____. *Worldwide Small Electrical Appliances Manufacturing Industry Report*. Woolwich, Maine: Author, 2009.

Bell, Sandra. *International Brand Management of Chinese Companies: Case Studies on the Chinese Household Appliances and Consumer Electronics Industry Entering US and Western European Markets*. Heidelberg, Germany: Physica-Verlag, 2008.

Castaneda, Christopher James. *Invisible Fuel: Manufactured and Natural Gas in America, 1800-2000*. New York: Twayne, 1999.

Harris InfoSource. *Consumer Appliances Industry Report*. Twinsburg, Ohio: Author, 2002.

Reis, Ronald A. *Becoming an Electronics Technician: Securing Your High-Tech Future*. 4th ed. Upper Saddle River, N.J.: Prentice Hall, 2000.

Snyder, Nancy T., and Deborah Duarte. *Unleashing Innovation: How Whirlpool Transformed an Industry*. San Francisco, Calif.: Jossey-Bass, 2008.

U.S. Bureau of Labor Statistics. *Career Guide to Industries*, 2010-2011 ed. http://www.bls.gov/oco/cg.

U.S. Census Bureau. North American Industry Classification System (NAICS), 2007. http://www.census.gov/cgi-bin/sssd/naics/naicsrch?chart=2007.

U.S. Department of Commerce. International Trade Administration. Office of Trade and Industry Information. Industry Trade Data and Analysis. http://ita.doc.gov/td/industry/otea/OTII/OTII-index.html.

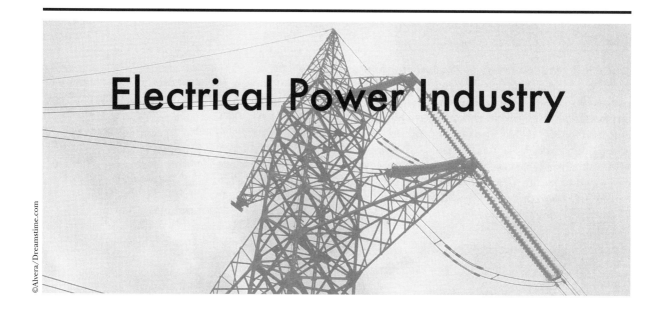

Electrical Power Industry

©Alvera/Dreamstime.com

INDUSTRY SNAPSHOT

General Industry: Energy
Career Cluster: Science, Technology, Engineering, and Math
Subcategory Industries: Electric Power Transmission, Control, and Distribution; Electric Utilities
Related Industries: Alternative Power Industry; Batteries and Fuel Cells Industry; Biofuels Industry; Coal Mining Industry; Electrical and Gas Appliances Industry; Nuclear Power Industry; Petroleum and Natural Gas Industry; Scientific and Technical Services
Annual Domestic Revenues: $399.5 billion USD (U.S. Census Bureau, 2007)
NAICS Number: 2211

INDUSTRY DEFINITION

Summary

The electrical power industry uses generators fueled by coal, oil, or nuclear fuel or powered by falling water or wind to produce electrical power, which it then distributes to users. In the United States and Canada, the majority of electrical utilities are connected to a continent-wide grid that allows companies to sell excess power or to purchase power when local demand is high. Utilities distribute electrical power to individual households and companies, billing customers for each kilowatt hour used. Although electric utilities encourage conservation, they must also plan for expanded demand caused by increased use of electric vehicles.

History of the Industry

The electrical power industry originated in the electromagnetic discoveries of nineteenth century physics. In 1800, the Italian count Alessandro Volta developed the voltaic pile or battery, the first device to reliably produce a steady electric current. Volta's discovery was almost immediately seized on by physicists and chemists. In 1800, the English chemist William Nicholson used the voltaic pile to separate water into hydrogen and oxygen. In 1807, British chemist Sir Humphry Davy isolated sodium and potassium by electrolysis. The use of electrical power to isolate elements from their compounds was one of the earliest and continuing industrial uses of electricity.

The connection between electricity and magnetism was established in 1821 by Danish physicist and chemist Hans Christian Ørsted, who showed that a magnetic field surrounds a current-carrying wire. In 1831, English chemist and physicist Michael Faraday demonstrated electromagnetic induction—the production of voltage when the magnetic flux through a loop of wire changes. This discovery made it possible to generate electrical energy whenever mechanical energy could be used to turn the coil of a generator.

The first rudimentary telegraph was developed by the American physicist Joseph Henry in 1831. It was rendered commercially viable by American artist and inventor Samuel Morse and found immediate application in the coordination of railroad applications. It was natural, therefore, that the first intercity telegraph lines would follow the railroad tracks between cities and that the existing system of telegraph poles would also carry telephone lines and electrical power. The first major effort at providing electric lighting to an urban area was the Pearl Street station built by Thomas Alva Edison in 1882. After the demonstration of a working elec-

tric lighting system, the demand for electricity boomed.

By the 1880's, the small community of electricity producers was split between those who favored direct current (DC) distribution and those who favored alternating current (AC). Because electrical energy must generally be produced as it is needed, there was strong incentive for standardization so that excess power could be traded between generating systems. The most vocal advocate of direct current was Edison, who was distrustful of the complicated mathematics needed to design alternating current circuits. Alternating current was advocated by George Westinghouse, who in 1886 had set up an alternating current lighting plant in Great Barrington, Massachusetts. Unlike direct current, alternating current could be transformed to a high voltage for transmission over long distances and then "stepped down" to a lower, safer voltage for local use. Direct current electricity lost a great deal of energy in transmission. Had Edison's direct cur-

A power plant operator monitors the steam turbine in an electric power plant using a control panel like this. (AP/Wide World Photos)

rent scheme been adopted, generating plants would have had to be stationed a few city blocks apart, and tremendous amounts of copper would have been needed for the transmission lines. A satisfactory alternating current motor was developed by Serbian engineer Nikola Tesla in 1887, setting the stage for the eventual use of alternating current nationwide.

With the widespread acceptance of alternating current transmission, electrical generators were constructed in places such as Niagara Falls, New York, where the energy of falling water could be used to turn the generators. The energy produced was then transmitted at very high voltage to industry and population centers. Soon, generators were placed at dam sites, and electrical power generation joined water management as the rational for dam construction. As utility companies grew, they found the need to burn coal, petroleum, and natural gas to produce steam to turn the turbines that powered additional generators. Nuclear power plant construction began in the 1950's. Environmental concerns have encouraged electricity generation by windmills and sparked research in using tidal energies to produce electricity.

The Industry Today

The overall process of generating electrical energy and distributing it to consumers can be di-

Electrical power is transported at very high voltage over long distances to substations. (©Alvera/Dreamstime.com)

vided into three stages. The first stage is the generation of electrical energy from some other form of stored or motion energy. These energy sources include falling water, wind, the tides, combustion of fossil fuels (coal, oil, or natural gas), and nuclear reactors. Almost all forms of generation involve applications of electromagnetic induction, in which a set of coils is rotated in a magnetic field. The second stage is the transmission of electrical power at very high voltage over possibly long distances to substations, where transformers reduce the voltage to a safer level. The third stage is the retail distribution of electrical energy to homes and businesses. Generally, electrical power is distributed by a 220-volt three-phase system. Individual households and businesses are served by electricity retailers, who meter the amount of electrical energy consumed and bill accordingly.

The electrical power industry consists of more than 3,200 electric utility companies that produce and distribute electrical energy across the country, together with about 1,700 nonutility companies that sell electrical power to industrial concerns and smaller utilities that do not market to

The Utilities Industries' Contribution to the U.S. Economy

Value Added	Amount
Gross domestic product	$255.2 billion
Gross domestic product	1.8%
Persons employed	559,000
Total employee compensation	$64.5 billion

Source: U.S. Bureau of Economic Analysis. Data are for 2008.

individual consumers. The corporate structure of the electrical power industry is quite complex. Many of the companies are owned by local governments, and others are investor-owned (stock) companies operating as regulated monopolies with their rate structures subject to review and approval by the government. Some operate as cooperatives, in which case the customers are the owners. There are nine federal electric utilities operated by government agencies, including the U.S. Army Corps of Engineers, the Department of the Interior, and the Tennessee Valley Authority. Government agencies such as the Tennessee Valley Authority have had an important role in making electrical power available to less-populated areas.

Nonutility producers of electricity include qualifying facilities, as defined by the Public Utilities Regulatory Act of 1987; independent power producers; and some combined heat and power plants located near industrial sites and not covered by the 1987 act. Qualifying facilities include combined heat and power plants that produce steam for industrial use and, as a by-product, electrical energy, which can be sold to utilities, and small power producers, companies that use renewable resources to produce electrical power not exceeding 80 megawatts.

The consumers of electrical power are conveniently divided into four sectors: residential, commercial, industrial, and transportation. The residential sector consists of individuals and families who use electricity for lighting and powering electrical appliances, as well as for heating and cooling their homes. The commercial sector includes retail stores, restaurants, hotels and motels, churches and synagogues, schools, and hospitals. The industrial sector consists of companies that use electricity in manufacturing and construction. A small percentage of the electrical energy produced in the United States is used for the electrolytic production of aluminum, chlorine, lye, and other important chemicals, as well as for chrome plating and galvanizing of iron. The transportation sector includes electric trains and trolleys.

The electricity distribution system in the United States and Canada consists of three large-scale power grids: the Eastern Interconnected System, the Western Interconnected System, and the Texas Interconnected System. There are limited interconnections between the Eastern and Western systems, and the Texas system is connected to the other systems by only a few direct-current lines. The large-scale grids allow utility companies to sell excess capacity to other producers and to purchase electricity as necessary. As a result, the electricity purchased by an individual household or business can

Inputs Consumed by the Utilities Industries	
Input	Value
Energy	$43.1 billion
Materials	$116.0 billion
Purchased services	$27.7 billion
Total	$186.8 billion

Source: U.S. Bureau of Economic Analysis. Data are for 2008.

At substations, transformers reduce the voltage to a safer level. (©Romica/ Dreamstime.com)

be a mix of hydroelectric, coal-generated, and nuclear power.

According to the U.S. Energy Information Administration, in 2007, coal-fired plants accounted for 52 percent of the electricity generated in the United States, natural gas for 21 percent, nuclear power for 19 percent, and hydroelectric power for about 3.5 percent. The percentages are sometimes quite different in other countries. France, for instance, gets more than half of its electricity from nuclear power, while in the oil-rich Arab states, oil is the major energy source.

INDUSTRY MARKET SEGMENTS

Roughly five thousand companies generate and distribute electrical power in the United States. Because the United States and international economies are so dependent on electrical power, it is not surprising to find that employees of the electrical power industry represent a broad spectrum of occupations. These employees include not only engineers, technicians, accountants, and customer service agents but also lawyers and economists who must deal with the complex regulatory environment and plan for the projected growth of the industry.

Small Businesses

Small businesses in the electrical power industry include small power producers and the smaller publicly owned or cooperative utilities.

Potential Annual Earnings Scale. A small power producer is likely to generate less annual revenue than a large municipal facility and may pay somewhat less, although depending on the position, salaries can range from $20,000 to $60,000 and beyond.

Clientele Interaction. Small power producers generally sell power to established utilities. Small utilities generally sell to individual households and businesses. Typically only one utility is given a franchise to sell electrical power to users in a given area, so people and businesses who are located in the area must purchase their power from that company. Customer service for a utility includes starting and stopping service, billing customers and receiving payments, maintaining a good public image for the company, and encouraging conservation so that the cost of delivering services is contained.

Amenities, Atmosphere, and Physical Grounds. Customer service personnel generally work out of offices accessible to the public. Because utilities are regulated as to the prices they can charge and the profit they can earn, office space will generally be as economical as possible. Technical employees may have a locker and a limited gathering space for use between calls.

Typical Number of Employees. The typical number of employees can range from one to a dozen at a small power producer and several dozen to hundreds at a small utility.

Traditional Geographic Locations. Small utilities typically have franchise areas with limited populations. They generally can be found in less-populated areas.

Pros of Working for a Small Utility. Because small utilities generally service a small area, their employees typically can work close to home. Customer service personnel will often find themselves working with their neighbors.

Cons of Working for a Small Utility. Workers at a small utility or power producer will generally have fewer benefits. Technical personnel and management must be on call during weather-related emergencies. Utility service to hospitals and police and fire departments must be maintained or restored as quickly as possible; therefore, personnel must be prepared to deal with emergencies as they occur, regardless of the weather or time of day.

Costs

Payroll and Benefits: Salaries for experienced professional power engineers can exceed $60,000 per year. Salaries for those providing other services range from $20,000 to $40,000 per year. An increasing number of small utilities and power producers outsource their payroll functions.

Supplies: In addition to the usual business supplies, power companies require computer systems, accounting software, power-monitoring equipment, and an inventory of spare parts, including power transformers. Generally, they must maintain a fleet of service vehicles.

External Services: Power companies may own some of the buildings they use and rent space in others. They may maintain cleaning and groundskeeping staff or outsource these functions.

Utilities: In addition to paying for gas, oil, and telephone and Internet access, small utility companies purchase electricity from larger utilities or nonutility providers for resale to customers.

Taxes: Electrical power firms pay business taxes to federal, state, and local governments. Some tax credits and incentives have been offered at the state and federal level to producers of renewable energy.

Midsize Businesses

Midsize electrical power companies include midsize utilities and some combined heat and power producers.

Potential Annual Earnings Scale. Salaries vary considerably, depending on the individual's position, but are generally somewhat higher than those offered at a small producer or utility.

Clientele Interaction. Midsize electrical power companies may serve an area of one or more counties and a variety of individual, business, and institutional clients. Effectively dealing with larger clients requires a technically educated customer relations team.

Amenities, Atmosphere, and Physical Grounds. Midsize utilities may have a more pleasant headquarters building than that of a small utility and will generally have bill payment locations in banks or supermarkets.

Typical Number of Employees. A midsize utility employs from one hundred to one thousand or more workers.

Traditional Geographic Locations. Midsize utilities are usually located in urban or suburban areas.

Pros of Working for a Midsize Utility. A midsize utility can provide better fringe benefits, such as health insurance and educational subsidies, than a small utility can.

Cons of Working for a Midsize Utility. Because a midsize utility has a larger service area, workers may be dispatched far from their home bases. Some employees must regularly be on call for emergencies.

Costs

Payroll and Benefits: Midsize electrical power companies have a professional staff of engineers, a technical staff with bachelor's or associate's degrees, a cadre of licensed electricians, and a number of unskilled workers who receive on-the-job training. Salaries range from $20,000 to more than $100,000 per year, depending on education and experience.

Supplies: In addition to the usual business supplies, midsize utilities generally must make a substantial investment in the equipment needed to maintain electrical service as well as in an inventory of spare parts. Computers are needed for record keeping.

External Services: Midsize utilities may hire contractors for janitorial services and groundskeeping.

Utilities: Midsize utilities pay for utilities such as gas, oil, and telephone and Internet access, and also pay for electricity to be resold to consumers.

Taxes: Midsize firms pay business taxes to federal, state, and local governments. Some tax credits and incentives have been offered at the state and federal level to producers of renewable energy.

Large Businesses

Large electrical power companies are primarily large-scale utilities, including those that provide nuclear power. They have revenues ranging from tens of millions of dollars to tens of billions of dollars. They may own several production facilities, for example, both a nuclear and a coal-burning plant. Some large companies do not provide electricity directly to individuals but sell only to utilities or major industries.

Potential Annual Earnings Scale. Pay varies greatly in large electrical power companies, depending on a person's position and experience, but it is generally better than in a smaller utility.

Clientele Interaction. Large utilities may own power-generating plants as well as directly service franchise areas. A staff of customer relations specialists must be maintained to handle customer complaints and work out rate schedules for large-scale users of electricity. Customer relations personnel may work with local governments to attract new businesses to the area and to project the growth of electrical demand in their service area.

Amenities, Atmosphere, and Physical Grounds. Generation facilities, particularly nuclear plants, are generally remote from major population centers. Hydroelectric facilities such as those at Niagara Falls and Hoover Dam offer an opportunity to work amid spectacular scenery. Because concern for safety is paramount at generating facilities, work spaces are generally clean, and on-site minor medical care may be provided. Generation facilities involve turbines driven by steam or falling water as well as the generators themselves, with high-tension wires to carry off the power produced.

Typical Number of Employees. A large utility generally employs more than two thousand workers.

Traditional Geographic Locations. Large utilities are often headquartered in cities, although the generating plants are located in more remote areas.

Pros of Working for a Large Utility. Large utilities are able to offer job stability with some opportunity for advancement. In addition, they typically offer good benefits, including quality health insurance and pension plans as well as subsidized education.

Cons of Working for a Large Utility. Large utilities, like many large companies, have impersonal work sites and often the competition for promotion can be fierce.

Costs

Payroll and Benefits: Large utilities and power plants have a professional staff composed of engineers, a technical staff with bachelor's or associate's degrees, and a number of unskilled workers who receive on-the-job training. Salaries range from $20,000 to more than $100,000 per year, depending on education and experience, with executives earning more. They also employ accountants, financial planners, and other business and administrative workers.

Supplies: In addition to the usual supplies needed by businesses and smaller utilities, large-scale utilities need electrical monitoring equipment. Those with nuclear plants need radiological monitoring equipment and waste storage and removal equipment.

External Services: Large utilities may hire contractors for instrument calibration and short-term construction jobs, or they may rely on in-house staff.

Utilities: Power-generating facilities pay for gas, oil, telephone and Internet access. They also buy electricity from other facilities as needed to supply their customers. To make energy, utilities must use energy. Electrical power plants may get their energy from falling water, coal, natural gas, or uranium. Hydroelectric plants generally do not have to pay for fuel, but coal-burning plants accept coal delivery from coal mining companies, usually by railroad, and natural gas plants must be connected through pipelines to petroleum refineries. Nuclear power plants purchase nuclear fuel rods as aluminum tubes containing purified uranium extracted from uranium ore.

Taxes: Large utilities pay business taxes to federal, state, and local governments. Some tax credits and incentives have been offered at the state and federal level to producers of renewable energy.

ORGANIZATIONAL STRUCTURE AND JOB ROLES

The electrical power industry is an important component of the energy industry, which includes producers of petroleum fuels, natural gas, and coal. It is vital to the prosperity of the nation. Although some energy conservation measures may reduce the overall need for energy, the rate of growth of demand for electricity is unlikely to contract in the foreseeable future. With the introduction of fully electric vehicles into the U.S. market, it is quite possible that the demand for electrical power will increase. The organizational structure is highly variable, as power-producing companies may be publicly or privately owned or function as cooperatives. The rates charged for electrical power must be approved by the appropriate local, state, or federal governing body. Interstate sales of electricity are regulated by the Federal Energy Regulatory Commission. This commission also must approve the construction of hydroelectric plants on navigable waterways. Nuclear plants are regulated by the U.S. Nuclear Regulatory Commission. Investor-owned utilities are generally answerable to state public service commissions. Environmental impact statements must be filed for any major increase in generating capacity. Large utilities may have a significant engineering and legal staff to deal with compliance issues as they arise.

The following umbrella categories apply to the organizational structure of the electrical power industry:

- Executive Management
- Engineers and Scientists
- Technical Operations
- Retail Operations

Executive Management

As in most industries, executive managers in the private sector of electrical power industry command the highest salaries and make the decisions that determine the long-term profitability of their companies. Executive managers in government-owned or cooperative utilities may earn somewhat less but enjoy greater job security. Executive managers generally have completed graduate degrees in management and may have academic backgrounds in engineering or economics. They have generally worked in various aspects of electrical power production before moving to senior executive positions. Executive management handles the general operations of the utility. Executive managers help establish rate schedules for customers and plan for corporate expansion. In the event of major storms or other interruptions of the power supply, executive managers have the responsibility of calling on crews to work overtime or to help out utilities in neighboring areas.

As businesses, electrical power companies have financial and accounting divisions, human resources departments, and groundskeeping and building maintenance departments. Many employ attorneys and other legal professionals to deal with regulatory issues. One area of particular concern to companies with power-generating facilities is security. All major power production facilities must be patrolled for possible sabotage. Nuclear plants must be constantly on guard against theft of nuclear material, sabotage, and terrorist activity. Electrical power companies must hire, train, and equip a substantial security force.

Executive management occupations may include the following:

- Chief Financial Officer (CFO)
- Controller
- Chief of Engineering
- Station Manager
- Legal Counsel
- Security Manager
- Groundskeeping and Building Maintenance Manager
- Human Resources Manager
- Administrative Support Manager

Engineers and Scientists

All electrical power plants convert some non-electrical form of energy to electrical energy. With the exception of hydroelectric facilities and wind farms, this means generating heat by burning fuel and using the heat to produce steam, which turns the blades of a turbine, producing rotational motion to turn the coils of a generator or dynamo.

The electrical power industry encompasses both generating facilities and transmission lines that take electrical energy to the substations, which subsequently deliver it to the ultimate consumer. The industry also includes combined heat and power generators that produce steam for industrial use and electricity as a by-product. The electrical power industry offers employment opportunities for engineers in most specialties as well as support staff of technicians and craftspeople. For the most part, engineers working in the power industry have passed the professional engineer examination for their field and state.

Engineer salaries range from about $40,000 to more than $100,000. Successful engineers can move to top management positions or become private consultants, commanding somewhat higher incomes. Civil engineers are involved in the design of power generation facilities as well as the company's commercial offices. Hydroelectric power plants have particular need for civil engineers to monitor water flows along rivers and water levels in dams. Materials engineers are needed to ensure the integrity of the turbine blades and of the other moving parts in the generator. They play an especially important role in nuclear power plants, where radiation shielding is a critical concern.

Mechanical engineers monitor the function of the generator and the turbine blades. The power industry employs several specialties within mechanical engineering. Hydraulic engineers deal with issues of fluid flow, including the flow of moving water through a hydroelectric plant or of steam generated in a boiler to turn turbine blades. Combustion engineers are needed in diesel-fueled, gas-burning, and coal-fired power plants. They are concerned with maintaining the heat-generating process within safe limits and with the discharge of the combustion products. Chemical engineers ensure the controlled flow of fuel to the combustion facility and the safe removal of the combustion products. Environmental engineers are needed to make sure that plant operations and waste disposal are in compliance with applicable environmental regulations.

Electrical engineers ensure that the power distribution system, particularly the all-important connection to the regional grid, is functioning properly. Electrical engineers monitor the output of the generator powered by the turbine and the system of conductors leading electrical energy out of the plant. Performance engineers are electrical or mechanical engineers who specialize in the tests and inspections needed to ensure that the power production and distribution systems are functioning properly.

Nuclear engineers are responsible for the reactor design and for making sure that it is operating within safe limits. They design and oversee the construction of new reactors and the modification of existing power plants. They also develop procedures for the handling of radioactive materials.

Computer engineers maintain or develop computer systems for generator operation as well as for normal business purposes, ranging from accounting to inventory control. Simulation engineers design simulators that allow power plant personnel to prepare for emergencies. To be prepared for any eventuality, power plant technical staff members must undergo extensive training on computer simulations. Writing the control software for electrical power plants requires knowledge of generator operations as well as programming skill and familiarity with the field of human factors psychology.

The employment of scientists by the electrical power industry is concentrated in the nuclear power component. The boundary between science and engineering is not sharp, and some individuals with degrees in physics, chemistry, computer science, or applied mathematics may be found working as engineers or engineer's assistants in the power industry.

Engineering occupations may include the following:

- Civil Engineer
- Materials Engineer
- Mechanical Engineer
- Environmental Engineer
- Hydraulic Engineer
- Combustion Engineer
- Electrical Engineer
- Computer Engineer
- Simulation Engineer
- Chemical Engineer

Technical Operations

The day-to-day operation of electrical power companies involves a host of technically educated professionals. These include power plant operators, distributors and dispatchers, maintenance supervisors, electrical and electronics installers, and line installers and repairers.

Power plant operators control the electricity-generating equipment at the power plant. In general, the power plant operator monitors a control board that displays the status of the boilers, turbines, and generators in the plant. Operators distribute the power demand among generators and follow the customer demand. With the aid of computers, they may increase the output of generators or take generators offline. There is very stiff competition for jobs as power plant operators, which pay between $40,000 and $65,000 per year. Power plant operators generally must go through several years of training before becoming fully qualified. A high school diploma is essential, and many power plant operators have appreciable college education. Some have bachelor's degrees.

Because boilers, turbines, and generators are working machines subject to the stress and strain of constant use, a cycle of inspection and scheduled maintenance must be established and followed. Special problems associated with nuclear power plants include shutdowns of the reactor for refueling, storage of reactor waste, and constant radiological monitoring to protect operating personnel and the environment. Maintenance supervisors manage the electrical and mechanical equipment of the power plant. They oversee the installation, maintenance, and repair of the equipment in the plant and its control systems. They are responsible for setting up maintenance and replacement schedules and seeing that they are followed. They bear considerable responsibility for the safety of the power plant as a workplace. They must have a working knowledge of electrical instrumentation as well as the ability to manage lower-level mechanics and technicians. Generally a bachelor's degree in electrical or mechanical engineering is required, along with five to ten years of power plant experience and at least two years of supervisory experience at a lower level.

The power distributor or dispatcher controls the flow of electricity through the transmission lines that lead from the generator to the substation. Power distributors have the responsibility of matching the power supply, bringing additional boilers into action when needed, and routing around generating units that may be shut down for repair. According to the U.S. Department of Labor, their salaries ranged between $38,000 and $83,000 in 2007. Although a bachelor's degree is not required for this position, power distributors must complete years of training as an apprentice and may need to achieve certification as a systems operator. Power distributors often belong to the International Brotherhood of Electrical Workers or the Utility Workers Union of America, both parts of the AFL-CIO.

Every utility company needs installers and repairers to maintain the electrical and electronic equipment essential to its operation. Installers and

OCCUPATION SPECIALTIES

Power Plant Operators

Specialty	Responsibilities
Generator switchboard operators	Control central electric generating plant switchboards to distribute and regulate power.
Hydroelectric-station operators	Control electrical generating units and mechanical and hydraulic equipment at hydroelectric generating stations.
Load dispatchers	Coordinate personnel in generating stations, substations, and lines of electric power stations.
Motor-room controllers	Control generation and distribution of electrical power from power station to plant facilities and maintain equipment.
Power-reactor operators	Control nuclear reactors that produce steam to generate electricity and coordinate auxiliary equipment operation.
Substation operators	Control current convertors, voltage transformers, and circuit breakers to regulate electricity flow through substations and over distribution lines.
Switchboard operator assistants	Compile gauge readings and perform other tasks as directed by the switchboard operator in an electric-generating plant. They clean and oil mechanical and electrical equipment and report malfunctions, and they may assist in tests to diagnose the cause of equipment malfunction.
Switchboard operators	Control converters, rectifiers, transformers, and generators to direct, distribute, and maintain power to chemical processing equipment.
Turbine operators	Control steam-driven turbogenerators in electric or nuclear power generating stations.

repairers generally have graduated high school and attended a vocational school or community college program in electrical technology. Electrical equipment provides the power for a device, while electronic equipment generally controls device performance. According to the Bureau of Labor Statistics, installers and repairers earn between $38,000 and $70,000, depending on experience and location. Linemen install and repair the vast network of cables over which electrical power is carried from the generating plant to the customer. In many communities, the cables are carried over utility poles that may also carry telephone wires. Becoming a lineman generally requires on-the-job training after completing a vocational or technical program. Linemen must be agile, not afraid of heights, and willing to work in all types of weather. Linemen earn from $27,000 to $67,000 per year for full-time work.

A lineman installs power lines. (©John Sartin/Dreamstime.com)

Technical operations occupations may include the following:

- Power Plant Operator
- Maintenance Supervisor
- Maintenance Worker
- Power Distributor/Dispatcher

- Electrical and Electronics Installer/ Repairer
- Lineman

Retail Operations

The vast majority of electric utilities sell electrical power to their customers, monitor the consumption, and bill monthly for the power consumed in kilowatt hours. Some utilities combine the delivery of water and natural gas with their electrical business. They may also be responsible for collecting certain fees, such as for trash collection and sewer services. Like other retail businesses, they maintain staff for accounting and billing, payment processing, and general customer service.

In general, electric utilities monitor power consumption at the customer's site, maintaining a staff of meter readers to record monthly usage, and billing residential and business customers accordingly. Meter readers must be familiar with their territories and able to drive themselves from site to site. Although extensive technical training is not required to be a meter reader, readers should be able to spot

OCCUPATION SPECIALTIES

Electrical Line Installers and Repairers

Specialty	Responsibilities
Cable installers-repairers	Install and repair underground conduit and cable systems.
Line repairers	Repair and replace power lines between generating stations, substations, and consumers.
Tower erectors	Erect transmission towers and install electric cables.

meters in need of repair and those that may have been tampered with or vandalized.

Utilities must issue bills to each customer and accept payment. In many communities, utility bill payments may be made at specified banks and retail stores as well as by mail or, increasingly, by computer over secure Web sites. The accounting function is highly automated, with payments entered as they are received. Because no one likes to pay utility bills, utility companies must generally maintain a staff of customer relations agents to receive complaints and work out payment arrangements for customers unable to pay in full. Customer service agents also are involved in setting up accounts as people move to a new address and discontinuing service at the previous address. Most utilities offer one or more cost-averaging plans for customers who prefer to pay the same amount each month, rather than face very high bills in summer or winter.

Most utility companies encourage conservation. Although this cuts into company revenue, it also eliminates the cost of expanding production, and in the case of nuclear or fuel-burning plants, the cost of complying with environmental regulations. Utilities advise their customers as to the cost advantage of compact fluorescent lightbulbs and the newer light emitting diodes (LEDs) over the old-style incandescent bulbs. They may also advise on

home insulation and on the coordinated use of illumination and heating and air-conditioning systems in big buildings to reduce costs overall.

Retail operations occupations may include the following:

- Meter Reader
- Billing Clerk
- Customer Relations Specialist
- Customer Service Agent

INDUSTRY OUTLOOK

Overview

The outlook for the electrical power industry shows it to be on the rise. The demand for energy in the United States is unlikely to decrease in the foreseeable future, and demand in the emerging nations of Asia is certain to increase. The electrical power industry is in growth mode, although there is some uncertainty as to the distribution of energy sources. A further uncertainty is attached to the deregulation or reregulation of the industry, which depends on legislative action. With more competition for the purchase of fossil fuels, an increased dependence on nuclear power seems inevitable. Nuclear power plants are scheduled for construction, but the problem of long-term storage of high-level nuclear waste persists, as does the problem of carbon emissions from conventional power plants. Another question is the extent to which electric-powered or hybrid vehicles will supplant gasoline- and diesel-powered vehicles. The possible emergence of new technologies may also affect the electrical power industry. Solar energy can supplant electricity from fossil fuels for home heating and cooling to some extent, but conversion of solar energy to electricity remains inefficient.

The electrical power industry is particularly sensitive to the electoral process. For example, in the 2008 presidential election, the advocates of expanded drilling for oil were pitted against environmental groups. Varying estimates have been made of the time that will be needed for more environmentally friendly technologies, such as wind farms and solar plants, to become a significant part of production capacity. Although nuclear power advocates point to the lower environmental impact of properly run nuclear plants, fear of possible nu-

Smart meters report electric consumption on an hourly basis, allowing utilities to charge differently for peak and off-peak usage. (©Richard Abplanalp/Dreamstime.com)

PROJECTED EMPLOYMENT FOR SELECTED OCCUPATIONS

Utilities Industry

Employment		
2009	Projected 2018	Occupation
18,130	16,700	Control and valve installers and repairers, except mechanical door
14,140	11,600	Electrical engineers
54,070	44,700	Electrical power-line installers and repairers
15,840	13,200	First-line supervisors/managers of mechanics, installers, and repairers
19,460	14,300	Meter readers, utilities

Source: U.S. Bureau of Labor Statistics, Industries at a Glance, Occupational Employment Statistics and Employment Projections Program.

clear accidents remains, along with still unresolved issues concerning the disposal of high-level radioactive waste.

The electrical power industry requires a technologically educated workforce. This is particularly true in the nuclear industry, where educational standards for reactor operators were significantly increased in the wake of the 1979 accident at the Three Mile Island Nuclear Generating Station. Although security issues may be of greatest importance in the nuclear side of the industry, any significant loss of electrical power-generating capacity could be damaging to the economy; therefore, all power generation facilities require security personnel. A number of types of power plants not yet in commercial operation may become practicable as the demand for electrical power grows. These include breeder reactors, which actually produce additional radioactive fuel as they generate electricity, and liquid metal reactors, in which a liquid metal such as sodium is used as the heat exchange medium instead of water. Uses of wind energy and solar energy are expanding. Solar energy for direct home heating may reduce the need for electrical power in many parts of the United States. Experi-

ments in the use of tidal energy are also under way.

Employment Advantages

The electrical power industry overall is in a controlled growth mode. Although the 2011 nuclear accident in Fukushima, Japan, may temporarily halt expansion in the nuclear power industry, many planned plants are likely to be built, if somewhat later than initially scheduled. As the demand for electrical energy grows, new power plants of all types will be constructed, and new technologies implemented. Significant new employment opportunities are likely to occur as the baby-boomer generation begins to retire. Highly skilled workers will find their skills transferable to new technologies as, for instance, solar or wind power stations come on line.

Scientific and technical staff in the electrical power industry therefore are likely to have many jobs open to them, even outside the traditional area of energy production. Students who prepare for engineering or science degrees or receive advanced technical training at a community college or in the military should be able to select from a number of attractive positions. Workers in all aspects of the electrical power industry can expect to participate in continuing education throughout their lifetimes.

Annual Earnings

Electrical power companies have generally functioned as regulated monopolies, which means that their profitability is unlikely to increase or decrease dramatically. However, as the industry became somewhat deregulated, the profit potential has become more uncertain. It is likely that power industry revenues will grow over time and that the fraction of electrical energy produced by nuclear power will increase, following the example of European countries. The cost of fossil fuels will almost certainly increase as industrialization and the standard of living rises in China, India, and other emerging nations. A marked increase in demand is possible as fully electric and hybrid electric vehicles capture more of the automotive market. The cost of hazardous reactor waste disposal or reprocessing is another economic variable. As spent nuclear fuel accumulates on site, there will be a push both for disposal at geologically safe sites and for reprocessing spent nuclear fuel. Transportation costs and security costs associated with transport of high-level waste by rail or truck must be considered.

In addition to their domestic operations, American companies have become involved in exporting electrical power technology, including nuclear technology, to other countries, particularly those in Asia and the Middle East. Technical workers may have interesting travel opportunities as plants are constructed in other countries or as equipment is designed for export.

RELATED RESOURCES FOR FURTHER RESEARCH

AMERICAN PUBLIC POWER ASSOCIATION
1875 Connecticut Ave. NW, Suite 1200
Washington, DC 20009-5715
Tel: (202) 467-2900
Fax: (202) 467-2910
http://www.publicpower.org

INTERNATIONAL BROTHERHOOD OF ELECTRICAL WORKERS
900 7th St. NW
Washington, DC
Tel: (202) 833-7000
Fax: (202) 728-7676
http://www.ibew.org

NUCLEAR ENERGY INSTITUTE
1776 I St. NW, Box 400
Washington, DC 20006-3708
Tel: (202) 739-8000
Fax: (202) 785-4019
http://www.nei.org

POWER AND ENERGY SOCIETY
Institute of Electrical and Electronics Engineers
345 E 47th St.
New York, NY 10017-2394

Tel: (212) 752-6800
Fax: (212) 752-4929
http://www.ieee.org

U.S. ENERGY INFORMATION ADMINISTRATION
1000 Independence Ave. SW
Washington, DC 20505
Tel: (202) 586-8800
http://www.eia.gov

UTILITY WORKERS UNION OF AMERICA
815 16th St. NW
Washington, DC 20006
Tel: (202) 974-8200
Fax: (202) 974-8201
http://uwua.net

ABOUT THE AUTHOR

Don Franceschetti has been a member of the physics faculty at the University of Memphis for more than thirty years. He received his bachelor of science degree from Brooklyn College in 1969 and his doctoral degree in physical chemistry from Princeton University in 1974. He came to the University of Memphis following research appointments in physics and materials science at the Universities of Illinois, North Carolina, and Utrecht (the Netherlands). He is a Dunavant University Professor. He has taught a wide range of physics courses and courses for physics teachers and has written extensively about the physical sciences and their history.

FURTHER READING

Baigrie, Brian S. *Electricity and Magnetism: A Historical Perspective*. Westport, Conn.: Greenwood Press, 2007.

Bodanis, David. *Electric Universe: How Electricity Switched on the Modern World*. New York: Three Rivers Press, 2005.

CareerBuilder.com. Salary Calculator and Wage Finder. http://www.cbsalary.com/salary-calculator.

Careers.org. Occupation Profiles: Descriptions, Earnings, Outlook. http://occupations.careers.org.

Friedel, Robert, Paul Israel, and Bernard S. Finn. *Edison's Electric Light.* Rev. ed. Baltimore: The Johns Hopkins University Press, 2010.

Galvin, Robert W., Kurt E. Yeager, and Jay Stuller. *Perfect Power: How the Microgrid Revolution Will Unleash Cleaner, Greener, and More Abundant Energy.* New York: McGraw-Hill, 2009.

Heppenheimer, T. A. "Nuclear Power: What Went Wrong?" *American Heritage of Invention and Technology* 18, no. 2 (2002): 46-56.

Jonnes, Jill. *Empires of Light: Edison, Tesla, Westinghouse, and the Race to Electrify the World.* New York: Random House, 2003.

Kaplan, Stan. *Power Plant Characteristics and Costs.* New York: Nova Science Publishers, 2010.

Levy, Salomon. *Fifty Years in Nuclear Power: A Retrospective.* La Grange Park, Ill.: American Nuclear Society, 2007.

Newton, David E. *Nuclear Power.* New York: Infobase, 2005.

PayScale.com. "Salary Snapshot for Nuclear Power Reactor Operator Jobs." January 29, 2010. http://www.payscale.com/research/US/Job=Nuclear_Power_Reactor_Operator/Salary.

Taylor, Allan, and James Robert Parish. *Career Opportunities in the Energy Industry.* New York: Ferguson, 2008.

U.S. Bureau of Labor Statistics. *Career Guide to Industries,* 2010-2011 ed. http://www.bls.gov/oco/cg.

U.S. Census Bureau. North American Industry Classification System (NAICS), 2007. http://www.census.gov/cgi-bin/sssd/naics/naicsrch?chart=2007.

U.S. Department of Commerce. International Trade Administration. Office of Trade and Industry Information. Industry Trade Data and Analysis. http://ita.doc.gov/td/industry/otea/OTII/OTII-index.html.

Environmental Engineering and Consultation Services

©Dreamstime.com

INDUSTRY SNAPSHOT

General Industry: Science, Technology, Engineering, and Math

Career Clusters: Business, Management, and Administration; Science, Technology, Engineering, and Math

Subcategory Industries: Consulting Engineer's Offices and Private Practices; Environmental Consulting Services; Environmental Engineering Services; Remediation Services; Sanitation Consulting Services; Site Remediation Consulting Services

Related Industries: Building Architecture Industry; Building Construction Industry; Business Services; Landscaping Services; Scientific and Technical Services; Waste Management Industry

Annual Domestic Revenues: $140.6 billion USD (Smith Travel Research, 2009)

Annual International Revenues: $344 billion USD (Research and Markets, 2009)

Annual Global Revenues: $484.3 billion USD (Research and Markets, 2009)

NAICS Numbers: 56291, 541330, 541620

INDUSTRY DEFINITION

Summary

Environmental engineering is considered as a subset of civil engineering. Environmental engineering and consultation services design, plan, assess, or perform engineering duties and gather information on the environmental consequences of proposed actions, in order to prevent, control, and remediate environmental hazards. Environmental engineers provide communities and policy makers with project management, permit acquisition, and other specialized environmental technology and services. Environmental consultants help businesses and municipalities prepare environmental impact statements and otherwise comply with environmental regulations. Environmental engineering is equivalent to sanitary engineering and is also called environmental health engineering or public health engineering.

History of the Industry

The earliest known practice of civil engineering is thought to have occurred in the period between 4000 and 2000 B.C.E. in ancient Egypt and Mesopotamia. During that period, humans departed from a nomadic lifestyle of mobile hunting and gathering and settled in constructed shelters. They still required transportation, however, and created wheel-based land vehicles, as well as sail-based water vessels.

Historians attribute the origins of large environmental construction initiatives to the construction of pyramids in Egypt between about 2700 and 2500 B.C.E. Other historic civil engineering constructions were the Parthenon in Ancient Greece (447-438 B.C.E.), the Appian Way of the Romans (about 312 B.C.E.), and the Great Wall of China (about 220 B.C.E.). The inventions of Archimedes in the third century B.C.E. constitute some of the first applications of mathematics and physics to problems of civil and environmental engineering. Environmental engineering began to develop in its own right with the construction and use of aqueducts, bridges, roads, dams, and harbors throughout the Roman Empire. The roots of the discipline grew with the architectural designs and construction expertise of artisans such as the carpenters and stonemasons of ancient and medieval times.

No clear distinction was originally made between civil engineering and architecture until the modern era. Civil engineering became a scientific term in the eighteenth century and rose to promi-

nence when the Institution of Civil Engineers was founded in London in 1818 and received a royal charter in 1828. Civil engineering thus became formally recognized as a profession. Attention came to be focused on what today would be recognized as several environmental activities pertaining to the construction of bridges, aqueducts, harbors, lighthouses, drainage systems, and river transport, as well as the manufacture of machinery for construction.

The first private college to teach civil engineering (including environmental engineering) in the United States was Norwich University, founded in 1819 by Captain Alden Partridge. The first degree in civil engineering in the United States was awarded by Rensselaer Polytechnic Institute in 1835. The first environmental engineering and consultation service in the United States was Tyree Organization, which was founded in Farmingdale, New York, in 1930. (It is still functional today, serving customers in the retail petroleum industry, with specializations in the excavation of contami-

Environmental engineers use technology to help companies reduce air pollution. (©Dreamstime.com)

nated soils, environmental testing, service station maintenance, and pump tank construction. The company also provides emergency response services, as well as engineering and compliance services for petroleum bulk storage, and operates from offices in California, Connecticut, Massachusetts, New Jersey, and New York.) Environmental engineering services progressed steadily thereafter, with the founding and establishment of several categories of small, midsize, and large environmental engineering and consulting companies.

The Industry Today

Environmental engineers focus today on the use of the principles of biology and chemistry to develop solutions to modern environmental problems. Information technology (IT) and automation with high-technology electronic innovations have become integral components of twenty-first century environmental engineering and consultation servcies. These technologies underlie diagnostics, operations, and environmental services generally. Companies are more actively involved in water and air pollution control, recycling, waste disposal, and public health issues than they were in the past.

Since 2003, a broad range of engineering and consultation services have emerged, tailored to electrical and telecommunication utilities and the mining industry. Services include design, electrical system studies, environmental permitting, testing, commissioning, and geographic information services (GIS), which are popular tools for environmental services and projects pertaining to surveying, construction, and transportation.

The environmental industry has advanced in the use of modern equipment, some of which improves on older versions. Engineers use such equipment to facilitate assessments and provide services several times faster and better than they could in the past and to enable environmental workers to undertake more challenging tasks. Workers in the field and those in laboratories and offices can easily and quickly communicate by mobile electronic devices, and staff can use computers to exchange information with other offices far and

An aerial view of a water treatment plant. (©Dijkmans Phillippe/ Dreamstime.com)

near and even to have discussions and conduct seminars by videoconferencing.

The industry now has computers, engineering software, mechanical and electrical tools, modern GIS instruments (for mapping lands) that did not exist in the past, storage tanks, centrifuges, electron and research microscopes, spectrophotometers, different recorders, chromatography equipment, monitoring and testing systems, varieties of laboratory equipment, and a host of other supplies in line with various companies' specialties. These tools make the modern environmental industry more useful, competitive, efficient, challenging, and exciting. For additional innovations, many environmental engineering businesses are now minimizing cost and environmental damage by adopting green IT policies that save energy. The U.S. Small Business Administration also conducts ethics Webinars over the Internet, teaching business owners about environmental ethics.

Environmental engineers conduct hazardous-waste-management studies, in which they evaluate the significance of hazards, advise on their treatment and containment, and develop regulations to prevent mishaps. They design municipal-water-supply and industrial-wastewater treatment systems, conduct research on the environmental impact of proposed construction projects, analyze scien-

The smoke and ash released by the eruption of a volcano in southern Iceland in April, 2010, caused the cancellation of many aircraft flights. (AP/Wide World Photos)

tific data, and perform quality-control checks.

Several environmental engineers and consultants have expanded their businesses to deal with local and worldwide environmental issues. Some companies study and attempt to minimize the effects of acid rain, global warming, automobile emissions, and ozone depletion, which are among the hottest environmental topics in the twenty-first century. They also become involved in the protection and preservation of wildlife. Many twenty-first century environmental engineers also work as consultants, helping their clients comply with regulations, prevent environmental damage, and clean up hazardous sites. Major modern environmental companies include CH2M HILL, Ecology and Environment, and environmental engineering and consulting divisions of large engineering and construction firms, such as Fluor and Bechtel.

Several small environmental engineering and consultation companies have been developed to provide a wide variety of environmental manage-

ment services for local communities and small establishments, such as food services, health care clinics, small bakeries, furniture and finishing factories, hotels, landscaping services, marinas, machine shops, retail stores, and service stations. Some small environmental businesses are independent subsidiaries of larger environmental engineering companies, and they serve as domestic firms with services to consumers. Many also provide a wide variety of assessments and solutions in construction, manufacturing, emergency response, remediation, risks to human health, and hazardous waste operations.

The environmental engineering industry today undergoes more scrutiny for compliance because of the growth in the number of businesses in operation. The tendency is to focus more on products and monetary gains, while relaxing important environmental laws that should be more strictly enforced because of increased manufacturing, excessive use of chemicals, more pollution, and too many disposables dumped as waste. Small environmental engineering businesses operating in the United States, for example, are advised to seek help from the Small Business Ombudsman (SBO) to learn how environmental protection laws work. The SBO is an office of the Environmental Protection Agency (EPA) with the mission of helping small businesses comply and cope with environmental laws.

As environmental businesses grow, they require more plans and skills to handle all their employees. Several companies that had few workers years ago now have to adjust their working conditions and plans to accommodate more qualified college graduates and other skilled workers who seek employment in the environmental field. The external assistance of the EPA and other experts in environmental assessment, consulting, and law is sought by several companies that provide seminars and training for their staffs. These environmental engineering organizations face the daunting task of ensuring all their employees receive adequate in-house training and refresher courses.

Some early environmental engineering companies, for example, those founded in the 1950's or 1960's, that have remained small or midsize and have always occupied the same buildings are renovating or moving into new buildings. These firms have felt the need to equip themselves with modern facilities and tools that conform to contemporary environmental standards. They must do so to demonstrate that, by improving their own situations, they can also supply clients with greater efficiency, better working conditions, more customer attraction, and higher business development commensurate with twenty-first century industrial progress.

Mandated taxation for environmental engineering and consultation industries is strictly adhered to by law, and voluntary incentives for workers have become essential to boost their morale and increase job satisfaction. Declaring a net loss has important tax consequences, because an environmental or other business can only declare a loss in two out of every five years. If a company declares a business loss more frequently than that, the Internal Revenue Service may review the business and reclassify it as a hobby, disqualifying it from writing off expenses of previous and future years.

As the world population increases and businesses grow larger, good stewardship of the environment by real estate and business concerns becomes important. Environmental engineers and consultants can thus expect to receive more business in the years ahead. Environmental professionals will teach clients the best recycling techniques and how to manage water, noise, and air quality.

Unexpected environmental upheavals in the form of wide-scale brush fires, hurricanes, tornadoes, earthquakes, volcanoes, and tsunamis pose greater challenges to the environmental industry. Some of these environmental problems defy all the known solutions. The April, 2010, volcanic ash that spewed into the atmosphere from Iceland virtually paralyzed air travel to and from Europe for a few days and adversely affected the entire world economy. All affected businesses could do was wait for winds to blow the ash out of their region. The explosion on the *Deepwater Horizon* and the resulting oil spill in the Gulf of Mexico during that same year demonstrated the limits of engineering technology to respond to deepwater oil drilling disasters.

Oil mars the beauty of this beach along the Gulf of Mexico after the April, 2010, explosion on an offshore drilling rig. (AP/Wide World Photos)

These types of events challenge experts to design and engineer appropriate twenty-first century solutions for large-scale environmental catastrophes.

INDUSTRY MARKET SEGMENTS

The environmental engineering and consultation industry comprises small companies that usually deal with environmental issues in smaller communities and on local levels, as well as larger companies that operate regionally, nationally, and internationally for a broad spectrum of clients. Most environmental firms are unlikely to remain permanently at only one end of the spectrum, since they often combine aspects of multidomestic operations with other aspects of global operations, depending on opportunities and national and global environmental needs.

Small Businesses

The Annual Council of Engineering Companies defined a small engineering firm in April, 2010, as one with one to thirty employees. Smaller firms tend to lack management information systems

Oil spill workers lay oil retention booms in Bay St. Louis, Mississippi, in May, 2010. (AP/Wide World Photos)

and thus have lower levels of resource availability for information-gathering. Some small businesses receive their environmental information from government organizations, literature, and in-house expertise. Small-business owners and marketers are always in search of high-impact, cost-effective methods of increasing revenue and gaining new customers. For strategic growth, some are marketing their services through mobile phones to grow business and reduce the high cost of advertising.

Potential Annual Earnings Scale. According to the U.S. Bureau of Labor Statistics (BLS), the average annual salary of an environmental engineer employed in the management, scientific, and technical consulting services industry was $81,690 in 2009. The top 10 percent of environmental engineers earned more than $115,750 in that year, while the bottom 10 percent earned less than $47,660. For environmental engineering technicians, the industry average annual salary was $41,550. The top 10 percent of earners earned more than $70,840, and the bottom 10 percent earned less than $27,160.

Clientele Interaction. Environmental engineering and consultation businesses emphasize personal relationships and client satisfaction. They must demonstrate professionalism during all phases of clientele interaction. Small companies assist private, public, and corporate clients to provide solutions to their development needs in local communities. Small environmental engineering and consultation companies vary in the level of services they can provide, depending on the size, scope, facilities, and objectives of each business. Some environmental management consultants are small businesses that serve only a piece of the industry in a given state or undertake specific, limited contracts in specified locations for clients.

Amenities, Atmosphere, and Physical Grounds. Small environmental engineering businesses provide the usual amenities and corresponding working conditions to ensure the quality of staff activities and interaction with customers. They are typically housed in small or midsize buildings that have adequate parking lots and equipped offices. They often include small research and testing laboratories. In addition to the necessary office furniture and storage facilities, technological amenities such as high-speed Internet access and fax, photocopying, printing, and scanning services are usually provided.

Typical Number of Employees. Small environmental consultancies may employ anywhere from one to thirty people.

Traditional Geographic Locations. Small environmental engineering companies are located in urban business or commercial districts. The majority do not have branches in other states, although some may have one or two separate offices at different locations in a city or in a nearby town, performing different functions for the same company. A few are located in isolated neighborhoods, either to take advantage of newly built facilities or to isolate operations involving hazardous materials.

Pros of Working for a Small Environmental Services Firm. Small environmental engineering and consultation businesses have relatively few workers, enhancing closer interactions and cooperative efforts. Opportunities for training, promotions, pay increases, and bonuses are more available to their small staffs than they might be to larger ones. Managers of small businesses frequently organize on-site training sessions involving air quality and health issues in the workplace, as well as certification programs through which staff can obtain credentials in indoor air quality and environmental business services. Online training solutions can also be obtained where on-site training is not possible.

Cons of Working for a Small Environmental Services Firm. Many small environmental business owners cannot afford to hire additional staff for considerable periods, especially when the economy is weak. In such instances, the existing staff may be stretched thin and experience stress. Workers must study more and be trained in additional skills in order to perform tasks in which a firm lacks the resources to hire specialists. Budget cuts and low profits could also adversely affect worker income.

Costs

Payroll and Benefits: Small consultancies often pay salaries on a per-project basis, though they often bill clients based on workers' billable hours. Owners and partners draw income from the businesses' profits. If there are no profits, they will not be paid. Benefits may be offered at the discretion of the employer.

Supplies: Small environmental engineering companies require a wide range of supplies, including office supplies, tools and hardware for installation and maintenance, varieties of chemicals, IT equipment (telephones, fax machines, and computers), and field supplies such as vehicles, cranes, excavators, spraying machines, surveying apparatus, sampling equipment (for soil, water, and air), testing kits, protective gear, and a host of other equipment and necessities for wide varieties of environmental services.

External Services: Small consultancies may contract other environmental consultants to provide expertise in a subfield their own employees lack. They may also contract Web design, advertising, public relations, accounting and tax preparation, and maintenance services. They may rent some equipment rather than purchasing it, and most businesses require insurance, including liability insurance.

Utilities: Common utilities for small environmental engineering and consultation properties include telephone, electricity, water, sewage, Internet access, cable television, and gas or oil.

Taxes: Small environmental engineering and consultation services must pay payroll taxes, as well as local, state, and federal corporate and property taxes. Partners and owners may report business income on their personal returns, in which case they must also pay self-employment taxes.

Midsize Businesses

The Annual Council of Engineering Companies in April, 2010, defined a midsize engineering firm as one with 31 to 250 employees. (This designation is further broken down into medium firms, with 31 to 100 employees, and medium-large firms, with 101 to 250 employees.)

Several midsize environmental consulting firms have experience in specific areas. Midsize companies such as Amory Engineers offer experience and expertise in a full range of engineering services, including system evaluation, master planning, facilities design, construction administration, and resident inspection. Their services also include land-use review and inspection services for municipal planning boards, zoning boards, and conservation commissions.

Potential Annual Earnings Scale. According to the BLS, the average annual salary of an environmental engineer employed in the management, scientific, and technical consulting services industry was $81,690 in 2009. The top 10 percent of environmental engineers earned more than $115,750 in that year, while the bottom 10 percent earned less than $47,660. For environmental engineering technicians, the industry average annual salary was $41,550. The top 10 percent of earners earned more than $70,840, and the bottom 10 percent earned less than $27,160.

Clientele Interaction. Midsize environmental engineering and consultation firms take on many or all aspects of projects, including delivering research, products, and services to clients in several states. They even undertake some overseas contracts. The commitment of the ideal midsize environmental engineering business is facilitated by emphasizing personal relationships along with quality and satisfaction of clients, and professionalism during all phases of clientele interactions. Each company must work closely with individual as well as corporate clients, locally, nationally, and internationally, across the environmental spectrum, including buildings, energy, air, water, land, and transportation sectors.

Amenities, Atmosphere, and Physical Grounds. The building facilities of midsize environmental engineering and consultation firms are larger than those of smaller businesses and are usually surrounded by more spacious physical grounds, and more parking spaces. Some businesses house their offices in multistory buildings located in busy urban areas or in isolated industrial facilities—especially if they have elaborate research and testing laboratories.

Midsize businesses require more facilities and amenities than small firms, corresponding with the greater volume of clients they serve and services they offer. Similar to large businesses, most midsize environmental engineering companies have a main headquarters in or near a big city for easier access and increased public patronage, as well as branches housed in smaller buildings in the same or different states, depending on the number of employees, types of projects, and nature of consultation services. A number of firms are also international in their operations, sometimes having building facilities overseas. Many midsize businesses have grown and evolved into more technological environmental companies with improved amenities and advanced techniques for engineering and consultation services.

Typical Number of Employees. Midsize environmental consultancies employ from 31 to 250 people. They tend to have more full-time specialized employees than do small environmental companies.

Traditional Geographic Locations. Since midsize environmental facilities serve larger communities, they are sited in urban areas, in or within the vicinity of large towns or big cities, where customers and environmental contracts are easier to obtain. As environmental companies expand their scientific and social services and engage in more research, testing, and construction, they become situated in isolated areas on the outskirts of cities or demarcated industrial locations in order to reduce or prevent harm to neighbors and passersby.

Pros of Working for a Midsize Environmental Services Firm. Midsize environmental firms' employees have greater chances of receiving more contracts, more customers, greater marketing opportunities, and consequently higher salaries than their counterparts at small environmental businesses. They enjoy greater job stability, since their employers have higher budgets and available facilities, plus higher volumes of clients. They also have better chances of gaining higher levels of environmental engineering experience and sharpened consultation capabilities in the process of exposure to more assignments and training sessions.

Many midsize companies have grown from small companies and desire continued growth. As a result, midsize companies invest significant funds in infrastructure that as small companies they could not afford and as large companies they will require to compete. The expansion process teaches employees to control costs, which becomes a strong factor that drives their engineering and consultation initiatives. Better plans are then made to undertake environmentally friendly projects that go along with decreased resource consumption and less cost.

Cons of Working for a Midsize Environmental Services Firm. Midsize environmental businesses strive to maintain growth and industry position, fearing that they could shrink as easily as they grew. Maintaining momentum can be a challenge for both partners and employees. The need to compete in an uncertain niche against both small and large firms can be difficult, requiring midsize firms frequently to redefine their roles and services in ways that small and large firms do not. Employees seeking to reach the height of their profession may not be satisfied at midsize firms.

Costs

Payroll and Benefits: Managers, administrators, and senior personnel at midsize firms receive annual salaries, while lower ranks such as janitors and grounds crews receive hourly wages.

Supplies: Midsize environmental engineering and consultancy companies need varieties of operational equipment and supplies for testing, research, installations, removals, construction, cleanup, and other services. Computers, engineering software, telephones, electrical generators, printers, fax machines, scanners, hardware for repairs and maintenance, engineering appliances, grounds and field supplies (such as excavators, wheelbarrows, loppers, chain saws, lawn mowers, and trimmers), chemicals, and office supplies are among the several essential supplies for functional activities. Appropriate vehicles (sometimes including helicopters) are needed to transport workers, equipment, and other supplies to the field and project locations.

External Services: The services of data analyzers, other laboratories, and environmental or scientific companies are often used to support operations, assessments, projects, and research at midsize firms. Other external services could include equipment, instrumentation, or machinery rental, installation, or maintenance. Landscaping contractors are hired to create and maintain appropriate and attractive grounds plus desirable horticulture. Companies may also contract staff seminar and training instructors, as well as tax experts, accountants, and auditors.

Utilities: Typical utilities for a midsize environmental company include electricity, water, sewage, gas or oil, telephone, cable, and Internet access. Several midsize environmental companies have their own gas or oil stations on the compound to meet demands of high gas and oil consumption.

Taxes: Midsize environmental engineering and consultation services must pay payroll taxes, as well as local, state, and federal corporate and property taxes.

Large Businesses

The majority of large environmental engineering and consultation businesses are located in multiple states and are national or international in their operations. The Annual Council of Engineering Companies in April, 2010, categorized large companies as those with more than 250 employees. The council recognizes a "very large" category of companies with more than 500 employees.

Potential Annual Earnings Scale. Large environmental businesses have annual earnings that run into the billions of dollars. Financial profits are dependent upon geographical location of the company and the extent of its operations, plus the variety of services offered nationally and even internationally. Earth Tech, for example, a leading environmental service provider with headquarters in Long Beach, California, is estimated to earn about $18 billion in U.S. revenues.

According to the BLS, the average annual salary of an environmental engineer employed in the management, scientific, and technical consulting services industry was $81,690 in 2009. The top 10 percent of environmental engineers earned more than $115,750 in that year, while the bottom 10 percent earned less than $47,660. For environmental engineering technicians, the industry average annual salary was $41,550. The top 10 percent of earners earned more than $70,840, and the bottom 10 percent earned less than $27,160.

Clientele Interaction. Large environmental engineering and consultation firms take on the entire scope of research, implementation, production, and services for clients in many states and even internationally, sometimes serving the U.S. federal government. They offer a wider variety of services than smaller firms, enabling clients to minimize or avoid time-consuming searches for the right services and consequently to give the company more patronage as a "one-stop shop." Commitment to excellence in all aspects of business and professional rapport with clients leads to repeat engagements, strong referrals from clients, and a successful track record of solving problems.

Amenities, Atmosphere, and Physical Grounds. Many large environmental engineering and consultation firms have a main headquarters for command and control, as well as branches at multiple locations, usually in more than one state or even overseas, for research, training, inspections, operations, and consultation services. Their buildings frequently resemble typical industrial facilities and are strategically located in urban or suburban areas. They are sometimes isolated from commercial areas or surrounded by other businesses, but many are situated on picturesque grounds on the outskirts of cities, with adequate free parking and smoke-free offices. The buildings have accessible, friendly working environments with attractive surroundings, waiting areas, offices, conference rooms, research and design laboratories, and sometimes cafeterias and recreational facilities.

These companies exhibit versatility by offering a wide variety of amenities that are often dependent on the varieties of engineering focus and consultation goals, as well as particular customers they seek to attract. Most workers work in offices, laboratories, or in the field. The place and hours of work vary greatly, depending on the requirements of each project. Workers in product development may spend much time building prototypes in workshops or laboratories, while research design typically takes place in offices.

Typical Number of Employees. Large environmental engineering and consulting corporations employ at least 251 people. Some employ many more than that. Houston-based Waste Management, an example of a very large environmental company, has thirteen hundred employees in its Los Angeles branch alone.

Traditional Geographic Locations. Large environmental facilities are sited in urban areas, in or near large cities that serve large populations. Many of their large buildings are closer to major roads and highways for easy access and are often situated in industrial areas, where they are accessible to manufacturers and other industrial businesses that require their services. Some firms have large headquarters facilities, as well as many smaller branch facilities across many states and overseas. Others have only a few branches in a few states but are equipped with enough staff to render services nationwide and internationally.

Pros of Working for a Large Environmental Services Firm. Large environmental engineering firms have the advantage of providing a wide range of environmental expertise and can thus offer jobs more quickly to applicants. Most large environmental companies are stable and in good financial

standing to offer more full-time and assured, lasting employment at high pay and good benefits.

Workers at large businesses have the opportunity to specialize, but they also have access to a wide range of tools, training, and environmental management services, which sharpen their skills and open career doors. Firms tend to increase their service offerings with higher pay scales, since they can afford to hire a wide variety of highly skilled and unskilled workers. Firms are large enough to provide a wide range of services using their enormous staffs and pool of expertise, tools, and technology. Moreover, their staffs are generally free to give projects the close attention they deserve.

Cons of Working for a Large Environmental Services Firm. Large firms are complicated bureaucracies. It can be difficult to feel noticed working at such a firm. At the same time, it can be easy to feel all too noticed when a superior requires help, or when several require help on conflicting projects simultaneously. The constantly changing methods and improving, innovative technologies that drive the environmental engineering industry can become overwhelming when one has to deal with them on a very large scale. Technology, science, and business advancements make the responsibility to help maintain clean air, water, and soils enormous for the staffs of large firms.

There is generally little risk of injury or illness due to strict precautionary measures for workers, but certain fields require working with potentially dangerous materials. Large contracts cannot escape the media, environmental groups, occasional lawsuits, and the limelight, which can be intimidating. Observing and enforcing regulations for all the tiny details of environmental operations on a large scale could be wearisome. Satisfying every client among hundreds could also be a daunting task. Promotion can be slow, since many qualified and diligent employees may compete for the same position.

Costs

Payroll and Benefits: Compensation and benefits managers of large environmental organizations plan, direct, and coordinate compensation and benefits. Large companies determine compensation levels based on job analysis and position descriptions. They often have complex salary structures to match their varied positions and required services. Managers, administrators, and senior personnel receive annual salaries, while lower ranks such as janitors and grounds crews receive hourly wages. Benefits are common at large firms, including retirement plans, health insurance, vacation time, sick time, and life insurance.

Supplies: Large environmental engineering and consultancy companies require operational equipment and accessories, laboratory equipment and supplies for indoor and outdoor research, numerous varieties of heavy and light equipment, computers, engineering software, monitoring and testing machines, instruments, and other materials. Appropriate strong vehicles are needed to carry people to near and remote locations and for transporting equipment to the field. Even helicopters in some instances are used to airlift staff, equipment, and supplies to remote locations or in emergency situations.

External Services: The services of data analyzers, other laboratories, and environmental or scientific companies are often used to support operations, assessments, projects, and research at large firms. Other external services could include equipment, instrumentation, or machinery rental, installation, or maintenance. Landscaping contractors are hired to create and maintain appropriate and attractive grounds plus desirable horticulture. Companies may also contract staff seminar and training instructors, as well as tax experts, accountants, and auditors.

Utilities: Typical utilities for a large environmental company include electricity, water, sewage, gas or oil, telephone, cable, and Internet access. Several large environmental companies have their own gas or oil stations on the compound to meet demands of high gas and oil consumption.

Taxes: Large environmental engineering and consultation services must pay payroll taxes, as well as local, state, federal, and international corporate and property taxes.

ORGANIZATIONAL STRUCTURE AND JOB ROLES

Environmental engineering and consultant services companies may be very small or very large, but they have the same core functions. At small firms,

all functions may be handled by an owner and partners plus a small support staff. Large firms may be highly compartmentalized and specialized, assigning a single task to each worker. All companies must develop the insight to recognize service opportunities driven by environmental needs and compliance with existing or anticipated environmental laws and regulations.

The following umbrella categories apply to the organizational structure of businesses in the environmental engineering and consultant services industry:

- Executive Management
- Customer Service
- Sales and Marketing
- Administrative and Office Support
- Technology, Research, Design, and Development
- Production and Operations
- Maintenance, Facilities, and Security
- Inspection
- Human Resources

Executive Management

Executive management personnel are responsible for planning, directing, and coordinating activities, research, and development in their organizations. They manage the overall functions of the organization, address systemic issues, and supervise the smooth and effective functioning of all departments. They handle the general operations of the company and ensure that all plans and regulations are duly carried out. They oversee the duties of various department heads. As an organization, the crucial step of combining approaches to sustainability and corporate social responsibility (CSR) into a unified strategy is essential for good executive management.

Executive managers generally earn the highest salaries in the establishment. The mean annual salary for an engineering manager at a technical services and consulting firm in 2009 was $125,260, according to the BLS. Chief executives earned an average of $196,100.

Executive management occupations may include the following:

- Owner/Partner
- Executive Director

- Administration/Office Manager
- Environmental and Permitting Manager
- Managing Environmental Consultant
- Program Manager
- Engineering Manager
- General or Operations Manager
- Project Manager
- Compensation and Benefits Manager
- Information Project Manager for Environmental Compliance
- Human Resources Manager
- Public Relations Manager
- Training Manager

Customer Service

Customer service personnel (or public relations personnel) plan and direct customer service and public relations programs designed to attract desirable customers and to create and maintain good customer relations and a favorable public image for employers or clients. They can also be engaged in fundraising aimed at planning and directing activities to solicit and maintain funds for special projects and charitable contributions. They work in partnership with clients to find creative, cost-effective solutions to environmental problems, leading to successful planning and solutions with minimal risk to budget and programs. They work with both public and private sector clients to assess the environmental impacts of strategic plans and programs. Being able to work with clients through the whole life cycle of an environmental project is key to effective production and operations.

The mean annual salary of a customer service representative in the industry was $33,890 in 2009.

Customer service occupations may include the following:

- Customer Service Manager
- Customer Service Representative
- Customer Service Director
- Public Relations Manager
- Director of Environmental Operations

Sales and Marketing

Sales managers direct the distribution or movement of products and services to customers. Sometimes, the sales and marketing unit includes financial managers who plan and coordinate accounting, banking, securities, investing, insurance, and other financial activities. Sales and marketing personnel coordinate sales distribution by establishing sales territories, quotas, and goals and establish training programs for sales representatives. They analyze sales statistics gathered by staff, to determine sales potential and inventory requirements, and monitor the preferences of customers.

Sales and marketing personnel employ their skills to deliver the best environmental practices and expert advice to their clients through sustainable design, solicitation, publicity, Web sites, special events, and community outreach. They usually have at least undergraduate degrees in business management, marketing, or related disciplines. The average salary of a sales manager in the industry was $124,690 in 2009. Financial managers earned an average of $131,220.

Sales and marketing occupations may include the following:

- Corporate Sales Manager
- Sales Director
- Senior Sales Manager
- Environmental Sales Manager
- Director of Environmental Operations
- Financial Controller

Administrative and Office Support

Office and administrative support supervisors and managers oversee the detailed activities of the support staff of an environmental engineering company in order to ensure on-time completion of scheduled work that meets the established quality standards of the organization. These managers plan and allocate work assignments to support staff working under them. They also issue deadlines to the support staff and promote their efficient performance with good supervision.

Secretaries and administrative assistants, who are vital components of the support staff, perform a variety of administrative and clerical duties necessary to run environmental organizations efficiently. They manage projects, plan and schedule meetings and appointments, and serve as information and communication managers for an office. They also handle travel and guest arrangements, conduct research pertaining to the environmental engineering industry, organize and maintain paper and electronic files, and disseminate information by using telephones, Web sites, e-mail, and mail services.

Although the core responsibilities for secretaries and administrative assistants have remained relatively unchanged, technological advances have introduced office automation and consequent organizational restructuring that have caused secretaries and administrative assistants to assume more of the responsibilities that were once reserved for managerial and professional staff. Secretaries and administrative assistants who work as support staff under office and administrative managers perform and coordinate the activities of office administrators. They also store data, retrieve data from various sources, manage databases, create spreadsheets, create presentations and reports, provide training and orientation for new staff, and integrate information for dissemination to staff and clients. They sometimes purchase supplies, negotiate with vendors, examine and maintain leased equipment, and manage areas of the business such as stockrooms.

Office or administrative support staff also include receptionists who are often the first business contacts encountered by visitors to consultancies. They sit in waiting areas or at front office desks to receive visitors and clients, answer telephone calls, answer visitors' inquiries about a company and its products or services, direct visitors to their destinations, sort and hand out mail, make appointments, file, keep records, enter data, and perform a variety of other office tasks such as faxing or e-mailing. Secretaries and administrative assistants use a variety of office equipment, such as computers, photocopiers, fax machines, scanners, telephone systems, and videoconferencing equipment.

Many environmental companies require office and administrative support supervisors and managers to have postsecondary training and, in some cases, associate's or even bachelor's degrees. A degree related to the environmental engineering industry may provide the jobseeker with an advantage in the application process. High school graduates who have basic office skills may qualify for entry-level secretarial positions through vocational education programs that teach office skills and typing or through one-year or two-year programs in office administration offered by business and vocational-technical schools, as well as community colleges. Many temporary-placement agencies also provide formal training in computer and office skills. Assistant training programs are available at many community colleges in bookkeeping, project management, transcription, Web design, and computer technology, alongside online training and coaching programs.

Word processing, writing, and communication skills are essential for all secretaries and administrative assistants. Many environmental employers increasingly require extensive working knowledge of computer software applications, such as desktop publishing, spreadsheets, project management, and database management. Employers also look for good interpersonal and customer service skills, since secretaries and administrative assistants need to be tactful in their dealings with people. Discretion, good judgment, initiative, organizational or management ability, and the ability to work independently are especially important for higher-level administrative support positions.

Secretaries and administrative assistants generally advance by being promoted to other administrative positions with more responsibilities in the environmental engineering organization. Qualified administrative assistants who broaden their knowledge of the environmental engineering operations, and enhance their engineering or consultation skills may be promoted to senior or executive secretary or administrative assistant, clerical supervisor, or office manager.

The mean annual salary of secretaries at environmental firms was $32,080 in 2009. Executive secretaries and administrative assistants earned an average of $47,110, while receptionists and information clerks earned an average of $29,590. Supervisors earned an average of $58,030.

Administrative and office support occupations may include the following:

- Administrative Support Manager
- Office and Administrative Support Supervisor
- Education Administrator
- General Office Clerk
- Secretary
- Executive Secretary
- Computer Operator
- Data Entry Clerk
- Information Clerk
- Bookkeeping, Accounting, and Auditing Clerk
- Administrative Assistant
- Receptionist

Technology, Research, Design, and Development

The technology, research, design, and development managers of an environmental engineering and consultancy company research current environmental problems and devise workable solutions involving current and innovative technology. They plan, direct, or coordinate the training and development activities of the staff and the organization in a manner that will give the business a competitive edge.

Workers in research and design typically work in offices, examine a client's needs, and specifically design practical and innovative solutions that protect environmental quality, enhance environmental awareness and responsibility, and make a valued contribution to business performance. Highly qualified environmental experts who are well versed in the development of imaginative and intelligent design are employed to strive for and achieve innovative, sustainable, and economical solutions while working at the cutting edge of technology.

Science and engineering technicians may enter the industry without a bachelor's degree, but some bachelor's degree holders begin as technicians before advancing to become researchers or pursuing additional education. Ph.D. graduates with postdoctoral experience are increasingly preferred by employers.

Wage and salary employment in environmental engineering research and development services in the United States is projected to increase by 25 percent between 2008 and 2018, according to Plunkett Research. Environmental scientists in the industry earned an average of $73,470 in 2009, while environmental science technicians earned an average of $42,980.

Technology, research, design, and development occupations may include the following:

- Head of Research and Development
- Senior Software Engineer

OCCUPATION PROFILE

Environmental Engineer

Considerations	*Qualifications*
Description	Uses engineering techniques to prevent, control, and remediate environmental problems.
Career clusters	Agriculture, Food, and Natural Resources; Manufacturing; Science, Technology, Engineering, and Math
Interests	Data; things
Working conditions	Work both inside and outside
Minimum education level	Bachelor's degree; master's degree; doctoral degree
Physical exertion	Light work
Physical abilities	Unexceptional/basic fitness
Opportunities for experience	Internship
Licensure and certification	Required
Employment outlook	Faster-than-average growth expected
Holland interest score	IRC

Note: See volume 1, "Publisher's Note," for an explanation of the Holland interest score.

OCCUPATION PROFILE

Energy Conservation and Use Technician

Considerations	Qualifications
Description	Provides technical assistance in efforts to conserve energy, usually by conducting tests and compiling data.
Career clusters	Agriculture, Food, and Natural Resources; Architecture and Construction; Manufacturing
Interests	Data; things
Working conditions	Work inside; work both inside and outside
Minimum education level	Junior/technical/community college
Physical exertion	Light work
Physical abilities	Unexceptional/basic fitness
Opportunities for experience	Apprenticeship; military service
Licensure and certification	Recommended
Employment outlook	Faster-than-average growth expected
Holland interest score	RIE

Note: See volume 1, "Publisher's Note," for an explanation of the Holland interest score.

- Senior Technical Project Manager
- Senior Director
- Training Engineer
- Technology Sourcing Specialist
- Firmware Developing Engineer
- Information Technology Project Manager
- Development Software Engineer
- Environmental Engineer
- Environmental Engineering Technician
- Environmental Scientist
- Environmental Science Technician
- Environmental Consultant
- Information Technology Technician
- Mechanical Engineer
- Geographic Information System (GIS) Analyst
- Engineering Intern
- Postdoctoral Researcher
- Web Developer
- Webmaster
- Research Assistant

Production and Operations

Environmental industrial production managers plan, direct, or coordinate the work activities and resources necessary to manufacture products of their companies in accordance with cost, quality, and quantity specifications. The operations management in an environmental organization is engaged in managing the processes that convert inputs of materials, labor, and energy into outputs of goods and services.

General and operations managers plan and coordinate the operations of their organizations. Duties include formulating policies, managing daily operations, and planning the use of materials and human resources. They ensure that business operations are efficient in terms of using as few resources as needed and effectively meeting customer requirements. Production and operations workers integrate diverse technologies, expertise, and deployment capabilities to create practical, superior products and services for clients. Opera-

OCCUPATION SPECIALTIES

Energy Conservation and Use Technicians

Specialty	Responsibilities
Calibration laboratory technicians	Test, calibrate, and repair electrical, mechanical, electromechanical, and electronic measuring, recording, and indicating instruments and equipment to conform to set standards.
Electromechanical technicians	Build, test, analyze, and adjust precision electromechanical instruments.
Electronics mechanics	Test faulty equipment, diagnose problems, and maintain records of repairs, calibrations, and tests.
Test technicians	Conduct tests and record results using engineering principles and test technology.

tions directors steer their companies to undertake productive, exciting, and challenging projects.

General and operations managers earned an average of $145,470 in 2009. Industrial production managers earned an average of $103,690.

Production and operations occupations may include the following:

- Industrial Production Manager
- Project Manager
- Training Manager
- General or Operations Manager
- Construction Operations Manager

Maintenance, Facilities, and Security

Maintenance and building engineering staff are charged with repairing malfunctioning building systems such as air-conditioning, plumbing, electrical hardware, and similar devices. They may also play an important role in renovation planning and implementation. Building maintenance personnel are alternately called engineers, environmental services personnel, and facilities managers. Most personnel in this department have vocational education and training, if not advanced degrees in engineering or related fields.

Security personnel oversee both physical security and the security of a firm's intellectual property. Building inspectors ensure that facilities are physically safe. Security officers are employed to ensure the security of employees and equipment, watch out for intruders or incidence of fires and other malfunctions and system failures, monitor surveillance cameras, conduct periodic inspections, and respond appropriately to emergency situations and important calls for assistance.

Security personnel receive training in environmental and public safety through vocational schools, undergraduate education, or other security certification programs. Some companies require them to obtain certification in cardiopulmonary resuscitation (CPR) and other first-aid techniques. The average salary for a security guard in the industry was $31,740 in 2009.

Maintenance, facilities, and security occupations may include the following:

- Chief Maintenance Engineer
- Heating, Ventilation, and Air-Conditioning (HVAC) Specialist
- Plumber
- Electrician
- Security Officer
- Investigator
- Building Inspector
- Network Security Specialist

Inspection

Environmental engineering inspection can be broadly classified into home, commercial, or environmental inspections, depending on the facility or place being inspected. In all cases, environmental inspection experts take a critical look to ensure that a customer is fully aware of any health and safety dangers and knows how to find solutions to existing problems and ensure compliance with environmental regulations. They are often called in by persons about to purchase, rent, or use buildings, land, or other relevant facilities.

The World Health Organization suggested in 2009 that up to 30 percent of new and remodeled buildings worldwide may be subject to excessive complaints related to indoor air quality (IAQ). When a consumer is buying any property, an environmental site assessment (ESA) expert will determine the potential for prior or current contamination of the site and determine whether soil sampling or other sampling is required to fully assess any potential contamination. A written analysis of the findings of interviews and recorded searches and field inspections will be provided in a way that allows informed decisions to be made by developers, lenders, and other interested parties.

Examples of typical building health hazards that require prompt inspection for detection and removal are asbestos (for homes built before 1980), low-quality water, lead (for homes built before 1978), radon (a radioactive gas that comes from the natural decay of uranium in the soil, and is present in all homes to some extent), and molds (especially for mold-prone and hidden or inaccessible environments). Construction and building inspectors earned an average of $61,260 in 2009.

Inspection occupations may include the following:

- Junior Inspector
- Materials Professional
- Engineering Technician
- Environmental Project Manager
- Environmental Engineering Inspector
- Environmental Science Technician
- Groundwater Technician
- Environmental Consultant
- Health and Safety Professional
- Remediation Cleanup Personnel
- Biologist
- Radiographer
- Construction Materials Technician (CMT)
- Soil Technician/Tester
- Environmental Health and Safety Consultant
- Water Quality Analyst
- Environmental Scientist
- Air Quality Engineer/Scientist
- Marine Naturalist
- Environmental Geologist
- Attorney
- Natural Resources Engineer
- Wastewater Engineer
- Laboratory Technician

Human Resources

The human resources department focuses on hiring environmental engineers who can design, plan, or perform engineering duties in the prevention, control, and remediation of environmental health hazards utilizing various engineering disciplines. They also hire environmental specialists for other projects such as waste treatment, site remediation, or pollution control technology. Human resources directors and managers are well trained in the field of human resources organization and management, through college-level education, special training, and work experience.

To cut costs and save time, some small businesses outsource human resources functions including payroll, taxes, unemployment, insurance, benefits, health and productivity, and accounting. Industry human resources managers earned an average of $102,900 in 2009.

Human resources occupations may include the following:

- Human Resources Director
- Human Resources Manager
- Compensation and Benefits Manager
- Human Resources Coordinator
- Administrative Assistant

INDUSTRY OUTLOOK

Overview

A 2009 IBS industry report stated that, as environmental legislation tightens, most businesses (and even households) are increasing their efforts to become green, backed by incentives and government funding. The greater public interest in the environment promotes significant growth opportunities for environmental businesses. According to PayScale, the most popular U.S. cities for environmental engineering jobs in 2009 were: Houston, New York, Atlanta, Dallas, Denver, Chicago, and Philadelphia. The largest U.S. employers of environmental engineers are URS Corporation, CH2M HILL, Camp Dresser and McKee, and Arcadia. Some 10 percent of employees had less than one year of work experience; 42 percent had one to four years of experience; 21 percent had five to nine years of experience; 17 percent had ten to nineteen years of experience; and 10 percent had twenty or more years of work experience. This report implies that the retention rate for employed environmental engineers has increased in the last ten years.

The remediation market was flat in 2009, as federal projects and backlog held off the effects of the recession for a number of remediation contractors. Projects and practices are turning green, with growing consciousness regarding energy costs and sustainability in the market. In a world that is increasingly being modernized by technology and innovation, many systems and activities are becoming automated, drastically affecting environmental and other industries by reducing human labor.

Jobs with the federal and state governments, and with organizations dependent on federal funds for support, will experience little growth over the next decade, unless budgets increase significantly. The federal government is expected increasingly to outsource environmental services to private consulting firms. This lack of funding will affect mostly scientists performing basic research.

The continual creation of congested urban communities and artificial environments, the accompanying myriad disposables, and the solid, chemical, and gas pollution will expand the scope and operations of the environmental industry. Environmental scientists who speak foreign languages and who are willing to work abroad enjoy the best opportunities for foreign employment. Environmental engineering jobs are projected by the BLS to grow by 31 percent between 2008 and 2018, much faster than the average of 11 percent growth across all occupations. More environmental engineers will be needed to help companies comply with environmental regulations and to develop methods of cleaning up environmental hazards. Energy and climate change have emerged as global risks and have significant future implications for business. Successful companies will minimize these risks through proactive strategies and innovative solutions of environmental consulting.

Employment Advantages

Environmental management and environmental consulting are broad fields that offer many advantages to employees seeking to diversify their skills. Additional sharpening of skills for employees is obtained through diligent, innovative, and special solutions to challenging environmental tasks, as well as on-site training or seminars in environmental issues in the workplace that could also enhance one's domestic environmental preparedness.

The diversity of the environmental industry in terms of the broad range of career paths offered continues to be a great benefit to those seeking professional advancement. The need to replace workers who retire will result in many job openings over the next decade.

The increasing need for companies to comply with environmental laws and regulations is expected to contribute to the demand for environmental engineers and scientists. Issues of asbestos and other building and construction-related hazards, water conservation, groundwater contamination and flood control, deteriorating coastal environments, and rising sea levels will also promote hiring and stimulate employment growth of environmental engineers and consultants.

As populations increase, development progresses, and people move to more environmentally sensitive locations, environmental engineers and consultants will be needed to assess building sites, new highways, factories, and farms for potential hazards and to address issues of pollution control and waste disposal.

Annual Earnings

According to the BLS, the U.S. environmental engineering and consulting industry includes about nine thousand companies, ranging in size from one-person businesses to global corporations. The industry is highly fragmented: The fifty largest firms account for less than 30 percent of industry revenue. Smith Travel Research estimates domestic revenues in the industry at $140.6 billion. Management Solutions International projects that U.S. real expenditures will increase to $398 billion in 2015 and to $442 billion in 2020.

RELATED RESOURCES FOR FURTHER RESEARCH

AIR AND WASTE MANAGEMENT ASSOCIATION
  1 Gateway Center, 3d Floor
  420 Fort Duquesne Blvd.
  Pittsburgh, PA 15222-1435
  Tel: (800) 270-3444
  Fax: (412) 232-3450
  http://www.awma.org

AMERICAN ACADEMY OF ENVIRONMENTAL
ENGINEERS
  30 Holiday Ct., Suite 100
  Annapolis, MD 21401
  Tel: (410) 266-3311
  Fax: (410) 266-7653
  http://www.aaee.net

ENTEC UK
  Northumbria House, Regent Centre
  Gosforth, Newcastle upon Tyne NE3 3PX
  United Kingdom
  Tel: 44-191-272-6100
  Fax: 44-191-272-6592
  http://www.entecuk.com

KEYSTONE ENVIRONMENTAL
  4400 Dominion St., Suite 320
  Burnaby, BC V5G 4G3
  Canada
  Tel: (604) 430-0671
  Fax: (604) 430-0672
  http://www.keystoneenviro.com

WATER ENVIRONMENT FEDERATION
  601 Wythe St.
  Alexandria, VA 22314-1994
  Tel: (800) 666-0206
  Fax: (703) 684-2492
  http://www.wef.org

ABOUT THE AUTHOR

Samuel V. Kisseadoo is a chartered biologist and professor of biology with more than thirty-three years of teaching and research experience in biology, ecology, plant sciences, and environmental science, in Africa, Europe, and the United States. He received a bachelor's degree from Kwame Nkrumah University of Science and Technology, Kumasi, Ghana, in 1977 and a master's degree from the same institution in 1982. In 1984, he received a second master's degree from the International Institute for Hydraulic and Environmental Engineering, Delft, the Netherlands, and in 1985, he received a third from the University of Aberdeen, Scotland. The City University of New York awarded him a master of philosophy degree in 1992 and a Ph.D. in 1993. Kisseadoo is one of the directors of the Hampton Land Conservancy (the first conservation organization for the city of Hampton, Virginia). He has written ten articles for Salem Press publications since 2004. His memberships include the Chesapeake Bay Foundation, the Society of Biology (United Kingdom), the Smithsonian Institution, the Ecological Society of America, the National Geographic Society, the New York Botanical Garden, the Botanical Society of America, and the Virginia Natural History Society.

FURTHER READING

Ausubel, J. H., and H. E. Sladovich. *Technology and Environment*. Washington, D.C.: National Academy of Engineering, 1989.
Committee on Industrial Competitiveness and Environmental Protection. *Fostering Industry-Initiated Environmental Protection Efforts*. Washington, D.C.: National Academies Press, 1997.
Davis, M., and S. Masten. *Principles of Environmental Engineering and Science*. 2d ed. New York: McGraw-Hill, 2008.
Hoover's. "Environmental Consulting." http://www.hoovers.com/environmental-consulting/—ID__385—/free-ind-fr-profile-basic.xhtml.
IBS Year-End Report, December, 2009. http://www.cisionwire.com/ibs/ibs-year-end-report-january—december-2009.

Jackson, S. A., et al. *Envisioning a Twenty-first Century Science and Engineering Workforce for the United States: Tasks for University, Industry, and Government.* Washington, D.C.: National Academies Press, 2003.

Masters, G. M., and W. P. Ela. *Introduction to Environmental Engineering and Science.* 3d ed. London: Prentice Hall, 2007.

National Academy of Engineering. *Frontiers of Engineering: Reports on Leading-Edge Engineering from the 2006 Symposium.* Washington, D.C.: National Academies Press, 2007.

PayScale.com. "Salary Survey for Industry: Environmental Consulting (United States)." April, 2010. http://www.payscale.com/ research/US/Industry=Environmental _Consulting/Salary.

Plunkett, Jack W. *Plunkett's Consulting Industry.* Houston, Tex.: Plunkett Research, 2010.

Richards, D. J., ed. *The Industrial Green Game: Implications for Environmental Design and Management.* Washington, D.C.: National Academies Press, 1997.

Richards, D. J., and G. Pearson, eds. *The Ecology of Industry: Sectors and Linkages.* Washington, D.C.: National Academies Press, 1998.

Sam, P. A. *International Environmental Consulting Practice: How and Where to Take Advantage of Global Opportunities.* New York: Wiley, 1998.

Schulze, P. C. *Measures of Environmental Performance and Ecosystem Condition.* Washington, D.C.: National Academies Press, 1999.

Smith, D. W., and D. S. Mavinic, eds. *Journal of Environmental Engineering and Science* 7, no. 6 (November, 2008).

U.S. Bureau of Labor Statistics. *Career Guide to Industries*, 2010-2011 ed. http://www.bls.gov/ oco/cg.

U.S. Census Bureau. North American Industry Classification System (NAICS), 2007. http:// www.census.gov/cgi-bin/sssd/naics/ naicsrch?chart=2007.

_____. The 2009 Statistical Abstract. Geography and Environment. http://www .census.gov/compendia/statab/2009/cats/ geography_environment.html.

U.S. Department of Commerce. International Trade Administration. Office of Trade and Industry Information. Industry Trade Data and Analysis. http://ita.doc.gov/td/industry/ otea/OTII/OTII-index.html.

Farming Industry

©Dreamstime.com

INDUSTRY DEFINITION

Summary

The farming industry plants, grows, harvests, transports, and markets crops to be used for food, animal feed, biofuel, textiles, and other purposes.

Some of the major industrial crops include grain, oilseeds, tobacco, dry beans, potatoes, vegetables, melons, fruits, and nuts. In the United States, the five most significant crops are the five that are heavily subsidized by the federal government: corn, rice, soy, wheat, and cotton. The industry encompasses many additional areas of labor beyond simply working the fields, such as agricultural science, engineering, business, and economics.

History of the Industry

The American farming industry dates back to European agricultural practices that were brought to the New World during colonial times. The southern colonies planted tobacco and cotton and used slave labor to grow them. This slave-based agriculture was central to the southern economy through the founding of the United States and lasted until the American Civil War brought an end to slavery in the 1860's.

The mid-to-late 1800's saw the introduction of more scientific agricultural practices that increased

The Farming Industry's Contribution to the U.S. Economy

Value Added	Amount
Gross domestic product	$132.1 billion
Gross domestic product	0.9%
Persons employed	732,000
Total employee compensation	$24.4 billion

Source: U.S. Bureau of Economic Analysis. Data are for 2008.

productivity and helped drive U.S. economic growth. The advancement of the farming industry was facilitated in 1887 by the establishment of state land-grant universities. These educational institutions taught and studied agriculture and established a federally funded system of agricultural experiment stations and networks in each state. In addition, as the Industrial Revolution progressed, the farming industry was rapidly mechanized during the late nineteenth and early twentieth centuries. Farmers employing such machines as tractors and combine harvesters could complete tasks at a speed and on a scale previously considered impossible. Mechanized agricultural production thus replaced manual labor wherever possible.

In the early 1930's, the farming industry was struggling in the face of economic and environmental hardships. The Dust Bowl ruined many farms, driving farmers off their land, during a time when the Great Depression had already caused a wave of farm foreclosures. In response, the U.S. Congress passed the Agricultural Adjustment Act of 1933, instituting an emergency program to aid farmers by protecting their equity and increasing the prices paid for farm products. Programs were also instituted to teach farm operators techniques to help protect soil resources.

Renewed demand for the industry was generated by World War II, and farm prices improved. By the mid-1940's, U.S. agriculture entered a sustained period of productivity gains. The development of railroad and highway networks and the increasing use of container shipping also were essential to the growth of mechanized agriculture.

They expanded the size of the market any given farm could reach by making long-distance shipping of produce affordable. This in turn made it possible for farmers to increase their profits by producing more food than their local regions could purchase, providing a motive to increase productivity beyond the scope of local demand.

Even with long-distance shipping, however, in the later twentieth century, agricultural productivity exceeded demand nationally, creating a surplus of agricultural commodities. The government sought to reduce this surplus, instituting policies designed simultaneously to increase demand and reduce supply. Surplus food, for example, was purchased by the government for use in school lunch programs to feed impoverished children.

In the late twentieth and early twenty-first century, agriculture has become an increasingly global industry. Exports continue to account for 20 to 30 percent of U.S. farm income, but American farm operators face new challenges, including the emergence of new foreign competitors, trade tensions over new technologies, and food safety issues.

Increased use of machines and the introduction of government price supports during the past century allowed farm operators to increase the size of their farms and gain efficiencies. Such advances in productivity through mechanization, plant developments, and new chemical fertilizers and pesticides led to fewer, larger, more specialized farms and a massive migration out of the farming industry.

Inputs Consumed by the Farming Industry

Input	Value
Energy	$30.6 billion
Materials	$134.8 billion
Purchased services	$37.8 billion
Total	$203.2 billion

Source: U.S. Bureau of Economic Analysis. Data are for 2008.

Also in recent decades, the farming industry has seen consumers becoming increasingly concerned about food safety, nutrition, quality, variety, and prices. Environmental interests have established relationships to help bring environmentally friendly production methods to agriculture. Government expenditures on food and nutrition programs and natural resource conservation have increased and become more integrated within the industry.

The Industry Today

The farming industry today is driven by demand from federal agricultural policy programs, food consumption trends, and the crop export market. The profitability of individual farm operators or companies depends on their ability to maximize crop yield, minimize input costs, and minimize risk. Larger farms and companies have the advantage of highly automated technologies and have access to the latest in seed and crop technologies.

However, more data indicate that small operations can compete effectively by producing specialty products.

U.S. farms that produce and market crops are becoming larger and more concentrated. There has been an increase in the number of farm operators contracting with large business operations called agribusinesses. These businesses purchase crops from many farms to achieve vast economies of scale. They allow contractors to reduce their risk levels, because the contractors are guaranteed a buyer and a set price for their crops. Other operators sell their products themselves, either to local distributors and suppliers or on commodities exchanges, where prices often are determined by worldwide supply and demand.

The farming industry increasingly encompasses and partners with highly technological businesses that are integral in the production and sales of farm products. These include companies developing farm machinery, fertilizer, pesticides, and her-

Farmers plow a field. Modern tractor cabs allow farmers to work in air-conditioned comfort and insulate them from the noise of the engine. (©Tommy Schultz/Dreamstime.com)

bicides. Some farmers, however, engage in pest management without the use of pesticides. For example, they may use natural predators, such as insects that eat other insects rather than crops, or introduce bacteria that only harm insects or substances that interfere with pests' reproductive cycles. Such techniques are often referred to as "organic" and are seen as aspects of the larger umbrella practice of organic farming.

In addition to organic farming, the industry employs a host of new and renewed methods of raising crops, including precision farming and bioengineering. Precision farming utilizes technology and data to make efficient decisions about raising crops. For example, precision farmers make detailed maps of their land and use electronic devices to monitor and manage crop conditions. Monitoring devices measure the amounts of water, weeds, and nutrients in the soil and overlay those data on maps created from satellite and aerial photographs. The Global Positioning System (GPS) is used to pinpoint the exact locations of land and nutrients. This information is used to determine where additional fertilizer, herbicides, and water may be required. By reducing unnecessary applications of chemicals, operators reduce their production costs. GPS technology also helps operators navigate equipment accurately through their fields.

Sensors on this equipment monitor yields, providing operators with even more information to determine where extra nutrients may be needed or which crops are ready for harvest.

Bioengineers modify the genetic code of plants to provide them with desirable characteristics or remove undesirable characteristics. Some crops are engineered to resist certain pests, tolerate drought, or contain additional nutrients. A growing number of farm operations, however, avoid the use of synthetic pesticides and herbicides and bioengineered crops altogether. These organic farms take advantage of the higher prices they can charge for certified organic grains, fruits, and vegetables. Since 1990, sales of organic products have grown 20 percent per year, and they are expected to continue climbing. The organic market has allowed some small farms to remain profitable. Organic farmers often need to know more than conventional farmers about the science of agriculture: They must know how plants grow and what helps them thrive. Most organic operators (and some conventional operators) adopt techniques that raise soil quality to naturally resist diseases, weeds, and insects. They might increase soil quality by planting high-nutrient crops in the off-season, for example, or by using conservation tillage practices, such as leaving remains of a crop to decompose in the soil after harvesting.

Advances in the farm industry have created many other disciplines related to agriculture. Agricultural scientists for example, advise farm operators regarding the optimal techniques to control weeds, apply pesticides, conserve water, or prevent soil erosion. Agricultural sales involves selling farm-related products, which requires knowledge of agriculture. There are many avenues one can take if one is interested in the farm industry in the twenty-first century. Opportunities exist, from owning or managing a large, capital-intensive farm to providing the technology to discover a specialty product that is in high demand. Whatever sector of the twenty-first century

This field of corn may be bioengineered corn rather than the "traditional" hybrid corn, and the kernels may be destined for an ethanol-producing plant. (©Dreamstime.com)

A traditional family farm, with a red barn and silos. About 91 percent of American farms are small farms, but they account for only 23 percent of U.S. agricultural production. (©Pat Bogusz/Dreamstime.com)

farming industry one embarks upon, one will need to possess a strong business aptitude and the ability to make money in an industry that is expensive to enter and that involves substantial risk.

INDUSTRY MARKET SEGMENTS

Contemporary farming operations are complex businesses that vary in size. Although this variance in acreage exists, the trend of small farms being combined into bigger farms continues. Some farm operations may comprise a few acres with a single owner-operator. Such farmers almost always need subsidiary income sources, and inded the average farmer earns only 10 percent of his or her annual income from farming. Large farms of several thousand acres may support twenty-five to one hundred workers.

Small Farms

Small farms generally have gross revenues of between $10,000 and $250,000 per year (although there are some reports that categorize small farms as those with less than $2,500 in annual earnings).

About 91 percent of American farms are small farms, but they account for only 23 percent of U.S. agricultural production. Many small farms are being combined into larger operations. Often, small-farm operators train for other occupations in conjunction with the small farming business, and small commercial farms tend to grow commodities that do not necessarily require a full-time commitment of labor, so their operators will have an opportunity to find other sources of income.

Potential Annual Earnings Scale. The average earnings for a small farming operation vary depending on the region where the farm is located, type of crops produced, weather patterns, and marketing trends. As is true of larger operations, a small farm may realize a profit one year and lose money the next. According to the U.S. Bureau of Labor Statistics (BLS), crop workers earned an average of $9.23 per hour, or $19,200 per year. Agricultural equipment operators earned $11.36 per hour, or $23,620 per year. Farmers and ranchers earned an average of $52,050 per year. Generally speaking, farmworkers and owners on small farms earn less than these averages.

Clientele Interaction. Almost all small farmers have some degree of direct interaction with their clients. Those who are contractors of large agribusiness concerns receive instructions and coordinate details of delivery with corporate representatives. Those who sell on commodity exchanges are usually involved in at least some aspects of the sales, and they may handle details with purchasers. In addition, many small farmers sell at farmers markets, where they spend hours each week interacting with individual consumers who attend markets not only to obtain quality produce but also to cultivate relationships with the people who grow their food.

Amenities, Atmosphere, and Physical Grounds. Working conditions for agricultural laborers and other farm employees vary. Much direct farm labor is physically strenuous and takes place outdoors in all kinds of weather. Harvesting fruits and vegetables, for example, may require much bending, stooping, and lifting. Farmers may enjoy the variety of the work, the rural setting, and the satisfaction of working the land. In the case of smaller farms, the amount of labor and time spent in these types of conditions is usually less than in larger operations. Other farm employees, such as soil agronomists or machinery engineers, may work more regular hours. Work on a farm does not lend itself to a regular forty-hour workweek. Work cannot be delayed when crops must be planted or harvested. Long hours and weekend work are common. For example, farmers and agricultural equipment operators may work six or seven days a week during planting and harvesting seasons.

Typical Number of Employees. It is not uncommon for all the labor on a small farm to be provided by members of the family associated with the operation. This labor pool can be anywhere from a single person to six or more people, including a spouse and children or even extended family. Some small farms do employ hired hands, however. In many areas, small farms employ custom services, which allows them to avoid the capital costs of buying specialized machinery.

Traditional Geographic Locations. While most farms are located in rural areas, urban farms also exist, so small farms may be located almost anywhere, from the countryside to plots of land adjacent to major metropolitan freeway systems to rooftops. The top five states for agricultural production are California, Texas, Iowa, Nebraska, and Kansas. Each state and region of the United States varies in crop type and variety, which are affected by the length of the growing season and the climate. The Midwest typically produces small grains, such as wheat, oats, and barley. California is a major producer of vegetables and melons, but the industry is very concentrated, as the top 10 percent of farms generate almost 90 percent of industry revenue. Of all U.S. farms, 15 percent produce grain or oilseed, accounting for two-thirds of all cropland revenue and 40 percent of all farm earnings. Because statistics of production are concentrated for fruits and melons and more fragmented for other crops, nearly every state has some form of small farm operations. However, the overall trend in all areas is toward consolidation of the industry in large farms.

Pros of Working on a Small Farm. On many small farms, family members work alongside one another, enjoying familial cohesiveness—especially when younger ages are involved. Farmers work outdoors and make a (partial) living off the land. Also, most farm operators work for themselves and value the independence of being self-employed. Most farmers got into farming because their parents and grandparents farmed, and they simply entered the family business. Many farm employees value the same things that farm owners do: the rural lifestyle, independence, and working outdoors.

Cons of Working on a Small Farm. Maintaining a small farm often requires long hours, as well as weekend work. Because there is relatively little income from the business, small farms often lack the resources to outsource labor needs, so farmers and their families and friends must do everything that needs to be done. Work cannot be delayed when crops must be planted or harvested, so farm operators must do what it takes to complete these tasks. For example, farmers, agricultural equipment operators, and farm mechanics may work six or seven days a week during planting and harvesting seasons.

The purchase of farm inputs, such as machinery, requires an increasing amount of capital and has resulted in fewer individuals being willing or able to take on the debt necessary to farm. Large cash outlays for farm equipment, increased specialization, and operators needing to produce larger quantities of a limited number of products have become far too stressful for many. Farmers also risk exposure to pesticides and other hazardous chemicals sprayed on crops or plants. However, exposure can be minimal if safety procedures are followed.

Costs

Payroll and Benefits: Most small-farm operators work for themselves with little or no staff overhead. Small-farm households depend heavily on off-farm income, so the nonfarm economy and job availability is important to them. Because of their off-farm income, median household income for small-farm households is comparable with the median income for all U.S. households. Farm households, regardless of the size of their farms, usually tend to have a high net worth, with their farms accounting for most of that value. It is not surprising that 94 percent of farm households in 2007 had a net worth equal to or greater than the median for all U.S. households.

Supplies: Farms require seed, fertilizer, herbicides, specialized equipment, maintenance tools, and fuel.

External Services: Small farmers may employ occasional contract laborers, but they tend to handle all general labor themselves. Contracted vendors may perform custom tasks, such as fertilizer and herbicide application, as well as custom harvesting. Farmers may also require the services of accountants or tax preparation experts.

Utilities: Farms must pay utility costs for homes and offices located on the property, as well as additional farm buildings and shops. These include electricity, gas, water, sewage, telephone, and Internet access.

Taxes: Farmers must pay income taxes, which vary year to year based on fluctuations in income and the depreciation of equipment, buildings, and other items used in the operation. They must also pay property taxes and possibly self-employment taxes.

Rent: Land that is rented from another party varies in cost depending on the region, and rent is often paid yearly or in two payments during the year, once before planting and once at the end of harvest. Some farmers receive loans from private financial institutions in order to pay rent during the planting season and repay the loans each year after harvest. Loans also are available from federal organizations; the U.S. Department of Agriculture's (USDA's) Farm Service Agency, for example, specifically earmarks funds for beginning farmers. Some farmers prefer not to own the land they farm. Instead, they lease land from absentee or older farm owners. Land leasing fees vary from region to region but can be anywhere from $30 per acre to several thousands per acre, depending on the soil value and the value of the specific crops grown in the region.

Midsize Farms

Midsize farms have traditionally been referred to as the heart of American agriculture. These farms, which tend to be independent family farms, generally have revenues of between $100,000 and $500,000. They make up the largest share of working farms, yet they are the most vulnerable economically. According to the USDA, the number of midsize farms decreased by approximately 20 percent between the early 1980's and 2001.

Potential Annual Earnings Scale. According to the BLS, crop workers earned an average of $9.23 per hour, or $19,200 per year. Agricultural equipment operators earned $11.36 per hour, or $23,620 per year. Farmers and ranchers earned an average of $52,050 per year; agricultural managers earned an average of $63,140; and farm labor contractors earned an average of $36,260.

Clientele Interaction. Farmers or farm managers must maintain good relations with purchasing agents, distributors, and other clients to ensure their continued business. Workers for midsize farms may sell some of the farms' produce at farmers markets or roadside stands, where they will have the opportunity to interact directly with consumers.

Amenities, Atmosphere, and Physical Grounds. Working conditions for agricultural workers on a midsize operation and other professions within the same scale of the farming industry vary. Much farm labor is physically strenuous—involving bending, stooping, and lifting—and takes place outdoors in all kinds of weather. In the case of midsize farms, the amount of labor and time spent in these conditions is usually greater than is the case for smaller operations—and sometimes even than is the case for the larger operations: Midsize farms compete with their larger competitors by keeping overhead costs to a minimum, so they may employ fewer workers and require more work of each. Operating machinery on a midsize farm can require long hours of tedious work. However, those who work directly with the soil may en-

Farming is capital intensive. A used 2010 John Deere 9770 series combine harvester was for sale on eBay for $280,000. (©Stephen Mcsweeny/Dreamstime.com)

joy the variety of the work, the rural setting, and the satisfaction of working the land.

Conditions for other farm industry workers, such as soil agronomists and agriculture machinery engineers, often involve more structured atmospheres and work schedules. Work on a farm does not lend itself to a regular forty-hour workweek. Work cannot be delayed on the farm when crops must be planted or harvested. During these busier times of the year, many sectors in the farm industry experience long hours and weekend work. For example, farmers, agricultural equipment operators and mechanics, and farm insurance agents may work six or seven days a week during planting and harvesting seasons.

Typical Number of Employees. Even on some midsize farms, it is not uncommon for all necessary labor to be provided by family members associated with the operation. Most midsize-farm operators enter the business because their parents and grandparents operated midsize farms, and they simply wish to continue the family business. Most enjoy the rural lifestyle, the independence, and working outdoors and would not trade their job for

any other. However, even in midsize farm operations, many of today's farmers work part time and train for or labor in other occupations. Many midsize farms use hired labor at times, even if they only pay a neighbor for a day or two when a family member is away or someone is sick. Midsize-farm operators are more likely to use custom services than are smaller farms, as this approach avoids the capital costs of buying specialized machinery. Labor needs are also very different among farms, depending on the type of crops being grown.

Traditional Geographic Locations. Midsize farms are found in practically all agricultural states, especially the top five: California, Texas, Iowa, Nebraska, and Kansas. The crops they produce vary by growing season and climate. The Midwest typically produces small grains, such as wheat, oats, and barley. California is a major producer of vegetables and melons, but the industry is very concentrated, as the top 10 percent of farms generate almost 90 percent of industry revenue. Of all U.S. farms, 15 percent produce grain or oilseed, accounting for two-thirds of all cropland revenue and 40 percent of all farm earnings. Because statistics of production are concentrated for fruits and melons and more fragmented for other crops, nearly every state has some form of midsize farm operations. However, the overall trend in all areas is toward consolidation of the industry in large farms.

Pros of Working on a Midsize Farm. Many midsize-farm operators have family ties to the industry and to their own farms. They have the opportunity to work alongside family members, encouraging family cohesiveness—especially when younger ages are involved. They like working outdoors and making a living from the land. Also, most farmers work for themselves and value the independence of being self-employed.

Cons of Working on a Midsize Farm. Farming often requires working long hours, including weekends. Midsize farms attempt to limit labor outsourcing, so farmers and their families and friends must do everything that needs to be done. Work cannot be delayed when crops must be planted or harvested, so farm operators must do what it takes to complete these tasks. The purchase of farm inputs, such as machinery, requires an increasing amount of capital, and fewer individuals are willing or able to take on the debt necessary to farm. The extent of the cash outlays required for farm equipment increase with size and specialization of a farm, and operators find themselves needing to produce larger quantities of a limited number of products to realize a profit.

As the size of the operation increases, so does the size of the machinery and the risk of injury. Exposure to pesticides and other hazardous chemicals sprayed on crops or plants places individuals at risk as well, and agriculture ranks among the most hazardous industries. Farmers are at high risk for fatal and nonfatal injuries, work-related lung diseases, noise-induced hearing loss, skin diseases, and certain cancers associated with chemical use and prolonged sun exposure. Farming is one of the few industries in which the family (who often share the work and live on the premises) is also at risk for injuries, illness, and death.

Costs

Payroll and Benefits: Most midsize-farm operators work for themselves with little or no staff overhead. Midsize-farm households often depend heavily on off-farm income, so the nonfarm economy is important to their bottom line.

Because of their off-farm income, median household income for midsize-farm households is comparable with the median income for all U.S. households. Farm households, regardless of the size of their farms, tend to have a high net worth, with their farms accounting for most of that value. Some 94 percent of farm households in 2007 had a net worth equal to or greater than the median for all U.S. households.

Supplies: Crop production supplies include seed, fertilizer, herbicides, equipment, maintenance tools, and fuel.

External Services: Farms may contract custom fertilizer applications, herbicide spraying, and custom harvesting, as well as accounting or tax preparation services.

Utilities: Farms must pay utility costs for homes and offices located on the property, as well as additional farm buildings and shops. These include electricity, gas, water, sewage, telephone, and Internet access.

Taxes: Farmers must pay income taxes, which vary year to year based on fluctuations in income and the depreciation of equipment, buildings, and other items used in the operation. They must also pay property taxes and possibly self-employment taxes.

Rent: Land that is rented from another party varies in cost depending on the region, and rent is often paid yearly or in two payments during the year, once before planting and once at the end of harvest. Some farmers receive loans from private financial institutions in order to pay rent during the planting season and repay the loans each year after harvest. Loans also are available from federal organizations; the USDA's Farm Service Agency, for example, specifically earmarks funds for beginning farmers. Some farmers prefer not to own the land they farm. Instead, they lease land from absentee or older farm owners. Land leasing fees vary from region to region but can be anywhere from $30 per acre to several thousands per acre, depending on the soil value and the value of the specific crops grown in the region.

Large Farms

Large farms generally have annual sales of more than $500,000, although, when using the gross cash farm income (GCFI) method of calculation, annual sales of greater than $250,000 place a farm in the large category. Some large farms still employ very few workers, while others may have one hundred employees or more.

Potential Annual Earnings Scale. According to the BLS, crop workers earned an average of $9.23 per hour, or $19,200 per year. Agricultural equipment operators earned $11.36 per hour, or $23,620 per year. Farmers and ranchers earned an average of $52,050 per year; agricultural managers earned an average of $63,140; and farm labor contractors earned an average of $36,260. Chief executives of agricultural companies earned an average of $161,700, while general and operations managers earned $94,130.

Clientele Interaction. The technical knowledge that a modern large-farm manager must possess is frequently considered far greater than that required of most businessmen with equal investment. The capital required to operate such a farm is beyond the reach of many owners. Operators and employees of large farms and related businesses need good communication and business skills. They are more likely to require some outsourcing of services and may interact with farm credit agencies, bankers, and accountants for their operation needs. As with any size operation, being able to manage people and resolve conflict is also important.

Amenities, Atmosphere, and Physical Grounds. Within a large farming business, the division of labor increases. Conditions for agricultural workers on a large operation vary. The operator-manager may spend more time managing and less time performing physical labor. The nature of the physical labor on the farm, though, remains largely the same as on smaller farms. It is physically strenuous and takes place outdoors in all kinds of weather. There is often much bending, stooping, and lifting. Moreover, more labor is required on large farms than on smaller farms. In addition, operating machinery on a large farm can mean long hours of tedious work, but those who work directly with the soil may still enjoy the variety of the work, the rural setting, and the satisfaction of working the land.

Conditions for other farm industry workers, such as soil agronomists and agriculture machinery engineers, often involve more structured atmospheres and work schedules. Work on a large farm does not lend itself to a regular forty-hour workweek. On large farms, there are many acres to cover, and work cannot be delayed when crops must be planted or harvested. During these busier times of the year, many sectors in the farm industry may need to work longer hours and weekends. For example, farm employees, agricultural equipment operators, and farm insurance agents may work six or seven days a week during planting and harvesting seasons. Large farms are still predominantly family operations. Nonfamily farms include those organized as nonfamily corporations.

Typical Number of Employees. The trend of substituting capital for labor is becoming more common among large farms, where large machines do the work of several people using smaller implements. Large farms are more likely than smaller farms to use custom services in order to ensure that work is completed in a timely manner, as many more acres are farmed within the growing season. Large American farms vary from a couple of individuals to over one hundred employees. Because of the amount of capital investment, management, and decision making required, operators are much less likely to work elsewhere part time. Large family farms are often organized as family corporations, and these account for a growing share of farm sales.

Traditional Geographic Locations. The top five states for agricultural production are California, Texas, Iowa, Nebraska, and Kansas. Nearly every state has some form of large farming operation. However, California is a major producer of vegetables and melons, and the top 10 percent of its farms reportedly generate almost 90 percent of industry revenue. Thus, the state houses a large concentration of large farm operations. Of all U.S. farms, 15 percent produce grain or oilseed, accounting for two-thirds of all cropland revenue and 40 percent of all farm earnings. Because production statistics are concentrated for fruits and melons and more fragmented for other crops, nearly every state has some large farm, but some states and particular crops involve a greater number of large farms than others. The overall trend in all areas of farming is toward consolidation of the industry in large farms.

Pros of Working on a Large Farm. Research has shown that large farms produce goods more efficiently than small farms. Large farms can reduce costs by taking advantage of volume discounts on their purchases. They can negotiate prices on fertilizer, seed, crop chemicals, petroleum products, machinery, and repair services. Large-farm operators also have an advantage in selling their products. Managers of large corn farms, for example, can contract directly with large processors for an entire year's production of a given quantity and quality for a specific date in the future, thus commanding a higher price. The middleman is eliminated, and production, handling, and processing can be prescheduled for greater efficiency. Large farms require a smaller investment in machinery and buildings per crop acre.

Cons of Working on a Large Farm. Farming often requires long hours, including weekend work. Work cannot be delayed when crops must be planted or harvested. For example, farm employees and agricultural equipment operators may work six or seven days a week during planting and harvesting seasons. The purchase of farm inputs, such as machinery, requires an increasing amount of capital, and fewer individuals are willing or able to take on the debt necessary to farm. Large cash outlays for farm equipment increase with size and specialization. Operators need to produce larger quantities of a limited number of products.

As the size of the operation increases, the size of the machinery does as well, as does the risk of injury. Exposure to pesticides and other hazardous chemicals sprayed on crops or plants place individuals at risk, and agriculture ranks among the most hazardous industries. Farmers are at high risk for fatal and nonfatal injuries, work-related lung diseases, noise-induced hearing loss, skin diseases, and certain cancers associated with chemical use and prolonged sun exposure. Farming is one of the few industries in which workers' families (who often share the work and live on the premises) are also at risk for injuries, illness, and death.

While large-scale industrial farming is the most efficient in terms of yield per dollar spent, taking advantage of this efficiency requires farmers to develop monocultures: That is, they must plant large quantities of the same crop, reducing biodiversity and reducing yield per acre. Nonindustrial, more personal farming is more efficient in terms of yield per acre because farmers can plant complementary crops on the same plot of land, yielding more food than any single type of crop planting can.

Costs

Payroll and Benefits: Sales attributed to large farms increased steadily from 51 percent in 1982 to 72 percent in 1997. According to the USDA's Economic Research Service, the largest share of this increase occurred in the classes of farms with sales between $1 million and $5 million. Most large-farm operators work for themselves with some staff overhead. On large farms, farmworkers can earn $50,000 to $60,000 per year. Benefits paid to these employees varies among farms. Farming households, regardless of the size of their farms, tend to have high net worths, with their farms accounting for most of that value. Some 94 percent of farm households in 2007 had a net worth equal to or greater than the median for all U.S. households.

Supplies: Crop production supplies include seed, fertilizer, herbicides, equipment, maintenance tools, and fuel.

External Services: Farms may contract custom services such as fertilizer application, herbicide spraying, and custom harvesting. Large farms may also contract advertising, legal, or accounting services as necessary.

Utilities: Farms must pay utility costs for homes and offices located on the property, as well as additional farm buildings and shops. These include electricity, gas, water, sewage, telephone, and Internet access.

Taxes: Farmers must pay income taxes, which vary year to year based on fluctuations in income and the depreciation of equipment, buildings, and other items used in the operation. They must also pay property taxes and possibly self-employment taxes.

Rent: Land that is rented from another party varies in cost depending on the region, and rent is often paid yearly or in two payments during the year, once before planting and once at the end of harvest. Some farmers receive loans from private financial institutions in order to pay rent during the planting season and repay the loans each year after harvest. Loans also are available from federal organizations; the USDA's Farm Service Agency, for example, specifically earmarks funds for beginning farmers. Some farmers prefer not to own the land they farm. Instead, they lease land from absentee or older farm owners. Land leasing fees vary from region to region but can be anywhere from $30 per acre to several thousands per acre, depending on the soil value and the value of the specific crops grown in the region.

ORGANIZATIONAL STRUCTURE AND JOB ROLES

The organizational structure and distribution of tasks on an individual farm is typically based on the size and geographic location of the operation. However, each particular farm within the industry is dependent upon various organizations and associated businesses for its success and viability. Job roles are largely the same on all farms, but on small farms all roles may be performed by only a handful of people, whereas larger farms may distribute tasks among more than one hundred people.

The following umbrella categories apply to the organizational structure of businesses in the farming industry:

- Business Management
- Farm Labor
- Sales and Marketing
- Technology, Research, Design, and Development

Business Management

In most farm operations, the owner-operator or partners (often a spouse, children, and sometimes employees) carry out the responsibilities of business management. Regardless of farm size, business management requires knowledge and experience to identify problems and recognize opportunities. For example, being able to recognize which alternative crop variety is best suited for a particular growing season is a constant endeavor in today's market. Business management also includes the development of short- and long-term planning through identifying goals, assessing needs, and developing strategic plans for farm operation. In some cases, especially with large operations, operators may hire or consult with outside managers who are knowledgeable in the industry. In such cases, operations are coordinated by farm management firms. Such managers may supervise small farms and even perform some of the manual labor. However, business managers on larger farms may oversee only nonlaborious facets of the business, such as selling crops, helping determine which crops to plant, developing planting and harvesting schedules, and deciding when temporary workers will be needed.

Agricultural economy is another sector within farm management. Utilizing modern analytical management skills and tools, agricultural economists conduct financial analysis, develop marketing plans, and set up optimal production schedules in food and fiber firms. Careers in this form of business management often have their origins in management or production operations or sales representative positions. These employees are then progressively assigned increased responsibilities for decision making.

Business management occupations may include the following:

- Farmer/Farm Owner
- Farm/Operations Manager
- Consulting Manager
- Agricultural Economist
- Accountant
- Crop Insurance Agent
- Farm Credit and Banking Service Specialist
- Purchasing Manager

Farm Labor

The majority of the work in the farming industry is performed in the fields. Farmers and workers plow fields, test and prepare soil, plant crops, tend crops (addressing irrigation and nutrient needs and combating pests and diseases), harvest crops and deliver them to market, and perform land management tasks (such as overseeing fallow fields, ensuring crop rotation, guarding against erosion, and so on) as necessary. They often must fit these tasks in with the other nonfarm labor necessary to support themselves, as farm income alone is commonly not enough for a farming family to live on. In addition, many farmworkers are migrants, traveling from region to region to follow the planting and harvesting seasons, or coming to an agricultural area only during seasons when work is available. These workers often endure extreme conditions for low pay, and they make modern farming possible.

Farm labor occupations may include the following:

- Farmer
- Farmhand
- Farm Labor Contractor
- Migrant Farmworker
- Agricultural Equipment Operator

Sales and Marketing

In most farm operations, the owner-operator or partners carry out the responsibilities of sales and marketing. Most food moves from farms to consumers through an efficient system that utilizes size and specialization of product. For example, grain-handling terminals, called grain elevators, are located along major railways and have continued to increase in size to help keep distribution costs to a minimum. Some of these massive concrete structures in the Midwest can fill hundreds of large railroad cars with grain. Most operators of mid-to-large operations devote their time to what they know best—planting, growing, and harvesting food—leaving the processing and marketing to agribusinesses. A large wheat operation in the Dakotas or Kansas may contract tens of thousands of bushels of wheat at a specific price per bushel at a local grain elevator terminal.

Selling directly to consumers and specialty markets is growing in popularity with small and midsize

OCCUPATION SPECIALTIES

Farmers/Farm Managers

Specialty	Responsibilities
Farm general managers	Operate farms for corporations, cooperatives, or other owners.
Fish farmers	Spawn and raise fish for commercial purposes.
Fur farmers	Feed and raise mink, fox, chinchilla, rabbits, and other fur-bearing animals for sale on the fur market.
Horse trainers	Train horses for riding or harness.
Livestock ranchers	Breed and raise livestock such as beef cattle, dairy cattle, goats, horses, sheep, and swine to sell meat, dairy products, wool, and hair.
Nursery managers	Supervise plant nurseries, which produce plants for sale to wholesale or retail customers.
Organic farmers/farm managers	Grow crops, control pests, and maintain soil health without the use, or with only limited use, of synthetic fertilizers and pesticides.
Poultry farmers	Raise chickens, turkeys, or other fowl for meat or egg production.
Shellfish growers	Cultivate and harvest beds of shellfish, such as clams and oysters.
Tree-fruit-and-nut crop farmers	Plant and cultivate fruit-producing trees.
Vegetable farmers	Plan and plant vegetables according to weather, type of soil, and the size and location of their farms.

operations. Farmers markets are an example of this type of marketing and are a growing resource for farms and food processors. Farmers markets provide large customer bases for farm products, as well as opportunities for farmers to develop their marketing skills and learn about customer preferences. They also allow farmers to network for other types of direct marketing, which, in turn, can increase profits. Farmers may also increase their profits and distribution opportunities by selling directly to institutional cafeterias, such as those at schools, senior centers, hospitals, and correctional facilities.

Food processing engineers are important contacts for farm sales and marketing staffs, as they research and develop products and processes using ingredients purchased from farms. They also devise processing, handling, and packaging equipment for farm industry sales and marketing. When assuming the role of project engineers, they supervise the design, construction, installation, and start-up of processes. As plant engineers, they keep factories running efficiently and well maintained. Some manage other workers, and others who work in technical sales and service often provide consultation.

Sales and marketing occupations may include the following:

- Farmer
- Sales Manager
- Farm Stand Cashier
- Farmers Market Worker
- Crop Storage Manager
- Seed Salesperson
- Crop Transporter
- Commodity Broker
- Export Sales Manager

Technology, Research, Design, and Development

Technological advances in plant breeding have resulted in a greater ability for farmers to choose crops with desirable traits, such as disease resistance and drought tolerance. Such traits can have enormous effects on the viability of crops and can ultimately increase yields. Investing in technology and research begins at the operator level and advances to services provided by large agricultural science research firms. New members of a farm operation should be prepared with college or vocational school degrees. Farm operators should be in the practice of reading farm publications and reports about new technology. On a yearly basis, and at every state and county level, a variety of workshops, field days, and conferences are held to update producers on the latest in plant technology and other issues in agricultural science.

Agronomists often interact with farm operators to meet their field-crop and soil-management needs. Through a good understanding of the industry's technology and research, agronomists study and help develop new varieties of crops, analyze soil structure, investigate soil chemistry, and study the interaction between water and soil. Agronomists are concerned about not only the economics of the farming industry but also the preservation of the environment. Agronomists can be involved with teaching at various levels, interacting with state departments of agriculture, and providing research throughout the country and the world.

Technology, research, design, and development occupations may include the following:

These storage grain bins await the soybeans ripening in the field. (©Linda Johnsonbaugh/Dreamstime.com)

OCCUPATION SPECIALTIES

Agricultural Scientists

Specialty	*Responsibilities*
Agronomists	Study how field crops such as corn, wheat, and cotton grow. They improve their quality and yield by developing new growth methods and by controlling diseases, pests, and weeds.
Animal and plant breeders	Breed animals and plants to develop and improve their potential.
Animal scientists	Conduct research on the selection, breeding, feeding, management, and health of domestic farm animals.
Dairy and poultry scientists	Conduct research on the selection, breeding, feeding, and management of dairy cattle and poultry.
Entomologists	Study insects and their relationship to plant and animal life.
Food technologists	Study the chemical, physical, and biological nature of food to learn how to safely process, preserve, package, distribute, and store it.
Horticulturists	Work with fruit, vegetable, greenhouse, and nursery crops and ornamental plants. They seek improved quality, yield, and methods to resist crop diseases.

- Agricultural Scientist
- Agriculture Mechanical Engineer
- Biochemist
- Entomologist
- Geneticist
- Soil and Plant Scientist

INDUSTRY OUTLOOK

Overview

The outlook for the farming industry shows it to be somewhat stable. This outlook stands in contrast to many years of decline in small farms and in farm-related employment. Despite the expectation that the number of self-employed farmers is expected to decline by 8 percent by 2018, agricultural manager jobs are projected to grow by about 6 percent—still slower than the average growth rate of all industries combined. Managers will be needed as owners of large tracts of land, who often do not live on their property, increasingly seek the expertise of agricultural managers to run their farms for them.

Market pressures on small and midsize family farms will continue to drive consolidation in the farm industry. The more prosperous farms are likely to grow in size in order to achieve greater economic returns on their investments. Larger farms may also continue to receive a greater portion of farm subsidies to help offset losses beyond the operators' control, such as drought, disease, and depressed markets. Despite this ongoing shift to larger farms, most farms continue to be organized as sole proprietorships, partnerships, or family corporations. Any direct ownership of large farms by publicly held corporations is likely to remain small. Through advances in technology, productivity will continue to improve and also result in less farm labor being required to produce crops. Low prices for many agricultural goods have not kept up with the increasing costs of farming. If these conditions continue, it will be difficult for many small farmers to survive. The difficulty of making a living exclusively from farming may continue to require farmers to seek other means of employment in addition to their farms.

There are factors on the horizon that are influ-

PROJECTED EMPLOYMENT FOR SELECTED OCCUPATIONS

Agriculture

Employment		
2008	Projected 2018	Occupation
2,300	2,600	Agricultural and food scientists
2,000	2,000	Agricultural inspectors
699,800	673,400	Agricultural workers
17,100	18,300	Animal care and service workers
8,300	8,300	Graders and sorters, agricultural products
246,500	260,700	Farm, ranch, and other agricultural managers

Source: U.S. Bureau of Labor Statistics, Industries at a Glance, Occupational Employment Statistics and Employment Projections Program.

encing the changes taking place in agriculture. More domestic consumers are purchasing agricultural products from farmers markets, community supported agriculture (CSA), and other local food distribution systems. Consumers are becoming increasingly health conscious, and the demand continues for organic produce. Such produce is grown mostly on small to midsize farms that can use nonchemical methods of pest control effectively. This type of production within the industry allows farms of small acreage to remain economically viable. Federal, state, and local government programs are increasingly available to provide assistance targeted at small to midsize farms.

Exports for agricultural products also are rising, reflecting international demand. Rising incomes in countries such as China, India, Indonesia, and Brazil have increased the demand for diversified diets in those countries, leading them to seek products beyond their traditional foods. An increased global consumption of biofuels and related research and technology for the development of en-

ergy self-sufficiency has added further strains to agriculture. This type of pressure on supply and price is strongly shown by the case of corn. This farm commodity dramatically affects the broader structure of global food markets, and at one point 25 percent of the corn crop was found to be used for ethanol production. In the future, whether corn will be used that intensely for fuel is critically dependent on the price of oil and also on the politics of biofuels. Cereals and oilseeds can also be used in multiple ways, and the competition for these commodities is expected to rise among businesses.

Climate change also threatens the productivity of the entire global food system. Some food supply and world economics experts foresee a looming food crisis that will first affect those populations that are already food-insecure and that may then spread to other populations. This could place a high demand on the farming industry in countries where high-efficiency agriculture continues to exist and thrive.

Employment Advantages

Those who work in the farming industry directly or indirectly enjoy the variety of the work. Many are exposed to rural settings and the satisfaction of being self-employed and working the land. Many small-farm operators work alongside family members, strengthening their families' cohesiveness. Food policy and sustainable agriculture are rapidly gaining traction as fields of great concern to many people, and many young people are passionately committed to finding ways to make sustainable farming pay. It remains unclear how many will succeed, but resources to help them are increasing. These include programs to develop cohesive local food production, processing, and distribution systems called foodsheds, as well as resources to enable small and midsize farms to compete with large farms. If these programs succeed, small-scale farming is poised to be an extremely exciting and fulfilling, albeit difficult, career choice.

Annual Earnings

The farming industry is ever changing and depends on several factors, including market pressures, alternative-fuel consumption, and politics.

In 2002, the U.S. industry realized gross revenues of $175 billion, according to the USDA's Economic Research Service. Renewed economic growth following the global recession of 2007-2009 may help farmers. This growth is expected to be slightly above the historical average long-term growth rate, so many markets, including agricultural markets, have the potential to expand, and such expansion may provide a foundation for gains in world demand for and trade in agricultural products. Long-term global demand for agricultural products in combination with the continued presence of U.S. ethanol could hold prices for corn, oilseeds, and many other crops at historically high levels. U.S. farm crop income is expected to increase from a net cash income of $76.3 billion in 2010 to a net cash income of $81.6 billion in 2019.

RELATED RESOURCES FOR FURTHER RESEARCH

NATIONAL PLANT DATA CENTER
2901 E Lee St., Suite 2100
Greensboro, NC 27401
Tel: (336) 370-3337
Fax: (336) 370-336
http://npdc.usda.gov

NATIONAL SOIL SURVEY CENTER
100 Centennial Mall North, Room 152
Lincoln, NE 68508-3866
Tel: (402) 437-5499
Fax: (402) 437-5336
http://soils.usda.gov

NORTH DAKOTA STATE UNIVERSITY EXTENSION SERVICE
NDSU Dept. 7000
315 Morrill Hall
P.O. Box 6050
Fargo, ND 58108-6050
Tel: (701) 231-8944
http://www.ag.ndsu.edu/extension

U.S. DEPARTMENT OF AGRICULTURE
1400 Independence Ave. SW
Washington, DC 20250
http://www.usda.gov

ABOUT THE AUTHOR

Jeffrey Larson is the director of physical therapy at the Tioga Medical Center in Tioga, North Dakota. He is a graduate of North Dakota State University and the University of Utah. He holds degrees in both athletic training and physical therapy. Larson has been evaluating and treating the rehabilitative needs of athletes of all ages and sports for more than twenty years. He is also a medical writer and founder of Northern Medical Informatics, a medical communications business that he operates with a focus on continuing education for allied health care professions, as well as consumer health education. Larson is a member of the American Physical Therapy Association and the American Medical Writers Association. In addition to his medical profession, he owns and operates a sixteen-hundred-acre wheat farm and ranch in northwestern North Dakota.

FURTHER READING

Crowell, Susan. "2007 Census of Agriculture: Agriculture's 'Middle' Slipping Away." *Farm and Dairy*, February 9, 2009. http://www.farmanddairy.com/uncategorized/2007-census-of-agriculture-agricultures-middle-slipping-away/11165.html.

Hoag, Dana L. *Applied Risk Management in Agriculture.* Boca Raton, Fla.: CRC Press, 2010.

Hoppe, Robert A., and Penni Korb. "Large and Small Farms: Trends and Characteristics." Chapter 1 in *Structural and Financial Characteristics of U.S. Farms.* Washington, D.C.: USDA Economic Research Service, 2004. http://www.ers.usda.gov/publications/aib797/aib797c.pdf.

"Hungry Planet." *Commonweal* 135, no. 10 (May 23, 2008): 5. http://commonwealmagazine.org/hungry-planet-0.

Jurena, Remy. *Agriculture in the U.S. Free Trade Agreements: Trade with Current and Prospective Partners, Impact and Issues.* New York: Nova Science, 2008.

Leval, Kim, et al. *The Impact and Benefits of USDA Research and Grant Programs to Enhance Midsize Farm Profitability and Rural Community Success.* Lyons, Nebr.: Center for Rural Affairs, 2006.

Mapes, Kathleen. *Sweet Tyranny: Migrant Labor, Industrial Agriculture, and Imperial Politics.* Urbana: University of Illinois Press, 2009.

Ricketts, Cliff, and Kristina Ricketts. *Agribusiness: Fundamentals and Applications.* 2d ed. Clifton Park, N.Y.: Delmar Cengage Learning, 2009.

U.S. Bureau of Labor Statistics. *Career Guide to Industries,* 2010-2011 ed. http://www.bls.gov/oco/cg.

U.S. Census Bureau. North American Industry Classification System (NAICS), 2007. http://www.census.gov/cgi-bin/sssd/naics/naicsrch?chart=2007.

U.S. Department of Agriculture. Economic Research Service. "Special Feature: The Shift to Large Farms." In *Structure and Finances of U.S. Farms: Family Farm Report,* 2007 ed. Washington, D.C.: Author, 2007. http://www.ers.usda.gov/publications/eib24/eib24g.pdf.

U.S. Department of Agriculture. World Agricultural Outlook Board and U.S. Interagency Agricultural Projections Committee. *USDA Agricultural Projections to 2019.* Washington, D.C.: Author, 2010.

U.S. Department of Commerce. International Trade Administration. Office of Trade and Industry Information. Industry Trade Data and Analysis. http://ita.doc.gov/td/industry/otea/OTII/OTII-index.html.

Federal Public Administration

©Dreamstime.com

INDUSTRY SNAPSHOT

General Industry: Government and Public Administration
Career Cluster: Government and Public Administration Occupations
Subcategory Industries: Executive Office of the President; Federal Judiciary; Federal Legal Counsel and Prosecution; General Federal Government Support; Independent Administrative Agencies; Internal Revenue Service; U.S. Cabinet Departments; U.S. Congress
Related Industries: Civil Services: Planning; Civil Services: Public Safety; Defense Industry; Local Public Administration; National and International Security Industry; Political Advocacy Industry; Public Health Services; Space Exploration and Space Science Industry
Annual Domestic Revenues: $2.6 trillion USD (United States Treasury, 2007)
NAICS Numbers: 92119, 92211, 92213, 923-926, 92111-92113

INDUSTRY DEFINITION

Summary

The federal public administration industry implements the policies and programs instituted by the federal government of the United States. When the president of the United States makes a broad proclamation concerning, for example, the implementation or enactment of a new law or policy, and when the U.S. Congress passes that act into law and the federal court system rules on the constitutionality or validity of that law, most citizens fail to comprehend the enormity of what has just occurred. Rather, they only read a short article or are presented with a short briefing of the process or newly enacted legislation. The human and other resources necessary to propose, implement, and analyze the laws and the policies of the United States are, however, quite staggering.

The three branches of the federal government—executive, legislative, and judicial—employ nearly 2 million people whose duties make the day-to-day operation of government programs possible. Careers in federal public administration may include, for example, monitoring and implementing budgets, drafting and analyzing legislation, collecting and analyzing statistics, developing and implementing public policy, and running or managing federal government agencies. The objectives of sound federal public

Nearly 2 million people are employed in the implementation of the policies and programs instituted by the federal government of the United States. (©Maria Dryfhout/Dreamstime.com)

administration include ensuring justice, liberty, and prosperity for the country, as well as improving the efficiency and efficacy of the federal government. Because federal government programs and objectives are funded primarily by tax dollars paid by citizens and businesses, a primary goal of federal public administration is to provide the best services at the lowest cost to taxpayers, thus maximizing efficiency and minimizing fiscal waste.

Employees of the government are often referred to as public servants or civil servants, terms that describe civilian, rather than military, government employees. Additionally, it is important to note that public administration is an academic field of advanced study. One can also work or teach in related fields, studying, for example, political science, public policy, or governance in general.

History of the Industry

Ancient cultures such as those of Egypt and Greece were among the first to categorize public affairs by office. The Roman Empire used a more detailed approach, establishing specific offices to collect taxes, conduct military and foreign affairs, and administer justice, among other functions. These ancient civilizations, however, did not have a specific field of study for those seeking to enter public service. By the beginning of the nineteenth century in England, those seeking careers in public administration were required to study, among other subjects, history and law. They were also required to pass entry examinations for their desired fields of service.

In the United States, most federal public servants were initially selected on the basis of the so-called spoils system, or patronage. Through this informal system, many federal civilian positions were filled as a way of rewarding those who had supported a winning political candidate. The United States was far from the first country to have such a system, as the patronage system was drawn from selection processes that had been prevalent in many countries, including England. Naturally, such a system was highly susceptible to corruption. It was also inefficient, as those best qualified for a certain position were not likely to be hired unless they actively had supported or contributed to a winning candidate's election. Moreover, those hired under the patronage system did not last long, as they quickly lost their positions after the next election in which their candidate was replaced.

As both the population and the size of the government increased, so, too, did the number of federal government positions needed to help administrate and regulate the growing business of the country and its citizens. In 1883, to remedy the deeply entrenched spoils system, the United States Civil Service Commission (USCSC) was established. This commission was designed to control entry into federal government employment through a merit-based selection process. Initially, the commission only achieved success with respect to the lower ranks of government employment. Not until the early 1900's did the commission achieve enough power to regulate employment for approximately half of the positions in federal government.

Over the next several decades, the USCSC gradually grew in power, until it controlled most low, middle, and management-level positions in the federal government. In 1978, the commission's power was split between two offices, the Office of Personnel Management and the Merit Systems Protection Board. Notably, many U.S. states have adopted merit systems similar to the federal system to regulate positions in state service. Approximately two thousand positions remain outside the jurisdiction of these two governmental bodies.

The president of the United States has the duty of appointing individuals to certain key positions, such as the directors of federal agencies, federal judges, and other key employees. Pursuant to the U.S. Constitution, the U.S. Senate has the duty to give "advice and consent" on the president's nominees and must vote on each nomination over which they retain that power. (Congress has the authority to establish by statute which appointees require senatorial consent and which appointees may be chosen solely by the president, by the judiciary,

or by cabinet secretaries.) Consequently, although a form of the spoils system may still be in effect for certain positions, the voice of the people, through their elected representatives, is still heard.

The Industry Today

The federal public administration industry employs approximately 1.8 million people in the United States, making it the nation's largest employer. In fact, federal workers account for approximately 3 percent of U.S. civilian employment. Although most federal agencies and offices are headquartered in Washington, D.C., 90 percent of federal public administration jobs are located outside the nation's capital. Excluding military service and other forms of classified work, almost every aspect of the business of the federal government is carried out by civil service employees. Simply stated, federal public administration employees make the workings of the government possible. Individuals are employed by the federal government not only in Washington, D.C., but also in every major U.S. city, as well as in small satellite offices in smaller cities and in towns throughout the country. Additionally, according to the U.S. Bureau of Labor Statistics (BLS), approximately ninety-two thousand federal employees work outside the United States.

Careers in public administration offer interesting and challenging work, a steady work schedule for most employees, competitive salaries, and benefits packages that are equivalent with, or better than, most benefits packages in the private sector. Specific career functions within federal public ad-

The Federal Government's Contribution to the U.S. Economy

Value Added	Amount
Gross domestic product	$578.5 billion
Gross domestic product	4.0%
Persons employed	5.174 million
Total employee compensation	$466.8 billion

Source: U.S. Bureau of Economic Analysis. Data are for 2008.

ministration include, for example, working in the Census Bureau, compiling and analyzing statistics concerning the population; analyzing soil for the Forestry Department; assisting immigrants in obtaining citizenship; implementing federal tax policy for the Internal Revenue Service; researching or drafting legislation for Congress; prosecuting federal crimes; and working as an economist for the Department of Commerce.

There are hundreds of distinct federal departments, agencies, and organizations spread across all three branches of the federal government. The executive branch, however, is by far the primary employer, accounting for about 98 percent of the nation's federal public administration employees. This government branch includes the Executive Office of the President, ninety independent agencies, and the following fifteen cabinet departments: Defense, which manages the branches of the armed forces; Veterans Affairs, which operates programs for veterans and their families and administers the hospital system and national cemeteries for veterans and military personnel; Homeland Security, which seeks to prevent terrorist attacks and implements immigration policy; Treasury, which prints currency and regulates financial institutions; Justice, which enforces federal laws and ensures public safety; Agriculture, which promotes agriculture and monitors the safety of domestic meat and poultry; Interior, which manages national parks and promotes conservation of natural resources; Health and Human Services, which regulates the Medicare and Medicaid health programs and ensures the safety of drugs and some

foods; Transportation, which plans and constructs highways, railways, and mass transit systems; Commerce, which conducts the census, compiles statistics, and regulates patents and trademarks; State, which represents national interests abroad, issues passports, and oversees the country's embassies and consulates; Labor, which enforces federal laws concerning wages, equal opportunity, and workplace safety, as well as regulating pension funds; Energy, which manages the use and development of energy and plans for future energy needs; Housing and Urban Development, which enforces equal housing laws and administers public housing projects; and Education, which distributes financial aid to students and schools and enforces the prohibition against discrimination in education.

Most of the government's independent agencies are charged with duties that fall within the jurisdiction of more than one government branch. Although most independent agencies are small, employing one hundred or fewer people, some are much larger and employ several thousand. Some of the best-known independent federal agencies include the Social Security Administration, which employs approximately sixty-two thousand people and which is charged with administering old age, disability, and survivor insurance programs; the National Aeronautics and Space Administration (NASA), which employs approximately eighteen thousand people and is responsible for space research and exploration; the Environmental Protection Agency (EPA), which employs approximately eighteen thousand people and is charged with reducing air, water, and land pollution; and the Office of Personnel Management (OPM), which employs five thousand people and functions as the federal government's human resources division.

These agencies alone employ tens of thousands of Americans, both domestically and abroad. There are, however, dozens of other agencies performing important services for the public that do not receive the press or notoriety of, for example, the Department of Defense. The Federal Housing Finance Agency (FHFA), the Election Assistance Commission (EAC), the Government Accountability Office (GAO), and the Library of Congress, for example, are all federal agencies charged with important duties.

Federal agencies employ a wide variety of individuals with diverse backgrounds. From mainte-

Inputs Consumed by the Federal Government

Input	Value
Energy	$18.0 billion
Materials	$87.4 billion
Purchased services	$360.0 billion
Total	$465.4 billion

Source: U.S. Bureau of Economic Analysis. Data are for 2008.

nance workers to high-level executives, anyone can seek a career in civil service. The federal government is prohibited from discriminating on the basis of race, color, religion, sex, national origin, disability, or age and seeks to attract minority candidates and individuals with disabilities. Moreover, the majority of public administration positions are career positions, as opposed to temporary positions. The retirement package offered by the federal government is competitive with those offered by many private companies.

INDUSTRY MARKET SEGMENTS

Unlike private businesses, there is no ownership element associated with employment in the field of federal public administration. The government owns and controls the resources, the terms and conditions of employment, the pay scales, and the benefit and retirement packages—all of which are funded in large part through taxes. Accordingly, one individual or a private organizational entity cannot own a federal agency. Notwithstanding this caveat, there are noteworthy differences that distinguish careers in small, medium, and large federal public entities.

Small Agencies and Offices

Small agencies are generally subagencies within large cabinet departments or independent agencies that operate semiautonomously. Some cabinet departments are themselves small, relative to the overall size of the federal government.

Potential Annual Earnings Scale. Employees of the federal government are paid according to the tables established by law. Most employees are paid according to the general schedule, a system of fifteen pay grades and ten steps per grade. Each position is assigned a grade, based on a combination of job duties and the education and experience levels of an entering employee. This grade determines base pay, which is then modified by a locality bonus based on the location of the position. As of 2010, the lowest based salary on the general schedule, GS-1, step 1, was $17,803, and the highest, GS-15, step 10, was $129,517. Including the locality bonus for the Washington, D.C., area, general schedule federal employees working in the nation's

capital earned between $22,115 (GS-1, step 1) and $155,500 (GS-15, step 10). In addition, separate tables establish the pay of government executives, judges, and senior scientists and professionals. Executives, such as cabinet secretaries and other high-ranking managers, earned up to $199,700 in 2010.

Clientele Interaction. Clientele interaction varies depending on the nature of the employment. For example, a geological surveyor in Montana may have significantly less clientele interaction than a physician employed in a veterans' hospital. Generally speaking, however, the smaller the agency or office, the larger the opportunity for interaction. If there are only fifteen employees in a satellite or regional office of a larger agency, each employee may perform more duties, and there may be fewer layers of bureaucracy between the agency and members of the public that it serves.

Amenities, Atmosphere, and Physical Grounds. Buildings owned by the federal government are generally designed for efficiency, not ambiance. Often, the same federal buildings house workers from different agencies. Many federal buildings are also of an advanced age, since it takes budgetary space and significant tax dollars to permit the construction of a new federal building.

The amenities in federal buildings are standard for the workplace. For example, these structures are capable of meeting the needs of the disabled and comply with all federal and state laws relating to safety and health. Furthermore, any supplies necessary to perform a job function, such as telecommunication equipment and office furniture, are supplied by the government and are periodically replaced or updated as needed. Because the resources are owned by the government, however, there often is a request period before supplies or resources may be replaced. Money must be secured from an agency's budget to fund such expenditures. In addition, ambiance is sometimes lacking when compared with that of private businesses.

The physical grounds of a small administrative agency, or of a satellite office of a larger agency, also vary on the basis of the location and the type of work that is to be performed at the office. A rural office that acts as a call center employing ten individuals likely will need significantly less space than a veterans' medical center staffing the same number of federal employees. The physical grounds oc-

The 2010 Annual Report to Congress on the White House staff lists the name and salary of every White House employee.
(©Dreamstime.com)

cupied by the agency could consist of a freestanding building or simply a single floor of a large government-owned or -leased building.

Typical Number of Employees. The typical number of employees depends on the needs of a particular agency and the number of citizens it serves in the relevant geographic area. For example, a small federal department such as the Department of Education employs only four thousand individuals, approximately three thousand of whom work in or near Washington, D.C. A small independent federal agency such as the Office of Personnel Management employs six thousand people, only one thousand of whom are located in the capital.

Traditional Geographic Locations. Whether small or large, the agencies of the federal government must be open and accessible to all citizens. Consequently, offices are located in cities, both large and small, in every state in the country. Satellite offices may also be found in small cities and even suburbs. For instance, it is common to find

passport agencies, which fall under the jurisdiction of the Department of State, in suburban towns. Additionally, the federal government has offices, known as embassies or consulates, in foreign countries that are staffed by federal employees who have chosen to live and serve abroad.

Pros of Working for a Small Federal Office or Agency. There are numerous advantages associated with working in the federal public administration industry. First, as with most federal jobs, both the salary and opportunity for advancement are well defined. Employees are aware of when they are scheduled for raises (assuming they perform their duties well) and, because salaries are listed on a pay scale that is widely publicized, employees are aware of the specific amount of the raise they can expect to receive. Compensation usually is competitive with private sector employment. Additionally, benefits and retirement packages are extremely competitive and are often superior to those offered by many private companies. Career federal public administration jobs are secure and offer a great life-to-work balance.

A particular advantage of federal public administration employment in a small office is that the opportunity for career advancement in that particular office may occur faster than it would in a larger office with more employees and, accordingly, more competition. Some job openings are filled internally. That is, postings for a vacancy are never advertised to the general public because there are qualified employees already employed at the hiring agency. Current employees likely need less training and assistance than new employees. Consequently, working at a small office can be very beneficial in terms of compensation, job duties, salary, promotions, advancement, and the opportunity to access internal job postings within that office.

Cons of Working for a Small Federal Office or Agency. Although there are many advantages to employment in the federal public administration industry, there are also some disadvantages. First, the opportunity for financial success and professional advancement can be finite. Most public administration positions in the federal government do not offer year-end bonuses that might be found in private sector employment. Similarly, managers do not always have the discretion to promote employees or to award raises simply based on an employee's performance; because of funding restrictions and bureaucratic issues, raises and other promotions are not always given when they are deserved. Consequently, some employees may feel undervalued or underpaid.

A particular disadvantage associated with working at a satellite or rural office is that employees may feel disconnected from their agencies. Because most agencies are headquartered in Washington, D.C., employees working in the main office are likely to hear information and news first and to feel much more connected to the business of the agency, unlike employees geographically separated from the headquarters of the agency and its key employees. Moreover, unless employees are willing to relocate for another job opportunity, they may find that their future employment prospects and opportunities for advancement at satellite offices are limited.

Costs

Payroll and Benefits: The federal government pays salaries and generous benefits to most employees, according to schedules determined by law and modified by congressional action. Congress generally passes cost-of-living adjustments for all employees that increase base salaries and modify locality bonuses.

Supplies: Federal agencies require extensive traditional office supplies and equipment, but they often do not require or obtain up-to-date equipment. Computer systems and software, for example, while required by all agencies, may be relatively old and even seem obsolete by the standards of private industry. In addition to these general requirements, specialized federal agencies may require highly specialized equipment, such as scientific testing supplies or secure communications devices.

External Services: The government employs almost every conceivable job description, but it also hires external contractors as necessary to fulfill its functions and maintain budgets. For

The public can view millions of dollars being printed during tours of the U.S. Bureau of Engraving and Printing in Fort Worth, Texas, and Washington, D.C. (©Dreamstime.com)

example, the Federal Protective Service, which is responsible for safeguarding more than nine thousand buildings, directly employs only 1,225 personnel. To fulfill its mandate, the service contracts more than 15,000 additional security guards.

Utilities: The federal government is a major consumer of utilities, including electricity, gas, telephone service, and Internet access.

Taxes: Federal agencies are generally exempt from taxation.

Midsize Agencies and Offices

Midsize agencies include larger independent agencies, as well as midsize cabinet departments.

Potential Annual Earnings Scale. Employees of the federal government are paid according to the tables established by law. Most employees are paid according to the general schedule, a system of fifteen pay grades and ten steps per grade. Each position is assigned a grade, based on a combination of job duties and the education and experience levels of an entering employee. This grade determines base pay, which is then modified by a locality bonus based on the location of the position. As of 2010, the lowest based salary on the general schedule, GS-1, step 1, was $17,803, and the highest, GS-15, step 10, was $129,517. Including the locality bonus for the Washington, D.C., area, general schedule federal employees working in the nation's

capital earned between $22,115 (GS-1, step 1) and $155,500 (GS-15, step 10). In addition, separate tables establish the pay of government executives, judges, and senior scientists and professionals. Executives, such as cabinet secretaries and other high-ranking managers, earned up to $199,700 in 2010.

Clientele Interaction. Because of the diverse nature of civil service positions, it is difficult accurately to gauge the degree of clientele interaction one may expect in a midsize agency or office. However, there are positions and classifications that operate solely on the basis of direct client interaction, such as physicians' assistants at the Department of Veterans Affairs and call center employees working at the Department of Labor, who assist individuals seeking their pension.

Amenities, Atmosphere, and Physical Grounds. The nature of employment in the federal public administration industry places employees generally on equal playing fields with respect to amenities and atmosphere. Although some federal buildings may be newer than others and, accordingly, may be more aesthetically pleasing, the amenities from one office to another are substantially similar. Physicians working at veterans' hospitals are generally accorded the same medical equipment and amenities whether they are based in Minnesota or Virginia. The services that must be provided to the public, regardless of the geographic location of a specific office, require that employees be similarly situated across the country with respect to amenities.

As the size of a federal agency or office increases, so do its attendant needs regarding physical space and room to accommodate many employees. In addition to headquarters, traditionally located in Washington, D.C., midsize agencies have satellite offices throughout the country, and even internationally, in order to meet the needs of both the agencies and the public. Entire federal buildings may be devoted to a specific, large agency. Midsize agencies may share office space with one another. For example, most midsize and large cities have

The U.S. Bureau of Engraving stopped printing postage stamps in 2005, when this function was assumed by private enterprises. (©Gale Verhague/ Dreamstime.com)

federal courthouses, which staff not only judicial branch staff but also federal prosecutors employed by the Department of Justice.

Typical Numbers of Employees. A midsize federal department, such as the Department of Health and Human Services, employs around sixty thousand people, with twenty-eight thousand of those employees working in the Washington, D.C., area, leaving slightly over half spread across the country. A midsize independent agency, such as the EPA, employs approximately eighteen thousand people, but only five thousand are located in the nation's capital. By way of example, the EPA has ten regional offices in the country, most of which are housed in federal office buildings.

Traditional Geographic Locations. The EPA is a good example of a midsize independent agency. By its nature, the agency must be spread out nationally to ensure the protection and conservation of natural resources. As a result, the EPA has regional offices in Seattle, San Francisco, Denver, Kansas City, Dallas, Chicago, Atlanta, Philadelphia, New York, and Boston. It also has smaller offices for specific purposes, such as conducting laboratory and field work, in smaller cities across the United States. Other midsize federal agencies have similar structures and distributions.

Pros of Working for a Midsize Federal Agency. As with most federal agencies, midsize agencies offer competitive hours, wages, and benefits that provide employees with high standards of living. The opportunity to access internal job postings can also be extremely beneficial. They also have more offices, employees, job classifications, and opportunities for advancement than do small agencies. Regional offices are numerous and often are located in some of the most desirable cities in the United States.

Another benefit of federal administrative employment, especially in situations in which the U.S. economy is experiencing an economic crisis or recession, is the retirement incentive package, sometimes referred to as the "golden handshake." Believing that phasing out older, higher-paid employees will save the government money in the short run, government officials occasionally offer incentive packages to eligible employees, including giving them the equivalent of more years of civil service, so that their monthly retirement paychecks will be higher than they otherwise would

have been. Although incentive packages exist in the private sector, they are more prevalent in the federal government and have a direct impact on more employees.

Cons of Working for a Midsize Federal Agency. Midsize federal agencies may be more likely than others to require more resources than they are allocated. Funding for new positions or promotion opportunities may suddenly become limited if funds are allocated elsewhere. Because the federal government operates under a fixed budget, a dramatic increase in the costs of running a particular agency—and especially the creation of an entirely new agency—will result in financial cuts elsewhere.

Costs

Payroll and Benefits: The federal government pays salaries and generous benefits to most employees, according to schedules determined by law and modified by congressional action. Congress generally passes cost-of-living adjustments for all employees that increase base salaries and modify locality bonuses.

Supplies: Federal agencies require extensive traditional office supplies and equipment, but they often do not require or obtain up-to-date equipment. Computer systems and software, for example, while required by all agencies, may be relatively old and even seem obsolete by the standards of private industry. In addition to these general requirements, specialized federal agencies may require highly specialized equipment, such as scientific testing supplies or secure communications devices.

External Services: The government employs almost every conceivable job description, but it also hires external contractors as necessary to fulfill its functions and maintain budgets. For example, the Federal Protective Service, which is responsible for safeguarding more than nine thousand buildings, directly employs only 1,225 personnel. To fulfill its mandate, the service contracts more than 15,000 additional security guards.

Utilities: The federal government is a major consumer of utilities, including electricity, gas, telephone service, and Internet access.

Taxes: Federal agencies are generally exempt from taxation.

Large Agencies and Offices

Large federal agencies represent immense employers and immense bureaucracies. They include major cabinet departments, as well as the entire legislative and judicial branches of the federal government.

Potential Annual Earnings Scale. Employees of the federal government are paid according to the tables established by law. Most employees are paid according to the general schedule, a system of fifteen pay grades and ten steps per grade. Each position is assigned a grade, based on a combination of job duties and the education and experience levels of an entering employee. This grade determines base pay, which is then modified by a locality bonus based on the location of the position. As of 2010, the lowest based salary on the general schedule, GS-1, step 1, was $17,803, and the highest, GS-15, step 10, was $129,517. Including the locality bonus for the Washington, D.C., area, general schedule federal employees working in the nation's capital earned between $22,115 (GS-1, step 1) and $155,500 (GS-15, step 10). In addition, separate tables establish the pay of government executives, judges, and senior scientists and professionals. Executives, such as cabinet secretaries and other high-ranking managers, earned up to $199,700 in 2010.

Clientele Interaction. As both the size of an agency and the size of a particular office increase, so, too, does the distance between most employees and the public they serve. At the headquarters of an executive department in Washington, D.C., much more resources are devoted to discussions of key issues, as well as politics and policy concerns, than at smaller satellite offices. Consequently, key employees in these large offices may find that they do not work with the public as much as they work with members of their own agency and in conjunction with other agencies.

Amenities, Atmosphere, and Physical Grounds. Many federal agencies are headquartered in historic government buildings in Washington, D.C. The main office of the Department of State, for instance, is housed in the Harry S. Truman federal building, only a few blocks from the palatial White House. The Ronald Reagan Building and International Trade Center, which houses the U.S. Agency for International Development (USAID), among other organizations, is one of the most beautiful federal buildings, visited by over 1 million tourists annually. The atmosphere in the largest offices is typically steeped in tradition, with American flags flying and pictures of national heads of state adorning the walls. Individual work spaces for average employees, however, likely are very similar with respect to atmosphere and amenities as those contained in other federal buildings, both large and small.

Because agency headquarters and other large federal buildings also serve as tourist destinations for those wishing to see the inner workings of government, the physical grounds surrounding the properties are very well cared for. Unlike smaller, satellite offices, many of these larger buildings are on display and photographed year-round, and they host events and functions related to the government.

Typical Numbers of Employees. The newly formed Department of Homeland Security, a large federal department, employs approximately 149,000 employees, 20,000 of whom are located in Washington, D.C. Similarly, the slightly smaller Treasury Department employs 109,000 individuals, 14,000 of them in Washington. Even though these agencies are headquartered in Washington, the small size of the city makes it impossible to staff a large percentage of an agency's employees there. Rather, between 10 and 20 percent of an agency's staff is commonly housed in the nation's capital.

Traditional Geographic Locations. Most federal administrative agencies have their headquarters in Washington, D.C. It is advantageous for nearly all major government agencies—and their respective heads—to work within blocks of one another. Because much of these leaders' time is spent in meetings—not only within their own agencies but also among agencies and the different branches of government—both the financial savings and the increased efficiency of proximity are significant. In addition to their Washington, D.C., headquarters, the largest agencies have several offices spread throughout the country, and even internationally when necessary, as in the case of the Department of Homeland Security and the Department of State, for example.

Pros of Working for a Large Federal Agency. Employees fortunate enough to work at the headquarters of major federal agencies work in the heart of the government. Important policy decisions and directives are made there, and they work in the same buildings with the most important employees in their agencies. These offices are extremely large, affording many opportunities for promotion and even access to newly created positions.

Cons of Working for a Large Federal Agency. Large agencies have even higher levels of bureaucracy than smaller agencies, and employees must face significant amounts of red tape. Their size also presents increased opportunities for corruption and inefficiency. Also, jobs, pay raises, and individual work assignments may be based not solely on competence, but also on individual relationships within the agency. Additionally, it is easy to get lost in the shuffle—it certainly would be difficult for individuals to stand out and make names for themselves among the fourteen thousand Treasury Department employees working in Washington, D.C., as opposed to among only a few dozen employees working in a smaller office.

Costs

Payroll and Benefits: The federal government pays salaries and generous benefits to most employees, according to schedules determined by law and modified by congressional action. Congress generally passes cost-of-living adjustments for all employees that increase base salaries and modify locality bonuses.

Supplies: Federal agencies require extensive traditional office supplies and equipment, but they often do not require or obtain up-to-date equipment. Computer systems and software, for example, while required by all agencies, may be relatively old and even seem obsolete by the standards of private industry. In addition to these general requirements, specialized federal agencies may require highly specialized equipment, such as scientific testing supplies or secure communications devices.

External Services: The government employs almost every conceivable job description, but it also hires external contractors as necessary to fulfill its functions and maintain budgets. For example, the Federal Protective Service, which is responsible for safeguarding more than nine thousand buildings, directly employs only 1,225 personnel. To fulfill its mandate, the service contracts more than 15,000 additional security guards.

Utilities: The federal government is a major consumer of utilities, including electricity, gas, telephone service, and Internet access.

Taxes: Federal agencies are generally exempt from taxation.

ORGANIZATIONAL STRUCTURE AND JOB ROLES

Any size agency or office of the federal public government needs to account for activities in the following areas. In smaller offices, one person may fulfill more than one role. In larger agencies, specialists fulfill unique requirements in specific groups. Regardless of size and scope, all functions must be fulfilled in order for an agency to operate efficiently.

The following umbrella categories apply to the organizational structure of federal administrative agencies:

- Executive Management
- Legal/Legislative Affairs
- Information Resource Management
- Public Affairs
- Human Resources
- Facilities
- Security
- Budget
- General Administrative Employment

Executive Management

The majority of executive managers of federal public administrative agencies are presidential appointees rather than career employees. They consult with the president to help form administration policy and implement the policies of their particular administration. When administrations change, they are replaced with other workers loyal to the administration. This sets such employees apart from the vast majority of federal civil servants, whose careers span multiple administrations and who do not make policy-level decisions.

Each cabinet department is headed by a secretary, while other executive managers may have titles such as administrator or director. These executives are supported by a host of other executive employees, some of whom hold career positions.

Combined, these executives bear ultimate responsibility, both for a department's successes and for its failures.

Executive management occupations may include the following:

- President of the United States
- Cabinet Secretary
- Deputy Secretary
- Undersecretary
- Chief of Staff
- Administrator
- Director
- Deputy Director
- White House Liaison

Legal/Legislative Affairs

Legislative affairs employees and other attorneys advise department and agency heads on all legal affairs, including negotiating and drafting contracts and drafting and interpreting statutes and pending legislation. They work closely with other departments when issues arise that may directly affect both departments. For these positions, experience "on the Hill," or working with Congress in some capacity, is generally required, since employees must understand not only the rule of law but also the political realities of the legislative process. Positions in this category are very competitive. For example, the Department of State reportedly receives over one thousand applications for the position of attorney, with only twelve to fourteen positions to fill.

Legal and legislative affairs occupations may include the following:

- Legal Adviser
- General Counsel
- Attorney
- Legislative Analyst
- Paralegal
- Administrative Assistant

Information Resource Management

Federal agencies, though mostly headquartered in Washington, D.C., must have both a national presence throughout the states and an international presence globally. In addition, because the government is accountable to the people, transparency is important to government operations, and such transparency in contemporary society requires electronic reporting of relevant data over the Internet. Thus, information and communication technologies are crucially important to the efficiency and success of any federal agency.

Chief information officers and chief technology officers provide the information technology services necessary for departments to carry out their missions. In addition to installing, repairing, and maintaining many different forms of technology, such experts also ensure the security of that technology. Among several important duties, information resource managment staff help design and install telecommunications and computer systems, provide technical assistance, and perform site surveys to determine structural and technical requirements.

Information resource management occupations may include the following:

- Chief Information Officer (CIO)
- Chief Technology Officer (CTO)
- Deputy Chief Information Officer for Business, Planning, and Customer Service
- Deputy Chief Information Officer for Information Assurance
- Principal Deputy Chief Information Officer for Operations
- Policy and Planning Analyst
- Security Analyst
- Systems Analyst
- Applications Software Analyst
- Systems Administrator
- Customer Support Representative
- Data Manager

Public Affairs

Public affairs staff oversee communications between their departments and the public. They write and disseminate statements, speeches, reports, communiques, documents, Web content, and other materials to inform the public of departmental operations. They also solicit, consolidate, analyze, summarize, and respond to comments from the public. They conduct press conferences; manage department Web sites; respond to letters, telephone calls, and e-mail from the public; arrange meetings between department employees and the public; and produce and coordinate audiovisual products for use by the public and the press.

Public affairs occupations may include the following:

- Assistant Secretary for Public Affairs
- Spokesperson
- Press Secretary
- Deputy Spokesperson
- Press Assistant
- Speechwriter
- Communications Director
- Deputy Communications Director
- Electronic Information and Publications Officer
- Public Liaison and Intergovernmental Affairs Officer

Human Resources

A federal department, much like a private corporation, seeks to hire the best candidates to implement its mission. Thus, dedicated human resources departments are vital to the efficiency of any administrative agency. These departments recruit, evaluate, promote, discipline, train, and dismiss employees. They administer payrolls and benefits and set retirement policies as well. Many of these functions are administered in part by the federal government's overarching human resources entity, the Office of Personnel Management, but other functions and subfunctions are handled by individual departments' human resources employees.

Human resources occupations may include the following:

- Human Resources Director
- Program Specialist
- Human Resources Specialist

Facilities

Each department must take account of its real estate, as well as maintain and manage the construction and repair of its buildings. Accordingly, it is necessary to have a dedicated team of employees to manage facilities. Facilities employees may be involved in general maintenance, space planning (evaluating usage patterns and projecting future requirements), engineering, strategic planning (forecasting facility needs years in advance), and

contract monitoring (ensuring that services the government has contracted for are being performed). They help manage and maintain the real property owned and leased by their departments, both in the United States and abroad, and are charged with maintaining all buildings in accordance with U.S. law.

Facilities occupations may include the following:

- Building Operations Director
- Overseas Building Operations Director
- Management Consultant
- Management Officer
- Facility Manager
- Contracting Officer

Security

Of paramount importance to any agency is security, as it relates not only to safeguarding important and sensitive information but also to protecting department employees who may work in dangerous situations. Agency heads must travel to foreign countries, some of which are not considered safe for civilian travel. Their schedules must be carefully coordinated to ensure that there is no possibility of danger or surprise. Additionally, the federal buildings in the United States that house most civilian employees must be guarded against terrorist attacks, both domestic and foreign. It is necessary to staff a dedicated security department to guarantee the safe, uninterrupted operation of each agency.

Security occupations may include the following:

- Special Agent
- Security Engineering Officer
- Civil Security Specialist
- Diplomatic Courier
- Uniformed Officer/Guard

Budget

Each department must operate within a prescribed budget. Budget specialists manage the finances of their departments, collecting fees, appropriating funds, securing reimbursements from other federal agencies, planning and presenting annual budgets, and effectively managing finite resources in order to achieve important policy and political goals. Because budget concerns affect all facets of a department's operations, this is an especially important area.

Chief financial officers and several other employees plan, formulate, present, and execute all budgetary matters. Notably, each agency does not set its own budget; rather, executive agencies submit prospective budgets to the Office of Management and Budget, and Congress has the ultimate authority over all budgetary appropriations (often referred to as "the power of the purse"). Accordingly, higher-level budget positions may be very political in nature. The complex interplay among different departments, as well as between the Executive Office of the President and the legislative branch of government, makes these positions very interesting and the work very challenging.

Budget occupations may include the following:

- Assistant Secretary of Resource Management
- Chief Financial Officer (CFO)
- Director for Program and Financial Control
- Budget Analyst
- Accountant
- Budget Officer
- Financial Specialist
- Auditor

General Administrative Employment

Although each department is charged with carrying out different policies and, as a result, employs individuals with different talents and skill sets, there are certain categories of employees that are necessary to staff almost every office nationally and abroad. Administrative employees, such as secretaries, administrative assistants, and receptionists, work actively, both with fellow employees and with members of the general public who are in need of assistance.

General administrative occupations may include the following:

- Secretary
- Administrative Assistant
- Paralegal
- Receptionist
- Telephone Representative
- Customer Service Manager
- Customer Service Representative

INDUSTRY OUTLOOK

Overview

The outlook for the federal public administration industry is consistently stable. Like many private businesses, however, the federal government is not immune from global economic troubles. In fact, in 2009, President Barack Obama called for lowering the annual pay raise for most federal workers to 2 percent for 2010, down from the 3.9 percent raise that federal employees received in 2009. When the entire private sector of employment, as well as millions of homeowners, are having difficulty making ends meet, such difficulties will eventually trickle down to generally stable civil service positions.

Notwithstanding any temporary concerns with federal public administrative employment, there is statistical evidence to support the contention that the industry in general will remain stable. First, and perhaps most important, many federal workers are set to retire in the near future. The Office of Policy and Management, using employment statistics from 2004, estimated that by the end of 2010, 58 percent of supervisory employees and 42 percent of nonsupervisory employees would be eligible to retire. Not all employees will retire as soon as they reach the age of eligibility, but these statistics are encouraging because they represent the end of employment for millions born in the first part of the baby-boom generation. These positions will need to be filled by younger employees in the near future.

In total, the number of both wage and salary workers in the federal government is projected to decrease by 4.6 percent during the years 2006-2016. However, the number of positions in human resources and conservation, as well as positions for registered nurses, for example, all are expected to increase through 2016. Classifications such as "word processors and typists," which are expected to decrease significantly—by 24.4 percent—are likely representative of a trend that exists both internal and external to the federal government; that is, there simply may not be a need for as many employees in such professions anymore, regardless of whether their employment is in the public or private sector.

The BLS projects that—because of increases in office automation, as well as the fact that the federal government has begun hiring and contracting

Not all federal jobs are in buildings as impressive as the one that houses the U.S. Supreme Court. (©Ken Cole/Dreamstime.com)

with private businesses to perform office and administrative support functions—the future need for federal government employees in that specific career sector will dwindle gradually. The forecasts cannot, however, take into account exactly what the future may hold. Few would have fathomed that the United States would have the need in late 2001 to create a new agency, the Department of Homeland Security, which would quickly become the third-largest federal agency.

The BLS predicts nationwide growth across five major job categories: security, enforcement, and compliance (positions such as police officers and airport screeners); medicine and public health (physicians and similar positions); engineering and science (scientists, chemists, and veterinarians); program management and administration (positions focused on agency efficiency and performance); and business (revenue agents and tax examiners for the Internal Revenue Service). As these fields grow in the private sector, they are likely to grow in the public sector as well.

Employment Advantages

Even though specific industries within the realm of federal public administration may be declining over the long term, and despite the fact that federal jobs as a whole are projected to decrease slightly, individuals seeking rewarding careers, the opportunity for advancement, and excellent health care and other important benefits should consider a career in federal public administration. Federal jobs exist in every city in every state, in a variety of agencies. A job in federal public administration can represent either a permanent career or a source of valuable experience that functions as a stepping stone to other work.

Because of the size of the federal government and the fact that many current employees will be retiring in the foreseeable future, it is certain that there will be many job openings across the country in every agency, even in career areas that are anticipated to decrease in importance over time. Especially in times of economic uncertainty, federal public administrative employment provides a high degree of job security, largely because the federal government is not as affected by economic fluctuations as is the private sector.

Annual Earnings

The federal government does not earn money in the sense that a private company, or an individual employee, earns money. The government operates primarily through the collection of taxes from individuals and businesses. For example, in fiscal year 2007, the federal government collected $2.6 trillion in revenue. As of 2007, there were approximately 1.8 million federal civilian employees. This statistic excludes employees of the U.S. Postal Service, as well as military employees. The average annual wage earned by a federal civilian employee in March, 2007, was $65,463. Accordingly, the federal government appropriated approximately $1.17 trillion, or about 45 percent of its 2007 revenue, to pay wages for federal civilian employees.

The 1.8 million federal civilian positions comprise thirty-two aggregate job categories, which differ significantly in their respective salary expectations. For instance, the highest-earning category—attorneys—earned an average of $111,304 annually, while the lowest-earning category—nursing assistants—earned an average of $33,134. Notwithstanding any economic difficulties that may persist beyond 2010, it is expected that federal public administrative employment will continue to be stable. Whereas many workers in the private sector have been laid off, or have had their hours, benefits, or pay reduced, federal workers received pay raises in 2010 and no significant reduction in force is anticipated.

RELATED RESOURCES FOR FURTHER RESEARCH

OFFICE OF CITIZEN SERVICES AND
    COMMUNICATIONS
    1800 F St. NW
    Washington, DC 20405
    Tel: (202) 501-0705
    http://www.usa.gov

OFFICE OF PERSONNEL MANAGEMENT
    1900 E St. NW
    Washington, DC 20415

Tel: (202) 606-1800
http://www.opm.gov

U.S. DEPARTMENT OF HOMELAND SECURITY
    245 Murray Ln. SW
    Washington, DC 20528
    Tel: (202) 282-8000
    http://www.dhs.gov

U.S. EQUAL OPPORTUNITY EMPLOYMENT
COMMISSION
    121 M St. NE
    Washington, DC 20507
    Tel: (202) 663-4900
    http://www.eeoc.gov

ABOUT THE AUTHOR

Andrew Walter is an attorney licensed to practice in the state of Connecticut. He received a bachelor of arts degree in international management, with a minor in English, from Gustavus Adolphus College in St. Peter, Minnesota, and a juris doctorate degree from Roger Williams University School of Law in Bristol, Rhode Island. He served as a law clerk for the judges of the Connecticut Superior Court, and he is currently employed as an attorney at the Connecticut Supreme Court, dealing with a variety of civil and criminal matters.

FURTHER READING

Frederickson, H. George, and Kevin B. Smith. *The Public Administration Theory Primer.* Boulder, Colo.: Westview Press, 2003.

Goldsmith, Stephen, and William D. Eggers. *Governing by Network: The New Shape of the Public Sector.* Washington, D.C.: Brookings Institution Press, 2004.

Lane, Jan-Erik. *Public Administration and Public Management: The Principal-Agent Perspective.* New York: Routledge, 2005.

Morgan, Douglas F., et al. *Foundations of Public Service.* Armonk, N.Y.: M. E. Sharpe, 2008.

Office of Policy and Management. "Key Events: Ninety-six Premerit Years, 1789-1883." http://www.opm.gov/BiographyofAnIdeal/PUevents1789p01.htm.

O'Leary, Rosemary, and Lisa Bingham, eds. *The Collaborative Public Manager: New Ideas for the Twenty-first Century*. Washington, D.C.: Georgetown University Press, 2009.

U.S. Bureau of Labor Statistics. *Career Guide to Industries*, 2010-2011 ed. http://www.bls.gov/oco/cg.

———. "Federal Government." In *Career Guide to Industries*, 2010-2011 ed. http://www.bls.gov/oco/cg/cgs041.htm.

U.S. Census Bureau. North American Industry Classification System (NAICS), 2007. http://www.census.gov/cgi-bin/sssd/naics/naicsrch?chart=2007.

U.S. Department of Commerce. International Trade Administration. Office of Trade and Industry Information. Industry Trade Data and Analysis. http://ita.doc.gov/td/industry/otea/OTII/OTII-index.html.

U.S. Department of State. "Department Organizational Chart: May, 2009." http://www.state.gov/r/pa/ei/rls/dos/99494.htm

Wiarda, Howard J., ed. *Policy Passages: Career Choices for Policy Wonks*. Westport, Conn.: Praeger, 2002.

Financial Services Industry

INDUSTRY SNAPSHOT

General Industry: Finance
Career Clusters: Finance; Marketing, Sales, and Service
Subcategory Industries: Credit Intermediation; Financial Planning and Consulting; Securities, Commodities, and Other Financial Investment Activities; Tax Preparation Services
Related Industries: Banking Industry; Insurance Industry
Annual Domestic Revenues: $342.6 billion USD (Fedstats.com, 2007)
Annual International Revenues: $858 billion USD (Fedstats.com, 2007)
Annual Global Revenues: $961 billion USD (Fedstats.com, 2007)
NAICS Numbers: 5223, 523, 541850

INDUSTRY DEFINITION

Summary

The financial services industry provides financial planning, investment strategies, tax preparation, and credit consultation services to businesses and individuals. This includes the selling and trading of stocks, bonds, securities, annuities, and other financial products, as well as consultations on issues such as portfolio management and retirement planning. Specialists offer personalized advice for clients who need it or simply execute transactions for those who choose their own products. Online trading and discount brokerages have made it easier than ever for clients to act as their own brokers. Other businesses in the financial services industry include credit counseling, tax preparation, and financial planning. Banking is a major component of financial services as a whole, but is covered in depth as a separate industry. Closely related but also treated separately is the insurance industry.

History of the Industry

A rudimentary stock market existed in France in the early fifteenth century, but the earliest organized stock market dates to 1605 in Amsterdam in the Netherlands. Wall Street, the legendary seat of the American financial services industry, was built in Manhattan in 1685 and was so named because it was constructed along a twelve-foot wall erected in 1653 to protect Dutch settlers from the invading British and the local Indians. By 1790, two dozen brokers and wealthy merchants formed the Buttonwood Agreement for the purpose of trading government securities on a commissioned sales basis. The Buttonwood Agreement evolved into the New York Stock Exchange.

After the War of 1812, financial offerings grew to include bank and insurance company stocks. Railroad stocks later became available, followed by stock in corporations opting to raise capital by going public.

A major turning point in the history of this industry was the stock market crash of 1929 and the Great Depression, events that shaped that generation's conservative financial mind-set. Their children and grandchildren too often took the other path, relying on credit to live above their means. In doing so, they set themselves up for financial disaster during the inevitable economic slowdowns. This was borne out in record numbers of bankruptcies and foreclosures in the late 2000's.

Early industry leaders such as Merrill Lynch, E. F. Hutton, Abbot, and Proctor and Paine offered a full range of brokerage services that included traditional stocks and bonds, mutual funds, futures, commodities, and annuities. Charles Schwab dramatically altered the industry when he opened his first discount brokerage house.

Deregulation of the financial industry opened the door to new business opportunities, and Schwab became an industry legend. He realized that not all investors required intensive assistance in making their purchases. Many already were choosing their investments and were required to pay brokers large fees simply for executing those buys. Schwab was among the first to see the potential of that untapped market and has consistently held the lion's share of the discount brokerage market. By the 1980's, franchise brokerage companies such as Edward Jones Investments had emerged as Schwab's competitors in that market and established a presence in small towns across the country.

Technology further changed the stock and bond industry in the 1980's. Online trading became another way for individual investors to manage their own portfolios. However, while computerized trading was beneficial, it also had the potential for disaster: The marker plunged more than five hundred points on October 19, 1987, in part because of flaws in computer programs that managed trades. Safeguards have been put in place to prevent a recurrence of that magnitude.

As the United States tax code became increasingly complicated, more people turned to professionals to prepare their returns. The industry giant H & R Block was founded in 1955 by brothers Henry and Richard Bloch. The company first offered bookkeeping services to small-business owners but soon realized there was an untapped market for income tax preparation for individuals as well. H & R Block has grown to include nearly fifteen thousand outlets worldwide, more than twelve thousand of which are in the United States.

The Industry Today

The financial services industry was harder hit than most by the 2007-2009 recession. People struggling to pay their mortgages had little or no money to invest. High unemployment rates in some states, including Michigan, Ohio, Louisiana, and Mississippi, led to unprecedented numbers of personal bankruptcies and foreclosures.

The industry was further damaged by the uneth-

Wall Street in New York is the symbolic head of the financial industry. (©Dreamstime.com)

ical and sometimes illegal practices of a few of the major players. In Wall Street jargon, a "bucket shop" is a brokerage business engaged in scams and fraudulent practices. "Turning accounts" refers to the unethical practice of making unnecessary transactions on a client's behalf for the sole purpose of generating commission income for the broker. Disclosures of insider trading also tarnished the industry.

Additionally, companies such as General Motors filed bankruptcy to reorganize, making their stock certificates worthless. In doing so, the company caused unrecoverable losses to shareholders. The Enron scandal and con artist Bernie Madoff's Ponzi scheme are infamous examples of financial malfeasance, but there also have been lesser-known abuses on a smaller scale. Combined, these factors have caused an erosion of trust in the industry that will take time to overcome.

However, despite its tarnished reputation, the industry as a whole is poised for average to above average growth in the years to come. When the economy stabilizes, investors again will look for places to put their money, and stocks, bonds, mutual funds, commodities, and other financial products again will become attractive vehicles. Shareholders will continue to buy and sell, while perhaps more closely monitoring the actions of their brokers and the companies in which they own stock. The industry will survive and thrive again because it

Inputs Consumed by Securities, Commodity Contracts, and Investments

Input	Value
Energy	$1.0 billion
Materials	$5.0 billion
Purchased services	$169.1 billion
Total	$175.1 billion

Source: U.S. Bureau of Economic Analysis. Data are for 2008.

performs a necessary service. The only way to achieve significant financial growth is through shrewd investments, and those who were hurt in the recession will want to protect themselves in the event it happens again. In inflationary times, investing wisely is a way to keep from losing financial ground.

Included among the industries fueling the financial services industry today are energy, particularly alternative energy; health care; and technology. Educational and religious organizations frequently update their facilities and issue bonds to finance the process. This creates new investment opportunities. Meanwhile, investors are shying away from former blue-chip companies that needed government bailouts to weather the economic downturn. Investors also are leery of banks for the same reasons.

As investors have become more savvy, online trading has greatly expanded, as has the use of discount brokerage houses. While this cuts into the employment opportunities in traditional brokerage businesses, it creates sales service jobs in the call centers where orders are taken and executed. Despite the smaller client pool, a knowledgeable full-service broker always will be able to find and retain clients. The ones who will be hurt most are those who lack elite sales skills.

To succeed in today's leaner industry, one needs at least a bachelor's degree. A higher degree is even more beneficial in

The Contribution of Securities, Commodity Contracts, and Investments to the U.S. Economy

Value Added	Amount
Gross domestic product	$196.1 billion
Gross domestic product	1.4%
Persons employed	871,000
Total employee compensation	$199.1 billion

Note: Employee compensation is greater than total value added, because this sector experienced a net loss in gross operating budget in 2008.
Source: U.S. Bureau of Economic Analysis. Data are for 2008.

The Contribution of Funds, Trusts, and Other Financial Vehicles to the U.S. Economy

Value Added	Amount
Gross domestic product	$53.6 billion
Gross domestic product	0.4%
Persons employed	89,000
Total employee compensation	$14.6 billion

Source: U.S. Bureau of Economic Analysis. Data are for 2008.

this highly competitive field. Education alone is not enough, however. The financial services industry requires workers who have self-confidence, a positive attitude, and the ability to persevere when times are tough. The markets always will have bull (high) and bear (low) cycles, and are not for the faint of heart. The broker must plan ahead to get through the tough times. Also required is the kind of personal integrity that demands knowing a client's threshold for risk and not exceeding it. Trading in financial products always is a gamble, and the broker needs to be ever mindful that he or she is gambling with the client's money.

Occupations within the industry not directly involved with the buying and selling of financial products are less subject to fluctuations in the mar-

Inputs Consumed by Funds, Trusts, and Other Financial Vehicles

Input	Value
Energy	$0.1 billion
Materials	$0.1 billion
Purchased services	$67.1 billion
Total	$67.3 billion

Source: U.S. Bureau of Economic Analysis. Data are for 2008.

kets and the economy in general. Financial planners or advisers who do not sell securities always will find clients among those seeking sound advice on retirement planning, for example, or setting up trusts to ensure the security of their spouses or children.

Companies and individuals doing tax preparation have not been hurt by the downturn. When money becomes tight, people turn to tax preparers more than ever for help in navigating the ever-changing tax code and making sure they take advantage of all possible credits and deductions. These professionals provide a needed service and will continue to flourish in both good times and bad. Along with the tax preparation, these companies often offer financial planning and financial consulting services. Those employees work year-round, as opposed to the seasonal nature of the income tax portion of the business.

Credit counseling professionals actually can benefit from a down cycle, as more people are overextended, and often need professional help to devise a debt repayment plan while working toward future financial solvency.

INDUSTRY MARKET SEGMENTS

Small Businesses

A small financial services industry business can be a local independent business, a franchisee, or a small branch office of a corporate giant. This can include an independent financial planning service provider, a discount brokerage, a tax preparation office, or a branch office of a full-service brokerage. A small-business owner draws clientele through a visible storefront location, word of mouth, local advertising, and involvement in community organizations. It is important that the businessperson is seen as rooted in the community. He or she also will rely heavily on referrals from other satisfied clients, and may offer free lunch events or seminars to market products and services.

Potential Annual Earnings Scale. Most of a financial services company's employees are in sales and thus work at least partly on commission; it is

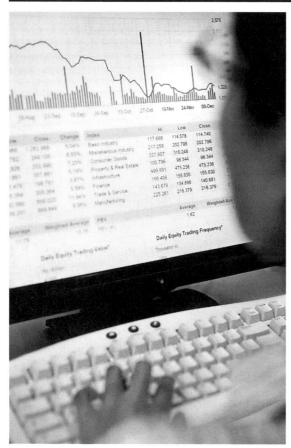

A stockbroker watches stock prices falling. (©Dreams-time.com)

difficult to estimate earnings, but they can easily exceed $100,000 per year with experience. Many earn significantly more. Support personnel can earn an hourly wage of $12 to $15 per hour or an annual salary of $20,000 to $40,000, depending on responsibilities and experience.

Clientele Interaction. In a small company or small branch of a large company, clientele interaction is high, as the only employees are those who sell financial products and a few administrative staff who also frequently interact with clients. The successful employee will be a people person, a good communicator, and able to make a good impression for the company.

Amenities, Atmosphere, and Physical Grounds. A small financial services business usually is located in a storefront building or leased office space in a professional office building or complex. Either way, it is comfortable and attractively

furnished to suggest to clients or prospective clients that the business is profitable. Because the job itself can be stressful, the serene environment also is essential for the employees.

A discount brokerage office will be more austere, to make a visual statement that the company is not getting rich at the expense of the client. By necessity, all offices will be equipped with the latest technology, as brokers need instant access to ever-changing prices and data. Desktop computers have replaced the old-fashioned ticker tape machines.

Typical Number of Employees. Usually from two to twenty-five people work in the small business, including the owner or franchisee, an office manager, sales brokers, and support staff. The smaller the office, the more these functions will overlap. Some of the administrative staff may be part time. The staff can be as small as a broker and assistant, with all the support functions handled at a corporate headquarters located elsewhere, a scenario not possible before the age of technology.

Traditional Geographic Locations. These businesses are found everywhere, from the largest cities and their outlying suburbs to the smallest towns. Financial services are needed everywhere. Businesses can be located in downtown financial district offices, small-town main streets, and suburban strip malls. Some, like H & R Block, rely on walk-in traffic and thus open offices in highly visible locations, like indoor malls and storefronts along busy streets. Companies that do most of their business by telephone often lease offices in professional buildings.

Pros of Working for a Small Financial Services Business. A small financial services company is a good fit for the highly motivated self-starter who works well without supervision. The owner of a small business has complete responsibility for its success or failure. Employees of smaller companies are able to learn all aspects of the business and gain valuable experience that can help them move on to jobs in larger, more competitive companies. Those who do best are happy to be in the thick of the action and not restricted by a narrow job description. Employers are closer to their employees in small businesses, and employees might be able to more easily negotiate flexible hours.

Cons of Working for a Small Financial Services Business. A small business, especially in the financial services industry, can be a high-stress working environment. The business in general is fiercely competitive, and economic fluctuations can wreak havoc on the industry. A small-business owner or manager works long hours and also may feel obligated to join civic organizations and volunteer in the community to create a positive image. Not everyone enjoys those activities. There is no specialization, so the person in charge must be knowledgeable about all the products offered.

Employees in a small financial services business have little chance for advancement within the company, and in time they may feel stifled. They also are likely to receive fewer benefits and earn lower salaries than workers in similar positions at larger companies.

Costs

Payroll and Benefits: Employees may be paid commissions, salaries, or an hourly wage. Bonuses often are another effective way to motivate sales employees. Benefits may include profit sharing, savings and investment plans, health insurance, vacation, and sick leave. At the owner's discretion, part-time employees may receive limited benefits.

Supplies: Supplies typically are limited to routine office supplies; computer, printer, and copier items; basic cleaning supplies; and break room supplies such as coffee for employees and clients.

External Services: These can include accounting and bookkeeping, advertising, legal, security, landscaping and lawn care, janitorial, snow removal, and the handling of routine or emergency maintenance issues. If the business is located in leased space in an office building or complex, the landlord may provide some of these services, particularly snow removal, lawn care, and security.

The Wall Street Bull is a 7,100-pound bronze sculpture in Bowling Green Park, near Wall Street. (AP/Wide World Photos)

Utilities: Small businesses in this industry need the basic utilities used by any similarly sized enterprise: electricity, gas, water, heat and air-conditioning, and telephone and electronic hookups.

Taxes: The business owner pays Social Security taxes on all employees, as well as the usual federal, state, and local income taxes. These are paid quarterly and based on projected earnings. There also may be local business or property taxes, and the owner pays personal income tax and any property taxes that are required locally.

Midsize Businesses

A midsize business, like a smaller one, is a single business, a franchise, or a branch office of a larger business. It can be a corporation, a partnership, or a sole proprietorship. These businesses are run by the owner or president, the franchisee, or the local branch manager. In large companies, managing a branch office often is a step toward further promotion and greater responsibilities in the corporate headquarters. This applies more to management than sales, as top sales producers need to stay geographically close to their clients.

Potential Annual Earnings Scale. The earnings potential at a midsize company depends on whether an employee is a commissioned sales representative or a salaried worker. Experienced sales brokers can easily earn $100,000 per year or more. Employees earn $25,000 to $65,000, depending on experience and responsibilities. Part-time clerical workers generally earn $15 to $20 per hour.

Clientele Interaction. Jobs in these companies require medium to high levels of clientele interaction. While many of the jobs require direct public contact, there are behind-the-scenes opportunities as well. Anyone involved in sales, whether directly or indirectly, needs excellent people skills. Selling intangible products requires superior sales and service skills, as well as the ability to foster the confidence of the customer.

Amenities, Atmosphere, and Physical Grounds. As in all financial product companies, the ambience should project wealth and stability and suggest the possibility of wealth for those who align themselves with the company. Tasteful decor is mandatory, and the building and grounds should be kept in immaculate condition. Employees work in comfortable, sometimes plush, surroundings, especially when clients visit regularly, as opposed to doing business by telephone or over the Internet. Here, too, the exception is the discount brokerage office, where it would be counterproductive to flaunt wealth.

Typical Number of Employees. Typically, midsize companies employ twenty-five to four hundred people in various duties involving management, sales, and administrative support. Other jobs specific to the industry include analysts who study a corporation's financial statements to determine whether it is sound for investors.

Traditional Geographic Locations. Midsize companies are found in large metropolitan areas and their suburbs, and in smaller towns as well. Financial services providers tend to gravitate toward visible locations, especially if they want to attract drop-in clients. When visibility is not an issue, well-kept office buildings are a good choice.

Pros of Working for a Midsize Financial Services Business. Employees have a greater opportunity to advance within the company than at smaller companies where there is no corporate ladder to climb. For example, brokers' assistants often are encouraged to take the classes necessary to become registered brokers so that they can legally execute transactions in a broker's absence. Some go on to become full-time brokers. A midsize business is a good arena in which to gain experience before joining a larger enterprise.

There are more categories of jobs available as midsize companies typically employ larger clerical staffs, accounting, grounds and maintenance workers, and need analysts and other workers specific to the industry. Those in salaried positions generally work normal business hours, with no need for overtime.

Cons of Working for a Midsize Financial Services Business. Those in sales positions tend to work long hours and are sometimes expected to entertain clients. They also might be expected to become active in civic and volunteer organizations in an effort to widen their pool of prospective customers. This is done on their own time. The work can be stressful in the extreme and requires persevering through hard times while dealing with disappointed or angry clients.

Jobs are more structured than in a smaller business, making it more difficult to gain knowledge of the business as a whole. Salaries tend to be lower than in larger companies, and, unless the midsize business is a branch office of a well-known company, not as prestigious.

Costs

Payroll and Benefits: Payroll and benefits usually compose the largest part of a midsize company's budget. Sales employees are commissioned, so their earnings justify the cost, as without them there would be no business. They may earn bonuses for achieving goals or exceeding quotas. Most of the workforce is on salary. Benefits usually include health insurance, vacation and sick leave, continuing education, profit sharing, and/or employer-matched savings and investment plans for all full-time employees. Part-time workers also might be eligible for limited or prorated benefits.

Supplies: Financial services businesses need all the usual office supplies and electronic equipment. They also need to stock routine cleaning and maintenance supplies.

External Services: Some services can be performed by outside contractors more cheaply than by employees. Purchased services can include legal, auditing, advertising, janitorial, snow removal, landscaping, and security. It is often more cost-effective for a midsize business to hire workers such as plumbers and electricians on an as-needed basis than to staff a maintenance department.

Utilities: Midsize businesses in the financial services industry require basic utilities such as telephone, Internet and electronic hookups, electricity, water, gas, and heat and air-conditioning.

Taxes: Owners must pay Social Security and payroll taxes on employees and submit all required quarterly statements. In addition to federal, state, and local income taxes, they must file and pay business income and any other relevant taxes. If the business is a branch office of a larger corporation, this is likely to be done by the tax and accounting specialists in the corporate headquarters, but the branch must maintain and submit accurate records.

Large Businesses

Large businesses—the industry giants—can be corporations such as Merrill Lynch, H & R Block, or Charles Schwab, or they can be a sizeable local or regional entities such as the New York Stock Exchange or the Chicago Board of Trade. These entities have instant name recognition, and their reputations make potential clients and/or investors feel confident about doing business with them.

Potential Annual Earnings Scale. Annual earnings for an experienced broker with a talent for sales are virtually unlimited. To reach this level, the individual must first earn the trust of investors with large portfolios and deliver services with complete integrity. Salaried employees from management down to the lowest-paid clerical worker enjoy earnings above the average in the industry. Top management usually receives an annual salary well over $100,000 or more, not including performance bonuses or stock options that make that figure significantly higher. At the other end of the spectrum, clerical workers can expect to be paid a minimum of $27,000 to $35,000 annually, a few thousand more than the industry average.

Clientele Interaction. This is an industry providing services to customers, so it follows that clientele interaction is high, especially for those in sales or sales support positions. Long-term success depends on personal integrity, excellent people skills, and solid product knowledge. But unlike small and midsize companies, the larger ones also provide numerous opportunities for those who prefer working behind the scenes.

Amenities, Atmosphere, and Physical Grounds. Corporate headquarters tend to be modern, with cutting-edge technology, and an ambience of wealth. They often are located in company-owned buildings, including big-city skyscrapers. Common areas, including lobbies and conference rooms, and offices visited by clientele are plush and kept in immaculate condition. Often there are no grounds to consider, but when the company is located in a campus-style setting, the landscaping also has to be flawless.

Typical Number of Employees. Large companies can employ several hundred to several thousand people in multiple locations. H & R Block, for example, operates more than 15,000 tax preparation offices, more than 12,000 of which are in the United States, although most of the jobs are seasonal. Edward Jones Investments has more than 12,000 broker offices, each of which has 200 to 300 employees. Merrill Lynch has more than 12,500 employees, while the Charles Schwab Corporation employs nearly 10,000, some in the San Francisco headquarters, others in branch offices both in the United States and abroad. The New York Stock Exchange has about 1,500 employees, and nearly 1,000 people work for the Chicago Board of Trade.

Traditional Geographic Locations. Large companies traditionally maintain a big-city presence, with satellite locations in smaller cities and in suburbs. Top sales producers usually do most of their work via telephone, so today's computer technology allows some to work in home offices with periodic visits to the office to meet with clients or management.

Pros of Working for a Large Financial Services Business. As in any industry, large companies attract those looking for upward mobility. An ambitious employee can work his or her way up through the ranks. The larger companies are more likely to provide company-paid continuing education opportunities that enable employees to climb the corporate ladder. There also is prestige in working for an industry leader. Salaries and benefits tend to be better. Should an employee need to make a geographic move for personal reasons, it often is possible to remain with the company and transfer to another office.

Cons of Working for a Large Financial Services Business. Because this is a highly competitive—even cutthroat—industry, the pressures are greater in larger companies. Those who are the most successful are likely to work fifty hours or more a week. The business also is very vulnerable to fluctuations in the economy. At a large company, management rarely takes a personal interest in employees. With a large pool of applicants eager to work for the company, marginal employees are more likely to be replaced than nurtured to reach their potential.

It is easy to get lost in the large number of employees, especially for those working in satellite locations far from the corporate headquarters, and far from the eyes of management. Top sales producers do not have this problem because their numbers give them visibility. Employees in other than sales positions may suffer from the out-of-

sight-out-of-mind problem and be overlooked for promotions.

Costs

Payroll and Benefits: Salaries, bonuses, and benefits are by far the largest budgetary item. Supplementing the usual benefits expected in any size operation, larger companies usually offer employer-paid educational benefits, and may pay for the individual broker's licenses required to do business. Company matching investment programs or profit sharing also is the norm, as are company-subsidized employee cafeterias. By offering better benefits and higher salaries, they can attract the higher-caliber workforce needed to maintain their stature.

Supplies: These companies use the same supplies as the smaller ones, but in larger quantities. Included are office supplies, printer and copier ink and toner cartridges, routine cleaning and maintenance supplies, restroom products, and cafeteria and break room supplies.

External Services: Large corporations might contract for services including legal, janitorial, landscaping, snow removal, trash removal, security, pest control, and cafeteria management. However, the larger the company, the more likely it is

Some financial products, such as mortgage-based securities, or derivatives, proved to be problematic for the financial industry. (©Dreamstime.com)

to employ people to handle the services that smaller companies choose to contract out.

Utilities: While large companies use proportionately larger quantities of electricity, gas, water, telephone, and Internet service, they essentially require the same utilities as their small and midsize counterparts.

Taxes: These companies pay Social Security, unemployment, and any other federal, state, or local taxes, along with quarterly federal, state, and local business income taxes. In addition, they pay taxes on company-owned properties and any other local taxes required to conduct business.

ORGANIZATIONAL STRUCTURE AND JOB ROLES

Every company, regardless of size, must perform some basic tasks to make sure the enterprise runs smoothly and complies with all industry regulations. In a small financial services operation the manager or franchisee will handle all or most of the responsibilities, acting as chief executive officer (CEO), securities broker, accountant, and janitor over the course of an average week. Midsize companies have employees charged with various, often overlapping duties. There is some flexibility here as the job descriptions are not as rigid as in larger corporations. Large companies have whole departments devoted to a single function, such as sales support, financial product analysis, accounts payable, or maintenance. In these companies the job descriptions tend to be exact and sometimes frustrating for an employee who enjoys a variety of tasks and new challenges. The larger the company, the more diverse job opportunities it can provide.

The following umbrella categories apply to the organizational structure of businesses in the financial services industry:

- Business Management
- Customer Services
- Sales and Marketing
- Facilities and Security
- Technology
- Occupations Specific to Financial Services

Business Management

A company's top management is charged with determining the direction a company will take, identifying its mission, and making the crucial decisions that support that mission. It establishes measurable goals and periodically tracks progress made toward achieving them. The larger the company, the more layers of management it requires to keep on track. It can be as simple as a single franchisee who does it all or as complicated as a board of directors to which a chief executive officer and/or president must answer. In that scenario, the CEO oversees the vice presidents, who oversee department managers in various areas of specialization. A vice president of finance would be responsible for the accounting, accounts payable, and payroll departments, for example.

Those who aspire to top management positions should have a graduate degree in their chosen area of specialization, such as a master's degree in finance or economics. Sometimes managers are hired from outside, but often they are promoted from within. In brokerage houses, top sales producers often are given the title of vice president, especially if they also manage a branch office. This is more than a courtesy title, as it demonstrates their value to the company and increases their credibility with clients.

Occupations in management include the following:

- Director
- Chief Executive Officer (CEO)
- President
- Vice President
- Sales and Marketing Manager
- Controller
- Human Resources Manager

Customer Services

If sales is the pulse of a financial services industry, customer services is its backbone. No financial services business could function without this department. These important members of the team hold the jobs that support the sales and marketing departments by interacting with clients and handling routine questions and problems. In the securities business, customer service employees perform the clerical duties, answer customer questions, and track sales. They serve the customer in any way that does not legally require the attention of a registered broker. In financial planning, tax preparation, and other similar companies, customer service is second only to sales and marketing as the department with the most clientele interaction. Jobs in this field require excellent communication skills, along with problem solving and attention to detail. It also is helpful to be able to multitask and perform well under pressure, as the customer service specialist often must placate disappointed or even disgruntled clients.

To obtain employment in customer services at a financial services company, one should have at least an associate's and preferably a bachelor's degree, although that is not always required. It is sometimes possible, particularly in a smaller company, to gain an entry-level position, then work up the ranks through on-the-job training or company-sponsored continuing education. A customer service manager in this industry is typically paid $50,000 to $75,000 annually, while customer service representatives receive from $28,000 to $35,000. The larger the company, the higher the salaries are likely to be, but the higher salaries inevitably come with higher levels of stress.

Occupations within the customer services department include the following:

- Customer Service Manager
- Customer Service Representative
- Order Writer
- Order Processor

Sales and Marketing

Sales and marketing are the lifeblood of the financial services industry and include multiple layers of employees, from the corporate marketing director to branch managers where appropriate, to sales representatives. Depending on the business, sales personnel also can be called stockbrokers, commodities brokers, or securities brokers. Some financial planners actually sell products such as trusts. Also included in this category are employees who sell their company's services to other businesses and individuals, including bookkeeping services, tax preparers, and credit counseling specialists.

Entry-level positions require a bachelor's degree, but those aspiring to managerial positions should also consider obtaining a master of business administration or other graduate degree. Along with at least a bachelor's degree, a broker must pass a six-hour exam to become registered to legally buy and sell securities. While formal education is the beginning, learning never stops. The markets are constantly changing, and only brokers who thoroughly understand the financial products offered and their attendant risks can successfully serve clients.

Occupations within the sales and marketing department include the following:

- Marketing Director
- Sales Manager
- Stockbroker
- Securities Broker
- Commodity Broker
- Sales Associate
- Administrative Assistant

Facilities and Security

A financial services company's offices must be maintained in a manner that suggests wealth and security. This means everything must be in good repair and immaculate. In a corporate headquarters building, a facilities manager oversees various departments, including maintenance, janitorial, security, landscaping, and in some cases even an employee cafeteria. The mail room also typically falls under the facilities umbrella. The largest companies will employ staff to cover all related needs, including licensed tradespeople. Departmental responsibilities can overlap.

In most industries, security means protecting the building, its contents, and the grounds. In a financial services business, security also means making sure sensitive data and client information are safeguarded. Although the threat of theft usually comes from outside the company, there also is the possibility of employee wrongdoing. The security officer may work in tandem with the technical staff to make sure the computer systems are not compromised.

In smaller companies, some security services may be provided by outside contractors, but someone in the company still needs to purchase those services and make sure they are performed satisfactorily. The smallest businesses will lease space in an office building that bears the responsibility for all but the office furnishings.

The complexity of the United States tax code causes many people to turn to professionals to prepare their income tax returns. (©Bruce Works/Dreamstime.com)

and in working order. Brokers must be able to depend on their computers for instant access to the often rapidly fluctuating financial data that once was transmitted via ticker tape. Computer technicians also may work with the security department to ensure that the company's computers are not compromised. Any company that deals in sensitive financial information is a target for hackers or other illegal activity.

Because computer technology is ever-changing, this department also is involved in the selection, purchase, and installation of new equipment. It is responsible, too, for training employees in the operation of the upgrades. In this and every industry there always will be jobs available for workers to create and maintain databases and for technicians to take care of the inevitable glitches.

Occupations within the technology department include the following:

- Information Technology Director
- Computer Operator
- Computer Technician

Occupations Specific to Financial Services

Motion pictures portray the trading floor of a stock or other exchange as a chaotic mix of hand signals, shouting, and general pandemonium. The reality looks pretty much the same. Everyone has a specific job and a responsibility to the clients he or she represents. Timing is key in an environment of wildly fluctuating prices.

In the financial services industry, researchers are used to study a corporation's financial statements and the stocks and bonds they offer. They calculate the risk factors, then make the results of those studies available to sellers of those products to enable them to make informed decisions for their clients. They also research companies going public and rate their financial products. When a company goes public, a brokerage house under-

An engineering degree is useful for a management position in facilities, and other workers such as electricians need to be licensed. Facilities managers earn, on average, $75,000 to $85,000 per year, while department heads under them earn less. The maintenance people earn the prevailing rate in their geographic location. When work is performed by an external provider, that company determines the pay scale.

Occupations within the facilities and security department include the following:

- Facility Manager
- Maintenance Manager
- Custodian/Janitor
- Groundskeeper
- Skilled Tradesman
- Chief Security Officer
- Investigative Personnel
- Mail Room Supervisor
- Mail Clerk
- Cafeteria Worker

Technology

These are the people who make sure all technical equipment and applications are state-of-the-art

writes the initial public offering, and that decision is made only after extensive research. All this research helps the broker advise clients on whether to buy, sell, or hold a particular financial product.

Credit intermediation specialists invest in financial products to generate earnings, and are not to be confused with credit consultants and credit counselors. A manager can earn $100,000 to $125,000 annually, while specialists start in the $40,000 to $50,000 range. Income tax preparers who work seasonally for companies like H & R Block earn on average $20,000 to $30,000. Independent tax specialists can earn up to $50,000. Income tax preparers should not be confused with certified public accountants (CPAs), who might do taxes in addition to their other work. They work full time year-round and earn considerably more.

Occupations specific to the financial markets industry include the following:

- Brokers' Assistant
- Trader
- Runner
- Product Researcher
- Credit Intermediation Specialist
- Tax Preparer

INDUSTRY OUTLOOK

Overview

The financial services industry was hard hit by the recession of 2007-2009. Multiple factors caused the industry to falter. Job losses left many people without discretionary income to invest. The stock market suffered major losses that greatly reduced investor trust. Whole industries, such as the banking and automotive industries in the United States, had to resort to federal bailouts, at great losses to shareholders. An economic turnaround will help, but it will take time to restore investor confidence. This instability was not limited to the United States; the late 2000's saw a slump affect the worldwide economy.

Despite these major setbacks, the industry as a whole is expected to experience average to above-average growth in the years 2010 to 2018. Investors still need to send their children to college, to plan for a comfortable retirement, and to strive to improve their financial situation. They will continue seeking advice from industry professionals to accomplish those goals. However, while jobs will continue to become available in financial services, there will be intense competition for every one of them. One way for a prospective employee to gain an advantage over other candidates is to work as a summer intern at a major financial services company. Familiarity with the company and its personnel can greatly improve hiring prospects, and at the very least, the intern will gain valuable experience to take to another firm.

The 2010-2011 *Occupational Outlook Handbook*, published by the United States Bureau of Labor, predicts 8 percent growth in the job market for financial managers from 2010 to 2018. A securities and commodity contracts or brokerage manager can expect $125,000 to $150,000 annually, not including significant potential performance bonuses. These jobs require postgraduate degrees. Over that period, more than 20 percent growth is expected in the field of financial analysis. Analysts and researchers will be in great demand and under great pressure to ensure that the products they recommend for sale are worthwhile. A postgraduate degree is a must, and salaries can range from $73,000 to $141,000, often with performance bonuses.

Sales agents in the field of securities (stocks and bonds), commodities, and other financial services are expected to see 9 percent growth in the job market, although some of this is attributed to unusually high turnover. Many would-be brokers fail to understand the market fluctuations and give up during the inevitable bear markets; others might not be willing to invest the amount of time it takes to become successful. A broker with a postgraduate degree can expect to earn $48,000 to $95,000 in the early years of his or her career. With experience, those earnings will increase substantially and are virtually unlimited. However, the work typically requires fifty- to sixty-hour workweeks.

Brokerage clerks represent one job category in the industry that is expected to slowly decline. They currently write orders, distribute dividends, deliver securities, and perform myriad duties that require close attention to detail. On average, brokerage clerks earn in the $38,000 range. As technology becomes more pervasive, there will be less need for the human touch in processing securities transactions.

Employment Advantages

The financial services industry is poised for growth. In the sales sector, significantly higher than average earnings are possible. Despite unfavorable publicity and cases of malfeasance, the vast majority who work in this field maintain high standards of integrity and foster trust in those with whom they do business. There still is prestige in working in the industry as well. However, these positions demand long hours, high stress tolerance, and the patience to build a solid client base over time.

Jobs in financial services are diverse. Nonprofits and companies in nearly every industry need financial experts. Brokerage houses employ researchers and other professionals in addition to those working in sales. Those who do those jobs enjoy high salaries, excellent benefits, and a comfortable working environment. The competition for jobs is fierce, so only those applicants who are best prepared will be hired. Internships and other work experience are crucial advantages for prospective employees. Another advantage for some is the income tax preparation field. Tax professionals can work from January through April and have the rest of the year to pursue their education or other career interests.

Annual Earnings

The financial services industry is greatly influenced by the state of the economy, both in the United States and worldwide. Because this is out of the control of the industry professionals, earnings can fluctuate greatly from one year to next, as clients and prospects can lose their jobs and have less money to invest. Some brokers and other industry workers are less affected by recessions and bear markets than others. They are the ones who specialize in clients who are retired, or are at a stage in life where they are not buying homes and other big-ticket items, and are thus better able to ride out the storm without changing their financial patterns.

PROJECTED EMPLOYMENT FOR SELECTED OCCUPATIONS

Securities, Commodity Contracts, and Related Activities

Employment		
2009	Projected 2018	Occupation
49,490	50,800	Brokerage clerks
62,700	74,900	Financial analysts
36,370	45,000	Financial managers
91,530	114,500	Personal financial advisors
154,540	168,200	Securities, commodities, and financial services sales agents

Source: U.S. Bureau of Labor Statistics, Industries at a Glance, Occupational Employment Statistics and Employment Projections Program.

As stated elsewhere, when the market is good, the industry as a whole offers somewhat higher earnings at all levels, and substantially higher for those selling stocks and other securities. Earnings in specific categories are addressed above, but in general industry personnel earn from around $25,000 at the lowest levels to virtually unlimited at the top. Remember, the market is cyclical, and always will be. There will also be lean years. Those on the lower rungs will not see their salaries reduced, but companies may be forced to lay off workers. Sales personnel need to put some money away to see them through the slow times.

RELATED RESOURCES FOR FURTHER RESEARCH

AdvisorOne
5081 Olympic Blvd.
Erlanger, KY 41018
Tel: (859) 692-2100
Fax: (859) 692-2000
http://www.advisorone.com

ADVISOR'S EDGE
1 Mount Pleasant Rd.
Toronto, ON M4Y 2Y5
Canada
Tel: (416) 764-3859
Fax: (416) 764-3943
http://www.advisor.ca

ASSOCIATION FOR FINANCIAL PROFESSIONALS
7315 Wisconsin Ave., Suite 600 West
Bethesda, MD 20814
Tel: (301) 907-2862
Fax: (301) 907-2864
http://www.afponline.org

BOND MARKET ASSOCIATION
360 Madison Ave.
New York, NY 10017-7111
Tel: (646) 637-9200
Fax: (646) 637-9126
http://www.bondmarkets.com

BROKER WORLD MAGAZINE
9404 Reeds Rd.
Overland Park, KS 66207
Tel: (913) 383-1247
Fax: (913) 383-1247
http://www.brokerworldmag.com

INDUSTRY TRADE DATA AND ANALYSIS
1401 Constitution Ave. NW
Washington, DC 20230
Tel: (800) USA-TRADE (872-8723)
http://ita.doc.gov

NEW YORK STOCK EXCHANGE
11 Wall St.
New York, NY 10005
Tel: (212) 656-3000
http://www.nyse.com

ON WALL STREET
1 State St. Plaza, 27th Floor
New York, NY 10004
Tel: (212) 803-8200
http://www.onwallstreet.com

ABOUT THE AUTHOR

Norma Lewis is the author of four nonfiction books, one an account of the Yukon gold rush for young adults, and the other three pictorial histories of the Southwest Michigan area she calls home. She is a prolific magazine writer. During the twenty years she has been writing, her travel articles have covered destinations, escorted group travel, solo travel, and recreational vehicle camping. Her work in children's and retirement magazines has received national awards. She holds a bachelor of science degree in business administration from Aquinas College, but left the corporate world for what she considers the best job in the world: freelance writing.

FURTHER READING

Addison, John A., et al. *Financial Services Leadership Strategies: Industry Leaders on Service Culture and the Impact of Technology.* New York: Aspatore Books, 2005.

Brighouse, David, and Janet Hontour. *Financial Services: The Commercial Environment.* Sterling, Va.: Global Professional Publishing, 2008.

Fitch, Thomas. *Career Opportunities in Banking, Finance, and Insurance.* New York: Checkmark Books, 2007.

Harvard Business School. *Guide to Careers in Finance.* Boston: Harvard Business School Press, 2002.

Mullen, David J. *The Million-Dollar Financial Services Practice: A Proven System for Becoming a Top Producer.* New York: AMACOM, 2007.

U.S. Bureau of Labor Statistics. *Career Guide to Industries,* 2010-2011 ed. http://www.bls.gov/oco/cg.

_____. "Management and Business and Financial Occupations." In *Occupational Outlook Handbook,* 2010-2011 ed. http://www.bls.gov/oco/oco1001.htm.

U.S. Census Bureau. North American Industry Classification System (NAICS), 2007. http://www.census.gov/cgi-bin/sssd/naics/naicsrch?chart=2007.

Fishing and Fisheries Industry

©Joe Klune/Dreamstime.com

INDUSTRY SNAPSHOT

General Industry: Agriculture and Food

Career Cluster: Agriculture, Food, and Natural Resources

Subcategory Industries: Aquaculture; Finfish Farming and Fish Hatcheries; Finfish Fishing; Shellfish Farming; Shellfish Fishing

Related Industries: Farming Industry; Food Manufacturing and Wholesaling Industry; Livestock and Animal Products Industry; Natural Resources Management

Annual Domestic Revenues: Fishing: $3.7 billion USD (IBISWorld, U.S. Fishing Industry Report, 2009); fish processing: $7 billion USD (Business Wire, 2005); distributing: $14 billion USD (Business Wire, 2005)

Annual International Revenues: $66.5 billion USD (GreenFacts Scientific Board, 2006)

Annual Global Revenues: $91.2 billion USD (GreenFacts Scientific Board, 2006)

NAICS Numbers: 1141, 11251

INDUSTRY DEFINITION

Summary

The fishing and fisheries industry raises and captures acquatic animals for use as food and for other applications. Fished creatures include finfish, shellfish, marine mammals, sea turtles, octopus, and squid. A variety of methods are employed to capture these creatures in the wild, from single-person angling with a hook and line to large commercial endeavors that harvest food using fleets of ships employing nets and traps. There are more than a dozen terms for different types of fishing vessels. In addition, aquaculturists raise fish and shellfish in aquatic farms rather than hunting them in open waters.

History of the Industry

The world's rivers and coasts have provided food for humans for millions of years. Scientists believe that humans began fishing during prehistoric times, perhaps 2.5 million years ago. Those early fishers might have used pieces of bone, wood, or stone to create fishhooks with fragments of bait. Archaeologists have found evidence that prehistoric European, American, and African coastal cultures gathered seafood, especially salmon and mollusks. The earliest known record of humans eating seafood is 380,000 years old. Some biologists have theorized that the human brain evolved in part as a result of diets including fish, which contain specific oils and proteins that help compose and maintain healthy brains.

While famous European cave art depicts horses and deer, ancient Egyptian art offers paintings of men hunting fish with spears and in boats. Naturally, people who lived along the shores of rivers or seas would gather what they could to supplement their diet with protein, in which fish and shellfish are rich. At some unknown point, ancient peoples discovered that fishes could be preserved in salt; salted preserved fish, such as pickled herrings and lox, is still eaten today. A related term to salting is "curing," which refers to the preservation of meat with salt, sugar, or other flavorings.

Science cannot determine when people first began using boats to fish. In South Korea, archaeologists have found a fishing boat dating from seventy-five hundred years ago, the oldest known vessel. Other ancient boats have been found in, remarkably, the desert of Kuwait, as well as in China (the world's most productive fishing nation), in Japan,

A trout hatchery provides albino and rainbow trout for stocking lakes. (©Richard Gunion/Dreamstime.com)

off the coast of Devon, England, and in the Great Pyramid of Egypt.

Fish spearing and harpooning were practiced in Europe as much as 300,000 years ago. Line fishing and netting came in later, in Mesolithic times (roughly 11,000-5000 B.C.E.). The Roman Empire, noted for its efficiency and ingenuity in a wide variety of methodologies from building and engineering to international trade, was a region successful in capturing, marketing, and distributing seafood. Increasingly sophisticated capture methods evolved during the Middle Ages in Europe: Vessels were built to larger sizes and capabilities, and fishing took place at farther distances offshore. Ecologists believe that herring and cod, two important staple fishes, began suffering from overfishing at this time. Archaeologists have found evidence that oysters and mussels formed a major part of the medieval European diet.

To offset harmful hunting, aquaculture was developed in the nineteenth century. Territoriality is an important concept in the fishing world. The United Nations Convention on the Law of the Sea, developed by scientists and diplomats, stipulates that countries own exclusive rights to their offshore resources, including fisheries, within an area extending twenty miles off their coasts. Earlier, these possessive rights had been considered to extend only three nautical miles from the coast, for an interesting reason: The Dutch legal writer Cornelis van Bijnkershoek (1673-1743) had argued that a reasonable distance for national control of the sea was the distance that a cannonball could be fired from shore.

Aquaculture farmers raise and tend fish and shellfish in inland or coastal, fresh or salty waters. Small fish farms usually use ponds or raceways (canals); larger fisheries are usually coastal. Canneries were built in the United States in the nineteenth century, although traditional methods of processing and packing seafoods predate the settlement of the Americas.

The Industry Today

As of 2009, there were an estimated 250 million fishers in the world (most in Asia, particularly China). Members of the fishing industry vary in size, from single-person or small-family efforts to large corporate endeavors. The largest aquatic resources remain along marine coasts and the high

An ocean salmon farm in Maine. (AP/Wide World Photos)

seas—the most productive areas being the Pacific Northwest, the Pacific Southeast, and the Atlantic Northeast—while poor peoples in many parts of the world still rely for food on rivers such as the Nile, Mekong, and Amazon.

Developed nations have fleets of ships as large as football fields on which commercial fishers use electronic equipment and satellite communications to track fish. As these vessels have enormous freezers to store tons of "catch" (the professional term for seafood that is harvested), employees may live onboard for six months. As of 2010, the industry harvested hundreds of billions of creatures every year, more than any other industry.

Industry followers estimate that the U.S. fishing and seafood industries consist of about twenty-five thousand commercial fishing vessels (mostly independently owned), seven hundred fish processors, and twenty-eight hundred distributors. Their total commercial value is approximately $14 billion. Most companies are privately held or are divisions of larger corporations.

International fishing efforts saw a dip in production and profits during the first decade of the twenty-first century, although fishing remains a flourishing business. In 2008, Ichiro Nomura, the assistant director-general of the Food and Agricul-

ture Organization of the United Nations Fisheries and Aquaculture Department, announced that the steadily growing endeavor of seafood farming would soon contribute half of the seafood consumed by humans worldwide. Aquaculture employees have, for many decades, tinkered with optimal food for the fishes they nurture. Nutreco Holding NV is the world's largest manufacturer of fish feed, and in 2009, it succeeded in replacing the normal predatory diet of salmon with soy foods and other vegetable-based products. This substitution made possible a significant reduction in business costs for fishery farmers, as fish feed makes up about 60 percent of the total cost in salmon farming alone. Scientists predict that future experiments with feed will greatly help the world's aquaculture economies, although such a radical change in salmon's diet necessarily also alters its nutritional content for consumers.

Fisheries are theoretically renewable resources, but countries around the globe report overfishing, in which fishers take such big catches that they deplete neighborhood stocks. The U.S. National Oceanic and Atmospheric Administration (NOAA) reports that, at the end of 2008, the number of threatened, endangered, or depleted protected species had reached twenty-four, a grim statistic.

This might not sound large, considering that the United States alone is estimated to have more than seven hundred different commercial species, yet it is a troubling figure.

A related concept is sustainability. Sustainability was defined in 1987 at the World Commission on Environment and Development as development that meets the needs of the present without compromising the ability of future generations to meet their own needs. Hunting a marine species to extinction can have dire and unpredictable results, and coastal nations exert efforts to prevent overfishing.

A small fishing boat off the coast of Alaska. (©Joe Klune/Dreamstime.com)

Every country with a fishing industry has enacted legislation concerning fishing. An important concept is "illegal, unreported, and unregulated" (IUU) fishing. This refers to fishing activities that violate national or international laws or rules, which were defined in 2007 by NOAA as follows:

(A) Fishing activities that violate conservation and management measures according to an international agreement, including capture limits or quotas, capacity restrictions, and bycatch (that is, marine animals caught unintentionally) reduction requirements;

(B) Overfishing; or

(C) Any fishing activities that endanger undersea mountains ("seamounts"), hydrothermal vents ("fumaroles"), and coral reefs.

In 2007, the NOAA spent $84.8 million on its Law Enforcement and Observers program, as well as $327 million on its Fisheries Research and Management program and $163.8 million on its Marine Mammal and Endangered Species Research and Management program. These numbers suggest how seriously the administration takes its regulatory responsibilities.

In the United States, federal laws regulate fishing in all U.S. territories, while other rules vary from state to state. For example, in 1994, in order to protect several species suffering bycatch status, Amendment Three of the Florida Constitution, otherwise known as the "net ban," outlawed the use of entangling nets in Florida's waters and restricted the use of other forms of nets, such as seines and shrimp trawls. The amendment was considered a pioneering measure and was enacted by a popular referendum. The law damaged the profits of fishers in the short term but favored the preservation of local renewable resources.

Climate change is another hazard for fishery stocks. The melting of the polar ice caps leads to warmer water and greater acidity in the oceans. Warm-water areas are becoming warmer, which leads to changes in fish behavior and to damages to coral reef ecosystems. Fishes in tropical and equatorial regions have begun to migrate northward and southward toward the poles, where they become invasive species. Fishing communities in these regions may find that their local hatcheries are decreasing, while fishers in colder climes must deal with the unpredictability of species behavior when invasion occurs. Extreme weather events, such as hurricanes and flooding that may be caused by climate change or by earthquake, jeopardize the lives and livelihoods of all people who work outdoors in the regions affected. For example, the devastating Indian Ocean tsunami of 2004 harmed fishing operations in fourteen countries for more than a year. In 2010, a catastrophic oil spill in the Gulf of Mexico endangered the livelihoods of thousands of Gulf Coast fishers, seafood restarateurs, and tourism companies; that region is home to one of the largest seafood industries in the United States, second only to Alaska.

After seafood is captured from fisheries or wild stocks, most of it is processed. Three stages of processing are handling (the initial stage of processing), packing, and manufacturing related products, such as fish oil, clam sauce for pasta, and pet food. The beginning step of processing can occur at sea—if the vessel contains a workroom with the proper tools and refrigeration—or at fish processing plants.

Processing companies of all sizes employ people as handlers: They sort, clean, cut, eviscerate, and scale (remove fish scales) or shuck (remove mollusk shells). The next step is to dress the products, which can include salting, filleting, blanching, precooking, spicing, and breading. Seafood may be preserved with salt and spices or by drying, smoking, or pickling in brine. Aquatic products may be delivered to grocery stores, restaurants, wholesalers, exporters, or directly to the public as fresh, canned or frozen fish, whole or filleted, as caviar, fish oil, or fish meal.

The popularity of seafood restaurants remains on the rise, as seafood is considered to be healthful. The United States is the world's third-largest consumer of seafood and related products. As of 2010, statisticians listed about four hundred seafood companies in the United States.

INDUSTRY MARKET SEGMENTS

Businesses in the fishing and aquaculture industry range in size from small, family-owned endeavors to larger, perhaps recreational businesses to vessels weighing over a hundred tons and employing several dozen employees. Ever-growing mariculture fisheries produce many millions of tons of

In 2010, a catastrophic oil spill in the Gulf of Mexico endangered the livelihoods of Gulf Coast shrimpers. (©Rimas Zilinskas/ Dreamstime.com)

seafood annually. Following the processes of harvesting, the industry proceeds to those devoted to preservation, delivery, and marketing, whether to seaside-dwelling individuals or to large chains of grocery stores, restaurants, and other purchasers (such as pet food manufacturers). The following sections provide a comprehensive breakdown of each of these different segments.

Small Businesses

Potential Annual Earnings Scale. The average earnings for a small fishing business, which is called an artisanal fisher business, vary from region to region, from subsistence level to feeding the family with some profit left over. It is impossible to announce average earnings from self-employed fishers in developing countries, as most of them do not report reliable income, if they report any at all. In the United States, the scale depends greatly on whether the fisher is working full time or seasonally, on the size of the crew, and on the capabilities of the vessel. The range can be between $16,000 and $40,000, taking those variations into account.

Clientele Interaction. Fishers meet consumers at the point of sale, for the most part. The market chain varies depending on the size of the catch, on whether the fisher has access to refrigeration, and on the distance to production centers and ports. In many parts of Africa, for example, after the fishes are caught, they will be dried or smoked to offset the roughly 30 percent of losses caused by insecure preservation methods. Small producers can sell their catch within their communities, usually in an open-air market or by home delivery.

Amenities, Atmosphere, and Physical Grounds. Artisanal fishers can boast of few amenities. In developing countries, the fisher works on a small boat, often entirely open-air, and thus is subject to the vagaries of the weather, as well as sunburn and other injuries, minor or major, depending on the size of the crew, which might be a single person or a two- or three-member crew. In developed countries, where a vessel plying coastal waters might have a modest dinghy (a small vessel with or without a sail, and with or without a covered area for a bridge), it will probably be made of sturdier materials than local wood and therefore less likely to risk capsizing or basic problems such as wood rot. Small-time fishers include the wealthy who

crew yachts, which offer more comforts; they might seek a catch chiefly for themselves but might also be small-time, local seafood vendors.

Typical Number of Employees. As in agriculture, most small fishing businesses employ fewer than six workers. Usually only one or two people work together on all aspects of the job. Unpaid family members make up a significant part of the business, such as handling and preparing the seafood for market. Most unpaid family workers assist with the fishing, but a small number might keep track of income and expenses or aid in selling the daily catch.

Traditional Geographic Locations. Fishing occurs wherever there is an intersection between human settlements and the sea; even landlocked countries may have fishing communities if they contain rivers and lakes. Fishing communities have a fascinating and picturesque variety: from the busy boatbuilding Village of Riverton, a community of about six hundred people on the banks of the Icelandic River in Manitoba, Canada, to guided trips for hunting large peacock bass on the Amazon River in Brazil to the courtyard houses of coastal fishing villages in Taiwan and many thousands more.

Pros of Working for a Small Fishing Business. Fishers work in their local fisheries or aquaculture facilities, so they have knowledge of the neighborhood resources. They know the behavior of the fishes, or the location of shellfish, and they know what to expect from the weather and seasons. No formal academic requirements exist. They acquire occupational skills on the job, many as members of fishing or farming families. Most workers employed in fishing can return to their homes at the end of the workday. They can set their own hours and work as much or as little as their ambition demands. They can oversee all aspects of the operation from capture to sale, and will usually be acquainted with their buyers.

Cons of Working for a Small Fishing Business. Fishing offers some of the most hazardous conditions to be encountered in any profession. Many fishers cannot fish daily but must rely upon seasonal conditions. Lobster fishers in Maine, for example, may reap large profits in one month but work only half the year. The work itself may be arduous and demanding, so fishers must be healthy and strong.

Costs

Payroll and Benefits: Small and subsistence-level fishers, especially in developing countries, do not need payroll offices as such. Sickness or other down-time factors result in no income. Job benefits may be meager or sporadic for the self-employed; as a rule, these jobs are not unionized, and workers must plan for their own futures. Deckhands are generally paid a percentage of the boat's catch.

Supplies: Fishing can require little more than a pole and hook or a net; even these are not necessary for the person who can harvest oyster reefs or dig for clams. In developing countries, fishing is often done from a small-draft boat, or a boat with little distance between the waterline and the keel. The small-business fisher might use rods, reels, hooks, lures, bait, fishing lines, or floats.

A seiner with a few crew members will tug a seine net behind it and use a power block (a specialized winch) to hoist its catch onto the deck; a trawler uses a trawl net. In the United States, even small vessels usually have sophisticated electronic sensing equipment that works in conjunction with sonar or echo sounding to inform fishing captains when fishes are present in the net, the species of the catch, and its size. Fishers also use navigational devices such as Global Positioning System (GPS) technology. They also have kitchens and refrigeration.

External Services: Small fishing businesses may require no external services or the occasional help from family or friends. In developed countries, a captain may seek an intermediary to process or sell the catch.

Utilities: At the artisanal level, a fisher might work from a simple dory or from a cruise or sail boat containing basic materials such as directional devices (maps and compasses) and ice coolers for preserving the catch on the return to port. An onboard computer and radio can be life-saving.

Taxes: Statisticians cannot provide global figures for taxation of small fishing businesses; in developing countries, taxes might be paid at the state or province level and at the federal level.

Midsize Businesses

Potential Annual Earnings Scale. Income varies greatly around the world, and the variables include the size of the catch (most fishers and industry employees earn a percentage of the revenues made from voyage to voyage), the local, national, or international market price of seafood, and the captains' discretion. As a rule, when fishers return to shore and sell their catch, the captain takes half of the earnings. He or she will have made a deal with the crew members, at the point of hiring, to share the monetary proceeds at a certain percentage (usually 10 percent, but it varies).

As of 2008, American fishers earned a median annual wage of $27,950; the least successful earned about $16,080, and the more successful earned between $33,580 and $45,930. The seasons are crucial to fishers: They normally earn the most in the summer and fall and the least during the winter, except in far northern climes. Alaskan crab fishers can earn as much as $20,000 to $40,000 per month during the peak season, though this is not the typical income. Fishers who live on ships for days or weeks are given free room and board, reducing their living expenses.

Salary ranges vary greatly depending on the responsibilities of the job: A beginning aquaculture employee might earn about $17,000 annually for taking care of fish and for cleaning and processing, whereas a marine biologist specializing in oceanography can earn between $55,000 and $100,000 per year. Workers in processing plants are usually paid by the hour, and with overtime and bonuses can earn up to $800 to $1,000 per week during the peak season.

Clientele Interaction. Fishers may collaborate with processing plants onshore, with wholesalers, with marketers and sales personnel, and with exporters; they may deal directly with onshore fish markets or with restaurateurs with whom they are personally acquainted. They must report catch statistics to regulatory agencies.

Amenities, Atmosphere, and Physical Grounds. Midsize fishing businesses' employees have a fairly happy situation, happier than that of artisanal workers—especially if they are in command of their vessels. Deckhands are expected to work hard and long hours, and they often retire at the end of the day to a section of the ship in which they share bunks with their crewmates. The working day might not be the normal nine-to-five hours of the landlocked civilian, either; if the call comes that a good fishing ground has been discovered in the middle of the night, then crews are expected to wake and report quickly to the deck and be ready to handle whatever job is before them, even if it is raining and they are relying on lamps and searchlights. If the sea waves are rolling high, it can be risky to work on deck. However, hundreds of biographies and autobiographies testify that morale remains high, and pride and camaraderie grow after particularly dangerous trips to sea. A person seeking a place on a midsize fishing vessel might complain, during the trip, about the crowded conditions, the few bathing facilities (if, indeed, there are any), the lack of variety in prearranged meals (which are mostly canned), and other perceived incivilities. However, in the United States and other countries, crews are likely to have showers, television, Internet connections, and some free time to enjoy them.

Typical Number of Employees. There really is no typical number of employees of midsize businesses. Each ship has a captain and is likely to have a first mate who assists the captain and who is responsible for the vessel when the captain is off duty. Boatswains supervise any number of deckhands, from a couple to a couple dozen.

Traditional Geographic Locations. The midsize fishing operation is most likely to be found in the developed world, especially in the United States, Europe, Australia, and many South American and Asian countries. Fishing takes place on ships rather than boats, though the size of the ship can vary. The Food and Agriculture Organization of the United Nations states that, in the twenty-first century, about 4 million commercial fishing vessels are reported to be in business. The sponge business is healthy in Florida.

Pros of Working for a Midsize Fishing Business. Fishing captains own their own vessels and can set their own hours. Workers hoping to move to a larger business can gain invaluable experience and expertise. Often, a captain will pay employees a basic wage as well as a percentage of the profits; the industry is similar to bartending and waiting tables in this regard. Ambition is well rewarded, and camaraderie is highly valued. Usually, just like any office workers, employees can return home at the end of the workday.

Cons of Working for a Midsize Fishing Business. The fishing industry is second only to timber-cutting in risk to life and health. More than four hundred commercial fishers died on the job between 1999 and 2008 in the United States alone. U.S. fatalities in the twenty-first century average 71 per 100,000 workers, with drowning the most common cause of death. Fishers and crabbers usually share quarters, up to six in a room. Work is risky because of slippery decks and high seas; crewmembers might be swept overboard; an overloaded ship can capsize.

Many fishers work sixteen-hour days, five days a week. The weather can be extreme and can be very cold in the Northern Atlantic and Northern Pacific, especially when the peak season for a given species falls during the winter (as it does for Alaskan crabbers). Handling and processing the catch is monotonous and can also be dangerous.

Costs

Payroll and Benefits: Fishing captains and crew members agree before each job on the terms of contracts that specify the percentage of profits that will be paid to each worker. Captains or vessel owners take the lion's share of the profits, but they are responsible for such expenses as maintenance of the vessel and the tools onboard, fuel, repairs, replacement of gear, licenses, fishing permits, and insurance. The income varies between crew managers and deckhands; bonuses might be handed out for hazardous duty or for overtime. A major benefit is that employees are often friends or family members who enjoy working together.

Supplies: Deckhands bring their own clothes, boots, and wet-weather gear, so they spend a few hundred dollars before leaving port. The vessel owner provides the safety equipment required by the Coast Guard and might charge the crew a percentage of the fuel, food, and other operating expenses. Deckhands purchase their own fishing licenses.

A midsize fishing endeavor will use vessels such as sixty- to seventy-foot-long launches powered by outboard motors or by inboard engines. The vessel should have a container for ice or chilled seawater, such as a cooler, fish hold, or refrigerator. Fishers who leave the shore will need vessels with fishing gear, such as lobster traps, nets for trawling shrimp, or seines for capturing finfish.

Navigational aids, such as GPS and charts, are

crucial, as are communication devices such as the radio. The deckhands may be responsible for operating oceanographic sensors, sonar, conductivity-temperature-depth systems, and other devices. Every crew member should wear a life jacket and know how to ready a life raft and use a first-aid kit in case of emergency.

Processing can occur onboard or onshore. Handling and processing supplies can include rendering devices such as handheld or automatic knives for gutting and filleting; band saws for cutting large frozen fishes; and salt-packing boxes, jars, or cans, though the latter requires a factory for canning, whether a commercial cannery or a community (or shared) kitchen. Smoked fish is produced by hanging the cleaned, cured, and dried fish above a woodsmoke fire in a room or building known as a smokehouse.

External Services: Sale of catch might occur at a neighborhood farmers market or even directly at the harbor where the vessel docks. The handling and processing of products is performed by the employees onboard, at seaside fish-chopping benches and tables, or at their homes or community factories such as canneries. Depending on the usual size of the catch, the captain might work with a repair facility, equipment sales and service, marine electronics, truckers, an exporter, or a marketing agency.

Utilities: Most vessels use power generators to provide electricity, sewerage, and security. They enjoy potable water, home- or ship-cooked food, television, shower stalls, and lodging for anywhere from days to weeks without the costs of usual onshore living expenses.

Taxes: In the United States, taxation on midsize fishing businesses varies from state to state; fishers may face both state and federal taxes, as well as sales taxes. Statisticians cannot supply a reliable number for worldwide tax figures.

Large Businesses

Many countries own fleets of enormous ships that serve as home to their crews for weeks or months. They ply the high seas, the ships have up-to-date amenities, and global production (annual size of the catch) is measured in the billions of tons.

In the area of seafood processing and distribution, U.S. industries are estimated to consist of about 650 processors and about 2,500 distributors;

they handle fresh or frozen fish and shellfish, as well as canned seafood. Other companies produce and sell related products, such as fish oil and pet food.

Potential Annual Earnings Scale. The earnings of large-scale fishing employees vary greatly, depending on the position, the company, experience, and benefits, as well as the geographic location of the business. As a rule, the larger the catch, the larger the paycheck. In 2010, the average salary estimated by various sources was between about $27,250 and $44,000 for fishers and fishing-industry-related positions. During peak seasons, even deckhands can earn $80,000 to $100,000 in a six- or eight-month workyear. Even entry-level factory trawler fish processors might earn $30,000 to $40,000 in six to eight months, depending on the size and species of the catch.

Clientele Interaction. With over ten thousand national seafood restaurants and hundreds of thousands of general restaurant chains that offer seafood, there are plenty of clients eager to buy shrimp, finfish, lobsters, clams, and other seafood. The catch is usually transferred to a processing plant or to a distributor, depending on whether it is processed out at sea or sold in whole form. Major companies such as Bumblebee Foods and StarKist rarely interact with civilian consumers face-to-face, even when shoppers are familiar with the brand names.

Amenities, Atmosphere, and Physical Grounds. The largest commercial fishing vessels use widely mechanized processes, and while their crews are subject to environmental conditions, they work among more comfortable living conditions than their colleagues in smaller businesses, as most of their ships are covered rather than exposed to the weather. Because a ship may remain months out at sea, it is in the captain's interest to ensure that conditions are as safe as possible in this dangerous profession. Crewmembers can enjoy many of their favorite pastimes during off-hours, as they would at home.

Seafood farms have traditionally operated inland or in coastal areas, which is certainly easier than wild-fishing, but twenty-first century entrepreneurs are discovering the advantages of using large pens in the open seas. The expenses caused by waste, pollutants, diseases, antibiotics, and other environmental disasters are obviated, and it is not necessary to monitor offshore cages on an hourly or daily basis.

Typical Number of Employees. Giant factory trawlers employ crews of over a hundred workers. Employers in the offshore fishing industry include giant floating processors (which process but do not catch fish) and tenders (which deliver fish to land and to offshore processors). There are also a number of "factory" or "catcher/processor" vessels that both capture and process fish at sea.

Traditional Geographic Locations. Large corporate businesses have fleets of ships and can voyage to great distances from coastlines, into the high seas. Alaska has held the title of the most productive fishing state since 1975, even though it competes with the much larger East and West Coasts. While Florida enjoys the most seafood restaurants, it is also a preferred destination for tourist and recreational fishers rather than huge businesses.

Pros of Working for a Large Fishing Business. Jobs at large companies can be very lucrative, for both fishers and fish processors, and there are always openings for young, energetic employees. Working for a few months out of the year allows employees to enjoy other work during off-peak seasons. Many positions are open to beginners who have studied merely two years at vocational schools, which offer hands-on experience. A wide variety of community colleges and universities offer courses in seamanship, vessel operations, marine safety, navigation, vessel repair and maintenance, and fishery technology. The U.S. Coast Guard also offers training courses. For fishers who enjoy teamwork, the camaraderie and morale can be high.

Many seafood farms also use state-of-the-art technologies (such as water purification and recycling of resources) and may enjoy the umbrella of government or other financial grants and tax incentives. Successful aquaculturists can produce hundreds of tons of seafood annually at a single fishery.

Cons of Working for a Large Fishing Business. Fishing is a grueling and potentially hazardous business, even on a large, technologically advanced ship. The high seas court the dangers of large waves and bad weather. Every vessel, small or enormous, has an open deck where employees do most of their labor, and large waves and wet decks require that deckhands use caution and look out for one another, in case someone is swept off-board.

Fish processing, with its use of knives and saws for slicing, gutting, and filleting, also carries risk of harm, even accidental amputation. It is a cold, wet, and monotonous job; these employees must remain alert at all times. If on-the-job injuries occur, the crew member must make do with what first aid the crew has to offer.

The industry is seeing aging in the workforce and difficulties with recruitment and retainment of younger workers. Fishers and crabbers usually share quarters, up to six in a room. Those who work on the sea for extended periods of time may miss their families.

Costs

Payroll and Benefits: The captain, vessel owner, or holding company manages payroll and determines benefits. Paychecks might be written for weekly or for monthly wages, depending on the company; usually, wages are paid out some time after the catch has been brought to its destination.

Supplies: Large fishing vessels have refrigeration equipment, factory freezer trawlers, and fish-finding equipment, including sonar, radar, temperature-probing equipment, night vision apparatuses, on-board computers, and many other systems and devices built in during the process of shipbuilding. These must be maintained and, perhaps, repaired. Survival suits, life rafts, and fire extinguishers are required. The U.S. Coast Guard supervises and regulates safety and security precautions. Every ship must carry an emergency position indicating radio beacon (EPIRB) in case the crew must radio for help, as well as medical kits that carry more than the usual first aid: antibiotics, morphine, and sutures.

External Services: Factory floaters are able, with their large crews, to do enormous amounts of work onboard; aquaculturists have also become technologically sophisticated in the last few decades. The At-sea Processors Association, to name just one, operates about twenty catcher-processor vessels. Still, they have market chains between catch and civilian shopper; the captains and crew think globally rather than locally. They might hire planners, marketers, wholesalers, exporters, retailers, and ecolabelers.

Utilities: Factory floaters and other very large industrial fishing ships come equipped with all of the utilities one would expect in an onshore business: computers for the leaders on the bridge and good amenities for the crew, including Internet service, television, shower stalls, and online or real-life activities for down-time workers.

Taxes: Taxation varies from the captain to the last person listed as deckhand or greenhorn. Legislation has been proposed that would provide a 75 percent tax credit for the purchase and maintenance of the numerous pieces of safety equipment needed on the average commercial fishing vessel.

ORGANIZATIONAL STRUCTURE AND JOB ROLES

Because the fishing and aquaculture industries vary widely from country to country and from community to community, it is difficult to provide an average picture of the business. The lives of the subsistence-level fishers in Africa are very different from the lives of American fleet captains. Civilian career opportunities, for students and apprentice fishers, usually begin at the deckhand level. Even the newly hired can earn promotions after only months of experience, depending upon their skills and ambition. The U.S. Coast Guard regulates requirements for experience, as well as physical and academic status. Those who want promotion can find satisfaction in learning the skills necessary for such departments as engineering, navigational, or supervisory positions on the bridge. The Department of Commerce, NOAA, and the Office of Marine and Aviation Operations offer a variety of fishing industry jobs in the Pacific Fleet; the Pacific Ocean is the region of most fishing operations.

The following umbrella categories apply to the organizational structure of businesses in the fishing and fisheries industry:

- Bridge
- Engineering
- Galley
- Factory/Processing
- Quality Assurance
- Distribution
- Sales and Marketing
- Surveying

Bridge

The hierarchy on a fishing vessel may take many forms, depending on its size. The bridge is run by the captain, who is responsible for the safety and actions of the crew and for decision making. The captain decides where to fish, maintains the ship's log, sets the course of the ship, commands the helm, and is responsible in the event that it is necessary to signal other ships. At the end of the trip, the captain determines where and how to return to port and is responsible for avoiding reefs, shoals, and other potential dangerous waters. The captain must be licensed by the U.S. Coast Guard.

Depending on the size of the vessel, there may be first mates and second mates, who are the highest executives after the captain. They help in supervising the crew and the overall good shape of the ship.

The boatswain is a position of power, as it is the supervisory controller of the deckhands. The boatswain (also known as and pronounced as bos'n) collaborates closely with the captain and first mate in decision making, but is basically in charge of the nets, tools, and other fishing devices on the deck. The decision to find the best area for fishing is shared between the captain and the boatswain, and the boatswain oversees the maintenance and use of nets and weights and other gear. Boatswains require a lot of experience, but if they excel, they are in line to earn the positions of second mates, first mates, and captains.

On a large ship there will likely be a purser, who serves a great variety of functions. Pursers enjoyed a bit of glamour and fame with the 1977 launch of a television program called *The Love Boat*; the purser was a popular character. Rather than facilitating romantic escapades, however, pursers on fishing vessels have the pragmatic jobs of maintaining payroll records and cargo manifests and paying crew members when a trip is over, as well as working as liaison to various government agencies in the form of delivering lists of crew member names. On a cruise ship, the purser is responsible for the passengers, but in any case he or she is in charge of the finances. This position fulfills the duties of human resources, as well: recruitment and retention of workers, seeking the best technologies and customer service, and related tasks.

According to the NOAA Workforce Management Office, a vessel's deckhands are responsible for maintaining the ship's exterior and interior spaces; maintaining and operating deck machinery and fishing gear; mooring and anchoring the ship; handling equipment; and standing watches. They may also build, rig, and maintain mission-related shore-side facilities such as electronic navigation towers, tide gauges, and visual stations. The deck department's crew includes the ordinary seaman (this job title includes both women and men) or the general vessel assistant, the able seaman deck utilityman, and the seaman surveyor. This unlicensed profession accepts high school graduates who are interested in the industry.

Bridge occupations may include the following:

- Captain
- Mate
- Boatswain
- Purser
- Deckhand
- Greenhorn

Engineering

According to the NOAA Workforce Management Office, a vessel's engineer is responsible for operating all of the ship's engineering systems, such as propulsion, fuel, electric power, refrigeration, ventilation, air-conditioning, and sanitation; maintaining all engineering systems in the ship and its boats; providing general engineering support for all departments and ship operations; maintaining inventories of equipment, tools, parts, and consumable supplies; and preparing a fueling plan and conducting fueling operations. Assistant engineers stand watches as the engineer in charge, direct the activities of assigned engineering watch personnel, and maintain and repair the engineering systems. These positions require a license.

Related, unlicensed positions include the fireman, the oiler, the engine utilityman, and the junior engineer, all of whom are responsible for making sure that the vessel and its employees work under safe conditions. The oiler and fireman take care of the heavy propulsion machinery. The junior engineer has usually had working experience in the roles of oiler or fireman, and must know how

to operate and repair auxiliary equipment. Applicants for these positions usually have to show working experience, but sometimes college course work in mathematics, various sciences, mechanical drafting, and mechanics can stand in stead of previous experience.

Engineering occupations may include the following:

- Chief Engineer
- Assistant Engineer
- Electrician
- Oiler
- Refrigeration Engineer/Cooling System Operator

Galley

The galley is the kitchen of a vessel. Before the vessel leaves port, the stewards go shopping for provisions. The chefs, or stewards, are responsible for planning, preparing, and serving healthy meals. They also maintain the galley, the messes (where crew eat together), storage areas, living areas, and other areas assigned in the contract and make sure these areas are neat and sanitary. Other tasks might include providing clean linens and other supplies that the crew needs.

This department does not require licensing but may require general experience gained onboard or in a restaurant, and/or education in a culinary school.

Galley occupations may include the following:

- Chief Steward
- Chief Cook
- Cook/Baker
- Second Cook
- Galley Assistant
- Housekeeper

Factory/Processing

The factory/processing department is operative only on a floating factory or other ship that includes a processing plant. The manager has a variety of responsibilities, including directing the processing plant or, alternatively, delivering seafood to and serving as a liaison with buyers who will process the products.

The manager is in charge of payroll and other payments relating to supplies, equipment, and other expenses; this position works with the captain in human resources activities such as supervising employees and ensuring that the vessel's procedures and equipment are the best possible.

Factory foremen (also known as fish processing supervisors) train and supervise employees in cleaning, eviscerating, and preparing fish for packing or canning. These supervisors are responsible for quality control during the various steps of processing, and may be in charge of hourly work schedules. They are concerned with the safety of the employees.

Seafood processors do the hands-on work of cleaning fish, shucking oysters, chopping lobsters, or handling whatever product the vessel brings aboard. They carry the catch into the department, which will have work tables and various tools, and begin sorting the catch. Larger ships may contain conveyor belts. On the largest ships, the catch may be very large indeed, so that speed is as important as artistry.

After the products are sorted, they must be washed and then speedily preserved: fish might be gutted and sliced (by hand or machine) into fillets, then chilled or frozen; oysters, shrimp, and other products will be put on ice and remain iced until delivery to a grocery store or seafood market. The processors face fairly strenuous labor. Handling the fish and using, for example, grinding machinery is only part of the job; they also might weigh the catch, carry racks of product from table or conveyor belt to boxes or other containers, prepare for canning, or actually do the canning.

These positions include "slimers" (the title suggests the messy nature of the job), packers, cleanup crew, machine operators, and office staff. The U.S. Bureau of Labor Statistics (BLS) estimates that food processors earned a median annual wage of $18,600 in 2008.

Factory/processing occupations may include the following:

- Factory/Processing Manager
- Factory Foreman
- Safety Manager
- Seafood Processor
- Fish Packer
- Fish Roe Processor
- Machinist
- Assistant Factory Technician

- Surimi Staff
- Surimi Technician
- Fishmeal Technician

Quality Assurance

The quality assurance manager holds a heavy responsibility, because consumers all over the globe are insistent on purchasing products that are not polluted, undersized, past their use-by date, or improperly preserved in any way.

Quality assurance occupations may include the following:

- Quality Assurance Manager
- Quality Assurance Technician
- Sanitation Crew
- Offloading Crew

Distribution

Once seafood has been captured, the products will be brought to shore either by the fishers themselves or by workers on what are called tender boats, who deliver the products to shore for the fishers. Then distribution can proceed in a wide variety of ways. Fish, crustaceans, and mollusks might be delivered to a cannery; in the Pacific Northwest, family-owned microcanneries have become a flourishing business. Shellstock shippers is the term for those who distribute mollusks such as oysters, mussels, octopus, squid, clams, scallops, and conch. Another big industry processes crustaceans such as lobsters, shrimp, and crayfish (or, popularly, crawfish).

Other companies manufacture fresh and frozen seafood dinners for grocery stores and restaurants; a majority of the latter offer at least one fish entrée on the menu. Salmon, grouper, snapper, and halibut dinners, as well as fish and chips, are enormously popular in the English-speaking world, not to mention many other European and Latin American countries. Frozen fishes, in blocks or fillets, as well as other ready-to-serve products such as raw or precooked oysters, lobsters, and shrimp, can be prepared and readied for distribution almost anywhere.

Raw aquatic products, from fish to crustaceans and mollusks, safely chilled from point of capture to point of preparation and sale, are snapped up by sushi restaurants. A small slice of fish is placed on a small ball of flavored rice, or the rice is surrounded by nori (a type of seaweed), and seafood (such as fish roe) is placed on the rice. Some seaweed, such as nori, is usually dried before it is consumed, but other seaweed, such as wakame, is eaten fresh in soups and other dishes. Seaweed collection is a large industry in Japan, with a large export trade, and smaller elsewhere.

The distribution role collaborates with both seller and buyer and, perhaps, a merchandising team/marketing agency.

Distribution occupations may include the following:

- Inventory Manager
- Importer/Exporter
- Distributor
- Freight Loader/Unloader
- Warehouse Manager
- Warehouse Worker
- Shipping and Receiving Clerk

Sales and Marketing

The fishing captain who knows that a market (grocery stores, restaurants, processing plants, and the like) is anticipating receiving captured products is a happy captain. It is difficult to describe a typical sales and marketing workforce because of the vast differences in sizes throughout the fishing industry.

At the smallest end of the spectrum, the captain or fisher is most likely to function as a seller and marketer; at the largest end, the captain works with international marketers, exporters, and distributors.

Sales and marketing occupations may include the following:

- Sales Manager
- Sales Representative
- Marketing Manager
- Marketing Representative
- Market Research Analyst

Surveying

According to the NOAA Workforce Management Office, a surveying department is responsible for collecting oceanographic and survey data; providing technical assistance to personnel in the research program; and perhaps maintaining oceanographic and survey instruments. Employees (who

may be federal employees) must have experience in working onboard or in an oceanographic survey program, in which they collected and annotated information and worked with monitoring instruments. The Survey Department gathers and records data about the catch and observes whether captured species are allowed by commercial fishing regulations. Observers may share use of the vessel radio to report to the regulatory agency, and they might be required to speak a foreign language if they are working abroad.

Surveying occupations may include the following:

- Chief Survey Technician
- Senior Survey Technician
- Survey Technician Assistant
- Survey Technician
- Junior Survey Technician

INDUSTRY OUTLOOK

Overview

The outlook for this industry shows it to be in decline. This decline appears slight when one looks at a drop of a few percentage points in global production and income, counted in the billions of dollars. However, factors such as the shrinking of fisheries and fish stocks, the aging of the overall workforce and difficulties with recruitment and retainment, competition with importers and with aquaculturists, poor management by such agencies as the National Marine Fisheries Service that police the industry, poor choices made by many fishers (from ignorance of or disregard for the laws) that lead to overfishing, climate changes that affect the oceans and coastlines, and coastal and marine pollution have left many small communities and many large companies staring at large or, in developing countries, even devastating slumps. During the twentieth century, fishers plundered their aquatic resources with abandon; in the twenty-first century, almost all sectors are now paying for the activities of the previous generations. According to the BLS, employment declines will continue also because of recently imposed and strictly regulated limits on fishing.

BumbleBee, a major seller of canned tuna and salmon, found in 2009 that it had to issue $220 mil-

Freshly caught skipjack tuna. (©Dreamstime.com)

and other areas limit the ocean-access possibilities to fishers who live in popular tourist-destination countries.

However, the outlook is not totally grim. The worldwide fishing and seafood production industries still remain one of the fastest growing food sectors; they employ around 200 million people globally, generating $80 billion a year.

While fishing in the wild has suffered diminished returns, aquaculture is on the rise, so seafood farmers have a happier outlook.

There is also the chartered ship industry for recreational fishers on inland rivers and in many American coastal regions, such as the Florida Keys. Commercial fishing is done only to a very slight extent in rivers, chiefly because of overfishing and increased regulations. Rivers are chiefly a natural resource for recreational fishers and guided tours, which encourage fly-fishing (the tourists throw their captured fish back into the water) and which usually

lion worth of notes to refinance debts, after seeing a rise in profits between 2003 and 2008. The slowdown was expected to continue through the following few years. Revenue in 2007 had been healthy, but the company downsized to lose about a thousand employees. StarKist had showed a 2.9 percent uptick from 2007 to 2008, but those profits were $70 million below those of 2003. Chicken of the Sea faced declining sales and negative publicity that resulted from a 2004 lawsuit, which alleged that the company failed to warn consumers about their products' mercury contents.

Countries abroad have also reported a variety of problems. In 2008, *The Guardian* published an article concerning anecdotal evidence that fishing captains in the United Kingdom were hiring Eastern Europeans rather than local employees in order to offset payroll costs. Many countries, in which captains own traditional engine-propelled boats that use diesel, find that regional or global crude oil prices make fishing trips expensive, sometimes prohibitively so. Privatized beaches in the Caribbean

PROJECTED EMPLOYMENT FOR SELECTED OCCUPATIONS

Fishing Industry

Employment		
2008	Projected 2018	Occupation
14,700	13,900	Fishers and related fishing workers
600	600	Cutters and trimmers (includes meat and poultry as well as fish)
200	200	Sailors and marine oilers
25,800	27,500	Supervisors (includes farming and forestry as well as fishing workers)

Source: U.S. Bureau of Labor Statistics, Industries at a Glance, Occupational Employment Statistics and Employment Projections Program.

return the tourists to their starting point on the same day.

Employment Advantages

There are always a great many and varied occupations in the fishing industry and its support industries. Inexperienced civilians ("greenhorns") travel in large numbers to Alaska and the Pacific Northwest to hire on as fishers and processors for a summer or simply to enjoy the adventure of gaining experience. The diversity of positions in all areas of fishing, aquaculture, and related fields offers job satisfaction to workers of all kinds, in the hands-on physical side or the office-based, regulatory and research side.

Tri Marine International, the top-earning North American seafood supplier in 2008, operates in countries around the world and is a major supplier of much-loved seafood, such as albacore, skipjack, yellowfin, bigeye, bluefin, and tuna. It oversees about ten refrigerated cargo ships that operate in the Pacific and Indian oceans, as well as both contracted and affiliated fishing boats. Its facilities include eight processing plants located worldwide.

Trident Seafoods, a major employer that was the second most flourishing North American seafood supplier after Tri Marine, is actually only a regional company in Alaska and the Pacific Northwest. Its employees capture salmon, crab, and assorted other fin- and shellfish, and do their own processing, canning, or freezing. Working for various retail and food service clients, Trident Seafoods operates a fleet of about thirty processing boats and trawlers, as well as about a dozen onshore processing plants. The company's brands include Trident, Louis Kemp, and SeaLegs brand of surimi (processed fish), which remain popular among shoppers. In 2009, Trident was healthy enough to purchase a bankrupt seafood company for about $4 million and to establish a new processing facility in Alaska.

Because the American dollar has weakened overseas, many vacationers choose to jaunt to inland aquatic resource activities such as recreational fishing. Leisurely tourist activities within the fifty states include fishing from chartered boats on rivers or lakes and wading through the Everglades to learn about wetland ecosystems. Tourism guides knowledgeable about local and regional aquatic resources are in increasingly high demand.

Specialist sight-seeing companies can employ all kinds of transport from speedboats to helicopters to cruise liners.

Fishing and aquaculture are industries that greatly reward ambition and provide gratification to the workers who know how much their labors are enjoyed by the average family sitting down to a good seafood meal.

Annual Earnings

The fishing industry earned global revenues of $91.2 billion in 2006, according to the GreenFacts Scientific Board. According to the BLS, in 2008 American fishers and workers in related fields (other than the self-employed) earned an average of $13.68 hourly and $28,460 annually, though managers earned about $42,740 and often much more. Fish cutters earned an average of $10.77 hourly and $22,400 annually. Fish packers might earn around $12.00 hourly. American fish and game wardens earned an average of $26.94 hourly and $56,030 annually. The twenty-first century downturn in revenues is expected to turn around within a decade or so of proper regulation and education of fishers in good practices of sustainability.

RELATED RESOURCES FOR FURTHER RESEARCH

AMERICAN FISHERIES SOCIETY
    5410 Grosvenor Ln.
    Bethesda, MD 20814
    Tel: (301) 897-8616
    Fax: (301) 897-8096
    http://www.fisheries.org

FOOD AND AGRICULTURE ORGANIZATION OF THE
    UNITED NATIONS
    Viale delle Terme di Caracalla
    00153 Rome
    Italy
    Tel: 39-6-570-53099
    Fax: 39-6-570-53152
    http://www.fao.org

FOOD INSTITUTE ONLINE
    1 Broadway
    Elmwood Park, NJ 07407
    Tel: (201) 791-5570

Fax: (201) 791-5222
http://www.foodinstitute.com

INTERGOVERNMENTAL OCEANOGRAPHIC
    COMMISSION
IOC/UNESCO Paris
1 rue Miollis
75732 Paris CEDEX 15
France
Tel: 33-1-45-68-39-84
Fax: 33-1-45-68-58-12
http://ioc-unesco.org

NATIONAL MARINE FISHERIES SERVICE
1315 East West Hwy.
Silver Spring, MD 20910
Tel: (301) 713-2334
http://www.nmfs.noaa.gov/fishwatch

NORTHWEST ATLANTIC FISHERIES ORGANIZATION
P.O. Box 638
Dartmouth, NS B2Y 3Y9
Canada
Tel: (902) 468-5590
Fax: (902) 468-5538
http://www.nafo.int

WORLDFISH CENTER
Jalan Batu Maung, Batu Maung
11960 Bayan Lepas
Penang, Malaysia
Tel: 60-4-626-1606
Fax: 60-4-626-5530
http://www.worldfishcenter.org

ABOUT THE AUTHOR

Fiona Kelleghan is a cataloging and metadata librarian at the University of Miami. Since about 1995, she has been responsible for cataloging federal and international government documents, including materials produced by such agencies as the Food and Agriculture Organization of the United Nations, as well as books and other materials for the University's Rosenstiel School of Marine and Atmospheric Science.

FURTHER READING

Banse, Tom. "First Microbreweries, Now Micro-Canneries Flourish." *OPB News* (Bellingham, Washington), November 9, 2009. http://news.opb.org/article/6177-first-microbreweries-now-micro-canneries-flourish.

Barrett, James, Alison Locker, and Callum Roberts. "The Origins of Intensive Marine Fishing in Medieval Europe: The English Evidence." *Proceedings: Biological Sciences* 271, no. 1556 (2004): 2417-2421.

Eilperin, Juliet. "World's Fish Supply Running Out, Researchers Warn." *The Washington Post*, November 3, 2006. http://www.washingtonpost.com/wp-dyn/content/article/2006/11/02/AR2006110200913.html.

Food and Agriculture Organization of the United Nations. *Aquaculture Development*. Rome: Author, 2001.

_____. *Report of the Expert Consultation on the Development of a Comprehensive Global Record of Fishing Vessels*. Rome: Author, 2008.

_____. *The State of World Fisheries and Aquaculture*. Rome: Author, 2008.

Haggan, Nigel, Barbara Neis, and Ian G. Baird, eds. *Fishers' Knowledge in Fisheries Science and Management*. Paris: UNESCO, 2007.

Morris, Steven, and Severin Carrell. "Enforcement and Voluntary Deals Prompt a Renaissance." *The Guardian*, March 25, 2008. http://www.guardian.co.uk/environment/2008/mar/25/fishing.food1.

Myers, Ransom, and Boris Worm. "Rapid Worldwide Depletion of Predatory Fish Communities." *Nature* 423 (2003): 280-283.

National Oceanic and Atmospheric Administration Workforce Management Office. "Vessel Employment: Career Opportunities in the Pacific Fleet." http://www.wfm.noaa.gov/about_us.html.

Pillay, T. V. R., and M. N. Kutty. *Aquaculture: Principles and Practices*. Ames, Iowa: Blackwell, 2005.

Stickney, Robert R., ed. *Encyclopedia of Aquaculture*. New York: Wiley, 2000.

U.S. Bureau of Labor Statistics. *Career Guide to Industries*, 2010-2011 ed. http://www.bls.gov/oco/cg.

U.S. Census Bureau. North American Industry Classification System (NAICS), 2007. http://www.census.gov/cgi-bin/sssd/naics/naicsrch?chart=2007.

U.S. Department of Commerce. International Trade Administration. Office of Trade and Industry Information. Industry Trade Data and Analysis. http://ita.doc.gov/td/industry/otea/OTII/OTII-index.html.

Wright, Sarah Anne. "Gone Fishing: Rugged Job Can Pay." *The Seattle Times*, February 8, 2004. http://community.seattletimes.nwsource.com/archive/?date=20040208&slug=fisherman080.

Zugarramurdi, Aurora, Maria A. Parin, and Hector M. Lupin. *Economic Engineering Applied to the Fishery Industry*. Rome: Food and Agriculture Organization of the United Nations, 1995.

Food Manufacturing and Wholesaling Industry

©Dreamstime.com

INDUSTRY SNAPSHOT

General Industry: Agriculture and Food

Career Clusters: Agriculture, Food, and Natural Resources; Manufacturing

Subcategory Industries: Animal Food Manufacturing; Animal Slaughtering and Processing; Bakeries and Tortilla Manufacturing; Coffee and Tea Manufacturing; Dairy Product Manufacturing; Farm Product Raw Material Merchant Wholesalers; Flavoring Syrup and Concentrate Manufacturing; Fruit and Vegetable Preserving and Specialty Food Manufacturing; Grain and Field Bean Merchant Wholesalers; Grain and Oilseed Milling; Grocery and Related Product Merchant Wholesalers; Seafood Product Preparation and Packaging; Seasoning and Dressing Manufacturing; Snack Food Manufacturing; Sugar and Confectionary Product Manufacturing

Related Industries: Beverage and Tobacco Industry; Farming Industry; Fishing and Fisheries Industry; Food Retail Industry; Food Services; Livestock and Animal Products Industry; Restaurant Industry; Veterinary Industry

Annual Domestic Revenues: At least $1 trillion USD (IBISWorld, 2009, and Plunkett's Research, 2010)

Annual Global Revenues: At least $1.6 trillion USD (Euromonitor International, 2007, and Plunkett's Research, 2010)

NAICS Numbers: 311, 4244-4245

INDUSTRY DEFINITION

Summary

The food manufacturing and wholesaling industry processes agricultural resources harvested from farms into products and distributes them to retail markets. A major global industry, food production occurs worldwide for both domestic consumption and export. Food engineers and scientists design technology and procedures that transform livestock and crops into commercial goods that meet government regulations for nutritional quality and protection from contaminants. Legislation addresses safety issues associated with this industry.

History of the Industry

Since ancient times, humans have processed agricultural resources to preserve them or make them suitable for consumption. For example, people learned before recorded history began to cook foods and to soak grains in

Tins in a production line in a salmon cannery. (©Bruce Amos/Dreamstime.com)

liquid to make them easier to eat and digest. Salting, smoking, and fermenting methods, moreover, were developed to preserve foods made from animals and plants. Records indicate that Romans preserved fruit in honey. By the Middle Ages, people used heat to dehydrate fresh agricultural goods. In late eighteenth century France, Nicholas Appert invented techniques using heat to sterilize food and seal it in corked glass bottles. He built a factory in 1810 to produce canned foods that could be stored for later consumption. The canning technologies developed by Appert and other nineteenth century inventors were essential to food manufacturing becoming a modern industry.

The Industrial Revolution caused European and American urban populations to expand significantly and made it possible for large-scale farms to produce an abundance of fresh ingredients. Urban dwellers were less equipped to produce their own food than rural populations, so the demand for food as a commodity increased. The supply of perishable foodstuffs increased at the same time. As a result, there was significant new demand for improved food manufacturing techniques that could process and transport food from field to consumer quickly and that could preserve perishable foods or transform them into less perishable commodities.

During the mid-nineteenth century, Louis Pasteur recognized that heat killed microorganisms, establishing principles for pasteurization that were eventually implemented to manufacture safe foods. Improved preservation methods enabled agricultural resources to be processed in the locations where they were abundant and then distributed to a broader market. These methods transformed the food manufacturing and wholesaling industry, opening new, distant markets for products that had previously been available only to local purchasers. The food industry became global, and new products became available in many markets for the first time. In addition to canning and preserving techniques, advances in mechanical refrigeration methods made this expansion possible because even perishable foods could be shipped long distances by ship and rail.

In the 1860's, the U.S. Civil War expanded the American commercial canning industry, as 30 million cans of food were manufactured each year to feed soldiers. Legislation regulated the quality and safety of manufactured foods. The U.S. Department of Agriculture (USDA), established in 1862, enforced these regulations through its Food Safety Inspection Service (FSIS). By the 1890's, Samuel Prescott and William Underwood were studying the bacteriology associated with canning food and were using mathematics to describe relationships between the amount of heat applied and the resulting reduction of microbe activity. Food manufacturing engineers applied that information to design effective food-sterilization procedures.

Upton Sinclair's book *The Jungle* (1906) revealed the dangerous and unsanitary conditions in some meatpacking houses and canneries. Established in 1906, the U.S. Food and Drug Administration (FDA) issued standards for food manufacturing. Some food manufacturers, such as Libby, McNeill, and Libby, promoted sanitation in their factories, requiring employees to change work clothing frequently in order to prevent them from contaminating the food they handled.

Twentieth century food manufacturing machinery benefited from scientific and technological advances. In the 1920's, Clarence Birdseye developed processes to manufacture and package frozen foods, which soon dominated the wholesale food market. In 1925, C. Olin Ball pioneered computer modeling of the heat processes used by food manufacturers to destroy harmful microorganisms, such as botulin. His FDA-endorsed mathematical mod-

els allowed manufacturers to determine the desirable thermal levels for food processing, and they have retained value into the twenty-first century.

By the late 1940's, many food manufacturers were exposing food to radiation to pasteurize it. They later used ultrahigh-temperature (UHT) methods. Better understanding of thermodynamic principles led to improved refrigeration technology. Food engineers devised ways to freeze-dry food, allowing companies to process and distribute popular consumer foods, including coffee. G. Howard Kraft patented a modified atmosphere packaging concept in 1960, which modern-day food manufacturers use to produce several billion packages annually.

Advances in computer technology enabled the Sara Lee factory in Deerfield, Illinois, to initiate comprehensive computer-controlled food manufacturing in 1964. That pioneering plant-automation system regulated several hundred production roles, including freezers in the company's warehouse and distribution systems. Other food manufacturers incorporated automation in their factories as those facilities were redesigned to replace

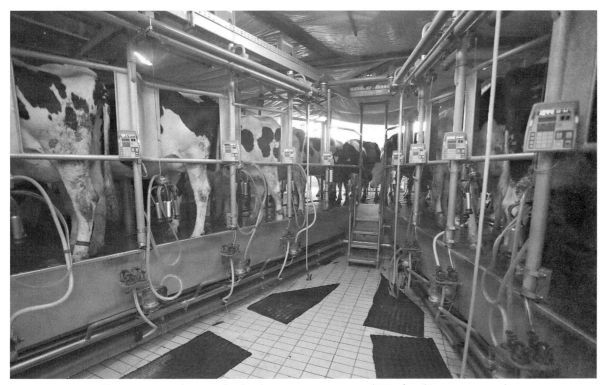

These cows are being milked with an automatic system. (©Picsfive/Dreamstime.com)

outdated technology. Starting in 1974, food supply chains used computerized Universal Product Codes (UPC). Researchers examined high-pressure techniques to impede harmful contaminants, resulting in industrial use of that technology by the 1990's.

The Industry Today

Twenty-first century food manufacturers and wholesalers pursue goals similar to those of their predecessors: improving food safety, quality, and variety. They strive to provide consumers with appealing foods that meet their expectations regarding nutrients, freshness, taste, and cost. By the early twenty-first century, many food manufacturers and wholesalers had become substantial corporations. Acquisitions, mergers, and takeovers consolidated the wealthiest food manufacturers and wholesalers. Manufacturers have often become identified with their most popular brands, which have thrived despite economic downturns. Many food manufacturers dominate their food specialties. For example, Tyson Foods manufactures the most poultry products globally. *Fortune* and *Forbes* magazines include food manufacturers on their lists of the world's most lucrative businesses.

Food engineers and scientists devise technological advances that are incorporated into contemporary food manufacturing. Powerful microchips enhance plant automation, allowing plants to process agricultural resources and package food more efficiently and swiftly. Engineers have developed biosensors that can locate harmful microorganisms in food. The use of heat remains a basic aspect of many modern food manufacturing techniques. Twenty-first century food manufacturers have refined heating methods to achieve more precise temperatures and shorter heating times for consistent production results.

Manufacturers have begun to use new methods to pasteurize food, including pulsed electric field (PEF) processing, magnetic resonance, irradiation, ultraviolet exposure, and high-pressure processing (HPP). These techniques have reduced the amount of heat used to destroy microorganisms, particularly bacteria, because thermal pasteurization processes often detrimentally alter food's chemical composition or structure. Foods pasteurized with these new techniques retain desired characteristics and nutrients, including vitamins.

The food manufacturing industry is reassessing its impact on the environment. Environmental awareness has contributed to food engineers de-

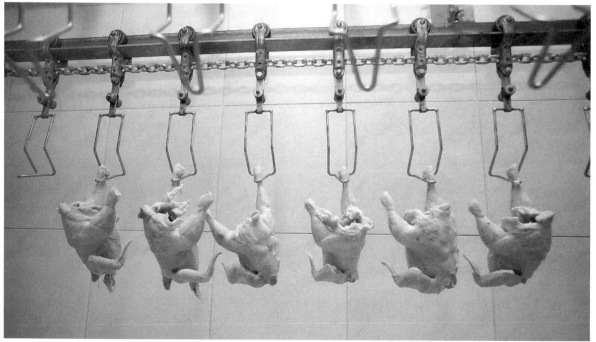

Chickens being processed. Tyson Foods manufactures the most poultry products globally. (©Picsfive/Dreamstime.com)

The Contribution of Food, Beverage, and Tobacco Product Manufacturing to the U.S. Economy

Value Added	Amount
Gross domestic product	$189.5 billion
Gross domestic product	1.3%
Persons employed	1.678 million
Total employee compensation	$87.8 billion

Source: U.S. Bureau of Economic Analysis. Data are for 2008.

veloping machinery and techniques that waste less energy and water. Many manufacturers recycle wastes produced during processing, attempt to achieve sustainable practices, and use packaging made from renewable materials. Some food packaging incorporates mechanisms designed to prevent or reveal tampering detrimental to food safety.

The Public Health Security and Bioterrorism Preparedness Act of 2002 requires manufacturers to record the sources and distribution chains of their products. Contemporary food manufacturers and wholesalers use electronic methods to compile inventories of food produced and shipped and to track the movement of ingredients and products within factories and to warehouses and retailers. The Institute of Food Technologists (IFT) has endorsed using electronic documentation of critical tracking events (CTEs) in the food supply chain, from agricultural resources to shipments. Because radio frequency identification (RFID) tracking tags on pallets are expensive, only about 40 percent of U.S. manufacturers use them, according to a 2006 *Food Engineering* survey.

In 2007, the FDA developed the Food Protection Plan in response to incidents of agricultural and foods contamination caused either maliciously by terrorists or by other sources. In October, 2009, fifty-five food manufacturers and distributors agreed to comply with the Foodservice GS1 U.S. Standards Initiative for identifying food businesses and products with Global Location Numbers and Global Trade Item Numbers to achieve better tracking of food products. The GS1 Global Data Synchronization Network (GDSN) aspired to secure 75 percent of manufacturers' participation by 2015.

Most food packaging meets government requirements for accurate labeling, although incidents of food fraud sometimes occur. Inspectors use deoxyribonucleic acid (DNA) tests and isotope ratio analysis to determine the source of misidentified foods. In March, 2010, the FDA intensified its efforts to penalize manufacturers that deceptively label food. The proposed FDA Food Safety Modernization Act would expand inspection of domestic and imported foods. In 2010, critics revealed that the FDA had not inspected 44 percent of the 51,229 food manufacturers in the United States from 2004 through 2008, demanding that the agency achieve more comprehensive oversight of the food industry.

Consumers' critical reactions to some technologies, such as the use of irradiation, have affected food manufacturing. Some manufacturers have responded to consumer demand for organic foods by processing agricultural materials that meet USDA and other standards to be certified organic. By 2005, the organic food manufacturing industry was generating approximately $14 billion annually. In 2009, the Ecological Food Manufacturers Association was established to assist food manufac-

Inputs Consumed by Manufacturers of Food, Beverages, and Tobacco Products

Input	Value
Energy	$17.3 billion
Materials	$460.9 billion
Purchased services	$78.8 billion
Total	$557.0 billion

Source: U.S. Bureau of Economic Analysis. Data are for 2008.

turers in adopting environmentally sustainable methods and resources.

Food manufacturers have also responded to public opinion regarding health issues, especially obesity in adults and children. In March, 2010, U.S. First Lady Michelle Obama spoke to Grocery Manufacturers Association members, asking food manufacturers to offer consumers healthier food choices. Starting in 2010, Campbell's Soup Company and Kraft Foods both decreased the amount of sodium in some of their foods. Food Network's *Unwrapped* and the History Channel's *Food Tech* delved into the industry, revealing to viewers the sources of their food, as well as manufacturing, packaging, and distribution processes and the workers employed at food plants.

Food manufacturing has been affected by a price crisis that occurred in the first decade of the twenty-first century, when wholesale prices for foods increased by approximately 25 percent. Prices for wholesale foods rose by 7 percent in 2007 alone, more than they had in any year since the 1980's, and wholesalers expect prices to keep increasing in the 2010's. Many manufacturers and wholesalers have turned their focus to inexpensive canned, frozen, and easy-to-prepare foods, which consumers affected by economic problems have sought for their affordability and convenience. Brands including Chef Boyardee, Hunt's, Peter Pan, and Banquet have experienced significant sales growth.

Recognizing that Internet sales represented one-fifth of total U.S. business revenues by 2010, the North Iowa Area Community College at Mason City established an associate of applied science degree in electronic agribusiness. This degree program is designed to prepare graduates for careers increasing electronic commerce related to the agriculture and food industries.

INDUSTRY MARKET SEGMENTS

The food manufacturing and wholesaling industry operates small to large businesses that create or distribute food to consumers. These businesses vary from sole practitioners who market specialty or boutique items, such as preserves or handmade cheese, through a handful of local stores in a given community to vast multinational corporations that own many subsidiaries and produce and distribute dozens of different food brands throughout the globe. Some 89 percent of food manufacturers employs fewer than one hundred people. The following sections discuss aspects of each of these varying segments.

Small Businesses

Small food manufacturers and wholesalers often produce foods for specialized markets and purposes, such as holiday candies or gourmet salad dressings. These businesses are sometimes affiliated with specific stores, tourism centers, hotels, restaurants, or groceries, which supply a steady source of clients. They strive to attract customers who will become loyal to their brands and appreciate unique food items.

Potential Annual Earnings Scale. Small food manufacturers pay employees varying wages depending on their skills, tasks performed, and production demands. According to the U.S. Bureau of Labor Statistics (BLS), food cooking machine operators earned an average of $26,200 in 2009, while bakers earned an average of $25,940, and butchers and meat cutters earned an average of $27,130. Food scientists and technologists earned an average of $59,790, and operations managers in food manufacturing firms earned an average of $107,650. Small businesses may pay less than these averages, and they often pay hourly wages or per-piece wages for pastry decoration and other hand-intensive labor.

Clientele Interaction. Small food manufacturers and wholesalers seek to provide food items, tastes, and qualities customers cannot find elsewhere. Owners and managers often are directly involved in making and distributing foods. Candy makers, for example, may personalize chocolates for customers by creating designs or decorations specific to individuals, groups, or occasions. Many small food manufacturers produce seasonal items and encourage customers to purchase those items from them each year. Some emphasize regional products, such as pecans grown in southern states. Small food manufacturers and wholesalers sometimes distribute cookbooks containing recipes that use their products.

Because customized orders are often expensive, small food manufacturers sometimes offer deals and discounts. They may create clubs, for example, in which customers receive a different food monthly by paying an annual fee, to please clients and ensure consistent business. Other offers might provide repeat customers special foods to celebrate birthdays or other occasions. Such personal attention usually enhances customer satisfaction. Electronic newsletters and blogs also provide manufacturers a means to interact with customers and tell about their business, provide recipes, and share photographs of workers, equipment, and processes used to make their food products. Some small food manufacturers incorporate elements of entertainment and hospitality in their businesses, providing visitors closer access to manufacturing processes than larger companies can permit. Visitors may enjoy watching such foods as cheeses and maple syrup being made.

Small food wholesalers seek contracts by visiting managers of grocery stores and other retail markets in their local area, emphasizing the uniqueness, quality, and affordability of the foods they offer. They often use electronic communications to distribute information about products and prices to retailers they identify as potential clients throughout the United States and globally.

Amenities, Atmosphere, and Physical Grounds. Small food manufacturers operate in a variety of settings, ranging from functional factories to attractive buildings adjacent to commercial stores. Regardless of their appearance, small food manufacturers share common elements. They stock their manufacturing space with equipment, including mixers, ovens, molds, pans, and machinery designed to perform specific tasks according to each manufacturer's needs. Some small food manufacturers have adjacent store and dining areas for customers to sample and buy their products. Small food manufacturing sites sometimes have glass windows in walls separating the manufacturing and public areas so people can observe workers making food items. Some manufacturers provide visitors with free souvenirs relevant to foods they produce.

Small food wholesalers keep products in one or several warehouses. They are often located near the manufacturers who produce the foods and beverages the wholesalers sell and ship to retailers. Buildings used for small food wholesaling are primarily utilitarian, including office and storage space. Parking areas provide space for vehicles and

the maintenance processes they require. Both small food manufacturers and wholesalers keep grounds surrounding their businesses neat, trimming grass and shrubbery and removing debris, for safety reasons and to convey a positive image to the public.

Typical Number of Employees. Small food manufacturers and wholesalers usually have small staffs, employing an average of twenty people or less to acquire ingredients and make, sell, or distribute food products. Owners and managers often work alongside employees. Some small food manufacturing and wholesaling businesses are family operations, employing relatives and friends. Businesses involving seasonal food items sometimes hire temporary workers to supplement full-time staffs.

Traditional Geographic Locations. Many small food manufacturing and wholesaling businesses are located in communities with low populations or rural areas in a variety of geographical settings. Some of these companies select their locations based on characteristics that make them conducive to manufacturing or selling their products, such as proximity to agricultural resources they need or to high-traffic areas, such as historical, tourist, or recreational sites.

Pros of Working for a Small Food Business. Employees of small food manufacturers and wholesalers often find their work enjoyable because they are able to interact with and receive feedback and appreciation from customers. Many workers also enjoy the sense of community that small businesses can cultivate. Most positions in these small businesses do not generally require college degrees. Special services, such as assembling gift baskets from manufacturers' foods and other artistic presentations involving food, enable employees to use their creativity. Some small businesses pay for employees to receive training in cake decoration or other skills. The seasonal nature of the market for many small-scale food products appeals to workers interested in part-time labor. Small businesses often give their staffs gifts of food they make and distribute. Experiences working in businesses of this size can prove beneficial to employees who decide to seek employment in larger companies.

Cons of Working for a Small Food Business. Small food manufacturing and wholesaling businesses may be understaffed, causing both owners and employees to be overwhelmed by high demand. Maintaining financial stability can be both difficult and stressful and can require owners or managers to find the time to gain knowledge of marketing, accounting, and other fundamental business subjects to keep their businesses operational. Some employees may not have the training needed to perform complex tasks involving decorating luxury foods adequately. Wholesaling jobs may require employees to complete training and certification to operate equipment such as forklifts and to drive commercial vehicles. Some positions require employees to work nighttime and early morning hours, and those baking or freezing foods, for example, may have to spend hours in hot or cold workspaces. Seasonal food production and distribution can interfere with employees' holiday plans. Business may slow between the holidays associated with many small food businesses' products.

Costs

Payroll and Benefits: Employees at small food manufacturing and wholesaling businesses may be paid hourly wages or salaries. These businesses often hire temporary or seasonal workers, who are paid hourly and generally do not receive benefits. Benefits for full-time staff, including sick and vacation time, vary according to agreements between employers and workers.

Supplies: Small food manufacturing and wholesaling businesses require diverse items to maintain their facilities and services, including ingredients, office supplies, cleaning materials, telecommunications equipment, baking and other industrial cooking equipment, and sterile food-packaging materials.

External Services: Many small food manufacturing businesses contract with suppliers to receive necessary agricultural resources and ingredients to make their food products. Both manufacturers and wholesalers often contract cleaning and maintenance services for their office spaces, external grounds, and production equipment and machinery; pest control services; and accounting and legal services. Contracted lawyers may oversee trademark acquisition and enforcement, arrange for inspections by officials, and ensure compliance with local, state, and federal licensing requirements. Manufacturers and wholesalers usually hire insurance agents to provide liability, property, and other insurance protection they need. They may contract for fuel services for vehicles.

Utilities: Small food manufacturers and wholesalers must pay for electricity, gas/oil, water, sewage, telephone, and Internet access.

Taxes: Small food manufacturing and wholesaling businesses pay property taxes and local, state, and federal income taxes. Wholesalers pay vehicle registration and licensing taxes, which may also apply to some small manufacturing companies. Manufacturers that sell their products directly to customers must collect sales taxes.

Midsize Businesses

Many midsize food manufacturing and wholesaling businesses are regional companies. Some produce and distribute brand-name foods that are familiar and popular mostly with consumers in their geographical region. Others manufacture and sell foods for nationwide distribution but operate at lower production and revenue levels than large food corporations achieve.

Potential Annual Earnings Scale. According to the BLS, food cooking machine operators earned an average of $26,200 in 2009, while bakers earned an average of $25,940, and butchers and meat cutters earned an average of $27,130. Food scientists and technologists earned an average of $59,790, and operations managers in food manufacturing firms earned an average of $107,650. Production supervisors in the industry earned an average of $50,380, wholesale sales managers earned an average of $107,260, and sales representatives earned an average of $57,210.

Clientele Interaction. Midsize food manufacturing and wholesaling businesses often emphasize the economic importance of their products to their immediate communities and surrounding areas, where many of their employees and customers live. They also note sentimental aspects of their products' ties to geographical places or beloved hometown figures to appeal to customers who have moved away and might be homesick for those foods. Some manufacturers provide discounts and services to ship their products to soldiers from the region who are serving overseas. Many manufacturers welcome groups from schools and other visitors to tour their facilities and learn about the products they make, providing opportunities to taste samples. Midsize food manufacturers and wholesalers frequently participate in scholastic business programs or offer internships to high school or college students.

Midsize food industries promote their brands by presenting company information, product descriptions, and order forms and contracts on their Web sites. Some midsize food manufacturers maintain social networking Internet sites to interact with their customers. They sometimes offer coupons or other deals to attract customers. Companies sometimes sell merchandise with their logos and print cookbooks containing recipes using their products. They occasionally offer special gift packages, combining such products as potato chips and dip, or provide tourist bureaus with foods to give away in promotions or to sell at community welcome centers.

Amenities, Atmosphere, and Physical Grounds. Most midsize food manufacturing and wholesaling industries consist of utilitarian structures where foods are processed and stored. Agricultural goods move through a variety of machines and tools designed for specific purposes, such as cutting, pressing, dipping, and other movements. Manufacturing plants often use long conveyer belts to move foods being processed to various stations where they undergo such treatments as drying, heating, or freezing and are pasteurized to remove contaminants. Buildings housing midsize manufacturers and wholesalers include freezers and shelving to store products.

Facilities usually include areas where employees can shower to prevent contaminating food-handling stations and can change into work clothing and safety gear. Some businesses maintain health stations where employees can be treated for any injuries occurring at work. Storage areas are provided for vehicles such as forklifts to move supplies and food within the processing and shelving sections of buildings. Parking lots and garages provide spaces for employees' and companies' vehicles. Docks en-

able trucks to access the buildings to unload or load supplies associated with food manufacturing or wholesaling. Speakers and intercoms transmit communications throughout plants.

Many midsize food manufacturing and wholesaling facilities are surrounded by fences and have guard stations at entrances to prevent inventory theft and unapproved visitors. Employees often have identification cards, some with bar codes or magnetic strips they can use to access production and storage areas. Most midsize food businesses emphasize cleanliness and safety over appearance within the spaces used for manufacturing. Public areas—where visitors view production processes, usually through glass walls, or buy foods and merchandise—often have designs relevant to the companies' products and provide facilities to accommodate visitors. Landscaping is usually attractive to convey a positive image.

Typical Number of Employees. Midsize food manufacturing and wholesaling businesses often employe fewer than one hundred people, but they may employ up to five hundred depending on their needs.

Traditional Geographic Locations. Agricultural communities in all regions of the United States are common sites for midsize food manufacturing and wholesaling businesses because of the proximity to resources needed to create food prod-

According to the American Egg Board, hens lay about five eggs per week. (©Dreamstime.com)

ucts. These industries often operate on the periphery of both urban and rural locations, depending on specific attributes those places offer. Midsize food manufacturers and wholesalers often choose sites near major transportation routes, including highways, interstates, railways, and rivers. Places with airports are essential for food businesses needing to ship by air.

Pros of Working for a Midsize Food Business. Midsize food manufacturing and wholesaling businesses endeavor to please their workers. Many companies provide training to prepare entry-level employees for their new positions and to teach all personnel about new technologies and procedures as needed. Food managers, engineers, and scientists also have access to educational opportunities to enhance their skills. These businesses often encourage employees to consider their workplaces and colleagues as forming communities: They host parties and picnics for employees and their families, honor employees at awards programs, distribute newsletters, and form committees for various projects in which employees can participate. Some midsize food businesses reward employees with such perks as stock dividends and recognize service anniversaries with gifts.

Cons of Working for a Midsize Food Business. Employees in midsize food manufacturing and wholesaling businesses are at constant risk from various hazards. Despite safety training and efforts to minimize accidents, some incidents do occur. Workers also experience physical problems such as carpal tunnel syndrome because of the repetitive motions involved in their tasks. Hearing loss is a concern because manufacturing requires the use of loud machinery. Some workers may be expected to monitor several tasks simultaneously and feel overwhelmed. The monotony and tedium involved with many workers' roles in manufacturing processes may bore or desensitize them, affecting their ability to pay attention to their assignments and possibly reducing the quality of the foods they produce. Some employees are must work night shifts or in hot or cold environments, depending on the manufacturing processes they are assigned. Some items may be subject to declines in production, recalls, or discontinaation as a result of food contamination, economic issues, or other problems: All these eventualities can result in reduced hours or layoffs for employees.

Costs

Payroll and Benefits: Employees in midsize food manufacturing and wholesaling businesses often work for hourly wages, especially if they are temporary workers. Overtime pay is available to employees working beyond their scheduled shifts. Managers and other higher-level employees usually receive annual salaries. Extra income or other forms of compensation reward some employees' job performance and their contributions to their companies' success. Such benefits as sick days, vacation time, and health insurance vary based on terms negotiated for each employee's contract. Employees in these businesses sometimes join labor unions, which monitor conditions relevant to their employment.

Supplies: Materials essential for midsize food manufacturing and wholesaling industries include ingredients, production machinery, safety equipment, cleaning supplies, telecommunications and computer technology, office supplies, and maintenance equipment for facilities and grounds.

External Services: Many midsize food manufacturing and wholesaling businesses purchase containers and packaging from other companies. They often contract for security cameras and personnel; pest control; maintenance and repair services for vehicles, machinery, and computers; and attorneys and business professionals to perform accounting, marketing, and other tasks, such as filing for brand trademarks. Many manufacturers consult with insurance experts to secure coverage for properties and any liabilities associated with workplace injuries and food safety. They sometimes arrange for consultants to assess whether businesses have adequately complied with health and safety laws and are ready for inspectors to evaluate their sites and performance. Fuel companies may provide these food industries with gasoline contracts to fuel vehicles.

Utilities: Midsize food manufacturers and wholesalers must pay for electricity, gas/oil, water, sewage, telephone, and Internet access.

Taxes: Midsize food manufacturing and wholesaling businesses pay property taxes and local, state, and federal income taxes. Wholesalers pay vehicle registration and licensing taxes, which may also apply to some small manufacturing companies. Manufacturers that sell their products directly to customers must collect sales taxes.

Large Businesses

Large food manufacturers and wholesalers are mostly corporations, often operating factories and warehouses in several geographical locations, including internationally. They usually produce or distribute major food brands, which form those businesses' identities. Approximately five hundred of the approximately twenty-eight thousand U.S. food manufacturers in 2006 were considered large businesses.

Potential Annual Earnings Scale. According to the BLS, food cooking machine operators earned an average of $26,200 in 2009, while bakers earned an average of $25,940, and butchers and meat cutters earned an average of $27,130. Food scientists and technologists earned an average of $59,790, and operations managers in food manufacturing firms earned an average of $107,650. Production supervisors in the industry earned an average of $50,380, wholesale sales managers earned an average of $107,260, and sales representatives earned an average of $57,210. The average chief executive of a food wholesaler earned $186,630, and the average chief executive of a food manufacturer earned $179,990. Employees of large firms typically earn salaries equal to or greater than these averages, although pay may vary significantly in different geographic areas.

Clientele Interaction. Most employees of large food manufacturing and wholesaling corporations have limited interactions with customers as a result not only of their scale of operation but also of safety and privacy concerns regarding their products. Some factories schedule tours for visitors, ranging from school groups to industrial professionals, and they may provide samples of their foods to the public in addition to selling merchandise and cookbooks featuring food brands they make or distribute. Large food manufacturers and wholesalers often establish Web sites to promote their products. Marketing includes coupons and discount offers.

Some large food corporations sponsor competitors in cooking contests; others sponsor entire cooking or recipe contests in which contestants must use their products. Many corporate food manufacturers and wholesalers invest in placement of their brands on television and in films to expand public awareness of their foods. Large food manufacturing and wholesaling businesses occasionally encourage the development of educational programs incorporating their products, such as documentaries examining how foods are manufactured. Many large food manufacturers and wholesalers offer internships for college students and young professionals to acquire experience working in big food industries.

Amenities, Atmosphere, and Physical Grounds. Large food manufacturers and wholesalers require big spaces for their processing plants, warehouses, and necessary structures and facilities for equipment and supplies. Many of these businesses cover substantial acreage. Their buildings are generally utilitarian and furnished with industrial machinery and equipment, such as vats and mixers, that sort, clean, and process agricultural materials into manufactured foods. Sanitary conditions, safety, and food quality are these businesses' primary concern, not appearances. Large food companies that permit public visitors incorporate areas for those visitors to watch manufacturing processes through windows that separate them from sanitized workspaces and workers.

Foods on conveyor belts sometimes pass through metal detectors to locate any harmful materials they acquire while being processed. Storage areas keep foods in freezers or on shelves in temperature- and humidity-controlled conditions. Large food manufacturers and wholesalers install such security and safety measures as alarms, speakers, and intercoms to transmit various communications and warn workers of dangers. Surveillance cameras monitor inside and outside areas. Fences circle the grounds of large plants. Guard buildings monitor movement through entrances and exits, preventing hazardous materials from being brought inside plants and detecting attempts to steal property. Many large manufacturers and wholesalers require employees to wear identification badges or use cards with bar codes or magnetic strips to enter restricted areas. Trucks deliver livestock and other resources to docks and also are loaded with manufactured foods.

Parking areas and maintenance buildings house vehicles. Grounds are usually maintained to enhance security, safety, and appeal for both employees and visitors. Employee areas at large food manufacturing and wholesaling facilities typically have locker rooms where workers can shower before putting on work clothes and safety equipment in order to wash away any contaminants on their bodies. Employee usually also have access to a dining area and places to exercise and relax. Health services are equipped to deal with routine matters as well as emergencies.

Typical Number of Employees. Large food manufacturing and wholesaling businesses may employ thousands of people at sites worldwide.

Traditional Geographic Locations. The vast physical size of most large food manufacturing and wholesaling businesses' buildings influences where they can be located. Some are built near cities, while others benefit from being in remote rural areas. Most are near transportation hubs for railroad, cargo ship, aviation, and trucking services. Some manufacturers and wholesalers use barges to move goods on rivers. Major food industries usually choose locations near agricultural resources, such as livestock yards and grain and soybean crops in the Midwest; poultry farms in the South; seafood and freshwater fisheries in coastal areas; and dairy, vegetable, and fruit farms in various areas.

Pros of Working for a Large Food Business. Employment at large food manufacturing and wholesaling businesses is accessible to entry-level workers who are unskilled and have minimal work experience and education. Many high school graduates and immigrants secure their first jobs with large food manufacturers or wholesalers. Most such businesses provide employees with training, and they often routinely provide workers safety education, rotate positions, schedule sufficient breaks, and install safer, more ergonomic equipment to meet Occupational Safety and Health Administration requirements. Large food corporations occasionally give employees clothing, food, or other items, frequently with brand logos, to recognize their contributions to company achievements and celebrate their employment anniversaries. Employees often enjoy participating in corporation-sponsored activities, such as sports teams, and belonging to large industrial communities.

Cons of Working for a Large Food Business. Large-scale food processing—especially seafood, dairy, and meat processing—is the most dangerous industry in the United States. Employees often suffer injuries, including occasional fatal injuries, from sharp tools and heavy machinery that operates at fast speeds, high pressures, and extreme temperatures. The machinery is also loud and often causes hearing problems. Standing for lengthy periods of time and engaging in repetitive arm and hand motions can harm muscles. The corporate culture at most large food industries can cause workers, especially entry-level workers, to feel insignificant and undervalued. They often envision few opportunities for advancement and salary increases, feeling stuck in their positions. As a result, employees may lack enthusiasm and commitment to their work, and the quality of their companies' products may suffer.

Costs

Payroll and Benefits: Employees at large food manufacturing and wholesaling businesses earn varied salaries based on positions held, credentials, tenure, and responsibilities. Administrators usually receive annual salaries, while most lower-level and temporary employees earn hourly wages. Employees also are sometimes compensated financially or with other incentives for achieving workplace goals and meeting inspection standards. Benefits such as health insurance and sick and vacation time vary according to workers' contracts.

Supplies: Large food manufacturers and wholesalers require bulk amounts of cleaning and office supplies. They need current technologies for communications and computer processes and equipment to repair and update machinery and ensure that it runs efficiently. Large manufacturing and wholesaling businesses acquire maintenance supplies for their buildings and grounds.

External Services: Some large food manufacturing and wholesaling corporations contract with suppliers to acquire employee uniforms and safety equipment. They may also contract with security services, pest control, and maintenance services for machinery, computers, vehicles, facility interiors, and grounds. They may have their own accounting and legal departments, or they may contract with legal and accounting services to oversee bookkeeping, marketing, trademark acquisition and enforcement, and other matters. Large food companies sometimes secure outside experts to ensure that they comply with safety and health regulations and can pass inspections. They also hire insurance agents to provide sufficient coverage for properties, inventories, and possible liabilities presented by injured workers and contaminated foods. Cleaners sometimes are contracted to launder employees' work clothing. Large food manufacturers often buy containers and packaging made by other companies. They usually purchase large quantities of vehicle gasoline from businesses specializing in fuels.

Utilities: Large food manufacturers and wholesalers must pay for electricity, gas/oil, water, sewage, telephone, and Internet access.

Taxes: Large food manufacturing and wholesaling businesses pay property taxes and local, state, and federal income taxes. Wholesalers pay vehicle registration and licensing taxes, which may also apply to some small manufacturing companies. If they sell any products directly to customers, they must collect sales taxes. They may also need to pay taxes in other countries if they have offices there, as well as tariffs and other trade fees for exported goods.

ORGANIZATIONAL STRUCTURE AND JOB ROLES

Food manufacturing and wholesaling businesses have similar organizational structures and employee tasks regardless of size. Unique situations due to manufacturers' and wholesalers' production and distribution goals and personnel qualifications often determine whether employees are assigned a specialized role or given responsibility for multiple positions. Small companies, especially sole proprietorships, may not have the luxury of choice: They may of necessity assign multiple roles to a single individual.

The following umbrella categories apply to the organizational structure of businesses in the food manufacturing and wholesaling industry:

- Business Management
- Customer Service
- Sales and Marketing
- Facilities and Maintenance
- Security

- Technology, Research, Design, and Development
- Production and Operations
- Distribution
- Groundskeeping
- Human Resources
- Information Technology
- Administrative Support

Business Management

Executives and other managers oversee overall operations and policies of food manufacturing and wholesaling companies. They establish goals and enact plans to achieve desired production, sales, and revenues. Managers often have specific assignments, supervising groups of workers or departments focusing on distinct processes. They secure consultants and experts in inspection and auditing to ensure their businesses meet all certification and safety requirements.

Food manufacturing and wholesaling managers usually have university degrees in business, food-related, scientific, or engineering fields. Some managers have master of business administration (M.B.A.) degrees to supplement technological or scientific degrees. Work experience and tenure at various corporation branches help managers advance. They usually earn the highest salaries at their businesses and receive bonuses and perks for outstanding performance, often measured by profits or the quality of the foods they produce.

Business management occupations may include the following:

- Owner
- Sole Proprietor
- President/Chief Executive Officer (CEO)
- Chief Financial Officer (CFO)
- Chief Operating Officer (COO)
- Vice President
- General or Operations Manager
- Plant Manager
- Warehouse Manager
- Department Director
- Legal Counsel

Customer Service

Customer service personnel in food manufacturing and wholesaling industries interact with clients and seek ways to expand sales by pleasing existing customers, responding to criticisms and requests, and attracting more buyers. They arrange plant tours and often work closely with marketing and sales personnel. They evaluate responses to surveys to assess customer satisfaction with their companies' products and services and report to management any problems affecting public opinion of those products. Some customer service personnel prepare educational materials for consumers, such as nutritional information, recipes, or suggestions for incorporating their companies' products into their diets.

Most customer service personnel have college or vocational degrees in business, public relations, or hospitality. Some also have food-related course work or employment experience. The ability to communicate well is essential for customer service positions.

Customer service occupations may include the following:

- Customer Service Director
- Customer Service Representative
- Public Relations Director
- Public Relations Representative

Sales and Marketing

Sales and marketing personnel promote their businesses' products to potential customers and retail markets. Marketing personnel develop publicity to advertise foods directly to potential retail customers, building the market for their products. Food manufacturers' sales staffs convince wholesalers to carry their products, and wholesalers' sales staffs convince retail stores to stock their products, based on the brand reputations and demand

---

OCCUPATION PROFILE

Manufacturer's Representative

Considerations	Qualifications
Description	Interests wholesale and retail buyers in carrying foods and other manufactured products by traveling to and visiting with prospective buyers.
Career clusters	Agriculture, Food, and Natural Resources; Architecture and Construction; Business, Management, and Administration; Human Services; Marketing, Sales, and Service
Interests	Data; people; things
Working conditions	Work inside
Minimum education level	On-the-job training; junior/technical/community college; bachelor's degree
Physical exertion	Light work
Physical abilities	Unexceptional/basic fitness
Opportunities for experience	Part-time work
Licensure and certification	Usually not required
Employment outlook	Average growth expected
Holland interest score	ESA

Note: See volume 1, "Publisher's Note," for an explanation of the Holland interest score.

built by advertising and marketing campaigns. Personnel travel to trade shows, conventions, and fairs to promote their products and attract clients. Sales and marketing personnel develop contacts with media, chambers of commerce, and other resources to help them determine the interests and needs of consumers, as well as those of retail outlets.

Sales and marketing personnel often have undergraduate degrees in business or marketing. Some of them have degrees in food science, nutrition, or other related fields, often with minors in business. Students seeking food sales and marketing positions sometimes acquire industry experience through internships and work-study programs while still in college, increasing their chances of both finding positions and succeeding in those positions upon graduation. Sales and marketing personnel usually receive annual incomes based on their qualifications and performance, as well as perks and bonuses to reward outstanding service. Some marketing personnel are graphic artists, photographers, or Web designers. Communication skills enhance sales and marketing personnel's work.

Sales and marketing occupations may include the following:

- Sales Director
- Marketing Director
- Sales Representative
- Marketing Representative
- Market Research Analyst

Facilities and Maintenance

Food manufacturers and wholesalers rely on a staff of maintenance and building engineering workers to service and repair systems, including electrical, water, refrigeration, and heating, ventilating, and air-conditioning (HVAC) systems, as well as industrial equipment and vehicles crucial for business operations. Some maintenance personnel have specialized assignments, while others are generalists. Maintenance personnel also include custodial workers who clean buildings and stock the soaps necessary to sanitize production workers' and other employees' hands. Some food industries also hire laundry personnel to wash and sanitize employees' uniforms and safety equipment. Facilities workers may also be responsible for pest control.

Most workers responsible for maintaining food industry facilities are required to have training or educational credentials, ranging from vocational course work to university-level engineering or technology degrees, and are expected to have licenses in their fields. Many seek additional training and certification to gain competence with new technologies. Technical maintenance personnel's credentials and skills usually determine their wages. Entry-level workers responsible for cleaning assignments usually are paid hourly wages, starting at minimum levels, and lack the educational background of technical maintenance personnel.

Maintenance and facilities occupations may include the following:

- Chief Engineer
- Facility Manager
- Heating, Ventilation, and Air-
  Conditioning (HVAC) Engineer
- Electrician
- Plumber
- Custodian/Janitor

Security

Food manufacturing and wholesaling companies require security personnel to protect both employees and food products. These personnel monitor workers' and visitors' activities inside plants, in restricted areas, and on surrounding grounds. They use surveillance equipment, such as cameras and audio devices, as well as patrolling production and warehouse facilities on foot or in small vehicles. Chemical and smoke sensors alert security personnel to biohazards and fires. Some personnel guard plant entrances, examining employee identification badges and inspecting vehicles for dangerous items that could contaminate foods or injure people. They also look for stolen items when people leave. All security personnel must be prepared to provide support when emergencies occur.

Some security personnel have received public safety training at vocational schools or universities, while others have backgrounds in law enforcement, fire safety, or military service. Most qualified security personnel are certified in their field. Many also acquire training and certification to use weapons and administer first aid. Security workers earn salaries based on their security ex-

The Federal Poultry Processing Inspection Act of 1957 mandated the inspection of all poultry slaughtered for human consumption. (©Picsfive/Dreamstime.com)

perience, responsibilities, and useful skills applicable to the food industry.

Security occupations may include the following:

- Security Guard
- Food Safety Inspector
- Food Safety Manager
- Biohazard Specialist
- Firefighter

Technology, Research, Design, and Development

Food manufacturers and wholesalers hire a variety of personnel to develop new products and improve manufacturing processes. Engineers design production factories and machinery. They also develop improved methods for storing and shipping food products. Food scientists investigate combinations of ingredients and chemicals to design food that tastes good or has other desired traits, including appealing texture or appearance and in-

creased shelf life. Nutritionists evaluate samples for nutritional value or deficiency. Quality control personnel inspect new products. Test groups provide opinions and insights that research and development personnel use to refine products.

These technical personnel usually have college degrees in engineering or scientific fields and are familiar with using laboratory equipment. Many have advanced degrees. They acquire licenses and certification when required. The food industry depends on highly trained technicians to design new foods, and the Department of Labor projects that jobs in these positions will increase by 16 percent between 2008 and 2018. According to the BLS, in 2009 food scientists and technologists working for manufacturers earned annual incomes averaging $59,790. The tenth percentile salary was $34,530, and the ninetieth percentile salary was $103,160. Researchers who create new products or flavors often receive extra monetary compensation for expanding their employers' lines. Industries have different agreements regarding intellectual property rights if technologies or formulas associated with an employee's work are patented or trademarked.

Technology, research, design, and development occupations may include the following:

- Vice President of Research and Development
- Food Engineer
- Food Scientist
- Nutritionist
- Biochemist
- Food Laboratory Technician
- Quality Assurance Specialist

Production and Operations

Food manufacturing and wholesaling industries rely on entry-level workers to conduct many crucial functions. Production workers perform approximately 54 percent of food manufacturing tasks in the United States. They are assigned diverse tasks, ranging from sorting vegetables to cutting up seafood. Some 34 percent of the food manufacturing workforce processes livestock, while 19 percent makes tortillas and bakery foods. Supervisors, often employees with more work experience and training than line workers, monitor production workers' performance and productivity. Inspectors evaluate the safety of products. Testers sample products for taste and quality before they are packaged for distribution.

Many entry-level production and operations workers lack specialized education or professional food industry experience. Manufacturers and wholesalers frequently train these workers to perform specific tasks. According to the BLS, the median hourly wage of all food production was $11.94, while the median for all production workers in all industries was $14.41. Food inspectors and quality assurance personnel, including USDA

OCCUPATION PROFILE

Millwright

Considerations	Qualifications
Description	Installs machinery and equipment according to layout plans, blueprints, and other drawings in an industrial establishment such as a food factory.
Career cluster	Manufacturing
Interests	Data; things
Working conditions	Work inside; work both inside and outside
Minimum education level	On-the-job training; high school diploma/technical/community college; apprenticeship
Physical exertion	Heavy work
Physical abilities	Basic fitness; must have trunk strength
Opportunities for experience	Apprenticeship; military service; part-time work
Licensure and certification	Usually not required
Employment outlook	Slower-than-average growth expected
Holland interest score	RES

Note: See volume 1, "Publisher's Note," for an explanation of the Holland interest score.

inspectors assigned to plants, often have completed food-related education and training, such as earning veterinary or agricultural degrees. Veterinarians are required to secure state licenses. Inspectors, often government workers, are certified to evaluate foods. Federally employed veterinarians earned annual salaries averaging $84,200 in 2009, while veterinary technologists and technicians earned $47,020 on average.

Occupations include the following:

- Production Manager
- Operations Manager
- Quality Assurance Director
- Quality Assurance Technician
- Supervisor
- Inspector
- Baker
- Butcher/Meat Cutter/Meat Trimmer
- Roasting, Baking, and Drying Machine Operator/Tender
- Food Batchmaker

Distribution

Distribution personnel deliver agricultural materials to plants to be processed into food and ship finished food products to customers. Distribution managers prepare manifests for shipments of raw goods and foods using various transportation modes traveling by land, air, and water. They secure agricultural permits and customs documents needed to transport food products over state and country borders and ensure that any tariffs are paid.

Distribution positions require differing qualifications. Many warehouse jobs are entry-level, involving moving inventory and loading and unloading vehicles. Workers often receive training after they are hired. They are paid hourly or yearly wages based on their assignments, with drivers often being compensated according to the mileage they cover. Physical strength and the ability to lift heavy weights often determine who works in warehouses. People who drive distribution vehicles usually are required to have training and licenses to operate commercial trucks. Distribution personnel often are trained and certified to use specific equipment, such as forklifts. Managers usually receive annual salaries, which are sometimes supplemented with bonuses and perks to reward performance.

Distribution occupations may include the following:

- Distribution Manager
- Heavy Truck Driver
- Light Truck Driver
- Train/Truck/Ship Loader
- Packer and Packager
- Freight Loader/Unloader

Groundskeeping

Groundskeeping workers keep the areas surrounding warehouses and plants safe. They clear drives, parking lots, and loading docks of debris, snow, ice, and other hazards that might injure workers and visitors or impede production and deliveries. In addition to practical tasks, groundskeepers design attractive gardens and landscapes to enhance companies' appearances. Occasionally, groundskeepers incorporate decorative examples of foods in which their companies specialize, such as corn stalks in landscapes at cereal companies. They sometimes build exercise trails for employees. They usually have experience using various gardening tools and basic knowledge of plants. Some may have horticultural training from high schools, vocational institutions, or colleges. Most have innate awareness of how to position plants and landscaping materials to beautify areas. Hourly or yearly wages vary according to workers' abilities and credentials.

Groundskeeping occupations may include the following:

- Head Groundskeeper
- Groundskeeper
- Landscape Architect
- Landscaper

Human Resources

Human resources personnel advertise available jobs, recruit candidates, assess applications, interview applicants, and hire successful candidates. They oversee employee training, administer payrolls and benefits, and help set and ensure employee compliance with company policy and procedures, including safety and food-handling procedures. They also respond to employee grievances and they may be involved in contract negotiations with collective bargaining units.

Human resources directors usually have human resources management or business degrees and previous work experience. Human resources managers in the food manufacturing industry earned annual salaries averaging $97,100 in 2009, whereas human resources specialists earned an average of $57,750 and human resources assistants earned an average of $35,080.

Human resources occupations may include the following:

- Human Resources Director
- Human Resources Manager
- Human Resources Specialist
- Human Resources Assistant
- Benefits Specialist
- Payroll Clerk

Information Technology

Information technology (IT) professionals maintain and design computer systems for use by food manufacturers and wholesalers. These systems include standard business computers and networks for use by administrative and management personnel, as well as specialized manufacturing computers. Computer programmers write code to direct automated production machinery, as well as designing custom databases to meet their companies' needs. They often oversee the computer control rooms that direct automated production processes. IT personnel maintain, repair, and update computers and ensure they are free of viruses, spyware, and other potential hazards. They may also manage their companies' Web sites. Some food manufacturers hire personnel skilled with visual and audio equipment to document procedures at their plants. Technicians also provide support services necessary for meetings at industrial sites or presentations, setting up audiovisual and other electronic equipment.

IT personnel usually have degrees or training in computer science or systems from universities or vocational schools. Some seek advanced degrees or training to secure certification in specialties or acquire knowledge of new technologies. Their salaries are based on their qualifications and responsibilities.

IT occupations may include the following:

- Information Technology Director
- Computer Programmer
- Software Engineer
- Network and System Administrator
- Database Administrator
- Webmaster
- Multimedia Technician

Administrative Support

Administrative workers perform the tasks associated with routine day-to-day business support. They fulfill a wide range of duties to aid managers and department heads and are crucial for manufacturers' and wholesalers' effectiveness. Some administrative clerks perform several tasks, while others specialize. They often document food resources brought in or shipped out of companies' buildings. Administrative workers deal with correspondence, answer phones, file invoices, prepare schedules, enter data in computers, and perform other clerical tasks. Receptionists greet visitors, record information about them, and provide them with identification badges.

Administrative workers have diverse educational and professional backgrounds. Some begin their careers in the food industry through temporary assignments. Many start as interns or in entry-level jobs and advance as they gain training, experience, and tenure.

Administrative occupations may include the following:

- Office Manager
- Administrative Assistant
- Bookkeeper
- Receptionist

INDUSTRY OUTLOOK

Overview

The outlook for the food manufacturing and wholesaling industry shows it to be on the rise. The industry thrives worldwide as decreasing percentages of nations' populations produce their own food. The United Nations emphasizes that more people live in urban areas than in rural areas, so the majority of Earth's population needs to purchase food it cannot produce. The BLS, meanwhile, notes that food manufacturing differs from nonfood industries because it is more resilient in the face of economic fluctuations. Indeed, one common response to economic downturns in industrialized nations is to eat fewer meals at restaurants and purchase more food for preparation at home. Most experts agree that these industries will sustain future growth.

In the early twenty-first century, food processing represents the biggest manufacturing industry in the United States, and it continues to grow to feed increasing populations. Mergers and acquisitions have contributed to some food manufacturers attaining substantial revenues. In 2001, when Kellogg bought the Keebler Foods Company, its revenues increased from $6 billion (earned in 2000) to $8.3 billion (2002). That corporation and other major food manufacturers credited revenue growth to their management adjusting strategies to stress value over volume. Kellogg mixed freeze-dried fruits in its cereals, appealing to health-conscious consumers, achieving $8.8 billion in sales by 2003.

In 2007, weakened economies resulted in some food manufacturers reporting net losses. A variety of factors contributed to these losses, including the H1N1 influenza, energy costs, and depreciating currencies. The losses were short-lived, however. According to *Food Processing*, twenty-six of the twenty-seven largest food manufacturers did not experience declining sales during the global financial crisis of 2007-2009. Some food manufacturers were unable to attain profits, however. Pilgrim's Pride declared bankruptcy in 2008, and Smithfield Foods closed plants and decreased production the following year. During 2008, the Food Institute announced that the number of food manufacturing mergers and acquisitions had decreased by 8.5 percent from the previous year. In *Global Economic Prospects, 2009*, the World Bank noted prices of food increased by 138 percent between 2003 and 2008.

Major food manufacturing corporations, such as General Mills, Kraft Foods, and Cadbury, continue to thrive. Many U.S. food manufacturers and wholesalers export products and operate plants in other countries to meet international demand.

Food manufacturers building new plants often expand to locations that offer economic incentives, as when ConAgra Foods built a new sweet potato processing plant in Louisiana that was projected to create several hundred new jobs by 2011. Technological advances have contributed to financial stability and growth.

As the recession affected consumers' budgets, food manufacturers produced affordable foods. Reuters noted that the food manufacturing sectors generating the most revenues were meat and dairy products, fruits and vegetables, and specialty foods. Manufacturers and wholesalers continuously survey markets to become aware of trends, such as low-carbohydrate diets, so they can produce foods to cater to those trends. The ability to adapt production to changing consumer behavior often ensures food manufacturers' success.

Food manufacturing revenues also benefit from consumers' health concerns. In the first decade of the twenty-first century, gluten-free food products realized annual sales of $1.5 billion in the United

---

PROJECTED EMPLOYMENT FOR SELECTED OCCUPATIONS

Food Manufacturing

Employment		
2009	Projected 2018	Occupation
49,440	49,100	Bakers
45,850	46,100	First-line supervisors/ managers of production and operating workers
81,880	85,300	Food batchmakers
106,470	101,400	Packaging and filling machine operators and tenders
92,690	96,900	Slaughterers and meat packers

Source: U.S. Bureau of Labor Statistics, Industries at a Glance, Occupational Employment Statistics and Employment Projections Program.

States. Production of "nutraceuticals" and functional foods earned over $75.5 billion for U.S. manufacturers in 2007, with sales projected to reach $167 billion in 2010. That subsector generated $2 billion in Canada and created twenty-five thousand jobs in that country.

By late 2008, many U.S. food wholesalers had merged and consolidated, while others declared bankruptcy. Small wholesalers, averaging $750 million in revenues annually, risked being taken over by larger wholesalers or foreign companies. C&S Wholesale Grocers, one of the U.S. industry's leading wholesalers, earned $19 billion in 2009, distributing food products to five thousand independent and chain grocery stores. Warehouse wholesalers, including Sam's Club, dominated much of the industry's sales. Many wholesalers gained more customers as increasing numbers of restaurants and food services purchased food.

Employment Advantages

The BLS projects that food manufacturing employment will decline by an estimated 0.1 percent from 2008 to 2018, a significant loss as the average industry will grow by 11 percent during the same period. Although automation will displace workers in various food manufacturing sectors, machines cannot perform all necessary manufacturing tasks. The need for humans to perform such tasks as processing livestock will ensure a steady supply of jobs for production workers. The quantity of those production positions will increase to meet a higher consumer demand for beef, fish, and poultry products. The food manufacturing industry will consistently need employees specializing in tasks requiring hand labor and human interaction with resources being processed.

The food manufacturing and wholesaling industry will need employees to perform more diverse roles at all levels of employment to meet increasing populations' food demands. Food manufacturing workers will be sought to fill positions vacated by retiring employees. First-job seekers lacking qualifications can often secure entry-level food industry positions that provide steady income and occasional perks. Increased use of automation technology creates demand for engineers, computer scientists, and repair personnel to develop, program, and service computer and machinery technology. Employees often benefit from training and certification offered by employers to aid in professional advancement.

Annual Earnings

Food manufacturing and wholesaling revenues have remained steady despite the global recession of 2007-2009. Market analysts emphasize that tallying exact monetary figures is difficult because food manufacturing and wholesaling statistics are often combined with agricultural statistics. The World Bank has stated that the food and agricultural industries represent 10 percent of the global gross domestic product (GDP), estimating their combined value at $4.8 trillion in 2006. In that year, U.S. food manufacturers' revenues of $372 billion represented more than 12 percent of the U.S. GDP. Canned foods accounted for $12.6 billion in revenues in the United States and $50.9 billion globally that year. Frozen food products in the United States generated $25.1 billion in revenues the next year.

Euromonitor International assessed global food industry revenues at $1.6 trillion in 2007. The food price crisis starting that year caused some manufacturers' and wholesalers' profits to decline. In 2009, *Fortune* magazine noted that successful large food manufacturers generated several billion dollars each in revenues, with Nestlé producing revenues of $104 billion. The 2010 *Plunkett's Food Industry Almanac* reported that U.S. companies' food sales during the previous year generated $579.3 billion domestically and $501.9 billion in exports, totaling $1.08 trillion. IBISWorld estimated 2009 U.S. wholesaling revenues at $241.5 billion.

RELATED RESOURCES FOR FURTHER RESEARCH

Food Engineering Magazine
  1050 Illinois Rte. 83, Suite 200
  Bensenville, IL 60106-1048
  Tel: (630) 694-4351
  Fax: (630) 227-0527
  http://www.foodengineeringmag.com

Food Marketing Institute
  2345 Crystal Dr., Suite 800
  Arlington, VA 22202
  Tel: (202) 452-8444

Fax: (202) 429-4519
http://www.fmi.org

GROCERY MANUFACTURERS ASSOCIATION
1350 I St. NW, Suite 300
Washington, DC 20005
Tel: (202) 639-5900
Fax: (202) 639-5932
http://www.gmabrands.com

INSTITUTE OF FOOD TECHNOLOGISTS
525 W Van Buren, Suite 1000
Chicago, IL 60607
Tel: (312) 782-8424
Fax: (312) 782-8348
http://www.ift.org

NATIONAL FROZEN AND REFRIGERATED FOODS
ASSOCIATION
4755 Linglestown Rd., Suite 300
P.O. Box 6069
Harrisburg, PA 17112
Tel: (717) 657-8601
Fax: (717) 657-9862
http://www.nfraweb.org

ABOUT THE AUTHOR

Elizabeth D. Schafer received a Ph.D. in the history of technology and science, specializing in agricultural history, from Auburn University in 1993. Her research focuses on agricultural engineers' work to develop more efficient machinery, equipment, and techniques to cultivate and harvest food and fiber crops. It also examines the role of veterinary science in controlling and eradicating animal diseases that cause public health risks by contaminating food and dairy supplies. She has contributed articles on food science and technology, nutrition, and veterinary history to numerous publications.

FURTHER READING

Basu, Saikat K., James E. Thomas, and Surya N. Acharya. "Prospects for Growth in Global Nutraceutical and Functional Food Markets: A Canadian Perspective." *Australian Journal of Basic and Applied Sciences* 1, no. 4 (2007): 637-649.

Belasco, Warren, and Roger Horowitz, eds. *Food Chains: From Farmyard to Shopping Cart.* Philadelphia: University of Pennsylvania Press, 2009.

Bowden, Rob. *The Food Industry.* London: Wayland, 2009.

Cubbitt, Ben. "Food Distribution: The Supply Chain Optimization Challenge." *Food Manufacturing* 19, no. 3 (March, 2006): 12.

Fraser, Jill Andresky. "A Return to Basics at Kellogg: How a Focus on Profitability, Cash Management, and Realistic Forecasting Spurred Innovation and Revival at One of America's Venerable Food Companies." *MIT Sloan Management Review* 45, no. 4 (Summer, 2004): 27-30.

Galvez, Farah R., and Sonia Yuson De Leon. *Food Technology and Globalization.* Manila, Philippines: Merriam Webster Bookstore, 2006.

Institute of Food Technologists. "Traceability (Product Tracing) in Food Systems: An IFT Report Submitted to the FDA." *Comprehensive Reviews in Food Science and Food Safety* 9, no. 1 (January, 2010): 92-175. http://www.ift.org/ Knowledge%20Center/Read%20IFT %20Publications/Science%20Reports/ Contract%20Reports/Traceability%20in %20Food%20Systems.aspx.

Kutz, Myer, ed. *Handbook of Farm, Dairy, and Food Machinery.* Norwich, N.Y.: William Andrew, 2007.

Maroulis, Zacharias B., and George D. Saravacos. *Food Plant Economics.* Boca Raton, Fla.: CRC Press, 2008.

Mattsson, Berit, and Ulf Sonesson, eds. *Environmentally Friendly Food Processing.* Boca Raton, Fla.: CRC Press, 2003.

Millstone, Erik, and Tim Lang. *The Atlas of Food: Who Eats What, Where, and Why.* Foreword by Marion Nestle. Rev. ed. Berkeley: University of California Press, 2008.

Morris, Charles E. "Seventy-five Years of Food Frontiers." *Food Engineering* 75, no. 9 (September, 2003): 54-63.

Murray, Sarah. "Food: The World's Biggest Industry." *Forbes,* November 15, 2007. http:// www.forbes.com/2007/11/11/growth-agriculture-business-forbeslife-food07-cx_sm_1113bigfood.html.

Nestle, Marion. *Food Politics: How the Food Industry Influences Nutrition and Health.* Berkeley: University of California Press, 2002.

Nützenadel, Alexander, and Frank Trentmann. *Food and Globalization: Consumption, Markets, and Politics in the Modern World.* New York: Berg, 2008.

Pehanich, Mike, and Dave Fusaro. "The Changing Fortunes of Food Manufacturing." FoodProcessing.com, September 7, 2007. http://www.foodprocessing.com/articles/2007/221.html.

Plunkett, Jack W., ed. *Plunkett's Food Industry Almanac, 2010: The Only Comprehensive Guide to Food Companies and Trends.* 7th ed. Houston, Tex.: Plunkett Research, 2010.

Trager, James. *The Food Chronology: A Food Lover's Compendium of Events and Anecdotes, from Prehistory to the Present.* New York: Henry Holt, 1995.

U.S. Bureau of Labor Statistics. "Animal and Food Scientists." In *Occupational Outlook Handbook*, 2010-2011 ed. http://www.bls.gov/oco/ocos046.htm.

———. *Career Guide to Industries*, 2010-2011 ed. http://www.bls.gov/oco/cg.

———. "Food Processing Occupations." In *Occupational Outlook Handbook*, 2010-2011 ed. http://www.bls.gov/oco/ocos219.htm.

U.S. Census Bureau. North American Industry Classification System (NAICS), 2007. http://www.census.gov/cgi-bin/sssd/naics/naicsrch?chart=2007.

U.S. Department of Commerce. International Trade Administration. Office of Trade and Industry Information. Industry Trade Data and Analysis. http://ita.doc.gov/td/industry/otea/OTII/OTII-index.html.

U.S. Food and Drug Administration. *Investigations Operations Manual.* Falls Church, Va.: FDAnews, 2004.

Food Retail Industry

INDUSTRY SNAPSHOT

General Industry: Agriculture and Food

Career Cluster: Agriculture, Food, and Natural Resources

Subcategory Industries: Baked Goods Stores; Commissaries; Confectionary and Nut Stores; Convenience Stores; Delicatessens Primarily Retailing a Range of Grocery Items and Meats; Fish and Seafood Markets; Fruit and Vegetable Markets; Meat Markets; Retailing Automotive Fuels in Combination with a Convenience Store or Food Mart; Retailing via Direct Sales to Residential Customers; Supermarkets and Other Grocery (except Convenience) Stores

Related Industries: Farming Industry; Food Manufacturing and Wholesaling Industry; Food Services

Annual Domestic Revenues: $719.5 billion USD (Gale Group, 2007)

Annual International Revenues: $1.461 trillion USD (Gale Group, 2007)

Annual Global Revenues: $2.1805 trillion USD (Gale Group, 2007)

NAICS Numbers: 424410, 424420, 424430, 424440, 424450, 424460, 424470, 424480, 424490, 445110, 445120, 445210, 445230, 445291-445292, 445299, 454390

INDUSTRY DEFINITION

Summary

The retail food industry sells food and nonfood items from fixed locations, ranging from small specialty shops and convenience stores to supermarkets, supercenters, and large bulk warehouse-type facilities. Gas stations that include convenience stores also sell a limited range of grocery products. Businesses such as delicatessens purvey a limited amount of retail foodstuffs to customers, besides serving as restaurants. Some grocery stores sell prepared foods. Retail food facilities contain specialized equipment, including shelves, bins, refrigerated cases, and freezers, to display food and nonfood items. Food also is sold directly to consumers via online Web sites. Items for sale include dairy products, baked goods, canned and frozen foods, fresh fruits and vegetables, fresh and prepared meats, fish, and poultry. Government regulations mandate proper storage and adherence to strict sanitary conditions.

History of the Industry

The nineteenth century general store, which sold everything from farm implements to clothing to food staples, can be considered the direct progenitor of the modern food retail industry. It in turn had evolved from frontier trading posts. Specialized food, dairy, and meat markets were the next type of outlet in this evolution, beginning about 1860. Most such food markets continued many of the customer policies used in general stores; these included personal service by clerks, liberal credit terms, and even payment by bartering of store goods for consumer-produced goods. The stock was presented to customers by clerks because shelves were inaccessible behind counters.

The first chain food store was almost certainly the Great Atlantic and Pacific Tea Company, universally referred to as the A&P. It began in 1859 as a tea shop and by the end of the American Civil War had twenty-five stores that sold groceries. By 1880, it had opened its one hundredth store. Another early chain was the Jones Brothers Tea Company, which began about 1872 and later became the Grand Union chain. Other well-known food companies that had their origins in the nineteenth century include Bohack's and the Great Western Tea Company, which became the massive Kroger Company.

Some of the largest chains grew via vertical integration, expanding through ownership of meatpackers, coffee-roasting plants, dairies, bakeries, and other subindustries. With somewhat less significant impact, expansion also has occurred the opposite way, with manufacturers and grocery wholesalers expanding into retail operations. Independent food stores of various sizes continued to operate, but as time progressed they captured a declining percentage of the market. Because of their lower prices, possible because of economies of scale, chain stores also became known as "economy" stores.

By the early 1910's, a few stores were advertising "self-service" while still providing the assistance of clerks for customers accustomed to such service. A Memphis, Tennessee, Piggly Wiggly market is considered to be one of the earliest self-service stores. By about 1920, self-service had be-

come an accepted part of the grocery business. Also becoming more common by then was the "combination" store, which provided groceries, produce, meat, and dairy products within one expanded facility for so-called one-stop shopping. By about 1930, this innovation had led in the eastern United States to the establishment of supermarkets that were four or five times larger than earlier grocery stores.

One of the first supermarkets—originally calling itself a "warehouse grocery"—was the King Kullen, founded by Michael Cullen in Jamaica, Queens, New York, in 1930. Big Bear was also among the first supermarkets, as was Alpha Beta, probably the most widespread of the early chains. For the first few years, supermarkets were not housed in specially built stores but operated from any spacious available property, including former garages, factories, warehouses, and even movie

Supermarkets remain a popular source of fruits and vegetables. Kroger is one of the largest food retail chains. (©Dreamstime.com)

theaters. Sometime during the 1930's, stores began being planned from the ground up. Some of the major twentieth century food retail chains included Grand Union, Albertson's, Safeway, Lucky, Vons, Supervalu, Winn-Dixie, Food Fair, Stop & Shop, Ralphs, and American. Many are no longer in business as independently owned chains.

The origin of the word "supermarket" is not clear, but one of its earliest uses was by the Cincinnati-based Albers Super Market in 1933. Its common definition is an aggregation of departments selling varieties of foodstuffs and a large number of other products in which the grocery area must be self-service. The various departments in early supermarkets might have been operated by individual owners who had banded together within a single facility. This is uncommon now, except in cooperative food stores (co-ops), where independent merchants routinely band together. They also may be known as affiliated independent retailers. A term that is no longer much in use is the "superette," a concept that is akin to today's convenience store.

About 1949, after a slow recovery from World War II, a lengthy period of consolidation began in the food retail industry. By 1967, the Federal Trade Commission (FTC) had issued an enforcement policy to address what it saw as overconcentration. This edict curtailed but did not end the mergers, which continue to this day. In the early years of the twenty-first century, the FTC again stepped in to halt mergers that it considered likely to unfairly limit competition. By the 1950's, food retailing constituted the largest percentage of any retail industry in sales, employing one out of every seven people working in all retail businesses.

Within the food retail industry, grocery sales constituted more than 88 percent of all sales by the end of the 1950's, a 22 percent increase over a thirty-year span. The 1950's had seen a resounding boom in supermarket openings; some even had floodlit premieres just like films of the day. In that decade, supermarket sales doubled from 35 percent of all retail food sales in 1950 to 70 percent at decade's end. Nonfood items, such as flowers, health and beauty aids, and greeting cards, were added to the stock of products, as was a greater selection of alcoholic beverages. In the thirty years between 1977 and 2007, food retail industry sales grew from $141 billion to almost $720 billion.

The birth of the convenience store is credited to an ice company owner in Dallas, Texas, in 1927. Because his business stayed open longer than local groceries—sixteen hours a day, seven days a week—he decided to add a few staples, such as eggs, milk, and bread, to his inventory. The convenience for customers increased his business, and other entrepreneurs followed suit. Various names—including "midget stores" and "bantam markets"—were used for this kind of business until the term "convenience store" came into general usage sometime after World War II.

The Industry Today

The retail food industry has historically operated on low profit margins, primarily because of competition. Its pretax profit generally has ranged from 1.3 to 2.5 percent of sales, depending on volume. In fiscal year 2003-2004, the percentage fell to a more than twenty-year low, with an estimated net profit after taxes of a mere 0.88 percent. By 2009, overall industry net profits were 1.43 percent, a loss from the previous year. The decline has been attributed to such factors as the poor economy, rising employee health care costs, the increasing costs of adhering to government regulations, and even credit card use fees. Independent retailers—those operating one to ten stores—actually garnered the highest profits, with a 1.9 percent return in 2009. However, because of the industry's ongoing consolidation, many independents during this period went out of business.

In 2008, there were more than 85,000 nonwarehouse grocery outlets, of which almost 26,000 were convenience stores that did not sell gasoline. In addition, about 120,000 convenience stores were attached to gas stations, a phenomenon more common in suburban and rural areas. It is estimated that there is one convenience store for every twenty-one hundred Americans. In those stores that are part of a gas station, an average of 65 percent of revenue comes from gasoline sales, groceries account for 12 percent, cigarettes 11 percent, beer and wine 4 percent, and prepared fast food (such as hot dogs and burritos) 2 percent. Most such places also dispense lottery tickets in states where they are legal. By 2005, there were more than 3,100 warehouse-type food outlets, including 680 Sam's Clubs. According to statistics of the Food Marketing Institute, in 2006 supermarkets alone

A shopper closely examines a loaf of bread at the supermarket. Generic or store-brand products are increasingly popular. (©Dreamstime.com)

had sales of almost $500 billion. In the same year, approximately one-half of every one hundred dollars spent in grocery stores was for perishable items.

Even some of the largest multibillion-dollar grocery chains remain regionally based and are not found in every state. Small to midsize chains, such as Trader Joe's, which have established a popular niche but offer a fairly limited stock of products, slowly are expanding into many regions of the United States. There are an increasing number of specialty stores that sell niche products such as organically grown "health" foods or ethnic foods. The growth in health food retailers springs from the growing desire of people to lead healthier lives. Stores even may specialize in only a single type of product, such as candy, cheese, nuts, or pastry. These stores generally charge higher prices but offer merchandise that may not be as readily available or of the same high quality elsewhere.

Most food-store chains offer goods under store-brand labels that usually cost less than similar national brand products. As early as 1930, almost 50 percent of all chains offered these "private" labels. In 1977, so-called generic brands were introduced in the United States by Jewel Food Stores, following a trial by the French giant Carrefours S.A. Containers often carried just a word or two describing their contents (like "cola" or "sweet peas") but bore either no brand name at all or one that was not recognizable to consumers. Such products sold for less than similar branded ones because there were few advertising costs, and some consumers had reservations about their quality. (Store ads carried slogans such as "Generics: Just plain good! Just plain cheap!") Within three years, almost fifteen thousand markets carried these no-frills products, and they accounted for up to 20 percent of sales in their categories.

Large chain operations such as Walmart and Target, which once dealt exclusively in nonfood items, increasingly are adding grocery sections. They usually do not purvey as much variety as large supermarkets, but they do provide convenience and lower prices because of their considerable buying power. By 2005, Walmart was deriving 28 percent of its sales from its grocery line, and by 2007, it had captured 17.5 percent of the grocery market share. With the start of the recession in 2007, many chains cut their prices. At the same time, food manufacturers began downsizing product packaging and contents, and consumers began paying as much for less.

Studies show that price and convenience are what customers value most, more than particular brands or stores. Markets that offer lower prices, discount cards, doubled coupons, and reward programs are more likely to retain long-term customers. Such incentives have replaced the once omnipresent variety of trading stamps (such as Green Stamps) that could be pasted in books and exchanged for many types of goods. The convenience of online shopping from such companies as the bulk-sales chain Costco also is a draw for consumers.

Also selling online is the mega-chain Walmart, currently the world's largest, although it does not offer food in all its stores. Some companies also offer limited home delivery. Items such as DVDs for sale and rent now are available in markets. It is estimated that the average full-service supermarket will derive 25 percent of its sales from canned goods and other edible packaged shelf items; 20 percent from a variety of nonfood items; 15 percent from meat, fish, and poultry; 11 percent from produce; 7 percent from the prepared foods or delicatessen section; 6 percent from dairy products; 6 percent from baked goods, either packaged or from an in-store bakery; 5 percent from frozen foods; and 5 percent from in-store pharmacies that fill prescriptions for medications. (Ratios for other types of food stores differ markedly.)

After Walmart, the Kroger chain, which also offers online sales, is the next largest retail food chain. By 2008, it had almost twenty-five hundred outlets located in more than thirty states. It operates under a variety of names and owns small convenience stores as well as huge markets. Like Walmart, Kroger's facilities offer a wide variety of services, including (at some locations) pharmacies, photo-processing services, and gasoline sales. It manufactures a large proportion of the products it sells, including dairy products and baked goods. In 2007, its net profit was 16 percent higher than the previous year.

Of the bulk warehouse-type businesses, Costco has membership stores in North America, Mexico, Asia, and other locations. In 2008, the company owned more than five hundred outlets, of which almost four hundred were in the United States. Its largest facilities contain up to 205,000 square feet, and its average outlet measures slightly more than 140,000 square feet. Its stores stock all manner of

A butcher stacks turkeys for Thanksgiving sales. The average Costco outlet measures slightly more than 140,000 square feet. (AP/Wide World Photos)

items, from furniture and appliances to food and tires. In fiscal year 2007, the company's net profit was almost $1.1 billion.

The cost of opening new stores has increased over the years. At the beginning of the twenty-first century, the cost to build, equip, and open a small business of twenty-four hundred square feet was at least $80,000. The cost of a large business with thirty-two thousand square feet required an investment of at least $850,000. Midsize locations fell somewhere in between. Labor costs at that time were estimated to be about 8 to 11 percent of sales. Food industry workers are more heavily unionized than the average of 14 percent for workers in other industries; in 2008, about 22 percent belonged to unions.

Unionized employees tend to be found in nationwide grocery chains; huge warehouse-type operations and smaller businesses are almost never unionized. Union membership and staffing requirements undoubtedly will be adversely affected in the future by further company consolidations.

Many of the jobs remain part time and relatively low paying, and as a result, these jobs tend to be filled by younger workers. According to the U.S. Bureau of Labor Statistics, in 2008 fewer than 14 percent of food retail industry jobs were held by workers fifty-five years of age and older, a smaller percentage than is seen in American industry as a whole.

There are several major types of food retail outlets that exist in the United States today. Of these, supermarkets, specialty shops, and warehouse-type facilities together compose the largest percentage by far.

Supermarkets. By industry standards, supermarkets are businesses that generate revenue in excess of $2 million per annum. They carry a full range of food and nonfood products and may offer prepared foods. They may be independently owned, but most probably are part of larger chain operations. Each store that is part of a large organization follows the corporate standards in matters such as design, product selection, and other operations. Independent markets may offer products unique to certain ethnic groups or have established other niches that enable them to withstand competition from chains. Most fall within a size range of thirty thousand to seventy thousand square feet.

Affiliates and Cooperatives. A grouping of independently owned stores, independent affiliates may band together to purchase from a central wholesaler for economies of scale. They may offer commonly held private labels. By industry standards, such affiliates do not exceed ten stores.

Cooperatives are somewhat similar to independent affiliates in that they are individually owned businesses that group together for economies of scale. They may offer commonly held private labels. Instead of purchasing from a central wholesaler, they most often own shares in it, and profits in part depend on the performance of each store. Cooperatives are more commonly found outside the United States.

A specialty store may deal in only one product or a type of product, such as health or ethnic food. They are sometimes called "gourmet" groceries. There are stores that sell only products made from olives, teas and coffees, cheeses, cakes, and gourmet meats. Greengrocers specialize in produce. Single specialty outlets usually are found in more upscale areas and most malls, while those selling ethnic foods can be located in compatible ethnic areas or increasingly anywhere such food is relished.

Hypermarkets. Mostly a European phenomenon, hypermarkets may run over 300,000 square feet and offer full department store facilities as well as groceries, gas stations, and other services. The origin of the format is credited to the French company Carrefours S.A. in the 1970's. Hypermarkets of about 225,000 square feet were tested in the United States by Walmart, but presumably because of their overwhelming size, they were not enthusiastically accepted.

Supercenters. Smaller than a hypermarket but larger than an average supermarket, supercenters generally range from 100,000 to 200,000 square feet. Such facilities—many owned by Walmart—are located in numerous U.S. localities; by 2007, Walmart had 2,250 supercenters. The company also has been the target of vocal protests because supercenters tend to drive small local stores out of business. Some cities have held elections to determine whether a supercenter should be built there. Statistically, nearby stores immediately tend to lose from 10 percent to 20 percent of their clientele when supercenters open.

Deep-Discount Stores. These stores offer a limited variety of grocery items, often private-label brands, at prices that are discounted relative to regular retail outlets. Their facilities tend to be quite spartan. Such chains as the Dollar Store and the 99 Cents Only Store may be the most ubiquitous examples of deep discount stores in the United States.

General-Line Grocery Stores. The closest type of food retail outlet to convenience stores is the general-line grocery, sometimes called the "limited assortment" grocery. It offers staples like milk and bread and a small selection of canned and frozen goods, but not meats or produce. General-line grocery stores are more common outside the United States.

Convenience Stores. Convenience stores provide a limited stock of basic supplies including foodstuffs and generally are open long hours, sometimes twenty-four hours daily. The majority of their sales are derived from cigarettes, beer, milk, candy, and soft drinks. They generally occupy between fifteen hundred and two thousand square feet. Two well-known chains are the Pantry and 7-Eleven, and there are many single-owner "mom and pop" stores in this category. In Latino areas, bodegas—which usually are not part of a chain—are plentiful. Convenience stores are found in most areas, even when there are supermarkets present, and are intended for those who need only a small number of items and want to get in and out quickly. For this advantage, customers generally pay a higher price per item than for comparable products in supermarkets. The stores attached to gas stations far outsell, in the aggregate, stand-alone convenience stores.

Warehouse Stores. The hallmarks of warehouse stores such as Costco and Sam's Club are huge size, utilitarian design, a membership fee, and merchandise sold in super-sized and/or large bundled-together quantities. Goods usually are shelved from floor to ceiling and may only include the most popular goods, usually numbering about one thousand different items, rather than a supermarket-type selection. Because the purchaser buys in bulk, the price per unit generally is lower.

INDUSTRY MARKET SEGMENTS

Small Businesses

Potential Annual Earnings Scale. Because a great many food retail industry jobs are part time and entry level, salaries for most positions are lower than the average for all industries. The workers in a small business are not likely to be unionized. The majority of nonmanagement workers earn between $9 and $15 per hour, but the average unskilled small-business employee will earn an hourly wage on the low end of the scale. Some nonunionized businesses pay even less than minimum wage. A small business will probably employ just an owner or manager and a small number of salespeople. If it is a one-store operation, the owners' earnings will vary according to the store's profits.

Clientele Interaction. In a small business, there is likely to be some personal relationship with individual customers. They may choose to be loyal to a business they know rather than shop around for somewhat lower prices. Although individually owned "mom and pop" stores are becoming less prevalent, except perhaps in heavily ethnic neighborhoods, specialty shops and ethnic markets may engender some of the same loyalty.

Amenities, Atmosphere, and Physical Grounds. Small retail food outlets rarely exceed fifteen hundred square feet, and 80 percent of the available space is for customer service, with the remaining 20 percent divided among backroom storage, a restroom, office space, and general work area. Some older stores may seem dark and cramped in comparison with newer facilities, which usually are attractively designed and well lit.

Typical Number of Employees. The number of employees depends on the store's hours; the average small independent business may have as few as two or three. If a store is open twenty-four hours, like some convenience chains, there will be at least three people on a day shift, including a manager, and one or two at night.

Traditional Geographic Locations. Many small general food businesses are clustered in lower socioeconomic areas that large chains do not find potentially profitable to enter. Specialty shops are more prevalent in wealthier areas where their higher prices do not matter and their "exotic" products are in demand. Ethnic markets mainly can be found in areas where corresponding ethnic

Many doughnut shops are mom-and-pop operations, but some are part of national chains. (©Nolte Lourens/Dreamstime.com)

populations are concentrated, but increasingly they are locating in higher socioeconomic locations as diverse groups of people develop a taste for their wares.

Pros of Working for a Small Business. Owners and employees of small businesses may get to know their customers by name and have personal relationships with them. Employees may have more say in how the business is run and can feel more integral to the operation, even making suggestions for improving service.

Cons of Working for a Small Business. In a small food store, prospects for long-term employment may be shaky, and benefits such as vacation time, health insurance, and sick leave are very limited. For the owner, who may have to take on all the duties in the business, there are long hours and little time off. Employees may only work part time and are not likely to be unionized. They generally earn less than comparable workers in other industries. Legally required expenses, such as for insurance and business licenses, reduce profits. Bad economic times may cause the business to close or to seek a less expensive location away from an established customer base.

Costs

Utilities: Utilities include water, gas, electric, telephone, and Internet service. If the property is not owned by the business operator, some or all of those expenses may be split as part of a lease agreement.

Taxes and Insurance: Small businesses are required to pay business, property, and other applicable taxes and collect sales taxes from their customers. They purchase business licenses and insurance, including fire, health, and liability as appropriate.

Rent: Rent is a major expense if the location is leased, particularly in a well-maintained downtown area or within a successful shopping center or mall. Flat fees or a percentage-of-sales fees are the usual lease arrangements. Escalator clauses are common. Rents are lower in downscale areas where profits also might be lower.

Midsize Businesses

Potential Annual Earnings Scale. Most midsize businesses are part of a chain and have at least one manager and multiple assistant managers.

The average manager earns about $19 an hour and may receive bonuses and profit sharing based on store performance. As a result, those in the more profitable stores will earn more than others in the same position at less profitable stores. Managers' salaries can rise to as much as $85,000 a year. Specialized workers such as butchers earn an average of $15 an hour. Less skilled workers earn on average about $10 an hour, depending upon whether they are unionized, and unskilled personnel such as baggers earn about $8 an hour or less.

Clientele Interaction. Because customers generally shop around for the best prices, store employees probably will not know most customers by name or even by sight. Employees who deal with the public are expected to be polite and helpful to everyone, even when customers are angry or unreasonable.

Amenities, Atmosphere, and Physical Grounds. Stores are likely to be well lit and invitingly decorated with professional displays and dependable temperature control. Aisles are wide and stock on shelves handily displayed.

Typical Number of Employees. The number of employees in a midsize store may number thirty to fifty or more, most of whom are part time.

Traditional Geographic Locations. Midsize facilities are found in urban and suburban areas. Ethnic markets usually are located in areas where there are sizable ethnic communities but increasingly are found in other areas as well.

Pros of Working for a Midsize Business. Workers in a midsize business are more likely to be union members and thus eligible for paid vacations, sick leave, and health insurance. Staff discounts often are available for employees who shop in the store. Physical surroundings usually are pleasant. Those who enjoy contact with the public are well suited to the food retail industry.

Cons of Working for a Midsize Business. Part-time or nonunion workers may be eligible for few benefits. Workers in chain stores are most likely to be covered by union contracts, but job security in independently owned stores is not as great, and average salaries are lower than in other industries. Midsize businesses may be more prone to takeovers from large chains, so job security may be affected. Injuries occur at a higher rate than average in the grocery industry. Long service hours may result in varied work schedules, including night and weekend shifts.

Costs

Utilities: Utilities include water, gas, Internet services, electricity, and telephone. For stores that are part of chains, these expenses are paid by corporate headquarters.

Taxes and Insurance: Owner-operated facilities pay local and state business taxes and collect sales taxes from their customers. Business licenses and health, fire, and liability insurance are part of doing business. For chain stores, such expenses are paid by the corporate headquarters rather than individual stores.

Rent: Midsize stores generally are built specifically for the business and may be either wholly owned or leased. In the latter case, flat-fee leases or a percentage of sales are the most common arrangements. Most midsize groceries are usually freestanding and not located within malls.

Large Businesses

Potential Annual Earnings Scale. A large facility may have an overall manager, assistant managers, and several department managers. The top manager may earn $20 or more per hour, receive bonuses based on the store's profits, and even have a profit-sharing arrangement. The manager's salary can be as high as $85,000 per year at national chains; convenience store managers earn less. Department or first-line managers can expect to earn about $17 per hour. Specialized workers such as butchers have the highest salaries among nonmanagerial personnel, averaging about $14 an hour. Pharmacists earn the most, possibly in excess of $100,000. Low-ranking personnel such as baggers earn the least, not much more than minimum wage, or about $8 per hour.

Clientele Interaction. There is little opportunity to get to know customers well in high-volume stores, but each employee is expected to treat shoppers with courtesy and respond quickly to their requests.

Amenities, Atmosphere, and Physical Grounds. Large businesses will most likely be well designed and inviting to shoppers, except in warehouse facilities. Climate control, product placement, and lighting usually are very good.

Typical Number of Employees. Because of their long hours of operation, large high-volume stores may employ seventy to one hundred workers, up to 80 percent of whom may work part time.

Traditional Geographic Locations. Large facilities are located in most urban and suburban areas but may not be found in places perceived as high-crime areas. Large grocery businesses usually are not found in malls.

Pros of Working for a Large Business. Full-time unionized employees are more likely to be found in large businesses. They have benefits such as health insurance, vacations, and sick leave. Employees often receive a store discount. The physical surroundings are usually pleasant. Those who enjoy interaction with the public will have amply opportunity for it. Because of government regulations, the health and safety of workers usually is well protected. Managers are provided with the valuable experience of supervising many employees and overseeing complex operations.

Cons of Working for a Large Business. In busy locations, work is likely to be hectic and nonstop. Some customers may be difficult to deal with. Salaries for less skilled workers in the food retail industry generally are lower than the average for all industries. Job security for nonunion workers may not be good. Because stores usually are open for long hours, workers may have to come in very early or work very late into the evening and on weekends and holidays. Injuries occur at higher rates in the grocery industry than the average for all other industries.

Costs

Utilities: Large stores will have major utility bills covering electricity, water, Internet service, gas, and telephone.

Taxes and Insurance: Payment of state and local taxes is required, and stores collect sales taxes from their customers. Business licenses and health, liability, and fire insurance are required. Corporate headquarters cover the expenses of individual stores that are part of the company.

Rent: Large stores are almost always constructed and wholly owned by the controlling corporation; if a store is leased, the rent is determined on a flat-fee or percentage-of-sales basis. Large stores generally are freestanding and not located within malls.

ORGANIZATIONAL STRUCTURE AND JOB ROLES

The organization of a retail food facility can vary considerably according to its size. A small store—regardless of whether it is independently owned, part of a convenience store chain, or a specialty shop—may have an owner or manager and perhaps one or two other employees. Larger facilities usually are divided into functional departments, each with its own manager, with an overall store manager who oversees all the various operations. There also may be assistant managers who are in charge when the store manager is not present. In turn, the facility's manager may be overseen by regional management.

The following umbrella categories apply to the organizational structure of small, midsize, and large food retailing businesses:

- Management
- Customer Services
- Sales and Marketing
- Facilities and Security
- Technology, Research, Design, and Development
- Regulation
- Centralized Operations
- Distribution and Supply

Management

The owner of a food store that is not part of a larger chain is responsible for all activities, including those involving ordering, displays, inventory, and sales. The manager supervises one or more employees and maintains the payroll. In larger facilities, certain activities such as display planning, payroll, advertising, and product ordering may be done at a regional company facility. The in-store manager is responsible for hiring, supervising, scheduling, training, and motivating employees and ensuring customer satisfaction. He or she oversees removal of outdated foodstuffs and the cleanliness of the facility in compliance with state and federal laws. According to 2010 statistics, 27 percent of overall store managers in regional or national grocery chains were women; 60 percent of all managers had at least ten years of experience.

Individual stores, depending on their size, will have an overall manager and assistant managers who may also be in charge of specific departments within the store. They also are referred to as first-line managers or department heads. Chains also have regional managers who supervise several stores. In addition, purchasing managers plan and direct the purchasing process. Category managers are similar to purchasing managers, but they specialize in specific areas such as soft drinks or snack foods. Marketing managers attempt to forecast sales and develop marketing plans based on consumer trends, customer feedback, and sales figures.

Occupations in the area of management may include the following:

- Manager
- Assistant Manager
- Department Manager

Customer Services

Because loyalty to individual market chains typically is not strong, customer service is an important component of the industry. Everyone who comes into contact with customers is held responsible for treating shoppers with respect and ensuring their satisfaction. In smaller stores, the owner, the manager, or a responsible employee will personally handle customers' concerns, provide assistance, and respond to problems. Larger markets and warehouse-type facilities have service areas where people can request refunds or exchanges, register complaints, and ask to speak to a manager. Such areas generally are staffed by employees who also perform other duties, but sometimes specific employees are posted there for an entire shift.

Among the positions that are involved in customer service are the following:

Cashiers. Along with stock clerks and order fillers, cashiers make up the largest segment of the food retail industry. Together these positions total almost 35 percent of all industry workers. They scan items being purchased, accept payment and make change, and produce a receipt. For items that are priced by weight, such as produce, and those that come without bar codes, they compute the correct price or key in product codes. They pack purchases in the absence of baggers. When necessary, cashiers may assist in other areas when union rules do not limit such activities.

Baggers. Sometimes called packers, packagers, or hand packers, baggers usually are the lowest paid employees in the industry. They place purchased items in sacks, assist shoppers in carrying packages to their vehicles, retrieve shopping carts from outside the store, return misplaced items to the shelves, and assist other store personnel as needed.

Butchers and Assistants. Butchers prepare meats, poultry, and fish by cutting, grinding, and trimming as appropriate, and they package and price their finished work for sale. They may prepare ready-to-eat foods. Most butchers and their assistants work in individual stores, but some may be located at processing facilities that prepare food for individual stores.

Bakers and Assistants. Bakers make bread, rolls, doughnuts, cakes, cookies, and similar products in stores or at centralized facilities. They create specialty items such as birthday cakes to order.

Salespeople/Counter Attendants. In stores with specialty shops that offer refreshments such as coffee, tea, and snacks, salespeople sell the products and may act as baristas. They also may prepare basic food such as sandwiches.

Produce Clerks. Responsible for keeping fruits and vegetables in fresh condition, produce clerks maintain optimum temperature and humidity levels in storage areas. They wrap items as necessary, keep produce moist in sales bins, and remove items that are no longer saleable because of deterioration.

Food Preparers. In stores that house delicatessens or other prepared-food sections, food preparers may assemble salads, fry chicken, and cook meats and other ready-to-eat foods. They assemble party platters and entire meals and prepare the edibles sold in-store.

Product Demonstrators. Usually hired on a sporadic and part-time basis, product demonstrators offer coupons and free samples of store items to entice customers to purchase the demonstrated products.

Chefs/Cooks. Very large stores and centralized facilities may have a head chef or cook who plans menus, sets prices, directs the preparation of foodstuffs, orders supplies, and maintains accounts.

Pharmacists. Pharmacists fill orders for medications and dispense them based on prescriptions and advise customers about over-the-counter health aids. They usually have technicians and aides assisting them.

Occupations in the area of customer services may include the following:

- Sales Clerk/Counter Attendant
- Cashier
- Bagger/Packer/Packager
- Produce Clerk
- Butcher/Meat Cutter/Meat Trimmer
- Bakery Clerk
- Delicatessen/Food Preparer
- Pharmacist
- Product Demonstrator

Sales and Marketing

Shoppers usually enter a food retail facility with specific needs in mind but can be induced to purchase more than they intended. This is known as "impulse" buying. Less essential goods such as candy, gum, breath mints, and magazines usually are placed adjacent to checkout counters where they are sure to be noticed. Staples may be placed in areas where shoppers will first have to pass shelves of less necessary items. Sometimes, the ends of shelves have impulse goods displayed because they are more readily visible from different areas of the store. Related items that are normally not shelved together, such as soft drinks and potato chips, may be featured together in special displays.

If possible, products are arranged so customers are drawn first to the sides of the store and then to the rear. This creates a circular traffic pattern that exposes shoppers to a greater proportion of the facility. Impulse goods are placed at eye level so they will be easily spotted. More vertical space is used to display certain items than horizontal space because this arrangement exposes customers to a greater variety of items. Heavy and bulky items are placed nearer the floor.

Individual stores cannot possibly carry every product available, so shelf space in markets is purchased by manufacturers to enable their goods to be featured and sold. In turn, the markets determine what is selling by keeping computerized records integrated with the cash registers. More space is given to hot-selling items, while lower-volume sellers and niche products generally receive less shelf or bin room. New products that come on the market also must compete for shelf space.

Until recent years, advertising for supermarket products generally was limited to newspapers. With the decline of that medium, paper advertising now is widely done through colorful flyers delivered once a week or more with the mail. Because all-purpose chain markets are more or less similar in pricing and merchandise, advertising usually focuses on sale-priced items. People are well aware of what convenience stores offer without advertisements. Specialty stores tend to generate most publicity through such outlets as Web sites, blogs, and other modern electronic methods of reaching potential shoppers. As with any business, word of mouth is a potent method of advertising for stores that sell "nonessential" products. Coupons and store discount cards also are methods for attracting customers.

To increase sales potential, some stores have prepared food or snack shops on the premises, usually leased to chains such as Starbucks or Coffee Bean. They may sell sandwiches and provide cater-ing service to large groups with party platters, particularly around holiday times. Large stores such as Costco may have fast food available within the store or at an outside kiosk.

Among the positions involved in sales and marketing are the following:

- Sales Clerk
- Stock Clerk/Order Filler
- Display Designer
- Computer Technician

Facilities and Security

With the trend toward larger store size, security is likely to remain a major concern despite increased electronic surveillance and other measures. The rate of loss through theft has historically run between 1 percent and 3 percent of sales and usually falls into one of three categories: thefts by employees, by customers, or by vendors. Of these, employee theft has historically been the largest

---

OCCUPATION PROFILE

Retail Salesperson

Considerations	Qualifications
Description	Sells and promotes food products on a retail basis.
Career clusters	Agriculture, Food, and Natural Resources; Business, Management, and Administration; Marketing, Sales, and Service
Interests	Data; people
Working conditions	Work inside
Minimum education level	On-the-job training; high school diploma or GED; high school diploma/technical school
Physical exertion	Light work; medium work
Physical abilities	Unexceptional/basic fitness
Opportunities for experience	Internship; part-time work
Licensure and certification	Usually not required
Employment outlook	Average growth expected
Holland interest score	ESA; ESR

Note: See volume 1, "Publisher's Note," for an explanation of the Holland interest score.

problem for retailers. The design of a store should try to minimize blind spots where shoplifting may occur. Other security measures such as cameras, exit alarm systems, and even undercover security personnel may be utilized.

Store design is also important for inviting customers in as well as deterring malefactors. The design of a store can be used to steer shoppers to areas they may not have been planning to visit. A well-planned design is particularly important for specialty stores that rely on passersby who may not have been intending to buy. Attractive window displays are generally not important in food retail outlets except for specialty stores. Lighting in all retail food outlets should be bright throughout the facility, and items that are on special display should be lit two to five times more brightly than the surrounding light source. Dependable refrigeration and temperature control is a must for all food stores.

Occupations in the area of facilities and security may include the following:

- Security Guard
- Cleaner
- Custodian/Janitor
- Interior Designer
- Architect

Technology, Research, Design, and Development

Technology plays a major role in the industry. In retail markets, integrated computer software keeps track of customer purchases while simultaneously updating inventory and ordering from suppliers. In the 1980's, a concept called Efficient Consumer Response (ECR) was instituted. It tracks purchasing patterns from store to store and therefore can allocate products to the individual stores where they are most needed. Its goal is to help stores avoid overstocking items while keeping enough inventory on hand to fill immediate needs.

The industry also makes use of the Internet. At the least, stores maintain Web sites to post their business hours, locations, and other basic information. Online selling has become an increasing part of the industry after a false start in the 1990's. By 2005, Internet sales accounted for almost $2.5 billion of the industry's gross sales; the Safeway chain saw Internet purchases double in two years. Leading the way was Britain's vast Tesco chain, which reported 150,000 online orders each week. Online sales were estimated to account for $100 billion in Europe and at least $85 billion in the United States by 2010. Consumers were less likely to shop online for perishable goods like produce.

Other technological advances include tracking delivery trucks to determine their locations and predict when deliveries will be made. Self-checkout technology was developed in 2002, combining bar code scanners, payment devices, and scales. This technology even allows for use of coupons. In an experimental stage is "scan-as-you-go," which begins to track purchases when a customer first selects an item. The ultimate goal is to eliminate checkstand delays and deter shoplifting.

Innovations that consumers take for granted today, such as shopping carts, also had to be developed. The first prototype of a cart, described as a folding chair on wheels, was developed in 1937 and patented by an Oklahoma man named Sylvan Goldman. Other ideas also were tested, including a cart set on tracks that ran parallel to markets' shelves. Twelve-digit bar codes using a Universal Product Code (UPC) that are used to quickly scan products at the checkout counter were another important innovation. Two developments from the 1960's—relatively inexpensive lasers and integrated circuits—made bar code use feasible. In Ohio in 1974, a package of chewing gum supposedly was the first product scanned and commercially sold, and the use of bar codes eventually became commonplace.

Automated self-checkout is available for customers who have few items. In many stores, this system has eliminated the so-called "express" line, but a majority of consumers still prefer to check out with a clerk. Another potential advance is the use radio frequency identification (RFID), which replaces bar codes with microchips. It enables the contents of a shopping cart to be instantaneously scanned. Both of these technologies eventually may eliminate many cashier positions.

Many software packages for such tasks as inventory control, accounting, ordering, and shopper tracking are commercially available. Computer analysis of customer demand makes it possible to reduce large stockpiles of inventories. If the design of displays is not done in-house, there are companies that specialize in designing optimum displays for different types of products within a store.

Technological occupations in food retailing include the following:

- Computer Technician
- Maintenance and Repair Worker
- Researcher/Scientist
- Product Tester

Regulation

The retail food industry is subject to local, state, and federal regulations, including those of the U.S. Occupational Safety and Health Administration (OSHA), especially in regard to sanitation and freshness. Wage and hour laws must be adhered to. However, in some nonunionized, low-profit-margin facilities such as bodegas or greengrocers, wages may be very low, hours long, and labor laws violated. Such places often hire low-skilled people who may have little other choice of jobs.

Occupations that may deal with aspects of governmental regulation include the following:

- Store and Regional Manager
- Compliance Specialist (usually a part of Human Resources departments)
- Inspector

Centralized Operations

Large chains have corporate headquarters where much of the administrative work, such as design planning, payroll, and human resources, is housed. Executives such as regional managers (sometimes called area or zone managers) oversee the operations of a number of stores within a large geographic area. Distribution warehouses stock products until they are needed in individual stores. There also may be factory-type facilities for bakery goods, meat processing, and so on. In large chains with warehouse facilities, warehouse workers unload, load, and keep track of stock to be delivered to individual stores. With the increasing automation in the food retail industry, these jobs may decline in number. Truck drivers pick up stock from warehouses and other central locations, deliver it to individual stores, and return outdated and superfluous merchandise not otherwise disposed of.

Occupations in the area of centralized operations may include the following:

- Regional Manager
- Purchasing Manager
- Purchasing Agent
- Marketing Manager
- Office Worker
- Truck Driver
- Warehouse Worker
- Factory Worker (at chains that manufacture some of their own products)
- Laborer
- Bookkeeper

Distribution and Supply

Large chains buy from a wide range of suppliers, and their purchasing power enables them to obtain the lowest prices. They generally do not favor long-term contracts. Walmart and its subsidiaries such as Sam's Club have their own distribution centers, more than 120 as of the late 2000's. Specialized stores tend to enter into longer-term contracts with a very few suppliers, presumably of high quality, such as growers of particular produce. Generally the retail business is responsible for arranging product shipment from its suppliers, and perishable items must be shipped safely and rapidly. Cooperatives and affiliated independents usually purchase through a central wholesaler that may charge them less than it would a major chain.

The primary occupations in food-retailing distribution and supply include the following:

- Wholesaler
- Warehouse Worker
- Farmer/Grower

INDUSTRY OUTLOOK

Overview

In the five years from 2003 to 2007, the food retail industry grew approximately 3 percent to some $719.5 billion in annual domestic revenues. Of this amount, supermarkets accounted for the largest portion—almost $405 billion, or about 56 percent—in 2007. Sales in supercenters amounted to more than 9 percent of the total revenue. Warehouse-style chains like Sam's Club and Costco continued to expand their market share. With the onset of the worldwide recession at the end of 2007, the rate of growth in the industry was expected to be very slow or even remain flat several years. Sales may reach $800 billion by 2012. Wages were expected to climb very slowly compared with other industries and perhaps experience little growth until 2018.

A factor in the slowdown may be that busy two-job families are increasingly buying their meals already prepared from a variety of specialized takeout chains and restaurants. With the growing interest in healthier diets and the burgeoning ethnic populations in the United States, general markets may try to subsume smaller stores by offering larger varieties of foodstuffs that appeal to a narrower and more specialized group of consumers. They will continue to expand the range of services they offer, including automated teller machines (ATMs), bakeries, prepared food outlets, liquor sections, and delicatessens. Store loyalty, except for specialty stores and niche chains such as Trader Joe's or Whole Foods, usually is low or absent in grocery chains. As of 2007, some 75 percent of consumers routinely shopped at five or more different stores looking for both lower prices and convenience.

Foreign-owned chains like Great Britain's Tesco now are attempting to enter the U.S. market. The financial success of this penetration will determine whether or not this trend continues. Conversely, U.S. firms have made forays into foreign markets, particularly in Latin America, and have bought up indigenous food retail chains. Using American-style management and retail techniques, these acquisitions increasingly resemble American stores. Some local stores have fought back by upgrading their service levels and the size of their facilities.

Expansion by American-owned interests in other markets sometimes has proved to be unsuccessful, particularly during the economic downturn that began in 2008. Walmart has been a leader in such expansion and by the beginning of the twenty-first century owned more than eleven hundred stores, including locations in Europe. The vast market in Asia would seem to be the next logical place for the entrance of the megachains, but the emergence of local competition may be strong, particularly in China.

Employment Advantages

Because employees are generally hired into entry-level positions, little or no prior experience is expected. Advancement in the retail food industry may be easier because on-the-job training is provided. Some positions, such as cashiers, may require at least a high school diploma, and higher management positions may require a college or technical school degree, but advanced schooling is not required for most positions. Because a majority of jobs are part time, flexible schedules may allow time for school or other activities.

About 30 percent of employees are under the age of twenty-four, so the industry is a youth-friendly environment. For those who enjoy working with the public, there is ample opportunity to do so. Even in a recession, people must purchase food, although their tastes may change. By 2007, according to the U.S. Census Bureau, the retail food industry employed 3.5 million people, not including conve-

PROJECTED EMPLOYMENT FOR SELECTED OCCUPATIONS

Food and Beverage Stores

Employment		
2009	Projected 2018	Occupation
99,940	99,400	Butchers and meat cutters
955,090	961,000	Cashiers
149,300	145,300	First-line supervisors/managers of retail sales workers
135,830	154,200	Food preparation workers
447,100	441,300	Stock clerks and order fillers

Source: U.S. Bureau of Labor Statistics, Industries at a Glance, Occupational Employment Statistics and Employment Projections Program.

nience stores attached to gas stations, so employment opportunities were ample. Turnover is high, especially among younger employees, thus creating openings for future workers.

Annual Earnings

The food retail industry is second in sales volume only to the motor vehicles industry. Just before the onset of the 2007-2009 recession, U.S. sales were almost $720 billion, a $15 billion increase over a five-year period. It was not a steadily rising trend line, however; for instance, in 2004, revenues decreased to $635 billion. Supermarkets continued to dominate the industry; 85 percent of their sales came from chains, and the remainder from independently owned markets. In 2004, wholesale clubs had sales of $32.6 billion and convenience stores $127 billion.

RELATED RESOURCES FOR FURTHER RESEARCH

AMERICAN WHOLESALE MARKETERS ASSOCIATION
2750 Prosperity Ave., Suite 530
Fairfax, VA 22031
Tel: (703) 208-3358
Fax: (703) 573-5738
http://www.awmanet.org

CAREERS IN FOOD
3800 S Fremont, Suite 200
Springfield, MO 65804
Tel: (877) 329-1693
Fax: (417) 447-0738
http://www.careersinfood.com

FOOD INDUSTRY SUPPLIERS ASSOCIATION
1207 Sunset Dr.
Greensboro, NC 27408
Tel: (336) 274-6311
Fax: (336) 691-1839
http://www.fisanet.org

FOOD MARKETING INSTITUTE
2345 Crystal Dr., Suite 800
Arlington, VA 22202
Tel: (202) 452-8444
Fax: (202) 429-4519
http://www.fmi.org

GROCERY MANUFACTURERS ASSOCIATION
1350 I St. NW, Suite 300
Washington, DC 20005
Tel: (202) 639-5900
Fax: (202) 639-5932
http://www.gmaonline.org

MEXICAN-AMERICAN GROCERS ASSOCIATION
405 San Fernando Rd.
Los Angeles, CA 90031
Tel: (323) 227-1565
Fax: (323) 227-6935
http://www.buscapique.com/latinusa/
buscafile/oeste/maga.htm

NATIONAL ASSOCIATION OF CONVENIENCE STORES
1600 Duke St.
Alexandria, VA 22314
Tel: (800) 966-6227
Fax: (703) 836-4564
http://www.nacsonline.com

NATIONAL GROCERS ASSOCIATION
1005 N Glebe Rd., Suite 250
Arlington, VA 22201
Tel: (703) 516-0700
Fax: (703) 812-1821
http://www.nationalgrocers.org/

UNITED FOOD AND COMMERCIAL WORKERS INTERNATIONAL UNION
1775 K St. NW
Washington, DC 20006
Tel: (202) 223-3111
http://www.ufcw.org

ABOUT THE AUTHOR

Roy Liebman is an emeritus librarian (full professor) of the California State University, Los Angeles, where he held several management positions during a thirty-five-year career. He is a 1958 graduate of Brooklyn College, a 1961 graduate of Pratt Institute (M.L.S.), and a 1978 graduate of the California State University, Los Angeles (M.A.). He is the author of five reference books to date, as well as having written numerous periodical articles, reference book essays, and more than two hundred book reviews covering a wide range of subjects. He wrote the script for a produced television documentary and has appeared as an interview subject in two other documentaries. He also previously held positions at the California Institute of Technology and the Brooklyn and New York Public Libraries, among others, and he is currently serving part time as a reference librarian at the Los Angeles Public Library.

FURTHER READING

Brownstone, Douglass L. *How to Run a Successful Food Specialty Store.* New York: Wiley, 1978.

Groceteria.com. "A Quick History of the Supermarket." Available at http://www .groceteria.com/about/a-quick-history-of-the-supermarket.

Lewis, Jerre G., and Leslie D. Renn. *How to Start and Manage a Retail Grocery Store Business: A Practical Way to Start Your Own Business.* Interlochen, Mich.: Lewis & Renn Associates, 1999.

Lewis, Len. *The Trader Joe's Adventure: Turning a Unique Approach to Business into a Retail and Cultural Phenomenon.* Chicago: Dearborn Trade, 2005.

Lichtenstein, Nelson. *The Retail Revolution: How Wal-Mart Created a Brave New World of Business.* New York: Metropolitan Books/Henry Holt, 2009.

Marion, Bruce W., et al. *The Food Retailing Industry: Market Structure, Profits, and Prices.* New York: Praeger, 1979.

Mueller, Willard F., and Leon Garoian. *Changes in the Market Structure of Grocery Retailing.* Madison: University of Wisconsin Press, 1961.

Pegler, Martin. *Food Retail Design and Display.* New York: Retail Reporting, 1994.

Regmi, Anita, and Mark J. Gelhar. *New Directions in Global Food Markets.* Washington, D.C.: U.S. Department of Agriculture, 2005. Available at http://www.ers/usda.gov/publications/alb794.

"A Short History of the Convenience Store Industry." Available at http://www .nacsonline.com/NACS/Resources/Research/History/Pages/default.aspx.

Speak, Hugh S. *Supermarket Merchandising and Management.* Englewood Cliffs, N.J.: Prentice-Hall, 1977.

U.S. Bureau of Labor Statistics. *Career Guide to Industries*, 2010-2011 ed. Available at http://www.bls.gov/oco/cg.

———. *Occupational Outlook Handbook*, 2010-2011 ed. http://www.bls.gov/oco.

U.S. Census Bureau. North American Industry Classification System (NAICS), 2007. http://www.census.gov/cgi-bin/sssd/naics/naicsrch?chart=2007.

U.S. Congress. House Committee on the Judiciary. *Competitive Issues in Agriculture and the Food Marketing Industry.* 106th Congress, 1st session, 2000.

Walsh, William. *The Rise and Decline of the Great Atlantic and Pacific Tea Company.* Secaucus, N.J.: Lyle Stuart, 1986.